Buddhism in South-east Asian Countries

Vol. 1

Buddhism in South-East Asian Countries

Dr. Indra Narain Singh

Prashant Publishing House
DELHI - 110094 (INDIA)

PRASHANT PUBLISHING HOUSE
C-34, 28 Foota Road, Gali No. 3
West Karawal Nagar, Delhi-110094
Phone : 9810396373, 22963970

Buddhism in South-East Asian Countries

First Published : 2009

ISBN : 978-81-908282-5-3

PRINTED IN INDIA

Published by Mr. R. K. Jha M/s. Prashant Publishing House, Delhi and Printed at H.S. Offset Press, Delhi.

PREFACE

Major world religion and philosophy founded in northeastern India in the 5th century BC Based on the teachings of Siddhartha Gautama, called the Buddha, Buddhism takes as its goal the escape from suffering and from the cycle of rebirth: the attainment of nirvana. It emphasizes meditation and the observance of certain moral precepts. The Buddha's teachings were transmitted orally by his disciples; during his lifetime he established the Buddhist monastic order (sangha). He adopted some ideas from the Hinduism of his time, notably the doctrine of karma, but also rejected many of its doctrines and all of its gods. In India, the emperor Ashoka promoted Buddhism during the 3rd century BC, but it declined in succeeding centuries and was nearly extinct there by the 13th century.

It spread south and flourished in Sri Lanka and Southeast Asia, and it moved through Central Asia and China (including Tibet), Korea, and Japan. In the 19th century, Buddhism spread to Europe and the United States, and it became increasingly popular in the West in the second half of the 20th century. Buddhism's main teachings are summarized in the Four Noble Truths, of which the fourth is the Eightfold Path. Buddhism's two major branches, Mahayana and Theravada, have developed distinctive practices and unique collections of canonical texts. In the early 21st century, the various traditions of Buddhism together had more than 375 million followers.

— *Author*

Acknowledgement

The present work has received encouragement, help and support from a large number of persons. It would be impossible to acknowledge my gratitude to everyone in this limited space.

I must above all especially express my idebtedness to Prof. Bhikshu Satyapal.

I wish to acknowledge with deep sense of gratitude, the unfailing encouragement and cooperation. I have received from my wife Aparajita, daughter Tanya and son Uday.

—Dr. Indra Narain Singh

Contents

Preface

1. Buddhism and Buddhists in China — 1

2. Buddhism in India — 65

Bibliography — 341

Index — 342

1

Buddhism and Buddhists in China

INTRODUCTORY

A well known missionary of Peking, China, was invited one day by a Buddhist acquaintance to attend the ceremony of initiation for a class of one hundred and eighty priests and some twenty laity who had been undergoing preparatory instruction at the stately and important Buddhist monastery. The beautiful courts of the temple were filled by a throng of invited guests and spectators, waiting to watch the impressive procession of candidates, acolytes, attendants and high officials, all in their appropriate vestments. No outsider was privileged to witness the solemn taking by each candidate for the priesthood of the vow to "keep the Ten Laws," followed by the indelible branding of his scalp, truly a "baptism of fire." Less private was the initiation of the lay brethren and _sisters,_ more lightly branded on the right wrist, while all about intoned "Na Mah Pen Shih Shih Chia Mou Ni Fo." (I put my trust in my original Teacher, SùJamuni, Buddha.)

The missionary was deeply impressed by the serenity and devotion of the worshipers and by the dignity and solemnity of the service. The last candidate to rise and receive the baptism of branding was a young married woman of refined appearance, attended by an elderly lady, evidently her mother, who watched with an expression of mingled devotion, insight and pride her daughter's initiation and welcomed her at the end of the process with radiant face, as a daughter, now, in a spiritual as well as a physical sense. At that moment an attendant, noting the keen interest of the missionary, said to him rather flippantly, "Would you not like to have your arm branded, too?" "I might," he replied, "just out of curiosity, but I could not receive the branding as a believer in the Buddha. I am a Christian believer. To be branded without inward faith would be an insult to your religion as well as treachery to my own, would it not? Is not real religion a matter of the heart?"

The old lady, who had overheard with evident disapproval the remark of the attendant, turned to the missionary at once and said, "Is that the way you Westerners, you Christians, speak of your faith? Is the reality of religion for you also an inward experience of the heart?" And with that began an interesting interchange of conversation, each party discovering that in the heart of the other was a genuine longing for God that overwhelmed all the artificial, material distinctions and the human devices through which men have limited to particular and exclusive paths their way of search, and drew these two pilgrims on the way toward God into a common and very real fellowship of the spirit.

A Buddhist monk was passing by a mission building in another city' of China when his attention was suddenly drawn to the Svastika and other Buddhist symbols which the architect had skilfully used in decorating the building. His face brightened as he said to his companion: "I did not know that Christians had any appreciation of beauty in their religion."

These incidents reveal aspects of the alchemy of the soul by which the real devotee of one religion perceives values which are dear to him in another religion. The good which he has attained in his old religion enables him to appropriate the better in the new religion. A converted monk, explaining his acceptance of Christianity, said: "I found in Jesus Christ the great Bodhisattva, my Saviour, who brings to fruition the aspirations awakened in me by Buddhism."

Just as it has been said that they do not know England who know England only, so it may be said with equal truth that they do not know Christianity who know it and no other faith. There are many in China like the old lady at the temple, who have found in Buddhism something of that spiritual satisfaction and stimulus which true Christianity affords, in fuller measure. The recognition of such religious values by the student or the missionary furnishes a sound foundation for the building of a truer spirituality among such devotees.

As will be seen in what follows, religion in China is at first sight a mixed affair. From the standpoint of cruder household superstitions an average Chinese family may be regarded as Taoists; the principles by which its members seek to guide their lives individually and socially may be called Confucian; their attitude of worship and their hopes for the future make them Buddhists. The student would not be far afield when he credits the religious aspirations of the Chinese today to Buddhism, regarding Confucianism as furnishing the ethical system to which they submit and Taoism as responsible for many superstitious practices. But the Buddhism found in China differs radically from that of Southern Asia, as will be made clear by the following sketch of its introduction into the Flowery Kingdom and its subsequent history.

THE ENTRANCE OF BUDDHISM INTO CHINA

Buddhism was not an indigenous religion of China. Its, founder was Gautama of India in the sixth century B.C. Some centuries later it found its way into China by way of central Asia. There is a tradition that as early as 142 B.C. Chang Ch'ien, an ambassador of the Chinese emperor, Wu Ti, visited the countries of central Asia, where he first learned about the new religion which was making such headway and reported concerning it to his master. A few years later the generals of Wu Ti captured a gold image of the Buddha which the emperor set up in his palace and worshiped, but he took no further steps.

According to Chinese historians Buddhism was officially recognized in China about 67 A.D. A few years before that date, the emperor, Ming-Ti, saw in a dream a large golden image with a halo hovering above his palace. His advisers, some of whom were no doubt already favorable to the new religion, interpreted the image of the dream to be that of Buddha, the great sage of India, who was inviting his adhesion. Following their advice the emperor sent an embassy to study into Buddhism. It brought back two Indian monks and a quantity of Buddhist classics. These were carried on a white horse and so the monastery which the emperor built for the monks and those who came after them was called the White Horse Monastery. Its tablet is said to have survived to this day.

This dream story is worth repeating because it goes to show that Buddhism was not only known at an early date, but was favored at the court of China. In fact, the same history which relates the dream contains the biography of an official who became an adherent of Buddhism a few years before the dream took place. This is not at all surprising, because an acquaintance with Buddhism was the inevitable concomitant of the military campaigning, the many embassies and the wide-ranging trade of those centuries. But the introduction of Buddhism into China was especially promoted by reason of the current policy of the Chinese government of moving conquered populations in countries west of China into China proper, The vanquished peoples brought their own religion along with them. At one time what is now the province of Shansi was populated in this way by the Hsiung-nu, many of whom were Buddhists.

The introduction and spread of Buddhism were hastened by the decline of Confucianism and Taoism. The Han dynasty (206 B. C.-221 A. D.) established a government founded on Confucianism. It reproduced the classics destroyed in the previous dynasty and encouraged their study; it established the state worship of Confucius; it based its laws and regulations upon the ideals and principles advocated by Confucius. The great increase of wealth and power under this dynasty led to a gradual deterioration in the character of the rulers and officials. The sigid Confucian regulations became burdensome to the people who ceased to respect their leaders. Confucianism lost its hold as the complete solution of the problems of life. At the same time Taoism had become a veritable jumble of meaningless and superstitious rites which served to support a horde of ignorant, selfish priests. The high religious ideals of the earlier Taoist mystics were abandoned for a search after the elixir of life during fruitless journeys to the isles of the Immortals which were supposed to be in the Eastern Sea.

At this juncture there arose in North China a sect of men called the Purists who advocated a return from the vagaries of Taoism and the irritating rules of Confucianism to the simple life practised by the Taoist mystics. When these thoughtful and earnest minded men came into contact with Buddhism they were captivated by it. It had all they were claiming for Taoist mysticism and more. They devoted their literary ability and religious fervor to the spreading of the new religion and its success was in no small measure due to their efforts. As a result of this early association the tenets of the two religions seemed so much alike that various emperors called assemblies of Buddhists and Taoists with the intention of effecting a union of the two religions into one. If the emperor was under the influence of Buddhism he tried to force all Taoists to become Buddhists. If he was favorable to Taoism he tried to make all Buddhists become Taoists.

But such mandates were as unsuccessful as other similar schemes have been. In the third century A. D. after the Han dynasty had ended, China was broken up into several small kingdoms which contended for supremacy, so that for about four hundred years the whole country was in a state of disunion. One of the strong dynasties of this period, the Northern Wei (386-535 A. D.), was distinctly loyal to Buddhism. During its continuance Buddhism prospered greatly. Although Chinese were not permitted to become monks until 335 A. D., still Buddhism made rapid advances and in the fourth century, when that restriction was removed, about nine-tenths of the people of northwestern China had become Buddhists. Since then Buddhism has been an established factor in Chinese life.

THE ESTABLISHMENT OF BUDDHISM AS THE PREDOMINATING RELIGION OF CHINA

Even the historical influences noted above do not account entirely for the spread of Buddhism in China. In order to understand this and the place which Buddhism occupies, we need to review briefly the different forms which religion takes in China and to note how Buddhism has related itself to them.

The World of Invisible Spirits

The Chinese believe _in_ a surrounding-world of spirits, whose origin is exceedingly various. They touch life at every point. There are spirits which are guardians of the soil, tree spirits, mountain demons, fire gods, the spirits of animals, of mountains, of rivers, seas and stars, of the heavenly bodies and of many forms of active life. These spirits to the Chinese mind, of today are a projection, a sort of spiritual counterpart, of the many sided interests, practical or otherwise, of the groups and communities by whom they are worshipped. There are other spirits which mirror the ideals of the groups by which they are worshipped. Some of them may have been incarnated in the lives of great leaders. There are spirits which are mere animations, occasional spirits, associated with objects crossing the interests of men, but not constant enough to attain a definite, independent life as spiritual beings. Thus surrounding the average Chinese peasant there is a densely populated spirit world affecting in all kinds of ways his, daily existence.

This other world is the background which must be kept in mind by one who would understand or attempt to guide Chinese religious experience. It is the basis on which all organized forms of religious activity are built. The nearest of these to his heart is the proper regard for his ancestors.

The Universal Sense of Ancestor Control

The ancestral control of family life occupies so large and important a place in Chinese thought and practice that ancestor worship has been called the original religion of the Chinese. It is certain that the earliest Confucian records recognize ancestor worship; but doubtless it antedated them, growing up out of the general religious consciousness of the people.

The discussion of that origin in detail cannot be taken up here. It may be followed in the literature noted in the appendix or in the volume of this series entitled "Present-Day Confucianism." Ancestor worship is active today, however, because the Chinese as a people believe that these ancestors control in a very real way the good or evil fortunes of their descendants, because this recognition of ancestors furnishes a potent means of promoting family unity and social ethics, and, most of all, because a happy future life is supposed to be dependent upon descendants who will faithfully minister to the dead. Since each one desires such a future he is faithful in promoting the observance of the obligation.

Consequently, ancestor worship, like the previously mentioned belief in the invisible spiritual world, underlies all other religious developments. No family is so obscure or poor that it does not submit to the ritual or discipline which is supposed to ensure the favor of the spirits belonging to the community. Likewise, every such family is loyal to the supposed needs of its deceased ancestors. In a very intimate way these beliefs are interwoven with the private and social morality of every family or group in Chinese society, and must be taken into account by any one who seeks to bring a religious message to the Chinese people.

Degenerate Taoism

Taoism is that system of Chinese religious thought and practice, beginning about the fifth century B. C., which was originally based on the teachings of Lao Tzu and developed in the writings of Lieh Tzu and Chuang Tzu and found in the Tao T'hing. It is really in this original form a philosophy of some merit. According to its teaching the Tao is the great impersonal background of the world from which all things proceed as beams from the sun, and to which all beings return. In contrast to the present, transient, changing world the Tao is unchangeable and quiet. Originally the Taoists emphasized quiescence, a life in accordance with nature, as a means of assimilating themselves to the Tao, believing that in this way they would obtain length of days, eternal life and especially the power to become superior to natural conditions.

There is a movement today among Chinese scholars in favor of a return to this original highest form of Taoism. It appeals to them as a philosophy of life; an answer to its riddles. Among the masses of the people, however, Taoism manifests itself in a ritual of extreme superstition. It recommends magic tricks and curious superstitions as a means of prolonging life. It expresses itself very largely in these degrading practices which few Chinese will defend, but which are yet very commonly practiced.

The Organizing Value of Confucianism

Confucianism brought organization into these hazy conceptions of life and duty. It took for granted this spiritual-unspiritual background of animism, ancestor-worship and Taoism, but reshaped and adapted it as a whole so that it might fit into that proper organization of the state and nation which was one of its great objectives. Just as Confucianism related the family to the village, the village to the district, and the district to the state, so it organized the spiritual world into a hierarchy with Shang Ti as its head. This hierarchy was developed along the lines of the organization mentioned above. Under Shang Ti were the five cosmic emperors, one for each of the four quarters and one for heaven above, under whom were the gods of the soil, the mountains, rivers, seas, stars, the sun and moon, the ancestors and the gods of special groups. Each of the deities in the various ranks had duties to those above and rights with reference to those below. These duties and rights, as they affected the individual, were not only expressed in law but were embodied in ceremony and music, in daily religious life and practice in such a way that each individual had reason to feel that he was a functioning agent in this grand Confucian universe. If any one failed to do his part, the whole universe would suffer. So thoroughly has this idea been adopted by the Chinese people that every one joins in forcing an individual, however reluctant or careless, to perform his part of each ceremony as it has been ordered from high antiquity.

The emperor alone worshipped the supreme deity, Shang Ti; the great officers of state, according to the dignity of their office, were related to subordinate gods and required to show them adequate respect and reverence. Confucius and a long line of noted men following him were semi-deified [Footnote: Confucius was by imperial decree deified in 1908.] and highly reverenced by the literati, the class from which the officers of state were as a rule obtained, in connection with their duties, and as an expression of their ideals. To the common people were left the ordinary local deities, while all classes, of course, each in its own fashion reverenced, cherished and obeyed their ancestors. It should be remarked at this point that Confucianism of this official character has broken down, not only under the impact of modern ideas, but under the longing of the Chinese for a universal deity. The people turn to Heaven and to the Pearly Emperor, the popular counterpart of Shang Ti.

Viewed from another angle, Confucianism is an elaborate system of ethics. In writings which are virtually the scriptures of the Chinese people Confucius and his successors have set forth the principles which should govern the life of a people who recognize this spiritual universe and system. These ethics have grown out of a long and, in some respects, a sound experience. Much can be said in their favor. The essential weaknesses of the Confucian system of ethics lie in its sectional and personal loyalties and its monarchical basis. The spirit of democracy is a deadly foe to Confucianism. Another element of weakness is its excessive dependence upon the past. Confucius reached ultimate wisdom by the study of the best that had been attained before his day. He looked backward rather than forward. Consequently a modern, broadly educated Confucianist finds himself in an anomalous position. He does not need absolutely to reject the wisdom which Confucianism embodies, but he can no longer accept it as a sound, reliable and indisputable scheme of thought and action. Yet its simple ethical principles and its social relationships are basal in the lives of the vast masses of the Chinese.

Buddhism an. Inclusive Religion

Upon this, confused jumble of spiritism, superstition, loyalty to ancestors and submission to a divine hierarchy Buddhism was superimposed. It quickly dominated all because of its superior excellence. The form of Buddhism which became established in China was not, to be sure, like the Buddhism preached by Gautama and his disciples, or like that form of Buddhism which had taken root in Burma or Ceylon. Except in name, the Buddhism of Southern Asia and the Buddhism which developed in China were virtually two distinct types of religion. The Buddhism of Burma and Ceylon was of the conservative H?y¡+ ("Little Vehicle" of salvation) school, while that of China was of the progressive Mahb.na ("Great Vehicle" of salvation) school. Their differences are so marked as to be worthy of a careful statement.

The Hinayana, which is today the type of Buddhism in Ceylon, Burma and Siam, has always clung closely to tradition as expressed in the original Buddhist scriptures. Its basic ideas were that life is on the whole a time of suffering, that the cause of this sorrow is desire or ignorance, and that there is a possible deliverance from it. This deliverance or salvation is to be attained by following the eightfold path, namely, right knowledge, aspiration, speech, conduct, means of livelihood, endeavor, mindfulness and meditation. To the beatific state to be ultimately attained Gautama gave the name Nirvana, explained by his followers variously either as an utter extinction of personality or as a passionless peace, a general state of well-being free from all evil desire or clinging to life and released from the chain of transmigration. Hinayana Buddhism appeals to the individual as affording a way of escape from evil desire and its consequences by acquiring knowledge, by constant discipline, and by a devotedness of the life to religious ends through membership in the monastic order which Buddha established. It encourages, however, a personal salvation worked out by the individual alone. The Mahb.na school of Buddhists accept the general ideas of the Hinayana regarding life and salvation, but so change the spirit and objectives as to make Buddhism into what is virtually another religion. It does not confine salvation to the few who can retire from the world and give themselves wholly to good works, but opens Buddhahood to all. The "saint" of Hinayana Buddhism is the _arhat_ who is intent on saving himself. The saint of Mahb.na Buddhism is the candidate for Buddhahood (Bodhisattva) who defers his entrance into the bliss of deliverance in order to save others. Mahb.na Buddhism is progressive. It encourages missionary enterprise and was a secret of the remarkable spread of Buddhism over Asia. Moreover, while the H?y¡+ school recognizes no god or being to whom worship is given, the Maha.n#(ame to regard Gautama himself as a god and salvation as life in a heavenly world of pure souls. Thus the Mahb.na type of thinking constitutes a bridge between H?y¡+ Buddhism and Christianity. In fact, a recent writer has declared that H?y¡+ Buddhists are verging toward these more spiritual conceptions. [Footnote: See Saunders, _Buddhism and Buddhists in Southern Asia,_ pp. 10, 20.]

After the death of Sù*amuni [Footnote: Sù*amuni is the name by which Gautama, the Buddha, is familiarly known in China.] Buddhism broke up into a number of sects usually said to be eighteen in number. When Buddhism came to China some of these sects were introduced, but they assumed new forms in their Chinese environment. Besides the sects brought, from India the Chinese developed several strong sects of their own. Usually they speak of ten sects although the number is far larger, if the various subdivisions are included.

To indicate the manifold differences between these groups in Buddhism would take us far afield and would not be profitable. It will be of interest, however, to consider some of the chief sects. One of the sects introduced from India is the Pure Land or the Ching T'u which holds before the believer the "Western Paradise" gained through faith in Amit¨(a. Any one, no matter what his life may have been, may enter the Western Paradise by repeating the name of Amit¨(a. This sect is widespread in China. In Japan there are two branches of it known as the Nishi-Hongwanji and the Higashi-Hongwanji with their head monasteries in Kyoto. They are the most progressive sects in Japan and are carrying on missionary work in China, the Hawaiian Islands and in the United States.

Another strong sect is the Meditative sect or the Ch'an Men (Zen in Japan). This was introduced by Bodhidharma, or Tamo, who arrived in the capital of China in the year 520 A.D. On his arrival the emperor Wu Ti tried to impress the sage with his greatness saying: "We have built temples, multiplied the Scriptures, encouraged many to join the Order: is not there much merit in all this?" "None," was the blunt reply. "But what say the holy books? Do they not promise rewards for such deeds?" "There is nothing holy." "But you, yourself, are you not one of the holy ones?" "I don't know." "Who are you?" "I don't know." Thus introduced, the great man proceeded to open his missionary-labors by sitting down opposite a wall arid gazing at it for the next nine years. From this he has been called the "wall-gazer." He and his successors promulgated the doctrine that neither the scriptures, the ritual nor the organization, in fact nothing outward had any value in the attainment of enlightenment. They held that the heart of the universe is Buddha and that apart from the heart or the thought all is unreal. They thought themselves back into the universal Buddha and then found the Buddha heart in all nature. Thus they awakened the spirit which permeated nature, art and literature and made the whole world kin with the spirit of the Buddha.

"The golden light upon the sunkist peaks,

The water murmuring in the pebbly creeks,

Are Buddha. In the stillness, hark, he speaks!"

Such pantheism and quietism often lead to a confusion in moral relations, but these mystics were quite correct in their morals because they checked up their mysticism with the moral system of the Buddha.

Still another important sect originated in the sixth century A. D. on Chinese soil, namely, the T'ien T'ai (Japanese Tendai), so called because it started in a monastery situated on the beautiful T'ien T'ai mountains south of Ningpo. Chih K'ai, the founder, realized that Buddhism contained a great mass of contradictory teachings and practice, all attributed to the Buddha. He sought for a harmonizing principle and found it in the arbitrary theory that these teachings were given to different people on five different occasions and hence the discrepancies. The practical message of this sect has been that all beings have the Buddha heart and that the Buddha loves all beings, so that all beings may attain salvation, which consists in the full realization of the Buddha heart latent in them.

There was a time when these sects were very active and flourishing in China. At the present time the various tendencies for which they stood have been adopted by Buddhism as a whole and the various sectaries, though still keeping the name of the sect, live peacefully in the same monastery. All the monasteries practice meditation, believe in the paradise of Amit¨(a, and are enjoying the ironic calm advocated by the T'ien T'ai. While the struggle among the sects of China has been followed by a calm which resembles stagnation, those in Japan are very active and the reader is referred to the volume of this series on Japanese Buddhism for further treatment of the subject.

When Buddhism entered China it brought with it a new world. It was new _practical_ and new spiritually. It brought a knowledge unknown before regarding the heavenly bodies, regarding nature and regarding medicine, and a practice vastly above the realm of magical arts. In addition to these practical benefits, Buddhism proclaimed a new spiritual universe far more real and extensive than any of which the Chinese had dreamed, and peopled with spiritual beings having characteristics entirely novel. In comparison with this new universe or series of universes which Indian imagination had created, the Chinese universe was wooden and geometric. Since it was an organized system and a greater rather than a different one, the Chinese people readily accepted it and made it their own.

Buddhism not only enlarged the universe and gave the individual a range of opportunity hitherto unsuspected, but it introduced a scheme of religious practice, or rather several of them, enabling the individual devotee to attain a place in this spiritual universe through his own efforts. These "ways" of salvation were quite in harmony with Chinese ideas. They resembled what had already been a part of the national practice and so were readily adopted and adapted by the Chinese.

Buddhism rendered a great service to the Chinese through its new estimate of the individual. Ancient China scarcely recognized the individual. He was merged in the family and the clan. Taoists, to be sure, talked of "immortals" and Confucianism exhibited its typical personality, or "princely man," but these were thought of as supermen, as ideals. The classics of China had very little to say about the common people. The great common crowd was submerged. Buddhism, on the other hand, gave every individual a distinct place in the great wheel _dharma,_ the law, and made it possible for him to reach the very highest goal of salvation. This introduced a genuinely new element into the social and family life of the Chinese people.

Buddhism was so markedly superior to any one of the four other methods of expressing the religious life, that it quickly won practical recognition as the real religion of China. Confucianism may be called the doctrine of the learned classes. It formulates their principles of life, but it is in no strict sense a popular religion. It is rather a state ritual, or a scheme of personal and social ethics. Taoism recognizes the immediate influence of the spirit world, but it ministers only to local ideals and needs. In the usages of family and community life, ancestor worship has a definite place, but an occasional one. Buddhism was able to leave untouched each of these expressions of Chinese personal and social life, and yet it went far beyond them in ministering to religious development. Its ideas of being, of moral responsibility and of religious relationships furnished a new psychology which with all its imperfections far surpassed that of the Chinese. Buddhism's organization was so satisfying and adaptable that not only was it taken over readily by the Chinese, but it has also persisted in China without marked changes since its introduction. Most of all it stressed personal salvation and promised an escape from the impersonal world of distress and hunger which surrounds the average Chinese into a heaven ruled by Amit¨(a [Footnote: Amit¨(a, meaning "infinite light," is the Sanskrit name of one of the Buddhas moat highly revered in China. The usual Chinese equivalent is Omi-To-Fo.] the Merciful. The obligations of Buddhism are very definite and universally recognized. It enforces high standards of living, but has added significance because it draws each devotee into a sort of fellowship with the divine, and mates not this life alone, but this life plus a future life, the end of human activity. Buddhism, therefore, really expresses the deepest religious life of the people of China.

It will be worth while to note some illustrations of the conviction of the Chinese people that there are three religions to which they owe allegiance and yet that these are essentially one. They often say, "The three teachings are the whole teaching." An old scholar is reported to have remarked, "The three roads are different, but they lead to the same source." A common story reports that Confucius was asked in the other world about drinking wine, which Buddhists forbid but Taoists permit. Confucius replied: "If I do not drink I become a Buddha. If I drink I become an Immortal. Well, if there is wine, I shall drink; if there is none, I shall abstain." This expresses characteristically the Chinese habit of adaptation. Such a decision sounds quite up to date.

The Ethical Culture Society of Peking, recently organized, has upon its walls pictures of Buddha, Lao Tzu, Confucius and Christ. Its members claim to worship Shang Ti as the god of all religions. An offshoot of this society, the T'ung Shan She, associates the three founders very closely with Christ. It claims to have a deeper revelation of Christ than the Christians themselves. A new organization, the Tao Yuan, plans to harmonize the three old religions with Mohammedanism and Christianity.

Buddhism has consistently and continually striven to bring about a unity of religion in China by interpenetrating Confucianism and Taoism. Quite early the Buddhists invented the story that the Bodhisattva Ju T'ung was really Confucius incarnate. There was at one time a Buddhist temple to Confucius in the province of Shantung. The Buddhists also gave out the story that Bodhisattva Kas'yapa was the incarnation of Lao Tzu, the founder of Taoism. An artist painted Lao Tzu transformed into a Buddha, seated in a lotus bud with a halo about his head. In front of the Buddha was Confucius doing reverence. A Chinese scholar, asked for his opinion about the picture, said: "Buddha should be seated; Lao Tzu should be standing at the side looking askance at Buddha; and Confucius should be grovelling on the floor."

A monument dating from 543 A. D., illustrates this tendency of Buddhism to represent its own superiority in Chinese religious life. At the top of the monument is Brahma, lower down is Sù*amuni with his disciples, Ananda and Kas'yapa on one face, and on the other Sù*amuni again, conversing with Buddha Prabhutaratna and worshipped by monks and Bodhisattvas. On the pedestal are Confucian and Taoist deities, ten in number. Thus Buddhism sought to rank itself clearly above the other two religions. From the early days Buddhism regarded itself as their superior and began the processes of interpenetration and absorption. In consequence the values originally inherent in Buddhism have come to be regarded as the natural possession of the Chinese. It does express their religious life, especially in South China, where outward manifestations of religion are perhaps more marked than in the north.

BUDDHISM AND THE PEASANT

In order that, one may realize the place that Buddhism holds in the religious life of the Chinese people as a whole, he must turn to the organizations through which it functions. It is sometimes difficult to estimate the place of Buddhism in China, because it so interpenetrates the whole cultural and social life of the people. It becomes their "way." To see how it touches the life of the average man or woman in various ways will, therefore, be illuminating. The most outstanding evidence of devotion are the many monasteries which dot the land in all Buddhist countries. China is less dominated by them than other lands, yet they form a very important reason for the persistence and strength of Buddhism there. One of the famous old shrines will represent them as a class and give evidence of their importance.

The Monastery of Kushan

Kushan Monastery, located about four hours' ride by sedan-chair from Foochow, is a famous shrine of South China. It occupies a large amphitheater about fifteen hundred feet above the plain, part way up Kushan, the "Drum Mountain," some three thousand feet high. From the top of the mountain on clear days with the help of a glass the blue shores of Formosa may be seen on the eastern horizon. The spacious monastery buildings are surrounded by a grove of noble trees, in which squirrels, pheasants, chipmunks and snakes enjoy an undisturbed life.

The ascent to the monastery begins on the bank of the Min River. At the foot of the mountain in a large temple the traveler may obtain mountain chairs carried by two or more coolies. The road, paved with granite slabs cut from the mountain side, consists of a series of stone stairs, which zig-zag up the mountain under the shadow of ancient pine trees. Every turn brings to view a bit of landscape carpeted with rice, or a distant view where mountains and sky meet. A brook rushes by the side of the road. Here it breaks into a beautiful waterfall. There it gurgles' in a deep ravine. The sides of the road are covered with large granite blocks which, loosened from the mountain side by earthquakes, have disposed themselves promiscuously. Their blackened, weather-beaten sides are incised with Chinese characters. One of them bears the words: "We put our trust in Amit¨(a." Another immortalizes the sentiments of some great official who has made the pilgrimage to the mountain. Near the monastery stand the sombre dagobas where repose the ashes of former abbots and monastery officials. Not far away on the other side of the road, hidden by trees, is the crematory where the last rem.ins of the brethren are consumed by the flames.

As one approaches the monastery he hears the regular sounds of a bell tolled by a water-wheel, reminding the faithful of Buddha's law. He sees monks strolling leisurely about and lay brethren carrying wood, cultivating the gardens, or tending the animals released by pious devotees to heap up merit for themselves in the next world. Just inside the main gate is a large fish pond, where goldfish of great size struggle with one another, and with the lazy turtles, for the round hard cakes purchased from the monks by the merit-seeking devotee.

The monastery itself consists of a large group of buildings erected about stone-paved courts, rising in terraces on the mountain side. The large court at the entrance leads to the "Hall of the Four Kings." As one enters the spacious door, he _is_ faced by a jolly, almost naked image of the "Laughing Buddha." This is Maitra®, the Mea siah of the Buddhists, who will return to the world five thousand years after the departure of Sù*amuni. In the northern monasteries Maitra® is often represented as reaching a height when standing of seventy feet or more, which indicates the stature to which man will attain when he returns to earth. On each side of the visitor are two immense images of the Deva kings. In Brahman cosmogony they were the guardians of the world. In this entrance hall of the Buddhist monastery they stand as guardians of the Buddhist faith. In the same hall looking toward the open court beyond is Wei To, another guardian deity of Buddhism. Somewhere near by is Kuan Ti, the god worshipped by the soldiers and merchants. Although a Confucian god, he was early adopted by Buddhist monks into their pantheon and made the guardian of their Order.

Beyond this entrance hall is a large stone-paved court. On the right side is a bell-tower whose bell is tolled by a monk who has kept the vow of silence for fourteen years. On the left is a drum-tower. On the right one finds a series of small shrines. A passage way leads to the library where numerous Buddhist writings repose in lacquered cases, some of them written in their own blood by devout monks. On the same side are guest halls, the dining room for three hundred monks, and the spacious, well equipped kitchen with running water piped from a reservoir in the hills above. A store where books, images and the simple requirements of the monks can be obtained is just above the dining room. On the left side of the court are large buildings used as dormitories far the monks, storerooms, and for housing the great printing establishment with its thousands of wooden blocks on which are carved passages from the Buddhist scriptures. Here also are kept the coffins in which the monks are to be burned.

On a terrace above the north side of the court rises the main hall, called the "Hall of the Triratna," the Buddhist Trinity, where three gilded images are seated on a lotus flower with halos covering their backs and heads. The center image is that of Sù*amuni, the Buddha. On his right is Yao Shih, the Buddha of medicine, and on the left, Amit¨(a. Quite often these images are said to represent the Buddha, the Law and the Community of Monks. On the altar are candlesticks and a fine incense burner from which curls of smoke arise. An immense lamp hangs from the ceiling. In the rear are banners with praises to Buddha given by pious devotees. The floor is tiled and covered with round mats made of palm fiber on which the monks kneel during worship. Before the mats are low stands for books. On each side of this main hall are the images of nine Buddhist saints (_arhats_), eighteen in all. Behind this large temple opens another court and on a terrace above it stands the hall of the Law with the images of Kuan Yin, the goddess of Mercy, and the twenty-four devas. Here also are small images of viceroys and patrons of the monastery.

The hillsides are dotted with numerous temples and shrines. There is one to Chu-Hsi, the great philosopher of the Sung dynasty, who was born in Fukien. In it are preserved a few characters indited by his hand. On the west side of the monastery are large buildings for the housing of animals released by merit-seeking devotees. Here cows, hogs, goats, chickens, geese and ducks spend their old age without fear of beginning their transmigration by forming the main portion of a Chinese feast.

The monastery is governed by an abbot, usually a man of good business ability, elected by the monks. Under him are the officers of the two wings or groups of attendants. One set looks after the spiritual interests, of the monks; the-other takes care of their material needs: The monks have worship about two o'clock in the morning and again at about four in the afternoon. The rest of the long day they spend in meditation, or study, in strolling about the mountain side or in sleep. Their life is separated from all stirring contact with the life of the world.

Monasteries Control F§«-shui

This monastery with its appointments is a good type of the monasteries all over China. It was founded at the request of the inhabitants of the neighborhood, because the dragons of the region used to cause much damage to the crops in the surrounding country. A holy monk came, founded the monastery, and by his good influence so curbed the dragons that the country-side has enjoyed peace ever since and the monastery has prospered. Since the fourth century of our era records show that by the building of monasteries in strategic place's holy monks brought rains and prosperity to various regions, or prevented floods and calamities from damaging the villages. In other words the monasteries are regarded as the controllers of _f§«-shui_ (wind and water). According to the Chinese philosophy winds and water are spiritual forces and may be so controlled by other spiritual forces that instead of bringing harm they will confer benefit upon the people. Floods and dry seasons are so frequent in China that any institution holding out the promise of regulating them would become firmly established in the affection of the people. The monasteries have taken this place.

One of the picturesque features of a Chinese landscape is the pagoda. These structures were introduced in the early stages of Buddhism to enshrine the relics of Buddha. It was said that Buddha's body consisted of eighty thousand parts, hence numerous pagodas were erected to shelter these relics. Inasmuch as a pagoda contained the relics of Buddha, it possessed magic power and so came to play a great part in the control of the winds and the rains. The pagoda in China has an odd number of stories varying from three to thirteen. The odd numbers belong to the positive principle in nature which is superior to the negative principle. The pagoda plays quite a part in the festivals of the people. On certain occasions the stories are hung with lanterns and the pagodas are visited by numerous throngs.

Prayer for Rain

Prayers for rain afford such a common illustration of the relation of Buddhism to the life of the peasant that a detailed presentation of such a service may be of seal value.

During a prolonged drought in some district of China, when the heat opens gaping cracks in the fields and the grain is drying up, the populace may visit their highest official and apprise him of the dire situation. He often forbids the slaughter of all animals for three days and, in case rain has not thereby come, he goes in person or sends a deputy to the nearest monastery to direct the monks to pray for rain.

(a) The Altar.—On such an occasion the great hall of the Law may be used for the ceremony. Quite often a special altar is erected in an enclosure near the monastery on a platform one foot high and twenty-five feet on each side, overspread by a tent of green cloth. In the center seats are arranged for the presiding monk and his assistants. On each of the four sides of the altar is placed an image of the Dragon King who is supposed to control the rain. If an image is not obtainable a piece of paper inscribed with the name of the dragon may be used. Flowers, fruits and incense are spread before the images. On the doors of the tent are painted dragons with clouds. The tent and altar are green and the monks wear green garments, because green belongs to the spring and suggests rain. For this ceremony the monks prepare themselves by abstinence and cleansing. The presiding monk is one of high moral character and religious fervor. While some monks recite appropriate sutras, two others look after the offerings, the incense, and the sprinkling of water during the ceremony to suggest the coming of rain. The services continue day and night, being conducted by groups of monks in succession.

(b) The Prayer Service._—The ceremonial is opened by a chant as follows: "Pearly dew of the jade heavens, golden waves of Buddha's ocean, scatter the lotus flowers on a thousand thousand worlds of suffering, that the heart of mercy may wash away great calamity, that a drop may become a flood, that a drop may purify mountains and rivers.

"We put our trust in the Bodhisattvas and Mahá,ttvas that purify the earth."

The chant ended, a monk takes a bowl of water and repeats thrice: "We put our trust in the great merciful Kuan Yin Bodhisattva." Then follows the chant:

"The Bodhisattva's sweet dew of the willow is able to make one drop spread over the ten directions. It washes away the rank odors and dirt. It keeps the altars clean and pure. The mysterious words of the doctrine will be reverently repeated."

This chant ended, the monks intone incantations of Kuan Yin, quite unintelligible even to them, but of magical value. While these are being uttered, the presiding monk and his attendants walk around the altar, while one of them with a branch sprinkles water on the floor. This symbolizes the cleansing of the altar and of the monks from all impurities which might render the ritual ineffective. When the perambulating monks have returned to their place, while the sprinkler continues his duties, the monks repeat the words: "We put our trust in the sweet dew kings, Bodhisattvas and Mahá,ttvas."

The Bodhisattvas have now come to the purified altar and while the abbot offers incense to them, the monks repeat the words:

"The fields are destroyed so that they resemble the back of a tortoise. The demons of drought produce calamity. The dark people [Footnote: A term denoting the Chinese.] pray earnestly while crops are being destroyed. We pray that abundant, limpid liquid may descend to purify and refresh the whole world. The clouds of incense rise."

This plaint is repeated thrice and is followed by an invocation:

"Wholeheartedly we cast ourselves to the earth, O Triratna, who dost exist eternally in the realm of _dharma_ of the ten directions."

The leader remains quiet a long time with his eyes closed, visualizing the Buddhas, the Bodhisattvas, the dragon kings, and the saints, all with their heavenly eyes and ears knowing that this region is afflicted with drought, that an altar has been constructed and that all have come to make petition. This meditation is regarded as of chief importance. It is followed by an announcement to the effect that the sutra praying for rain was given by the Buddha, that a drought is afflicting the land, that the altar has been erected in accordance with the regulations and that prayer is being made for rain. But fearing that something may have been overlooked, the magic formula of "the king of light who turns the wheel" is read seven times so as to remedy such oversight.

The altar having thus been cleansed of all impurities, the rain sutra is opened and the one hundred and eighty-eight dragon kings are urged by name in groups of ten to take action. The formula is as follows:

"We with our whole heart invite such and such dragon kings to come. We desire that the heart and wisdom which knows others intuitively will move the spirits above to obey the Buddha, to take pity on the people below and to come to our province and send down sweet rain."

When the dragons have all been duly invited, the monks chant suitable magical formulas, while the leader sits in meditation visualizing these dragon kings and their tender solicitude for the people in distress. The monastery bell is sounded and the wooden fish is beaten, while drums and cymbals add their effect. The whole is intended to draw the attention of the dragon kings to the drought. Then the fifty-four Buddhas are invited in a similar manner in groups of ten, the sixth group consisting of four. A similar form of address is used and similar magical formulas are recited with the noisy accompaniment. The ceremony concludes by the expression of the hope that the three jewels (Buddha, the Law and the Community of Monks) and the dragon kings will grant the rain.

Upon the altar are four copies of an announcement to the dragon kings and Buddhas. On the first day three copies are sent to them through the flames, one to the Buddhas, one to the dragon kings and one to the devas. One copy is read daily and then sent up at the thanksgiving ceremony. The announcement is as follows:

"We put our trust in the limitless, reverent ocean clouds, the dragons of august virtue and all their host, all dragon kings and holy saints. Their august virtue is difficult to measure. In accord with the command of Buddha they send liquid rain. May their quiet mercy descend to the altar; may they send down purity and freshness, spreading over the ten directions. We put our trust in the company of dragon kings of the clouds, the saints and the Bodhisattvas."

The offerings are made only in the morning inasmuch as the Buddhas, following ancient custom, are not supposed to eat after the noonday meal. Great care is taken that the altar shall not be desecrated by any one who eats meat or drinks wine. The magic formulas of great mercy are uttered or the name of Kuan Yin is repeated a thousand times. The monks, take turn in these services which continue day and night until rain comes.

(c) Its Meaning.—In the religious consciousness of the people is the idea that the drought is a punishment for sin. The altar is made pure and acceptable and sin is removed in various symbolic ways. This fits in with the idea that man is an intimate part of the world order. His sin disturbs the order of nature. Heaven manifests displeasures by sending down calamities upon men. Men should cease their wrongdoing which disturbs the natural order and should also wash away the effects of their sins. The services for rain with their magic formulas help to clear away the consequences of sin and to predispose Heaven to grant its blessings again.

Monasteries Are Supported Because They Control F§«-shui

The prayers for rain are an important part of the Chinese peasant's world order. Drought is the manifestation of Heaven's displeasure at the infraction of Heaven's laws. It calls for self-examination and repentance. Thus the monastery opens up the windows of the universal order as this touches the humble tiller of the soil.

The Buddhist monasteries not only hold services in time of drought, but also in time of flood and at times when plagues of grasshoppers afflict the land, or when diseases afflict human beings. Their adoption of Chinese customs led them to have special ceremonies at the eclipse of the sun and moon, although they knew the cause of the eclipse. Peasants and officials support the monastery because of these services regulating the wind and water influences and through them bringing the people into harmonious relation with the great world of spirits.

BUDDHISM AND THE FAMILY

One of the criticisms of the Chinese against Buddhism is that it is opposed to filial piety. According to Mencius the greatest unfilial act is to leave no progeny. In spite of this charge Buddhism has done much for the family. It has taken over the ethics of the family, filial piety, obedience and respect for elders, and has made them a part of its system. Transgression of these fundamental duties is visited by dire punishments in the next world. The faithful observance is followed not only by the rewards of the Confucian system, but results in the greatest rewards in the future life.

Kuan Yin, the Giver of Children and Protector of Women

Buddhism has done more. Out of its atmosphere of love and mercy toward all beings has developed Kuan Yin, the ideal of Chinese womanhood, the goddess of Mercy, who embodies the Chinese ideal of beauty, filial piety and compassion toward the weak and suffering. She is especially the goddess of women, being interested in all their affairs. Her image is found in almost every household and her temples have a place in every part of China.

A brief history of this deity will enable us to understand the significance of the cult. Kuan Yin started as a male god in India, called Aval?ö¬ara, who was worshipped from the third to the seventh century of our era. He was the protector of sailors and people in danger. In the course of time, either in China or in India, the god became a goddess. Some think that this was due to the influence of Christianity. In China both forms survive, though the goddess is better known. A Buddhist once said that a Bodhisattva is neither male nor female and appears in whatever form is convenient.

Kuan Yin is a very popular goddess. Her experiences in Hades are dramatically presented by traveling theatrical companies. Her deeds of mercy are portrayed in art. Her well known story runs as follows:

Kuan Yin was the daughter of the ruler of a prosperous kingdom located somewhere near the island of Sumatra. Her birth was announced to the queen by a dream. The little girl ate no meat nor milk. Her disposition was very good. Her intelligence was most extraordinary. Once she read anything she never forgot it.

At the age of sixteen her father tried to betroth her to a young prince. She refused and decided to give herself to a life of fasting and abstinence. Angered b-v her obstinacy the father ordered her to take off her court dress and jewels, to put on the garb of a servant and to carry water for the garden. The garden never looked so beautiful. The daughter also looked well and showed no signs of weariness, because the gods assisted her in her work.

Relenting a little the king sent an older sister to urge Kuan Yin to accept the husband he had found for her. When she refused, he sent her to a monastery and charged the abbess to treat her harshly, so that she might be forced to return home. Expecting to win the king's favor, the abbess put the most unpleasant tasks on the girl. But again the gods assisted her and made her work light, so that her tasks were always well done and the young woman was cheerful.

One day the report came to the king that his daughter was associating with a young monk discussing heterodox doctrines and that she had given birth to a child. This news so enraged the king that he burned the monastery, killing many monks. The princess was captured and brought before him. Inasmuch as she was obdurate, the king ordered her to be executed. The executioner's sword, however, broke into a thousand pieces without doing her any injury. The king then ordered her to be strangled. A golden image sixteen feet high appeared on the spot. The princess laughed and cried: "Where there was no image, an image appeared. I see the real form. When body flesh is strangled, then appear the lights of ten thousand roads." She went to purgatory and purgatory at once changed into paradise. Yama, in order to save his purgatory, sent her back to the world. She appeared at Puto, an island off the coast of Chekiang near Ningpo. Here she rescued sailors and performed many miracles for people in distress.

In the meantime the father, who had committed many sins, became sick. His allotted time of life had been shortened by twenty years. Moreover, an ulcer grew on his body for every one of the five hundred monks he had killed when he burned the monastery. A miserable, loathsome old man, he came to an old monk, who was really the princess in disguise, and asked for help. The monk told him that an eye and an arm of a blood relative made into medicine was the only cure for his trouble. The two living daughters were willing to make such an offering, but their husbands would not permit them to do so. The old monk urged the monarch to take up a life of abstinence, to rebuild the monastery he had burned, and to provide money for services to take the five hundred monks whom he had killed through purgatory. He also said that a nun in the convent would offer an arm and an eye. When the monarch entered the monastery, he found hanging before the incense burner an arm and an eye. These were boiled, mixed with medicine and rubbed on the king's body. He soon became well. Further inquiry revealed that these members belonged to his daughter.

This is the story of the most popular goddess in China. She is worshipped by her devotees on the first and fifteenth of every month, on the nineteenth of the sixth month, when she became a Bodhisattva, and on the nineteenth of the ninth month, when she put on the necklace. A month after marriage every young bride is presented with an image of the Goddess of Mercy, an incense-burner and candlesticks.

This goddess is worshipped whenever trouble comes to man or woman. Her names signify her willingness to listen to all prayers. She is the "one who regards the voice," i.e., prayer; "one who hears the prayers of the world;" "one who regards and exists by himself as sovereign;" "the ancestor of Buddha who regards prayer;" "one who frees from fear;" "Buddha the august king;" "the great white robed scholar;" "great compassion and mercy."

Kuan Yin, the Model of Local Mother-Goddesses

This conception is the creation of the social and religious consciousness of the women in China. It reveals their aspirations for mercy, compassion, filial piety and for the beauty that crowns a well developed character. Such an ideal does not mean that these have been realized in all the numerous homes of the Chinese, but it manifests their sense of such an ideal to be realized in life and their ardent longing for its realization.

Mother-goddesses are found all over China and they have all of them been influenced by Kuan Yin. Some of them have originated with actual women who were deified after death. Here is the story of one of these goddesses who presides over the censer in a small temple in Formosa. She was born in the province of Kuangtung. At the age of seven she was adopted by a family as the future wife of their eighteen-year-old son. One day while crossing a river he was drowned. This was a great blow to her. When she was fourteen years old the father of the family died. The two women, thus left alone, wept bitterly day and night. The comfort of relatives was of little avail. The mother was becoming emaciated with grief. The daughter, unable to bear the strain any longer, washed herself, burned incense before the ancestral tablet of her betrothed, and then took this vow:

"I am willing to remain a virgin, to apply myself to carrying water and working at the mortar and to serve my mother-in-law. If I cherish any other purpose and change my chastity and obedience, may Heaven slay me and earth annihilate me."

When the mother heard this vow she stopped her weeping. Inasmuch as they had no uncle to look after them, they worked day and night. A relative of her future husband gave her one of his sons as an adopted son. The child died after a few months. This was a great grief. Then the mother died. The daughter sold her possessions to obtain money for a proper burial. She had only a coarse mourning cloth for her dress. After a while she adopted a child as her son. When he grew up she found him a wife who served her as faithfully as she had served her mother-in-law. When she was eighty years old, she dreamed that the golden maid and jade messenger of Kuan Yin stood beside her saying: "The court of Heaven has ordered you to become a god (sh©«." She died soon after this. She said of herself:

"Shang Ti took compassion upon me during my life, because with a firm heart I kept my chastity and served my mother-in-law with complete obedience. Therefore he gave me the office of Kuan Pin. I have performed my duties in several places. Now I am transferred to Formosa."

This story and many others like it mirror the moral ideals of the women of China in the midst of their struggles for help and light and guidance.

Exhortations on Family Virtues

The Buddhists issue a large number of tracts. These are very commonly paid for by devotees who make a vow that, if their parent becomes well, they will pay for the printing of several hundred or thousand of these tracts for free distribution. In these tracts are usually many stories illustrating the rewards of filial piety. The story is told in one of them about a Mrs. Chin whose father-in-law being ill was unable to sleep for sixty days. His condition grew worse. Mrs. Chin knelt before Kuan Yin's altar, cut out a piece of flesh from her arm and cooked it with the father's food. His health at once improved and he lived to the age of seventy-seven. Another story is told in the same tract of a woman who cut out a piece of her liver and gave it as medicine to her mother-in-law.

These Buddhist tracts take up all the moral habits which make the family and clan strong and stable and surround them by the highest sanctions. A tract picked up in a Buddhist temple at Hangchow purports to be the revelation of the will of Buddha. It urges sixteen virtues. The first is filial piety. The tract says:

"Filial piety is the chief of all virtues. Heaven and Earth honor filial piety. There is no greater sin than to cherish unfilial thoughts. The spirits know the beginning of such thoughts. Heaven openly rewards a heart that is filial."

The second one mentioned is another important family virtue, namely, reverence:

"The saints, sages, immortals and Buddhas are the outgrowth of reverence. The greatest sin is to lack reverence for father and mother. When brothers lack reverence for one another, they harm the hands and feet. When husband and wife lack reverence, the harmony of the household is ruined. When friends do not have reverence, they bring about calamity."

Then follow similar exhortations on sincerity, justice, self-restraint, forbearance, benevolence, generosity, absence of pride, covetousness, lying, adultery, mutual love, self-denial, hope for the consolations of religion and for an undivided heart ruled by peace. These are virtues quite essential to the integrity of the family. They are taught, not in the abstract but by the exhibition of shining examples, by vivid representations of the rewards both here and hereafter, and by pictures of awful punishments. So by precept and example, by threat of punishment here and hereafter and by declaration of reward in the future Buddhism has tried to maintain the family virtues of the Confucian system and has attempted to permeate them by the spirit of sacrifice. Still it has always been the sacrifice of the weak for the strong, of the young for the aged, of the low for the high, of women for men.

Services for the Dead

Buddhism very early took over the relatively simple services for the dead and developed them into an elaborate ritual which made very vivid the spiritual universe which Buddhism introduced. In the sixth century a service was held in behalf of the father-in-law of Emperor Ning Ti (516-528 A. D.) for seven times every seven days. He feasted a thousand monks every day, and caused seven persons to become monks. On the hundredth day after the death he feasted ten thousand monks and caused twenty-seven persons to become monks.

Since that time services on every seventh day after the decease until the forty-ninth day, when a grand finale ends the ceremonies, have been very popular.

The object of such services is to conduct the soul of the dead through purgatory, in order that it may return to life or enter the Western Paradise. This is done by making a pleasing offering to the guardians and officers of purgatory, and to the gods and Bodhisattvas whose mercy saves people. Numerous missives are consigned to the flames, informing the rulers of the nether world about the soul of the dead; offerings of gold and silver, of various articles of apparel, of trunks, houses, and servants are made, all, however, made out of bamboo frames covered with paper. Various powerful incantations are recited which force open the gates of purgatory and let the soul out.

The services may be crowded into one day or they may be held on every seventh day until the forty-ninth day, i.e., seven sevens. Various explanations are given' for these services.

During the first week the soul of the dead arrives at the "Demon Gate Barrier." Here money is demanded by the demons on the ground that in his last transmigration the deceased borrowed money. Accordingly large quantities of silver shoes [Footnote: The silver used for this purpose is molded, in accordance with ancient usage, in the shape of shoes and carried about in that form by merchants.] must be sent to the dead so that he may settle all claims and avoid beating and inconvenience. During the second week the soul arrives at a place where he is weighed. If the evil outweighs the good, the soul is sawn asunder and ground to powder. In the third week he comes to the "Bad Dog" village. Here good people pass unharmed, but the evil are torn by the fierce beasts until the blood flows. In the fourth week the soul is confronted with a large mirror in which he sees his evil deeds and their consequences, seeing himself degraded in the next transmigration to a beast. In the fifth week the soul views the scenes in his own village.

In the sixth week he reaches the bridge which spans the "Inevitable River." This bridge is 100,000 feet high and one and three-tenths of an inch wide. It is crossed by riding astride as on a horse. Beneath rushes the whirl-pool filled with serpents darting their heads to and fro. At the foot of the bridge lictors force unwilling travelers to ascend. The good do not cross this bridge, but are led by "golden youth" to gold and silver bridges which cross the stream on either side of this "Bridge of Sighs."

In the seventh week the soul is taken first to Mrs. Wang who dispenses a drink which blots out all memories of the earthly life. Then the individual enters the great wheel of transmigration. This is divided into eighty-one sections from which one hundred and eight thousand small and tortuous paths radiate out into the four continents of the world. The soul is directed along one of these paths and is duly reborn in the world as an animal or as a human being or passes on into the Western Paradise.

In imitation of this bridge a bridge is built of tables in front of the home of the dead. At the end the tables are placed upside down and a lantern placed on each table-leg. At night this bridge is illuminated. A company of monks repeat their prayers and incantations, while others mount upon the bridge to impersonate devils. The pious son with the tablet of his deceased parent comes to take his father over the bridge. When his way is disputed by the demons, he falls on his knees and begs and gives them money, negotiating the passage at last with the aid of a large quantity of silver.

Another ceremony is the breaking through purgatory. Five supplications duly signed are addressed to the proper authorities, four being suspended at each of the four sides of the table and one at the center. Tiles are then placed over the table or on the ground. After incantations have been repeated to the accompaniment of the sounding of the bell and the wooden fish, the supplications are burned and the tiles are broken as a symbol of breaking through purgatory and of releasing the soul.

Thus Buddhism has taken over the most important function of ancestor worship, has extended it and made it more significant to each individual as well as to the family.

BUDDHISM AND SOCIAL LIFE

How the Laity is Trained in Buddhist Ideas

A common way of emphasizing moral ideas among the people by Buddhist teachers is the use of tracts purporting to have a divine origin. The following gives the substance of such a tract:

Not long ago in the province of Shantung, there was a sharp and sudden clap of thunder. After the frightened people had collected their wits, they discovered a small book written in red in front of the house of a certain Mr. Li. Mr. Li picked up the book, copied it and read it reverently. He gave a copy to Mr. Ma, the prefect, but Mr. Ma did not believe in the book. Thereupon Maitra®, the Messiah of the Buddhists, spoke from the sky as follows:

"These are the years of the final age. The people under heaven do not reverence Heaven and Earth, they are not filial to father and mother, they do not respect their superiors. They cheat the fatherless, impose upon the widow, oppress the weak; they use large weights for themselves and small measures for others. They injure the good. They covet for their own profit. They cheat men of money, use the five grains carelessly, kill the cow that draws the plow. This volume is sent for their special benefit. If they recite it they will avoid trouble. If they disbelieve, the years with the cyclical character _Ping_ and _Ting_ will have fields without men to plant them and houses without

men to live in them. In the fifth month of these years evil serpents will infest the whole country. In the eighth and ninth months the bodies of evil men will fill the land.
*"Those who believe this book and propagate its teachings will not encounter the ten sorrows of the age: war, fire, no peace day and night, separation of man and wife, the scattering of the sons and daughters, evil men spread over the country, dead bones unburied, clothing with no one to wear it, rice with no one to eat it, and the difficulty of ever seeing a peaceful year. Sù*amuni foreseeing this final age sent down this volume in Shantung. The Goddess of Mercy saw the sorrows of all living beings.*
*Maitra® commanded the two runners of T'ai Shan, the god of the Eastern Mountain, to investigate the conduct of men and as a first punishment to increase the price of rice, and then besides the ten sorrows already mentioned above, to inflict the punishments of flood, fire, wind, thunder, tigers, snakes, sword, disease, famine and cold. The rule of Sù*amuni which has lasted twelve thousand years is now fulfilled, and Maitra® succeeds to his place."*

These sorrows may be escaped by reciting this sutra whose substance we find above. If it is repeated three times the person will escape the calamity of fire and water. If one man passes it on to ten men and ten men pass it on to a hundred, they will escape the calamities of sword, disease and imprisonment, and receive blessings which cannot be measured. He who in addition to repeating the sutra practices abstinence will insure peace for himself. He who presents one hundred copies to others will insure his personal peace. He who presents a thousand copies will insure the peace of his family. He who is attacked by disease, may escape it by taking five cash of the reign of Shun Chih (1644-1661 A. D.), the first emperor of the Ch'ing dynasty, one mace of the seed of cypress, one mace of the bark of mulberry, boil in one bowl of water until only eight-tenths of the water remain, drink and he will become well.

In this way the five Buddhist commandments for the laity not to kill any living creature, not to steal, not to commit adultery, not to lie, and not to use intoxicating liquor are propagated and made real to the common man. The method is quite efficient. Whole provinces have been put into a panic by such prophecies.

Effect of Ideals of Mercy and Universal Love

The command not to kill any living being has had considerable influence in China. There are volumes of stories telling of the punishments which will be visited upon those who disobey and of the rewards of those who release living animals. Every monastery has a special place for animals thus released by pious devotees.

There is a popular story about a fishmonger of the T'ang dynasty who was taken sick and during his illness dreamed that he was taken to purgatory. His body was aflame with fire and pained him as though he were being roasted. Flying fiery chariots with darting flames swept around him and burned his body. Ten thousand fish strove with one another to get a bite of his flesh. The ruler of the lower regions accused him of killing many fish and hence his punishment. For a number of days he was hanging between life and death. His relatives were urged to perform some works of penance. They had his fishing implements burned. With reverent hearts they made two images of Kuan Yin, presented offerings and repented. The whole family performed abstinence, stopped killing living things, printed and gave away over a hundred copies of the Diamond Sutra, and ferried over a large number of souls through purgatory. As a result of their efforts the sick man became well.

The following comment was made on the above story by a scholar. If its premises are granted, the conclusion is inevitable:

> *"If the fiery chariots are seal, why does not man see them? If they are false, how is it that man feels the pain? But where do the fiery chariots come from? They come from the heart and head of the one who kills fish. The fire in the heart (heart belongs to the element fire) causes destruction. The chariot fire also causes destruction."*

This attitude of mercy has been extended to human beings. There are numerous tracts against the drowning of little girls in those regions where this custom is prevalent. One tells the following story: In the province of Kwangtung there lived a Mrs. Chang who daily burned incense and repeated Buddha's name. One day she and her husband died. Much to their surprise and consternation Yama (the potentate of hell) decided that Mr. Chang must become a pig and Mrs. Chang a dog. Mrs. Chang accordingly went to Yama and said, "During life we honored Buddha and so why should we become animals after death?" Yama said, "What use is it to honor Buddha? During life you drowned three girls whom I sent into life. People with the face of a man and the heart of a beast, should they not be punished?" The husband accordingly took on a pig's skin and the wife a dog's. Then by a dream they revealed to their brother Chang number two that, although they repeated Buddha's name, they were not permitted to be reborn as men, because they had drowned little girls.

Perhaps the extent of this spirit, of mercy and its possibilities may be illustrated by the reverence for the ox. While there is a great deal of cruelty in China to animals and men, it is rarely that one sees an ox abused. Up to the advent of the foreigner an ox was not killed for meat. In many places in China today the slaughter of an ox would bring the punishments of the law upon the butcher. No doubt this reverence is due to the great Indian reverence for the cow. The law of kindness has been extended to other animals, taking the rather spectacular form of releasing a few decrepit animals and allowing them to spend their last days in a monastery compound. There are many kindly things done in China. The dead are buried, the sick are provided with medicine. Every year numerous wadded garments are given away to poor people. Various groups carrying on a humble ministry of helpfulness have found a real inspiration in the ideals held before them in Buddhism, the rewards promised and punishments threatened.

Relation to Confucian Ideals

Why have not these ideals exercised a larger influence in China? The answer is quite simple. The activities of the monks have been strenuously opposed by the Confucian state system. The philosopher, Chang Nan-hsiian, a contemporary of Chu-Hsi, states concisely for us the differences betwen Confucianism and Buddhism in his comment on a passage in the _Book of Records._

"Strong drink is a thing intended to be-used in offering sacrifices and entertaining guests,—such employment of it is what

Heaven has prescribed. But men by their abuse of such drink come to lose their virtue and destroy their persons—such employment of it is what Heaven has annexed its terrors to. The Buddhists, hating the use of things where Heaven sends down its terrors, put away as well the use of them which Heaven has prescribed.

"For instance, in the use of meats and drinks, there is such a thing as wildly abusing and destroying the creatures of Heaven. The Buddhists, disliking this, confine themselves to a vegetable diet, while we only abjure wild abuse and destruction. In the use of clothes, again, there is such a thing as wasteful extravagance. The Buddhists, disliking this, will have no clothes but those of a dark and sad color, while we only condemn extravagance. They, further, through dislike of criminal connection between the sexes, would abolish the relation between husband and wife, while we denounce only the criminal connection.

"The Buddhists, disliking the excesses to which the evil desires of men lead, would put away, along with them, the actions which are in accordance with the justice of heavenly principles, while we, the orthodox, put away the evil desires of men, whereupon what are called heavenly principles are the more brightly seen. Suppose the case of a stream of water. The Buddhists, through dislike of its being foul with mud, proceed to dam it up with earth. They do not consider that when the earth has dammed up the stream, the supply of water will be cut off. It is not so with us, the orthodox. We seek only to cleanse away the mud and sand, so that the pure water may be available for use. This is the difference between the Buddhists and the Learned School." [Footnote: _Shu King,_ Pt. V, Bk. X, p. 122.]

This statement reveals at once the opposition of the sect of the Learned and the influence which Buddhism exerted upon its members.

Buddhism while enjoying occasional favor from the state was often zealously persecuted. In 819 Han Yii issued his celebrated act of accusation. In 845 the emperor Wu Tsung issued his decree of secularization. At that time 4600 monasteries and 40,000 smaller establishments were pulled down and 265,000 monks and nuns were sent back to lay life. Their rich lands were confiscated. Under the Ming dynasty, as well as under the Ch'ing dynasty, Buddhism enjoyed a precarious existence. Whether Buddhism would have improved the moral conditions of the Chinese; if it had been given a free hand, is difficult to affirm. Still its failure is at least partly due to the opposition of Confucian orthodoxy.

The Embodiment of Buddhist Ideals in the Vegetarian sects

The state persecutions of Buddhism forced it to leave temporarily its institutional life and trust itself to the people. These persecutions were usually followed by a revival of piety and religion among the people. The Buddhist teachers gathered about themselves a large number of lay devotees who formed societies which practice religious rites in secret. These sects have preserved the genuine Buddhist piety, not only in times of persecution, but at times when the Buddhist organization under imperial favor was departing from its simplicity.

A number of these sects have continued under different names for several centuries. For example, the Tsai Li, a society now enjoying a quiet existence in North China, is successor to the White Lotus society. The latter started in the fifth century. Its members sought salvation in the Pure Land of Amitabha. In the eleventh century it enjoyed imperial favor. During the Mongol dynasty it fought against the throne with rebels and placed one of its leaders, Chu Y?ang, a monk, on the throne, who became the founder of the Ming dynasty. The sect was soon proscribed and its members persecuted by the government. During the Ch'ing dynasty it took part in a rebellion and was ruthlessly exterminated. At present it goes under the name of _Tsai Li,_ i.e., within the Li or principles of the three religions. It is a mediator among the three religions. There are thirty-one organizations of this sect in Peking and branches throughout North China. The society forbids the use of wine and opium, though it does not forbid the use of meat. It usually has a Buddhist image, Kuan Yin or some other. It uses Buddhist prayers and incantations. The outstanding doctrines held during its long history have been the hope of salvation in the Western Heaven of Amit¨(a, the early coming of Maitra®, the Buddhist Messiah, and the large use of magic formulas and incantations.

Another sect which embodies Buddhist ideals is the Chin Tan, the sect of the philosopher's stone or pill of immortality. Its founder was the writer of the Nestorian tablet and so the sect is related to Christianity. It exalts the teaching of universal love. This is one of several examples of a supposed contact between Buddhism and Christianity.

These sects of which the two above are examples are present in all parts of China. They obey the five Buddhist commandments for laymen. The members spend much time in fasting and prayer, and in the repetition of Buddhist books. Their lives as a rule are simple and sincere. They are preparing for rebirth in the land of Amit¨(a, or are expecting the early coming of the Buddhist Messiah to set this world right. In the meantime, by means of incantations, personal regimen and cooperative action they are doing all they can to usher in a better state.

Pilgrimages

Pilgrimages are very popular in China. The famous Buddhist shrines are Wu T'ai Shan in Shansi, Puto on the coast of Chekiang, Chiu Hua Shan in Anhwei, and Omei Shan in Szechuan. These, one on each side of China, represent the four elements of Buddhist science, wind, water, fire and earth. They are also the centers of the worship of the four great Bodhisattvas, Wenshu, Kuan Yin, Titsang and Puhsien. Besides these large centers there are many others to which pilgrims direct their footsteps.

In the spring of the year, when the god of spring covers the earth with a green mantle, when the sky and winds call, many start on their pilgrimage. Many go singly and laboriously, kneeling and bowing every few steps. Others go in happy companies, chaperoned by a pious, village dame, who has organized the group. Some go because their turn has come. They are members of a guild which has a fund devoted to pilgrimages by its members. Some go for the performance of a vow made to Kuan Yin, when the father was sick unto death and the goddess prolonged his life. To others it is the culmination of a pious life. All go for the joy which travel in the spring gives.

Puto, an island off the coast of Chekiang, is the goal of many pilgrims from all parts of China. In, the monasteries on the island are about two thousand monks. In the pilgrim season this number is increased to ten thousand monks and thousands of lay pilgrims.

A group of pilgrims was going along merrily. The sun was bright, lighting up the white caps on the deep blue sea. Spring was rioting all about. One member was an abbot from Hangchow. A small, humble-looking man with a few straggling long hairs where the mustache usually grows, was a lay Buddhist from Wuchang. One was a bright young monk from Tientsin. Last, but almost omnipresent and always bubbling over, was a servant of the abbot from Hangchow. He was in the presence of divinity and his whole life was heightened for the time being. "Why did you come!" they were asked. "We came to worship the holy mother, Kuan Yin." When they entered a shrine each purchased three sticks, of incense and two candles and reverently placed them before the image of the goddess, kneeling and bowing. Then they sat and partook of the tea offered by the attendant. After paying a small gratuity, they went on to the next shrine.

On the way a large black snake as thick as an arm lazily crossed over the road. They stood, reverent and awestruck, until he disappeared in the grass, remarking that this was a good omen. When crossing a sand dune piled up by the winds the abbot from Hangchow remarked that this was called the flying sand, wafted there by the goddess who took pity on some travelers who had been compelled to cross a narrow strait in order to come to a cave. This cave, called Fan Yin Tung, is one of the rifts made by an earthquake and washed out by wind and waves. Below it rushes the tide; from above the sun sends down a few rays. Each pilgrim after offering incense looks into the darkness to see whether he can behold in the dark cavern an image of some Buddha. One sees Kuan Yin and is acclaimed as having had a good vision. Another sees the Laughing Buddha. All exclaim that he has been the most fortunate of all, for this Buddha is the Messiah to come and he who beholds him will be blessed. So from place to place they wander, chatting and seeing the sights of the island. Thus thousands are doing in various parts of China, and in this way strengthening the hold of Buddhism upon themselves and their communities.

BUDDHISM AND THE FUTURE LIFE

Before the advent of Buddhism the Chinese had only a vague idea regarding life after death. The Land and Water Classic mentions the Tu Shuo mountain in the Eastern Sea, under which spirits of the dead live, the entrance guarded by two spirits, Sh «Tu and Y? who are in general control of the demons. In some parts of China the names or pictures, of these spirits are placed on the doors of a house to guard it. The Taoists early developed the idea of a western paradise presided over by the Queen of the West, located at first in the K'un Lun mountains and later in the islands of the Eastern Sea. This heaven, however, was limited to Taoist hermits and mystics. Buddhism made a complete purgatory and heaven known to every one in China.

The Buddhist Purgatory

This is really Buddhism's most noteworthy addition to China's religious equipment; Buddhism lays much stress upon the experiences of a soul immediately after death. Its punishments are well known to every individual. The temple of the City Guardian found in every walled city has a replica of the court in purgatory over which he presides. In the temples of T'ai Shan there is an elaborate exhibit of the tortures inflicted on culprits in purgatory. Every funeral service conducted by Buddhists or Taoists is intended to conduct the soul of the dead through purgatory and pictures vividly the progressive experiences from the first seventh day to the seventh seventh day. On the the seventh month, on the fifteenth day [about August] a special service is held for the souls of the dead in purgatory. Furthermore, every community has a general service [about October] for the souls of those who died a violent death or who have no one to look after them. During the war many services were thus held for those who died on the battlefields of Europe. At such services the scenes in purgatory are vividly portrayed by pictures and figures. The temples distribute tracts with pictures of purgatory so that women may see them and understand. On the stage are often acted powerful plays whose scenes are laid in Hades. This propaganda is perhaps the most efficient of its kind.

Purgatory is depicted as consisting of ten courts each surrounded by small hells, where the soul undergoes punishment and cleansing. The fifth court, which may be taken as an example of the other courts, is in charge of Yen Lo or Yama. Yama was once in charge of the first court, but his tender heart pitied the souls who came before him and sent them back to earth. Because of this leniency he was placed in charge of the fifth court.

When a soul has passed through the first four courts and it has been discovered that there is no good conduct to its credit, it is led to the fifth court and examined every seven days regarding past conduct. In order to get back to the world of men, it eagerly promises to complete various unfinished vows, such as to repair monasteries, schools, bridges, or roads, to clean wells, to deepen rivers, to distribute good books, to release animals, to take care of aged parents, or to bury them suitably. But it is plainly told that the gods know its artifices, and that now these unfinished tasks can never be completed. The gods have reached the unanimous opinion that no injustice is being done. Accordingly there is no appeal, but each soul is led by attendants with bulls' heads and horses' faces to a tower whence they may see their native village. Its front is in the shape of a bow with a perimeter of twenty-seven miles; its height is four hundred and ninety feet. It is guarded by walls of sword trees.

Good men, whose deeds of omission are balanced by the good they have done, return to life. Only souls judged to be evil see their village from this tower. These can see their own families moving about, and can hear their conversation. They realize how they disobeyed the teachings of their elders. They see that the earthly goods for which they have struggled are of no value. Their plottings rise up with lurid reality. They see how they planned a new marriage although already married, how they appropriated fields, state property, and falsified accounts, putting the blame on persons who were dead. While they observe their village they behold their erstwhile friends touch their coffin and inwardly rejoice. They hear themselves called selfish and insincere. But their punishment does not stop here. They behold their children punished by magistrates, their women afflicted with strange diseases, their daughters ravished, their sons led astray, their property taken away, the ancestral house burned and their business ruined. From this tower all passes before them as a lurid dream and they are stricken in heart.

About the fifth court are sixteen small hells where the soul is punished. In each one are stakes buried in the ground and fierce animals. The hands and feet of the guilty one are bound to a stake, his body is opened with small knives, and his heart and intestines quickly devoured.

In each of these sixteen hells is a certain type of sinner: (1) Those who do not reverence the gods and demons and who doubt the existence of rewards and punishments; (2) those who hurt and kill living beings; (3) those who break their vows to do good; (4) those who resort to heterodox practices and vainly hope to attain eternal life; (5) those who upbraid good men, fear the wicked and hate men because they do not die speedily; (6) those who strive with other people and then put the blame upon them; (7) men who force women; and women who seduce young men, and all who have libidinous desires; (8) those who gain profit for themselves by injuring others; (9) the stingy and those who absolutely disregard others, whether alive or dead, giving them no help in dire need, when they can do so without injury to themselves; (10) those who steal and put the crime upon others; (11) those who requite favors with hate; (12) those whose hearts are perverse and poisonous, who instigate others to do wrong even if they may not have carried out their suggestion; (13) those who tempt others by deceit; (14) those who involve others in their squabbles and in gambling and then themselves win out; (15) those who stubbornly persist in their false ideas, do not repent, and slander others; (16) those who hate good and virtuous men.

Besides these sixteen sorts of sinners the fifth court deals with other types of wicked people; those who do not believe in rewards and punishments after death, who hinder good causes, who burn incense without a sincere heart, speak of the sins of others, who burn books that urge men to be good and worship the Great Dipper, but persist in eating meat; those who hate men; who repeat sutras and incantations, and take part in religious ceremonies, but do not fast beforehand; who slander the Buddhist and Taoist religions; who know how to read, but refuse to read the ancient and modern exhortations regarding rewards and punishments; who dig into graves and destroy their marks, who purposely set fire to trees and underbrush, or are careless with fire in their own houses; who shoot arrows at animals with the intent, to kill; who urge and tempt the sick and weak to enter into contests of any kind with themselves; who throw tiles and stones over neighboring walls, poison fish in the river, fire guns, or make nets or traps for birds; who sow salt on the ground, who do not bury dead eats and snakes very deep and thus cause death to those who dig; who cause men to dig the frozen ground in winter or spring (the vapors of earth chill such diggers to death); who tear down adjoining walls and compel their neighbors to move the kitchen stove; who appropriate public highways, lands, close wells and stop gutters. Those who have committed any of the above sins are taken, to the tower whence they can see their own village and then are consigned to the great crying hell, Rr-ava, that is, the fourth of the Buddhist hot hells. [Footnote: Buddhism distinguishes hot and cold hells. In a country like India severe cold is a serious torture.] Thence they go to their respective small hells. When their time has expired, they are examined in order to see whether they have any other sins which need punishment.

Those who have committed any of the above sins may not only escape punishment, but may have their punishment in the sixth court lessened, if they fast regularly on the eighth day of the first month and take a vow not to commit these sins. Some sins, however, cannot be arranged for in such a way, such as the killing of living beings and hurting them; the associating with heretics; committing fornication with women and then poisoning them; committing adultery, violence, envy, or injuring the good name of others; stealing, requiting favors with hatred, and hearing exhortation but not repenting. These are major sins.

Its Social Value

The social value of purgatory is quite plain from the description of the fifth court and of the sinners who are punished therein. Purgatory is the social mirror of China, wherein the consequences of all unsocial acts are pictured in such a vivid way as to deter the individual from committing them. It is effective in China, not only because of the realistic presentation, but because the opinion of the community is against such acts and in favor of repressing them on every occasion.

The Buddhist Heaven

Buddhism brought into China not only a fully developed purgatory but also a heaven which all may enter. The sovereign of the western heaven is Amit¨(a (or in Chinese O-mi-to-fo), with whom Kuan Yin, the goddess of Mercy, is usually associated. Amit¨(a is explained as meaning "boundless age." The original meaning is "boundless light," which suggests a Persian origin with Mannichean influences. The translations of the Amit¨(a sutras were wholly made by natives of central Asia.

Amit¨(a is one of the thousand Buddhas; he is regarded as the reflex of Sakyamuni and is connected also in his earthly incarnation with a monk called Dharmá*ra. This monk desired to become a Buddha. This wish he presented to L?'varar¡* asking him to teach him as to what a Buddha and a Buddha country ought to be. L?'varar¡* imparted this knowledge. Then the monk after meditation returned having made forty-eight vows that he would not become a Buddha, until all living beings should attain salvation in his heaven.

The eighteenth vow expresses his ideal:

"O Bhagavat, if those beings who have directed their thought towards the highest perfect knowledge in other worlds, and who, after having heard my name, when I have obtained Bodhi (knowledge), have meditated on me with serene thoughts; if at the moment of their death, after having approached them surrounded by an assembly of monks, I should not stand before them worshipped by them, that is, so that their thoughts should not be troubled, then may I not obtain the highest perfect knowledge."

A few extracts from the _Amit¨(a Vy?? will illustrate the Buddhist idea of life in this Pure Land:

"In the western region beyond one hundred thousand myriads of Buddhist lands there is a world. Great Happiness by name. This land has a Buddha called Amit¨(a. The living beings there do not suffer any pain, but enjoy all happiness. Therefore, it is called the land of Pure Delight... the land of Pure Delight has seven precious fountains full of water containing the eight virtues. The bottom of these fountains is covered with golden sand. On four sides there are steps made of gold, silver, crystal and glass, precious stones, red pearls, and highly polished agates. In the pools are variously colored, light emitting lotus flowers as large as cart wheels, delicate, admirable, odorous and pure..."

"The Buddha of this land makes heavenly music. It is covered with gold. Morning and evening during six hours it rains the wonderful celestial flowers (Erythrina Indica). All the inhabitants of this land on clear mornings after dressing offer these celestial flowers to the hundred thousand myriads of Buddhas of the regions who return to their country at meal time. When they have eaten they go away again."

"This country possesses every kind of wonderful varicolored birds, the white egret, the peacock, the parrot, the s'rarika (a

long legged bird), the Kalavingka (a sweet voiced bird)... All these birds, morning and evening during the six hours, utter forth a beautiful harmonious sound. Their song produces the five _indrya_ (roots of faith, energy, memory, ecstatic meditation, wisdom), the five _bala_ (the powers of faith, energy, memory, meditation and wisdom), the seven _bodhyanga_ (the seven degrees of intelligence, memory, discrimination, energy, tranquillity, ecstatic contemplation, indifference), and the eight portions of the correct path _marga,_ (the possession of correct views, decision and purity of thought and will, the ability of reproducing any sound uttered in the universe, vow of poverty, asceticism, attainment of meditative abstraction of self-control, religious recollectedness, honesty and virtue), and such doctrines. When all beings of this land have heard the music, they declare their faithfulness to the Buddha, Dharma and the Sangha (the Buddha, the Law and the community of monks)."

As to those who enter this land it says:

"All living beings who hear this should make a vow to be born in that land. How can they reach the Pure Land? All very good men will gather in that place... He whose blessedness and virtue are great can be born into that country. If there is a good man or woman who, on hearing of Amit¨(a, takes this name and holds it in his mind one, two, three, four, five, six, or seven days, and his whole heart is not distracted, to that man at death Amit¨(a will appear. His heart will not be disturbed. He will at once enter into life in the land of Pure Delight of Amit¨(a. I see this blessing and hence utter these words. Those living beings who hear these words should make a vow to be born in that land."

The Harmonization of These Ideas with Ancestor Worship

The extension of life beyond the grave in purgatory, or in the Pure Land and through transmigration was readily accepted in China. Both the new ideas and the disciplines through which to realize them were eagerly adopted, and have held their place to this day. In other lands the creation of a heaven and a hades has weakened the grip of ancestor worship and ultimately displaced it. In China the opposite result has obtained, due, no doubt, to the fact that the family system and along with it the supreme duty of filial piety were fostered by the state and Buddhism and its teachings were permitted only in so far as they bolstered it up. Another reason lies in the agricultural basis of China's civilization, reenforced by the great difficulty of communication, which tended to make the family system dominant in China. Today, the improvement of communication and the introduction of the industrial system of the West with the individual emphasis of modern education are factors which are weakening the family system and with it ancestral worship.

THE SPIRITUAL VALUES EMPHASIZED BY BUDDHISM IN CHINA

Near the House of Parliament in Peking is located a small monastery dedicated to the goddess of Mercy, Kuan Yin. Before her image the incense burners send forth curling clouds of smoke. The walls are decorated with old paintings of gods and goddesses. The temple with its courtyard has the appearance of prosperity. Its neat reception room, with its tables, chairs and clock, shows the influence of the modern world. Here a monk in the prime of life spent a few months recently lecturing on Buddhism to members of parliament and to scholars from various parts of China. Frequently the writer used to drop in of an afternoon to discuss Buddhism and its outlook. Usually a simple repast concluded these conversations, the substance of which forms the greater part of this section.

The Threefold Classification of Men Under Buddhism

"What does Buddhism do for men?"

"There are in the world at least three classes of men. The lowest class live among material things, they are occupied with possessions. Their life is entangled in the crude and coarse materials which they regard as real. A second, higher class, regard ideas as realities. They are not entangled in the maze of things, but are confused by ideas, ascribing reality to them. The third and highest class are those who by meditation have freed themselves from the thraldom of ideas and can enter the sixteen heavens."

Salvation for the Common Man

"What can Buddhism do for the lowest class?"

"For this class Buddhism has the ten prohibitions. Every man has in him ten evils, which must be driven out. Three have to do with evil in the body, namely, not to steal, not to kill, not to commit adultery; four belong to the mouth, lying, exaggeration, abuse, and ambiguous talk; three belong to the mind, covetousness, malice, and unbelief."

"Is not this entirely negative?"

"Yes, but it is necessary, for during the process of eliminating these evil deeds, man acquires patience and equanimity. Buddhism does not stop with the prohibitions. The believer must practice the ten charitable deeds. Not only must he remove the desire to kill living beings, but he must cultivate the desire to save all beings. Not only must he not steal, but he must assist men with his money. Not only must he not give himself to lasciviousness, but he must treat all men with propriety. So each prohibition involves a positive impulse to virtue, which is quite as essential as the refraining from evil."

"What energizing power does Buddhism provide?"

"First, is purgatory with its terrors. The evil man, seeing the consequences of his acts upon himself, becomes afraid to do them and does that which is good. Then there is transmigration with the danger of transmigration into beasts and insects. Again, there are the rewards in the paradise of Amit¨(a. Moreover, there is even the possibility not only of saving one's self, but by accumulated merit of saving one's parents and relatives and shortening their stay in purgatory."

The Place of Faith

"Can any man enter the western paradise of Amit¨(a?"

"Yes, it is open to all men. The sutra says: 'If there be any one who commits evil deeds, and even completes the ten evil actions, the five deadly sins and the like; that man, being himself stupid and guilty of many crimes, deserves to fall into a miserable path of existence and suffer endless pains during many long ages. On the eve of death he may meet a good and learned teacher who, soothing and encouraging him in various ways, will preach to him the excellent Law and teach him the remembrance of Buddha, but being harassed by pains', he will have no time to think of Buddha.'"

"What hope has such a man?"

"Even such a man has hope. The sutra says: 'Some good friend will say to him: Even if thou canst not exercise the remembrance of Buddha, utter the name of Buddha Amitabha.' Let him do so serenely with his voice uninterrupted; let him be (continually) thinking of Buddha, until he has completed ten times the thought, repeating 'Namah O-mi-to-fo,' I put my trust in Buddha! On the strength of (his merit of) uttering Buddha's name he will, during every repetition expiate the sins which involve him in births and deaths during eighty millions of long ages. He will, while dying, see a golden lotus-flower, like the disk of the sun, appearing before his eyes; in a moment he will be born in the world of highest happiness. After twelve greater ages the lotus-flower will unfold; thereupon the Bodhisattvas, Aval?ö¼aras and Mahasattva's, raising their voices in great compassion, will preach to him in detail the real state of all the elements of nature and the law of the expiation of sins."

"Does faith save such a man?"

"Yes, not his own faith, but the faith which prompted the vow of Amitabha. Amit¨(a's faith in the possibility of his salvation gives him supreme confidence that he will attain salvation. All he needs is to have the desire to be born in that paradise and to repeat the name of Amitabha."

Salvation of the Second Class

"How do those of the second class attain salvation?"

"The men of the second class regard ideas as realities. They are not entangled in the maze of things, but are confused by ideas, regarding them as real. These men do not need images and outward sanctions, but they need heaven and purgatory though regarding them as ideas. By performing the ten good deeds they will obtain a quiet heart, having no fear, and become saints and sages. Among men, saints and sages occupy a high rank, but not so among Buddhists. By merit of good works merely they enter the planes of sensuous desire, the six celestial worlds located immediately above the earth."

Salvation for the Highest Class

"And the third class?"

"This class has many ranks. There are those who by the practice of meditation (four _dkyanas_) [Footnote: Dhyana means contemplation. In later times under the influence of the idea of transmigration heavens were imagined which corresponded to the degrees of contemplation.] can enter the sixteen heavens conditioned by form.

By the practice of the four _ar?hy¡+s_ [Footnote: That degree of abstract contemplation from which all sensations are absent.] they enter the four highest heavens free from all sensuous desires and not conditioned by form. These heavens are the anteroom of Nirvana."

"What is the driving power in all this?"

"It is _v?a_ or energy."

Heaven and Purgatory

"Do heaven and purgatory exist?"

"Heaven and purgatory are in the minds and hearts of men. Really heaven is in the mind of Amit¨(a and purgatory exists in the illusioned brains of men."

"Does anything exist?"

"Nâ)rjuna says: 'There is no production, no destruction, no annihilation, no persistence, no unity, no plurality, no coming in and no going forth.'"

Sin

"Does sin exist?"

"In the mind of the real Buddhist sin and virtue are different aspects of the all. Sin is illusion; virtue is illusion, There is a higher unity in which they are reconciled."

Nirv¡+

"Do you know of any one who attained Nirv¡+?"

"Yes, I have experienced it. It is not a state beyond the grave. It is a state into which one can enter here."

"Can you express this experience in words?"

"Impossible. I can only indicate the shore of this great ocean. At first I was in great distress and agony, as though carrying the illusions of the world. Then came a great peace and calm, ineffable, serene, and surpassing the power of language to express."

The Philosophical Background

"What is behind this universe!"

"Underlying this universe of phenomena and change there is a unity. It is the basis of all being. It is within all being and all being rests in it. It is because of this common background that men are able to apprehend it. This universal basis we call _dharma,_ or law. Its characteristics are that everything born grows old, is subject to disease and death; that the teachings of Buddha purify the mind and enable it to obtain supreme enlightenment; that all Buddhas by treading the same way of perfection will attain the highest freedom."

"You speak of the Buddhist Trinity."

"Yes, we have the Dharmaka.. This is the essence-body, the ground of all being, taking many forms, Buddhas, Bodhisattvas, spirits, angels, men and even demons. It is impersonal, all-pervasive. It may be called the first person. The second person is the Sambhogaka., the body of bliss. This is the heavenly manifestation of Buddha. The third person is the Nirm¡+ka.. This is the projection of the body of bliss on earth."

Some identify this trinity with that of the Christian faith. While there is a resemblance, we should note that the first person of the Buddhist trinity would correspond to God as the absolute or the impersonal background of universal Being. The second corresponds to the glorified Christ and the third to the historic Jesus. There is no counterpart either to God the Father or to the Holy Spirit.

"Do you believe in the salvation of all beings?"

"Yes, all have the Buddha heart. All living beings will finally become Buddhas."

Then turning to a friend of mine the speaker said: "What have you done in Buddhism?" The friend answered: "I have written and translated many books." "I do not mean that," he answered. "What _work_ have you done?" The friend confessed that he had not done much else. Then he said: "Every morning when you awake, reflect deeply and profoundly upon your state before you were born. Think back to that state where your soul was merged with Buddha. Find yourself in that state and you will find ineffable enlightenment and joy."

The sun was setting behind the Western hills. The blare of trumpets sounded on the city wall. Outside of the door was the whirling sound of Peking returning home from its mundane tasks and joys. We joined the rushing, restless crowd and still we felt the calm of another world. Has not Christianity a message of balm and peace for these sons of the East who are so sensitive to the touch of the eternal and sublime?

What Buddhism Has to Give

An important government official obliged to deal with many vexatious requests and demands declared: "I could not get through my day's work, if I did not spend an hour every day in meditation, just as Buddha did when he became enlightened." He was asked what he did when he meditated or prayed. "Nothing at all." "Well, about what do you think?" "Of nothing at all. I stop thinking when I engage in religious meditation. Life makes me think too much. I should lose my sanity, if I did not stop thinking and enter into the 'void', whence we all came and into which we all are going to drop back."

His Christian inquirer still was unsatisfied by the Buddhist's description of his prayer life, and pressed further for details. "What happens when you meditate or pray?"

"Nothing happens, I tell you, except, that I experience a peace which the passing world cannot give and which the passing world cannot altogether take away. The secret of religion is simply to realize that everything is passing away. When you accept that fact, then you become really free. The Christian world seemed to have been tremendously impressed by the slogan of the French soldiers at Verdun, 'They shall not pass!' Perhaps the German soldiers did not pass just then or there. But the French soldiers themselves are all passing away. And everything in the world is passing away. What our Buddhist religion teaches us is: 'Let it pass!' You cannot keep anything for very long. And prayer or meditation is simply to practice yourself in that thought deliberately. Oh, it is a wonderful peace when you fully believe that gospel, and enter into it every day. Vanity of vanities, everything is vanity! Why worry? We do altogether too much worrying. To pray means simply to quit worrying, to quit thinking, to enter into the indescribably passionless peace of Nirvana."

Here seemed to be an ardent Buddhist. When asked what he thought as the difference between a Buddhist and a Christian, he answered promptly:

"Yes, there is my wife. She is a very good woman. All the neighbors come to her, when there is any one sick or in trouble. So I say to her: 'Wife, I should think you would make a first-class Christian.' But I think she lets herself be worried by altogether too many troubles. She is all the time thinking and fussing and planning. To be sure, it is mostly about other people, But then she does have the children and the house and the relatives and friends and neighbors to look after. Perhaps she really cannot be a Buddhist. Perhaps it is all a matter of temperament. Oh, but I tell you it is great to be a Buddhist, because it gives you such a wonderful peace."

PRESENT-DAY BUDDHISM:

Periods of Buddhist History

The history of Buddhism in China may be divided into four periods. Buddhism entered China, as we have seen, in the second century B.C. The first period, that of the translation and propagation of the faith, ended in 420 A.D. The second period, that of interpenetration, lasted to the beginning of the T'ang dynasty, 618 A.D. The third, the period of establishment, ended with the close of the five dynasties, in 960 A.D. The fourth period, that of decay, has extended to the present day.

The Progress of the Last Twenty-five Years

There are signs of a revival of Buddhism in China. Whether this is a tide, or a wave, only the future can reveal. In 1893 Dharmapala, an Indian monk, stopped in Shanghai on his way back from the Congress of Religions in Chicago. It was his purpose to make a tour of China, to arouse the Chinese Buddhists to send missionaries to India to restore Buddhism there, and then to start a propaganda throughout the whole world. He addressed the monks of Shanghai. Dr. Edkins, the veteran missionary, acted as his interpreter. Dharmapala was surrounded by a horde of curious monks who were more interested in his strange appearance and in the cost of his garments than they were in his great ideals. They were also feeling the iron heel of the Confucian government and at once inquired about the attitude of the government toward such an innovation. Dharmapala did not go beyond Shanghai.

Japanese Buddhists, especially the members of the Hongwanji sect, have taken a deep interest in Chinese Buddhists. Count Otani once visited the chief monasteries of China. Numerous Japanese Buddhists have made such visits. In 1902, the Empress Dowager, fired by a reforming zeal, decided to confiscate Buddhist property and to use the proceeds for the spread of modern education. The Buddhist monasteries put themselves under the protection of Japanese monks in order to hold their property. When by 1906 the Empress Dowager saw the consequences of her edict, she at once issued a new edict, reversing the former one, and the Japanese monks took their departure.

The Japanese Buddhists have been fired by missionary zeal for China. In many of the large cities of China are the temples of the Hongwanji sect. Established primarily for the Japanese, these temples are intended to serve as points of departure for a nation-wide missionary work. The twenty-one demands made upon China included two significant items in the last group which the Chinese refused to sign: "Art. 2: Japanese hospitals, churches and schools in the interior of China shall be granted the right of owning land." "Art. 7: China agrees that Japanese subjects shall have the right of missionary propaganda in China."

Under Japanese influence there was established in 1907 at Nanking, under the leadership of Yang, a lay Buddhist devotee, a school for the training of Buddhist missionaries. The students were to go to Japan for further training, and the more promising ones were to study in India. This project was discontinued after the death of Yang on account of the lack of funds.

When the republic was established Buddhism felt a wave of reform. The monasteries established schools for monks and children. A magazine was published which appeared irregularly for several numbers and then stopped. A national organization was formed with headquarters at Peking. A survey of monasteries was begun. The activities in lecturing and propaganda were increased, but Yuan Shih-kai issued twenty-seven regulations for the control of Buddhist monasteries, which markedly dampened the ardor of the reformers. The world war which accentuated the spirit of nationalism had the added effect of stirring up Buddhist enthusiasm. There are at present signs of new activity among them in China.

Present Activities

While Buddhism may be standing still or even dying in certain parts of China, it is showing signs of new life in the provinces of Kiangsu and Chekiang and in the large cities. Such revival in centers subject to the influence of the modern world shows that Buddhism in China as in Japan has sufficient vitality to adjust itself to modern conditions. Let us consider some of these activities.

(a) The Reconstruction of Monasteries._—During the T'ai Ping rebellion, which devastated China in 1850-1865, the monasteries suffered with the towns. Not only were the monasteries burned to the ground, but their means of support were taken away and the monks were scattered. There are still many of these ruined monasteries in the Yangtze valley and in southern and western China. Quite a number of them have been rebuilt. Perhaps the most notable example is that at Changchow which was destroyed during the rebellion. Today it is the largest monastery in China, having about two thousand monks. In Fukien several new monasteries have been built in the last few decades. In the provinces of Chekiang and Kiangsu, in the large cities and about Peking there are building activities, showing that the monasteries are feeling a new wave of prosperity.

T'ai Hsu, one of the leaders' of modern Buddhism, is holding up an ideal program for Buddhism in this time of reconstruction. He proposes that there should be 576 central monasteries, 4608 preaching places, 72 Buddhist hospitals and 72 orphanages.

(b) Accessions._—Regarding the number of monks it is almost impossible to obtain any reliable figures. A conservative estimate, based upon partial returns, makes the number of monks about 400,000 and that of nuns about 10,000. The impression among the Buddhists is that the number of monks is increasing. That is quite probable in view of the rebuilding and repairing which is now in progress.

More significant is the number of accessions from the learned class. Many officials, disheartened by the present confused political situation, have sought refuge in the monasteries. Some of them are now abbots of monasteries and are using their influence to build them up. All over China there are Confucian scholars who are giving themselves to the study of Buddhism and to meditation. Some of the Chinese students who have studied in Buddhist universities in Japan are propagating Buddhism by lecture and pen.

(c) Publications._—Quite as significant is the increase in the publication of Buddhist literature of all kinds. Many of the monasteries have printing departments where they publish the sutras needed for their own use. In addition, there are eight or more publishing centers where Buddhist literature is printed. The most famous are Yang's establishment at Nanking, the Buddhist Press in Yangchow and that in Peking. In these establishments about nine hundred different works are being published. The most noteworthy recent publication has been that of the Chinese Buddhist Tripitaka in Shanghai.

Among these publications are a few modern issues. The Chung Hua Book Company has published several works on Buddhism. Other books have been issued for the sake of harmonizing Buddhism with western science and philosophy. In this enterprise Japanese influence is visible. In 1921 a Shanghai press published a dictionary of Buddhist terms containing 3302 pages, based on the Japanese Dictionary of Buddhism. Other works also show the influence of Japanese scholarship.

Among the publications have appeared two magazines. One published at Ningpo, is called "New Buddhism." This is struggling and may have to succumb. The other is known as the "Sound of the Sea Tide," now published in Hankow. Moreover, in all the large cities there are Buddhist bookshops where only Buddhist works are sold. These all report a good business. This literary activity reveals an interest among the reading classes of China. Few such books are purchased by the monks. The Chinese scholars read them for their style and for their deep philosophy, but also for light and for help in the present distracting political situation of their country.

(d) Lectures._—Along with publication goes the spread of Buddhism by lectures in the monasteries and the cities of China. A few years ago Buddhist sermons, however serious, were only listened to by monks and by a few pious devotees. Today such addresses are advertised and are usually well attended by the intellectuals. Often many women are found listening. Monks like T'ai Hs?Yuan Ying have a national reputation. Not only monks, but laymen trained in Japan are delivering lectures on the Buddhist sutras. The favorites are the Awakening of Faith and the Suddharma Pundarika sutra.

(e) Buddhist Societies._—With the lectures goes the organization of Buddhist societies for all sorts of purposes. There is a central society in Peking which has branches in every province. The connection is rather loose. Buddhism has never been in favor of centralization. Nor for that matter would the government have allowed it. The chief ends aimed at by these societies are fellowship, devotion, study, propagation, and service. Such societies, often short lived, are springing up in many quarters. They meet for lectures on Buddhism or to conduct a study class in some of the sutras. Occasionally the more ambitious conduct an institute for several months. Some spend part of the time in meditation together. Several schools for children are supported by these societies. They also encourage work of a religious nature among prisoners, distributing tracts and holding services. Such activities are especially appreciated by those who are to suffer the death penalty. The societies are also doing publishing work. The two magazines are supported by the members of the larger societies.

(f) Signs of Social Ambition._—Social work is a prominent feature of some of these Buddhist societies. They have raised money for famine stricken regions, have opened orphanages, and assist in Red Cross work. One of the largest Chinese institutions for ministering to people who are sick and in trouble is located at Hankow. Around a central Buddhist temple is a modern-built hospital, an orphanage and several schools for poor children. It may not maintain western standards of efficiency, but it certainly represents the outreach of modern Buddhism.

Perhaps their most far-reaching advance has been made because of the realization that leaders are needed and that they must be trained. Several schools for this purpose have sprung into existence. Such schools are necessarily very primitive and are struggling with the difficulties of finding an adequate staff and equipment and of obtaining the best type of students.

Another sign of new life has been the making of programs for the future development of Buddhism. One of the most comprehensive appeared a short time ago. For the individual it proposes the cultivation of love, mercy, equality, freedom, progressiveness, an established faith, patience and endurance. For all men it proposes (1) an education according to capacity; (2) a trade suited to ability; (3) an opportunity to develop one's powers; (4) a chance for enlightenment for all. For society it urges the cultivation of cooperation, social service, sacrifice for the social weal, and the social consciousness in the individual. On behalf of the country it urges patriotism, participation in the government, and cooperation in international movements. For the world it advocates universal progress. As to the universe it specifies as a goal the bringing of men into harmony with spiritual realities, the enlightenment of all and the realization of the spiritual universe.

A Buddhist writer sums up the aims of new Buddhism as follows:

> *"Formerly Buddhism desired to escape the sinful world. Today Buddhism not only desires to escape this world of sin, but longs to transform this world of sin into a new world dominated by the ideals of Buddhism. Formerly Buddhism was occupied with erecting and perfecting its doctrines and polity as an organization. Today it not only hopes to perfect the doctrines and polity, but desires to spread the doctrines and ideals abroad so as to help mankind to become truly cultured."*

The Attitude of Tibetan Lamas

Not only the Chinese Buddhists, but the Lamas of Mongolia and Tibet are feeling the impulses of the new age. Quite recently an exhibition was held in the Lama temple at Peking which attracted thousands of visitors. Its object was to obtain money to repair the temple, and thus to give its work a fresh impulse. That these impulses are not necessarily hostile to Christianity is shown by a letter written by the Kurung Tsering Lama of Kokonor district to the Rev. T. S?sen of Szechuan:

"I, your humble servant, have seen several copies of the Scriptures and, having read them carefully, they certainly made me believe in Christ. I understand a little of the outstanding principles and the doctrinal teaching of the One Son, but as to the Holy Spirit's nature and essence, and as to the origin of this religion, I am not at all clear, and it is therefore important that the doctrinal principles of this religion should be fully explained, so as to enlighten the unintelligent and people of small mental ability.

"The teaching of the science of medicine and astrology is also very important. It is therefore evident if we want this blessing openly manifested, we must believe in the religion of the only Son of God. Being in earnest, I therefore pray you from my heart not to consider this letter lightly. With a hundred salutations."

Enclosed with this letter was a poem written in most elegant language.

"O thou Supreme God and most precious Father, The truth above all religions, The Ruler of all animate and inanimate worlds! Greater than wisdom, separated from birth and death, Is his son Christ the Lord shining in glory among endless beings. Incomprehensible wonder, miraculously made! In this teaching I myself also believe—As your spirit is with heaven united, My soul undivided is seeking the truth Jesus the Savior's desire fulfilling, For the coming of the Kingdom of Heaven I am praying. Happiness to all."

The Buddhist World Versus the Christian World

Looking back over the last twenty-five years we see rising quite distinctly a Buddhist world growing conscious of itself, of its past history and of its mission to the world. This Buddhist, world has much more of a program than it had twenty-five years ago. Its object is to unite the Mahay¡+ and the H?y¡+ branches of Buddhism and to spread Buddhist propaganda over the world. At present the leadership of this movement is in Japan. It is in part a political movement. There is no question that Christianity is not at all pleasing to the Japanese militarists. It is regarded by them as the advance post of western industrialism and political ambition. Quite naturally such leaders desire to make the Buddhist world a unit. It is also a social movement. The spirit of the Japanese Buddhist has been brought to consciousness by the new position of Japan. Japan is seeking to take its place in the world as a first rate power. By this not only will Japan's industry and commerce profit, but its spiritual values must also be adapted to the world. The movement then has its spiritual side. Japanese travelers and people are going to all parts of the world. They carry with them the religious ideals which have been shaped by Buddhism. Buddhism in the past was one of the great religions of salvation with an inspiring missionary message. It is again awakening to this task of evangelization. Under the leadership of Japanese scholars and religious statesmen the Japanese are seeking to unite the Buddhist world so that it shall become a force in the new world. Japan is thus trying to give back what it has received in the past.

At present in Buddhist countries there is a strong force working against this movement. Nationalism is a new force to be reckoned with. Still even with the spirit of nationalism permeating every group, the Buddhist world is getting together and will strive to make its contribution to the life of the whole world.

THE CHRISTIAN APPROACH TO BUDDHISTS

Questions Which Buddhists Ask

Buddhists are approaching Christianity. In many places a spirit of inquiry and interest in the Christian religion is met. It is not necessary that there should be a Buddhist world permanently over against a Christian world. The questions which Buddhists ask a missionary indicate an interest in vital themes. Some of them are as follows:

We put our trust in the three Precious Ones. In what do you trust? Is not your Shang Ti (name for God used in China) a being lower than Buddha and just a little higher than a Bodhisattva? Is not Shang Ti the tribal god of the Jews? Do you believe in the existence of _purgatory?_ What sufferings will those endure who do not live a virtuous life? Do you believe in the reality of the Western Paradise? How can one enter it? There being three kinds of merit, by what method is the great merit accumulated? How is the middle and the small merit accumulated? What are the fruits of these proportions of merit and what are they like? Tell me how to believe Christ. What work of meditation do you perform? Is not Buddhism more democratic than Christianity, because it holds out the possibility of Buddhahood to all beings? Is not Buddhism more inclusive, because it provides for the salvation of all beings?

Knowledge and Sympathy

These questions make it plain that the worker who is to deal with Buddhists should have a broad background of general culture. He must be thoroughly humanized. He should have a good knowledge of the history of philosophy and religion, including the work of the modern philosophers. A knowledge of the life of Buddha and of the doctrines of the H?y¡+ or Southern Buddhism, as well as the tenets of the Mahay¡+ should be in his possession. The psychology of religion should interpenetrate his historical learning; the best methods of pedagogy should guide his approach to men. Of course he must speak the language of the Buddhist, not only the spiritual language, but his everyday patois. He will find it an advantage to know some Sanskrit. While this requirement is not very urgent at present, it will rapidly become a necessity for doing the best work.

This knowledge should be interpenetrated by a genuine sympathy, that is, imagination tinged with emotion. The worker should be able to view doctrines, values and actions from the point of view of the Buddhist and his past history. He must have a genuine interest in and a great capacity for friendship. The Buddhists are very human, responding to friendship very quickly. Such friendship forms a link between the man and the larger friendship of Christ.

Emphasis on the Aesthetic in Christianity

A Chinese Christian leader described his idea of a church as a place removed from the din of the street, approached by a walk flanked with trees and flowers and adorned within by symbols speaking to the heart of the Chinese. He longed for the mystic silence and the beauty of holiness which would open the windows of the world of spiritual reality and throw its light upon the problems of life. He was asked, "Would you adapt some of the symbols of the Chinese religions?" He said, "Many of those symbols are neutral. They suggest religious emotion. Their character depends upon the content which the occasion puts into them. If the content is Christian then the symbols and emotions will become Christian."

Christianity is a religion of beauty. The beautiful in architecture, symbol and ritual, expressing the spiritual universe of the past, present and future, makes a strong appeal to the Chinese heart. It may well be emphasized in the future as never before.

Emphasis on the Mystical in Christianity

Not long ago a Buddhist in one of the large cities of China was converted. He found great joy in the experience which revived him and gathered into unity the broken fragments of his life. He attended church regularly and participated in the prayer meetings. Gradually he discovered that he was not being nourished. He felt his joy slipping away from him and his divided life reinstating itself. He went to Buddhism for consolation. He is not hostile to the church. He appreciates the help he received, but he said that he came for consolation and peace and found the same—hard orthodoxy and morality so familiar to him in Confucianism.

While the case of this man may have individual peculiarities, it may be made the starting point for a discussion of the situation in many churches in China. The early message to the Chinese was doctrinal. The false notion of many gods had to be displaced by the idea of the one true God. With this idea of the true God a few other tenets of the Christian religion are often held as dogmatic propositions to be repeated when questions are asked. The great sin preached is the worship of idols.

The second part of the Christian message is salvation by faith in Jesus Christ. This salvation is other-worldly to a large extent. The extreme emphasis upon it has made of the church an insurance society, membership in which insures bliss in the world beyond.

The third part of the message has been concerned with moral acts, abstinence from opium (liquor and tobacco in some churches), polygamy, and the gross sins. Attendance upon church services, contribution for the support of the church, and the refusal to contribute to idolatry have also been required.

The emphasis to a large extent was doctrinal, moral and individual. The result has been a body of people free from the gross sins, but also innocent of the great virtues and individualistic in their outlook upon this world and the next. This emphasis is needed, but in addition there should be the cultivation of the presence of God in the soul by appropriate means. The Christian Church of China should develop a technique of the spiritual life suited to the East.

The formation of habits of devotion should be emphasized. Intercessory prayer should be given a larger place. Contemplation and meditation should be regarded not merely as an escape from the turmoil and strife of the world, but as a preparation for the highest life of service and sacrifice. Buddhist mysticism united the whole universe and was the great foundation of Chinese art, literature and morality. The spiritual world of Christianity must likewise seep through into the very thought of Asia and inspire the new art, literature and morality which will be the world expression of a Christian universe.

Emphasis on the Social Elements in Christianity

To the aesthetic and mystical emphasis must be attached a social emphasis. Buddhism is often criticized as not being social. It is a highly socialized religion. It has had a large influence upon social life in the East. This social life is different from ours. We see its wrongs and weaknesses. Likewise do the Buddhists see the materialism and injustice of our social life. Christianity must relate itself to the modern world as it is rising in China and seek not merely to remedy a few wrongs or heal a few diseases, but must release the healing stream into the social life of the East. This will be done and is being done through the Church community which has become conscious of itself, realizing its needs and wants, seeking in an intelligent and systematic way to rehabilitate itself. It is not so much the external unrelated efforts that accomplish the thing needed, but it is rather the community life stirred by ideals and fired by a new dynamic which begins the work of reformation.

Emphasis on the Person of Jesus Christ

(a) As a Historical Character._—The great asset of the missionary among Buddhists is the historical person of Christ. In contrast to many of the Bodhisattvas, the saviours of the Buddhists, Jesus is a historical character. His life among men was the life of God among men.

(b) As the Revealer._—God is like Christ. Christ reveals God as the complete, the perfect person. He possessed the pure spiritual personality. The chief characteristic of this personality is love. This love conscious of itself finds its highest joy in the well-being of others. This love of God produced human life which, springing from the lowest form, broke through the material elements and is capable of attaining the highest development.

Christ reveals to man his heavenly relationship. Man created in the likeness of God stands in the highest relation of one person to another through love. He likens this relation to that of father and son. He lifts man to the fellowship with the divine. Yet such a fellowship that man preserves his personality.

Christ reveals man in his relation to men as a brother and the form of love which shall control the relation of man to God as well as man to man.

Christ revealed and founded the Kingdom, a society of the saved, dominated by the spirit of the founder and making this spirit of love and service the organizing power in the world.

(c) As the Saviour._—Mahay¡+ Buddhism emphasized saviourhood. Christ is the saviour of men. In Buddhism the stress is placed upon the merit of the saviour and the saved. There is no question that merit has some value. Yet Christ does not save us by merit, nor do we help to save one another by merit. Salvation is a moral and spiritual process. It is concerned with the biology of the soul. The salvation that we preach is not the salvation by knowledge, or meditation, or merit, but by the interpenetration of Christ's spirit in ours, by the mystic and moral union of our life with his. As Paul says: "That I may know Him and the power of His resurrection and the fellowship of His suffering." Yet He is not the saviour of the individual alone. He saves the community, the church. Only as His spirit permeates and dominates the community does he find his true self and the real salvation.

(d) As the Eternal Son, of God._—The Mahay¡+ system does not emphasize the historicity of Amitabha or of the

> Bodhisattvas. Spiritual truth is the development of the soul. It is not limited by time and place. Likewise Christianity must emphasize the eternal character of Jesus Christ. "The Logos existed in the very beginning, the Logos was with God, the Logos was God." To the Mahb.nist this spiritual history is more real than any fact conditioned by time and place.

The Christian worker must learn to understand the import of the Gospel of John. He must see in Jesus Christ "The real Light, which enlightens every man." He must be able to convince himself that the Christ is the fulfillment of the highest aspirations of the Mahb.na system.

How Christianity Expresses Itself in Buddhist Minds

In 1920 a number of Buddhist monks, under the leadership of Rev. K. L. Reichelt formed a Christian brotherhood. The members of this small brotherhood decided that they must subscribe to vows and they took the four following:

"I promise before the Almighty and Omniscient God, that I with my whole heart will surrender myself to the true Trinity, God the Father, the Son and the Holy Spirit. I will with my whole heart have faith in Jesus Christ as the Saviour of the world who gives completion to the profoundest and best objects of the higher Buddhism. I will live in this faith now and ever after.

"I promise solemnly before God with my whole heart to devote myself to the study of the true doctrine and break wholly with the evil manners of the world and show forth in my public and private life that I am truly united with Christ.

"I promise that I in every respect will try so to educate myself that I can be of use in the work of God on earth. I will with undivided heart devote myself to the great work; to lead my brethren in the Buddhist Association forward to the understanding of Christ as the only One, who gives completion to the highest and profoundest ideas of Higher Buddhism.

"I promise that until my last hour I will work so that out of our Christian Brotherhood there may grow forth a strong church of Christ among Buddhists. I will not permit any evil thing to grow in my heart, which could divide the brotherhood, but will always try to promote the progress of every member in the knowledge of the holy obligations laid down in these vows and our constitution."

Such men ought, to make choice Christians.

Christianity's Constructive Values

Buddhism in the course of its long history developed certain religious ideas and values which we find in Christianity. It faced the fact of sin and placed it in the heart. It diagnosed the fundamental instincts of men, sex-appetite, will-to-achieve, and pugnacity. These must be overcome. It regards them as delusions which must be eliminated. Christianity also deals with these instincts. It is under no delusion as to their strength. There are certain tendencies in Christianity which have tried to annihilate them. The central tendency of Christianity, however, recognizing their power for good, seeks to sublimate them and make them serve the individual and society. This attitude of the two religions toward these instincts is fundamentally different. The attitude of Christianity has been justified even in Buddhist lands where the religious life of the people has followed the same line that Christianity advocates.

Early Buddhism tried to dissolve man's personality. Later Buddhism corrected this and perhaps has appealed too much to the desire on the part of the individual to enter a heaven which is merely a replica of the earth. Christianity starts with a personal God and holds up before the believer the goal of perfection for his own personality. It finds man without a self and confers a real selfhood upon him.

Early Buddhism taught that salvation is accomplished by the individual alone. It denies the possibility and the necessity of help from a divine source. Subsequent history has proved this to have been wrong. In India, Buddhism has been displaced by Hinduism, and in China, and Japan, the Mahb.na has developed the idea of salvation through another. The great stream of Buddhism has recognized that man by himself is helpless. He must have the help of a divine power in order to obtain salvation. Christianity asserts that salvation is possible only through the intervention of God. The incarnation, the life, death and resurrection of Jesus and his work in the world through the Holy Spirit on the one hand are the expression of God's solicitude for man, and, on the other hand, correspond to the deep need which men of all ages have felt, for a power above themselves. From the early stages of magic to the highest reaches of religion we find this constant factor recognized by human groups all over the world. They bear witness to a power above themselves to whom they continually appeal. In Christianity we find this main tendency enunciated most clearly. The individual cannot save himself. Mankind cannot save itself. Both must rely upon the assistance of the divine power which started this universe on its way and which is the ever present creative force.

Christianity, moreover, has established the community of believers including all classes and conditions of men. Herein each one may realize him&if. Herein also he may realize the kind of community which is friendly to his highest aspirations for himself. Herein he has the opportunity to transmute the instincts above mentioned into forces which make for the larger development of his own person and the well-being of the community.

Accordingly, as Christians face Buddhists, they can do so with the consciousness that this great religion has been reaching out after the light which shines brightly in our Christian religion. They have the assurance not only that they have a message which brings fulfilment to the ideas of the Mahb.na, but also that it has prepared the way for the hearts of the Chinese to receive the highest message of Christianity.

2

BUDDHISM IN INDIA

INTRODUCTION

Language in History and Modernity

It was a quiet, cool January dawn in the South-Indian city of Tiruchirapalli in the year 1964. A can in his hand, a man named Chinnasami left his home—leaving behind his aging mother, young wife, and infant daughter—and walked to the city's railway station. On reaching there, he doused himself with its contents and set himself on fire, shouting out aloud, *"inti ol1ika!tamil1 vâl1ka!"* (Death to Hindi! May Tamil flourish!). Chinnasami's example was not lost. A year later, to the date, history repeated itself but not necessarily as farce: five other men burned themselves alive "at the altar of Tamil." Three others died just as painfully—not in a raging blaze, but by swallowing insecticide—also for the sake of Tamil, they declared in their own last words.

These dramatic acts were reported by the mainstream news media in India, sometimes in a matter of fact fashion, sometimes with derision, but invariably as yet another example of the "frenzy" and "fanaticism" that speakers of Tamil habitually display when it comes to their language. American newsmagazines like *Time* and *Newsweek* briefly noted the acts, translating them for the benefit of their readers by reporting that "in the style of Vietnamese monks," these men had "turned [themselves] into human funeral pyre[s]." The Vietnam analogy came home to roost in South India: the monks immolated themselves for their religion, but no one had yet burned themselves for their language, it was suggested. That pride of place goes to speakers of Tamil. *Utòal manònòukku, uyir tamil1ukku,* "body to earth, life for Tamil": in stories and poems about these men which have circulated since, so is their "sacrifice" for their language commemorated.

How do I, a late-twentieth-century-historian, make sense of these deaths? Disciplined by history, I would naturally demand, What is it that led so many men and women to proclaim that they would live and die for their language? Why did they so passionately confess that a life without Tamil is not worth living, that they would forsake material gains and worldly pleasures, even the ambrosia of the gods, for its sake? Trained by my discipline to always historicize, these deaths—as indeed the lives of these women and men—have nonetheless taught me to appreciate the hubris of the historical will to elucidate, as they have laid bare the inadequacies of the very language of history itself to write about matters such as these. Yet historicize I must, if only to rescue these men and women from charges of "frenzy" and "fanaticism." And so I will return to their stories, later, but only after resorting to history.

And yet it would seem that history as a discipline has no place for acts such as Chinnasami's or, for that matter, for the language for which he sacrificed himself. While it is hardly news that languages have histories, "the odd thing about the *questione della lingua* [the language question] is how rarely historians ask it," Gramsci's attempt to theorize it notwithstanding (Steinberg 1987: 199). This is especially true for colonial and post-colonial India where the language question—that complex of issues relating to language, politics, and power—has hardly been interrogated by disciplinary history despite its obvious importance for the political cultures of the emergent nation-state.

The historian is a rare presence in scholarly debates on the national language crisis, the internal partitioning of the nation into linguistic states, or the pedagogical dilemmas of multilingualism. This is partly because of a (Orientalist) preoccupation with caste and religion, those two gatekeeping concerns of South Asian studies on identity politics (Ramaswamy 1993: 684-85). But just as clearly, it seems that because our historical conceptions come to us in and through language, historians have tended to treat it, the linguistic turn notwithstanding, as a transparent medium of communication of information rather than as an ideological formation that itself has a politics which has to be historicized.

Yet, even as I try to make a case in this study for (Indian) historians to take the language question seriously, I do so with the troubled knowledge that disciplinary history has been complicit in the Europeanization of alternate life-worlds and imaginations. For the knowledge procedures and institutional practices of history have universalized the European historical experience as the desirable norm, against which all other histories, Indian included, appear inadequate and incomplete (Chakrabarty 1992). Nevertheless, as Dipesh Chakrabarty insists, we cannot give up on history, for it is one of the fundamental modalities of our times, "in the establishment of meaning, in the creation of truth regimes, in deciding, as it were, whose and which 'universal' wins." What we can—and must—do instead, as Meaghan Morris recommends, is to resist the writing of histories of places like India "as a known history, something which has already happened elsewhere, and which is to be reproduced, mechanically or otherwise, with a local content" (quoted by Chakrabarty 1992: 17-20). Histories which seek to corrode the universalizing imperative of Europe's knowledge practices ought to heed all those "scandalous" moments of "difference" which "shock" and "disrupt" the homogenizing flow of history-as-usual:

> Subaltern histories, thus conceived in relationship to the question of difference, will have a split running through them. On the one hand, they are "histories" in that they are constructed within the master code of secular History and use the academic codes of history-writing (and thereby perforce subordinate to themselves all other forms of memory). On the other hand, they cannot ever afford to grant this master-code its claim of being a mode of thought that comes to all human beings naturally, or even to be treated as something that exists out there in nature itself. Subaltern histories are therefore constructed within a particular kind of historicized memory, one that remembers History itself as a violation, an imperious code that accompanied the civilizing process that the European Enlightenment inaugurated in the eighteenth century as a world-historical task.

The "unassimilable," the "untranslatable," the "different"—these then are the stuff of histories written in a post-colonial moment. The goal is not the illusory quest for the authentic, but a narrative refusal to seek recognition through collapsing the "difference" of India's histories into the "sameness" of Europe's.

And so, when I raise the *questione della lingua*, and demand that Indian historians heed it, I do so with the full realization of its European origins. And yet, the work of colonialism and modernity has ensured that this is no longer a question that just belongs to Europe but is also a dilemma for the worlds that it colonized. To ask the language question, but to answer it and write it differently for a colonial and post-colonial context—these then are the burdens of this book.

Language and Devotion

How then do I write *differently* the (hi)stories of Chinnasami and his fellow speakers who claimed a willingness to die for Tamil? Although Chinnasami's immolation by itself is a spectacularly singular act, defying easy translation into universal categories, the attitudes that produced it could be conveniently assimilated into the metanarrative of nationalism, as yet another instance of "linguistic nationalism." Indeed, this is typically how the few scholarly works that deal with the question of Tamil, if only tangentially, gloss it—as "Tamil nationalism," or its variant, "Tamil revivalism," and as such, an entity that is forged in the shadows of metropolitan Indian nationalism, itself declared a "derived" version of the normative European form (Chatterjee 1986). It would be hard to deny the importance of ideologies of nationalism, derived or not, for much that happens in late colonial and post-colonial India. We hear repeatedly in the words of many a speaker of Tamil, from at least the later decades of the nineteenth century, the logic of Herder, Fichte, and other prophets of (European) linguistic nationalism:

Language is breath;
Language is consciousness;
Language is life;
......
Language is the world;
Without language, who are we?
(Bharatidasan 1978: 132)

That the cunning of Europe ensures that Herder & Co. speak in such clear Tamil tones only reminds us of the regimes of repetition and mimicry that colonialism sparked among subject populations. Yet, as Homi Bhabha observes, colonial mimicry is marked by a profound ambivalence, for "in order to be effective, mimicry must continually produce its slippage, its excess, its difference." Mimicry in the colony, "on the margins of metropolitan desire," is always "a subject of difference that is almost the same, but not quite" (Bhabha 1994: 85-92). But how do we narrate the lives of those who lived in the colony so as to keep alive this ambivalence of mimicry, this tension between the "almost the same" but the "not quite," which dismembers European norms and forms, as Bhabha reminds us? Equally crucial, how may we write their stories so as to displace the universal narrative of nationalism, a narrative whose normative "silent referent" is always (western) Europe, that paradigmatic site of the modern nation-state (Chakrabarty 1992)? For inevitably in such a narrative, "Tamil" nationalism is a (distorted) variant of something that has already happened elsewhere, but reenacted with local content.

This is not the only problem with the analytic of nationalism for writing a different history. Even as the nation-state has become so ubiquitous in this century that, as Benedict Anderson (1983: 14) observes, "everyone can, should, will 'have' a nationality, as he or she 'has' a gender," there has been a tremendous surge in scholarly works on nationalism. Indeed, that single term, "nationalism," has become theoretically overburdened, rendering it incapable of capturing the many incommensurable differences that separate the story of one nation from another. And yet, nationalisms "do not work everywhere the same way: in a sense they must work everywhere in a *different* way, this is part of the national 'identity' " (Balibar 1989: 19). This is especially true when it comes to the complex nexus between linguistic identity and nationalism. Herder, Fichte, and others may have declared that "those who speak the same language...belong together and are by nature one and inseparable whole" (Kedourie 1961: 69). But nationalism is not everywhere predicated on linguistic passions, nor does language loyalty necessarily or always induce a singular nation-state, if we recall the Swiss in the very heart of Europe, modern Latin America as it emerged from the former Spanish and Portuguese empires, or even Arabic in parts of its diaspora, to cite a few random examples (Seton Watson 1977). In other words, passions of the tongue do not readily map onto the passions of the nation. As Prasenjit Duara has recently suggested in his *Rescuing*

History from the Nation, "although nationalism and its theory seek a privileged position within the representational network as the master identity that subsumes or organizes other identifications, *it exists only as one among others* and is changeable, interchangeable, conflicted, or harmonious with them" (1995: 8, emphasis mine). In this book, I hope to "rescue history from the nation" by displacing the latter as the locus of this particular history I write, and by refusing to subordinate, all too quickly, the sentiments and notions of all those who lived and died for Tamil under the rubric of "nationalism." Which is why I propose a new analytic to theorize the discourses of love, labor, and life that have coalesced around Tamil in this century, discourses which can only be partially contained within a metanarrative of nationalism, or even a singular conception of the nation, as we will see.

My access to this analytic—and hence to a different take on the language question—is through a Tamil word, *par1r1u,* which speakers of Tamil routinely use in their talk about the language. Typically, the term appears with the word *tamil1* in the compound *tamil1ppar1r1u,* the hinge on which hangs the structure of affect and sentiment that develops around Tamil. So, its speakers are told to cultivate *tamil1ppar1r1u,* to demonstrate *tamil1ppar1r1u,* and to not sacrifice *tamil1ppar1r1u* for worldly gains. Those who practice *tamil1ppar1r1u* are *tamil1ar,* "Tamilians" by the same token, anybody who does not show *tamil1ppar1r1u* is not a Tamilian. The lexical meanings of *par1r1u* include adherence, attachment, affection, support, love, and devotion. Out of these, I have chosen "devotion" to gloss *par1r1u,* and the term "Tamil devotion" to denote *tamil1ppar1r1u,* as well as other similar sentiments that Tamil speakers express for the language: *an1pu,* "affection" *pâcam,* "attachment" *kâtal,* "love" *ârvam,* "passion" and the like.

This then is a book about the poetics and politics of *tamil1ppar1r1u,* "Tamil devotion"—those networks of praise, passion, and practice centered on Tamil. And it is about the lives of those women and men who declare themselves to be *tamil1ppar1r1âlòar* or *tamil1an1par,* "devotees of Tamil." I analyze how the language has been transformed into an object of devotion in the course of the social mobilization and political empowerment of its speakers. I explore the consequences of this for the ontology of Tamil, as well as for the formulation of cultural policies around it. And I consider how language devotion produces the modern

Tamil subject—*tamil1an1*, the "Tamilian"—an entity whose subjectivity merges into the imagined self of Tamil. *enkòum tamil1, etilum tamil1,* "Tamil everywhere, everything in Tamil": this is the leitmotif of *tamil1ppar1r1u* at its climactic moment. "If we live, we live for Tamil; if we die, we die for it," declared one of its devotees (Puthumai Vanan 1968: 7). Another insisted, "[Our] mind is Tamil; [our] entire body is Tamil; [our] life is Tamil; [our] pulse is Tamil; [our] veins are Tamil; [our] flesh, muscle, everything is Tamil; everything in [our] body is Tamil, Tamil, Tamil" (S. Subramanian 1939: 15-16).

Body, life, self: all these dissolve into Tamil. Devotion to Tamil, service to Tamil, the sacrifice of wealth and spirit to Tamil: these are the demands of *tamil1ppar1r1u* at its radical best.

As we will see, there are considerable differences among Tamil's devotees over the meaning of their language, and over how best to practice *tamil1ppar1r1u*. Nonetheless, I consider them as members of one singular community because they all agree upon one foundational certainty: the natural and inevitable attachment between Tamil and its speakers, an attachment that is repeatedly presented in devotional talk as inviolable, eternal, sacral. The goal of this study lies not so much in exposing the illusory nature of this certitude as in illustrating how, and in what manner, *tamil1ppar1r1u* is able to generate and sustain it in the first place. What ideological devices and strategies of persuasion are deployed by Tamil's devotees to convince their fellow speakers of the natural and unshakable bond(s) between themselves and their language? What are the institutional practices through which such a certitude is disseminated among Tamil speakers so as to appear self-evident and commonsensical? What are the ways in which its logic is used to mount resistance against putative foes, and to garner power? And finally, how is this certitude deployed to produce the modern Tamilian, whose subjectivity is anchored by Tamil and has no existence independent of it?

My use of *tamil1ppar1r1u* to interrogate the language question thus is not a nativist gesture, for I make the concept do theoretical work for me in ways which exceed the many tasks that speakers of Tamil have themselves assigned to it in their prolific discourses. Neither is it meant to alienate non-Tamil-speaking readers, despite its alterity (heightened no doubt by the diacritical marks that grace its English transliteration!). Nevertheless, its frequent presence in these pages marks the difference accompanying the ideologies of Tamil that cannot be readily assimilated into preexisting categories such as nationalism. By leaving it untranslated in many instances, and by glossing it in English in others, I seek to remind the reader (and me) of the ironies of writing about Tamil devotion in English, as I wish to draw attention to the inevitable hybridity that accompanies academic exercises like this one, which are conducted between cultures, between languages. But above all, following the cue of many who have written on the politics of translation, *tamil1pparlr1u* allows me to "inscribe heterogeneity" in these pages, even as its assertions betray, as we will see, the colonial and post-colonial space which it inhabits (Niranjana 1992).

So, what kind of theoretical work does the analytic of devotion perform in this study? Most obviously, by hijacking it from the domain of religion to which it has been conventionally confined in South Asian studies, I wish of course to suggest that devotion is not solely directed towards deities and religious personages in India. Instead, piety, adoration, and reverence have routinely centered on sovereigns and parents; more recently, on politicians, movie stars, and other figures of popular culture; and most distinctively in our time, on the nation. Remarkably, through the intervention of its supporters, Tamil, too, joins their ranks, and even subversively displaces them—so much so that, as *tamil1pparlr1u* gathers strength as the century wears on, it is increasingly asserted that Tamil alone ought to be the sole and legitimate focus of the unconditional devotion of its speakers. This indeed is the dream, and demand, of the most fervent of its adherents. The analytic of devotion allows me to demonstrate how sentiments that accumulate about Tamil among its speakers resonate with attitudes expressed towards deities, sovereigns, and parents. In fact, central to the work of *tamil1pparlr1u* is the wholesale annexation of genres of praise, vocabularies of reverence, and habits of adulation which have been conventionally reserved for such notables.

Further, the analytic of devotion enables me to track the myriad micronetworks of statements and practices through which Tamil has been transformed, over time, in specific historical, political, and social circumstances, into an object of passionate attachment.

Despite what its devotees might claim, Tamil (or for that matter, any language) does not have an inherent, natural, even God-given capacity to generate loyalty, love, longing; it is made to do so, and to serve specific ends. Such structures of sentiment that tie a language to its adherents are crucial to the politics of its empowerment. Yet they are too hastily passed over by a social science scholarship that has its sights set on demonstrating how languages have been used as agents of social and political mobilization, or as catalysts for nationalist activity. In such analyses, we learn little about how specific languages are transformed into sites of such loyalty, reverence, and love. How indeed do they acquire the capacity which *enable* them to act as symbols or catalysts, or, just as crucially, *disable* them from doing so? To remember Chinnasami, once again, *how* does Tamil acquire the power to move him to burn himself alive in its name?

The politics of language empowerment, however, are never independent of its poetics, those rhetorical norms and strategies of persuasion through which its adherents attempt to convince their fellow speakers about the glories of their language, the urgency of its cause, and the need to surrender their wealth, bodies, and souls for it. Such networks of talk are especially crucial for *tamil1ppar1r1u,* for the hold that Tamil appears to exercise over its devout follows not least from the deployment of the persuasive power(s) of the language itself. Its devotees repeatedly confess to the joys of hearing the very sound of Tamil, and comment on its *men1mai* (softness), *in1imai* (sweetness), *nunòmai* (fineness), and so on. The potency of Tamil devotional talk lies not just in the scholarly breadth it displays or in the logic of its arguments, but just as crucially in its strategic use of alliterative phrases, affective figures of speech, catchy idioms, rhetorical flourishes, and the like. My analysis of Tamil devotion therefore follows the suggestion that "linguistic practice, rather than simply reflecting social reality, [is] actively...an instrument of...power....Words [do] not just reflect social and political reality; they [are] instruments for transforming reality." (Hunt 1989: 17).

Attention to linguistic practices is particularly necessary in colonial situations where new language hierarchies emerge to displace older ones, as European languages, linguistic forms, and literary genres capture prestige, profit, and power (Cohn 1985; Fabian 1986; Rafael 1988). As elsewhere in the British empire,

Tamil devotion, too, paradoxically relies on English to stimulate *tamil1ppar1r1u*, a reliance that noticeably diminishes by the 1920s and can rightfully be seen as one of its more visible successes. The attitudes of Tamil's devotees towards English, the language of their colonial masters, are quite equivocal and contradictory. While many of them—as is typical of bilinguals spawned by colonial systems—are clearly at ease in going back and forth between the two languages, there are many differences in the structure and logic of arguments, the representational devices, and the strategies of persuasion they deploy in doing so. Rather than reflecting some essential qualities inherent to either language, such differences are themselves traces of the different ideological work performed by the two languages, Tamil and English, within *tamil1ppar1r1u.* All this of course only reminds us that linguistic practices such as these are never just about languages. Instead, our choice of languages and the myriad ways in which we use them are intimately reflective of our sense of selves and the worlds in which we live, the economies of prestige and power within which we function, and the politics of our beings.

Finally, I turn the lens of devotion on *tamil1ppar1r1u* itself, to reveal how despite the claims of Tamil's devotees, there is no singular, homogeneous language that consolidates itself as the focus of their love and adulation; there is no singular, homogeneous community that emerges in their imaginings; and there is no singular path to practicing what they praise and preach. Its apparent singularity as a sentiment notwithstanding, *tamil1ppar1r1u* itself is multiple, heterogeneous, and shot through with difference.

Language, Colonialism, and Modernity

Tamil's devout have been quick to assimilate Chinnasami and his fellow self-immolators into a pantheon of devotees which stretches back into the hoary mists of time and includes mythical sages, legendary kings, even the gods themselves. For like the nation, that other entity produced in modernity, *tamil1ppar1r1u,* too, is driven by the imperative to clothe itself in timeless antiquity, so that devotion to Tamil appears to be as ancient as the language itself. Yet Tamil devotion—in the sense in which I have identified it as networks of praise, passion, and practice through which the language is transformed into the primary site of attachment, love, and loyalty of its speakers—is a more recent phenomenon whose foundations were laid in the nineteenth century with the consolidation of colonial rule in what was then the multilingual Madras Presidency. Writing the Tamil question differently also therefore means a resistance to assimilation into a nativist antiquity. For, continuities with the past notwithstanding, Chinnasami's act, and the stories of his fellow devotees who proclaimed their willingness to place their life and limb at the service of the language, has to be located within new regimes of imagination, institutional practices, and technologies of meaning production that were ushered in, however skewed, with colonialism and modernity. And what were some of these?

First, although it has been transformed into a subject of sustained devotion fairly recently, Tamil attracted praise from at least the second half of the first millennium C.E. But much of this praise was episodic, scattered, even oblique. The language was rarely the primary subject of such eulogies, for the fundamental concern of even its most ardent admirer was with ensuring the literary worth of its poetry, or the salvational potential of its hymns, rather than with Tamil per se. Indeed, it is only in the latter half of the nineteenth century that Tamil emerges as an autonomous subject of praise (Krishnan 1984). Further, in the pre-nineteenth-century verses of praise, the power of the language was complexly entangled with the power(s) of divinities and extraordinary beings, rather than with the power of "the people." Tamil was eulogized, but not because it ensured communication between its speakers, enabled the schooling of the citizenry, or facilitated the governance of the populace. Instead, it was held in awe for its demonstrated ability to perform wondrous miracles and command the all-powerful gods (Ramaswamy 1996).

This is not to say, in a reworking of the old secularization argument, that an enchanted world in which Tamil was divine and salvational gave way, with modernity, to a disenchanted one in which it is bureaucratized and rationalized. On the contrary, the language continues to be assigned a salvational task within the regimes of Tamil devotion, as we will see. Yet the terms on which Tamil is rendered salvational vary, as does the logic. In *tamil1pparlr1u,* the ideological work done on the language places the people who speak it at the very center of the project, as an imagined community. It is the task of ensuring that Tamil commands the adulation and veneration of its speakers, rather than the attention of the gods, which consumes its modern devotees. We get a glimpse of this new people-centered ideology in the Tamil-speaking region from around 1879:

Tamil gave birth to us; Tamil raised us; Tamil sang lullabies to us and put us to sleep; Tamil taught us our first words with which we brought joy to our mothers and fathers; Tamil is the first language we spoke when we were infants; Tamil is the language which our mothers and fathers fed us along with milk; Tamil is the language that our mother, father, and preceptor taught us....[T]he language of our home is Tamil; the language of our land is Tamil.

As we will see later, the imagining of Tamil as the favorite of the gods lingers on well into this century, but it has to contend with a new sentiment ushered in with modernity in which languages are seen as the personal property of their speakers (Anderson 1983: 66-69). Hence the insistent use of collective pronouns, such as "our" and "their," in modern discourses on language. This people centered ideology of modernity inaugurates a *patrimonial* imagination in which language is constituted as a tangible, material possession that is transmitted from one generation of its speakers to another who relate to it as a property owning "collective individual" (Handler 1988: 140-58). Since it is their patrimony, its speakers are enjoined to ensure the well-being of their language, for in this lay the future of the community whose very existence is now predicated on its possession. Propelled by such a logic of possession—of language as personal property—*tamil1ppar1r1u*, too, declares that speakers of Tamil "have" a language; it renders them the new masters of Tamil, masters who are called upon, ironically, to "serve" the language with their body and life.

Chinnasami and his fellow devout also lived and operated in a world in which print culture had become normalized (Venkatachalapathy 1994). This was a hybrid culture; put in place in the seventeenth and eighteenth centuries by sundry European missions and colonial establishments, it then bloomed prodigiously after 1835 with the legalization of Indian ownership of presses. From around 1812, the College of Fort St. George in Madras, with its coterie of British administrator scholars and their Tamil-speaking subordinates, began to publish Tamil grammars, editions of ancient literary works, prose translations and commentaries, and so on (Zvelebil 1992: 159-64). By the 1890s, when *tamil1ppar1r1u* began to manifest itself, it was quite clear that print and prose were fundamental technologies through which it would be practiced. Well into the next century, the devout struggled to find funds for their printing presses, subscribers for their journals, and readers for their books. But they did not give up their confidence in this new miraculous technology that allowed them to circulate their ideas about their language among the populace, however limited its literacy. Speeches made in Tamil revival organizations and literary academies, at public rallies, even street poetry and processional songs, were invariably translated into print. Print helped in the standardization and homogenization of Tamil, and granted it a visible continuity with an ancient remote past that it resurrected. It ushered in new discursive styles, modes of punctuation and syntax, genres of literature, transformations in script, and new ways of relating to the language—as something seen and read, rather than merely heard. Like the modern nation, the devotional community was at its core a print community, a network of Tamil speakers who were also now readers and consumers of the language, "connected through print" (Anderson 1983: 47-49).

Finally, as Tamil emerges as a subject of devotion in the late nineteenth century, it also becomes a subject of history. In 1903, V. G. Suryanarayana Sastri (1870-1903) posed a novel question—"What is the history of a language?"—and then replied: "The emergence of sounds to express thought, and the formation of words; speech and its development into language; alphabets and their use in writing; grammatical conventions and language formation; word conventions and textual traditions—these are the contents of the history of a language" (Suryanarayana Sastri 1903: i-ii).

Recognizing the existence of such histories in Europe, Suryanarayana Sastri appropriated the new European sciences of comparative philology and historical linguistics to publish his *Tamil1mol1iyin1 Varalâr1u* (History of the Tamil language), arguably the first secular history of the language in Tamil. A little prior to this, M. Seshagiri Sastri had published a philological analysis of the language (1884). Indeed, comparative philology elicited much admiration among the devout. As one of them, D. Savariroyan (1859-1923), declared:

The science of Comparative Philology—the invention of German writers enables one to understand the secrets of languages, their points of resemblance or divergence. It discloses as in a mirror, the origin and growth of a language, its primary and secondary stages, its manifold transformations, its word-formation and its grammatical structure. The cultivation of such a study confers innumerable benefits on the languages and without doubt we also shall be partakers of these advantages according to the degree to which we cultivate it.

This fascination with comparative philology and historical linguistics was clearly compensatory, a response to colonial comments on the absence of "historical," "comparative," and "scientific" work in India prior to the arrival of European technologies of knowledge. So, the missionary Robert Caldwell (1814-1891), author of *A Comparative Grammar of the Dravidian or South-Indian Family of Languages* (1856), acknowledged the "earnestness" and "assiduity" with which "native" grammarians had hitherto studied their languages, but observed with regret that they did not have the "zeal for historic truth" that is the "special characteristic of the European mind":

They have never attempted to compare their own languages with others—not even with other languages of the same family. They have never grasped the idea that such a thing as a family of languages existed. Consequently the interest they took in the study of their languages was not an intelligent, discriminating interest....Their philology, if it can be called by that name, has remained up to our own time as rudimentary and fragmentary as it was ages ago. Not having become comparative, it has not become scientific and progressive....If the natives of southern India began to take an interest in the comparative study of their own languages and in comparative philology in general...[t]hey would begin to discern the real aims and objects of language, and realise the fact that *language has a history of its own, throwing light upon all other history.*

The "comparative" study of languages, the genealogical links between languages of the same "family," the "history" of language, and the "progress" of language: these provided the agenda for the numerous linguistic studies carried out in colonial India, "the happy hunting ground of the philologist," from the late eighteenth century. Colonial ideologies were driven by the assumption that "mastery" of India's languages would secure the "mastery" of India; it would enable British "command" and "native" obedience; and it would ensure "the vast and noble project of the Europeanization of the Indian mind." The "grand work" of British rule was thus inevitably accompanied by the colonization of Indian languages, a project involving "descriptive appropriation" and "prescriptive imposition and control" (Cohn 1985; Fabian 1986: 76). India's numerous languages were collected, classified, standardized, enumerated, and thus dramatically transformed from "fuzzy" and "uncounted" entities into neatly bounded, counted, and mapped configurations (Kaviraj 1992). The result was an arsenal of grammars, manuals, dictionaries, and glossaries culminating in the grand, multivolume authoritative *Linguistic Survey of India* (1903-28). Caldwell's *Grammar*—the most cited English-language narrative in Tamil devotional discourse—belonged to this arsenal and authorized many of the founding assumptions of Tamil devotion. It popularized the key term "Dravidian" (based on the Sanskrit word *drâvidòa,* itself a transmutation of *tamil1*) as the umbrella category for Tamil and the other languages of South India whose origins and structure, as demonstrated using the "scientific" principles of comparative philology, were quite different from Sanskrit and its "Indo-European family of tongues" of the North. Partha Chatterjee (1993: 7) has recently suggested that the modernization and standardization of Bengali from the mid-nineteenth century was carried out by an emergent bilingual intelligentsia "*outside* the purview of the [colonial] state and European missionaries." Yet India's languages, Bengali included, were (re)appropriated by their speakers only after they had been incorporated into a colonial economy of distinctions, hierarchies, and meanings. Thus Tamil's devotees waged their battles on a colonial (and colonized) terrain where Sanskrit loomed loftily as a "classical" tongue, and Tamil was reduced to a mere "vernacular" where Sanskrit was the language of the "fair" and "noble" Aryans, Tamil the tongue of the "menial" and "dark skinned" Dravidians; and so on. Colonial knowledges of India were certainly "dialogically" produced through interactions with "native" categories, traditions, and informants. In the process, however, many a "native" notion was fundamentally altered in meaning as well as in use, the modern concept of "Dravidian" being an excellent case in point (Irschick 1994).

Above all, the colonization of language meant its historicization: language has a history of "its own," a history that, like many others in the nineteenth century, was imagined organically. So languages are born, grow, produce literatures, spawn civilizations, and even die, if not tended to appropriately. The histories of various languages were laid out in linear narratives which sequentially charted their evolution through time. Produced as they were in a colonial context, many such narratives about India's languages were steeped in the rhetoric of decline and degeneration. A glorious past was inevitably followed by the dismal present; under the aegis of the British and enlightened "natives," India's languages could be rescued, "revived," and "improved," paving the way to a bright future. This logic of decline and of improvement drives Tamil devotionalism as well, which attempts to historicize Tamil by locating its "origins," "development," and "spread." Such a historicization is invariably accompanied by a comparison of its "progress" with that of other languages; not surprisingly, it culminates in the lament that Tamil was utterly doomed, and that something had to be done to save it. When this historicizing imperative converges with the patrimonial imagination about Tamil, an entirely novel horizon of sensibilities crystallizes that I characterize as *modern*. The life of the language is now perceived as inextricably intertwined with the lives of its speakers as an imagined community: their pasts, present, and futures are inseparable. So declared one of Tamil's devotees in 1915: "O Tamil pandits! O Tamil people! Be warned! Guard your language. Language is the life of its community of people. If the Tamil language is destroyed, the excellence and glory of the Tamilians, too, will be destroyed....Let your tongues only speak Tamil; let your quills only write Tamil; let your hearts only desire Tamil" (Subramania Siva 1915: 202).

It is because Chinnasami and his fellow devout are subjects of such an imagination that their stories inevitably differ from those of any speaker of Tamil who loved and praised the language prior to modernity.

Language and Gender

The globalization of the nation form and its cultures of modernity enabled the universalization of the concept of language as "mother tongue," the site where culture becomes nature. The mother tongue is a construct that emerged at a particular historical moment in the complex transformation of Europe's linguistic landscape from the middle of the second millennium, as Latin was progressively withdrawn from the public domain and the "vernacular" was elevated as the language first of the state and then eventually, by the nineteenth century, of the nation (Seton Watson 1977). The historicity of the construct, however, has scarcely been explored. Consider the following statement by the American literary critic Walter Ong:

> Why do we think so effortlessly of the first language we learn as our "mother" tongue?...The concept of "mother" tongue registers deeply the human feeling that the language in which we grow up, the language which introduces us as human beings to the human life-world, not only comes primarily from our mother, but belongs to some degree to our mother's feminine world. Our first language claims us not as a father does, with a certain distance that is bracing...but as a mother does, immediately, from the beginning, lovingly, possessively, participatorily, and incontrovertibly. Mother is closer than father: we were carried in her womb. In her and from her we were born. Our world is a fragment of hers.

Yet neither Ong nor other scholars who routinely use the term "mother tongue" interrogate the historical conditions under which the "first language" comes to be so "effortlessly" attached to "our mother's feminine world," from philology to pedagogy. Why in so many contemporary societies whose patriarchal foundations have been only further updated with modernity, and where everything from property inheritance to the generational transmission of one's very name is reckoned through the father, does the figure of the mother come to be associated with language? The association seems especially surprising given the importance accorded in modernity to language as the essence of the national spirit. Even for feminist theorists of language, this has not been a matter of concern (Cameron 1990), nor has it been one for scholars of South Asia. This is particularly striking because the category of the "mother tongue"—and its equivalent in Indian languages—appears to have gained salience only from the second half of the nineteenth century in the subcontinent, but has since become ubiquitous. Today, speakers of Tamil invariably use this term, and its Tamil gloss, *tâymol1i* (lit., "mother language"), to refer to their language. Consider how one of its admirers defines Tamil as *tâymol1i:* "Tamil is the *tâymol1i* of the Tamil community. The newly born child calls the woman who gave birth to it, *'ammâ'* [mother]. She, too, coos over her child and calls it *'kanònòç'* [precious one]. So, because Tamil is the language with which the mother is hailed, and it is the language which the mother herself uses, it is our *tâymol1i*" (Sivagnanam 1970: 2).

The echoes here of Ong's statement from the other side of the world are loud and clear. As we will see, Tamil's devotees, as indeed others in India, struggled to secure official recognition, from the colonial state, of their language(s) as "mother tongue." What was at stake in doing so? Why does the new people centered ideology of language and the patrimonial imagination ushered in with modernity resort to the figure of the mother? In attempting to answer such questions for Tamil, this study opens up for critical scrutiny the feminization of languages in modernity, a feminization that has been so naturalized as to have sealed off the "mother tongue" from history.

Tamil devotion would remain simply a rehearsal of Europe's linguistic history if all that happens to Tamil in the course of being drawn into various structures of modernity is its recasting as "mother tongue," *tâymol1i.* Yet this is not the only kind of feminization that the language undergoes within the regimes of *tamil1ppar1r1u.* For lurking in the shadows of the "mother tongue," but frequently disrupting its hegemonic claim on Tamil, is Tamil1ttây (lit., "Mother Tamil"), the apotheosis of the language as goddess, queen, mother, and maiden. Indeed, in the discourses of Tamil's devotees, there is a ready slippage between *tamil1* Tamil1ttây; *tâyppâl,* "mother's milk" *tây,* "mother" and *tâymol1i,* "mother tongue," all of which over time come to be synonymous with each other. Like other figures of difference, Tamil1ttây operates subversively to disrupt the flow of hegemonic discourses and ideologies, compelling the "mother tongue" to reveal the convergence between "language" and "motherhood" that has come to be so naturalized. The work of Tamil1ttây thus offers a striking illustration of the displacement and disarticulation of European notions at the very site of their colonial deployment.

My first introduction to Tamil1ttây came in 1988 when I chanced upon an anthology of poems called *Mol1iyaraci*, "Queen language." Its very first selection, drawn from an 1891 play, *Man1ôn1manòîyam*, by P. Sundaram Pillai (1855-97), represented the earth as a woman whose beautiful face is *paratak kanòtòam* (India) and whose radiant brow is the southern peninsula. The *tirâvitòa nâtòu* (Dravidian land) adorns that brow as an auspicious *tilakam* (sacred mark). The poem then declared:

- O great goddess Tamil (*tamil1 anòanku)!*
- Like the fragrance of that *tilakam*, your fame spreads in all directions, and delights the whole world.
- Spellbound in admiration of your splendid youth and power, we offer you our homage.

The poem went on in this vein for several more verses (Velayutam Pillai 1971: 1-3). My interest in it was further piqued when I discovered that its first verse was institutionalized in June 1970 as the Tamilnadu state's "prayer song." The government's reasons for doing this are telling:

It is observed by Government that many prayer songs are being sung at the commencement of functions organized by Government or attended by Ministers. In order to ensure uniformity in the singing of prayer songs, the Government have been for some time considering whether a theme might be chosen for being rendered as a prayer song, which will have no religious or sectarian association. After very careful consideration, the Government have decided that the piece containing six lines from Thiru. [Mr.] Sundaram Pillai's "Manonmaneeyam" which is an invocation to the Goddess of Tamil, would be an appropriate theme for being rendered as a prayer song.

In his reminiscences, M. Karunanidhi (b. 1924), the Tamilnadu chief minister who ordered the institution of the prayer song, observes that there were orthodox Tamilians who objected to this official recognition accorded by the state to the "Goddess of Tamil." Yet despite this, the government stood by its decision. Soon after, in April 1971, the adjoining union territory of Pondicherry, the predominantly Tamil-speaking former French colony, also instituted an anthem in praise of Tamil1ttây based on a 1939 poem by the well-known poet and native of Pondicherry, Bharatidasan (1891-1964) (Krishnamurthy 1991: 139-40).

Over the next couple of decades, both governments faced many problems in implementing their orders and getting their constituents to sing these songs correctly. Many Tamilians do not even realize that Tamil1ttây is the embodiment of the language they speak when they invoke her in these songs. Nevertheless, what intrigues me is that the governments of both these Tamil-speaking regions chose to make Tamil devotion into an everyday public and performative act in this way. Why personify the language, and why resort to the female figure? How is the female body deployed in devotional discourse(s), and to what ends? Why does the figure of the mother come to dominate from among a whole range of female subject-positions?

Just as intriguing to me has been the virtual lack of recognition accorded to Tamil1ttây by scholars. Elsewhere, I have suggested that this may be due to the many ambiguities that surround the figure in the intellectual and cultural discourses and practices of the region (Ramaswamy 1993: 687-90). But it is precisely because it is a figure—of speech, worship, and identity—which manifests itself episodically that I am intrigued by the cultural, political, and ideological work to which Tamil1ttây has been put by her devotees. How does one write the history of a concept that is not ubiquitous, consistent, or immediately apparent? Fellow scholars in Tamilnadu frequently expressed incredulity and even skepticism over my interest in Tamil1ttây. "There is no such thing as Tamil1ttây," one of them told me; "she is only a figment of our imagination," another assured me. I found it difficult to reconcile such statements with my innumerable encounters with her in essays, poems, songs, textbooks, newspaper reports, and public speeches. If Tamil1ttây is so inconsequential, why did these texts dwell in such loving detail and at such length on her various attributes, marvel over her many past achievements, and lament over her current state of decrepitude? If she is only a figment of the imagination, how would we account for the colorful posters and newspaper cartoons which have made visible what is arguably a mere metaphor? And what about her wooden and stone statues and metal images which have transformed literary imagination into material substance? Coming of age as a historian at a time when the clarion call of my discipline has been to make the hidden, the submerged, and the suppressed "visible," I asked myself how one writes the history of something that is visible but not seen.

For her devotees, Tamil1ttây is a singular figure with her own unique biography, a repertoire of deeds that cannot be reproduced, and a range of powers unfathomable. There is literally no one like her. Yet it is clear that she joins a pantheon of comparable female icons of the nation such as Bhârata Mâtâ, "Mother India" Britannia of England; Marianne of France; Guadalupe of Mexico, and the like (Agulhon 1980; Gutwirth 1992; Mosse 1985; Ryan 1990; Sarkar 1987; Warner 1985; Wolf 1958). Some other Indian languages have been similarly feminized (King 1992). Nevertheless, because she is a figure who cannot be easily assimilated or translated into a ready-made narrative of language-and-nationalism organized around the founding concept of "mother tongue," Tamil1ttây allows me to interrogate and write the language question differently. So, in spite of her interstitial and episodic presence in the narratives of her own devotees, Tamil1ttây emerges as one of the principal protagonists of this book.

Preview

Tamil's devotees tell numerous stories about their language. The many variations and differences in these stories are informed, however, by one foundational narrative, which goes like this. Once upon a time, long long ago, Tamil1ttây had reigned supreme, lavishly patronized by great Tamil kings. That had been an age of peace, prosperity, and happiness. There had been no inequities based on caste, creed, or gender. Learning, culture, and civilization had flourished. Today, however, ignored by her "children," "Tamil1ttây has been cast into prison....[S]he has several ailments. She languishes away, devoid of the fine food of poetry....How many wounds, how many scabs, how many boils, how many pustules, how many scars, plague our mother! Tamil1ttây's beautiful body—her glorious form—is now riddled with bloody wounds. And what of her heart?" (Kalyanasundaranar 1935: 30-31).

Her devotees identify their land and community with the body of Tamil1ttây: "O Mother! Your land shrinks! Your sons diminish! Your body, too, shrinks!" (Suddhananda Bharati 1936: 10). In turn, the salvation of the body politic lies in ridding the body of Tamil1ttây of its wounds, scars, and centuries of neglect. Her devotees repeatedly insist that if Tamil1ttây prospers, so too will Tamilians, and so too will their land and community. In the mystical poet Suddhananda Bharati's utopian vision of a new Tamil homeland restored to the reign of Tamil1ttây and Tamil learning:

> *Thre is gold and greenery everywhere;*
>
> *The smile of our illustrious queen who reigns over the cool Tamil grove, is like the glow of the morning light that destroys darkness...[!]*
>
> *Countless poets sing their songs!*
>
> *The cuckoos fill the air with sweet Tamil music!*
>
> ......
>
> *The land holds high its head; our own arts and sciences shoot up like mountains!...*
>
> *The parched land is now a pleasant grove!*
>
> ......
>
> *Holding her auspicious scepter, our mother reclines gloriously on her priceless throne of knowledges....*
>
> *And celestials pray for her long life thus, "Long live Tamil sweeter than nectar!...*
>
> *May you grace us so that Tamil learning flourishes and the entire world flourishes with it!"*
>
> *(Velayutam Pillai 1971: 80-81)*

This narrative of the golden past of Tamil, its degenerate present, and its utopian reign in the future provides the driving imperative for Tamil devotional practice, which draws its strength from the desire to restore Tamil and Tamil1ttây's lost honor and pride. This imperative manifests itself in the repeated plea that Tamil speakers should wake up from their centuries of "sleep" and, filled with a new consciousness (*unòarcci*), bring about the "improvement" (*valòarcci*) of Tamil. Only thus could they fulfill their filial debt to their language/mother and reestablish the rule of Tamil (*tamil1 âtòci*) (Kothandaraman 1986).

Clear as this agenda may appear, it was constrained from the start by the multiple and often countervailing conceptions that prevailed about the language among its devotees, and it is these that I first detail in chapter 2. I follow this, in chapter 3, with an analysis of Tamil1ttây, a figure that appears on the surface to bring unity to the multiple imaginings about Tamil, but that on closer scrutiny dissolves into the contrary images of goddess, mother, and maiden. My aim in this chapter is to demonstrate that just as Tamil is multiply configured, and Tamil1ttây is multiply imagined, so too is language devotion multiply manifested, as religious, filial, and erotic, all struggling for prominence and domination.

From love, I move to questions of labor in chapter 4. Here, I explore how the differing agendas of the various imaginations about Tamil come into play in public policies and politics, and I track the many dilemmas that trouble its devotees as they translate their "talk" of *tamil1pparlr1u* into *tamil1ppanòi,* "service" and "work" for Tamil. And then at last in the penultimate chapter 5, I turn to the lives and stories of those devotees, which are offered as models of emulation for all good and loyal Tamil speakers. My concern here is to chart the production of what I characterize as the "devotional subject," an entity wrought in the cauldron of Tamil devotionalism whose history is the story of the language, and whose life cannot be imagined independently of Tamil. At the turn of this century, the devotional subject is one among a large number of possible subject-positions occupied by speakers of Tamil. By the middle of this century, not least because of the myriad activities of *tamil1pparlr1u,* there is a dramatic shift: the devotional subject is the only legitimate subject, for to be Tamilian meant that one *has* to be a devotee of Tamil; there is no other subject-position possible or desirable for its speaker, in the view of the ardent enthusiast. I explore this at some length in my concluding chapter 6, where I consider how the "Tamilian" becomes a subject of Tamil as the language itself becomes subject to *tamil1pparlr1u.*

Love, labor, and life as these are articulated in the discourses of Tamil devotion around the figure of Tamil1ṭtây: these, then, are the primary concerns of this study. It is with the help of Tamil1ttây and the practices of *tamil1pparlr1u* that coalesce around her that I set out to explore the language question in Tamil India differently—as a history that appears almost the same, but is not quite.

ONE LANGUAGE, MANY IMAGININGS

One Language, Many Imaginings

In his important reflections on language and nationalism, *Imagined Communities,* Benedict Anderson concludes evocatively: "What the eye is to the lover..., language—whatever language history has made his or her mother tongue—is to the patriot. Through that language, encountered at the mother's knee and parted with only at the grave, pasts are restored, fellowships are imagined, and futures dreamed" (1983: 140).

In this statement, as elsewhere in the vast scholarly literature on nationalism, languages are assumed to have singular, homogeneous, and stable identities that their speakers carry with them from mother's knee to the grave. Yet this in itself is perhaps one of nationalism's lasting myths, installed by its own strategies of rationalization and standardization of language. The many adventures of Tamil within the discourses of *tamil1ppar1r1u* suggest rather that attachment to a language is rarely singular, unanimous, and conflict-free. A language may carry a singular name—its "proper" name—but this does not necessarily translate into a singular body of sentiments that connect it to its speakers. Instead, as languages are subjected to the passions of all those interested in empowering them, they attract multiple, even contrary, imaginings. The power that they exercise over their speakers is correspondingly varied, multiplex, and historically contingent.

The putative unity suggested by the name "Tamil" notwithstanding, there is no monolithic presence which reigns in the regimes of Tamil devotion that so assiduously transform the language over time into an object of adulation, reverence, and allegiance. Instead, it is imagined in different ways in different contexts by different devotees. In four such regimes of imagination—the "religious," the "classicist," the "Indianist," and the "Dravidianist"—Tamil is variously conceived as a divine tongue, favored by the gods themselves; as a classical language, the harbinger of "civilization" as a mother tongue that enables participation in the Indian nation; and as a mother/tongue that is the essence of a nation of Tamil speakers in and of themselves. *Tamil1ppar1r1u* is thus not a static monolith, but evolves and shifts over time, entangled as it is in local, national, and global networks of notions and practices about language, culture, and community.

What follows in this chapter, then, is a discursive history of Tamil from the 1890s to the 1960s. By "discursive history" I mean the history of the discourses that gathered around Tamil as it became the focus of talk and practice. "Discourse" has become one of the most frequently used but casually understood terms of our times. My own sense of it has been influenced by Foucault's. Although I do not necessarily agree with many aspects of his work nor explore all its consequences, I do follow his assumption that discourses are "practices that systematically form the objects of which they speak," and I agree with his insistence that production of discourses (= "knowledges") cannot be divorced from the work of power (Foucault 1972: 49). Accordingly, I focus on statements not primarily to analyze their truth-value, their accuracy, or the extent to which they correctly reflect the "beliefs" of their producers; instead, my concern is to consider how propositions are advanced and arguments built; to uncover the ideological devices used and conceptual moves made in this process; and to determine how certain notions about language, culture, community, and history acquire a hard materiality with the circulation and recirculation of such utterances through talk as well as institutional practices. For devotees of Tamil, undoubtedly, *tamil1ppar1r1u* is a state of mind, an exemplary habit, a way of life—indeed, the only possible condition of being. It may be all these, but I analyze it as a network of discourses which forms, and reforms, the focus of its attention, the Tamil language.

Further, I also treat *tamil1ppar1r1u* as a network of competing "projects." The concept of "project," too, has been much-used but little defined in recent scholarship. Like Nicholas Thomas, I find the concept useful, for it draws our attention "not towards a totality such as a culture, nor to a period that can be defined independently of people's perceptions and strategies, but rather to a socially transformative endeavor that is localized, politicized, and partial, yet also engendered by longer historical developments and ways of narrating them" (1994: 105). As Thomas writes,

> A project is neither a strictly discursive entity nor an exclusively practical one: because it is a willed creation of historically situated actors it cannot be dissociated from their interests and objectives, even if it also has roots and ramifications which were not or are not apparent to those involved. And a project is not narrowly instrumental: the actors no doubt have intentions, aims, and

aspirations, but these presuppose a particular imagination of the social situation, with its history and projected future, and a diagnosis of what is lacking, that can be rectified....This imagination exists in relation to something to be acted upon...and in tension with competing...projects, yet it is also a self-fashioning exercise, that makes the maker as much as it does the made. And projects are of course often projected rather than realized.

Not least of the reasons I find such a notion of the project attractive is because it allows me to consider Tamil's devotees not as mute ciphers but as interested beings grappling with the many new ideas—and some old ones—about their language ushered in with modernity, even as it draws attention to the discursively situated contexts of their articulations and practices.

Religiously Tamil: The Language Divine

Through much of the nineteenth century in many parts of India, the quest for foundational principles for the "reform" of society in the aftermath of colonial conquest led to a retreat into "religion" and "tradition," imagined as sites outside the sphere of the colonial state, and hence pure and untouched. What followed was a fundamental redefinition of religious identities, the polarization of communities on religious principles, and the yoking of religious traditions to the various political and cultural projects of modernity (K. Jones 1989). These came to pass in the context of a colonial regime which singled out religiosity as the essential, inherent, and eternal trait of the Indian, just as materialism and science were the province of the West. For India, therefore, true modernity "would lie in combining the superior material qualities of Western cultures with the spiritual greatness of the East" (Chatterjee 1986: 51).

Living as they did in the crosswinds of colonial modernity, many of Tamil's devotees, too, fell victim to the assumption that religious fundamentals would provide salvation to a populace imagined in decline. The means to such a salvation lay in divine Tamil, "the tongue vouchsafed by God to fulfill his purpose in this world" (Devasikhamani 1919: 24). (Re)assertions of Tamil's divinity (*teyvattan1mai*) accompanied a wave of religious revivalism which surfaced in the Madras Presidency in the closing decades of the nineteenth century, primarily centered around a reworking of Shaivism, declared the most ancient and authentic religion of those Tamilians who were not Aryan Brahmans. Neo-Shaivism, as I shall refer to this reformulated religion, began to make its presence felt from around the 1880s through the publishing and organizational activities of some its principal exponents, such as P. Sundaram Pillai, J. M. Nallaswami Pillai (1864-1920), P. V. Manikkam Nayakar (1871-1931), K. Subramania Pillai (1888-1945), Nilambikai Ammai (1903-45), and, most prolific of all, Maraimalai Adigal (1876-1950). These reformers typically hailed from the ranks of the new elites spawned by colonialism everywhere in India: they were educated, urban, middle-class, upper-caste "non-Brahman" professionals and government employees. They may have disagreed with each other on finer points of terminology or doctrine, but they were unanimous in their demand for the removal of "polytheistic" religious practices, claimed to have been introduced into a pristine Shaivism by Aryan Brahmans from the North through their linguistic vehicle, Sanskrit. Their program was puritanical and elitist as well in its advocacy of vegetarianism and teetotalism, and in its call for the excision of "irrational" customs and rituals (animal sacrifices, the worship of godlings, and the like) which were the very stuff of village and popular religion. For the true "Tamil religion" (*tamil1ar matam*), they insisted, was the monotheistic, "rational" worship of Shiva using pure Tamil rituals based on Tamil scriptures performed by Tamil ("non-Brahman") priests through the liturgical medium of divine Tamil (Alarmelmankai 1914; Maraimalai Adigal 1930a, 1974b; K. Subramania Pillai 1940; Swaminatha Upatiyayan 1921).

Neo-Shaivism emerged to counter what was perceived as the disparagement of Dravidian beliefs in colonial narratives, as well as in neo-Hindu formulations produced primarily in northern India. Numerous internal contradictions and changes through time notwithstanding, British colonialism operated on the fundamental assumption that India was primarily Hindu, and that Hinduism, in turn, was made up of at least two principal streams which were historically, philosophically, and racially different from each other. On the one hand, there was the high and morally uplifting religion of the "Aryans" locked away in ancient Brahmanical texts written in Sanskrit, which a whole century of Orientalist research had construed as authentic and pure Hinduism. On the other, there were the "aboriginal," "barbaric," "material demonologies" of the "pre-" or "non-" Aryan tribals, village folk, and uneducated masses, which, by the 1880s, were increasingly identified by many as "Dravidian." Dravidian religion was generally caricatured as "fear ridden," "hideous," and "wholly degrading, intellectually, morally, and spiritually" (e.g., Elmore 1915: 149-52; Whitehead 1921: 152-58). It was deemed "primitive" because of the absence of recognizable scriptural or philosophical traditions such as those possessed by the "civilized" Aryans, and because of its reliance on shamanistic rituals, animal sacrifices, and animistic ceremonies involving petty village deities and bloodthirsty mother-goddesses.

Such colonial speculations also generated an evolutionary theory of Indian religious history (Inden 1990: 117-20). The dark, feminine, materialistic, and sensual religion of the aboriginal Dravidians was conquered by the philosophically and intellectually advanced, virile, white gods of the Aryans. Over the centuries, it was conceded, the two religions did intermesh, the influence of the superior Aryan modifying the "crude animism" of the primitive Dravidian for the better. This had not happened, however, without taking a toll, for latter-day Hinduism reveals the extent to which a pristine Aryan religion had itself come to be eroded by the superstitious and animistic practices of the Dravidian "substratum" (Caldwell 1856: 518-28; Elmore 1915; Whitehead 1921). Nevertheless, "whatever be their present-day union or interminglement, it is difficult to imagine any original connection of the Aryan Brahmans and their subtle philosophies, with the gross demonolatory of the Dravidian peoples who surround them" (Government of India 1912: 51).

Such a theory was extremely useful for a body of thought that we now identify as "neo-Hinduism," which struggled to salvage Hinduism from a colonial scrutiny that savagely denounced some of its aspects, while lavishing praise on others. Like colonialism in whose shadows it was forged, nineteenth-century neo-Hinduism, too, reduced "India" to a Hinduism whose pure and authentic manifestations were limited to the Sanskritic scriptural tradition characterized as "Aryan" (Halbfass 1988: 197-262; K. Jones 1989). In many a neo-Hindu narrative, the progressive admixture of the aboriginal Dravidians had caused the "fall" of Hinduism from its glorious Aryan beginnings, a decline that was only further exacerbated with the invasions of the Muslims. Although not all neo-Hindus or Indian nationalists unanimously participated in the denigration of the Dravidian, they nonetheless shared a lasting conviction that India could be saved by returning to the imagined purity of a pristine Sanskritic Aryanism (Leopold 1970).

By the turn of this century, several neo-Hindu organizations had established themselves in the Madras Presidency; one of the most influential among them was the Theosophical Society, which moved its headquarters to Adayar in 1882-83. The society was heavily patronized by English-educated Tamil Brahmans who found its validation of scriptural and Aryan Hinduism, appropriately scientized and modernized, particularly satisfying (Irschick 1969: 26-54; Suntharalingam 1974: 290-311; Mani 1990). While Brahmans all across India generally prospered under colonial rule, Tamil-speaking Brahmans had especially reaped rich rewards. Barely 3 percent of the population, they disproportionately dominated the bureaucracy and various professions such as education, journalism, law, and medicine, as well as associational politics, into the 1920s, primarily by getting a head start in English and university education (Visswanathan 1982). But even more perniciously, Brahman domination was ensured by a colonial legal culture which institutionalized Brahmanical social theory as the very foundations of the Raj (Derrett 1968: 225-320; Washbrook 1989: 241-44). As a consequence, all those caste Hindus who were not Brahman—almost three fourths of the populace of the Presidency—were unilaterally considered "Shudra," the lowest of the Sanskritic fourfold hierarchy. Such a characterization came to be increasingly resented by the later decades of the nineteenth century by upper-caste "non-Brahman" landholding and merchant elites, growing numbers of whom, especially among Chettis and Vellalas, were also acquiring English education and competing for urban jobs, as well as for political privilege, within a colonial state structure that was undergoing increasing bureaucratization and centralization (Barnett 1976: 22-27; Washbrook 1976: 280-87). So P. Sundaram Pillai, one of the founding fathers of neo-Shaivism, complained thus in 1896 to a fellow Vellala, Nallaswami Pillai:

> Vellalas who form the flower of the Dravidian race have now so far forgotten their nationality as to habitually think and speak of themselves as Sudras....In fact to tell them that they are no more Sudras than Frenchmen and that the Aryan polity of castes was the cunningly forged fetters by which their earliest enemies—

the Aryans of the North—bound their souls which is worse than binding hands and feet, might sound too revolutionary a theory, though historically but a bare fact.

Many a Brahman intellectual was quick to respond to such charges. M. Srinivasa Aiyangar, amateur historian and litterateur, countered:

Within the last fifteen years, a new school of Tamil scholars have come into being, consisting mainly of admirers and castemen of the late lamented professor...Mr. Sundaram Pillai....Their object has been to disown and to disprove any trace of indebtedness to the Aryans, to exalt the civilization of the ancient Tamils, to distort in the name of historic research current traditions and literature, and to pooh-pooh the views of former scholars, which support the Brahmanization of the Tamil race.

Not least of the consequences of the turn-of-the-century culture wars between these elite products of the "new" education and of the colonial bureaucratic and professional systems was that by the 1920s Brahmans as a community were declared enemies of Tamil and of its speakers. Manickam Nayakar, a devotee of Tamil who also claimed that "his best and tried friends are mostly Brahmans," was compelled to declare in 1917 that "the general disposition of many a Brahmin is to disown his kinship with the rest of his Tamil brethren, to disown his very mother Tamil and to construct an imaginary untainted Aryan pedigree as if the Aryan alone is heaven-born....[T]heir general trend is to assume that they are themselves Aryans and not Tamilians, and to take as an axiom that Tamil and Tamils owe everything to Sanskrit" (Manickam Nayakar 1985: 75). Indeed, as we will see, although individual Brahmans continued to proclaim their *tamil1ppar1r1u* into the 1920s, their devotion was always suspect, tainted as it was by their community's support of Sanskrit, increasingly deemed alien to Tamil and its culture.

In such a charged climate, the ascendancy of the Brahman dominated Indian National Congress in the early 1900s, and the entry of the Theosophical Society into nationalist politics from 1913, only fueled the growing fears of the Vellala and Chetti elite that under the guise of "nationalism," Brahmans would hijack the nation and turn it into a Sanskritic, Aryan, and above all Brahman domain. In such a nation, Tamilians who were not Brahmans would continue to be ritually and socially denigrated as "Shudra," "the sons of concubines" (Maraimalai Adigal 1963, 1974a: 44-45). It is thus not surprising that the earliest efforts to constitute an alternate non-Aryan, non-Sanskritic, and non-Brahmanical religion as the embodiment of all that was truly and originally Tamil were most actively sponsored by these Vellala and Chetti elites. Synecdochically representing the entirety of the "non-Brahman" populace of the region, they vigorously argued that it was only such a "Tamilian religion" that would stem the continuing empowerment of an Aryan-Sanskritic-Brahman-Hinduism which inevitably spelled doom for Tamil and its speakers in the emergent nation. In turn, these "non-Brahman" elites received the support of the colonial state, itself-seeking allies to counter the growing influence of the Congress. The consequence was an informal alliance between them and the colonial administration, which is reflected in the pro-British stance of the Justice Party (founded in 1916-17 to represent "non-Brahman" interests) and in the eulogies of British rule and English that surfaced within neo-Shaivism (Maraimalai Adigal 1967a, 1974a: 45-46).

The Polarization of Tamil and Sanskrit

So, from the turn of this century, neo-Shaivism engaged in a complex set of maneuvers. On the one hand, it had to counter the damaging caricatures of Dravidian religion in colonial narratives. On the other, these very texts also contained much ammunition that could be deployed for its battle against neo-Hinduism and its surrogate, Indian nationalism: the declaration that Dravidian religion far preceded Aryan arrival, not just in the Tamil-speaking country but all over India; the suggestion that Tamil-speaking Brahmans had never participated in this religion; the pronouncement of ancient Tamilian society as egalitarian, untainted by the hierarchical and oppressive caste system of the Aryans; and above all, the possibility that that most important Hindu deity, Shiva, might be Dravidian in origin (Elmore 1915: 13-14; Gover 1871: 1-15). Neo-Shaivism appropriated such colonial propositions, fused them with statements drawn from pre-colonial Shaiva narratives, and proposed the following tenets of the emergent "Tamilian religion," *tamil1ar matam* (also called by some, "Dravidian religion," *tirâvit#a matam*): Shaivism is the true and original religion of all Tamilians who are not Brahman. It is also the most ancient religion of India, predating Sanskritic Hinduism by many centuries. Its principles are enshrined in the devotional and philosophical texts of divine Tamil, and it would be in vain, therefore, to seek it in the demonistic rituals of the populace (as the colonials were wont to). Further, it was not the Dravidians who corrupted a pristine Hinduism (as neo-Hindus were inclined to suggest); on the contrary, it was Brahmanism and Aryanism that had debased the original Tamilian religion and diverted it from its hallowed path of monotheism, rationalism, and egalitarianism into the "gutters" of polytheism, irrational rituals, and unjust social hierarchies (Maraimalai Adigal 1930a: vii-viii; Savariroyan 1900-1901: 269). The removal of such impurities brought in by Sanskritic Brahmanism would lead to the retrieval of pristine Shaivism, the restoration of a pure Tamilian subjectivity, and the growth of self-respect and pride among speakers of Tamil. And it is for this project that Tamil was enlisted by neo-Shaivism, its divinity reemphasized and popularized in the process. Cleansed of its Sanskritic impurities, the divine language would be the beacon that would throw light on all that was originally Tamil/ Dravidian. It would sift and separate the pure Tamil Shaiva texts from all those masquerading as such.

The writings and speeches generated by neo-Shaivism show that this was not an easy or consistent project, not least because there was little agreement over what constituted the original Shaivism, and because it was difficult—in certain cases impossible—to dismantle the complex linkages that had developed between Tamil and Sanskrit over the centuries of their coexistence from the early first millennium C.E. In the early decades of neo-Shaiva activity, from around the 1880s to around 1905, there were few explicit statements against Sanskritic Hinduism per se. The focus instead was on countering the negative characterizations of Dravidian religion by asserting its distinctiveness, its uniqueness, its rootedness in high philosophy, and its parity with the Sanskritic tradition. "Moderate" neo-Shaivism, therefore—as exemplified by the writings of J. Nallaswami Pillai, for instance— visioned Tamilian religion as part of a larger Hindu complex, but oriented around divine Tamil and its scriptures rather than around Sanskrit.

Gradually, however, such assertions gave way to overt antagonism towards Sanskritic-Brahmanical-Aryan-Hinduism, and even to calls for a complete break from the latter by the 1920s.

This transformation took place in the context of changes in the curriculum of Madras University, which, starting in 1906, became the site of an acrimonious debate over the compulsory study of Sanskrit and the elimination of the "vernaculars" the growing demand for "Home Rule" by the Besant led factions of the Congress, beginning in 1915; the British promise of "self-government" by stages in 1917; the many attempts after that by the colonial state to play off the "non-Brahman" against the Brahman in electoral politics; and finally, the iconoclastic atheism of E. V. Ramasami (1879-1973) and his followers (Irschick 1969; Nambi Arooran 1980: 35-139; Washbrook 1976: 274-87). In the "radical" neo-Shaivism that crystallized in response to these events, and is perhaps best exemplified by the later religious writings of Maraimalai Adigal, a Tamil-speaking Dravidian "non-Brahman" Shaiva community was clearly posited against Sanskritic, Brahmanical, Aryan Hinduism (Maraimalai Adigal 1930b, 1974b; K. Subramania Pillai, 1940: 45-47). Talk of parity between Tamil and Sanskrit gave way to assertions of the superiority of the former. Legends and stories that had accumulated over the centuries about Tamil's divine powers were recycled and embellished, and the very legitimacy of Sanskrit was questioned in this process.

One such story, based on an incident in the life of the nineteenth-century mystic Dandapanisami, is especially popular in neo-Shaiva tellings. When challenged by a Brahman who invoked the superiority of Sanskrit because the *Veda*s were in that language, Dandapanisami declared that unlike them, the Tamil scriptures did not advocate the sacrifice of goats and the consumption of meat. The argument between the two notables continued for a while, and it was finally decided to settle the matter by calling upon the deities. They placed in front of the spear of Lord Murugan three chits with the following messages: "Tamil alone is eminent," "Sanskrit alone is eminent," and "Both are eminent." A virgin maiden was asked to choose among the chits and she picked out the one that declared, unambiguously, "Tamil alone is eminent." Dandapanisami rejoiced, brushed his eyes reverentially with the chit, and then placed it in his mouth. Subsequently, he composed his famous verse on Murugan which praised him as the lord who himself had declared Tamil's superiority over Sanskrit. He then went on to write the

Tamil1alank#âram, a hundred-verse eulogy of Tamil recounting its various miraculous abilities and supernatural powers (Velayutam Pillai 1971: 124-61). In the same vein, another of Tamil's admirers, years later, narrated a story his mother had told him about one of his ancestors who had had the power to cure the sick and the dying with the help of Tamil hymns. One day, a cobra, with its hood raised, wandered into the room where he sat, offering his prayers in Tamil. It drank some milk and slithered away, leaving him unharmed. "Is it not clear from this that Tamil has supernatural powers!" he asked rhetorically of his readers. Such stories, of which there are many, reminded Tamil speakers that the Tamil scriptures were infinitely superior in their moral and ethical content, and in their salvific potential, to the Sanskrit *Veda*s. It was a Brahmanical conspiracy that denied the divinity and ritual efficacy of Tamil, designated it as a "Shudra" language, and appropriated all its treasures, including the mighty Shiva himself, for Sanskrit (Maraimalai Adigal 1936a: 105-6; K. Subramania Pillai n.d.: 15-17).

By the time radical neo-Shaivism was under full steam in the 1920s, it was declared unequivocally that Tamil, and not Sanskrit, was the *only* appropriate ritual language for all pious Tamilians. Indeed, Tamil is the world's first divine language, and the religion it expounds the most eminent: "In the whole wide world, there is no greater god than Paramashivam [Shiva]; no religion loftier than Shaivism; no land more superior to the Tamil land; no language more divine than Tamil...and no people more auspiciously pure than Tamilians" (Swaminatha Upatiyayan 1921: 20).

Taking advantage of the technologies and communication possibilities generated in the colonial milieu, neo-Shaiva associations and publications took this message of Tamil's divinity to the public. They urged Tamil speakers to make divine Tamil the center of their renewed religious lives, the core of their (recast) beings. Prior to the neo-Shaiva revival, the cause of divine Tamil and of Shaivism had largely been the purview of religious specialists, temples, and monasteries. Now, lay intellectuals and activists—who were career bureaucrats, lawyers, academics, and even civil engineers—established societies for propagating the message of neo-Shaivism in various cities and towns across the Tamil-speaking parts of the Presidency. They published books and journals, conducted religious and Tamil classes, arranged conferences, and ran local libraries (Nambi Arooran 1980: 20-21; Ramaswamy 1992b: 84-89). Many of these societies as well as their journals were short lived, and suffered throughout their careers for want of support and subscription. Yet there are success stories as well, such as the Tirunelvçli Ten1n1intiya Caivacittânta Nûr1patippuk Kal1akam, founded in 1920. Both this organization and its journal *Centamil1c Celvi* (founded in 1923) continue to exist today, albeit not without their share of problems. Although neo-Shaiva organizations eschewed direct participation in associational politics, they threw their influence behind many causes dear to *tamil1ppar1r1u* such as the demand for education in Tamil, the numerous protests against Hindi, and the movement for renaming Madras state as Tamilnadu, the land of Tamil.

Being Religious, The Tamil Way

Movements for religious reform in colonial India have been extensively studied, and a recent volume clearly shows that spoken, rather than scriptural, languages were the sites of some of the most intense debates and discussion in this regard (K. Jones 1992). Yet, while we have a growing understanding of the recastings of religious doctrines, practices, and conceptions of community, the changes undergone by the languages through which such reconfigurations were attempted have been left largely unexamined. *Tamil1ppar1r1u*'s divinization of Tamil to authenticate its project(s) reminds us that the medium itself has to be empowered in order to empower the message, to invoke an overused but nevertheless appropriate cliché. Neo-Shaivism declared that Shaivism and divine Tamil are the two "eyes" with which modern Tamil speakers would regain their lost vision and be redeemed. Divine Shiva and his divine Tamil go together, hand in hand, and cannot be separated: each lends power and authority to the other.

Neo-Shaivism emerged to counter what was perceived as the recasting of India as predominantly Aryan, Sanskritic, Brahmanical, and Hindu by both colonialism and neo-Hinduism. Such a countering was necessary because of the fear that "non-Brahman" Tamil speakers would inhabit such an India only in the fissures: ritually denigrated, socially demoted, and symbolically cast out, as "Dravidians" and "Shudras." Yet speakers of Tamil had once been the dominant people of the subcontinent, a preeminence they had lost with the arrival of Sanskritic Aryan Brahmanism. In Maraimalai Adigal's version of this imagined history, "the religion of the land, that is Shaivism, underwent a marked change." Yet, he wrote, this was a change that was limited to the "outer rim," for "in its center, it remained as pure as crystal and as impenetrable as a hard diamond. What is bound and true to its core, what is perfect and complete in itself, requires no change, requires no improvement" (Maraimalai Adigal 1930c: iii).

Neo-Shaivism attempted to recover this imagined pure center and use it as the foundation on which to (re)constitute a true Tamilian religious subjectivity untouched by Brahmanism, Aryanism, Sanskrit, and Hinduism. Cleansed of its Sanskritic impurities, Tamil, the language in which its pure and original scriptures were deemed written, was the means through which this center could be reached. The language had perforce to be (re)divinized for this project, for it had to take on and counter the power of divine Sanskrit. Other religious groups in earlier times had advocated the divinity of Tamil, but not always at the expense of Sanskrit, and not in such a sustained and prolific manner using the modern technologies of print and communication (Ramaswamy 1996). In the changed circumstances of the late colonial period, when a devolving state rewarded communities that could establish their timeless distinctiveness and religious autonomy, there was much to be gained by claiming the existence of a unique Tamilian/Dravidian community, bonded together from time immemorial by its own distinctive religious traditions that were embodied in its own sacred language. Such a claim necessarily called for a delegitimization of Sanskrit and a radical distancing from its scriptures and tradition. Such a project also perforce needed the projection of Tamil as divinity, the ranking favorite of the gods themselves.

Civilizing Tamil: The Language Classical

The search for authentic first principles as the foundation on which to rebuild a modern community did not lead all of *tamil1ppar1r1u* towards religion and Shaiva scriptures. Instead, with the help of the secular sciences of comparative philology, archaeology, ethnology, and history, a new source for these was located in ancient Tamil heroic and love poems of the so-called Cank#am age of the early centuries C.E. Hitherto completely outside the horizon of contemporary scholarly awareness, these poems were "discovered" and published between the 1880s and 1920 primarily because of the efforts of C. W. Damodaram Pillai (1832-1901) and U. V. Swaminatha Aiyar (1855-1942). The story of this "discovery" in all its fascinating detail has yet to be told, but it is important to register some of its manifold effects on *tamil1ppar1r1u.*

Most immediately, with this "discovery," the antiquity of Tamil literature, dated up until then in colonial histories to the late first millennium, was now pushed back, at the very least, to the early centuries C.E., and in the writings of some devotees to the beginning of time itself. These poems not only deepened the antiquity of Tamil literature, but quite as crucially, within a few years of their being made public, they came to be valorized as the repositories of an ideal and perfect Tamil society, prior to its colonization by either the British or, more enduringly, by the Brahmanical Aryans from the North. They were combed to generate nostalgic portrayals of an ancient Tamil people who were adventurous and heroic; who roamed the high seas in pursuit of gold and glory; who were "hospitable and tolerant in religion," "egalitarian" and "rationalist," fun-loving but contemplative and philosophical as well (Kanakasabhai 1966). Most significantly, these poems were tangible proof that Tamilians were speakers of the only "living" "classical" language and the proud possessors of a great "civilization," the most ancient in the world. Devotional narratives, regardless of their ideological differences and political commitments, are saturated with the pride that their authors experience in being the modern day inheritors of this ancient literature. In his memoirs, S. Ilakuvan (1910-1973), a Tamil college teacher who was imprisoned in 1965 for his participation in the anti-Hindi protests, has this to say about the effect on his young mind when he learned in college about the antiquity of Tamil and the wealth of its literature:

The glories of the ancient Tamil land and the eminence of Tamilians captured my heart. I became convinced that classical Tamil (*uyartan1ic cemmol1i*) had to have been the mother of all the languages of the world. I was saddened that our great and glorious Tamil country has today lost its name, and languishes away as a small part of Madras [Presidency]. I resolved that my life's mission lay in restoring the rights of the Tamil land, and the preeminence of Tamil. The battle for Tamil is the battle of my life. Similarly, M. P. Sivagnanam (1906-1995), who hailed from an indigent working-class family and could afford only a primary school education, studied these poems on his own when he was in a colonial prison in the early 1940s. He writes of his experience on reading one of the anthologies of the Cank#am corpus, the *Pur1anân1ûr1u:*

> I gained consciousness of belonging to a community called Tamilian when I first read the *Pur1anân1ûr1u.* Before that, I knew I was a Tamilian. But it was only on reading the *Pur1anân1ûr1u* that I realized that the Tamil-speaking people had their own unique history, their own unique customs, their own distinctive political traditions, and their own nationality. Tamilians have had their own unique motherland (*tâyakam*) and its name is Tamilnadu, I realized. Tamilnadu had been ruled for thousands of years by Tamilians. It struck me that no empire from the North had ever subjugated Tamilnadu or Tamilians during the Cank#am period. When I learned that men and women lived as equals in those days, my heart rejoiced. I forgot myself when I read the poems about the heroism of the mothers who sent off their young, innocent sons to the battlefield thronging with spears. I thanked God with all my heart for the good fortune of being born in such a Tamil land.

Again and again, there are similar examples of the wonder and admiration that the poems of this ancient literary corpus elicit from Tamil's devotees. They have been invoked as models for personal belief and behavior, as inspiration for public and political action, and as the founding charter for an ideal society of the future in which Tamil would reign supreme, once again.

The Tyranny of Civilization

An undiluted enchantment with the Cank#am age undoubtedly floods the entire devotional community. But its poems were of special interest to a particular regime of *tamil1ppar1r1u* that I characterize as "counter Orientalist classicism." This regime's fundamental agenda lay in securing acknowledgment—from the world at large, but especially from the colonials and from the Aryan North—of the "civilizational" status of Tamil culture. It went about this task by demanding recognition of an ancient truth that had been grossly overlooked by Orientalism, colonialism, *and* metropolitan nationalism: namely, that Tamil, too, like Sanskrit, was glorious, polished, and perfect. It is *centamil1*, "refined Tamil." Yet Orientalism and the colonial state had classified it as a "vernacular," as a corrupt derivative of Sanskrit, and denied its great texts the status of "literature." Classicism thus sought to rescue Tamil from its current lowly status as a mere "vernacular" (*un#n#ât#t#u mol1i*) and to have it reinstated in all its glory as a "classical" language (*uyartan1ic cemmol1i*) that was, like Sanskrit, Greek, and Latin, the vehicle for a lofty, unique, and refined literature, culture (*pan#pu*), and civilization (*nâkarîkam*) (Suryanarayana Sastri 1903: 132-34). The historian Nambi Arooran (1980: 70-110) has skillfully charted the growing demand among Tamil scholars and politicians from the early decades of this century for recognition of Tamil as a classical language on par with Sanskrit (and Arabic and Persian) in the curriculum of Madras University. I would suggest that there were other gains to be made in securing such a recognition, besides ensuring the victory of "non-Brahman" (Tamil) over "Brahman" (Sanskrit) in the struggle for power in the region. A less tangible, but nonetheless potent, consequence lay in the possibility that Tamil speakers, too, might now demand membership to that select club of "civilized" cultures of the world whose languages had been deemed "refined" and "classical."

It has been suggested that "the colonies of the European empires were in the nineteenth and early twentieth centuries the context of a new and doomed efflorescence of European discourse about virtue, race, and civilization, even while that discourse was in a process of radical reconsideration in Europe as the alternative ontology of 'political economy' advanced" (Kelly 1991: 11). Tamil devotionalism as conducted in the classicist idiom offers one striking illustration of such an efflorescence, although I will reserve judgment (for now) on whether this was necessarily "doomed." Unlike neo-Shaivism, which retreated into the domain of an (imagined) uncolonized religion to conduct its project of resistance and renewal, classicism took its battle right into enemy territory. For the concept of "civilization" was no innocent classificatory device through which Orientalist and colonial knowledges neatly organized the messy world of culture(s). Instead, it was a fundamental technology of rule in which colonial dominance was secured by institutionalizing a hierarchy of differences, not only between the "West" and the "Orient," but between the various regions, cultures, and communities of the subcontinent as well, on a developmental scale ranging from savage barbarism to civilized perfection. Language was one tangible index by which such differences of cultural and moral worth were measured. The "inflectional" Indo-European, representing the summit of linguistic (and racial) achievement, was the standard by which the "tonal," "isolating," and "agglutinative" languages that were not Indo-European were evaluated: the latter were declared incapable of expressing complex, abstract, refined thought. Correspondingly, their speakers were "primitive," "barbarous," and morally deficient (Curtin 1964; Metcalf 1994; Spadafora 1990).

Such notions were embedded in numerous discourses on language, race, and progress that came to the attention of Tamil's devotees. Consider the following unflattering portrayal of the "Turanians," a linguistic and racial group into which, through much of the late nineteenth century, many colonial narratives placed Tamil speakers:

> We may say generally that a large number of them...belong to the lowest Paleozoic strata of humanity[,]...peoples whom no nation acknowledges as its kinsmen, whose languages, rich in words for all that can be eaten or handled, seem absolutely incapable of expressing the reflex conceptions of the intellect or the higher forms of consciousness, whose life seems confined to the glorification of animal wants, with no hope in the future and no pride in the past. They are for the most part peoples without a literature and without a history[,]...peoples whose tongues in some instances have twenty names for murder, but no name for love, no name for gratitude, no name for God.

And consider the response by one of Tamil's devotees, Nallaswami Pillai, to such a characterization:

> Did we not all read in our school-days that the Tamilians were aborigines and savages, that they belonged to a dark race, a Turanian one, whom the mighty civilising Aryans conquered and called Dasyus, and that all their religion, language and arts were copied from the noble Aryan. Even a few years ago, a great man from our sister Presidency held forth to a learned Madras audience how every evil in our society, whether moral, social or religious, was all due to the admixture of the civilized Aryan with the

barbarous Tamilian. Classicism, like neo-Shaivism, thus set out to contest all such claims—Orientalist as well as metropolitan Indian—that denigrated Tamil speakers as "barbaric" and "primitive," and that unilaterally declared that the "civilized" Aryan was inevitably superior to the "aboriginal" Dravidian. This battle, however, was fought not on the ground of religion but on the terrains of "literature" and "history," those domains whose very possession spelled the difference between peoples who led moral and civilized lives and those who barely subsisted on immoral "animal wants." In this war, the weapon was the "classicality" (*uyarttan1iccemmai*) of Tamil with which its devotees would demonstrate the originality, autonomy, and antiquity of their culture and history; the distinctiveness of their language from Sanskrit; its crucial role as a parent of many languages; and its status as the fount of an ancient civilization as glorious as, if not more glorious than, the Sanskritic one (Maraimalai Adigal [1948]; Suryanarayana Sastri 1903).

Like neo-Shaivism, classicism, too, was an oppositional discourse that was conducted largely by an educated, urban, and professional middle-class, attracting academics (historians, litterateurs, philologists, and Tamil scholars), schoolteachers, lawyers, and bureaucrats. Unlike neo-Shaivism, however, a number of Brahman admirers of Tamil, among them V. G. Suryanarayana Sastri, T. R. Sesha Iyengar (1887?-1939), and U. V. Swaminatha Aiyar, joined the ranks of devotees who were nominally Christian, such as D. Savariroyan and G. Devaneyan (1902-81), as well as upper-caste "non-Brahmans" like P. Sundaram Pillai, Maraimalai Adigal, and Somasundara Bharati (1879-1959), and those of Sri Lankan origins such as Damodaram Pillai and V. Kanakasabhai (1855-1906). Like neo-Shaivism, classicism primarily conducted its activities through literary and historical societies, the most famous among them (which continue to exist today, although fairly truncated) being the Maturait Tamil1c Cank#am, "Madurai Tamil Academy," founded in 1901 (henceforth Madurai Tamil Sangam); the Karantait Tamil1c Cank#am, "Karanthai Tamil Academy," founded in 1911 (henceforth Karanthai Tamil Sangam); and the Shaiva Siddhanta Kazhagam. Like their neo-Shaiva counterparts, with whom they frequently shared members, their contrary views of Tamil notwithstanding, these associations promoted the cause of Tamil in educational institutions, petitioned for the establishment of a Tamil University, encouraged the battle against Hindi, and so on. But most of all, they focused upon editing and printing ancient manuscripts, publishing periodicals and books, holding literary festivals, running libraries, and conducting classes for the study of classical Tamil. As such, they represent the antiquarian and scholastic aspirations of *tamil1ppar1r1u.*

The Contest with Sanskrit

Classicism, too, was concerned, like neo-Shaivism, with demonstrating the antiquity (*ton1mai*) and primordiality (*mun1mai*) of Tamil, as well as its uniqueness (*tan1imai*) and purity (*tûymai*). These were not established, however, by linking Tamil to the world of the gods, as in neo-Shaivism. Instead, it was argued that Tamil is the first language of the first humans to flourish on the face of this earth, prior to the emergence of any other language or people (Devaneyan 1966; Maraimalai Adigal 1948). Indeed, classicism drew upon the secular science of comparative philology to dispute ancient religious stories (which neo-Shaivism had revived) about the divine origins of Tamil, insisting instead that the language was not bestowed upon the world by Shiva, but emerged to fulfill the need for human communication (P. T. Srinivasa Aiyangar 1985: 13-15; Suryanarayana Sastri 1903: 51-57).

In all such matters, classicism, too, of course contended with the hegemonic influence of Sanskrit, not so much as a "divine" language but as India's paradigmatic classical tongue. A century of colonial linguistic practice had only reinforced the ancient Sanskritic dogma that all languages (of India) are corruptions of a primordial, eternal Sanskrit. British scholar administrators and their Brahman teacher-assistants based in Calcutta's Asiatic Society and College of Fort William had declared Sanskrit as the fount of Indian "vernaculars," the sole generator of high Hindu civilization, and the only language worthy of comparison with the lofty Greek and Latin. This is a story that has been already told many times (Kejariwal 1988; Kopf 1969).

What has been less noted is the resistance to such formulations that arose almost from the beginning of colonial rule among British administrators and missionaries based in South India. Skeptical about the clubbing together of the languages spoken in "their" part of the subcontinent with the northern tongues, these men were especially critical of the characterizations of Tamil or Telugu as "vulgar derivatives" of Sanskrit. This skepticism was first voiced in Alexander Campbell's *Grammar of the Teloogoo Language* (1816) and in Francis Ellis's introduction to that grammar. Tamil and Telugu, it was argued, form "a distinct family of languages, with which the Sanscrit has, in latter times especially, intermixed, but with which it has no radical connection" (Ellis 1816: 2). In the 1840s and 1850s, other philological analyses reinforced such assertions, frequently referring to Tamil in this process as "copious," "elegant," "refined," and "cultivated" (Asher 1968; Singh 1969: 78-88). In 1855, Tamil was even declared "a rival of the ancient Sanskrit" (Bower 1855: 158). All such scattered observations were consolidated in 1856 in Robert Caldwell's *Comparative Grammar of the Dravidian or South-Indian Family of Languages,* which used the word "classical" to characterize *centamil1,* "correct Tamil" (Caldwell 1856: 31); authorized the name "Dravidian" to refer to the "family of languages" of South India, distinct from Sanskrit and its Indo-European family of tongues (28-37); insisted that Tamil "can dispense with its Sanscrit altogether if need be, and not only stand alone but flourish without its aid" (31); and suggested that prior to the arrival of Aryan Brahmans, the "elements of civilization" already existed among the Dravidians (77-79).

Tamil's devout found much that was flattering in Caldwell's *Grammar,* which lent the authority of comparative philology (and the West) to the claims of autonomy and distinctiveness of Tamil made in its pre-colonial texts that *tamil1ppar1r1u* resurrected. Yet Caldwell's hallowed status notwithstanding, all his ideas were not wholeheartedly embraced, pace recent scholarly evaluations of the missionary's impact on Tamil cultural politics (Dirks 1995, 1996; Ravindiran 1996). Indeed, many devotees resented his claim that the term *tamil1* had derived from the Sanskrit words *dravid#a* or *drâvid#a* (Chelvakesavaroya Mudaliar 1929: 9; Damodaram Pillai 1971: 3-6, 34-35; R. Raghava Aiyangar 1979: 4-13). Others objected to his attempts to establish affinity between the Dravidian and "Scythian" families of languages, insisting instead that the former was completely distinctive and autonomous (T. Chidambaranar 1938: 5; Devasikhamani 1919: 26). Many also set aside his suggestion that Dravidians had migrated into India, proposing instead an autochthonous origin which placed them in the subcontinent from the beginning of time (T. Chidambaranar 1938: 10). Finally, there were even those who resisted Caldwell's classification of Tamil as a "Dravidian" language, insisting that the word *dravid#a* had been used in the past for Tamil-speaking Brahmans alone (Damodaram Pillai 1971: 34-39; Devasikhamani 1919: 9; Somasundara Bharati 1912:1). Their resistance is not surprising, for in spite of some eulogistic portrayals of Dravidian culture in the writings of some colonials (like C. D. Maclean and Gilbert Slater), which the devotees found useful to invoke, the dominant colonial image of the Dravidian, as created through census records, administrative manuals, and district gazetteers, is captured in this unflattering picture of the 1891 *Census:*

> This was a race black in skin, low in stature, and with matted locks; in war treacherous and cunning; in choice of food, disgusting, and in ceremonial, absolutely deficient. The superior civilisation of the foreigner [the Aryan] soon asserted itself, and the lower race had to give way.... The newcomers had to deal with opponents far inferior to themselves in civilisation, and with only a very rudimentary political organisation, so that the opposition to be overcome before the Arya could take possession of the soil was of the feeblest.

In such statements, which were also picked up by many a metropolitan nationalist narrative to pursue the agenda of salvaging Indian pride by taking refuge in Aryanism, the white, virile, civilized, energetic, and superior Aryan is starkly contrasted with the dark, feminine, menial, and aboriginal Dravidian. Correspondingly, the latter's language, too, is "aboriginal," uncivilized, and inferior. So the 1901 *Census of India* observed: "In India, the Indo-Aryan languages—the tongues of civilization...—are continually superseding what may, for shortness, be called the aboriginal languages such as those belonging to the Dravidian, the Munda, or the Tibeto-Burman families....[I]t may be added that nowhere do we see the reverse process of a non-Aryan language superseding an Aryan one" (Government of India 1903: 248-49). This particular statement in the *Census* was authored by George Grierson, who headed the ambitious *Linguistic Survey of India* project for the colonial state (published 1903-28). It is telling that the underlying premise of this authoritative survey was that the "civilized" Aryan languages are inherently superior to the "aboriginal" non-Aryan. So, commenting on the progressive shrinkage in the spread of Dravidian languages, Grierson noted, "Aryan civilization and influence have been too much for [them]" (Government of India 1903: 279). And in the *Linguistic Survey*, although the "importance" of Tamil is recognized, and the antiquity of its literature noted, it is not unambiguously adorned with the mantle of classicality and civilization, as is Sanskrit (Grierson 1906: 298-302).

All the same, slowly but cautiously from the 1920s on, the colonial state began to concede the antiquity and "copiousness" of Tamil, and its status as a "cultivated" language. Dravidian speakers of today, the *Census of 1931* admitted, have "a culture of very great antiquity[;]...speakers of Dravidian languages [were] the ancient inhabitants of Mohenjadaro and perhaps the givers of culture to India" (Government of India 1933: 454-55). The *Census* was here alluding to the recently discovered archaeological remains of the Indus Valley in Mohenjadaro and Harappa, which pointed to a sprawling prehistoric urban civilization rivalling Mesopotamia and Egypt. To the delight of many a Tamil devotee, this prehistoric civilization was declared to have been possibly Dravidian by some colonial archaeologists. Thus Maraimalai Adigal quoted John Marshall in 1941:

> They (the orientalists) pictured the pre-Aryans as little more than untutored savages (whom it could have been grotesque to credit with any reasoned scheme of religion or philosophy). Now that our knowledge of them has been revolutionized and we are constrained to recognize them as no less highly civilized—in some respects, indeed, more highly civilized—than the contemporary Sumerians or Egyptians, it behoves [*sic*] us to re-draw the picture afresh and revise existing misconceptions regarding their religion as well as their material culture....The Indus Civilisation was Pre-Aryan and the Indus language or languages must have been Pre-Aryan also. Possibly, one or other of them...was Dravidic.

Maraimalai then proceeded to overwrite Marshall's tentative conclusion with the following sweeping pronouncement:

> If Sir John Marshall had had a first hand knowledge of the Tholkappiam and some other ancient classics of Tamil, he would have easily shown in corroboration of what he stated as regards the pre-Aryan antiquity of one of the Dravidian languages, that

Tamil, alone, and not any other, as he vaguely affirmed, must have been the language spoken and cultivated by the pre-Aryan inhabitants of the Indus Valley.

Maraimalai Adigal was not alone in making such a bold assertion. More than a decade earlier, in the late 1920s, soon after Marshall's report on the Indus Valley excavations was first published, fellow devotees T. R. Sesha Iyengar and M. S. Purnalingam Pillai had already insisted that "future discoveries and dispassionate researches" would confirm Dravidian authorship of the Indus civilization and "the remote antiquity" of Tamil culture (Purnalingam Pillai 1945: 26; Sesha Iyengar 1989: 32-61). They were able to make such assertions confidently, emboldened as they were by the many claims of classicism which challenged the dominant Orientalist wisdom about Tamil's place in India's past, and which proceeded to write an alternate script in which history began not in the North with the Aryans, but in the South with the Dravidians.

Opposing Orientalism

Classicism's status as an oppositional discourse is most apparent in the frequently expressed lament that the achievements of Tamil speakers in India's history had been totally ignored by scholars, especially those based in the North. As Sundaram Pillai dramatically declared in 1897: "The history of Indian Civilization is the old story of the Giant and the Dwarf. The victories in it are the victories of the vaunting Aryan, while the wounds are the wounds of the bleeding pre-Aryan" (quoted by Nallaswami Pillai 1898-99: 113).

The first step lay in overthrowing this "Aryan bigotry and pride" and rewriting the script of India's history so as to show how "Dravidian forebears enriched, strengthened and improved the culture of Aryan India" (Sesha Iyengar 1989: 63). Two basic strategies were adopted for such a rewriting. In the one that I call "compensatory," the aim was to demonstrate that "Hindu" or "Indian" civilization had emerged from a "harmonious commingling of the cultures of the Dravidian and the Indo-Aryan" (Sesha Iyengar 1989: 63). Tamil, it was insisted, "was quite as classical" as Sanskrit, and its literature "is no less ancient, noble, and vast." Tamil and its literature were thus validated by espousing a parity with Sanskrit, whose value was never questioned. Neither is the divide between "Aryan" and "Dravidian," seen as distinctive but complementary halves of "India," nor the legitimacy of the Brahman. As can be expected, compensatory classicism was a strategy that was favored typically, though not always, by devotees who were nominally Brahman, such as R. Raghava Aiyangar (1870-1946), M. Raghava Aiyangar (1878-1960), T. R. Sesha Iyengar, and Swaminatha Aiyar. Their commitment was to a syncretic Indian civilization jointly produced by the "genius" of Tamil and the "genius" of Sanskrit, both of which are necessary and complementary (P. T. Srinivasa Aiyangar 1985: 85).

From the start, but especially by the 1920s, this strategy was challenged by another that I call contestatory, paradigmatic examples of which may be found in the writings of Suryanarayana Sastri, Savariroyan Pillai, M. S. Purnalingam Pillai, Maraimalai Adigal, G. Devaneyan, K. Appadurai (1907-89), and K. A. P. Viswanatham (1899-1994), among others. Contestatory classicism asserted the superiority of Tamil over Sanskrit, rather than the parity of the two. Sanskrit, after all, was a "dead" language in contrast to the everlasting Tamil (*kan1n1ittamil1*). The "barbarian" Aryans had developed into "civilized beings" on coming into contact with the "highly civilized Dravidians" rather than the other way around. For in the ancient past, Tamilians were settled agriculturists, whereas the Aryans had been mere nomadic pastoralists. Tamilians lived in splendid cities and traded with distant lands, while Aryans were still grazing herds. Tamilians were monotheistic and philosophical, whereas Aryans were polytheistic and ritualistic. Tamil had not evolved from Sanskrit, as the Orientalists maintained; on the contrary, classical Sanskrit itself developed under the influence of Tamil (Maraimalai Adigal 1963, 1966; Purnalingam Pillai 1985: 4-5).

Thus contestatory classicism reversed Orientalism's claim that the true genius of India lay in its Aryan past, asserting instead that it is to Tamil and Tamilian culture that Indian civilization owes all, for, in Sundaram Pillai's words, "what is ignorantly called Aryan philosophy, Aryan civilization, is distinctively Dravidian or Tamilian at bottom" (quoted by Nallaswami Pillai 1898-99: 112). In the logic of contestatory classicism, Aryan Brahmans had not only been responsible for bringing about the end of the Dravidian golden age, but they had also stolen all that was originally and truly Tamil and passed it off as their own

(Maraimalai Adigal 1963, 1966; Savariroyan 1900-1901). Misinformed by such crafty Brahmans, Western scholars had got India's history all wrong. So instead of beginning in the North and with "the Aryan Conquest," Sundaram Pillai suggested that the "scientific historian" should begin his study in the South, which was after all, "India proper" (quoted by Nallaswami Pillai 1898-99: 113).

Tamil and the Nostalgia for Civilization

From early in this century, Tamil's classicist devotees went about the task of setting the record straight. The result has been a new—and, from the devotee's perspective, an infinitely more satisfactory—script for the Tamil (and Indian) past. In "the hoary past" (going back millions of years ago, in many accounts), there had been an ancient mega-continent (consisting of present-day Australia, Africa, and southern Asia) where Tamil had flourished. This was the land referred to as "Kumarikkan#t#am" in ancient Tamil texts and attested to as "Lemuria" by Western scientists. Classicism offered brief but nostalgic portrayals of Kumarikkan#t#am, imagined as the home of the first two Tamil academies that produced countless literary masterpieces. This state of prelapsarian bliss came to an end with a series of floods, which destroyed the original Tamil civilization and which compelled Tamil speakers to fan out and civilize different parts of the world, taking their language with them. "Traces of this wide dispersion are found in Palestine, Egypt, Italy, Scandinavia, and far-off Erin in the names of places with the suffix *ur,* in the modes of life pursued, in the resemblances of the Tamilian myths to those of Greece and to the northern sagas" (Purnalingam Pillai 1945: 4). So, the urban remains of the Indus Valley and the great poems of the Cank#am age were only the later remnants of a much more ancient Tamilian civilization, established at the very beginning of time. Orientalism had thus got wrong not only the history of India, but that of the world as well, for it was the Tamil-speaking land which was the "cradle" of the "whole human race" and of "human civilization" (K. Appadurai 1975; Devaneyan 1966; Somasundara Bharati 1912).

The consolidation of industrial modernity in the West has frequently sparked nostalgia for a life in nature, away from city lights and urban sprawls, amid fresh fields and rolling pastures.

Tamil1ppar1r1u, I have insisted, is a discourse of modernity. But it was conducted in the milieu of a colonial culture whose own ideology of the civilizing mission deemed that the natives lacked "culture" and "civilization." Tamil's modern devotees, therefore, yearn not for nature but for culture and for civilization. The archaeological remains of the Indus Valley and the poems of the Cank#am age, not to mention the antediluvian continent of Lemuria, enabled them to claim that Tamil speakers, too, had "civilization," just "like the Greeks," but even earlier. In 1967, C. N. Annadurai (1909-69), a devotee of Tamil who was also the chief minister of the state of Tamilnadu, gave a speech at Annamalai University in Chidambaram in which he extolled the virtues of the Cank#am poems and the antiquity of "Dravidian civilization." He then called upon the students to carry "the message that our classics contain to the entire world and declare that what was *the most ancient here is what is being introduced today as the most modern*" (quoted in Ryerson 1988: 141-42, emphasis mine). Reversing the logic of Europe's civilizing mission, *tamil1ppar1r1u* thus claimed that Tamil speakers did not need to be granted civilization, for they had possessed it all along, long before any one else, and indeed had bestowed it upon the rest of the world. But such a claim has come with its own costs. For in its anxiety to secure membership in the select club of the civilized, *tamil1ppar1r1u* reinforced Europe's civilizational model of the world. So, ironically, the "uniqueness" of Tamil and its "civilized" state is claimed by demonstrating its similarity with other "civilized" cultures, by insisting Tamil speakers were, after all, "the Greeks of the East" (Purnalingam Pillai 1985: 5-6).

LANGUAGE AND THE NATION: INDIANIZING TAMIL

In the 1890s, around the same time that neo-Shaivism and classicism emerged, a third imaginary also surfaced in the discourses of *tamil1ppar1r1u,* which I call "Indianist." Over the next few decades, it moved from strength to strength, gathering reinforcement from metropolitan Indian nationalism as well as compensatory classicism at home. By the 1930s, however, this regime had to contend with the assertions of both radical neo-Shaivism and contestatory classicism against Hinduism, Brahmanism, and Sanskrit, all of which Indianism deemed necessary to Tamil devotion. More contentiously, it locked swords with the Dravidianist regime of *tamil1ppar1r1u* that was provoked by the Madras government's attempt to institute the compulsory study of Hindi in 1937-38. Dravidianism introduced into Tamil devotion the political and cultural philosophy of E. V. Ramasami, C. N. Annadurai, and their populist Dravidian movement, which the Indianist regime branded as contrary to the spirit of Indian nationalism and hence illegitimate.

In contrast to neo-Shaivism and classicism, however, both Indianism and Dravidianism were overtly political projects concerned with transforming the nature of power relations in the Tamil-speaking region. But here the similarity between the two ends. For Indianism, it was British colonialism and English that had to be replaced by the Indian nation with its family of "national" languages, of which Tamil would be the language of the region, while Hindi would be the "official" language of communication with other Indians. For Dravidianism, on the other hand, "India" itself occupied the space vacated by the colonial, whose legitimacy was only ambivalently questioned. Indeed, the Dravidianist's scathing denunciations of the "imperialism" of India (identified with the North, Aryan Brahmans, Sanskrit, and Hindi) were as passionate as the Indianist's attacks on colonialism. This important distinction notwithstanding, both the Indianist and the Dravidianist are critically concerned with Tamil as the language of politics, and not merely as the language of religion and ritual, or literature and civilization. Their agenda was to ensure that Tamil ruled (again) within *tamil1akam*, "home of Tamil." Therefore, it was not enough to establish learned academies and publish books which proclaimed the glories of divine or classical Tamil. In addition, its devotees had to fight for its institutionalization as the language of government, education, and everyday public communication. As T. V. Kalyanasundaram (1883-1953) demanded in 1924, "What is the condition of our mother tongue, Tamil, today? Where is Tamil1ttây? Does she adorn the seat of government? Does she preside over our associations? Does she flourish in our legislative chambers? Can we at least see her in our schools and colleges? Can we spot her in those political bodies that claim to fight for our rights? At the least, is there a place for her in Tamil newspapers?" (Kalyanasundaranar 1935: 19).

Rather than relying on religious or literary revivalism, as did neo-Shaivism and classicism, these regimes therefore encouraged

Tamil enthusiasts to aggressively engage state structures and institutions, and to intervene in political processes, for it was in and through politics that Tamil could be empowered. And in turn, empowered by the claims of Indianism and Dravidianism, many devotees of Tamil went on to become state legislators; members of various government committees on language, education, and cultural policies; even chief ministers by the late 1960s. With Indianism and Dravidianism, *tamil1ppar1r1u* finally enabled its practitioners to secure power, privilege, even profit.

Indianism's prime exponents in the devotional community were V. O. Chidambaram Pillai (1872-1936), especially before the 1920s; T. V. Kalyanasundara Mudaliar prior to the 1940s; V. Ramalinga Pillai (1888-1972), R. P. Sethu Pillai (1896-1961), and M. P. Sivagnanam; and Brahmans like C. Rajagopalachari (1878-1972), V. V. Subramania Aiyar (1881-1925), Subramania Sivam (1884-1925), Suddhananda Bharati (1897-1990), and of course, the most paradigmatic of them all, Subramania Bharati (1882-1921). Generally from upper caste, middle-class, middle-income families—Sivagnanam is a striking exception here—they were professional journalists, lawyers, teachers, litterateurs, poets, and politicians; and in their private lives, they were reformed but devout Hindus. In contrast to Dravidianists, who imagined (away) India in very Tamil terms, these devotees framed their concern with Tamil in terms of India. India, in turn, was sometimes an abstract territorial space; at other times, it was personified, like Tamil, as the goddess and mother, Bhârata Mâtâ, "Mother India." So, the opening lines of one of Subramania Bharati's most popular poems on Tamil incorporates the phrase *vande mâtaram* (homage to [our] mother) from the famous hymn that the Bengali Bankim Chandra Chatterjee had composed in honor of Bhârata Mâtâ:

Long live the glorious Tamil!
Long live the fine Tamil people!
Long live the auspicious Indian nation !
......
Vantç Mâtaram! Vantç Mâtaram!
(Bharati 1987: 50)

It is not accidental that the "mother" whom this verse reverenced is not Tamil1ttây but Bhârata Mâtâ, for Indianism was driven by the terrible anxiety that *tamil1ppar1r1u* would lead Tamil speakers to forget India. Thus Tamilians were chastised in a poem by Ramalinga Pillai first published in 1922:

> *Intiyattây [Mother India] languishes in sorrow, and you speak of your own community!*
>
> *That is disgraceful!*
>
> *O Tamilian, break the chains that enslave that venerable woman...!*
>
> *Long live the Tamil land!*
>
> *May our Tamil language flourish, so that our Intiyattây who supports us may find fulfillment.*
>
> *(Ramalinga Pillai 1988: 29)*

Negotiating gingerly between loyalty to Bhârata Mâtâ and devotion to Tamil1ttây, between the shoals of pride in the nation (*tçs#âpimân1am*) and pride in their language (*pâs#âpimân1am*), Indianism reminded Tamil speakers that the liberation of Tamil would have to proceed in tandem with the liberation of India. In his reminiscences, the mystic-poet Suddhananda Bharati recalls how as a young man, his passions were directed as much against the emergent Dravidian movement as against the British, and how he and his young friends countered the cry of "Down with Brahman Rule" with the alternate cry of "Vantç Mâtaram." When we are enslaved to the British, what is the point of saying that we are slaves to Aryanism? he asks. "Relinquishing our home to a foreigner, siblings fight with each other over food. Meanwhile, the foreigner seizes all our food and goes away, leaving us with our squabbles" (Suddhananda Bharati 1950: 143-46). In the Indianist vision, therefore, Tamil speakers had to work together with their Indian "siblings" to throw off the shackles that fettered both Bhârata Mâtâ and Tamil1ttây, instead of fighting with each other. Swayed by the impassioned rhetoric of the Dravidian movement, they ought not to forget that this was their primary goal, Sethu Pillai reminded them on the very eve of Indian independence: "In fifteen more months, we are going to rule over our own nation. India is going to belong to Indians. Similarly, is there any doubt that Tamilnadu will belong to Tamilians?...Tamil1ttây in all her former glory and splendor will reign in our hearts" (Sethu Pillai 1968: 1-2).

Not surprisingly, Indianism launched few attacks on Brahmans, Aryanism, or Sanskrit. On the contrary, it produced sympathetic accounts of Brahman contributions to Tamil and its culture, many of whose authors were not Brahmans (Kalyanasundaranar 1935: 37-38; Ramalinga Pillai 1953: 44-48; Sivagnanam 1979: 96-101). Some of its proponents even cast aspersions on (colonial) neologisms such as "non-Brahman" and "Dravidian," whose very legitimacy and historicity they questioned (Bharati 1988: 229, 263; Ramalinga Pillai 1947, 1953: 40-51; Sivagnanam 1979: 63-68). Further, there was always a place for Sanskrit within Indianism's economy of sentiments about Tamil: "In Tamilnadu, Tamil ought to be preeminent. All over India, may Sanskrit flourish, as it always has. To accomplish the unification of our Indian nation, everyone should know Sanskrit. Nonetheless, in Tamilnadu, Tamil should flourish with great eminence" (Bharati 1988: 229).

Given this linguistic division of labor, some even recommended that Sanskrit should be the national language of India (Nuhman 1984: 57-59; Padmanabhan 1982a: 274-76; Rajagopalachari 1962: 51). Correspondingly, Indianist prose was also heavily Sanskritized, especially in the hands of its Brahman practitioners. This lack of hostility towards Sanskrit extended to other Indian languages as well. In the Indianist vision, India is a land where, "along with the glorious Tamil, there flourishes Sanskrit and Urdu and Persian, the unique Telugu, Kannada with its sweet words, lofty Marathi, and fine Malayalam, Gurjaram [Gujarati], Hindi, and eighteen such languages" (Venkatesvara Ayyar 1918: 3). This congenial vision, of course, was severely tested after independence with the struggle over linguistic states and the securing of borders with neighbors, as well as over the Indian state's Hindi policy in the 1950s and 1960s, as we will see.

But in general, Indianism's strategy was to gloss over all internal sources of contention and difference in favor of closing ranks against the real enemy, the English-speaking colonial. Tamilians were reminded, repeatedly, that it was English—rather than Sanskrit or Hindi or any other Indian language—which was responsible for the current sorry state of their beloved Tamil. Kalyanasundaram thus rebuked the Anglophiles who discarded Tamil1ttây and worshipped Ânk#ilattây (Mother English) instead. "Their birth mother starves; the other mother is well-fed. What a sign of our times!" (Kalyanasundaranar 1935: 21). In his autobiography, Suddhananda Bharati writes that from early in his life, he had to resist pressures brought upon him by his Brahman family to study English. He asked of them, "Why should I study English in order to be a servant to someone else? I am a Tamilian. I will only study Tamil." His resistance to English was fostered partly in response to an environment in which he saw so many young men mortgage their family homes and property to chase after an English education, only to wander around jobless afterwards. What did they acquire, he asks, "by giving up their mother and running after the other woman?" All they can say proudly is " 'I do not know the *Gîtâ*, but I do know Gibbon....' Is Tamil not enough for the Tamilian?" (Suddhananda Bharati 1950: 54-69; see also Bharati 1988: 180-85).

The Indianist dilemma is quite apparent in Suddhananda Bharati's story, however. He tells us that his youthful resistance to English soon gave way to an appreciation for its necessity for Tamilians if they wanted to be citizens of the world (Suddhananda Bharati 1950: 94). Indeed, he soon became "infatuated with English" he often gave public lectures in it, and even taught English to schoolchildren. Even the most anti-English of devotees was aware that English was necessary not just for learning the ways of the West, but also for communicating with other Indians until a suitable national language had been selected. As that latter project ran aground on the reefs of "Hindi imperialism," many devotees who in their early years wrote passionately against English, like Kalyanasundaram and Rajagópalachari, became its advocates, albeit reluctantly, from the 1940s.

In attempting to persuade Tamil speakers that "India" or its languages would not harm Tamil, Indianism came to rely heavily on the emotive metaphor of the mother. Consider the following statement:

The sons of Bhârata Mâtâ speak several languages....Our Indian sons adorn their Intiyattây [Bhârata Mâtâ] with these languages. In adorning her thus, is their unity harmed or affected? Those who say that the existence of so many languages is harmful speak from ignorance. Born from the womb of India, these brothers may speak various languages but are united by the same spirit of love and devotion for their nation....Therefore, the existence of so many languages in the nation is a sign of excellence.

The Indianist logic was the logic of the family, itself reconstituted as the foundational site of unity, cooperation, and harmony. Could siblings, born from the same mother's womb and reared on her milk, harm each other? So Ramalinga Pillai reminded his fellow speakers that they should not forget: "However many languages there are in the Indian nation, for several thousands of years, the Indian people have been drinking the same mother's milk, and are members of the same culture" (Ramalinga Pillai 1953: 53).

Indianism, of course, presented Tamil speakers with two mothers, Tamil1ttây and Bhârata Mâtâ. It was not a choice between one or the other, as Dravidianism would have it. Instead, in the Indianist imagination, while Tamil1ttây's womb and milk unites all Tamil speakers as *Tamilians,* the womb and milk of Bhârata Mâtâ transfigures them into *Indians,* and ties them with other Indians in webs of sibling solidarity. It is through sharing Bhârata Mâtâ's womb and milk that Tamilians, the children of Tamil1ttây, symbolically become part of the Indian body politic.

It is also the logic of the family and of motherhood that generated that very crucial notion that Indianism (and Dravidianism) popularized among Tamil speakers: namely, that Tamil is their *tâymol1i,* "mother tongue," the language of their home and mother. Part of the challenge that Indianism faced, of course, was to reconcile Tamil's homely status as "mother tongue" with neo-Shaivite attempts to promote its divinity, and classicist efforts to secure its classicality, a task that was not all that easy.

Indianism and Divine Tamil

Like neo-Shaivism, but unlike classicism or Dravidianism, the Indianist regime was willing to accept that Tamil is a divine language (Bharati 1988: 117; Ramalinga Pillai 1953: 13-18). Unlike neo-Shaivism, however, this did not lead it to question the legitimacy of Sanskrit and of Aryan Brahmanical Hinduism. Consider how Tamil1ttây introduced herself in one of Bharati's poems published in 1919:

The primordial Shiva gave birth to me;

The Aryan son Agastya saw me and took delight;

That Brahman endowed me with a grammar, complete and perfect. (Bharati 1987: 529)

All the same, even if Indianism thus upheld Tamil's divinity, it did not make this into a fundamental part of its own agenda, as did neo-Shaivism. For there was concern that dwelling on Tamil's divinity would hinder its transformation into a modern language of governance, education, public communication, and politics. As early as 1892, one of its devotees—T. Saravana Mutthu, librarian of the Presidency College, Madras—demanded, "How does it benefit Tamil if we vehemently insist that God created Tamil?" (1892: 3-4). The educationist P. Sivaswami Aiyar similarly suggested in 1917 that "instead of relying on the belief that Tamil was a divine gift and that its vocabulary was copious and its diction rich and self-contained, serious attempts should be made to incorporate into Tamil, from other languages, if necessary, terms that were easy to understand" (Irschick 1969: 304). Recognizing the growing skepticism among many about Tamil's abilities to communicate the modern sciences of the West, Bharati's Tamil1ttây observed to her "children" in 1919:

"Tamil will die a slow death
The languages of the West will triumph in this world."
So says the simpleton;
Alas! what an accusation!
Go forth in all eight directions!
Bring back here the wealth of all learning!
By the grace of my father, and the penance of our learned scholars, this great taint will be effaced,
With lofty fame I shall last forever in this world!
(Bharati 1987: 531)

It is perhaps not surprising that Bharati saw the task of modernizing and scientizing Tamil as a joint enterprise, made possible through Shiva's grace and human scholarship, for as he insisted elsewhere, Tamil's divine origin was not just fantasy but historically attestable (Bharati 1988: 117). Like Bharati, Indianism was ultimately ambivalent about Tamil's divinity, an ambivalence that is also reflected in its attitude towards religion. As did so many "secular" nationalists in colonial and post-colonial India, devotees of Indianist persuasion upheld the inherent equality of all Indian religions. All the same, Hinduism in particular—in its reformed new "universalist" version which condemned caste hierarchies and irrational rituals, and recommended an action oriented practice of spiritual truths—received special attention. For Bharati, as indeed for others like him, Hinduism was the best religion of the world and Tamil speakers its most eminent practitioners. Correspondingly, a true devotee of Tamil was not exclusively Shaivite (as in neo-Shaivism), nor polemically atheistic (as in Dravidianism), but clearly and proudly a "Hindu." As Bharati insisted in 1917:

> A man who has pride in Tamil (*tamil1apimân1am*) is one who embraces Hinduism (*hintu tarmam*). That alone will illuminate the path of the devotee of Tamil. For the man who does not care for the *Tçvâram*, the *Tiruvâcakam*, the *Tiruvâymol1i*, the *Tirukkur1al#*, and the *Kamparâmâyan#am* has no claim to be a devotee of Tamil. One who knows these texts will realize that it is through Hinduism that this world will find salvation.

Thus in contradistinction to radical neo-Shaivism, which adopted an oppositional stance towards Sanskritic Aryan Hinduism in the name of a "Dravidian" Shaivism, Indianism linked the cause of Tamil to an inclusivistic neo-Hinduism (Halbfass 1988: 403-18; Ramalinga Pillai 1953: 39). Indeed, to counter Christian missionary influence in schools (and later, the Dravidian movement's atheism), Indianism advocated a thorough grounding in Tamil and Sanskritic scriptures for Tamil children as part of its "national education" (*tçciya kalvi*) scheme.

All the same, such an embrace of religiosity brought its own share of problems for Tamil's devotees, as it did for others in modern India. Indianism did celebrate the existence of diverse religious beliefs among Tamil speakers, although it employed a distinctly Hindu idiom in such a celebration (Bharati 1937: 35-36; Ramalinga Pillai 1988: 28-29). Nonetheless, there was also considerable anxiety that such a diversity itself could, and did, give rise to sectarian divisiveness and tensions. Not surprisingly, in these circumstances, Indianism placed its hopes in Tamil as the bond which would tie together all Tamil speakers, be they Hindu, Muslim, or Christian. In a public speech that he gave in 1928, Kalyanasundaram pointed out: "If we wish to bind the people born in this [Tamil] nation in the net of unity, there is only one instrument, and that is the Tamil language.... We may be attached to different religions, but we cannot forget we are all Tamilians" (Kalyanasundaranar 1935: 25-26).

Kalyanasundaram was able to say this with confidence because he and his fellow devout were simultaneously creators as well as subjects of the founding certitude of *tamil1ppar1r1u:* in contrast to caste and religion, which divided one Tamil speaker from another, their language, especially in its incarnation as "mother tongue" and as Tamil1ttây, bonded them together in the "net of unity," as firmly and surely as the love of their mother(s).

Indianism and Classical Tamil

In the same manner that it affirmed Tamil's divinity, Indianism also confirmed its classicality, especially because the burgeoning classicist scholarship was so convincingly demonstrating to Tamil speakers that while their "mother tongue" might not yet be "scientific," it was certainly more ancient and venerable than English or any other European language being paraded around as a paragon of modernity. So Bharati (1937: 62) declared in 1919 that he had read and appreciated "the exquisite beauties" of Shelley, Victor Hugo, and Goethe, but no "modern vernacular of Europe can boast of works like the *Kural* of Valluvar, the *Ramayana* of Kamban and the *Silappadhikaram* (Anklet Epic) of Ilango."

Like the other regimes of *tamil1ppar1r1u*, the Indianist, too, represented the age of the Cank#ams as free of sectarian strife and caste oppression, when the philosophy of "all towns are our towns, and all men are our kinsmen" had reigned (Kalyanasundaranar 1935: 28-36; Ramalinga Pillai 1953: 57-59). Its concern with these poems as with other works of Tamil literature, however, was not so much antiquarian as it was utilitarian. The hope was that these would help modern Tamil speakers liberate themselves from their enchantment with English.

If they were exposed to the greatness of their past through the medium of their own language, they would truly appreciate the value of Ilango and Kamban, instead of lauding Shakespeare and Tennyson (Bharati 1937: 62; C. S. Subramaniam 1986: 252-60; Kalyanasundaranar 1919: 122-26). Accordingly, many of Tamil's Indianist devotees, like Subramania Aiyar, Chidambaram Pillai, and Sivagnanam, undertook the publication of accessible (and in many instances Sanskritized) interpretations of ancient Tamil works, which were also popularized through literary conferences, street plays, and movies (Sivagnanam 1970: 97-104, 109-15).

While there was a general consensus that it was important to stress Tamil's classicality so as to bolster the pride and self-respect of its speakers today, there was also concern that an excessive emphasis could detract from the equally urgent task of transforming it into a modern language of rule, education, and everyday communication. And this utilitarian thrust to the Indianist project led it to rebuke, even denigrate, "panditic" and scholarly Tamilians who, it was claimed, resisted efforts to help change Tamil into a useful contemporary language, in their single-minded pursuit of its classicality (Bharati 1987: 527-28; Nuhman 1984: 16-33; C. S. Subramaniam 1986: 264-65). For Indianism, a true Tamil devotee was one who made Tamil suitable for school textbooks, and one who would ensure that it was the language used by its speakers in their assemblies and associations. "The Tamil devotee (*tamil1apimân1i*) is one who produces new knowledges, new literatures, and new life in Tamil," in Bharati's words (Thooran 1986: 256-57). The absence of modern, scientific literatures in Indian languages, devotees like Bharati insisted, perpetuated Indian enslavement to English through dependence on the Western mastery of the sciences. The aim therefore was to learn as much as possible from English, in order to displace it from its throne and replace it with Tamil, suitably modernized and scientized.

Their faith in the inherent greatness of Tamil notwithstanding, many of its devotees wondered about its ability to communicate modern, scientific thought. From the turn of this century, these enthusiasts had to face Anglophile critics who claimed that "wallowing in sentimentalism," supporters of Tamil were sacrificing the youth of the country to their "superstitious beliefs in the vernaculars." A contributor to the *Educational Review* in 1916 insisted, "The fact is that our vernaculars are in a most crude state so far as scientific exposition is concerned. It is no answer to say that we have very good poetry and some grandiloquent prose, in the vernaculars. A language that is well-equipped for poetic expression is not necessarily so for a scientific thesis. Kalidasa and Bhavabhuti may well feel handicapped if they were set to translate a modern elementary textbook of science" (quoted in Irschick 1969: 304-5). The challenge therefore lay in scientizing Tamil, in transforming it from a language of great poetry and piety into one of modern science and technology.

A similar challenge was faced by language reformers and modernizers in other parts of the subcontinent, as indeed in other regions of the world (Fishman, Ferguson, and Dasgupta 1968). But in Tamil India, those committed to the creation of scientific vocabularies had to contend not only with all the problems of colonial modernity (such as borrowing from the West without sacrificing pride in the indigenous, embracing the secular without surrendering the religious, and so on), but also with the many languages that rivalled for attention as the reservoir from which to draw for "improving" Tamil—English, Sanskrit, and classical Tamil being the principal contenders. By the 1930s, devotees of Indianist persuasion came to clash with others on this matter because in their logic, Sanskrit was the one language that had the power to displace English, a contention that gave rise to considerable ire, as we can imagine.

This was not the only problem that Indianist devotees faced, for they also sought to ensure that in the process of modernizing and scientizing Tamil, they authorized a language that could easily be used by "the people," its principal consumers. Indianism's clarion call, as captured in Bharati's exhortation "to write as one speaks," meant that the Tamil used in textbooks, newspapers, and political speeches ought to be understood, in the words of V. Ramaswamy (1889-1951), by the rickshaw puller on the street. So Bharati's preface to his famous 1912 poem *Pâòcâli Capatam* (The vow of Panchali), insisted: "Simple words, a clear style, easy rhythms that can be readily comprehended, and simple tunes that the common folk will appreciate—he who composes a poem along these lines today will be breathing new life into our mother tongue" (quoted in Nuhman 1984: 92). Yet the modern Tamil authorized by Indianism in the name of "the common folk" continued to be Sanskritic in its lexicon, betraying both the upper-caste and upper-class prejudices of its practitioners, as we will see.

Indianism and the "Mother Tongue"

In all these struggles—to counter the excessive influence of Tamil's divinity and classicality, to wean Tamil speakers away from their infatuation with English, to create new vocabularies for use in scientific education and modern government, to fashion a language that would be understood by "the common folk"—Indianism relied extensively on Tamil's status as "mother tongue."

In the Indianist regime, as indeed in Dravidianism, the speaker's relationship to Tamil is cast in the intimate and familiar terms of a child's interactions with its mother, rather than with some distant abstraction called "the classical tongue" or "the divine language." Early in this century, Bharati (1937: 29) observed that "nations are made of homes." For both these regimes, however, the nation is not merely made of homes; symbolically and discursively, it *is* home, a domain of selfless love and sibling solidarity, a realm of nonpolitics (Chatterjee 1989).

The language of the home acquired potency and validity for Indianism, precisely because it was imagined to be *not* the language of the colonized, Anglicized, public sphere. Untarnished by the West, it was the language of every Tamil speaker's heart, mind, and true self, and hence the means through which anticolonial resistance could be launched. The home, however, was also the abode of the mother, imagined as the true bearer of all that was noble and spiritual about Tamil (and Indian) culture. Just as crucially, the mother was also the vehicle through whom Tamil, the "mother tongue," would continue to be reproduced, even as in the outer, material world, away from the home, Tamil speakers, especially their menfolk, would perforce have to employ English. Not surprisingly, there was much agony among the devout over the alarming escalation in the use of English by women and girls, especially within the intimate and hitherto uncolonized space of the home. Why are we surprised, they asked, that there is no respect for Tamil when "even our women in their kitchens rejoice that they speak English" (Vasudeva Sharma 1928: 18)? An editorial in the nationalist daily *Cutçcamittiran1* (23 August 1917) similarly lamented that if this alarming trend were to continue, "we will be spoiled in every way."

Although the construct of "mother tongue" frequently erupted in neo-Shaiva and classicist discourses, generating paradoxical formations such as "our divine mother tongue" or "our classical mother tongue," it was with Indianism from the turn of the century that the term assumed both popularity and political saliency. English, it was argued, would only turn Tamil speakers (and other Indians) into clerks and accountants; their "mother tongue," however, would transform them into patriots and citizens. As Kalyanasundaram declared in 1924, "The nation in which the mother tongue does not flourish will never achieve freedom.... The first step towards freedom is respect for the mother tongue" (Kalyanasundaranar 1935: 21).

Indianism was particularly concerned that such a "respect" for Indian languages was being denied by the colonial state's classification of these as "vernaculars"—"the language of the slaves." Thus S. Satyamurthy, a leading spokesman for the Congress Party, declared to the Madras Legislative Council in November 1928: "Vernacular means the tongue of slaves. I do not think we ought to insult our languages by calling them 'vernaculars' or tongues of slaves. Of course, the answer of the Englishman would be, 'My vernacular is English.' But he never uses the word 'vernacular' in connection with his mother tongue."

Therefore, where classicism protested the categorization of Tamil as a "vernacular" by seeking recognition for its classicality, Indianism did so by insisting on its status as *tâymol1i* (mother tongue)—as the language of the people, of their homes, and of their mothers. Consider the following statement from an essay entitled "Tâymol1i," written by Kalyanasundaram, that appeared in his *Navacakti* in 1924:

> Every man reveres the woman who gives birth to him, the nation (*nât#u*) where he was born, and the language he speaks, by referring to these as his "mother." As much as the love he has for the mother who carried him, ought to be his love for the nation that delivers him, and the language that rears him. A man who does not revere his nation and his language is like the sinner who does not reverence his own mother. Indeed, the language that one speaks is the very wellspring of the love for one's mother, and of devotion to one's motherland. A man who is not devoted to the mother tongue he speaks is a man who has reviled his own mother and his own nation.

So endemic does the identification of language with motherhood become with Indianist discourse that even when Tamil1ttây herself was not specifically invoked, Tamil and mothers came to be spoken of in identical terms. In his memoirs Sivagnanam, an autodidact who remembers learning much of his Tamil at his mother's knee in her kitchen, writes, "As far as I am concerned, when I say Tamil is my 'mother tongue,' it is not rhetorical. It is really true. My knowledge of Tamil is my mother's gift. For that reason, Tamil *is* my mother tongue" (Sivagnanam

1974: 868). For its devotees, there was nothing more natural than referring to their language as "mother tongue" because it was literally something they acquired from their mothers. It was, as Sivagnanam reminds us, their mothers' gift.

Indianism and Hindi

From early in the century, in the Madras Presidency as in other parts of the subcontinent, there were many who were concerned with the problem of developing a national language so as to overcome the dependence on English for interregional communication. Hindi was an early favorite candidate among many Tamil speakers, as it was in its own "home" in northern India (Dasgupta 1970). In 1906, in an article he published in *Intiyâ*, Bharati endorsed the view that since Hindi was already spoken by eighty out of India's three hundred million, Tamil speakers, too, should embrace it. Yet, he lamented, no steps had been taken to promote it in the South (C. S. Subramaniam 1986: 443-44). Soon after, in a 1908 letter to the nationalist Tilak, Bharati wrote that he and his friends had started a small Hindi class in Madras city (Padmanabhan 1982: 48-49; see also Nuhman 1984: 55-61). In subsequent decades, other devotees of the Indianist persuasion backed the cause of Hindi and countered Dravidianism's demonization of the language by reminding their fellow speakers that supporting it did not necessarily amount to the "murder" of their mother, Tamil (Kalyanasundaranar 1935: 21; Sivagnanam 1974: 136-41). Convinced that the regional Congress Party was dedicated to the twin causes of promoting Tamil at the regional level and Hindi at the national level, devotees inclined to Indianism supported that party.

Yet the promotion of Hindi as key to national unity and integration posed many dilemmas for Indianism, caught as it was between devotion to "Tamil" and "India." Over the years and especially in the decade following independence, many an Indianist became increasingly suspicious of the Congress Party's aggressive Hindi policy, which was perceived as endangering Tamil, as Dravidianists had long maintained (Sivagnanam 1974: 138-41, 416-18, 505-7). They came to appreciate the realities of functioning in a multilingual polity in which, contrary to their conviction that all languages are equal "children" of Bhârata Mâtâ, one of them would be the privileged "imperial state language." Ramalinga

Pillai captured their conflicting sentiments when he wrote that Tamil speakers were famed the world over for inviting other languages into their home and honoring these. However, he asked, to what extent should they let their own language and culture suffer in this process (Thaninayagam 1963: 12)? What would happen to Tamil and its glorious literature, others demanded, if state funds were redirected towards the support of Hindi? For, as Somasundara Bharati, professor of Tamil and a Congress supporter in his early years, insisted, "clothed with prestige and privileges peculiar to an imperial state language, Hindi is sure to become a dangerous rival to Tamil." Not surprisingly, he wondered if an old "evil," English, was being replaced by a new one, and whether Tamil would continue to suffer in this process (Somasundara Bharati 1937: 17).

Although opposed to compulsory Hindi education, many Indianist devotees like Kalyanasundaram and Sivagnanam continued to extend their allegiance to the Congress's policies into the 1940s, in reaction to the powerful anti-Hindi and anti-India demonology of Dravidianism, and in the face of the Dravidian movement's growing demand for retaining English as the common language. As colonial rule gave way to Congress rule, however, they became convinced that the cause of Tamil would be compromised by the larger cause of the (Hindi-dominated) Indian nation and its needs. Not surprisingly, by the late 1940s, Kalyanasundaram joined forces with the Dravidian movement to oppose Hindi (Kalyanasundaranar 1949). Similarly, in 1946, Sivagnanam formed an interest group called the Tamil1 Aracu Kal1akam, "Association for Tamil Autonomy" (henceforth Tamil Arasu Kazhagam), whose main agenda was to put pressure on the Congress to promote the increased use of Tamil in administration and education, to work towards the creation of an autonomous Tamil state out of a composite Madras Presidency, and to ease up on its pro-Hindi policy. As Sivagnanam wrote in April 1947 on the eve of Indian independence, "The Tamilian is prepared to be Indian. However, he is first and foremost a Tamilian. Only secondarily is he Indian" (Sivagnanam 1981: 105). By 1954, his organization was forced to part ways with the Congress, and in 1967, Sivagnanam even entered into an electoral alliance with the Dravidian movement—the same movement against which through much of the 1950s he had conducted so many campaigns

(Sivagnanam 1974: 368-69, 535-55). Most indicative perhaps of Indianism's radical transformation through its dealings with the Hindi question is C. Rajagopalachari's changing stance. The chief promoter of Hindi who made its study mandatory in the late 1930s in the Madras Presidency, he began to insist "English ever, Hindi never" from the late 1950s, and even made electoral deals with his Dravidianist rivals by the 1960s (Rajagopalachari 1962).

The Congress and Indianized Tamil

In 1967, the Congress, the party that prided itself on delivering India from colonialism and that had ruled Madras for the two decades since independence, suffered a stunning defeat at the polls and has never returned to power in the state since. For many a Tamil devotee, the Congress's defeat was its just deserts, for had it not shown, over the years, that it was the enemy of Tamil and Tamil1ttây? Supporters of the Congress have tried to counter such a charge. It was the Congress, more than the non-Brahman elite's Justice Party, that used Tamil from early in this century in party work and popular mobilization. It was under Congress rule that Tamil was extended as medium of instruction in high schools in 1938, and university education in 1960-61. The Congress government also set up, in 1959, the Tamil Development and Research Council entrusted with producing, Tamil school and college textbooks in the natural and human sciences, accounting, mathematics, and so on. It also helped finance a series of children's encyclopedias in Tamil, "lucid commentaries" on Cank#am poetry, and an "authentic history of the Tamil people" in 1962-63. And finally, in 1956, it was the Congress that passed the law instituting Tamil as the official language of the state (Karthikeyan 1965-66; C. Subramaniam 1962). Yet, as its critics have been quick to point out, few of these measures seemed to have made any difference to life in the Tamil-speaking land. So, Mohan Kumaramangalam wrote in 1965:

> In practice, the ordinary man finds that the Tamil language is nowhere in the picture....In Madras city, English dominates our life to an extraordinary extent....Corporation property tax, electric consumption and water tax bills are only in the English language; all communications of the Collector are in English; in virtually all trade, including the smallest consumer goods, bills, receipts, etc. are made out in the English language. I think it will be no

exaggeration to say that a person can live for years in Madras without learning a word of Tamil, except for some servant inconvenience!

As many of its supporters rightly point out, the Congress government's record on *tamil1ppan#i,* "service to Tamil," is not as terrible or as bleak as its critics portray it. Nevertheless, it pursued Tamil policies that were largely Indianist in complexion at a time when the growing Dravidianist discourse was very persuasively pointing to "India" as the source of many of the Tamil speaker's problems, and at a time when even Indianists within the devotional community were turning away from the Congress. Its Indianist predilections meant that the "improvement" of Tamil under Congress rule proceeded side by side with at least tacit support for the Indian state's Hindi policy. The Congress also resisted a number of devotional demands out of fear that these would open the "Pandora's box" of linguistic "balkanization": the renaming of Madras state as "Tamilnadu," the authorization of Tamil as primary liturgical language in temples, the use of pure Tamil instead of Sanskritized Tamil in school textbooks and administrative manuals, and so on. Above all, Congress policies, like orthodox Indianism's, were premised on the fundamental assumption that "Tamil" and "India" were intertwined, an assumption that it felt compelled to uphold if only to counter the separatist agenda of the Dravidian movement. It would be sacrilegious to think exclusively of Tamil as deserving the absolute allegiance of all its speakers. Thus the Congress, and even the Indianist regime, were never animated by the spirit of total and unconditional celebration of Tamil that characterized Dravidianism's attitude towards the language. In the words of one devotee of Tamil whose own sentiments were contestatory classicist and Dravidianist, "None of the Congress Ministers of Tamil Nad was either a Tamil scholar or a Tamil lover. The Congress leaders of Tamil Nad as betrayers of Tamil, cannot represent the State any more. Blind cannot lead the blind, much less the keen sighted" (Devaneyan 1967: 25). In 1967, the Tamil electorate came to the same conclusion.

LANGUAGE OF THE NATION: DRAVIDIANIZING TAMIL

And so, finally, I turn to the Dravidianist regime that crystallized in the 1930s, gained momentum through the 1940s and 1950s, and peaked in the mid-1960s. Its primary terrain of activity was a series of anti-Hindi protests which dramatically drew together diverse elements of the devotional community in opposition to the regional and central governments that sponsored Hindi, itself-caricatured as an evil and demonic force out to destroy pure and sweet Tamil (and its speakers). Contemporaries and participants alike marvelled that the common cause against Hindi threw together religious revivalists like Maraimalai Adigal with such avowed atheists as Ramasami; Gandhians like Kalyanasundaram with men like Annadurai who preached secession from India; university professors and elite antiquarians, such as Somasundara Bharati and Purnalingam Pillai, with populist street poets, pamphleteers, college students, and young men like Chinnasami who immolated themselves. Indeed, the poet Bharatidasan, the paradigmatic Dravidianist, had himself been a self-declared devotee of "India" up until the 1920s, and had published some passionate poems on Bhârata Mâtâ before his conversion to Dravidianism and anti-Hindi politics by the 1930s (Ilango 1982; Ilavarasu 1990). Other events of these decades—the creation of linguistic states out of the erstwhile Madras Presidency, the securing of appropriate borders with neighboring states, the struggle to rename Madras state Tamilnadu—also compelled devotees otherwise inclined, such as Sivagnanam, to turn to Dravidianism. Dravidianism is thus the crisis idiom of *tamil1ppar1r1u*, the regime par excellence for mobilizing—albeit temporarily and sometimes reluctantly—diverse, even opposing, devotees under one umbrella, around events that were deemed to be threatening to the future of Tamil and Tamil1ttây.

The most passionate and radical of all the regimes, Dravidianism routinely elicited from its adherents declarations of willingness to give up their wealth, their lives, and their souls for Tamil. It also produced some antagonistic, even violent, attitudes towards other languages and their speakers, as for instance in the following verse published by Bharatidasan, which is fairly typical: "Our first task is to finish off those who destroy [our] glorious Tamil! / Let flow a river of crimson blood!" Its emphasis on fierce, public displays of devotion meant that images of battlefields, of blood, and of death proliferate in Dravidianist discourse. True Tamilians are those—like Chinnasami—who show their commitment to their mother/tongue by putting their very bodies on the line, and dying for it, if need be. More so than the other devotional regimes, Dravidianism's driving imperative was a vision of the Tamil community as an autonomous racial and political entity (*in1am*), even nation (*nât#u*), whose sacral center is occupied solely by Tamil, from which all its members claim shared descent. So, where neo-Shaivism constituted Tamilian solidarity around the shared worship of Shiva and divine Tamil, and classicism emphasized a common ancient, literary past, Dravidianism focused on descent and kinship. Tropes of motherhood, siblingship, shared blood, the home, and the like mark its discursive style, as they do Indianism's. The significant difference between the two, of course, is that Dravidianism made a commitment to only one entity—namely, Tamil. As Tamil1ttây herself insisted, sometime in the early 1960s: "Do not forget that you are all children who emerged from my womb. I *am* your mother. The learned call me Tamil1ttây. You are called Tamilians (*tamil1ar*). You and I have been inextricably bound together for ever and ever through language. That language is what the good scholars call Tamil....If we look closely, we have a home. That its name is Tamilnadu gives [me] great happiness" (Pancanathan n.d.: 9).

In this statement as elsewhere in Dravidianism, descent is reckoned solely from Tamil, which is not merely one among a "family" of languages *in* a putative Indian nation, as it is in Indianism, but is *the* language *of* the nation, imagined variously as "Tamilian" or "Dravidian." No doubt, by the 1970s Dravidianism became more accommodating on the question of India. But the fundamental imperative of this regime continued to be the establishment of the absolute rule of Tamil through the complete Tamilization of the political apparatus and its accompanying ideology, in a territorial space designated as Tamil or Dravidian, which at least into the early 1960s was seen as independent of, and indeed in opposition to, "India."

The political philosophy of Dravidianism was provided by a broad swathe of ideas associated with "the Dravidian movement" (*tirâvit#a iyakkam*). This movement made its impact on the Dravidianist regime when the elitist "non-Brahman" associational politics of the Vellala dominated Justice Party (1916/17-44) was supplemented by the populist call for radical social reform by E. V. Ramasami and his Self-Respect League (founded in 1926) and the Tirâvit#ar Kal1akam, "Association of Dravidians" (the DK, established in 1944). Although many Self-Respecters were concerned with Tamil (e.g., Velu and Selvaraji 1989), Ramasami himself was extremely critical of *tamil1pparlr1u,* especially of its valorization of the divinity, antiquity, and motherhood of Tamil. This did not stop Dravidianism from lionizing him and selectively appropriating his ideas of rationalist materialism, iconoclastic atheism, radical anti-Brahmanism, and Dravidian nationalism, for he provided the most polemical and sustained attacks on Indian nationalism, which this regime found useful. Ramasami's obvious dilemma was that Tamil devotion threatened his vision of a Dravidian nation that would incorporate all "Dravidians" of southern India, and not just Tamil speakers. Such a vision had to contend with the resistance of those putative "Dravidians" who were speakers of Telugu, Kannada, and Malayalam. In addition, it was compromised by Tamil speakers who did not necessarily want to participate in a multilingual polity, even if it was "Dravidian." And indeed, as the Dravidian movement itself split, when Annadurai parted company with Ramasami and his DK in 1949 to found his own party, the Tirâvit#a Mun1n1çr1r1ak Kal1akam or "Dravidian Progress Association" (DMK), the inherent tensions between the alternate conceptions of the "Dravidian" and "Tamil" nation came to the fore. By the late 1950s, as the DMK entered the domain of electoral politics, its agenda was primarily formulated in terms of a Tamil nation (albeit one often referred to as "Dravidian"), confined to the territorial spəce of a Tamilspeaking area, rather than coeval with the more ambitious nation that Ramasami envisaged comprising the speakers of all Dravidian languages.

Like the Dravidian movement, Dravidianism, too, had to contend with the tensions between an exclusive Tamil-speaking nation and a more inclusive Dravidian nation. It adopted various strategies to deal with this, such as suggestions that "Tamil" and "Dravidian" are the same; that since Tamil is the "mother" of all Dravidian languages, the latter are merely extensions of the former; and so on. So, like the other regimes, Dravidianism had its share of contradictions. Notwithstanding these, as a consequence of its discourse, Tamil comes to be firmly "Dravidianized," even as the "Dravidian" category, which had been gaining political and cultural visibility in the region since the 1880s, was unequivocally associated with Tamil. In contrast to neo-Shaivism and classicism, Dravidianism advocated political radicalism and activism as the means to achieve the reign of Tamil: "We have talked enough....[W]hen are you going to show your sacrifice to [Tamil1ttây]? We are waiting every moment for the honor of being arrested." Under the influence of Dravidianism, *tamil1ppar1r1u* took to the streets, sometimes quite violently. Petition politics gave way to protest politics, increasingly radical and populist. Antiquarian and elite notions about Tamil and Tamil1ttây, hitherto confined to learned academies and scholastic journals, came to be invoked in street songs, polemical plays, and political speeches at populist anti-Hindi rallies; they were circulated in daily newspapers and street pamphlets, and plastered across billboards and wall posters. Dravidianism typically catered, like the Dravidian movement itself, to the Everyman, generically designated in its texts as *tamil1an1*, "Tamilian" (Barnett 1976: 114-15). It attracted its following from devotees who were predominantly from middle and lower castes, and from middle or low-income families with limited or no formal education, like Chinnasami and his fellow self-immolators. At the same time, the DMK's support of literature and language also attracted numerous well-educated Tamil scholars and academics to Dravidianism. In turn, many DMK leaders have been devotees of Tamil. They have assumed titles—*ar1iòar* (scholar) Annadurai, *kalaiòar* (the artist) Karunanidhi, *nâvalar* (the eloquent) Nedunceliyan—which display both their scholarly aspirations and the close links between populist ideology and high literature in the political culture of the region (Barnett 1976: 56-86). Dravidianism's paradigmatic exponents were undoubtedly well-known poets and politicians like Bharatidasan, Annadurai, "Pulavar" Kulanthai (1906-72), Perunchitran (1920-95), Mudiyarasan (b. 1920), Karunanidhi, and the early Kannadasan (1927-81). But encouraged by the Dravidian movement's populism and by Dravidianism's assertion that Tamil belonged to "the people," the Everyman, who remained anonymous or relatively unknown, took to writing and publishing poems, short stories, and essays on the language and on Tamil1ttây. Of all the regimes of *tamil1ppar1r1u*, Dravidianism was thus the one that was truly populist, in spirit as well as constituency.

Dravidianism's fundamental agenda, of course, was to establish the absolute preeminence of Tamil in all spheres of life and being, and to ensure that devotion to the language (and its community) was not diluted by any other passions—for the Indian nation, for the gods of the Hindu pantheon, or even for the families and mothers of individual devotees. For Tamil is everything; it is the life (*uyir*), breath (*âvi*), and consciousness (*un#arvu*) of every true Tamilian. In its purest form, there were no divided commitments in Dravidianism, no subordination of Tamil to Shiva, to literature and learning, or to India. Tamil was not a means through which to construct something else, be it an alternate religious or civilizational formation, or allegiance to India. In and of itself, it ought to be the very center of everything in the devoted Tamil speaker's life. Without it, there is nothing. So Bharatidasan wrote in a poem suggestively entitled "Living for Tamil Is the Only Life":

O Tamil! Homage to you!

......

Your well-being is ours as well.
Your victories are ours as well.
We may as well be dead if we live for ourselves.
Living for Tamil is the only life!

For the Dravidianist devoṭee, Tamil was so much a part of the Tamilian's very essence that it would be impossible to separate the language from its speaker. So Bharatidasan insisted:

We can turn mountains into pits;
We can dry up the ocean bed;
We can fly speedily through the skies.

......

We can even bring the dying back to life.
The Tamilian cannot be separated from Tamil
Even for a moment, by anyone.

This conviction, that Tamil and its speaker devotee had so blended into each other that it would be impossible to separate them, is echoed in other poems as well. Consider this verse by Kannadasan addressed to Tamil1ttây:

Would I ever forget you? Would I cease to sing about you?
Even if they set me on fire,

In the burning flames of the fire,

The world will see only you, O dear mother of mine!

(Kannadasan 1968: 89)

Elsewhere, in 1954, in lines that eerily anticipate Chinnasami's immolation a decade later, the poet wrote, "even in death, Tamil should be on our lips. Our ashes should burn with the fragrance of Tamil. This is our undying desire" (Kannappan 1995: 22).

Given such sentiments, Dravidianism was particularly concerned with all alternate objects of passion that might draw its speakers away from Tamil, such as "India," their gods, and their families. It therefore focused as much energy to convince Tamil speakers of the illegitimacy of these other entities as to emphasize that it is Tamil that sustains their life and consciousness.

Dravidianism and India

While Indianism emphatically asserted that the liberation of Bhârata Mâtâ and Tamil1ttây would have to proceed in tandem, Dravidianism, particularly in its early years, and most especially as expressed by its more radical exponents, saw in the very establishment of the Indian nation the downfall of Tamil. A poem that was published in the *Tirâvit#an1* on 31 August 1947, a fortnight after India was officially liberated from colonial rule, declared: "The foreign Bhârata Mâtâ (*an1n1iyap pâratattây*) has attained glory. / Our own dear Tamil1ttây has been greatly disgraced."

Dravidianism, at its peak, portrayed the newly emergent Indian nation as an imperialist formation, as a tool in the hands of Brahmans and Banias (North Indian merchants), and as an instrument with which the material interests of Dravidians would continue to be subordinated to Aryan Indians (Annadurai 1974: 39-48, 1985: 22-23; Pancanathan n.d.; M. S. Ramasami 1947: 5-6, 19-20). Consider the following verse from a 1947 pamphlet revealingly entitled *Songs of Separation for the Dravidian Nation:*

The Brahmans and Banias have united;

We are all children of Bhârata Mâtâ, they lie to us[.]

......

Our own Tirâvit#attây [Mother Dravida] is our mother;

Bhârata Mâtâ who belongs to the duplicitous, is a deceitful mother;

If the Dravidians realize this, they will have no trouble.

If we let down our guard, the Northerners will loot and plunder.

(M. S. Ramasami 1947: 14)

Indianism, we have seen, offered Bhârata Mâtâ to Tamil speakers as a mother who would reproduce them as "Indians." In the logic of Dravidianism, however, she was clearly a false mother who sought to lure gullible Tamilians away from their true mother with promises of milk, nourishment, and even jobs. So, in 1958, Bharatidasan, who in his early years had waxed passionately on Bhârata Mâtâ and even declared her his true mother, published a poem in which he ridiculed the Tamilian who is confused about his "real" mother. The poem is addressed to Tamil1ttây:

"O glorious Tamilian! What is the name of your nation?"

When I ask thus, he sheepishly says "India," O mother!

How will this child ever improve if he confuses the evergreen

Tamil nation with India, O mother!

Will he ever change, the one who does not recognize his mother as mother, and declares the evil that destroys his motherland as mother, O mother!

Sitting in [his] mother's lap and nursing on the breast milk of Tamil, how can this child not know [his] mother's name, O mother!

Tamil *is* [his] mother tongue, and Tamilnadu is his motherland.

Does not the Tamilian realize this?

So, while Indianism sought to naturalize "India" by presenting it in the familiar terms of the home and the mother, the Dravidianist logic lay in demonizing it as a "deceitful" or "evil" mother, and substituting Tamil1ttây in its stead as the authentic, *sole* mother of all true Tamil speakers.

Dravidianism's antagonism towards India came to the fore in the numerous protests against Hindi, presented in its discourses as a blood-sucking demoness, lowly maid, seductive temptress, and false mother out to destroy the noble, righteous, but endangered Tamil1ttây. Such Manichean images were deployed to create fear and hatred of Hindi, and to generate sentiments of love, loyalty, and filial piety for Tamil, which its loyal speakers were obliged to protect with life and limb. Just as crucially, the regional state government (in the control of the Congress) and the Indian nation were also rendered into objects that deserved the Tamilians' deepest opprobrium and the withdrawal of their support, emotional *and* electoral. Dravidianism thus seized upon the linguistic fact that Hindi was related to Sanskrit, and translated the assertions of radical neo-Shaivism and contestatory classicism against Aryan Brahmanism into political action against the Indian nation. For Dravidianism, the battle against Hindi was not only inevitable and natural; but necessary and morally legitimate; it was a "holy war" (*ar1appôr*) fought against evil and on behalf of the good and righteous (Ramaswamy, forthcoming). Although Hindi was in effect legislated out of Tamilnadu government schools in 1968 by the DMK, and although all kinds of accommodations with the North have been made since the 1960s, to this day the threat of Hindi has continued to be effectively used to reiterate the autonomy and uniqueness of a Tamil space within a larger Indian whole, to summon up the specter of non-Tamil elements entering the pure Tamil body politic, and to remind Tamil speakers of the dangers that await them if they cease supporting the Dravidian movement and its Tamil cause.

Dravidianism and Hinduism

In the years between the late 1920s and 1950s, when the influence of the iconoclastic and atheistic Ramasami was at its peak and before the DMK actively entered the fray of electoral politics, Dravidianism also sought energetically to dissociate Tamil from all religious affiliations. Like radical neo-Shaivism, it castigated Hinduism as a Brahmanical, Sanskritic, and Aryan conspiracy hatched to destroy Tamil and Dravidian society. So, for Dravidianism, a true Tamilian/Dravidian is one who is emphatically *not* a Hindu. "A Hindu in the present concept may be a Dravidian, but the Dravidian in the real sense of the term cannot and shall not be a Hindu" (quoted in Harrison 1960: 127). Tamil speakers were therefore repeatedly called upon to destroy all (Hindu) irrationalisms and foolish beliefs, and to rescue themselves from *ârya mâyai,* "Aryan illusion" (Annadurai 1969). Thus Bharatidasan, who in the 1920s had written passionate poems on Hindu deities and continued occasionally to publish religious verse into the 1930s, insisted in the 1950s that "there is no god" and told the Tamilian that his duty lay in weaning away his hapless fellow speakers from their false belief in divinities.

And here is where Dravidianism parted company with neo-Shaivism: for in its attacks on religion, it did not spare either Shiva or the reformed "rational" version of Shaivism that Maraimalai Adigal and others were attempting to popularize (Sivathamby 1978: 30-31; Venkatachalapathy 1990). Neo-Shaivism may have insisted that Shaivism is the authentic Tamilian religion, radically different from Aryan Brahmanical Hinduism, but Dravidianism was not convinced about this. Nor was it ready to brook neo-Shaivite resistance to reforming and rationalizing the Tamil script, believed by many devout Shaivites to be Shiva's own handiwork (Sivathamby 1979: 71). Dravidianism was also not willing to define the Tamil/Dravidian community as Shaiva, for what would then happen to Tamilians/Dravidians who were nominally Vaishnavas, Christians, and Muslims? So Tamil is the life, the consciousness, and the soul of the Tamilian. It is indeed everything, but it certainly is not "divine Tamil," for to imagine it as such would entangle it with the irrationalisms, inequalities, and idiocies of Hinduism. Tamil speakers, too, consequently would be subordinated and demeaned in an inherently Brahmanical order of things, and they would lose all their "self-respect." In a revealing speech of 1944, Ramasami offered the following advice to his fellow Dravidians: "You may well ask, 'If we give up Hinduism, what religion can we profess to have?' Have courage and claim that religion which will not demean you as untouchable and lowly in society. If there is objection to this, you may always say you are Dravidian and that your religion is Dravidianism. If you have problems even with that, say that your religion is humanity" (Anaimuthu 1974: 446).

Contrary to Marguerite Barnett (1976: 274), who has suggested that "within the Dravidian ideology there was no coherent alternative to religion or Hinduism," I would argue that especially within the Dravidianist regime of *tamil1ppar1r1u,* various efforts were made to create alternatives to both religion and Hinduism. Given the complex entanglements between Tamil devotion and Hinduism, however, such efforts were not entirely successful, nor were they as autonomous as Dravidianism would have desired. Minimally, those devotees of Tamil who turned to active electoral politics as members of the DMK distanced themselves from

Ramasami's iconoclastic irreverence for Hindu scriptures, gods, and images. By the 1950s, both the DMK and Dravidianism generated a curious combination of agnosticism ("we do not ask whether there is god or not"), monism ("there is only one god and one community"), populism ("god lives in the smile of the poor"), and humanism ("we must develop that kind of outlook which treats all humanity as one"). This medley of diverse beliefs that Anita Diehl (1977: 29) has shrewdly characterized as "pragmatic, agnostic humanism" opened up a space for the steady incorporation of all kinds of elements from popular as well as the devotional religious practices of the region into the ideology of Dravidianism, such as the celebration of the harvest festival, Pongal; the worship of Murugan; and the apotheosis of Valluvar and his *Tirukkur1al#* (Ramanujam 1971: 168, 175; Ryerson 1988: 108-93).

One other important strategy is followed by Dravidianism in filling up the space vacated by Hindu gods. Consider this 1959 poem by Bharatidasan, addressed to a *tampirân1*, "Shaiva monk preceptor," in response to the opposition of the orthodox to the growing demand for use of Tamil as ritual language in temples:

Is it religion (camayam) that is important, O *tampirân1*[?]

It is fine Tamil that is indeed eminent, O foolish *tampirân1*[.]

Why do you hate Tamil, O *tampirân1*[.]

Why do you hate your mother, O *tampirân1*[?]

Even if religion is destroyed, Tamilians will flourish[.]

If good Tamil is destroyed, can there be a Tamil community[?]

Do service to Tamil! O *tampirân1*[.]

Tamil is the life of the Tamilian! O foolish *tampirân1*[.]

Is it God who is great[?] O *tampirân1*[!]

It is glorious Tamil that is indeed great[!] O foolish *tampirân1*[.]

Even if God disappears, the Tamil community will flourish[.]

If Tamil dies, its community, too, will die, O *tampirân1*[.]

Do you intend to destroy the Tamil creed (*tamil1ner1i*) by invoking Shaivism (*caivaner1i*), O foolish *tampirân1?*

Service to Shaivism is not great, O *tampirân1*[.]

It is auspicious service to Tamil that is eminent, O *tampirân1*[.]

......

Only one thing is greater than [our] mother(s)! O *tampirân1!*

Is that not Tamil, O foolish *tampirân1?*

There are few clearer statements than this of Dravidianism's attempt to displace conventional gods and the religious beliefs associated with them, and to substitute Tamil in their stead. Indeed, Dravidianism sacralized Tamil, even while refusing to participate, at least overtly and consciously, in its divinization. Dravidianism's ambivalence towards religiosity and Hinduism notwithstanding, Tamil was offered to its speakers as an iconic object that deserves all the adulation, adherence, and service they had hitherto reserved for their gods. In this process, even within Dravidianism, Tamil was imagined as desired by the gods, and was every now and then deified. So, in his controversial 1945 poem, *Tamil1iyakkam* (The resurgence of Tamil),Bharatidasan asked whether Tamil, "which is life itself," is not dear to the gods (Bharatidasan 1969: 27). On a more personal note, in his autobiography the poet Mudiyarasan, who identifies himself as an ardent follower of Ramasami and Annadurai, asks, "I consider Tamil as god (*kat#avul#*). How can I be an atheist (*nâttikan1*)?" (Mudiyarasan n.d.: 86-87). A similar sentiment undergirds the DMK government's institution of the homage to Tamil1ttây as the state song in 1970. The government may have announced that it was doing this because the song had no "religious or sectarian associations," an assertion it was able to make because it carefully edited out Sundaram Pillai's original title, *Tamil1t teyva van#akkam,* "Homage to *Goddess* Tamil." Nonetheless, in its official statement (in English), Tamil1ttây herself is referred to as "goddess of Tamil," and the hymn is characterized as "prayer song."

Dravidianism and the Tamil Family

Dravidianism did not just have to delegitimize the "other mother," Bhârata Mâtâ it also had to ensure that flesh-and-blood Tamil-speaking mothers themselves did not pose a threat to the absolute devotion and loyalty owed to the sacralized language. This was a very complicated task, for motherhood was the ground on which both Indianism and Dravidianism constituted *tamil1ppar1r1u.* Indeed, Dravidianism was not content with merely establishing similitude between language and one's mother; more strikingly, it insisted that language *is* that mother:

When I was a child, you snuggled me and placed me on your lap;

You placed flowers in my hair, and adorned me, and admired my beauty;

You are the sweet mother who protected me, in the shade and in the heat;

O my ancient Tamil! May you live long!

(Ulakanathan 1969: 4)

Similarly, the well-known DMK rhetorician R. Nedunceliyan, who later became a key member of the government, insisted in 1960 that there was no difference between one's mother and Tamil:

There is *no distinction at all* between our mother who bore us for ten months, gave birth to us, watched over us, sang lullabies to us, and fed us milk and guarded us, and our Tamil language which taught us about good conduct and tradition, and granted us good values and knowledge, and which is the very reason that we live well and in prosperity. We have the same attachment to our language as we have for our mother; we have the same devotion to our language as we have for our mother; we have the same love for our language as we have for our mother. He who disregards his language...is like he who disregards his mother and forsakes her.

Dravidianism may have invited speakers of Tamil to imagine it as their mother. At its most dramatic, however, it elevated Tamil to a position of absolute preeminence, even transcending the status and authority of one's birth mother. For instance, the poet Pulavar Kulanthai declared passionately:

I will never refuse to obey my [own] mother's words;

But if harm befalls my precious Tamil1ttây,

I will not fear to set aside my own mother's words.

I will chop off the head of [Tamil1ttây's] enemy,

Even if [my] mother prevents me.

(Pulavar Kulanthai 1972: 21)

By extension, this kind of loyalty extended to fellow Tamil speakers as well, as is apparent from Bharatidasan's much-cited declaration: "I will not leave alone the man who scorns the greatness of Tamilians / *Even if [my] mother prevents me*" (Bharatidasan 1958: 5, emphasis mine).

Indeed, Dravidianism even insisted that service to Tamil and to Tamil1ttây should take priority over the Tamilian's family—over spouses, children, and parents. So Perunchitran demanded as late as 1975: "Are the troubles of your own mother more important than the terrible suffering of our glorious Tamil1ttây? /.../ Are the words of your own mother sweeter than our Tamil language, which is like ambrosia?" (Perunchitranar 1979: 109).

Yet in thus subordinating the family to Tamil, Dravidianism only overtly and consciously articulated a sentiment that was widespread in the devotional community as a whole. As we will see later, in the life stories of individual devotees as these are narrated in memoirs and biographies, their families are typically superseded in favor of devotion to the Tamil cause. The family, which is a primary site for cultivating devotion to the language, is ultimately transcended within the regimes of *tamil1ppar1r1u*. Such a transcendence is deemed necessary, for not even the family can—or can be allowed to—intervene between the devotee and his language.

The DMK and Dravidianized Tamil

Deriving considerable political capital from its self-appointed role as the guardian of Tamil and from demonizing the Congress as an agent of "evil" North Indian interests during the prolonged anti-Hindi protests of the 1950s and 1960s which it spearheaded, the DMK swept the state polls in 1967. Two days after the party's victory was assured, its leading newspaper, *Nam Nât#u*, carried the headline, "Tamil1ttây's Desire of Many Years Fulfilled." The *Muracoli*'s front-page cartoon showed Tamil1ttây, a smile on her face, placing a crown on Annadurai, her "chief son." And it was declared that Tamil1ttây's victory was the fruit of penances undergone by her followers for Tamil's sake: "In order that Tamil1ttây be enthroned, in order that Tamil1ttây should abide with honor, so that Tamil1ttây may be crowned...so many became prey to gunfire, so many drowned in an ocean of red blood, so many martyrs set themselves on fire, so many great ones passed away. This we know. Today, we see Tamil blooming everywhere. You must all go to the Legislative Assembly. You will hear good

Tamil there." The DMK takes great pride that so many of its leaders—Annadurai, Nedunceliyan, and Karunanidhi, among others—have been hailed as great scholars of Tamil and of literature in their own right. So, for many Dravidianists, the DMK's victory finally fulfilled Bharatidasan's dream, voiced years earlier in 1945, that "only the Tamilian who knows Tamil should rule as the chief minister of Tamilnadu" (Bharatidasan 1969: 19).

Regardless of what its opponents may say or statistics may reveal, the DMK has promoted itself as selflessly dedicated to the Tamil cause. Party literature as well as government publications provided details of the measures that it undertook to promote the language: the increasing use of "chaste" and "good" Tamil in administrative and public facilities; the publication of Tamil encyclopedias, scientific manuals, and textbooks; the increasing support of Tamil scholars and Tamil studies both within and outside Tamilnadu; and so on—programs pursued by the Congress government as well to varying degrees. In addition, under the DMK, Hindi was in effect legislated out of state schools in 1968; steps were taken, although not successfully, to introduce Tamil as the exclusive language of higher education and as medium of worship in high Hindu temples; and the state itself was renamed Tamilnadu, "land of Tamil." DMK cultural policy also focused on creating a new literary and historical canon, by drawing upon the findings of *tamil1ppar1r1u*, especially upon contestatory classicism and Dravidianism. Not surprisingly, the poems of the Cank#am corpus occupy a hallowed place in this canon, Karunanidhi himself offering a new interpretation in 1987 (Karunanidhi 1987a). Similarly, the *Tirukkur1al#*, the new "scripture" of Dravidianism, is valorized, as is the *Cilappatikâram*, as exemplars of the "secular," "egalitarian," and "chaste" essence of true and pure Tamil culture, free from the influences of Sanskritic Aryan Brahmans with their priestly ways.

Correspondingly, a new pantheon of secular icons surrounding the presiding deity, Tamil1ttây, has sprung up. It includes Tiruvalluvar, the author of the *Tirukkur1al#* Kattabomman, who died a martyr's death during the late-eighteenth-century British expansion into South India, and who is considered a paradigmatic symbol of Tamil heroism (Ramaswamy 1994); and Kannagi, the heroine of the *Cilappatikâram*, who is imagined as the ideal Tamil woman, renowned for her chastity and wifely fidelity (J. Pandian

1982). Similarly, Ramasami and Annadurai were lionized for giving Tamil speakers their "self-respect," and many DMK narratives contain laudatory poems on their achievements. And it was under DMK rule that Chinnasami and his fellow devotees who burned themselves alive were immortalized. New mythologies and praise poems on all these figures were written and circulated. Their life stories were narrated and offered as paradigms for Tamil speakers to emulate. Commemorative memorials were set up, and festivals conducted in their honor. In 1968, the government used an academic gathering in Madras, the Second International Conference of Tamil Studies, to treat the populace to a spectacular celebration of Tamil, featuring giant floats of Tamil1ttây, Tiruvalluvar, and other Tamil icons. The party's leaders must believe that such acts carry symbolic as well as political capital, for as recently as 1984, its election manifesto chose to present its achievements to the electorate in the following terms:

In order that Tamil1ttây's jeweled crown should shine,

We built the historic temple to Valluvar whose fame reaches the very skies;

And the world-famous new town of Poompukar with its *Cilappatikâram* museum, seven stories high!

And a fort in the memory of Virapandya Kattabomman at Panjalamkurichi.

We enabled all these, not just one, not just two, but plenty! plenty!

And yet, as critics as well as supporters of the DMK are quick to ask, have such gestures really helped the cause of Tamil? I quote Sivagnanam, who, despite his recent rapprochement with the DMK, lamented thus:

A museum commemorating the *Cilappatikâram* and a memorial celebrating Kattabomman have been built. The names of ministers and homes have been changed. Street names have been changed, and so have the names of towns. But Tamil's fortunes have not changed. Formerly, Tamil1ttây was worshipped three times a day. Today, she is worshipped six times a day. She is worshipped with great pomp and splendor. But the chains that fetter her arms and legs have not been destroyed....Tamil will not grow by changing the names of streets, towns, and gardens.

Dravidianism and its Discontents

And this is a lament that we continue to hear to this day, even after about a century of Tamil devotional activity. Sivagnanam's statement points to a fundamental problem with which the Tamilnadu state has had to contend, especially in the past three decades or so, when it has been under the rule of political parties which are ostensibly dedicated to the Tamil cause. In addition to confronting the crucial issue of which Tamil to promote—"classical" Tamil, "pure" Tamil, the "people's" Tamil, and so on—there has been growing awareness that the socioeconomic and political realities of Tamil's status as a regional language within the linguistic economy of a multilingual nation-state, itself embedded within a larger global environment in which English dominates as the world language, preclude the active implementation of public policies that will ensure the supremacy of Tamil in all spheres at all times, the ideal of Dravidianism (on this, see Tamilkudimagan 1990). Strapped by financial and political constraints, it has been easier for the state to indulge in symbolic activities, such as changing street names and instituting official anthems, rather than to ensure high quality education in Tamil studies, or to create job opportunities that would convince Tamil speakers that the study of Tamil is a viable end in itself. Tamil's devotees undoubtedly recognize the value of the symbolic act, but Sivagnanam's lament also reminds us that Tamil devotionalism demands much more, especially from a party that claims to be ruling on behalf of Tamil1ttây. From the start, Dravidianism, like Indianism, placed its hopes in the political process. The establishment of a Tamil state and the Tamilization of the political apparatus, it was proclaimed, would ensure the triumph of Tamil, everywhere and in everything. And yet, this has not happened. This is a tragedy that casts its long shadow not just on Dravidianism, but on the rest of the Tamil devotional community as well.

This has not been the only cross that Dravidianism has had to bear. The Congress's policies caused the increasing disenchantment of devotees of Indianist sentiment and compelled several to embrace Dravidianism. Similarly, the empowerment of the DMK has accompanied the progressive Indianization of the message of Dravidianism, as its radical separatist vision and its credo that Tamil is everything have been progressively diluted in favor of the Tamil community's coexistence with India. Numerous compromises made by the DMK government on linguistic and cultural policies may be cited to support this claim, but perhaps the most illuminating here is the sanitized version of Sundaram Pillai's 1891 hymn that was instituted as the state "prayer song" in 1970.

Of course, the state song is still loyal to Dravidianism's "secular" recasting of Tamil1tteyvam, "Goddess Tamil," as Tamil1ttây, "Mother Tamil." The lines from the 1891 hymn that likened Tamil1ttây to the primordial lord Shiva—which neo-Shaivism kept alive through the next century—are excised, on the grounds that an appropriate prayer song for a modern Tamil community should have no religious or sectarian associations. This significant erasure is not surprising given radical Dravidianism's antagonism to the divinization of Tamil and to Hinduism. And yet, the government order explicitly refers to Tamil1ttây as the "goddess of Tamil," a slippage that is not accidental. For it indexes the progressive accommodation with religiosity that characterizes DMK cultural policy through the 1950s and 1960s. It also reminds us that within Dravidianism itself, Tamil increasingly took on the mantle of conventional Hindu deities, even as it displaced them.

Next, the recast anthem comes close to compensatory, rather than contestatory, classicism's stance on Tamil, for the government also deliberately excised the much-quoted lines of the original hymn that had referred to Sanskrit as a "dead" language and had declared the superiority of the ever-enduring Tamil (*kan1n1ittamil1*). In his reminiscences, Chief Minister Karunanidhi maintains that these lines were not incorporated into the state prayer song because "it is not appropriate to disparage or ridicule other languages, and to use inauspicious words such as 'ruined' or 'dead' in a hymn in praise of Tamil1ttây to be recited at government functions" (Karunanidhi 1987: 233). Yet, as we have seen, both contestatory classicism and Dravidianism built their arguments on the assumption that Sanskrit was a "dead" language whose very presence had sucked the life out of Tamil.

Finally, Sundaram Pillai's hymn was selected over numerous others precisely because it simultaneously acknowledges the legitimacy of both *tirâvit#a nât#u* (Dravidian nation) and *paratak kan#t#am* (Indian nation). Indeed, the government insisted that the state's prayer song would in no way supplant the Indian national anthem: while the former would be sung at the commencement of official functions, the latter—and no other—would be recited at their conclusion. Thus the modern Tamil community—as envisioned by the DMK government in this hymn—has been symbolically framed in terms of its dual "Dravidian" and "Indian" heritages, a position that clearly conforms more closely to the Indianist, rather than to the radical Dravidianist, imagining of Tamil. In what ought to have been Dravidianism's paradigmatic moment of triumph—the institution of a daily celebration of Tamil and Tamil1ttây by the DMK—it appears as if it is Indianism, and its vision of Tamil as part of the Indian whole, that wins out.

THE MANY FACES OF TAMIL

This chapter has taken its cue from a number of recent studies which claim allegiance to a new area of scholarly inquiry called "language ideology." As the anthropologists Kathryn Woolard and Bambi Schieffelin note, language ideology provides a "much-needed bridge between linguistic and social theory, because it relates the micro-culture of communicative action to political economic considerations of power and social inequality" (Woolard and Schieffelin 1994: 72). My own analysis here has allied itself with one subset of concerns in this burgeoning field in its focus on "ideologies of language," those networks of representations and significations about language which emerge within particular literary, social, political, and religious formations. However natural and timeless they might appear, conceptions about a language among its interested speakers are rarely neutral or innocent; they are produced at specific historical moments, they are generally linked to efforts to create or retain power and control, and they change through time. Such conceptions are "partial, contestable, and contested, and interest laden": disguising their historicity, they present themselves as eternally true; hiding their cultural specificity, they masquerade as universally valid and commonsensical (Woolard and Schieffelin 1994: 58; see also Joseph and Talbot 1990).

I have suggested that the endowing of Tamil with various extraordinary attributes—divinity (*teyvattan1mai*), classicality (*uyarttan1icemmai*), purity (*tûymai*), antiquity (*ton1mai*), motherhood (*tâymai*), and so on—has to be located within larger social and political projects conducted by its numerous devotees. Other languages in other places—Afrikaans, Arabic, English, Hebrew, to name a random few—have been similarly empowered. But few have been studied in any historical depth to reveal the extent of ideological work necessary to transfer them into sites of privilege, potency, and power (for examples of this, see Alter 1994; Ferguson 1968; R. Jones 1953; Roberge 1992). My analysis of such work done on Tamil suggests that although consensus eventually emerges around such certain key contentions, this is a process that is riddled with contradiction and contrariety. The very importance of Tamil for its adherents has meant that there is much at stake in the manner in which it is constituted, and hence its imaginings are subject to many negotiations within the community united in devotion to it. *Tamil1ppar1r1u* is neither a wholly homogenous nor an entirely consensual activity, because the principal entity at its center is itself not conceived in a singular manner. Instead, Tamil's devotees bring their own varying visions and shifting agendas to bear on their imaginings about their language and its role in their lives. As a consequence, Tamil devotion flourishes as a multifaceted enterprise, fissured by countervailing purposes and contrary passions, as we have seen.

But important questions remain. If the language has been subjected to all these alternate imaginings, as I have suggested, how are its devotees able to mobilize so many of their fellow speakers to rally around it? What is it that led many of them to claim as they did that they lived for its sake, and would die for it? Indeed, what is it that compelled them to speak and write with so much passion and fervor about its state of being—its past glory, its present ignominy, and its future fate? To answer such questions, I turn to the figure of Tamil1ttây.

3. FEMINIZING LANGUAGE

Tamil as Goddess, Mother, Maiden

Tamil's devotees do not merely relate to it as their language. They are able to breathe so much life and inject so much passion into practicing *tamil1ppar1r1u* because Tamil to them is more than an intangible abstraction. Instead, embodied in the figure of Tamil1ttây, it is a near and dear being—their personal goddess, their devoted mother, even their beloved lover—who commands their veneration and adulation, and deserves their love and loyalty. Yet, like the language she embodies, Tamil1ttây appears differently to different devotees at different moments in their lives, and is thus variously represented as *teyvam,* "goddess" *tây,* "mother" and *kan1n1i,* "virgin maiden." Consequently, she does not have a singular persona. Indeed, this is how Tamil devotion, fundamentally a network of patriarchal discourses conducted largely by men, solves the "problem" of having a female figure enshrined at the very heart of its enterprise. She is first isolated and abstracted from the "real" world in which Tamil-speaking women of all shades have been disempowered through much of this century; she is then endowed with a plenitude of powers and possibilities which transform her into a strikingly exceptional Woman, not readily confused with the flesh-and-blood women on whom she is also obviously modelled. Though she may be thus empowered, her potential to exceed the control of her (male) creators is contained through her fragmentation. The plethora of multiple personae that she is endowed with works to prevent her consolidation as a threatening, all-powerful being, even as it simultaneously opens up the possibility that her various selves may be deployed in contradictory ways for the different projects of her devotees. Tamil1ttây thus is yet another classic example of the objectification of woman as a thing "to be appropriated, possessed, and exchanged in the social relations of cooperation and competition among men" (Uberoi 1990: 41). Although we will see later that some Tamil-speaking women have their own way with her, Tamil1ttây, like other exemplary female icons, is far from cutting a feminist figure in her guise as tame goddess, benevolent mother, and pure virgin. Visible and valorized she may be, but she is very much a figment of the patriarchal imaginations of modernity in colonial and post-colonial India.

THE POETICS AND POLITICS OF PRAISE

The founding narrative which popularized the habit of imagining Tamil as goddess, mother, and maiden is P. Sundaram Pillai's 1891 hymn, "Tamil1t teyva van#akkam," "Homage to Goddess Tamil." Sundaram Pillai, of course, occupies a hallowed niche in the pantheon of *tamil1ppar1r1u* as a truly loyal son of Tamil1ttây. As his fellow devotees exclaim, was it not remarkable that although he lived all his life in Kerala, a non-Tamil-speaking region, he confessed to Tamil1ttây, "I may reside in [the land of] Malayalam, but I think of [only] you as my mother" (Sundaram Pillai 1922: 23)? Born in 1855 in Allepey into a middle-income Vellala family of traders, Sundaram Pillai had a master's degree in philosophy. Aside from a brief bureaucratic stint as commissioner of separate revenues for Travancore (1882-85), he taught history and philosophy at the Maharaja's College in Trivandrum until his death in 1897. His historical researches on Tamil literature secured for him membership in the Royal Asiatic Society and the coveted title of Rao Bahadur from the colonial state (Pillai et al. 1957).

In writing his hymn on Tamil1ttây, Sundaram Pillai took great care in locating it within a prior Shaiva tradition of deifying Tamil (Sundaram Pillai 1922: 9; Kailasapathy 1970: 102-9). Like his seventeenth-century predecessor, Karunaiprakasar, he refers to Tamil as deity and even boldly establishes a parity between the mighty Shiva and his Tamil1tteyvam, both of whom are deemed "primordial," "everlasting," and "boundless." Nonetheless, Sundaram Pillai was indeed inaugurating a new sensibility when he explicitly feminized Tamil as goddess, mother, and maiden. Aside from a few verses, the feminization of the language was quite underdeveloped prior to his hymn, but since then it has gained an immense following. Furthermore, large numbers of subsequent poets, especially those influenced by the Dravidian movement, have abandoned the conventional practice of beginning their works by calling upon the traditional Hindu deities to shower their benedictions on them. Instead, they more typically appeal to Tamil1ttây as their sole muse and guardian deity (Kailasapathy 1970). In doing so, they broadcast their allegiance to the Tamil cause and secure membership for themselves in the Tamil devotional community, even as they elevate the language to a status commensurate with that of the gods.

Equally striking, since Sundaram Pillai's time many devotees have not just been content with short invocatory verses on Tamil1ttây; instead they have also produced long and elaborate praise poems on her, many of which have been—and continue to be—published in literary journals and popular newspapers, or printed in anthologies (e.g., Nagarajan 1980; Somasundara Pulavar n.d.; Velayutam Pillai 1971). Indeed, praise poetry is one of the principal technologies through which devotion to Tamil1ttây is produced and circulated. For while there are a number of devout prose writings in which Tamil1ttây figures, it is praise poetry written in Tamil that is her favored niche.

Praise poetry has a long history in the literary cultures of the region, and it may be traced back through the devotional verses of the second millennium to the royal panegyrics of the ancient Cank#am corpus. Most such praise poems focused on deities, sovereigns, and spiritual notables, although occasionally other subjects of praise, like Tamil itself, materialized (Krishnan 1984; Ramaswamy 1996). As literary practice, praise poems enabled poets to articulate sentiments of love and adulation for their chosen subjects, to recount the salvific powers and glorious actions of the deity or the sovereign, to dwell lovingly upon his or her beautiful form and appearance, and the like. Many conventional genres of praise—such as the *tirupal#l#iyel1ucci*, the *tirutacânk#am*, the *pil#l#aittamil1*, the *tûtu*, and so on—have been extremely productive over the centuries, offering standardized templates that a poet could readily deploy in the praise of a chosen subject or patron (Zvelebil 1974: 193-219).

Remarkably, such genres, which were predominantly reserved for deities or sovereigns in the premodern praise literature, are used from the early decades of this century to laud Tamil. Thus, there are many examples of *Tamil1ttây pal#l#iyel1ucci*, "the awakening of Tamil1ttây from sleep" *Tamil1ttây tirutacânk#am*, "the ten constituents of [the kingdom of] Tamil1ttây" and of *Tamil1ttâyppil#l#aitamil1*, "Tamil1ttây as extraordinary child." There are innumerable versions of *Tamil1ttâymâlai*, "garland of Tamil1ttây" at least two poems written in the ancient *âr1r1uppat#ai*, "guide," genre in which poets direct their fellow speakers to the presence of a glorious and bountiful Tamil1ttây whom they had forgotten; and two poems featuring Tamil as messenger, *tûtu* (Amirtham Pillai 1906; Arangasami [1977]; Parantama Mudaliar 1926; Somasundara Pulavar n.d.: 8-10, 35-43; Sundara Shanmugan 1951; Velayutam Pillai 1971: 56-61, 83-84; Pekan 1986). Additionally, popular and folk genres such as the *kur1avaòci* and the *villuppât#t#u* have also been appropriated in narratives such as the *Tamil1aracikkur1avaòci* (The fortuneteller song on Queen Tamil) and *Tamil1 Val#arnta Katai* (The story of Tamil's growth) (Navanitakrishnan 1952; Varadananjaiya Pillai [1938]). At the very least, all this suggests the energy with which modern devotees of Tamil have colonized high as well as popular forms, so that a space may be cleared for their chosen one among the more conventional objects of adulation in the Tamil life-world. Through the deployment of such poetic genres and praise strategies, they have endowed their language with the powers and charisma that have gathered around gods, sovereigns, and notables over the centuries—the right to command allegiance, demand loyalty, and mobilize followers. In turn, her devotees are encouraged to relate to Tamil1ttây as they have interacted with these figures—with a mixture of adulation, reverence, and deep love.

Praise, Arjun Appadurai suggests, is a "regulated, improvisatory practice" that creates a "community of sentiment involving the emotional participation of the praiser, the one who is praised, and the audience of that act of praise" (A. Appadurai 1990: 94). The praise poem on Tamil1ttây personalizes the language, presenting it to its devotee as a tangible being who is familiar, even intimate—a personal god, patron sovereign, guardian muse, object of desire, and increasingly, mother figure. The praise poem also knits together the language and its devotees into a community of adulation and worship, each act of praise allowing them an opportunity to dwell lovingly upon the wonders and powers of their beloved Tamil. Finally, the praise poem allows its authors to renew their faith in themselves and in each other as devotees of Tamil1ttây. The praise of Tamil1ttây through poetry thus is more than just a literary or political gesture, signifying one's adherence to Tamil; it is, also, crucially, a *ritual* act through which *tamil1ppar1r1u* is continually renewed and reaffirmed. It is therefore not surprising that many such praise poems, particularly by hallowed devotees such as Sundaram Pillai, Subramania Bharati, or Bharatidasan, are recited over and over again in devotional circles, especially at times that call for a heightened demonstration of piety and loyalty.

All this is not to say that poetry is the only form of expression in Tamil devotion. Certainly, its devotees wrote a great deal about Tamil in prose, especially on matters relating to language and cultural policy, on the promotion of Tamil in education, government, and public activities, and so on. In such prose narratives, however, especially when they were written in English, it is comparatively rare to find Tamil1ttây. Instead, Tamil generally appears in prose as a nonpersonified language—not as an animate being, as it frequently does in its poetry. This in itself is perhaps not surprising, for prose narratives on Tamil were often produced for the consumption of the state, in the process of petitioning the government for various favors. In contrast, poetry on Tamil1ttây is typically generated for the consumption of its speakers. Indeed, especially in the colonial period, the state appears to have been remarkably disinterested in this whole sphere of activity that was so prolific and widespread among Tamil's devout. So the striking dependence on poetic discourse in Tamil devotional circles was more than just a literary habit, dictated by the norms of a culture in which poetry, rather than prose, was until fairly recently the privileged mode of literary expression. Rather, the recourse to Tamil poetry was also a strategic practice through which its devotees expressed and constituted their devotion to their language through a medium (Tamil) that is considered their very "own," through a form (poetry) that is deemed authentically and deeply "Tamil," and through forums (such as community based literary and revivalist activities) that were outside the interests of the state. Poetry made possible intimate, even veiled, discourse about the language, allowing participation only to those who were familiar with its imagery, meters, rhetorical nuances, and so on. Thus poetry enabled Tamil's devout to practice what I would characterize as "intimate politics" in which affect and passion were deployed to establish the boundaries of a community united in devotion to the language.

And yet, although poetry had been the preferred mode of pre-colonial literary work, with the onset of modernity and its privileging of prose as rational, objective, and scientific, poets were increasingly pushed to the margins of social prestige and economic well-being in many parts of colonial India, and certainly in the Tamil-speaking region. Paradoxically, this itself may account for poetry's popularity as a discursive form among Tamil's devotees. Because prose, especially prose in English, was so closely associated with the existing power structures, poetry, I suggest, emerged as the favored form for the disenfranchised and the disempowered. Concomitantly, poetry also presents itself as a form of expression for those who want to oppose the existing system and the dominant ideology. In her marvellous ethnography on the ideology of poetry in Bedouin society, Lila Abu-Lughod suggests as much and notes that among the Bedouins, "poetry is, in so many ways, the discourse of opposition to the system[,]...[a] symbol of defiance" (1986: 233-59). I appropriate her suggestion, applying it as well to the production of poetry by *tamil1ppar1r1u,* which has clearly been a discourse of opposition conducted around sentiments of decline, loss, and disempowerment. On the one hand, poetry is widely believed to encapsulate the best of Tamil's literary tradition; it is associated with the Tamil past, especially the past of the ancient Cank#am age when poets, we are repeatedly told, commanded even kings. Poetry, it is nostalgically believed, is a deeply and authentically Tamil form. On the other hand, at least in the past century or so, its very subordination to prose within the regimes of colonial modernity meant that it emerged not just as a means but as a site of resistance to dominant ideologies, as well as to the new literary and linguistic forms that threatened what was perceived as authentically Tamil. For all these reasons, when Tamil's devotees want to write most passionately, intimately, and fiercely about their language, they turn to poetry.

In the praise poetry on Tamil and Tamil1ttây since the time of Sundaram Pillai, there is no singular conception of *par1r1u,* "devotion," that reigns. Instead, like the language and like Tamil1ttây, devotion, too, is multifaceted, and here I examine three of its modalities. In what I wish to call its "pietistic" mode, it is Tamil1ttây's persona as *teyvam,* "goddess," that is foregrounded, and the devotee casts himself as a pious worshipper. The predominant sentiment of this modality is reverence for a divine being, the relationship between the language and its *pious* devotee modelled on the ritual relationship between an omniscient goddess and her subordinate worshipper. I characterize the second of the modalities as the "somatics of devotion." Here, the emphasis is on Tamil1ttây's persona as *tây,* the "mother" of her devotees, who correspondingly cast themselves as her "children." In this modality, the relationship between the language and its *filial* devotee is biological and corporeal, modelled on the genealogical and familial bonds that tie a mother to her child. Here, devotion takes on a distinctly filial flavor, predominantly expressed in the domestic idiom of the family and the home. And then, there is a third modality that I characterize as the "erotics of devotion." Here, it is Tamil1ttây's persona as woman that is highlighted, the devotee casting himself as a desiring man. In this modality, the relationship between the language and its *desiring* devotee is charged with eroticism, although Tamil1ttây's status as *kan1n1i,* "virgin maiden," obviously complicates an already ambivalent situation. I have analytically distinguished these modalities of devotion (pietistics, somatics, and erotics), these three aspects of the devotee (pious, filial, and desiring), and these three personae of Tamil1ttây (goddess, mother, and maiden). But in much of the discourse of *tamil1ppar1r1u,* they are all quite intertwined, making Tamil devotion a very fraught and complicated affair indeed.

TAMIL AS DEITY: PIETISTICS OF TAMIL DEVOTION

In Sundaram Pillai's founding hymn, Tamil1ttây figures prominently as a goddess, variously invoked as *teyvam, an#ank#u,* and *tây*. Poems featuring Tamil1ttây as deity are generally more frequent in the religious and Indianist regimes of *tamil1ppar1r1u* (Bharati 1988: 117; Ramalinga Pillai 1988: 19, 474; Velayutam Pillai 1971), although many a Dravidianist poet who vigorously challenged the divinization of the language also occasionally slipped into this imagery. Consider a poem by Mudiyarasan entitled "Tamil1 En1 Teyvam" (Tamil is my deity). A dedicated Dravidianist, the poet consciously distances himself from religiosity in his personal reminiscences, but he did not hesitate to write about Tamil thus:

Residing in my heart that is your temple (kôvil), offer me grace;

Adorned in your garland of poetry, offer me protection;

Resting on my tongue, grant me good sense;

In verse and word, I will be strong.

......

I worship you every day and talk about your fame everywhere;

The world deems me a mad fellow (*pittan1*), a fanatic (*ver1iyan1*);

Don't you see?

(Mudiyarasan 1976: 27-28)

There are clear resonances here with the rhetorical modes and vocabulary of (Hindu) religiosity, so that even in a poem produced under the ideological mantle of the Dravidian movement, the relation between the language and its devotee is one of divine piety and reverence.

In this modality, Tamil1ttây may be a goddess, but she is not imagined as a transcendent remote divine being. Instead, true to the spirit of the devoṭional, *bhakti* Hinduism of the region, she is an immanent figure who is intimately and personally connected with the lives of her devotees. Indeed, one of the most striking features of the pietistics of *tamil1ppar1r1u* is the immediacy of bonds between the goddess and her worshippers; the truly devout can not only feel her presence, they can also see her, even touch her. Further, as in *bhakti* Hinduism, she is not only god to her pious devotee, but she is also his parent, guide, sovereign, friend, lover, and child. At different moments in his life as her pious worshipper, she may manifest herself to him in these various roles. As such a worshipper, Navaliyur Somasundara Pulavar (1878?-1953), a Tamil teacher at the Vattukottai school in Jaffna, Sri Lanka, declared:

> Like [our] mother, shes gives us food;
>
> Like [our] father, she gives us learning;
>
> Like our wife, she creates pleasure at home;
>
> Like our child, she gives sweet words pleasant to our ears.
>
> (Velayutam Pillai 1971: 86)

This multiplicity in her persona as *teyvam* notwithstanding, Tamil1ttây is above all a personal god, and the pious devotee relates to her on those terms. When he contemplates her, he does so oblivious to the presence of any other deity or being. Many praise poems are replete with references to actions (*van#ank#utal, parâvutal, pôr1r1utal*) that are typically used in the reverencing of Hindu divinities: "so that we may attain well-being, let us place on our head the flowerlike feet of our youthful goddess Tamil (*paintamil1tçvi*)," or "let us bow at the feet of our ancient goddess Tamil" (Velayutam Pillai 1971: 34-35). Tantalizing as these utterances may be in indexing an attitude of worshipfulness, it is not clear if the pious devotee actually offered *pûja*, that paradigmatic Hindu act of divine worship, to his goddess Tamil, thus casting into doubt whether Tamil1ttây, even in her overtly divine manifestation, is ever treated unambiguously as a Hindu divinity within *tamil1ppar1r1u*.

Crucial to the pietistics of devotion is the deliberate adoption of strategies of archaization and "subterfuges of antiquity" (Kaviraj 1993: 13). Although there are certainly ancient precedents to her present incarnation, Tamil1ttây is clearly a modern creation, not older than a century or so. But this is not what her pious devotee maintains. He claims that like the language she embodies, Tamil1ttây is a primeval deity. And the poems about her only support such a claim, so striking a throwback are they to ancient literary forms of veneration and adoration in the baroque motifs they use, their aesthetic structure, and their rhetorics. Through such strategies of archaization, her pious follower certainly establishes his own literary reputation as a skilled, learned poet; but just as crucially, he bestows a halo of venerable and formidable antiquity upon Tamil1ttây herself. And in a culture where the aura of primordiality carries with it a power that is as immense as it is intangible, this itself contributes towards the power of the goddess.

Tamil1tteyvam: Portrait of a Goddess

So what are the various ways in which Tamil1ttây has been constituted as primeval deity, the beloved of the gods, and the most bountiful of all beings?

"You were there, even before the mighty Himalayas emerged, and Kumari Nadu submerged!"

A fundamental strategy for establishing the antiquity of Tamil1ttây is by placing her in the company of the gods, as their companion, confidante, and friend. For some of her pious following, she, like the gods themselves, has no beginning. Sundaram Pillai hinted at this by comparing her with the primordial Shiva. Somasundara Bharati, too, referred to her as *mutalilal#ôr*, "one who has no beginning," and *mûppumilal#*, "she who is ageless" (Velayutam Pillai 1971: 23). Abstracted from the vagaries and contingencies of secular time, Tamil1ttây thus lives in cosmic time. Yet, being a modern himself and very much aware of the power of historical memories, the pious devotee also links her to ancient historical personages of the Tamil-speaking countryside. So he fashions for her a biography assembled from stories and legends of the Shaiva canon and from the newly emerging "facts" of ancient Tamil history. Tamil1ttây was created by Shiva (sometimes with the aid of the goddess Earth, but at other times single-handedly), and delivered to the world (through the intervention of that paradigmatic Tamil god, Murugan, in some versions) by the mythical sage Agastya. From his abode in the Potiyam mountains (in the Western Ghats), Agastya adorned her with her very first "jewel," the legendary grammar called *Akattiyam*. Subsequently, she matured as a child in the antediluvian academies of the Pandyan kingdom, which flourished under the benevolent patronage of Shiva himself. She slowly moved out of cosmic time into history as she came of age in the last of the academies in Madurai, proudly fostered by the "triumvirate" (*mûvçntar*), the famed Pandya, Chera, and Chola kings celebrated in the Cank#am poems. From then on, as an ever-virginal maiden, she enjoyed the patronage of various Tamil rulers. During this time, she was gifted with some more spectacular "ornaments" which adorn her body—the five great epic poems (*paòcakâviyam*), the *Tirukkur1al#*, the *Tiruvâcakam*, and so on. This is, of course, a biography with no end, for, being a deity, she has no end.

"There is no one like you! This is indeed the truth"

Not only is Tamil1ttây the most ancient and primordial of all beings, she is also incomparable. "O goddess Tamil! There is no other deity like you," declared Somasundara Pulavar (Velayutam Pillai 1971: 87). Incomparable she may be, but the pious devotee does invoke her likeness to the five elements (fire, water, earth, air, and ether), to the everlasting *karpaka* tree, to the sun and the moon, and so on. He also compares her to tasty fruits, beautiful flowers, and flavorful foods. So, Tamil1ttây is hailed as "the sea of ambrosia," as "the golden creeper, ripe with sweetness," as one "who shames the sweet sugarcane." In early medieval religious poetry where gods are routinely praised thus, it has been suggested that such visual and taste-oriented metaphors exemplify the devotee's intimate sensory experience of the divine presence (Cutler 1987: 199). This may also be true for Tamil's pious devotee, who yearns to capture Tamil1ttây's wondrous qualities and present these to his fellow speakers in terms both familiar and desirable. But more often than not, he declares helplessly that words are inadequate to capture her greatness, her fame, and her beauty. "O mother, who will find it easy to talk about all your excellent virtues?" asked A. Venkatachalam Pillai (1888?-1953), chief poet of the Karanthai Tamil Sangam and first editor of its *Tamil1p Pol1il*. And Thudisaikizhar Chidambaram (1883-1954), who worked for a while in the colonial police service, a job he gave up to dedicate himself to Shaiva revivalism, wondered plaintively, "Is it even possible for someone like me to sing your greatness?" (Velayutam Pillai 1971: 11, 66).

"She encircles the resounding world"

Flourishing as she has from remote antiquity, Tamil1ttây is also sovereign of the world, and of all the peoples who live in it, and of all the languages they speak. For had she not preceded all of them, and indeed, was she not responsible for their creation? So, the eight cardinal directions echo to the sound of her victorious drums and the songs of her fame (Velayutam Pillai 1971: 78-80). In picture posters produced by organizations like Kampan1 Kal1akam in Karaikkudi (henceforth Kamban Kazhagam) and by notables in Annamalainagar, as well as on the covers of magazines like *Tamil1 Vat#t#am* (1967), Tamil1ttây thus appears seated on a globe, her "throne" (figs. 1-3). From early in the century, *tamil1ppar1r1u* had claimed that since Tamil1ttây had formerly ruled the world, there was little doubt that she would reign supreme, once again, in the future. For her devotees seeking to mobilize their fellow speakers around the cause of Tamil1ttây, such an imagining of Tamil as an ecumenical language of the world served to keep alive the aura of its ancient sovereignty in an age of disenchantment and decline.

"You are sovereign of the fine Tamil world"

In the spirit of divine and kingly cultures of the region in which gods are kinglike, and sovereigns are godlike, Tamil1tteyvam is also imagined as Tamil1 Araci, the queen of the fine Tamil world (*nar1tamil1ulakam*), the empress of the entire Dravidian land (Vedanayakam Pillai 1879: 285). Poems composed in the *tirutacânk#am* (the auspicious ten limbs) genre enumerate the ten "royal limbs" of her kingdom—her sovereign title, land, capital city, river, mountain, vehicle, army, drum, garland, and banner. Tamil1ttây's "army" is the might of her poetry; her "royal mount," the tongue(s) of her glorious poet(s). The three branches of Tamil—literature (*iyal*), music (*icai*), and drama (*nât#akam*)—make up her "royal drum" she wears Tamil poems around her neck as her victorious "garland" her "royal banner," appropriately enough, is the flag of knowledge made up of all the goodness of the incomparable Tamil; and so on (Velayutam Pillai 1971: 83-84).

Yet Tamil1ttây is clearly conceived by her admirers to be more than a goddess of learning and knowledge. The Herderian notion circulated through colonial knowledges, that language provides the legitimate foundation for distinctive nation-states, is enrolled into her constitution as a goddess of polity as well, as a queen who rules over the Tamil land and community. Most typically, Tamil1ttây's "kingdom" extends from the Venkatam (Tirupati) hills in the north, to Cape Kumari in the south, and from coast to coast, the traditional *tamil1akam* (Tamil home) of the ancient Cank#am poems. Some devotees, especially of contestatory classicist inclination, were more ambitious and maintained that she was queen of all of India. Thus in the Kamban Kazhagam poster (fig. 2) as well as in the frontispiece of the 1947 edition of Velayutam Pillai's anthology, *Mol1iyaraci* (Queen of languages), Tamil1ttây is seated on a map of (prepartition) India. In such visuals, she clearly challenges the authority of Bhârata Mâtâ, who is generically shown standing on a map of India with her arms stretched out to encompass the east and the west, her head in the Himalayas, her feet resting in the South (fig. 4). For contestatory regimes of *tamil1ppar1r1u*, it is Tamil1ttây, however, who should legitimately occupy the land now appropriated for Bhârata Mâtâ.

At the same time, her pious devotee also takes care to establish Tamil1ttây's intimate connections with the Tamil-speaking landscape. So, rivers like the Tamaraparani and the Kaveri are imagined as ornaments that snake their way across her body; the two mountain ranges (Western and Eastern Ghats) are visualized as her arms; the cool and fragrant southern breeze (*ten1r1al*) is likened to her sweet breath; and so on. A sacred geography thus emerges around her persona: Potiyam, the mountain home of the sage, Agastya, is hallowed as her "birth" place; Madurai, that seat of Tamil learning, is where she reigned as queen; the Vaigai River is where she performed many of her miracles that demonstrated her supernatural powers; and so on. Like Tamil itself, the land where it is spoken and over which Tamil1ttây rules is sacred as well (Velayutam Pillai 1971: 73-98).

"You are knowledge itself"

Her pious devotee also insists that Tamil1ttây's "kingdom" is not just the earthly spread of the Tamil land (or India, or the whole wide world). Instead, she is queen of something even more superior, the kingdom of knowledge. In the words of R. Raghava Aiyangar, a leading member of the Madurai Tamil Sangam and the first editor of its journal, *Centamil1:*

> *O sweet Tamil1ttây! May you flourish forever here and offer grace to your devotees!*
>
> *You produced the poetry of Kapilar and other poets of the good academy in the southern land.*
>
> *You fed the world with the* Kur1al# *of Valluvar.*
>
> *You destroyed darkness with mighty Kamban.*
>
> ......
>
> *You stand as source of all learning.*
>
> ......
>
> *You caused learning to grow among women.*
>
> ......
>
> *You created scholars to nourish our minds.*
>
> ......
>
> *O fine Tamil1ttây! Look at all you have accomplished!*
>
> *(Velayutam Pillai 1971: 41-42)*

The world's best knowledge, of course, is in Tamil; its poets are the finest, and so is its literature. The more contestatory devotee insists that Tamil1ttây's learned productions are far superior to anything that other languages, especially Sanskrit, can offer. Sundaram Pillai himself set the tone in his paradigmatic 1891 hymn when he asked polemically why should the (Sanskritic) *Manusmr#ti,* which advocated a different norm for each caste, be forced upon Tamil speakers when they have their own *Tirukkur1al#?* Why do we need the *Veda* when we have the *Tiruvâcakam,* which melts the stoniest of hearts (Sundaram Pillai 1922: 22-23)? Since his time, of course, others have continued to declare that their Tamil1ttây's auspicious words are more glorious than the words of the *Veda,* the *Vedânta,* the *Bhagavad Gîtâ,* and other such hallowed texts of Sanskritic Hinduism.

For the less contestatory devotee, however, Tamil1ttây appears to have been a Saraswati-like figure. Indeed, that paradigmatic Sanskritic goddess of learning and wisdom is sometimes portrayed as Tamil1ttây's friend, who commands poets to sing to her in Tamil so that she, too, may enjoy that wondrous language

(Velayutam Pillai 1971: 89). At other times, Tamil1ttây is herself referred to as *kalaimakal#* (= Saraswati), and in many a visual and iconographic representation, the similarity between the two goddesses is quite striking. Given the antagonism towards Sanskritic Hinduism that characterizes so many of the regimes of *tamil1ppar1r1u*, Tamil1ttây thus appears to displace Saraswati in the affections of many a pious devotee. As such, she, and not Saraswati, was the fount of all learning, the mother of all languages, and the inspiring muse for scholar and devotee alike.

"She is the goddess who commands the gods who guard us"

Nothing more clearly suggests the desire of her pious devotee to move Tamil1ttây into the space occupied by his traditional gods than the many verses in which she is credited with performing various miraculous deeds conventionally attributed to Shiva, Vishnu, and other deities of the Hindu pantheon. So Chidambaram declared that Tamil1ttây, too, performed the three cosmic deeds of creation, maintenance, and destruction for which Shiva is famed (Velayutam Pillai 1971: 66). C. Venkatarama Chettiyar (b. 1913), who taught Tamil at Annamalai University, wrote that the three branches of Tamil embodied "this precious world which was formerly spanned by the three steps of that lofty Lord of Lakshmi [Vishnu]" (Velayutam Pillai 1971: 44). That her pious devotee could go to great lengths to make such claims is clear from a long poem in which Chidambaram addresses Tamil1ttây:

You dispatched the Lord of all devotees as messenger!

......

Is there anything more to be said of your greatness?

......

You transformed poison into ambrosia!

You made the rock thrown into the ocean to float as a raft!

You coaxed the murderous elephant to bow down to that great devotee!

You transformed a mere pile of bones into a woman!

......

You caused palm-leaf manuscripts to float on the floodwaters!
you protected them from being scorched by the worst of fires!

......

You opened the doors [of the temple] of Tirumaraikadu!
You cured the hunched back of the great Pandyan!
You taught the heretical Jains to learn the wonders of the great Shiva!

......

My! My! What greatness! What wonder!
(Velayutam Pillai 1971: 66-67)

These lines may sound arcane and esoteric, but they remind us, once again, that the power of Tamil1ttây in this modality is constituted by deliberately archaizing her, by placing her in another time, in a world of mysterious but wondrous acts and beings. They also confirm what every pious devotee would like to hear, that his goddess would do anything for those who were devoted to her—quench the anger of a murderous elephant who was threatening to kill one of her adorers, cure the chronic fever of another, even play the role of a lowly messenger so that the love life of one of her worshippers would thrive. Indeed, this is a fundamental aspect of the structure of piety that is constituted around the divine Tamil1ttây: in return for services rendered to her by her devotees, she would protect them, grant them miraculous favors, and shower wealth and grace on them. In short, she would do anything for those who were truly her adoring dependents.

But most crucially, these lines recall incidents from the life stories of famous devotees of Shiva in which the latter tests the devotion of his followers to punish those who were cruel to them, to reveal to them his compassion, and to grant eternal bliss to his truly devout (Peterson 1989). And yet, these same incidents are invoked in the modern discourses of *tamil1ppar1r1u* with a significant, even cosmic, difference. For here, Tamil1ttây is the inspiring force behind Shiva's activities, the true author of these wondrous deeds, and the paradigmatic savior of the world.

"The supreme one who has no beginning and no end, ardently desires you"

Although her pious devout, especially orthodox Shaivites, are careful to not let Tamil1ttây's powers overtly challenge Shiva's, some of them do not hesitate to point out that not only Shiva but also Vishnu and the other gods are at her bidding, enthralled as they are by her beauty, virtue, and learning. They declared that "in order to see [her], the lord Vishnu himself, with the northern *Vedas* in tow, followed [her]," and they reminded each other that Shiva's cosmic weariness flees when Tamil sounds fill his divine ears with pleasure. Shiva may be Tamil1ttây's father-creator, but that great lord may also desire her. So filled was he with longing to hear her words that he left his celestial abode and came down to earth to preside over the Tamil academy of Madurai. So eager was he to have her near him that he ordered the recital of Tamil hymns every day, not finding comfort in the Sanskrit *Vedas* (Velayutam Pillai 1971: 4-6, 66-68, 108-15).

Because she is the beloved of the gods, her pious devotee calls upon the more established divinities to protect her, or prays to them to grant grace so that he himself could serve her better. Thus the opening invocatory verse to the *Mol1iyaraci* anthology declares, "I pray to Murugan who dwells in the grove, so that I may be born in the Tamil land where words flourish." The pietistics of *tamil1ppar1r1u* thus appears to have a curious contradiction. On the one hand, her pious adorer imagines Tamil1ttây as a supreme, omniscient being who is not just the beloved of the gods, but even commands them and inspires them to perform their various godly deeds. On the other hand, because many who participated in this modality were also for the most part quite religious themselves, they never do totally abandon their faith in the established gods of the Hindu pantheon. Instead, they continue to pray to them so that their own personal goddess, Tamil1ttây, may also benefit from the good will of those great beings.

"I am your devotee; you are my refuge"

For the pious devotee for whom she is his personal deity, Tamil1ttây is the source of everything in this world—of knowledge and happiness, of wealth and prosperity, of bliss and light, indeed of life itself. She is the destroyer of darkness and of false illusions. She cures her followers of anger and jealousy, and grants them true vision. She cures them of afflictions and weeds out their troubles. At her feet, even the worst sinners find salvation. By her very presence, she destroys the sins of her devotees. She is indeed their ultimate refuge. A. Kantasami Pillai (1885-1969), a professor of Tamil, declared:

O Tamil1ttây, may you flourish blissfully as a sovereign queen!

You gave birth to us, and embracing us, fed us nectar from your beautiful breasts;

You taught us to speak as infants, and also the full meaning of numerous words;

You caused our evil habits to flee, and firmly established in their stead good conduct that is dearer than life and fame....

You taught us to respect ourselves, and teaching us about the experiences of the past and the present,

You have shown us the road to eternal release!

(Velayutam Pillai 1971: 4)

Similarly, R. Raghava Aiyangar wrote eloquently that "with the help of [your] divine ladder of priceless books, we can climb straight up to the heavens" (Velayutam Pillai 1971: 41). Even more dramatically, for Somasundara Pulavar there was only one cure for the endless disease that is life, and it lay at the feet of his noble Tamil1ttây (Velayutam Pillai 1971: 93). The pious devotee is indeed convinced that Tamil1ttây may be the most omniscient of gods, and the most powerful of sovereigns, but she has the compassion and the tenderness of one's own mother. She therefore never forsakes even the most humble and most lowly of her adherents. She is infinitely forgiving—even overlooking the faults of those who turned their backs on her, so benevolent and compassionate a being is she (Velayutam Pillai 1971: 12). There is little doubt, therefore, as A. Varadananjaiya Pillai (1877-1956), a member of the Karanthai Tamil Sangam and author of several praise works on Tamil1ttây, insisted, that it was she who was going to abide with them for ever and ever, even accompanying them to the world beyond the present one (Velayutam Pillai 1971: 26-28).

Tamil1ttây is thus both the means to their salvation and salvation itself. By constituting her in such terms, these pious devotees were only expressing in religious terms the foundational message of *tamil1ppar1r1u* that Tamil is everything to its speakers—their body, their life, their spirit, and, ultimately, their soul itself.

Profiling the Pious Devotee

So, who are the true adorers of Tamil? For this modality, they are those who think of Tamil1ttây as their *teyvam* and have faith and confidence in her divinity, her compassion, and her supreme abilities. The pious devotee chastises his fellow speakers for failing to reverence Tamil1ttây, or for ridiculing and scorning her. "There are base people who do not know about the depth of your excellence! Grant me grace, so that I do not become one of them." Because her detractors' minds were filled with confusion, they say harsh things about her. "What indeed is the worth of their knowledge?" her adorers demanded (Velayutam Pillai 1971: 61-62).

Since her pious devotee believes that Tamil1ttây is an omniscient being, the source of his life and wisdom, and his ultimate refuge, he is also convinced that his salvation, and that of his fellow Tamilians, lies in securing her grace (*arul#*). Her *arul#* would cure Tamil speakers of laziness and sloth, and grant them manliness and courage; it would destroy all illusions and rid them of all sins, past and present; and it would release them from the cycle of births. So her devotee beseeches her to open her eyes and grant him grace. Indeed, one of his favorite poetic genres is the *tirupal#l#iyel1ucci* (the awakening [of the lord] from sleep), for he is convinced that ignored by her followers, Tamil1ttây has gone to sleep, and thus no longer offers them grace. As Diana Eck notes, "In the Hindu view, not only must the gods keep their eyes open, but so must we, in order to make contact with them, to reap their blessings" (1985: 1).

Thus, crucial to the structure of piety that develops around Tamil1ttây is the belief that both she and her speakers must "awaken" and "open their eyes" it is only then that she would be able to grant grace, and they could receive it. All would then be well with the (Tamil-speaking) world.

Just as he longs to receive her *arul#,* the pious devotee also yearns to experience her, with his mind, heart, and all his senses. So he imagines her as residing on his tongue. He longs to "immerse" himself in her and blend with her very being (Velayutam Pillai 1971: 61-62). There is an erotic subtext to the piety of the devout in *tamil1ppar1r1u,* as there is in so much of devotional Hinduism. Indeed, some of her adorers are so overcome when they contemplate her beautiful and splendid form that, they confess, "[Our] bodies brim with ecstasy; our hair quivers in excitement; [our] tongues stammer with love; and [our] bones melt" (Velayutam Pillai 1971: 68; see also Sivalinga Nayanar 1940). In Varadananjaiya Pillai's words:

Our hands in prostration, our minds throbbing with joyousness,
the hair on our bodies quivering in excitement,
Brimming with ecstasy, we offer you our prayer!
May you live long, O Tamil1ttây! O mother of ours!
May you flourish for ever and ever and ever.
(Velayutam Pillai 1971: 82)

This kind of ecstatic piety supplements the more overt but secular sexual economy of the erotic modality of Tamil devotion, as we will see. Increasingly, as the imagining of Tamil as a familial mother figure came to dominate *tamil1ppar1r1u*, desire for Tamil1ttây could only exist in the interstices. But within the modality of pietistics, erotic sensibilities were granted some latitude, for divine sexuality continued to have a kind of currency that was not so readily conceded to maternal sexuality within the new bourgeois codes of morality that were put in place in colonial South India.

The Ideology of Pious Devotion

At its heart, the structure of piety produced by this modality turns around a dyadic relationship between the language, imagined as a benevolent, bountiful, and omniscient goddess, and its devotees, who cast themselves in the role of pious, submissive, and helpless worshippers, totally dependent on her for succor, inspiration, and salvation. She is the protector, and they are the protected; she is the muse who inspires, and they are the poets who breathlessly yearn to be inspired. Imagined thus as an omniscient perfect being, the language she embodies is correspondingly omniscient and perfect as well.

This modality is therefore particularly favored by the religious regime of *tamil1ppar1r1u* that treats Tamil as a perfect, complete language of plenitude which had unfortunately fallen on hard times, because of the evil ways of other languages, because of being ignored by its own speakers, and so on. The principal agenda of this regime, as of classicism, is the restoration of all of Tamil's "wealth" (*celvam*) that had been tainted or lost over time. There is less concern here with renovation, as there is in Indianism and Dravidianism, for how could one improve something that was already so perfect?

Perhaps the most striking feature of this modality is the passion and fervor with which her pious devotees appear to believe that in their Tamil1ttây, they are faced with a divine presence so perfect and so powerful that they themselves could do nothing but sing her praises and spread her word. It is she who has to give them grace and lead them to salvation; it is she who is the agent, the active principle. Tamil's devotees, I have repeatedly emphasized, are clearly moderns, living in a century when they have been exposed, in varying degrees, to all kinds of modern technologies, knowledges, and ways of being. Yet, when writing about their language in this mode, they consciously deny to themselves the most modern and secular of all attitudes, that of placing themselves as the center of their cosmos. Instead, they choose to insert their divinized language into that spot, throw themselves at her mercy, and await her grace.

TAMIL AS MOTHER: SOMATICS OF TAMIL DEVOTION

"Is there anything comparable to the mother's love?" So asks Sivagnanam in his reminiscences (1974: 30). Not really, as far as Tamil's devout were concerned, and in their imaginings, the incomparable Tamil was increasingly likened to their incomparable mothers. The representation of Tamil as mother, variously invoked as *tây, ammâ, mâtâ,* and *an1n1ai,* was particularly acute in the modality of somatics which gained ground as the Indianist and Dravidianist regimes gathered momentum from the 1920s on. Although Tamil1tteyvam is also hailed as *ammâ* and *tây* (not surprisingly, considering that goddesses and mothers are symbolically and emotionally intertwined in the Hindu life-world), the mother who figures in the modality of somatics is essentially a familial, domestic, and secular being. Rhetorically and aesthetically as well, the modality of somatics was populist rather than archaizing, relying on the imagery of the quotidian and the vocabulary of the spoken language rather than on the high literary Tamil typically used by the pious devotee.

Within the discourses of *tamil1ppar1r1u,* the confluence of "language" and "motherhood" may be traced back to the late nineteenth century. So, in 1879, S. Vedanayakam Pillai (1826-89), author of the first Tamil novel, unambiguously declared, "Tamil gave birth to us; Tamil raised us; Tamil sang lullabies to us and put us to sleep" (Vedanayakam Pillai 1879: 285). A few years later, in the 1887 foreword to his edition of the Cank#am anthology, the *Kalittokai*, Damodaram Pillai pleaded with his readers to financially help him salvage ancient manuscripts, asking of them, "Is not Lady Tamil (*tamil1 mâtu*) your mother?" (Damodaram Pillai 1971: 69). In 1891, Sundaram Pillai dedicated his play, *Man1ôn1man#îyam*, with its well-known invocatory hymn on Tamil1ttây, to his *tamilmâtâ*, "Mother Tamil" (Sundaram Pillai 1922: 12). A year later, T. Lakshmana Pillai wondered if those who considered Tamil as their *mâtâ* and *tây* (mother) would come forward to honor her, and Suryanarayana Sastri insisted that his Tamil could not be compared to a barren mother (*malat#i tâyâr*) (Lakshmana Pillai 1892-93: 154, 185-86; Suryanarayana Sastri n.d.: 59). As the next century advances, this occasional practice of referring to Tamil as "mother" coalesces into a well-entrenched linguistic and cultural habit. Increasingly, the *analogy* between language and motherhood is displaced by the *convergence* of the two domains, so that Tamil *is* the mother of the filial devotee. In essay after essay, poem after poem, devotees speak and write about their beloved Tamil as they would about their mothers, and vice versa (Maraimalai Adigal 1967b; Purnalingam Pillai 1930: 56-58; see also Ramaswamy 1992a).

In the modality of somatics, the language and its devotee are held together not so much through the supernatural powers of a divine being as through the emotional powers invested in the maternal body. Where the pious devotee praises her miraculous abilities and awe inspiring deeds to elicit the devotion of the Tamil speaker, the modality of somatics relies instead on various parts and substances of Tamil1ttây's body: her fertile womb, her nurturing milk, her pitiful tears, her scarred face, and her fettered limbs. In contrast to the modality of pietistics, where the bond between the language and its devotee is registered in intangibles such as the granting of *arul#* (grace), the filial devotee emphasizes the sharing of corporeal substances like milk and blood. Thus he insists that since Tamil1ttây's womb had given birth to speakers of Tamil, and her milk had raised them, in return her "children" ought to serve her by putting their own bodies at her disposal. In turn, those bodily parts and substances that foreground such bonds of birth are the most frequently invoked. While the pious devotee expresses his devotion on a religious terrain, the filial devotee registers it in uterine terms. Speakers of Tamil are

Tamilians not necessarily because they worship Tamil1ttây, but because they have been borne by Tamil, and nurtured and raised on it. They are all thus "siblings," because they have shared the womb and milk of Tamil. Occasionally, Tamil1ttây appears as *cevilittây*, "foster mother." But more often than not, she is explicitly identified as the birth mother, *în1r1atây*. So the intimacy between the language and its speakers in this modality is constituted by bringing Tamil1ttây right into their homes, as their mother who gave birth to them and raised them to be loyal and devoted Tamil speakers.

In maternalizing Tamil1ttây thus, her filial devotee drew upon the model of the "new mother" produced in bourgeois imaginations in so many regions of colonial India. She is a domestic paragon, furnished with a modern education but still retaining a modicum of religiosity and presiding over her neat and disciplined home, and her by now largely nuclear family (Chatterjee 1989; R. Kumar 1993: 32-52; Ramaswamy 1992a). In pre-colonial Tamil literature as well as in modern folklore, mothers are benign as well as threatening, nourishing as well as destructive, compassionate as well as fierce and malevolent (Shulman 1980: 223-67; Trawick 1990). In the discourses of *tamil1ppar1r1u*, however, Tamil1ttây is unambiguously compassionate, nourishing, pacific, and benign. This may seem surprising because she is always represented as a virgin, and the virginal or single mother/goddess, it has been suggested, frequently displays vengeful, punitive behaviors (Erndl 1993: 153-58). For both Indianism and Dravidianism, however, with their agendas of transforming Tamil speakers into a productive, enlightened, and educated community imagined as a harmonious and united family, an uncontrollable, threatening, and violent mother figure was not only embarrassing but counterproductive as well. Great care was therefore taken not to cast Tamil1ttây in the image of the many fierce mother-goddesses that her filial devotee was undoubtedly familiar with from both high and popular Hindu religious practice. Instead, she was modelled on the "new" mother who they hoped would eventually come to reign in Tamil-speaking homes—disciplined but compassionate, educated but modest and feminine, and respectable and virtuous.

All the same, the empowering of Tamil by appropriating the figure of the mother has had its advantages and its disadvantages for *tamil1pparlr1u.* On the one hand, Tamil's filial devotee is only too pleased to tap into the enormous reservoir of affective powers associated with motherhood in this region, especially since that reservoir had been significantly replenished in a colonial culture where mothers were constituted as the custodians of the authentic, pure, and uncolonized community. On the other hand, the devotee also had to be careful that his beloved language, in thus benefitting from its association with the mother, would not be entirely consumed by that very crucial figure of the life-world of its speakers. Increasingly, as the century wears on, the filial devotee was inclined to declare the superiority of Tamil1ttây's motherhood over that of his human mother. *Tâyin1um cir1antat Tamil1*, "Tamil that is superior to [our] mother," is a sentiment frequently encountered in devotional discourses from the 1930s on, especially in the Dravidianist idiom. As Margaret Trawick (1990: 156) rightly notes, "Many children in Tamilnadu grow up with more than one 'mother' and experience more than one household as home." The filial devotee, however, had to ensure that Tamil1ttây and her "home" were never just one among many for his fellow Tamil speakers, but the most important of them all.

Tamil1ttây: Portrait of a Mother

Filial anxiety and concern lace the sentiments of affection, love, and admiration for Tamil1ttây in the modality of somatics. Typically, she is featured as a once-glorious but now-endangered mother—frail, pitiful, and in desperate need of help from her sons: "O young Tamilians! What is the condition of our Tamil1ttây today? She stands without jewels and gems; she has lost her radiance; her crown has vanished; her fragrance is gone; she stands dejected and in tears; she grieves in sorrow; she is emaciated" (S. Subramanian 1939: 1).

Both Indianism, in its struggle against English and British colonialism, and Dravidianism, in its battle against Hindi and North Indian imperialism, circulated various images of Tamil1ttây as abandoned and desolate, the pitiful state of her body calling attention to the endangered state of Tamil. Consider the following poem by Bharatidasan, published in 1960:

O Tamil1ttây, you struggle for life in an ocean of grief
Grasping at the smallest stick, seizing it as if a giant raft!

O Tamil1ttây, buffeted around by fierce storms,
you clutch at worms in the soil, as if at roots!
O Tamil1ttây, writhing in the scorching heat,
You hurry to the stagnant pool as if to a waterfall.

Such images of a suffering Tamil1ttây are also supplemented by allusions to her decaying, diseased body. Sivagnanam exhorted his listeners at an anti-Hindi rally held in Madras in 1948: "It is Tamil1ttây who gave birth to us. When we were infants, it is in Tamil that we would have called out to our mothers, *ammâ, ammâ.* If such a loving mother's face is scarred by pox marks, and if we have the strength to prevent this, do we stand by doing nothing?" Years earlier, in a public talk he gave to the Karanthai Tamil Sangam in 1927, Maraimalai Adigal, too, pleaded, "Do not allow the pox marks of Sanskrit to scar Tamil1ttây's fine body." His plea was greeted with loud claps and cheers of "Long live Tamil! Long live pure Tamil! Long live Tamil1ttây! Long live Maraimalai Adigal!" (M. Tirunavukarasu 1959: 527). The modality of somatics thus thrives on the patriarchal imagining of the woman-as-passive-victim, dependent on her male kin to protect, honor, and save her.

The Violated Body of Tamil1ttây

Most potently, aiming to provoke the filial passions of Tamil speakers, her devotees circulated stunning images of Tamil1ttây being violated. She is incarcerated in dark dungeons; her golden body is trapped in iron manacles; her enemies suck up her blood; they hurl spears at her breast; they threaten to decapitate her, and so on. In the late 1940s, for instance, as the tensions over the creation of linguistic states out of Madras Presidency escalated with the impending loss of chunks of Tamil-speaking border areas to neighboring states, Sivagnanam ended his editorial in his journal *Tamil1 Muracu* on 15 April 1947: "O Tamilians! P. N. Rao's plan hangs like a sword over our Tamil1an1n1ai's [Tamil1ttây's] head. The Malayalees with their craving for land are waiting to chop off her feet. If we do not hasten, Tamil1an1n1ai will certainly be murdered. After we lose Venkatam and Kumari, our Tamil land will look like a mother with both her head and feet amputated" (Sivagnanam 1981: 112).

Being moderns, of course, her filial devotees are very much aware of the power of mass media and the visual image. Numerous cartoons published in Dravidian movement newspapers during the anti-Hindi protests of midcentury presented the reading public with striking visual enactments of various acts of violation of Tamil1ttây's body. One such cartoon, printed in several key Dravidian movement newspapers and magazines, showed the premier of the Presidency, Rajagopalachari, the archsupporter of the Hindi cause in the 1930s, attacking with a dagger a bejeweled Tamil1ttây, who stands undefended, carrying in her hands the ancient literary texts, the *Tirukkur1al#* and the *Tolkâppiyam* (fig. 5). Another, published in the 1950s in the DMK paper *Ar1appôr,* depicts a man personifying "North Indian Hegemony" cutting off a weeping Tamil1ttây's tongue with a sickle. Yet others showed Tamil1ttây locked up in prison, or shedding tears over the bodies of her children shot down by the police during anti-Hindi demonstrations.

Perhaps the most dramatic of these cartoons was published in *Kut#i Aracu* in 1937 on the eve of the first major anti-Hindi protests (fig. 6). Entitled *"Âccâriyâr Sâkasam: Tamil1an1n1ai Mân1apank#am,"* "Rajagopalachari's Bravado: The Dishonoring of Tamil1ttây," it depicts a woman of obvious distinction, wearing a crown and a halo, and carrying a scepter. She stands with tears flowing down her face, surrounded by a group of men, one of whom, clearly identifiable as the premier, Rajagopalachari, is attempting to disrobe her.

The accompanying text tells the reader that although many of her venerable sons in the Madras Legislative Assembly watched with growing anger as Tamil1ttây was being thus treated, they were too cowardly to do anything about it and stood by with their heads hanging in shame. The text ends on an appeal: "O true Tamilians! What are you going to do now?" The cartoon revived, of course, the well-known incident recounted in the ancient Sanskrit epic, the *Mahâbhârata,* of the disrobing of Draupadi by her Kaurava cousins as her Pandava husbands look on helplessly. A few years earlier, Subramania Bharati, in his poem *Pâòcâli Capatam* (Draupadi's oath; 1912-24), had drawn upon the story to allegorize the dishonoring of the nation/mother (Bharati 1987: 193-309). Given the antipathy to Sanskritic Hinduism within the Dravidian movement which spearheaded the anti-Hindi protests, the plot here follows a different course: rather than the lord Krishna coming to Tamil1ttây's rescue, as he does with Draupadi, it is the vastness of her own learning and the respect of her people that ultimately save her honor in the cartoon.

Of the many messages packed into this cartoon, the most striking is the act of *mân1apank#am,* "dishonoring," carried out through the disrobing of Tamil1ttây in a public space as hallowed as the state's legislature. This is not the singular instance of the use of this theme in *tamil1ppar1r1u,* although it is unique in the explicitness with which it singles out a man, and a very identifiable public figure at that, as perpetrating the crime. A year after the publication of the cartoon, at the Velur Women's Conference held on 26 December 1938, Narayani Ammal, a Tamil scholar who would be incarcerated for participating in the anti-Hindi protests two months later, reminded the assembled women that like Draupadi of yore, Tamil1ttây was in danger of losing her honor to Dushasana (Sanskrit and Hindi). "I hope her screams reach your ears," she concluded. More unusually, in a poem by Vanidasan (1915-74), a disciple of Bharatidasan, Hindi is identified as a *vççi,* "(female) prostitute," and charged with the offense of "snatching away the mother's garment." In general, however, her devotees leave ambiguous the gender or the identity of the entity which disrobes Tamil1ttây. Consider this excerpt from the proscribed text *In1pat Tirâvit#am* (Sweet Dravidian land), particularly striking because its author, Annadurai, did not generally employ the gendered vocabulary typically used by many of his fellow Dravidianists. Addressing the disloyal son who has turned his back on his "dishonored" mother (here signifying the Tamil land rather than language), Annadurai wrote: "How can you stand by and watch [our] enemy turn your motherland (*tâyakam*) into a *vel#l#ât#t#i* [maid/concubine]? Does not your blood boil when you see [him] uncoiling her braid, rubbing off the vermilion on her forehead, peeling off her clothing, and kicking her with [his] feet?" (Annadurai 1989: 91).

These lines are particularly dramatic for the care with which they systematically specify the manner in which the mother's body is violated and dishonored, stopping just short of suggesting actual rape. Indeed, it is important—but heartening—to emphasize that in none of the narratives I have collected on Tamil1ttây is there any explicit description of her rape. Although one could argue that the very possibility of rape that such vivid imagery suggests is just as threatening, its explicit absence contrasts with the reality of rape that has haunted women's lives in colonial and post-colonial India, as well as with allusions to the "rape" of a feminized land or nation in other parts of the world (Kolodny 1975; R. Kumar 1993: 127-42; Montrose 1992). Given the enormous emphasis that her devotees place on their Tamil1ttây being a virgin, and given the ritual and symbolic power accorded to the sexual purity of the woman, the rape of Tamil1ttây would have been both inappropriate and unproductive, for it would render the figure unavailable, even useless, for continual deployment within the sexual and patriarchal economies of *tamil1pparlr1u.* Instead, even while hinting at the potential for rape that lurks behind the disrobing of Tamil1ttây, her devout followers deploy the sentiments of shame and outrage associated with the violation of the mother's body. The image of disrobing is particularly effective in a culture where such a high premium is placed on honor, and where women's sexual purity and virtue underwrite the honor of their male kin in particular. The dishonor associated with public disrobing is especially heightened in this case because it involves the hallowed figure of the mother. The mother's public disrobing suggested not just the dishonor inflicted upon her individual self but, more damagingly, the dishonor visited upon all those who shared her flesh and blood—namely, her Tamilian "children," most especially her sons. So, the poet Vanidasan wrote in 1948, "The mother's honor is the Tamilian's honor. Think of saving yourself!" It is telling that in all such instances, as has been noted by Radha Kumar in another context, the violation of the female body is not specifically presented as an act of violence against women (R. Kumar 1993: 37). It is instead, very quickly, translated into the violation of the community and its honor.

The Fertile Womb of Tamil1ttây

Because the modality of somatics constructs its structure of devotion on the terrain of uterine bonds, the womb of Tamil1ttây is of particular importance to the filial devotee. So wrote a poet named Tamilkkovan in a poem entitled "My Life Is Yours":

O beautiful Tamil1ttây! The other day, I was born from your womb!

......

I am your son who brings you victory!

O mother, if someone scorns you
Of what use is my birth and life?

Her womb, of course, produced not just Tamilkkovan but all other speakers of Tamil as well, who are therefore transformed into each other's "siblings" by virtue of this somatic fact. It is her womb that unites them all as members of one "family." So Suddhananda Bharati (1938: 104) reminded his fellow speakers that wherever they may be and in whatever state, they ought to remember that "they are children of one mother's womb (*vayir1u*)." Tamil1ttây's womb thus functioned as a mnemonic device, reminding all speakers of Tamil of the bonds of birth that tied them to their language which had laboriously and patiently borne them all. As Tamil1ttây herself reminded them, "Do not forget that you are all children who emerged from *my* womb (*mat#i*). I am *your* mother....You are all called Tamilians" (Pancanathan n.d.: 9). In turn, one of her devotees, Viracolan, reiterated, "O mother, in embryonic form conceived, in fetal form enlivened, we were firmly planted in your womb (*vayir1u*). Then we were delivered to the world." So, her womb in this discourse serves somatically to confirm the facticity of birth as speakers of Tamil and as constituent members of the Tamil "family."

Her womb is also deployed by her devout to eliminate other mothers—such as Bhârata Mâtâ or Ânk#ilattây (Mother English) or Hindi—who may offer nourishment to Tamilians, raise them up, or secure them jobs. Nevertheless, the fact that their wombs had not given birth to Tamil speakers meant that their motherhood was, at worst, false and, at best, inferior to that represented by Tamil1ttây. For Indianism, obviously, Bhârata Mâtâ's womb mattered just as Tamil1ttây's. As Bharati insisted in his 1907 poem "Vantç Mâtaram" (Homage to Mother [India]): "Those who are born from the same mother's womb / Are they not brothers though they may squabble with each other?" (Bharati 1987: 51).

Years later, Ramalinga Pillai reminded his fellow speakers:

This venerable Intiyattçvi [Bhârata Mâtâ] gave birth to three hundred and thirty million children!

......

For how many days did she carry us?
How many troubles did she face for us?

We forgot all her difficulties; she endured all our faults!
Millions and millions of foreigners came here to plunder;
She put up with millions of them, and took care of her children!
......
Such a noble lady we forgot.
......
Will not her womb that gave birth to us burn?
Will not her tender heart grieve?
When her own children to whom she gave birth forsake her, how can a woman endure that?
(Ramalinga Pillai 1988: 309-10)

In the logic of Indianism, Bhârata Mâtâ's womb enables Tamil speakers to be reborn as "Indians." In that capacity, they owed her filial duty and love. To forget this meant the "betrayal of the mother's womb," causing it to "burn" and allowing it to be "violated" (Ramalinga Pillai 1988: 303-16). The maternal womb becomes the ground on which contrary allegiances thus come to be negotiated, with Dravidianism making a commitment to only Tamil1ttây's and Indianism to Bhârata Mâtâ's as well (see also Lakshmii 1990).

Tamil1ttây (as indeed Bhârata Mâtâ) may be a virgin, but her womb was immensely fertile and fruitful. In the imaginations of some of her more ambitious devotees, her womb had given birth to not just Tamilians but to other languages and their speakers as well. Perhaps the earliest use of this notion was Sundaram Pillai's famous hymn, which declared that Tamil1tteyvam's *utaram,* "womb," had given birth to the four other Dravidian languages: Kannada, Telugu, Malayalam, and Tulu (Sundaram Pillai 1922: 22). By 1891, when Sundaram Pillai published this hymn, many of Tamil's devotees were familiar with Robert Caldwell's assertions that Tamil was the oldest and most cultivated member of the Dravidian "family" of languages. Yet Caldwell also insisted that Tamil was one "dialect" among the many Dravidian dialects, and not "the original speech" from which they had all descended. It certainly was not, in his reckoning, the "mother" of the Dravidian family (Caldwell 1856: 26, 52, 61). Sundaram Pillai, however, not only so declared it but even used that most maternal of somatic parts, the womb, to secure this claim. Since his time, of course, the notion that Tamil's womb generated all Dravidian languages has acquired an enormous materiality, especially in Dravidianism, whose more ambitious exponents stake a claim on the bodies of all Dravidians (and not just Tamil speakers) on the ground that they are after all Tamil1ttây's children and owe loyalty to her (e.g., E. V. Ramasami 1948: 30).

The Nourishing Milk of Tamil1ttây

For her filial devotee, Tamil1ttây's milk (*pâl*) is just as significant as her womb. As early as 1879, Vedanayakam Pillai described Tamil as "the language which our mothers and fathers fed us along with milk" (Vedanayakam Pillai 1879: 285). In 1891, Sundaram Pillai's *Man1ôn1man#îyam* featured a dramatic monologue in which the hero, Jeevakan, declared that it is through mother's milk that pride in one's language and one's land is imbibed. By the turn of this century, the assumption that Tamil was mother's milk had become so naturalized that in 1913, when the senate of Madras University proclaimed that the "vernaculars" would no longer be compulsory for students, the *Òân1apânu* protested by comparing this resolution with one that would dictate that it was no longer mandatory for mothers to raise their children on their own milk. And in 1914, V. V. Subramania Aiyar, an Indianist devotee of Tamil, insisted that it would be impossible for anyone to produce great works of literature in a language that had not been taken in with the mother's milk (Subramania Aiyar 1981: 20). Over and again during this century, Tamil has been invoked by its devotees as "the milk of our youth," the "fine milk," "the glorious mother's milk," and the like (Ramaswamy 1992a: 49-51). The 1931 *Census* even lent the blessings of the colonial state to such an imagining by defining the "mother tongue" as "the language which [one] had taken in with mother's milk" (Government of India 1932: 287).

Sometimes, Tamil is imbibed through the human mother's milk, a suggestion that has had important, even conservative, implications for Tamil women's identity (Ramaswamy 1992a; see also Lakshmi 1990). But more often than not, her filial devotee insists that it is Tamil1ttây herself who raises her children on her nourishing milk. Thus, borne by Tamil1ttây's womb, and having shared her milk, Tamil speakers are rendered "siblings," members of the same "family." By midcentury, so entrenched were such assumptions that Ramasami's rationalist attack on the feminization of Tamil was launched under the title *Tâyppâl Paittiyam* (The madness over mother's milk) (E. V. Ramasami 1962: 7-17). This powerful attack, however, has not detracted either its devotees or others from continuing to compare Tamil to mother's milk, a hit song from the recent film *An#n#âmalai* (1992) being a case in point.

If Tamil is mother's milk, then foreign languages, like English, are likened to "bottled milk," even "tonics." Their virtues are infinitely inferior to those of mother's milk/Tamil, which they may supplement but never replace. So, in 1956, during the debate in the Madras Legislative Assembly on replacing English as the official language of the state with Tamil, one of the members passionately declared: "Today our mother tongue reclines royally on the throne of government. For a child, its mother's milk is far more necessary than bottled milk. Even if the children who grow up on bottled milk survive, there are excellent substances (*cattu*) in their mother's milk. Children who drink their mother's milk have fine dispositions as well."

It is interesting that the legislator, P. G. Karuthiruman, used the Tamil word *cattu* to refer to the substances contained in mother's milk, for some of the meanings of that word are truth, virtue, goodness, and moral excellence. These are precisely the fine qualities that every true speaker who was reared on Tamil is supposed to imbibe. Accordingly, the filial devotee insists that it is Tamil1ttây's milk that cultivates in the Tamil speaker *mol1ipparl1rl1u* (devotion to language), *nât#t#upparl1rl1u* (devotion to nation), *ân#mai* (manliness or courage), and *tan1mân1am* (self-respect) (Iyarkaiselvan 1959: 8). Not surprisingly, Tamil's enemies (like Sanskrit or Hindi) were characterized, especially in Dravidianism, as languages that poison the purity of Tamil1ttây's milk (Bharatidasan 1948: 4; Perunchitranar 1979: 57).

In premodern Tamil literary culture, mother's milk was typically associated with purity, coolness, and creativity (Shulman 1980: 93-104). In her ethnography of contemporary Tamil family life, Margaret Trawick (1990: 93-94) has suggested that the importance of mother's milk derives from the belief that it is the substantial repository of mother's love (*an1pu*). These are all characteristics that her filial devotee would readily associate with

Tamil1ttây's milk. But there are also ideological uses to which the mother's milk has been put in the discourses of Tamil's modern adherents. For one, imagining Tamil as mother's milk enables the language to be symbolically incorporated into the bodies of its individual speakers to become part of their very essence. As such, it would be impossible to separate the language from its true and loyal speaker, as Bharatidasan declared on many occasions. Equally important, the inscription of Tamil as mother's milk allows the filial devotee to remind his fellow Tamilian of the duty (*kat#amai*) he owed Tamil1ttây, as in the following call issued during the 1938 anti-Hindi protests by C. Velsami: "When one sees Tamil1ttây suffering, can any heroic Tamilian who has been born in Tamilnadu, and raised here, and has joyously drunk her sweet milk—can he have the heart to watch her suffering?"

Like the mother's womb, the mother's milk, too, serves simultaneously as a mnemonic device that somatically reminds all Tamil speakers of the facticity of birth into the Tamil community and as a mobilizing device—*an1n1aiyin1 pâl kat#amai,* "obligation to mother's milk"—that seeks to arouse them into taking action out of recognition of this "fact."

The Pitiful Tears of Tamil1ttây

Finally, I turn to the tears of Tamil1ttây, which, of all her bodily parts and substances, most clearly indexed her current state of utter distress. Especially from around the 1930s on, discourses of *tamil1ppar1r1u* abounded with allusions to the weeping Tamil1ttây, to the tearful Tamil1ttây appealing to her children to help her, to Tamil1ttây sitting in a corner, wailing away, and so on. Soon after the self-immolation of Chinnasami, Aranganathan, and Sivalingam in 1964-65, a DMK newsmagazine, *Muttâram,* carried a striking cover with the faces of these youths in the foreground. The backdrop is the close up of the face of a woman—most likely, Tamil1ttây—with large drops of blood-red tears flowing down her cheeks (fig. 7). That Tamil1ttây's tears are meant to not just create affect, but also to incite and mobilize is clear from the following passage from Karunanidhi's memoirs in which he describes the first large-scale political protest spearheaded by the DMK against the Congress and its Hindi policy. In 1953, the DMK called upon the Congress government to change the name of a town called Dalmiapuram in Tiruchi district (named after a North Indian cement magnate) to its Tamil original, Kallakudi. So, on 15 July, Karunanidhi and a group of his DMK followers reached the railway station of Dalmiapuram, erased the Hindi name on the station board, and painted the Tamil name of Kallakudi in its stead. They then proceeded to lie down on the railway tracks; in the resulting altercation between the police and the protesters, two men lost their lives, and many were severely wounded. Consider how Karunanidhi represents this event to his readers:

We have reached the battlefield. We have reached the place where our glorious Tamil1ttây stands insulted. We have reached the place where our once magnificent mother now stands, shedding tears. Our wonderful mother who nurtured and raised us on glorious Tamil…huddles wearily, her limbs fettered in the enemy's chains. They have put up a railing of guns around her shackles which we came to destroy. Our mother stands shaking and weeping! "Look at her from afar. Do not touch her. Savor her suffering form," so says the government.

Having set the stage thus, Karunanidhi turns to describe the death of the first young man, Natarajan:

O mother! O Tamil1ttây! Look at your son Natarajan to whom you gave birth. You used to be adorned with gold and jewels once upon a time! Today, you are adorned by the corpses of your martyred sons. Is this fair? Look at his corpse which soaks your lap with blood. You gave birth to millions of children. Now you have the fate of lighting their young bodies on their funeral pyres.…O mother! Weep! Cry out! It is only if you cry, it is only if you shed your tears that we can gather together an army that will bring down the reign of cowards.…Weep, mother, weep. O glorious Tamil1ttây, you once upon a time wore a smile; now you shed tears of blood.…But your tears will not be in vain.

"Your tears will not be in vain": in the logic of Tamil devotion, especially Dravidianism, on reading (or hearing) statements like these which were circulated through street poetry and political speeches at anti-Hindi rallies, her "children" would rush to the rescue of their mother, wipe away her tears, and restore her, and the language she embodied, to well-being. The tears of Tamil1ttây came to somatically index the sad state of the body politic in Tamil devotion. Indeed, in neighboring Sri Lanka, where Tamil nationalism has been driven by a rather different set of imperatives, a 1977 pamphlet on the suffering of Tamil speakers on the island under Sinhala domination is entitled *The Tears of Tamil1ttây* (*Tamil1ttâyin1 Kan#n#îr*). Nowhere does the work mention Tamil1ttây, yet it is clear that for its author, her tears were enough to recall for his readers the state of utter desolation of Tamil speakers in Sri Lanka (Puttoli 1977).

Profiling the Filial Devotee

More than the modality of pietistics, the modality of somatics has a conscious mobilizing agenda—not surprisingly, since it was the mode most favored by Dravidianism with its militant stance on *tamil1ppar1r1u*. So, images of the distressed, diseased, and violated mother were circulated not just for rhetorical effect but also to incite her "children" to take up arms and come to her rescue. Tamil1ttây herself implored thus in 1965:

> *O Tamilian, my dear son to whom I gave birth!*
>
> ......
>
> *Where have you gone, leaving to suffer your mother who bathed you, fed you, sang lullabies, nurtured you, showered you with love?*
>
> ......
>
> *Your mother has been cast into prison!*
>
> *Will you not rescue her from there?*
>
> *Your mother has been shackled!*
>
> *Will you not break her chains?*
>
> *Did I not feed you fine food?*
>
> *Was not the milk that you drank heroic milk?*
>
> *O son who has forsaken me! O Tamil son who has gone off to sleep!*
>
> ......
>
> *Your mother is calling out to you! Can you not hear her whimpers and*
>
> *see her tears?*
>
> *Are your ears deaf? Are your eyes blind?*
>
> *Where are you, my son! Where are you?*

Those Tamil speakers who refused to respond to such an impassioned plea laid themselves open to charges of betraying their own mother, even matricide (E. M. Subramania Pillai 1951-52: 161-63). During the anti-Hindi protests of 1938, Suddhananda Bharati declared: "The Tamilian who rejects Tamil rejects his own mother. The Tamilian who does not reverence Tamil has forgotten his own mother. Can you ever forget the mother who gave birth to you? Our ancient mother stands in dishonor among the languages of the world, and sheds tears. Will not her sons come forth and wipe away their mother's tears?" (Suddhananda Bharati 1938: 110). Equally dramatically, the poet Pulavar Kulanthai insisted that "the murder of Tamil is like the murder of one's mother" (Pulavar Kulanthai 1972: 35). In this modality, it was not enough for Tamil speakers to put their literary and scholarly talents at Tamil1ttây's disposal; they had to be prepared to surrender their bodies as well. In its economy of devotion, along with the sharing of the mother's womb and milk, the shedding of the son's blood has a great deal of currency. So, Perunchitran was willing to declare in 1965 in a poem he wrote in a Kadalur prison:

When they tell me

This body, and all the blood and sinews and feelings that it contains, belongs to Tamil1ttây and to the Tamil people,

I lose all my fatigue!

(Perunchitranar 1979: 66)

Similarly, an essay published in the *Ân1antapôtin1i,* a literary journal that was largely Indianist in sentiment, asked, "O youthful Tamilian! Does not your mother's Tamil blood run in your heart? Do you not love your mother?...Wake up....Let your Tamil blood boil over and rouse you" (Mutthu 1938: 336).

Such statements, of which there are innumerable examples, graphically illustrate the extent to which the somatics of devotion operated, discursively and symbolically, at a gut level. Seeing Tamil1ttây in tears, the Tamil son is reminded of the mother whose womb had borne him, whose milk had nourished him, and whose blood runs in his veins. This memory leads him to shed his own blood to prove his *tamil1ppar1r1u:*

I will push back the hostility of other languages beyond the oceans

"May the Tamilians stand loftily! Long live Tamil!"
I will thus beat my drum.
......
Even as I am being cut down, and as the blood spurts out from my fierce wounds,
I will fall down on my Tamil soil, crying out "Tamil!" "Tamil!"
(Pulavar Kulanthai 1972: 11-12)

Her impassioned devotee is of course ready to shed not just his own blood but also that of the numerous enemies of his Tamil1ttây. So declared a twenty-three-year-old youth at an anti-Hindi rally in Madras city in 1938: "If the Tamilians have any heroism, the blood of several thousands of members of the Aryan race must be shed. The blood of the Aryans must be shed and a river of blood should flow in this country. The leaders may not have faith in violence, but we have faith in violence....[T]housands of youths will arise for planting our red flag, and giving up their lives for the sake of Tamil."

Tamil devotion has certainly contributed to literary and linguistic efflorescence in Tamilnadu and undoubtedly helped the political empowerment of the disenfranchised and the colonized. All the same, it has also underwritten an economy of violence and death, an economy in which dying for Tamil and Tamil1ttây is superior to living without her. That such an economy did not exist merely in the discursive spaces of devotional narratives but actually came to touch the lives of Tamilians, especially in the 1960s, is apparent from the stories of Chinnasami and numerous others who sacrificed themselves in the battle for Tamil.

Further, in its somatic mode, *tamil1ppar1r1u* relied heavily on regimes of violence directed against the female body in order to elicit the allegiance and loyalty of the Tamil speaker to Tamil1ttây. Indeed, Tamil devotion in this mode appears to need such images of the violated female body for the particular strategies of persuasion and incitement that it employed to whip up the passions of the "sleeping" Tamilian. Figures of the violated mother are deployed again and again, not so much to draw attention to acts of violence against women as to highlight the plight of the language and the dishonor wreaked upon the community of its speakers.

The Ideology of Somatic Devotion

In contrast to the pietistics of *tamil1pparlr1u,* in which Tamil1ttây reigns as an all-powerful sovereign goddess holding in thrall her worshippers, in the modality of somatics she is a diseased and *powerless* personage, helplessly dependent on her children for restoring her to her former state of health and glory. She is no longer the protector and the patron of her devotees; instead, it is they who have to come to her aid. This difference in the manner Tamil1ttây is imagined in the two modalities captures in turn the difference in the way the language and its devotees related to each other in the religious and classicist regimes, as opposed to the Indianist and Dravidianist imaginaries. The latter two were essentially populist and pragmatic, concerned with improving the language, revamping it with new vocabularies and new genres, and closing the gap between its literary and spoken forms. In spite of their inherent faith in Tamil, devotees who participated in these regimes were aware that much had to be done to transform Tamil to make it a suitable language for politics, education, and modern communication; and they were particularly anxious that invocations of its ancient greatness and wonders often detracted their fellow speakers from this all-important task. They were also painfully aware that rather than just relying on the talents of literary pandits and great Tamil scholars, Tamil would only improve if every Tamil speaker in every Tamil-speaking home joined the cause. For all these reasons, for devotees who were of Indianist or Dravidianist persuasion, the image of Tamil as an endangered, emaciated, and powerless mother was much more appropriate than that of Tamil1ttây as a glorious, perfect, and all-powerful goddess queen.

Moreover, the pious devotee cast Tamil1ttây as an all-powerful goddess who is the primeval generator of thought, of the arts and the sciences, and of civilization itself. In contrast, in the somatics of devotion, such a Tamil1ttây is replaced by a mother figure, celebrated for her reproductive and domestic role in the idealized Tamil family. Consider the following from an essay on Tamil published in 1938 during the first wave of anti-Hindi protests:

Who is the woman who comforted you with her sweet words when you were young and tired? Who is the glorious woman who assuaged your hunger with milk when you were infants? Who is the fine woman who rocked you to sleep in your cradles with her sweet words? Who is the woman who taught you to speak your first words so that your parents and kinsmen rejoice? Who is the woman who guided you and helped you when you played happily in the streets?....She is indeed the fine and incomparable Tamil1 An1n1ai [Tamil1ttây].

Here, in contrast to the pietistics of *tamil1ppar1r1u*, the language is celebrated for its biologically *reproductive* role as collective mother of Tamil speakers—for parenting, rearing, and nourishing them—rather than for its culturally *productive* role as the fount of literature and high civilization. Thus goddesses and queens, who provided the dominant models for imaging the language in the elite religious and classicist regimes (and in the modality of pietistics), were displaced by the Tamil woman, celebrated as an ever-youthful, fertile mother who confirmed that all Tamil speakers were each other's "siblings" and members of the same "family" because they had shared the same womb and drunk the same milk.

Indeed, the somatics of *tamil1ppar1r1u* reminds us that identity claims in modernity do not rest merely on abstract formulations or on symbolic statements of fraternity, solidarity, and unity. They also crucially rely upon sensory symbols and visceral entities that call attention to the bonds of birth, to the sharing of substances, to the very commonalties that emerge from belonging to what Benedict Anderson has so persuasively characterized as the "imagined" community. In Anderson's formulation, the nation is one such imagined community "because the members of even the smallest nation will never know most of their fellow members, meet them, or even hear of them, yet in the minds of each lives the very image of their communion" (Anderson 1983: 15). Extending Anderson, I would propose that bodily images of shared womb and milk, of the blood and tears of the members of the community, and indeed of the mother figure herself are devices that are deployed to enable this act of communion that so critically and intimately binds together all members of the imagined community as one "family." Even as such bodily metaphors, images, and substances determine membership *in* the community, they also serve as boundary maintaining devices by identifying those who are *not* in the community. So, it is clear that for Tamil's devotees, those who did not recognize that they were born from Tamil1ttây's womb and raised on her milk, and those who were not moved to come to her aid when they saw her shackled body or her tears of sorrow, were emphatically *not* Tamilian. They were discursively written out of the Tamil community and symbolically cast out.

TAMIL AS MAIDEN: EROTICS OF TAMIL DEVOTION

Like so many other love stories, Tamil devotion, too, has its triangle of desire constituted by three protagonists: Tamil1ttây, imagined as a beautiful, desirable, but emphatically virginal mother; the male devotee, typically portrayed as young, heterosexual, virile, and desiring; and the female devotee, young and heterosexual like her male counterpart, beautiful and desirable like her mother/language, but destined to be a married mother entrusted with the task of reproducing the language and its community. By virtue of being constituted as a hallowed mother figure to whom absolute devotion and loyalty is owed, Tamil1ttây obviously does not enter the field as an equal player, and she frequently interrupts the sexual and familial bonding of her human devotees. Nevertheless, the devotional triangle is not just disruptive but productive as well, which is not least of the reasons that it flourishes. For the circulation of desire among the three protagonists, however complicated and conflictual it may seem on the surface, only ensures that the language and its devotees are indelibly interlocked in structures of pleasure and service which further increases their longing for each other. The work of the modality of erotics reminds us that Tamil devotion is not just about loss, pain, suffering, and death, but also about enjoyment and pleasure. Passions of the tongue may be pious and filial, but they are erotic as well.

At the core of the structure of sentiment that is constituted by the modality of erotics is the desiring male devotee's undiluted pleasure in Tamil and in Tamil1ttây, rather than his awed reverence or filial anxiety. The Tamil word that is generally used for expressing this pleasure is *in1pam* (and its cognate, *in1imai*). This polysemic word means joy, delight, sweetness, and bliss, but in a large number of contexts, it signifies sensual pleasure and romantic love. So, the numerous verses and essays entitled *in1pattamil1*, "sweet Tamil," or *tamil1in1pam*, "pleasures of Tamil," are certainly replete with images of Tamil's innocent beauty and delights, the pleasures of hearing its mellifluous sounds, the joy of-speaking the language and reading its literature, and so on

(Bharatidasan 1986: 87-89, 94; Sethu Pillai 1968). But consider the following 1938 verse by Bharatidasan, recited during the anti-Hindi protest marches of that year:

Our bodies, our wealth, our very breath,

We will surrender to our sweet Tamil (in1pattamil1)*!*

Even the pleasures woman alone gives do not compare to our great Tamil!

We will declare!

(Bharatidasan 1948: 9)

This explicit comparison by the poet of the pleasures (*cukam*) offered by a woman and by Tamil is not fortuitous, as evidenced in several poems written by male poets with titles such as "Tamil1 en1 Kâtali" (Tamil is my beloved) and "Tamil1 En1 Man1aivi" (Tamil is my wife) (Mudiyarasan 1976: 34-39; Nagarajan 1980: 26-34). Thus, in "Tamil is my beloved," Mudiyarasan, one of the better-known poets of the Dravidian movement, declared passionately:

In order to acquire you, I wander all around;

If you reject me, how can I endure this life?

Is it not your sweet passion that drives me to frenzy?

O delicious language of mine! Gather me up and embrace me!

(Mudiyarasan 1976: 35)

Or consider this verse in which there is a striking slippage from Tamil as "mother" to Tamil as "wife":

[You] are the mother who fed us milk;

You are the food that sates our hunger;

You are the song that gives so much delight (in1imai)*;*

You are the light we bring into our Tamil homes with the bond of marriage (tâli)*;*

O Mother/Goddess Tamil (tamil1an#ank#ç)*!*

So, just as Tamil1ttây comes to occupy a space inhabited by their conventional gods and human mothers, she also competes, as a woman, with their human spouses and lovers in the imagination of many a male devotee. The desiring devotee dwells on her physical attributes as a beautiful, sensuous woman, praising her "glorious, golden body," "abundant breasts," "lustrous lips," and so on. He rejoices that her "dark spear-shaped eyes" beckon him, that her "glowing face" rivals the luster of the moon, that her "narrow waist puts lightning to shame," and the like. He pronounces ecstatically that "his heart surges with the nectar of pleasure" when he beholds her, and that the pleasure (*cukam*) she gave him when she embraced him in the moonlight caused him to tremble (Mudiyarasan 1976: 34-36; Velayutam Pillai 1971: 84-89). Many such statements are highly stylized, of course, and follow the conventions of erotic Tamil literature. However, occasionally we also get more personalized glimpses of the devotee's desire for his beloved Tamil1ttây. T. K. Chidambaranatha Mudaliar (1882-1954), a well-known Tamil scholar and expert on the medieval poet Kamban, recalls that as a young boy studying in high school in the 1890s, he heard a public lecture by Swaminatha Aiyar at a local college in Tiruchirapalli. The lecture was on the glories and greatness of Tamil. Chidambaranathan remembered it well in 1935:

The reverend Aiyar listed the beautiful jewels worn by our Lady Tamil (*tamil1makal#*):

The Cûl#âman#i adorns her head;

The Cintâman#i is on her breast;

The Kun#t#alakçci hangs from her ears;

The Val#aiyâpati encircles her arms;

Her waist wears the Man#imçkalai;

And her ankles are adorned with the Cilappatikâram.

As soon as he recited this, I became completely entranced (*mayank#ip pôyvit#t#çn*). That night, all I could do was dream about this—that Lady Tamil (*tamil1an#ank#u*) was approaching me, and bewitching me with her every step and turn with the beauty of her jewels.

Yet Chidambaranathan and his fellow male devotees could only dream of Tamil1ttây as such, for their desire for her, however passionate, could never be consummated, lurking as it had to in the interstices of the two dominant structures of imagining their beloved: she was their mother, and she was a perpetual virgin. Indeed, one of the most frequent ways in which Tamil1ttây is described in Tamil devotional discourses from its very inception is as *kan1n1ittây*,"virgin mother," a deliberate contradiction which only emphasized her extraordinary exceptionalism (K. Appadurai 1944: 28-29, 33; Kathiresan Chettiar 1959-60: 170; Pancanathan n.d.: 25; Sharif 1990: 8-9; S. Subramanian 1939: 36-37). Tamil1ttây's bodily intactness underscored the inviolability of the language she embodied, its purity and autonomy as well as its self-sufficiency, even its divine wholeness. Immensely fruitful though her womb may be, the insistence that she is a virgin meant that her sexual purity (*tûymai*) is not compromised by her fertility and productiveness (*val#amai*). As one devotee proudly noted, "Our Tamil1an1n1ai [Tamil1ttây] flourishes as a virgin, as queen of chastity (*kar1pu*)" (Tamilmallan 1984: 62). Cast as an asexual figure confined to perpetual virginity and hallowed motherhood, Tamil1ttây is rendered sexually "safe," an object of filial longing at best, of unconsummated desire at worst. The dilemma this poses for the desiring devotee is best expressed by Ramalinga Pillai in a poem suggestively entitled "Kan1n1it Tamil1," "Virgin Tamil":

> *She came towards me, adorned with blossoms,*
> *Filling me with such delight* (in1pam)*;*
> *Transported to the world of gods, I rejoiced;*
> *O, how can I describe my bliss!*
> *Gold and gems she may not have;*
> *Even so, she was filled with beauty;*
> *With her sweet gentle smile,*
> *she filled my mind with pleasure* (in1pam).
> ......
> *Enchanted by her virginal beauty,*
> *I reached forward to tightly embrace her!*
> *Seeing then that she was my mother, I shrunk back, and fell at her feet, my body doubled up in shame!*
> *"Filled with alien thoughts, I totally forgot the mother who gave birth to me.*
> *Alas! I lost my mind."*
> *So I grieved in distress.*

Underlying the medley of ambivalences here—of shame and guilt, of desire and revulsion, of grief and joy—is the (sexual) unavailability of Tamil1ttây, however desirable she may be. Her state of perpetual virginity transforms Tamil1ttây into a passive, undesiring female herself, erasing all traces of active sexuality from her being, but it also meant that the male devotee's desire for her went unrequited. It remained as fantasy, never to be consummated. In Tamil devotion therefore, as indeed in so many ideologies, female virginity proves to be both disempowering and empowering: disempowering because it marks the female body as undesiring; empowering because it suggests impenetrability, self-sufficiency, and unavailability.

The emptying of active sexuality from Tamil1ttây's being is critical to the work of the devotional triangle of desire, for this is what allows the Tamil-speaking woman to enter the male devotee's regimes of pleasure. As the flesh-and-blood embodiment of Tamil1ttây, she acts as her surrogate but without the imperative to maintain a virginal status. In fact, the very reproduction of Tamil required the woman to abandon her virginity through a chaste monogamous marriage to the male Tamilian (Ramaswamy 1992a). All the same, because the male Tamilian is also devoted to Tamil in these narratives, there is a concern that the primary commitment to Tamil1ttây should not be compromised by the necessary sexual bonding with these human surrogates. So, in a long poem published as recently as January 1993 in a daily newspaper, the hero declares to his beloved that only after he had destroyed Hindi, which was threatening to enslave and wipe out Tamil, would he even "think about [her] beautiful breasts, and caress and enjoy [her]!" Similarly, years earlier, during a December 1956 debate in the Madras Legislative Assembly on instituting Tamil as the official language of the state, one of the members burst into a story about two lovers, in which the woman waits impatiently for the arrival of her beloved only to find out that he had been delayed on his way over to meet her. The hero tells her: "I was hurrying along thinking about you. At that time, I heard someone making a speech in sweet Tamil (*in1pattamil1*); hearing that, I forgot myself and stayed on." The legislator, V. Balakrishnan, goes on to tell his (predominantly male) audience that this is why we have been told that *in1pattamil1*, "sweet Tamil," has more *kâtal*, "(romantic) love," to offer us than even our *kâtali*, "female lover." The explicitness of the analogy here between the woman and Tamil as *kâtali* is all the more remarkable because it is made in the state's legislative chambers and in the context of promoting the cause of Tamil as official language.

Caught between his language/mother and his wife/lover, the male devotee looks for ways in which he could have them both. One solution for accomplishing this, which Bharatidasan offers in one of his poems, is for the male devotee to work together with his beloved in serving Tamil. So the hero tells his lover:

I have been born for you, truly, my beloved!
You have been born for me, O cuckoo bird, my shining beam!
......
I gave myself to you....
You gave yourself to me....
......
[My] mother hailed me....
She hailed you....
Our mother's land, our Tamil
We have to rescue from ruin!
This is in1pam! *This is* in1pam!
What else do we desire but this?

Thus the male devotee calls upon his beloved to give up their mutual pleasure in each other for the sake of Tamil1ttây. Here, we see that the devotional triangle works not so much to disrupt the dyadic relationship between the male and female devotee as to rewrite the very meanings of "pleasure" and "desire" themselves: the poem begins with a celebration of the sexual union of the male devotee with his beloved and ends with a call to jointly sublimate that pleasure in each other in service of the language. Through such an act of sublimation, the language and its devotees, male and female, come to be ever more tightly bound to each other through bonds of pleasure and desire—fueled, denied, and rekindled.

This is of course not the only way out. The male devotee also confesses that if he indeed had to abandon himself to a sexual relationship with a human lover, it could be with none other than a Tamil-speaking woman, imagined as the very living embodiment of Tamil—a surrogate Tamil1ttây cast in her image, but without the ambivalent burdens of virgin motherhood. Many poems suggest this, some even maintaining that it would be an act of betrayal and disloyalty for the Tamilian male to marry anyone other than a "true" and "pure" Tamilian woman, but there is one text I want to focus upon here, entitled *Kâtalikku* (For my beloved). Published in 1961, the work is cast in the form of a series of letters written by an ardent male adorer of Tamil1ttây to his human beloved, who appears to be severely vexed over his intense attachment to the language/mother which frequently takes him away from her side. The purpose of the letters appears to have been not only to convince her of the worthiness of his work for *tamil1ppar1r1u* but also to convert her to its cause, because only then, it is clear to him, could he consummate his relationship with his beloved. So, in the penultimate letter he declares in response to her question, "Do you want me? do you want Tamil?": "Dearest! I need you; I need Tamil as well; I need both you and Tamil. I need you as one who has herself blended with Tamil....Dearest! For me, you are sweet Tamil (*in1pattamil1*)." He then goes on to compare different parts of his beloved's being and body to the different aspects of Tamil and its literature, writing, "In your youth—your beauty—your dark eyes—your fine brow—your eyelids—your black hair—...in the very movement of your limbs, I see only precious Tamil....[Y]ou are living Tamil. I want you. I want only you as the very embodiment of Tamil (*tamil1 kalanta nî tân1 vçn#t#um*)" (Arulsami 1966: 80-86).

In this narrative as well, the work of the devotional triangle is productive. The hero is an ardent devotee who, passionately dedicated as he was to the cause of Tamil, is drawn to the Tamil-speaking woman precisely because in her, he sees the flesh-and-blood embodiment of his dear Tamil1ttây. The narrative also works to successfully constitute him as an object of desire of the female Tamil speaker: she starts out as a reluctant lover, not entirely enchanted with either him or *tamil1ppar1r1u*. By the end of the narrative, in the final letter of this exchange, his narration of his work for Tamil wins her over to him and to its cause (Arulsami 1966: 87-88).

These fascinating instances clearly suggest that Tamil devotion cannot be confined to its more obvious pious and filial manifestations alone. The modality of erotics, however, exists only in the interstices of *tamil1ppar1r1u*, erupting every now and then, tantalizingly, in the writings of Tamil1ttây's desiring devotee(s). This may seem surprising in light of the vigorous traditions of pre-colonial erotic poetry in the Tamil-speaking region as indeed in other parts of India. But these traditions did not fare particularly well with the introduction of new Victorian and bourgeois norms of sexual morality which took deep root in colonial India, under the scathing missionary, Orientalist, and colonial scrutiny of "Hindu" sexuality (Metcalf 1994: 92-105; Sinha 1995). This colonial scrutiny was itself reflective of a major realignment in notions of respectability and "correct" sexuality within ideologies of nationalism from the early decades of the nineteenth century in modern Europe (Mosse 1985). For twentieth-century South India, the conflicts between older forms of sexual expression and its newer, more "respectable" bourgeois manifestations have scarcely been documented. But it does appear that the colonial critique only heightened puritanical norms and sexual ethics that the upper castes of the region routinely supported in pre-colonial times. The Dravidian movement, in its own attacks on Brahmanism, celebrates what it identifies as the authentic Tamil form of premarital love and sexual union, *kal#avu*, which is held up as the desirable alternative to the "arranged" intra caste marriage dictated by Brahmanical norms. At a rhetorical level, the movement certainly promotes freer expressions of love and sexuality. Nevertheless, it too practices its own politics of virtue in which the chastity, modesty, and sexual fidelity of the Tamil woman underwrite not just the honor of the Tamil man but also the purity and honor of Tamil culture, land, and language (Lakshmi 1990; M. S. S. Pandian, Anandhi, and Venkatachalapathy 1991). So M. Rajamanikkam declares, "As we safeguard the purity of women, we ought to guard the purity of [our] language" (quoted in Tirumaran 1992: 159). Caught between the new norms of bourgeois respectability and older, deeper conventions of female chastity and sexual virtue, the modality of erotics has a troubled and shadowy presence in the discourses of Tamil's devotees. Consequently, the erotic and sensuous persona of Tamil1ttây is displaced by the compassionate and nurturing image of de-sexualized and spiritualized motherhood.

ON THE FEMINIZATION OF LANGUAGE

Its devotees may empower their language by drawing upon three different models of femininity—an all-powerful goddess, a compassionate but endangered mother, and a desirable but unattainable maiden. But eventually and hegemonically, it is the maternal image that came to dominate devotional imaginations, overwriting the divine and the erotic. Why? And why feminize the language at all? In the pre-colonial poetic traditions to which Tamil's modern devotees are indebted in myriad ways, the feminization of Tamil was largely underdeveloped, although not entirely absent. And the language was not associated with motherhood. In the rare instances when it was personified, its gender was either unspecified or even male. Yet, from the late nineteenth century on, the personification of Tamil relied extensively on the female form, and especially on the female form clothed in maternal garb. Such a feminization of the language, however, was neither idiosyncratic nor exceptional, but symptomatic of a fundamental regendering of culture and community under colonial rule and modernity. Two complex imaginaries converged to provide the terrain on which this took place: a dominant colonial identification of all things Indian as feminine (or effeminate); and bourgeois nationalist discourses of modernity conducted around the hallowed figure of the mother.

Their many contrary impulses notwithstanding, colonial discourses fundamentally contrasted the natural "masculinity" of British imperial culture with the inherent "femininity" of (Hindu) India, the former being preordained to rule and command, the latter to obey and follow. This in turn was the gendered expression of the Orientalist imaginary that undergirded colonial rule, in which the natural and inherent superiority of the rational, secular, industrious, progressive (masculine) West prevails over the irrational, spiritual, passive, and unchanging (feminine) East (Metcalf 1994: 92-112; Said 1978; Sinha 1995). It was not only India that was feminized thus. At least since the time of James Mill, the Indian woman, too, metonymically came to represent "Indian" culture and civilization, just as, in another context, the (white) European woman was a sign of her culture and civilization. Identified as it was in colonial discourses as the site of the authentic India, the female domain assumed a new significance in anticolonial and countercolonial discourses which mounted their resistance on the same terrain. When imagined as the repository of all that was uncolonized, Indian women became the embodiment of all that is truly and purely Indian. Correspondingly, all that is deemed authentic, true, and pure is by definition feminine, domestic, and private, for the male, public world was tainted by its association with colonialism (Chatterjee 1989).

The language of that public world was of course English, whose very dominance had consigned India's languages to the inner, private domain of the home and the family—the domain of the woman. Inhabiting the same domain as the woman, India's languages, too, were perforce feminized in the discourses of the colonized. Like the woman with whom they now shared space, they became embodiments of all that was imagined to be authentically Indian. Sivagnanam best captured this transformation, although he confined his remarks to Tamil, in a speech he gave to an anti-Hindi conference in Madras in 1948, soon after Indian independence: "Formerly, when the British empire sought to destroy Tamil by introducing English, men took to its study for jobs and status. At that time when Tamil was neglected and relegated to the kitchen, it was Tamil women who guarded it with their own arms. Now that English rule has come to an end, our women who have hitherto been protecting Tamil are now returning Tamilttây back to us." The easy slippage in the last sentence from "Tamil" to "Tamilttây," from Tamil as language to Tamil as woman, is possible because in Sivagnanam's imagination, as in that of numerous other Indians like him, it is women who are the "custodians" of India's languages, watching over them until they could be reclaimed and restored to their former glory (by men).

And yet Indian women themselves—as indeed women in so many other parts of the world—had been radically reconfigured by bourgeois discourses of modernity, for if woman was idealized as the repository of all that was glorious and wonderful in one's culture, she was also firmly put into her place, in the home and amid her family as "mother" (Mosse 1985: 90-91). Many studies have demonstrated that the consolidation of nationalist ideologies in different regions of the world was accompanied by an "extravagant celebration of motherhood" (Margolis 1984: 28). This was especially true in western Europe, which provided the model for so many ideologies that crystallized in colonial India. There, bourgeois nationalist discourses were marked by the discursive and symbolic separation of the "home" from "work," and of the "nation" from the "world." The home and the nation were hallowed as noncompetitive, depoliticized arenas, and as sacral repositories of moral values and virtue. The reproduction of these arenas, as such, was ensured by insisting that women are "by nature" self-sacrificing, virtuous, unambitious, and nonpolitical beings, destined to be child bearers and nurturers. As George Mosse notes (1985: 97), "Women as national symbols exemplified order and restfulness.

Woman was the embodiment of respectability; even as defender and protector of her people, she was assimilated to her traditional role as woman and mother, the custodian of tradition, who kept nostalgia alive in the active world of men." Such a representation was only further consolidated within nationalist ideologies seeking to put the nation on a pedestal as an iconic object of platonic affection and unconditional devotion, for how much more successfully could this be done than by recasting the nation itself as a selfless, compassionate, and de-sexualized Mother, disaggregated from the public realms of politics, self-interest, and sexual competition (Badinter 1981; Davin 1978; Margolis 1984; Poovey 1988: 1-23)?

In colonial India as well, at different times in the nineteenth century, the "woman's question" loomed large in the writings of newly westernized and middle-class (Hindu) elites. Mostly centered in the urban hubs of Calcutta, Bombay, and Madras, they sought to counter the colonial censure of Indian culture and tradition by "reforming" their women and transforming them into virtuous, educated "companions." By the turn of this century, this reforming zeal yielded to a "new" nationalist patriarchy, as the nation came to be valorized as a "home" and "family" whose health could be guaranteed by ensuring the re-signification of largely middle-class women as the educated mothers of its future citizens (Chatterjee 1989; R. Kumar 1993; Lakshmi 1990). The woman-as-wife or sexual being was subordinated to the woman-as-mother or reproductive being, for as one Swami Jagadiswarananda insisted in 1933, "motherhood is the fulfillment of wifehood" (quoted in Visweswaran 1990: 67). As Visweswaran rightly notes, motherhood emerged as "a strategy of containment" that was both oppositional and hegemonic: "Oppositional because it resisted the British 'sexing' of all Indian women as potential 'wives,' opting for a spiritual, de-sexualized woman, 'the mother.' Hegemonic because the other side of the British equation of the sexual Indian woman, was the asexual, spiritual Victorian woman" (Visweswaran 1990: 66).

Thus, in Indian nationalist discourses, while the home is presided over by the woman as mother, the nation as home is presided over by her archetype, Bhârata Mâtâ, a nationalist icon like Britannia or Marianne, but one who also embodies the difference of Indian spirituality and tradition. For nationalist thought in Tamilnadu, Subramania Bharati's statement in his essay "The Place of Woman" marks this convergence of the woman in her guise as mother and India as Bhârata Mâtâ:

Nor is it without significance that the country of spiritual liberation, India, should, at this hour of her mighty awakening, have adopted as her most potent spell, the words "Vande Mataram," i.e., "I salute the Mother." That means that the first work of a regenerated India will be to place the Mother, i.e., womankind, on the pedestal of spiritual superiority. Others speak of their Fatherlands. To us, the Nation is represented by the word "Mata" [mother].

In projects like *tamil1ppar1r1u,* which were conducted in the outlying regions of the emergent nation, this nationalist valorization of India as mother was supplemented by the celebration of language as mother, itself at odds with Bhârata Mâtâ in the Dravidianist imagination, as we have seen. Given the cultural politics of Tamilnadu, where a large number of Tamil's devout asserted that they were victimized not just by British colonialism but by North Indian "imperialism" as well, the Tamil-speaking home and its mother—and their language—were doubly burdened. They not only had to define authentic Tamil subjectivity against the colonial West; in addition, and even more urgently in the decades following Indian independence, they were enrolled into the project of guarding the purity and fidelity of Tamil speakers from what in many accounts was considered a more enduring enemy, the Aryan Sanskritic Brahmanic North.

So, the representation of the language as Tamil1ttây; as *tâymol1i,* "mother tongue" *tâyppâl,* "mother's milk" or simply *tây,* "mother" surfaced in a late colonial situation in which motherhood came to be privileged, not only as the *sine qua non* of women's identity but also as the foundational site on which pure and true subjectivities and communities could be imagined and reproduced.

In the fractured colonial context in which the (Tamil) male was increasingly tainted by his association with the outer, non-Tamil-speaking colonized public domain, the home-family-domestic nexus was imagined as the site where an essential "Tamil" unity, spirituality, and wholeness continued to be maintained. As the woman in her incarnation as "mother" came to be marked as the very human embodiment of this wholeness, spirituality, and unity, the (Tamil) language she spoke (= "mother tongue") correspondingly also found itself reconstituted in her image, taking on her persona of femininity, spirituality, and de-sexualized motherhood. Of course, given the powerful anti-Hindu and even antireligious sentiments of many of her devotees, great care was taken—although not with unconditional success, as we may recall—not just to de-sexualize Tamil1ttây but to de-spiritualize her as well. So the image of Tamil1ttây as deity and desirable maiden is progressively overshadowed by her reincarnation as a familial and secular *tây*, "mother."

Its devotees themselves offer two kinds of explanations for why they have imagined Tamil as mother. It is customary, they tell us, to think of one's language as one's mother; it is "ancient Tamil tradition" (Government of Tamilnadu 1990: 49; Purnalingam Pillai 1930: 56-58). As we have seen, however, this "tradition" was neither ancient nor customary. The devotees also insist that their language, like their mothers, gives birth to Tamil speakers, and nourishes and raises them. Like their mothers, their language, too, abides with them for ever and ever. In a world where there was nothing more assured than the love of a mother for her child, K. Appadurai asked what could one say about "the love of the mother of all of Tamilnadu who bore not only our bodies, but also bore the mothers who bore us, and bore the mothers of the mothers who bore us?" (1944: 20). For Tamil's devotees, it was natural to valorize the one bedrock of their existence as a community, that is, their language, by assimilating it to that foundational figure which they claimed guaranteed their existence as individuals, namely, their mother.

The new ideologies of motherhood that confirmed motherly love as foundational were thus enrolled in reinforcing the new ideologies of modernity in which language was seen as foundational to community and nation. In the discourses of *tamil1ppar1r1u*, there are multiple roles played by this foundational metaphor of the nourishing and compassionate mother. It *familiarizes* and *familializes* the relationship between Tamil speakers and their language by couching it in the comfortable everyday terms of the home and the family. The metaphor also *naturalizes* this relationship by constituting a sense of originary and selfless love that Tamilians, as her "children," necessarily and naturally owe to their language/mother. It *de-historicizes* the bonds between the language and its speakers by presenting them as timeless, essential, and beyond the vagaries of history. Above all, it *depoliticizes* the relationship by enabling the abstraction of the community of speakers of Tamil from politics, and by re-signifying it as a "family" whose members were united as harmonious siblings bonded together through sharing Tamil1ttây's womb and milk.

VISUALIZING TAMIL1TTÂY

The struggle over the multiple linguistic imaginings and the many conceptions of femininity that have gone into the constitution of Tamil1ttây came to the fore when the devout attempted to fashion for her a consistent and credible iconographic presence. In January 1981, almost a century after her first appearance in the poetry of her admirers, a statue of Tamil1ttây was officially installed in Madurai, on the occasion of the Fifth International Tamil Conference, by the Tamilnadu chief minister, M. G. Ramachandran. One critic scoffed at the government's attempt to pass off an archaic female figurine as Tamil1ttây (Ilantiraiyan 1981: 67-68). Another wrote:

It is a matter of great sorrow that they have made a statue, called it Tamil1ttây, and have even conducted an inauguration ceremony around it. There cannot be anything more foolish than this. In these days when we say that we should not have any statues of even our gods, *they have turned what is merely imagination into solid form.* They have sown the seeds of great danger for future generations who will come to believe that all this is true. This is foolishness of the highest degree. Formerly, during the nationalist movement, this is how the Congress wove its lies around figures such as Cutantira Tçvi [Goddess Freedom], Bhârata Mâtâ, and so on, by creating statues for them and painting their pictures. *There is nothing wrong in imagining that Tamil, or our nation, is our mother, and in praising them as such.* But to then turn around and create statues for them is not very rational.

This critic objected not so much to the feminization of the language as mother as to the transformation of "mere imagination" into concrete reality. That such an objection should have emerged is perhaps not surprising, for it is hard to miss the irony of an overtly material form of Tamil1ttây receiving the blessings of a government that was putatively dedicated to implementing the ideology of the Dravidian movement. At least since the 1920s, that movement had attacked the rationality and sensibility of a Hindu culture that generated multilimbed, multiheaded material manifestations of what ought to be a singular, formless godhead (Annadurai 1969: 42-43; Ryerson 1988). Thus Ramasami asked every true Dravidian to solemnly pledge, "I will not worship images anymore; I will not go to temples where images of divine forms are placed" (Anaimuthu 1974: 317). And Bharatidasan declared, "God has neither figure nor name....It is not a Tamil principle to worship stone or copper" (quoted in Ryerson 1988: 82-83). Yet, and the irony continues, some of the earliest material and visual manifestations of Tamil1ttây appeared during the anti-Hindi protests of the late 1930s that were spearheaded by Ramasami and his Self-Respect movement. In 1938, Dravidian movement newspapers carried visuals of Tamil1ttây being assaulted by C. Rajagopalachari (figs. 5, 6). And when Ramasami himself was arrested in 1938, thousands of his followers protested by carrying in a procession a giant statue of Tamil1ttây in a posture of mourning through the streets of Madras (Visswanathan 1983: 236).

Indeed, it was not until the 1930s that the verbal habit of imagining Tamil as Tamil1ttây was supplemented by visual practice. By that time, visual and material representations of Bhârata Mâtâ were fairly common, even in Tamilnadu (Baskaran 1981). Occasionally, drawings of Tamil1ttây began to appear in literary magazines, often accompanying poems or essays on her; on mastheads of Tamil devotional journals; and sometimes in advertisements for shops or publishing houses that carried her name (fig. 8). Consumption of these visuals, as of the journals that they appeared in, would have been by a largely urban, scholarly elite, interested primarily in Tamil literature and poetry and hence by no means a popular audience. More recently, she has also been featured on covers of books on language issues and on Tamil poetry (Bharatidasan 1992; Govindarajan 1988; Nagarajan 1980;

Sivagnanam 1978). And, over the years, many Tamil revivalist and literary organizations as well as individual devotees—the Kamban Kazhagam in Karaikkudi; a group of notables headed by Professor A. Alagappan of Annamalai University; and, more recently, the Tamilnadu state—have printed and circulated large color posters, very much like the posters of Hindu goddesses and popular personalities that one frequently encounters in modern homes and public spaces everywhere in India (figs. 1, 2, 9) (Guha-Thakurta 1991). Statues of Tamil1ttây are less frequent. Giant floats carrying Tamil1ttây's statue were part of the grand state-sponsored public processionals of the Tamil conferences held in Madras in 1968 and Madurai in 1981. A statue in wood adorns the entrance foyer of the library of the Tamil University in Tanjavur. Large stone statues of Tamil1ttây may be found in Madurai and Karaikkudi. Significantly, there are no statues of Tamil1ttây in Madras, the political capital of the region. This in itself is a sign not just of the state's ambivalence towards religious and female iconography, but also of its very different attitude towards language and Tamil devotion, as we will see later.

These statues and pictures show clearly that Tamil1ttây's iconography as generated by *tamil1ppar1r1u* is a melange of traditional and nouveau forms, of conflicted dependence on religious and secular imagery, and of an ambivalent reliance on old esthetic devices to iconize what is after all a brand-new personage. Their best efforts to the contrary, her devotees have found it often difficult to escape the vise of Hindu religious as well as Indian nationalist imagery. For one thing, unless she is clearly identified as "Tamil1ttây," it is very easy to confuse her visually with the hundreds of other goddesses and female divinities that are popular in this region. For another, in the cartoons in which she was featured in the 1960s, she could easily be mistaken for—or deliberately be read as—an everyday Tamil woman (fig. 10). While in quite a number of the visuals that are printed in magazines and journals she is left unnamed, leaving it to the reader to figure out from context who she is, in a large majority of cases she is named specifically as Tamil1ttây. The fact that her devotees have to regularly resort to identifying Tamil1ttây through inscribing her name suggests, at the very least, that no iconographic canon has as yet crystallized around her, as it has around well-known deities such as, say, Lakshmi or Ganesha who arguably do not need to be identified as such. At the same time, given the low literacy rates in the region, the use of writing to identify her visuals has obvious implications for who has, and who does not have, ready access to Tamil1ttây.

Naming is not the only strategy that her devotees have used to identify their Tamil1ttây visually. They have also tried, with mixed success, to generate a repertoire of distinctive iconographic features that would give her a visual presence that cannot be readily confused with other well-known goddesses. First and most clearly, an important feature of Tamil1ttây's iconography is that she is almost invariably shown carrying a sheaf of cadjan leaves in her left hand. Ironically, given the important role played by print capitalism in disseminating the assertions of Tamil devotion, there are very few visuals which show her with a printed book. The use of cadjan leaves instead of the printed book underscores the archaizing strategies in devotional poetry, conveying to the viewer the impression that she is an ancient and hoary figure. At the same time, when the leaves are left unnamed, as they are in a large number of cases, Tamil1ttây could be easily mistaken for Saraswati, whose iconographic tradition also has her holding such palm-leaf manuscripts. In a number of cases, however, the leaves in Tamil1ttây's hand are identified specifically as the *Tirukkur1al#*. Additionally, the Annamalainagar poster of Tamil1ttây (fig. 1), as well as pictures of her published in journals like *Tamil1t Ten1r1al* (1 July 1948) and *Nakkîran1* (15 January 1960), visually translate the poetic notion that the many "gems" of Tamil literature are jewels that adorn Tamil1ttây's body. In particular—and here one may note the clever play on the titles of these various texts—the *Cilappatikâram* jingles on her feet as anklets, the *Man#imçkalai* encircles her waist as a jeweled belt, the *Kun#t#alakçci* hangs from her ears as gold rings, the *Val#aiyâpati* adorns her arms as bracelets, and the *Cîvaka Cintâman#i* crowns her head as a diadem.

Other iconographic features drawn from Tamil literary and historical traditions serve to bestow upon Tamil1ttây a visual presence that distinguishes her from that "other" mother, Bhârata Mâtâ. In the Annamalainagar poster, Tamil1ttây sits on a throne inscribed with the symbols of the fish, the bow, and the tiger, which are claimed to represent the ancient Pandya, Chera, and Chola kingdoms, the oldest in the recorded history of the region (fig. 1). The same symbols may be seen in the official Tamilnadu government statue and in the poster released by the state (fig. 9). The Annamalainagar poster, as well as the Kamban Kazhagam's, also links her visually with the three "branches" of Tamil, *iyal* (literature), *icai* (music), and *nât#akam* (drama), by incorporating images of a literary manuscript, a lute, and drums (figs. 1, 2). In many visual and material manifestations, Tamil1ttây holds a musical instrument in her hand; once again, the similarity here with Saraswati, the Sanskritic goddess of music, is unmistakable. Yet her followers insist that Tamil1ttây's musical instrument is not Saraswati's *vîn#â* but the much more ancient *yâl1* mentioned in Cank#am poems.

In general, there is unusual unanimity in presenting Tamil1ttây visually as a young woman, albeit one who often appears rather matronly. This is in keeping of course with her dominant image as a *kan1n1i* (maiden), and with the assertion that Tamil is an evergreen, ageless, undying language (*kan1n1ittamil1*). So far, I have only found two exceptions to this general pattern. First, in a cartoon that appeared in a DK journal, *Pôrvâl#*, during the anti-Hindi protests of 1948, Tamil is cast as an old woman who contemptuously looks at the newborn babe, Hindi, with which the Indian state was planning to displace her. The cartoon resorts to the image of the old woman to juxtapose the venerable antiquity of Tamil with the upstart immaturity of the "infant" Hindi. And second, in illustrations accompanying a set of poems written in the *pil#l#aittamil1* (extraordinary child) genre and published in 1981, Tamil1ttây is featured, in keeping with the requirements of that genre, as a little infant and young girl, albeit one who has the face of a grown woman. These exceptions aside, in the majority of cases in which she appears as a young woman, Tamil1ttây is generally depicted sedately seated and chastely clothed, which suggests, if we follow George Mosse's comparable discussion of Marianne of France, the imperative to associate her with stability and bourgeois respectability (1985: 91). In quite a few cases, Tamil1ttây wears a sari and blouse in the modest style that comes to be associated with the middle-class woman. But equally strikingly, in a large number of instances, including the official state poster, she appears in garments truer to a more archaic iconographic tradition—tight-fitting short upper bodice, no top cloth, and figure-hugging clothing from the waist down (figs. 9,

11). This is typically how the devotional assertion that Tamil is an ancient "classical" language has been visualized; the body of Tamil1ttây is archaized by clothing her in the (imagined) garbs of an ancient Hindu goddess or literary heroine. Here, parenthetically, one may note Mosse's observations about the comparable archaizing of the clothing and accoutrements of European icons of the nation, such as Germania and Britannia. "Like all symbols," he comments, "the female embodiments of the nation stood for eternal forces. They looked backward in their ancient armor and medieval dress [suggesting] innocence and chastity, a kind of moral rigor directed against modernity—the pastoral and the eternal" (Mosse 1985: 98).

Despite the ambivalently developed but nevertheless manifest eroticization of the Tamil1ttây figure, I have not come across a single visual representation of her as an object of (sexual) desire, with one potential exception: the 1967 cover of the literary journal *Tamil1 Vat#t#am,* which features a sensuous, beautifully adorned Tamil1ttây seated rather seductively on a globe (fig. 3). In all her other visual appearances, Tamil1ttây is a remarkably de-sexualized figure with little indication of her poetic persona as a desirable woman. The female allegorical figure, Madelyn Gutwirth suggests, "operates to reify female untouchability." The "mute remoteness" and "emptiness of expression" worn by many a statue of Tamil1ttây, their voluptuousness notwithstanding, hardly make them suitable objects of desire (Gutwirth 1992: 256-57). The absence of visuals of a sensuous Tamil1ttây only underscores the precarious life of the modality of erotics within the world of Tamil devotion.

The alternate conceptions of the language generated by the religious and classicist imaginations on the one hand, and Indianism and Dravidianism on the other, visually manifest themselves in the contrary images of Tamil1ttây as a glorious, bejeweled woman in some of her pictures, and as a disheveled woman in a state of disarray in others. In general, the latter is restricted to the various cartoons generated during the anti-Hindi protests of the midcentury in contexts that were clearly populist. These cartoons thus show Tamil1ttây in various stages of distress—as weeping behind bars, bending over the bodies of her dead children, cowering in a corner with tears running down her face, and so on (figs. 7, 10). One striking visual which was published in February 1965 even has a weeping Tamil1ttây holding the charred body of Aranganathan in her arms. At the end of the Hindi struggle in 1967 with the coming of the DMK to power, Tamil1ttây recovers her beatific stance, once again, as she is portrayed happy, smiling, and back on her throne.

Another important area of visual contestation is over Tamil1ttây's representation as a queen on the one hand, and as an everyday Tamil mother/woman on the other. In the former, her limbs are adorned with jewels; she wears a crown, or is being adorned with one; and she carries a scepter: she is clearly the sovereign of her putative kingdom. But during the 1950s and 1960s, Tamil1ttây was more often than not featured as an everyday woman, clad in a sari and blouse (fig. 10). Some of these visuals mark her distinctiveness by bestowing a halo around her or placing a small crown on her head. Nevertheless, she could quite readily be mistaken for a generic Tamil-speaking woman, especially when the pictures do not name her. So cartoons of Tamil1ttây crying over the bodies of her children fade into newspaper pictures of women shedding tears over the death of their near and dear ones. The feminization of the language is so pervasive that texts and essays on Tamil, or on "our mother tongue," routinely begin to carry the figure of a woman either playing with her children or reading to them. Such images only visually reinforce the notion that the Tamil-speaking woman, especially in her guise as mother, is after all a surrogate Tamil1ttây.

But undoubtedly the biggest area of contestation in the visual politics around Tamil1ttây, as in the written and spoken discourses on her, surrounds her representation as "goddess." The reliance on the canons and materials of Hindu iconography has meant that the over-riding impression imparted by the various statues and some of the posters of Tamil1ttây is that she could well be a goddess: she wears the crown that many Hindu divinities typically wear; she holds her right hand in the typical gesture of offering grace to her devotees; she sits on a large lotus, or her feet rest on it, as is typical of many goddesses; and her face often carries the same look of remoteness and transcendence that marks the countenance of many a deity. The real distinctive marker, however, of whether a particular picture or statue intends to present Tamil1ttây as a goddess lies in the number of arms she is endowed with. As is well-known, the supernatural quality and the power of Hindu deities find iconographic representation in the multiple arms they bear. Typically, deities with great power are shown with four arms, while minor deities, female consorts, and godlings have two. The mother-goddess is generally portrayed with four arms, sometimes more.

In general, the large majority of these pictures and statues, especially those produced under the mantle of the Dravidian movement and Dravidianism, show Tamil1ttây with two arms. She is not a supernatural, superhuman figure participating in all the irrationalities of Hindu religiosity; instead she is a near and dear mother. The seductive maiden on the cover of the 1967 issue of the *Tamil1 Vat#t#am* is four-armed, however, and so is the Tamil1ttây of the poster issued by the Kamban Kazhagam (figs. 2, 3). The statue of Tamil1ttây that the latter sponsored is also four-armed, the four arms signifying, I was told, the three branches of Tamil learning (*iyal, icai,* and *nât#akam*) and grace (*arul#*) (fig. 11). This very same statue was recast again in 1981 as the official, government sponsored figure of Tamil1ttây installed in Madurai. But the state's statue shows Tamil1ttây with only two arms; in all other respects, it is identical to the four-armed statue of the Kamban Kazhagam. The two additional arms were left out on specific orders from the highest levels of the government—even from the chief minister himself, I was told (compare figs. 9 and 11). This concession to Dravidianist iconoclasm aside, it is telling that the state's visual representation of Tamil1ttây is in all other respects truer to her religious persona as goddess than to her secular incarnation as mother. For the state would very much like to capitalize on the enormous attention that Hindu divinities continue to command among the populace, in its own effort to pass itself off as a devotee of Tamil1ttây, albeit a reluctant one.

Today, the Kamban Kazhagam's four-armed statue of the goddess sits in a "temple" to her that has been built in the southern town of Karaikkudi (fig. 12). The foundation for the temple was laid in April 1975 with the blessings of the DMK government of M. Karunanidhi, which also sanctioned the hefty sum of five lakh rupees for the project. The temple was finally opened to the public in April 1993. Its central sanctum houses, in addition to Tamil1ttây, the images of her two most ancient "sons," the grammarians Agastya and Tolkappiyar. Three subsidiary sanctums carry the images of Ilango, Tiruvalluvar, and Kamban, three of Tamil's most famous poets. The temple itself is shaped in the form of a triangle, the three angles signifying the three most ancient kings—the Chera, the Chola, and the Pandya, Tamil1ttây's oldest patron sons; alternatively, they also represent the three branches of Tamil, *iyal* (literature), *icai* (music), and *nât#akam* (drama). Although the structure is referred to as a *kôvil*, the sponsors are very clear that it is not a "temple" in the religious sense; the image of Tamil1ttây is not an object of worship, nor are Hindu religious rituals performed. This is a temple that commemorates, in their vision, the language that belongs to the entire world; accordingly it is open to all who revere Tamil. Indeed, during the dedication of the temple in 1993, it was clear that everybody assembled there was careful to distance themselves from all overt signs of religiosity. In his speech, Karunanidhi, who officially opened the temple to the public, even pointed out there should be no mistake about his extending his approval to an image that had four arms. Rather than signifying irrational divinity, the four arms represented the four languages that Tamil had given birth to: Kannada, Malayalam, Telugu, and Tulu. Tamil1ttây was not a goddess to be worshipped but a guardian who will guide us, he insisted. For his part, Kunrakudi Adigal (1925-95), the controversial head of the Shaiva *mat#am* (monastery) at Kunrakudi, also concurred, making clear his hopes that Tamil speakers visiting the temple would renew themselves as Tamilians and resolve to write, speak, and think in Tamil, always.

All the effort invested in creating for her a distinctive iconographic presence notwithstanding, there is no single, standardized image of Tamil1ttây that reigns today. Even as it underscores the many quandaries inherent in translating into visual and material media what is after all an abstraction, the absence of a singular pictorial representation provides a powerful visual reminder of the multiplicity of conceptions about the language, and the many models of the feminine, that have gone into the imagining of Tamil1ttây within the poetic and prosaic productions of her devotees. And as with the verbal discourses on Tamil1ttây, in iconographic practice as well the struggle has been waged on several fronts, producing a range of variations in her visual persona. That out of all this a single standardized hegemonic image has not emerged is not necessarily a sign of failure; on the contrary, the existence of this multiplicity and fluidity—what Paul de Man has characterized as a "surplus of meaning" (Gutwirth 1992: 255)— sures the iconographic availability of Tamil1ttây, as goddess, queen, mother, and maiden all rolled into one, that future devotees can continue to cash in on.

4. LABORING FOR LANGUAGE

The State of Tamil Devotion

From its inception, Tamil devotion meant that speakers of Tamil had to be at the service of the language, to labor in its name and on its behalf. Glossed in devotional narratives as *tamil1ppan#i*, "Tamil work," or *tamil1tton#t#u*, "Tamil service," this labor is presented as honorable, virtuous, and meritorious. It is mandatory for all those who claim to be Tamilians for it is an obligation (*kat#amai*), even a debt (*kat#an1*), that they owe, by virtue of being speakers of Tamil, to their language. Sundaram Pillai set the tone for this when he presented his 1891 play, *Man1ôn1man#îyam*, with its invocatory hymn to the goddess Tamil, as "tribute" (*kat#amai*) to his *tamil1mâtâ*, "Tamil mother," and called upon his fellow Tamil speakers to fulfill their debt (*kat#an1*) to her by rescuing from obscurity ancient Tamil works and creating new literatures (Sundaram Pillai 1922: 9-12). Since then, again and again devotees have represented their work on behalf of the language as *ar1appan#i*, "meritorious work," or *tirutton#t#u*, "auspicious service." Indeed, in 1959, Bharatidasan even explicitly declared that it was not service to God that was important, but service to Tamil (*tamil1ttirutton#t#u*).

While there was general consensus among its devotees that talk about Tamil had to be translated into work, and that *tamil1ppar1r1u* in and of itself was incomplete without *tamil1ppan#i*, there was much less agreement, as can be expected, on what constitutes appropriate labor, on what kind of Tamil one should serve, and on who ought to be involved in this. In the logic of neo-Shaivism and classicism, laboring for Tamil meant the establishment of learned literary academies, as well as the publication and circulation of ancient religious texts and literature. Indianism and Dravidianism, on the other hand, proposed that it was through seizing political power that Tamil's fortunes would turn. For devotees like Maraimalai Adigal, the cleansing of Sanskrit from the speech of the elites would by itself lead to the revival of the language, whereas for a Bharati or a Bharatidasan, it was the people's speech that ought to be the basis for a rejuvenated Tamil. Moreover, there was much disagreement over identifying the putative enemies of Tamil against whom its devotees had to labor. Was it Sanskrit, English, or Hindi? Was it the Brahman or the colonial? Was it the scholastic Tamil pandit or the uneducated Tamil mother? If these were all threatening Tamil, what was the best way to prioritize the tasks ahead? Should the work of Tamil improvement precede the Tamilization of the political apparatus, or should it be the other way around? The questions were many, the problems manifold.

Laboring for Tamil also meant that its devotees had to contend with the state. Should *tamil1ppan#i* be conducted by individual devotees and their associations, or should the state be the principal agency? Although they did occasionally interact with some of its institutions in the pursuit of their agendas, both neo-Shaivism and classicism largely steered clear of the state. Indianism and Dravidianism, on the other hand, were directly concerned with changing the nature of power relations and the structure of political authority. They aimed to get rid of the British and Brahmans, respectively, and to place in their stead loyal and pure Tamil speakers in positions of power and authority. The state, in turn, has vacillated in its relationship to *tamil1ppar1r1u.* During the late colonial period, prior to the accession of the Justice Party to power in 1920, the state basically stayed aloof from devotional activities or, at most, played a mediating role between various conflicting interest groups and agendas. In the 1920s and 1930s, however, with the Justice Party and the Congress at the helm, the state began to accommodate, although not without resistance, various devotional demands, especially in the domain of education (e.g., demands for the institution of Tamil as medium of instruction and as subject of study in schools and colleges, the establishment of a Tamil University, and other such measures that Nambi Arooran [1980: 70-139] has analyzed). In the years following 1947, when several of Tamil's devotees were elected to political office and even became chief ministers, not only did this imperative to accommodate accelerate but the state was compelled to progressively "Tamilize" itself, sometimes through conscious involvement in devotional efforts, at other times through actively implementing distinctively pro-Tamil policies in various public, governmental, and educational arenas. And yet, in its Tamilization the state has been reluctant at best, and even recalcitrant at times. Indeed, the state has often assumed the role of a follower rather than a leader, and it frequently appears to be succumbing to pressures from the devotional community, rather than staking out its own autonomous trajectory.

There are obviously many reasons why the state's work for Tamil has been riddled with reluctance, contradiction, and failure, and why it has rarely met the high expectations of the devotees of the language. The most compelling of these reasons are their very different conceptions about language. The everyday, administrative functioning of the modern state demands the adoption of what we may characterize as a "rationalist-bureaucratic" imagination in which language is treated as an *object:* as an "instrument" of communication and education, a "tool" for governance, and a "vehicle" for the transmission of ideas, thought, and knowledge. On the other hand, the emotional and cultural life of its devout was underwritten by a passionate attachment to Tamil, imagined as the very life, spirit, and soul of every Tamilian. For its followers, Tamil was not just an inanimate object but a near and dear *person* whose well-being is likened, again and again, as we have seen, to the well-being of one's own mother. This is not to say that the state, particularly in its post-colonial manifestation, was unaffected by this symbolic investment in Tamil1ttây: it makes several gestures in this direction, as we have seen. Nor does it mean that the devotional community did not have its own share of the rationalist, instrumentalist conception of language. Nevertheless, the state's attitudes and intentions towards Tamil are quite different from its devotees', and this difference manifested itself repeatedly in the realm of policy making. Certainly, language and cultural policies in Tamilnadu have been highly contested because of the multiple, contrary meanings with which Tamil has been invested over the decades by its devout. But these policies are also riddled with contradictions because of the different conceptions about the language that drove the state, in contrast to those that reigned in the community of its devotees.

WORSHIPPING WITH TAMIL: LANGUAGE AND LITURGY

In the 1950s and 1960s, more than half a century after *tamil1ppar1r1u* reared its head, the state took up for legislation an issue that was dear to neo-Shaivism from at least the 1920s on. This issue, glossed as *tamil1 aruccan1ai* (Tamil worship), turned around the use of Tamil and its religious texts in temples in Tamilnadu where Sanskrit was still the dominant liturgical language. Neo-Shaivism insisted that in ancient Shaiva religion, it was Tamil, rather than Sanskrit, that was used as language of worship. But then "[Brahmans] introduced the words of their northern language in which one can see very little trace of any kind of divinity, empowered them, and denigrated our great and glorious Tamil scriptures, the *Tçvâram* and the *Tiruvâcakam,* as 'songs of the Shudras' " (Maraimalai Adigal 1967a: 150).

Moreover, Brahmans were not just content with empowering Sanskrit in this way; they also ensured that it was only after they had chanted the *Veda*s, had received the deities' blessings, and were out of earshot that Tamil hymns were even recited. They had thus displaced the divine Tamil from its own temples with the upstart Sanskrit (Kandiah Pillai 1947; K. Subramania Pillai 1940: 97-106; Swaminatha Upatiyayan 1921: 22-24). The language of liturgy therefore emerged within the practice of *tamil1ppar1r1u* as a key site on which was waged the battle between Brahmanical Hinduism and Tamil Shaivism, between Sanskrit and Tamil scriptures, and above all, between Brahman and "non-Brahman" as ritual specialists and social elites.

Although the relative importance of Tamil and Sanskrit in temple worship has varied from sect to sect, the two languages have been an integral part of the region's institutionalized scriptural Hinduism from the late first millennium C.E. (Cutler 1987:187-94; Peterson 1989: 54-56). Over the centuries, periodic doctrinal and sectarian conflict had erupted around the question of language and liturgy (A. Appadurai 1981: 77-82), but beginning in the 1920s, with neo-Shaivism taking on an increasingly radical stance, the call came for completely excising Sanskrit and its scriptures from Tamilnadu temples and replacing these with Tamil and its scriptures. Along with this also came the demand, as was voiced in 1943 by the Tamil1 Un#arcci Mânât#u, the "Tamil Consciousness Conference," for de-Sanskritizing the names of deities, temples, and temple towns and replacing them with their original or former Tamil names (Ilankumaran 1991: 175). One enthusiast even urged that throughout Tamilnadu, all temples ought to follow only one uniform Tamil liturgical text and priests should be taught to remember that they are Tamilians, should be assured that conducting worship in Tamil would bring in more remuneration, and should be granted honors if they perform good *aruccan1ai* in Tamil. For the loyal devotee of Tamil, devotion to the (Hindu) gods could not, and should not, be allowed to compromise devotion to Tamil.

By the 1940s and 1950s, populist organizations like K. A. P. Viswanatham's Tamil1ar Kal1akam (Society of Tamilians) and Sivagnanam's Tamil Arasu Kazhagam had extended their support to the neo-Shaiva demand for Tamil *aruccan1ai* (Sivagnanam 1960: 53-54, 1974: 448). Paradoxically, political parties, like the DK and the DMK, also stepped into this arena of ritual and liturgical politics by the 1950s. As we have seen, the Dravidian movement and the Dravidianist idiom of *tamil1ppar1r1u* poured rationalist scorn on Brahmanic Hinduism and neo-Shaivism alike. All the same, by the 1940s Dravidianism began to support the demand for *tamil1 aruccan1ai* (Sundara Shanmugan 1948: 12, 30; Velu and Selvaraji 1989: 78). As the poet Bharatidasan eloquently observed in 1945, every day in temples across Tamilnadu, the Tamilian relinquished "Tamil honor" by acquiescing to the use of Sanskrit hymns in worship (1969: 27). For the DK and the DMK in the 1950s, *tamil1 aruccan1ai* assumed saliency as another issue with which to contest both Brahmanical power and the Congress government. Thus at a public meeting in 1957, S. Gurusami, the editor of the DK newspaper *Vit#utalai,* declared that Brahmans had used Tamilian labor to build their huge temples and carve their sculptures, and had then prevented Tamilians from offering worship there. Instead of the richness of Tamil, the "filth" of Sanskrit filled these temples, and E. V. Ramasami, Tamilians were told, would soon lead a protest to help Tamil, the language of *aruccan1ai.*

The iconoclastic Ramasami himself, as we will see, spared no words in denouncing neo-Shaivism's divinization of Tamil. Yet, as early as 1926 he demanded, "Why should we worship our deities in an alien language?" and in his usual irrepressible fashion, he asked in 1972, on the eve of his death, "What business has a god in Tamilnadu if he does not want Tamil?" (quoted in Diehl 1977: 71). His atheistic agenda for completely ridding all traces of religiosity from Dravidian consciousness notwithstanding, through the 1950s and 1960s Ramasami promoted the cause of

Tamil as liturgical language as a means through which Tamil speakers would regain their self-respect. He argued that it would free them from servitude to Aryan Brahmanism and Sanskrit (Anaimuthu 1974: 1043-44). Indeed, for Ramasami and the DK, *tamil1 aruccan1ai* was only one of several fronts on which to conduct their war against Brahmanical Sanskritic Hinduism, which included the breaking of Brahman monopoly on priesthood, the opening of the *sanctum sanctorum* in temples to all castes, and the public burning of Sanskrit scriptures.

Neo-Shaivism and Dravidianism, contrary ideologies though they may be, thus came together to support *tamil1 aruccan1ai,* united by their common cause against Brahmans and Sanskrit. Ironically, however, the neo-Shaiva agenda for instituting Tamil as liturgical language was realized in practice not by insisting upon its divinity, but by invoking its status as "mother tongue" and hence a language intelligible to its speakers. This is the argument that was used, for instance, by Kunrakudi Adigal, one of the key spokesmen on this issue. For him, Tamil *aruccan1ai* was a weapon with which to counter not just Sanskritic Brahmanism's hegemony but the Dravidian movement's atheism as well. In 1953, at a time when Ramasami's campaigns against religion and Hinduism were gaining momentum, he argued that it was Sanskrit's "unintelligibility" that rendered it incomprehensible to the Tamil populace and that, not surprisingly, promoted irreligiosity among them. "If the *pujaris* [priests] were to cast off their superiority complex and to conduct *archanais* [worship] in a language understandable to the average devotee, there would be no anti-god demonstration in the street" (quoted in Presler 1987: 115-16). As if to prove this point, in 1971, when Karunanidhi was chief minister, he declared that following a nearby temple's 1953 switch to Tamil *aruccan1ai,* the number of its patrons as well as the temple's revenues had dramatically escalated.

Karunanidhi made this statement in Coimbatore, in support of the DMK government's attempts in 1970 and 1971 to authorize the use of Tamil as primary language of worship, at a time when many temples across Tamilnadu were actually already doing so, under various guises. Although it is his government that is most closely associated with the *tamil1 aruccan1ai* issue, this had been a matter of concern for the state for the past couple of decades. At least since the late nineteenth century, its avowed policy of religious neutrality notwithstanding, the colonial state had steadily increased its jurisdiction over temples. But its predominant concern continued to be regulation of temple administration and finances, and the language question did not invite legislation (A. Appadurai 1981; Mudaliar 1974). During the 1950s and 1960s, however, the Congress-led state could no longer ignore demands for Tamil *aruccan1ai,* and the Hindu Religious and Charitable Endowments Department (HRCE) "quietly promoted," as Franklin Presler notes, the increasing use of Tamil hymns in temples. Yet during these years, there was no attempt to substitute Tamil for Sanskrit, only to "strengthen Tamil's place alongside Sanskrit rituals" (Presler 1987: 115). This did not save the Congress government from being pressured to do away entirely with Sanskrit, replacing it with worship solely in Tamil. Responding to such demands, M. Bhaktavatsalam, the minister for the HRCE—and not a Brahman—declared in 1959 that when he listened to the *aruccan1ai* being offered in Tamil, he was not inspired, did not understand it, and found it "boring." Another Congress member in the Assembly, P. S. Krishnaswami Ayyangar, a Sri Vaishnavite Brahman, insisted that if Tamil were instituted as the liturgical language, non-Tamil devotees who came to temples would find it difficult to comprehend their gods' worship—the assumption here, of course, being that Sanskrit could be understood by one and all. The government's position was that since religious "tradition" (*campratâyam*) should not be interfered with by the state, and since it did not matter which language was used to offer worship, "traditional" (i.e., Sanskritic) forms of worship ought not be abolished. So, Bhaktavatsalam declared in the Legislative Council: "Worship has to be offered according to tradition and custom. It is not proper to change that order. There is no point in raising the issue of Sanskrit or Tamil in worship. The demand for bringing in Tamil to do *aruccan1ai* is a meaningless agitation. *Aruccan1ai* means the recitation of names of the deity. What difference does it make [whether the name is in Sanskrit or Tamil]?...This is a meaningless agitation."

Yet, the government's position to the contrary, the protest against the use of Sanskrit in temples had been launched in the first place precisely because "tradition" had been radically reinterpreted over the past few decades; because it made all the difference whether something was named in Sanskrit or Tamil;

and because religion and language could not be dissociated from each other, as neo-Shaivism had repeatedly insisted from the turn of the century.

The Congress government no doubt resisted the demand for *tamil1 aruccan1ai,* partly because of its reluctance to oppose Sanskritic Hinduism, but also partly because in this, as in other matters concerning Tamil in the 1950s and 1960s, it tried to counter the growth of "linguism" and regionalism (as sponsored by the Dravidian movement) that were perceived as threats to Indian nationalism (the basis for its own power). As the Congress was compelled to take a stand on Tamil in variance with large sectors of the Tamil devotional community, the language of liturgy became one of the key issues on which the party was rendered vulnerable to demonization as an enemy of Tamil.

The "quiet encouragement" of the Congress government in strengthening the place of Tamil alongside Sanskrit in temples gave way to its active promotion with the coming to power of the DMK in 1967. In mid-1971, the government formalized its informal support by issuing a series of orders which declared that "the Tamil Nadu people desire that in all temples *archanais* should be performed in Tamil" (quoted in Presler 1987: 116). In August 1971, Sanskrit was demoted from its status as the normative liturgical language and was declared optional. Its place was now taken by Tamil. In spite of resistance mounted against such orders by many Brahman priests as well as by organizations such as the Madras Temple Worship Protection Society, there were numerous well-publicized performances of Tamil *aruccan1ai* in many temples, conducted in the presence of members of the DMK government (Presler 1987: 116). Though the government nowhere overtly banned the use of Sanskrit or compelled the sole use of Tamil, at least one deputy commissioner interpreted its order in such terms. This sparked off a major uproar, resulting in the eventual staying of all Tamil *aruccan1ai* orders by the Supreme Court in August 1974. The *Centamil1c Celvi,* which for decades had been publishing essays promoting the use of Tamil in temples, had the following comment:

In Tamilnadu, there is resistance to Tamil music; there is resistance to Tamil as official language; there is resistance to Tamil as medium of instruction in colleges; there is resistance to reconverting the names of places and towns to pure Tamil; there was resistance to naming Madras state as Tamilnadu; there is resistance to the conduct of domestic rituals in Tamil; there is resistance to pure Tamil. When we have resistance like this everywhere, it is no surprise that there is so much opposition to worship in Tamil.

What are some of the implications of the controversy over Tamil *aruccan1ai* for the public practice of Tamil devotion? First, neo-Shaivite claims about the illegitimacy of Sanskrit for religious practices in the Tamil-speaking region received the sanction, albeit ambiguously and fruitlessly, of the Tamilnadu state. Chief Minister Karunanidhi defended his actions thus: "If the right to perform the *archanai* in Tamil is denied, Sanskrit considered as Devabhasha [language of God], and along with that God and religion also, will be driven out from Tamil Nadu to north India....If the gods in south India cannot tolerate Tamil *archanais*, let the gods move to north India" (quoted in Presler 1987: 130). Similarly, the minister in charge of implementing the *aruccan1ai* policy declared, as neo-Shaivism had from the beginning of this century, that "it was wrong to say that God could follow only Sanskrit" (quoted in Presler 1987: 116).

Furthermore, neo-Shaivite assertions of the divinity of Tamil also received the blessings of an ostensibly "secular" state that was in the control of a party, the DMK, which at various times had vociferously declared its opposition to religious beliefs of any kind. In Karunanidhi's words, "A section of the people claim that Tamil language has no divinity and hence there is nothing sacred about it. *It is only to controvert this view,* the Tamil Nadu Deviga Peravai and the HRCE Department have introduced Tamil *archanais*.

The Tamil *archanai* only move is born more out of our love and attachment to Tamil than ill will or hatred towards any other language" (quoted in Presler 1987: 118, emphasis mine). Its detractors claimed that the DMK's actions followed from the fact that it was a antireligious party "with no faith in God"—God and religion being identified here, of course, with Sanskrit and the Sanskritic tradition. Yet the DMK's support of *tamil1 aruccan1ai* was clearly part of its overall policy of Tamilizing the public sphere. Indeed, contrary to its detractors' claim, it was also in line with the many accommodations that that party had made since at least the 1960s with various aspects of high Hinduism through a corresponding Tamilization of that religion, as I noted earlier.

Moreover, in many religious systems, including scriptural Hinduism, the magical power of a sacred language is predicated on its unintelligibility to the lay worshipper. Quotidian, "profane" languages that are readily comprehensible are believed to not have the same ritual efficacy (Tambiah 1985: 22-30). Indeed, Dakshinamoorthy Bhattar, a priest who challenged the government's orders, argued that the efficacy of ritual depended on the particular sounds of Sanskrit and that there would be "disaster" if he "dared to perform the *archanai* in Tamil" (Presler 1987: 117; see also Harrison 1960: 130). And much to the dismay of many a Tamil devotee, it was not only a Brahman priest who argued thus, but also Gnanaprakasar Tecikar, a respected "non-Brahman" Tamil scholar. But the state's argument was not couched in the vocabulary of ritual efficacy. For regardless of the doctrinal and metaphysical premises on which neo-Shaivism asserted the divine potency and ritual powers of Tamil, the state's *aruccan1ai* orders derived their eventual legitimacy from the democratic logic that the language of worship ought to be understandable and intelligible to the people, that it ought to be the "mother tongue." Sanskrit's legitimacy was undermined not by questioning its divine status (as neo-Shaivism did), but by declaring its "unintelligibility" among the people. By the same token, Tamil was ordered in its place not just because it was divine, but because it had the "love and attachment" of the people and was their "mother tongue." Here, the Tamil *aruccan1ai* issue appears to provide another illustration of the "demoticization" of liturgical languages—such as Hebrew or Latin or Arabic—that has inevitably accompanied the nationalization and democratization of political and social systems with modernity (Anderson 1983: 68-69). Yet Sanskrit was not threatened by an ordinary "demotic" tongue but by another "sacred" language that had also been recently empowered as "mother tongue." This is what makes the demand for Tamil liturgy unusual.

Finally, the Tamil *aruccan1ai* controversy gave the lie to the state's assertion that "language is not the essence of religion" (quoted in Mudaliar 1974: 223). The Congress government had resisted the demands to replace Sanskrit with Tamil in the 1950s on this basis. It is "meaningless," Bhaktavatsalam had insisted, to raise the language issue in matters of worship. Interestingly, in 1974 the Madras High Court defended the DMK led state's legislation by invoking the same principle (Mudaliar 1974: 223): "It cannot be taken that unless religious matters are expressed in a particular language they cease to be religious" (quoted in Presler 1987: 117). Yet, as neo-Shaivism had asserted again and again, was it even possible to contemplate god without divine Tamil? Even the DMK minister in charge of the state's religious policy declared in the Legislative Assembly in 1971 that it was god himself, filled with "Tamil consciousness," who had enabled the institution of Tamil *aruccan1ai.* From the point of view of many a devoted Tamilian, god and Tamil could not be separated at will or through state legislation.

CLEANSING TAMIL: LANGUAGE AND PURITY

One evening, when she was barely thirteen, Nilambikai was taking a stroll in their garden with her famed father, Maraimalai Adigal (who at that time still went by his Sanskritic name, Swami Vedachalam). He began to sing a verse from Ramalinga Adigal's famous *Tiruvarut#pâ* but when he came to the second line of the verse, Vedachalam stopped and said to his daughter: "Is it not wonderful that Ramalinga Adigal has sung this song so beautifully in pure Tamil (*tûyattamil1*)? But, instead of using the Sanskrit word *tçkam* in the second line, would it not have been better if he had used the pure Tamil (*tan1ittamil1*) word, *yâkkai?* Because Sanskrit words have been allowed in Tamil, it has lost its beauty and Tamil words have gone out of use." Father and daughter resolved, from that day on, to speak and write only in *tan1ittamil1* (lit., "exclusively Tamil," but more generally glossed as "pure Tamil") (Nilambikai 1960: iii).

This incident is cited as the originary moment of what comes to be called *tan1ittamil1 iyakkam,* the "pure Tamil" movement, and is dated by most scholars to 1916, though the roots of Maraimalai Adigal's own personal predilections in this regard may be traced back to the late 1890s. The movement has invited considerable criticism and resistance, even within the devotional community. Nonetheless, it still continues to have its share of enthusiasts who publish books and journals advocating its virtues, and who seek, with varying degrees of success, to make *tan1ittamil1* into an everyday habit in contemporary Tamilnadu. For the ardent purist, there is no difference between "Tamil" and *tan1ittamil1* good Tamil is always already *tan1ittamil1,* the only language in the world that is capable of flourishing without the aid of other languages (Nilambikai 1960: 40-51). This has meant that for purists, even their fellow devotees who do not follow the ideals of *tan1ittamil1* are, by definition, enemies of Tamil; they are not the true "sons" of their language/mother (Ilankumaran 1991: 130-36, 168-69). "Those who oppose *tan1ịttamil1* are murderers of Tamil," the purists declare unequivocally (quoted in M. Tirunavukarasu 1959: 520).

Soon after the incident in the garden, Vedachalam Tamilized his name (and those of his children), and from then on referred to himself, at least in his Tamil publications, as Maraimalai Adigal. Vedachalam was not the first to do this. A few years earlier, in 1899, another Tamil enthusiast, V. G. Suryanarayana Sastri, had published a collection of sonnets in which his name appeared in its Tamil form as "Paritimâl Kalaiòar." Although this was the only occasion in which Suryanarayana Sastri used his *tan1ittamil1* name, his act is much-cited in purist circles, not just because of his fame as a Tamil scholar but also because he was Brahman (Tirumaran 1992: 118-23). Since that time, many of Tamil's adherents have Tamilized their given Sanskritic names and have bestowed *tan1ittamil1* names on their children (Kailasapathy 1986: 30). The pure Tamil movement, however, advocates more than just symbolic acts such as the Tamilizing of personal names and, by extension, the names of towns, streets, deities, temples, and so on. It is equally concerned with transformations in written and spoken Tamil, with the conscious refusal, in both public and domestic contexts, to rely on words that are deemed non-Tamil. As early as 1906, the Tamil scholar and Murugan devotee Pamban Swami (1851-1929) published a book of verses called *Cçntan1 Centamil1,* in which care was taken not to allow even one Sanskrit word to appear (Tirumaran 1992: 123-26). And with the more concerted efforts of Maraimalai Adigal and his followers, this trend picked up momentum from the 1920s—with varying degrees of success, of course (Maraimalai Adigal 1930a: xxv-xxvi, 1934: 11-12). It has been estimated that even at the height of Maraimalai Adigal's enthusiasm for *tan1ittamil1* in the 1930s, at least 5 percent of the words in his texts continued to be Sanskritic (Nambi Arooran

1976: 345-46). Nevertheless, even impressionistically-speaking, the marked decline in the use of foreign words, especially of Sanskritic origin, in Tamil literary, scholarly, and even bureaucratic circles over the past half century is quite striking. The *tan1ittamil1* movement, however, has paid less attention to excising foreign syntactic patterns and Sanskritic rules of compounding and suffixes, Sanskritic phraseology, and so on, all of which have arguably had a more enduring impact on Tamil literary and speech styles (Annamalai 1979: 48; Kailasapathy 1986: 30-31).

Even the most ardent of purists would readily admit that it has been impossible to totally cleanse Tamil, not least because no real criteria have been developed to determine what constitutes a "pure" Tamil word. Purists castigate the continued use of non-Tamil words in short stories, novels, newspapers, and cinema, and they lament that the earlier enslavement to Sanskrit has now been supplemented by dependence on English, especially in popular speech and culture. Such laments remind us that language purification efforts, not just in Tamilnadu but elsewhere in the world, are elite literary enterprises. Typically, they appear as an imposition of a norm from above, rather than as a manifestation of a need or sentiment from below. Purists like Maraimalai Adigal even insisted that it is indolence and lack of discipline among its speakers that was responsible for Tamil's "corruption," and that it was the duty of disciplined, alert literati to rectify this "problem." "Defiling one's speech by mixing up with it extraneous elements simply indicates laxity of discipline, looseness of character, and lack of serious purpose in life," he scolded (Maraimalai Adigal 1980: 32). Not surprisingly, when couched in such terms, language purification efforts have certainly not caught the popular or populist political imagination, and they are frequently chastised for going against the flow, for trying to set the clock back, and for reviving archaisms (Jernudd and Shapiro 1989; G. Thomas 1991). As one critic declaimed in the *Madras Mail* in 1927:

A shortsighted nationalism compels such folk to strive to keep all immigrant words out....Fortunately such purists do not control the growth of a language. That is the work of the common people. The purists may frown at slang, they may grumble that the language is being debased by slipshod and lazy talkers and writers, but fifty per cent of what they condemn eventually finds its way into the language, to be defended by a later generation of purists as violently as the earlier fought for its exclusion. Language cannot be successfully cribbed, cabined and confined.

All the same, these movements have emerged with such frequency all over the modern world because they are rarely concerned with language alone. Instead, they are crucially intertwined with questions of identity, of definitions of self and other. Maraimalai Adigal, for instance, deplored the habit of "imitation" among his fellow speakers, especially those belonging to urban upper castes. This habit had led them to use Sanskrit words instead of their Tamil equivalents. Such imitation was only a linguistic reflection of the social and religious enslavement of Tamilians to Sanskritic Brahmanism. Carrying this logic further, *tan1ittamil1* adherents who follow in Maraimalai Adigal's footsteps, such as Nilambikai, Devaneyan, Ilakuvan, and Perunchitran, proposed that Brahman power in Tamilnadu would be subverted if Tamilians stopped using Sanskrit words in Tamil writing and speech.

Yet efforts to cleanse Tamil have not always been directed just against Sanskrit; nor have attempts to use pure Tamil necessarily been motivated by hostility towards other languages (Varadarajan 1966: 99-130). Indeed, the range of opinions offered by Tamil's devotees about the feasibility, the desirability, and the necessity of *tan1ittamil1* captures quite effectively the multiple imaginations about the language that prevailed among them. The *tan1ittamil1* movement associated with Maraimalai Adigal and his followers was largely an expression of contestatory classicism and radical neo-Shaivism. Their efforts to cleanse Tamil were propelled by hostility towards Brahmanism and its literary and ritual vehicle, Sanskrit. Even among them, however, numerous differences prevailed (Ilankumaran 1991: 129-37, 189-90; Tirumaran 1992: 153-208). For instance, the neo-Shaiva support for pure Tamil was linked to a religious project of Tamilizing Shaivism and of a return to pre-Sanskritic rituals and worship (Nilambikai 1960; Swaminatha Upatiyayan 1921). On the other hand, contestatory classicism's secular concern with purifying Tamil emerged from its agenda of restoring literary Tamil to its imagined state of pure classicality. Indeed, for contestatory classicism, the medieval religious texts which are the foundational scriptures for neo-Shaiva revivalism were themselves responsible for the flood of Sanskrit words that inundated Tamil literature after the pristine Tamil of the Cank#am poems (Devaneyan 1972; Tirumaran 1992: 189-204). Dravidianism, too, lent its support to the contestatory classicist project, motivated principally by the political imperative of countering (Sanskritic) Indian nationalism. However, given its own populist agenda, it was cautious about unilaterally embracing purification efforts with their inherently classicizing, archaizing, and prescriptive consequences. Thus Dravidianist prose eliminates Sanskrit words wherever possible, but not at the cost of distancing Tamil from the everyday language of the people. Indeed, among many in the Dravidian movement, like Ramasami and Annadurai, there was even hostility to pure Tamil advocates and their attempts to impose scholastic, high caste linguistic norms on the populace (Sivathamby 1979: 71-73).

But this is the not only reason that Maraimalai Adigal's *tan1ittamil1* movement has not been greeted with cheering enthusiasm by many Tamil scholars and adherents. For some proponents of compensatory classicism, attempts to cleanse Tamil of Sanskrit words was not just unnecessary but even undesirable (Swaminatha Aiyar 1991d: 52-53; Vaiyapuri Pillai 1989: 4-6; see also Tirumaran 1992: 274-77). And here, one may recall an interesting 1941 essay in which U. V. Swaminatha Aiyar defended the use of Sanskritic terms for food, such as *pôjan1am* and *nivçtan1am,* instead of their Tamil equivalent, *côr1u,* on the grounds that the former constituted the true "Tamil tradition" (*tamil1 marapu*). Swaminatha Aiyar's argument certainly betrays an overtly classist and paternalistic stance, for he proposed that while it was all right to use the Tamil word, *côr1u,* with a poor servant, it was not appropriate to do so with a notable (Swaminatha Aiyar 1991a). Not surprisingly, this essay elicited an angry response from at least one fellow devotee, K. A. P. Viswanatham, who was clearly anguished that the venerable Tamil scholar appeared to be more devoted to Sanskrit than to Tamil (Viswanatham 1941: 360). At one level, Swaminatha Aiyar's essay is clearly in line with compensatory classicism's agenda of presenting Tamil and Sanskrit as twin contributors to an Indic literary civilization. At another level, this exchange also shows that purists had to struggle against both upper-caste (Brahman and high "non-Brahman") and upper and middle-class linguistic dependence on Sanskritized Tamil.

Absence of explicit hostility towards Sanskrit also marked Indianism's efforts to cleanse Tamil (Ramalinga Pillai 1953;

Sivagnanam 1960). Between July and November 1915, a little prior to Maraimalai Adigal's explicit "conversion" to the pure Tamil cause, Subramania Sivam, Chidambaram Pillai, and others whose *tamil1ppar1r1u* found its expression in imagining an Indianized Tamil advocated the need for a *tan1ittamil1* style that would be free of foreign words, including Sanskrit and English; they even announced a prize (of five rupees) for anyone who would submit essays in pure Tamil. One of their statements specifically targeted Sanskrit as the "first enemy" of Tamil. Ironically—and showing the Sanskritic inflection of Indianist prose—their appeals continued to use the Sanskrit word for language, *pâs#â*, rather than the pure Tamil *mol1i* and were replete with other Sanskritic words.

These appeals by Sivam (and other Brahmans) have been interpreted by some apologists as proof that devotees who were nominally Brahman were not necessarily enamored with Sanskrit to the detriment of Tamil (Sivagnanam 1970: 91-93). All the same, Indianism's attempts to overcome the marked dependence on Sanskrit words was motivated less by religious, antiquarian, or political imperatives, as was the case with neo-Shaivism, contestatory classicism, and Dravidianism, than by its populist concern with supporting the "language of the people" (Sivathamby 1979: 48-67).

But the Tamil of most Tamil speakers for much of this century has been shot through with Sanskrit (and words from other languages). So, since Indianism also sought to ensure, like Dravidianism, that the "natural," "living" language of the people prevailed, it did not fetishize the elimination of Sanskritic words, confining itself instead to the discontinuation of arcane literary terms, both Sanskrit *and* Tamil, favored by orthodox pandits and scholars.

Further, in contrast to Maraimalai Adigal's *tan1ittamil1* movement, Indianism's call for cleansing Tamil was clearly anticolonial rather than anti-Brahman. Its predominant concern was with ridding English words from Tamil, and the expunging of Sanskrit was put on hold, for the time being at least. Indeed, responding to a criticism by a "Son of India" published in the nationalist daily *Cutçcamittiran1*, and realizing that essays submitted to his prize competition were unable to disentangle themselves from Sanskrit, in November 1915 Subramania Sivam went back on his earlier declaration of July 1915:

We have only insisted that we should write in a Tamil that is free of English. We have never said that we should have a *tan1ittamil1* that is free of Sanskrit....There is little doubt however that Tamil is a unique language (*tan1ipâs#ai*). Nevertheless, because of the interactions between Tamilians and Aryans for a long time, Tamilians have become habituated to innumerable Sanskrit words. If we thought it was possible to easily write essays these days in a *tan1ittamil1* that is free of Sanskrit, would we announce that we would reward someone for this?

Thus, for Indianism the elimination of colonialism and its language, English, took precedence over the task of de-Sanskritizing Tamil. In direct contrast, Maraimalai Adigal explicitly declared in 1927 at a presentation to the Karanthai Tamil Sangam that liberation from Aryanism and its language, Sanskrit, constituted the first "*cuyarâjyam*" ("independence") for Tamilians (M. Tirunavukarasu 1959: 528). Years later, Devaneyan Pavanar also insisted that Tamilnadu did not win its freedom with the withdrawal of the British. Only the withdrawal of Sanskrit would constitute true independence for Tamilians (Devaneyan 1972: 339). Contrary to what their critics may claim, however, these purists did not support the intrusion of English words into Tamil. Nonetheless, for them, unlike the Indianists, Sanskrit was the more enduring foe.

All these conflicting agendas for cleansing Tamil of "foreign" words came to a head in the 1930s, when its devout started to seek state patronage for the creation of appropriate vocabularies and glossaries for pedagogical purposes, and especially for instruction in the sciences (Nambi Arooran 1976: 339-40). As early as 1916, several devotees in Salem town had organized themselves into a Tamil Scientific Terms Society, and the first issue of its journal, edited by C. Rajagopalachari, confessed: "The greatest difficulty that confronts those who wish to produce books in the languages of the country...is, we believe, the absence of adequate and precise terms for scientific ideas and the chaotic state in which attempts to build up such terms are left to remain" (quoted in Irschick 1969: 303-4). Faced with this "difficulty" and "chaos," many turned, to the dismay of purists, to Sanskrit as the source for new scientific vocabularies. So, in 1932, the state sponsored glossary of scientific terms (*kalaiccol*) for pedagogical use was highly derivative from Sanskrit and also relied heavily on English. This only confirmed the purists' suspicion that the state was in the clutches of

Brahmanical elements who were enemies of Tamil (Ilankumaran 1991: 191-93; Tirumaran 1992: 244-46).

The release of this glossary galvanized many purists to organize, and in 1934, under the auspices of the Cen1n1ai Mâkân#at Tamil1c Cank#am (Madras Presidency Tamil Sangam), based in Tirunelveli, they formed a collective called the Kalaiccolâkkak Kal1akam (the Committee for Scientific Terms). They organized several conferences, ran a short lived journal called *Tamil1ttây*, and in 1938 published a glossary with around ten thousand technical terms in physics, chemistry, mathematics, geography, and other subjects. Along with coining *tan1ittamil1* terms, the glossary also eliminated the special *grantha* letters that had been incorporated into the premodern Tamil script to register Sanskritic phonology. Although the 1938 text was a real triumph for the *tan1ittamil1* cause, the state's glossaries and vocabularies for the next two decades continued to be dependent on Sanskrit and English (Ilankumaran 1991: 194-97, 202-6; E. M. Subramania Pillai 1951-52). Not surprisingly, into the 1950s purists lamented that "even though *tan1ittamil1* has the approval of the common people, it has not secured a place in government" (Tirumaran 1992: 167). Some DMK legislators even suggested that under cover of creating new administrative terms, the (Congress) government had given a new lease to Sanskrit words and erased authentic Tamil words from the people's life. Struggling under the sheer weight of centuries of administrative routines, the state's lukewarm response to *tan1ittamil1* efforts was undoubtedly motivated by its primary concern with ensuring bureaucratic efficiency and convenience of usage. At the same time, the party in power, the Congress, favored an Indianized Tamil and was especially hostile towards any anti-Sanskrit purification attempts.

This became particularly clear during the debates in the later half of the 1950s and the early 1960s over the Tamilization of the language of administration. Allapichai, a Congress legislator in the council, warned the government to keep out of state committees on administrative and pedagogical terminology "linguistic fanatics," who would only create vocabularies which might please ancient grammarians and purists, but would be incomprehensible to "the people." C. Subramaniam, the Congress minister for education, indeed put the ball back into the court of the purists by declaring in 1956: "The Tamil language has power (*cakti*).

Those who allege that exposure to the words of other languages will lead to its destruction, will block its development, and will tarnish its excellence must have no faith in the power of our Tamil language." Devotee cum legislator Muthukannappan responded, "We cannot forcibly bring in words from another language....[I]f we do so, Tamil1ttây is powerful. She will destroy these words, or she will subdue those other words. Everybody should recognize her power." Nonetheless, through the 1950s the Congress-led state put up a good deal of resistance to demands for ushering in the reign of (*tan1i*)Tamil. These included the replacement of the Sanskritic term *âkâúvân#i* for radio by the pure Tamil term, *vân1oli*, and the Tamilizing of personal honorific terms, *úrî* and *úrîmati*, as *tiru* and *tirumati*.

It was not until the DMK came to power in 1967 that such demands were fulfilled, and the pure Tamil cause received a boost, although purification efforts are not particularly high on the agenda of either the Dravidian movement or the Dravidianist idiom of *tamil1ppar1r1u*. Among the DMK government's first actions was to put up a giant sign, appropriately illuminated with neon lights, on the ramparts of the secretariat building in Madras, which read, in pure Tamil, *tamil1aka aracu talaimaic ceyalakam*, "head offices of the government of the Tamil land." The state motto in Sanskrit, *satyemeva jayate*, was translated—although not replaced—as the (*tan1i*) Tamil *vâymaiyç vellum*, "truth always triumphs" (Ramanujam 1971: 26). Sanskritic designations for various government officials, members of the state legislature, state departments, and so on were all replaced with pure Tamil equivalents, and today, in public functions conducted by the government as well as in official publications of all kinds, it is rare to encounter obviously Sanskritic or English words (although they are not entirely absent).

Since 1967, the Tamil that one hears on the radio, as well as on television, is comparatively free of non-Tamil words. State committees appointed by the DMK government for creating pedagogical and administrative terminologies, as well as for producing textbooks, have been dominated by purists, thus ensuring that pedagogical Tamil and bureaucratic Tamil are as pure as they can be (Annamalai 1979: 50). And indeed, the 1971 glossary of administrative terms released by the state seemed at last to be taking the right step in the direction of fulfilling the purist's dream that in the streets of Tamilnadu, it is (*tan1i*)Tamil that ought to reign.

What are some of the implications of the *tan1ittamil1* movement for the pursuit of *tamil1ppar1r1u?* Most immediately, it offers another striking example of how discourse about Tamil in the devotional community has translated itself into practice, and how this process has been plagued by so many problems, not least because of the multiple notions about the language that concurrently prevail. Tamil's devotees who have participated in the movement attempt to cleanse their own speech and writing styles; they use Tamil instead of Arabic numerals, and they follow a putative Tamil dating system that commences with the birth date of Tiruvalluvar, fixed by Maraimalai Adigal at 31 B.C.E. Over the past few decades, many have conducted public campaigns among merchants and shopkeepers in cities like Madurai and Coimbatore to Tamilize the names of commercial establishments (Tirumaran 1992: 255-56). In 1987, the state joined in this campaign by issuing similar orders (see Tamilkudimagan 1990 for the public response to this). Critics wonder if such efforts to Tamilize life and culture in Tamilnadu is akin to fighting a battle that has already been lost—first to Sanskritization, but these days more enduringly to Anglicization and westernization. They parody the neologisms of *tan1ittamil1* and criticize them for getting in the way of the "real" tasks of modernizing education, restructuring the economy, erasing social inequities, and so on. And they question its tyrannical and homogenizing tendencies that spell death for the creative and "natural" flow of language and literary culture (Tirumaran 1992: 273-320).

Yet, such criticisms notwithstanding, the pure Tamil movement has succeeded in *disabling* all those who had claimed that Tamil was incapable of expressing thoughts that could only be expressed in Sanskrit or English, and who maintained that Tamil cannot flourish without the aid of other languages; conversely, it has *enabled* those who wanted to use Tamil words but had been unable to do so because of the domination of words of other languages. From the 1930s on, *tan1ittamil1* adherents have published dictionaries and glossaries of "pure" Tamil words (including both neologisms as well as rehabilitated ancient ones) for use in public as well as domestic contexts. They have also provided Tamil speakers with lists of pure Tamil personal names as well as names for their houses, suggestions on how to write letters and publish invitations for special occasions without resorting to non-Tamil words, and so on (Nilambikai 1952).

All this does not minimize the reality that Tamil speakers of all class, caste, and professional backgrounds by and large continue to depend on words borrowed from other languages—Sanskrit, Telugu, Persian, Arabic, Hindustani, and English—for the myriad tasks of modernity. This only foregrounds the tragedy of not just the pure Tamil movement but of language purification efforts everywhere in the world. In seeking to cleanse languages, such movements attempt to resist and undo the reality of hybridity that characterize the societies in which they emerge (Vaiyapuri Pillai 1989: 4-12). Not surprisingly, it is this attempt to homogenize and singularize the language to conform to some imaginary pure originary moment that has invited the displeasure of critics. So, V. Ramaswamy, the well-known essayist and founder-editor of the literary journal *Man#ikkot#i*, asked: "What is Tamil? *paccaittamil1* is Tamil, so too is vulgar (*koccai*) Tamil. Marketplace Tamil is Tamil as well. A child's youthful prattle, too, is Tamil. Even the mixed *man#ipravâl#a* [Sanskritized] Tamil is Tamil" (quoted in Tirumaran 1992: 280).

But for the *tan1ittamil1* devotee, such a suggestion would be sacrilegious, as would be the corollary to this statement: the speakers of all these various forms of the language have the right to call themselves "Tamilians." Indeed, the *tan1ittamil1* movement attempts to transform Tamil speakers not just into subjects of Tamil but into subjects of a particular kind of Tamil—*tan1ittamil1*—that is deemed to be its only right and possible form. If Tamil devotionalism aims to ineluctably connect the subjectivity of Tamil speakers to the language, *tan1ittamil1* goes further and links this subjectivity to a particularly narrow and rigid definition of Tamil. The *tan1ittamil1* project is thus concerned not merely with cleansing the language but also with singularizing and homogenizing the subjectivity of its speakers, for ultimately, it is only the speaker of pure Tamil who is worthy of being called a Tamilian.

"WHAT'S IN A NAME?": RECHRISTENING MADRAS STATE

From the earliest days of *tamil1ppar1r1u*, the territorial space in which Tamil was spoken was referred to as either *tamil1akam*, "home of Tamil," or *tamil1nât#u*, "land/nation of Tamil," an area that in the colonial period was named "Madras." Since neither had an overtly political agenda, neo-Shaivism and classicism were not particularly concerned about conducting their devotional activities in a territorial space which both was ruled by a foreign power and was signified by a foreign word. But for Indianism and Dravidianism, with their obvious interest in ensuring the rule of Tamil in all spheres, it was sacrilegious that the very land in which the language was spoken did not officially bear its true Tamil name. Quoting from a primary school textbook, S. B. Adithan (1905-81) wrote indignantly in 1958: " 'The nation we inhabit is called India. In it, we inhabit the southern portion that is South India, called Madras State....' Here, we do not even see the term 'Tamil Nadu.' What is wrong in teaching that the land we inhabit is called 'Tamil Nadu'? Do they fear that if they use the term 'Tamil Nadu,' our impressionable Tamil children will develop attachment to Tamil Nadu?" (Adithanar 1965: 5).

To many a devotee of Tamil, this incongruity became especially inexcusable after 1956 when the multilingual Madras Presidency was dismantled, leaving only the Tamil-speaking region to continue on as Madras state. Prior to this date, adherents of Indianist inclination had been willing to wait till the Indian state had honored the demand for linguistic states, which were created only after a protracted struggle from the late 1930s through the mid-1950s. In turn, in 1938 the Dravidian movement had launched its battle cry, "Tamilnadu for Tamilians," a cry that by the early 1940s transmuted itself into "Dravidanadu [Dravidian nation] for Dravidians." For the next decade or so, until they had sorted out the many differences over whether they were fighting for the autonomy of Dravidians of the putative Dravidanadu, or just for the Dravidians of Tamilnadu, the DK and the DMK used both terms, Dravidanadu and Tamilnadu, interchangeably. After the States Reorganization Act of 1956, the dream of a multilingual Dravidanadu was abandoned, and followers of the Dravidian movement joined proponents of Indianism in their demand for renaming the state—with one major difference, of course (Karunanidhi 1989: 316-17, 519-21). For Dravidianism, at least until the early 1960s, the state renaming was linked to a separatist project for creating an independent Tamil nation. The Indianist regime, on the other hand, always steadfastly maintained that the renaming of the state as Tamilnadu was not contrary to the spirit of Indian nationalism. Indeed, it was a celebration of India's multilingual plurality.

These differences did not deter devotees of rival factions from coming together, with the common cause of ensuring that the state be renamed. In the late 1950s, the two political parties most enthusiastically concerned with this issue were the Nâm Tamil1ar (We Tamils) and Sivagnanam's Tamil Arasu Kazhagam. The We Tamils party was founded in 1958 by a wealthy London trained barrister, S. B. Adithan, the publisher of the popular Tamil daily *Tin1atanti.* The party's principal agenda was the founding of a sovereign Tamilnadu. The many ideological differences he had with Adithan and his own ambivalences over *tamil1ppar1r1u* notwithstanding, Ramasami lent his considerable influence to the We Tamils, his vision of a sovereign Dravidanadu having been rendered unfeasible (Anaimuthu 1974: 1878-79; E. V. Ramasami 1961). In 1960, the We Tamils conducted statewide protests for the secession of Madras and the establishment of a sovereign Tamilnadu. The protests were marked by the burning of maps of India (with Tamilnadu left out), and they led to the arrests of Adithan, Ramasami, and numerous others (Sundararajan 1986: 32-35). Soon after, in early 1961, Sivagnanam, an Indianist devotee of Tamil who was ideologically opposed to men like Adithan and Ramasami on many fronts, spearheaded the protests launched by his party, Tamil Arasu Kazhagam, outside government offices and the legislature in Madras, as well as in several other cities all over the state, leading to the arrest of hundreds (Sivagnanam 1974: 851-65).

These protests and arrests themselves followed the tragic death in Virudhunagar of a sixty-year-old Gandhian and lifelong social reformer, Shankaralinga Nadar (1895-1956), on 13 October 1956, after a prolonged fast of seventy-seven days. Foremost among his list of demands was the renaming of Madras state (Sundararajan 1986: 68-76). The Congress government ignored Shankaralingam's demands, and even the DMK later formally distanced itself from his act. But his sacrifice did not go unnoticed among Tamil's devout (Karunanidhi 1989: 282, 711; Pancanathan n.d.: 29-31; Sivagnanam 1974: 809-10). Indeed, a decade later when Madras was formally renamed Tamilnadu, Annadurai reminded his fellow members in the Legislative Assembly of Shankaralingam's martyrdom for the Tamil cause, and in 1970, when Karunanidhi became chief minister, a monthly pension was granted to the dead man's wife (Karunanidhi 1987b: 225).

Shankaralingam's death, prior to the 1957 general elections, did not visibly alarm the Congress party, but the protests of 1960-61 led by the We Tamils and the Tamil Arasu Kazhagam did elicit a response, highlighting as they did the growing threat of the Dravidian movement on the very eve of the 1962 elections. In early 1961, the government partially relented and, after a lengthy debate in the legislature, agreed that within Tamilnadu, when communications were conducted in Tamil, the name "Tamil Nad" would henceforth designate Madras state. For communications with other states, the central government, and the rest of the world, especially as these were conducted in English, the state would continue to be referred to as Madras. In consigning the English name, "Madras," to use in the world outside the Tamil-speaking region, which would henceforth be designated by the Tamil name, "Tamilnadu" (albeit misspelled "Tamil Nad"), the state's legislation at least conceded the devotional community's demand that in the intimate sphere of the home and the family, it is Tamil that should reign.

But the respite purchased with this gesture was only temporary, for many of the devout and the rival political parties that backed them continued to keep the pressure on the government. In 1963, the matter was debated at length in the Indian Parliament where, following the submission of a nonofficial bill, Annadurai offered an impassioned defense for unilaterally adopting the name "Tamilnadu" on all fronts. The bill was turned down, on the grounds that the request had to be made officially by the state government. However, in 1964 the Congress government of M. Bhaktavatsalam, already pushed to the wall by the rising wave of anti-Hindi sentiment in the state, once again rejected renewed demands. It was not until the DMK came to power that things changed. One of its very first acts was to pass a resolution in July 1967 confirming the change of name, and on 14 January 1969, Madras state was officially rechristened Tamilnadu. So, after more than a decade of petitioning and debating, and after many centuries of having been a literary and cultural reality, "Tamilnadu" became a political reality as well. When Annadurai "raised his voice to say 'Hail, Tamil Nadu,' every member, including Congressmen followed suit. How could any Tamilian remain unmoved?"

(Ramanujam 1971: 26). Through the maze of petitions and protests, it is clear that the Congress—the "nationalist" party that under colonial rule took pride in contesting English, and that fostered linguistic consciousness in the Madras Presidency as a counter to British power—increasingly pushed itself, and was in turn thrust, into a corner from which it vigorously defended the legitimacy of the colonial inheritance. Its spokesmen insisted that they were in favor of retaining the old colonial name as a matter of expediency; in no way should this be mistaken as an absence of "love" for Tamil on the Congress's part. "We have foreign monuments and roads and streets named after foreign persons.... We have indeed so much else of the hangover of the past that we cannot take a big broom and sweep them away." There were several grounds on which this paradoxical defense of the colonial "hangover" was mounted. First, the Congress insisted that in contrast to "Madras," the name under which "we have lived for centuries," the name "Tamil Nadu" had no foundation in the literature and history of the region. The Congress persisted in this argument over the years. So, in May 1963, T. S. Pattabhiraman declared in the Rayja Sabha:

> There has been Bengal and there must be Kerala historically. But there has been no Tamil Nad historically. It is only the creation of politicians, of political parties of a recent date. There was nothing in existence as a unified Tamil Nad till about five hundred years ago. It was "Pandya Nad" or "Chera Nad" or "Chola Nad." There has never been historically a "Tamil Nad." And why do you want to create a new one, when historically it is not justified? It is not justified politically. It is not justified democratically.

Not surprisingly, this argument about the alleged illegitimacy of "Tamil Nadu" and the implicit historical legitimacy of "Madras" provoked angry responses. The most notable of these were Annadurai's documentation of the deep historicity and antiquity of the term during the parliamentary debate in 1963 and Sivagnanam's similar effort in the Madras legislature in 1967. "The name Tamilnadu did not appear yesterday or today. We hear of the name from the time of Tolkappiyar 2,500 years ago," skeptics were told. As its detractors did not fail to point out, the absurdity of the government's position was apparent from the fact that the ruling party's regional wing had renamed itself *Tamilnadu* Congress in the 1920s. Indeed, throughout the debates in both Madras and New Delhi, all parties concerned, including the Congress, liberally used the term "Tamilnadu" when they referred to Madras state. As one critic of the government remarked astutely, "Their very speeches nail down this point. What [we] seek to do is to give *de jure* recognition to a *de facto* fact that is there."

Second, the Congress insisted that the word *nât#u* in the compound "Tamilnadu" was inherently dangerous, for it suggested that Tamil speakers might want a separate nation (*nât#u*) of their own and did not want to be a part of *pârata nât#u*, "India." Bharati may have referred to the Tamil space as *centamil1nât#u*, "glorious Tamilnadu." But "that might have been appropriate in song, and for arousing devotion towards one's *nât#u*. Today, however, we are independent and rule ourselves under a parliamentary system.... Is Tamilnadu our *nât#u* or is it India that is our *nât#u?* How can we say that this is our *nât#u* and that too is our *nât#u?*"

Here, Chief Minister Bhaktavatsalam was deliberately playing upon the multiple meanings that have historically coalesced around the word *nât#u*, the most recent of which, of course, was the modern sense of "nation" that Bharati, Kalyanasundaram, and others had popularized from the turn of the century. This was a strategic move on Bhaktavatsalam's part, for it was bound to remind everyone that the parties demanding the renaming had been only a few years ago also demanding secession from India in the name of a sovereign Tamilnadu. Given that Madras was in the throes, in the early 1960s, of the most violent of anti-Hindi protests, renaming the state Tamilnadu would be tantamount to surrendering to "antinationalist" forces, in the view of the government. Further, such a renaming would also alienate the many non-Tamil-speaking peoples who still lived in the state and considered it their home. Would this mean that they would have to leave the state? "The 'We Tamil' Party will say that only Tamilians should reside in Tamil Nad and all others should get out. This will be opening the Pandora's box."

Third, and most consistently and steadfastly, the government repeatedly asserted that much was invested in the name "Madras," for it was the name by which everybody in the world knew the state. "When our eminent people go to America, to Germany, and to France, they are recognized only if they say they are from

Madras." What would happen to the reputation and fame of the state if Tamilians gave up its familiar name and adopted a new name such as "Tamilnadu"? supporters of "Madras" asked repeatedly. Another Congress member pointed out—most injudiciously, under the circumstances—"Just because 42 per cent of the people in India speak Hindi, we do not call it Hindi Nad." More astutely, in 1964 Bhaktavatsalam reminded everyone that by retaining the colonial word, the government was not declaring its devotion to the English language; instead, it was staking a claim on the very name "Madras," at a time when there was such danger of losing the city that bore that name to neighboring Andhra Pradesh. It is our way of saying to the Andhras that Madras is "ours," not "yours," he declared. Indeed, it is telling that until the very end, even when the renaming resolution was submitted by the DMK in 1967 and every other party supported it unanimously, the Congress representative, Karuthiruman, suggested that perhaps members should consider the hyphenated term "Tamilnadu-Madras state," which in his view conveyed a desirable union of the English and Tamil names. In effect, the Congress, this most "anticolonial" of political parties in the state, was implicitly declaring that modern Tamil speakers as a political and territorial community could only have a presence in the world by allowing themselves to be mediated through a colonial category.

There are good political reasons why the Congress doggedly refused to accede to the demand for renaming, even though prior to 1947, it had just as vigorously sponsored the cultivation of linguistic consciousness and regional pride to neutralize colonial power. "I do not see any reason why, when we [Indians] are in power, we should not give effect to what had been done when we were not in power," one of its critics wondered. But the reasons would have been apparent to everyone, as the demand for renaming was most enthusiastically voiced by parties which were clearly in opposition to the Congress, and whose strength was on the rise in the various regions of the nation. That itself was a sign that linguistic and regional pride (as sponsored by these oppositional parties) would challenge the nation (and the Congress party). The establishment of linguistic states, the internecine struggles between them over borders and resources, the switch to regional languages for their administration, and the resistance from various quarters to Hindi all pointed towards the fragmentation that threatened the union of India, as well as Congress power. As one Congress member put it, "It will be opening the Pandora's Box, once you begin to give recognition for a language as the basis for renaming a state." Pushed against the wall by the upsurge of linguistic sentiments, the Congress was repeatedly forced to take a stand that went against its own reputation as a defender of linguistic consciousness in the colonial period. So the same party that had vigorously upheld de-Anglicization and vernacularization, and that had renamed the Parliament "Lok Sabha" and India "Bharat," now held out against the demand for renaming Madras: "they want the names to be changed after the language; *just because* it was named by the British people, they want to change it." The (mock) incredulity in this member's tone betrays the Congress's realization that the "Pandora's box" of linguistic pride that it had helped open, as an anticolonial strategy, had to be now tightly reclosed if the union (and Congress power) were to be maintained, even if this led it to mount a defense of English and the colonial inheritance.

Thus the Congress was compelled to make its case on pragmatic grounds: everybody in the world knows us as Madras; why should we risk losing our reputation by changing our name? When there were "so many problems of importance concerning the daily life of the people with which we are trying to grapple," the demand for renaming was not just inconsequential but even distracting:

> It is perhaps necessary to remind ourselves that in this House we are trying to tackle fundamentals. Once we find proper solutions to basic questions affecting our life, the life of the society, its economics, its goals, political and social, the rest will take care of themselves. When we solve our economic problems, when we solve our cultural problems, these changes in names of places and of roads and of persons will adjust themselves to the changing conditions.

The Congress's materialist pragmatism sharply contrasts with the devotees' "sentimental" attachment to the name "Tamilnadu." The government may well have asked, "What is in a name?" but for Tamil's devotees, and various other supporters of the renaming, this particular name was everything, for it was the one "named after our language." When asked "What do you gain by renaming [Madras] as Tamil Nadu?" Annadurai replied: "We gain satisfaction sentimentally; we gain the satisfaction that an ancient name is inculcated in the hearts of millions and scores of millions of people. Is that not enough compensation for the small trouble of changing the name?" By renaming Madras as Tamilnadu, "something is changed in our thinking, in our soul, in our fiber," he concluded. Similarly, a few years later, Sivagnanam declared, "Nobody has a right to refer to me by someone else's name....I should be referred to by the name of my language, my ethnicity, and my land." For its devotees, the very "fundamentals" of life and livelihood were invested in Tamil. The honor shown their language by renaming their state after it was far from an incidental matter that would follow after the "basic questions affecting life" had been tended to. For Tamil, as they had repeatedly asserted, was life itself.

ENTHRONEMENT OF TAMIL: DILEMMAS OF RULE

In December 1956, on the very eve of the 1957 general elections, the Madras legislature passed a bill instituting Tamil as the official language of the state (*ât#ci mol1i;* lit., "language of rule"). The implications of the bill were potentially momentous for the course of *tamil1ppar1r1u,* for it was declared that progressively over the next few years, all the official proceedings of the Madras government, so far dominated by English, would be entirely conducted in Tamil. Certain important caveats notwithstanding (such as the continued use of English in courts, especially at the higher levels), the bill seemed to fulfill a long cherished dream of the entire devotional community: namely, Tamil ought to reign, once again, in its own land. As one member, R. Krishnaswami Naidu, enthusiastically declared in the Legislative Assembly, "All our troubles have now ceased as Tamil1ttây reclines in royal style on her auspicious throne." Another member echoed this sentiment, proclaiming that "from now on, we will progress and advance."

Embedded in these as well as in many other declarations made in the legislature in the 1950s and 1960s was the implicit recognition that until the state intervened in Tamil improvement activities that had hitherto been conducted largely by the devotional community, the language and its speakers would not really prosper. As Gajapathy Nayakar, a Tamil scholar who was also a member of the Legislative Council, declared, resorting to the logic of gender endemic to *tamil1ppar1r1u:* "It is only when a man marries a woman that family life can be conducted. In the same manner, we should think of the state as man, and the language as woman. It is only out of their union that proper rule will ensue."

And yet, over the next few years the state itself repeatedly admitted its inability to ensure the rule of Tamil in its own land and in the community of its speakers. Only a few years after he presented the Tamil as Official Language Bill with such enthusiasm in 1956, C. Subramaniam was compelled to confess: "As a first task, we restored her rightful throne back to Tamil1ttây. We did this believing that if our Tamil1ttây were enthroned, we would be filled with happiness, and that happiness would give us the enthusiasm to attend to our other tasks. However, even though we have now installed Tamil as our lofty language of rule, we have been unable to implement it" (C. Subramaniam 1962: 24). What accounts for the state's helplessness in Tamilizing itself, and what does this state of helplessness imply about the cause of *tamil1ppar1r1u?*

Here, it is instructive to consider the debate on the bill in the legislature in December 1956, for this itself anticipated many of the problems the state faced over the next few decades in implementing its provisions. First, this was one of the rare occasions in which the figure of Tamil1ttây entered arenas of government and found a presence in official discourse. It is telling that Subramaniam, the education minister, offered the bill as a ritual tribute to Tamil1ttây, declaring that members should set aside their political differences and join in her "enthronement ceremony" (*mut#icût#t#uvil1â*). He was not alone in invoking her name, and the speeches made by other members were liberally sprinkled with references to the "liberation" of Tamil1ttây and her "enthronement." Both metaphors clearly suggested that Tamil1ttây, the former queen of the Tamil kingdom who had been displaced from her throne by rival languages and had been reduced to the status of a lowly maid (*pan#ippen#*), had now been restored to her rightful place in the hierarchy of power and command. In enabling her reinstatement, not only did the legislators fulfill their own "debt" (*kat#an1*) as her subjects/children, but they also signaled their intention to ensure that despite the continued presence of other languages (English and Hindi, most notably) in the Tamil home/kingdom, Tamil would reign supreme. It would rule as the language of power, while the others would merely be languages of communication with the rest of India and the world. The Official Language Act might well be the fruit of the decades of hard work put in towards Tamil's liberation by its devotees, as Subramaniam graciously acknowledged in his opening remarks. All the same, the act would be the instrument with which the importance of Tamil would be impressed upon recalcitrant sections of the society, through the agency of the state. Ironically, therefore, at what ought to have been a moment of great triumph for its devotees, the act clearly represented the realization that love or passion for Tamil would not ensure that it prosper as much as would material and pragmatic considerations. Jobs and the exercise of power were now dependent on knowing and using the language: "If Tamil comes in as language of rule, and if we insist that it is the language everyone has to learn in colleges, how many will want to read Shakespeare and Milton?...Desire for the Cank#am poems will bloom. Tamil, too, will flourish." Political power and material needs perhaps would secure for Tamil what love and passion had so far not accomplished.

Second, from the start, the state openly acknowledged that for the time being, the enthronement of Tamil was more symbolic than real. It was all well and good to "love" Tamil, but logistically, the rule of Tamil would take time, enthusiasm, and resources to implement. "If we decide suddenly that everything has to be in Tamil, that will only give rise to confusion," Subramaniam informed legislators in December 1956. L. Raghava Mudaliar warned his fellow legislators that devotion to the language (*mol1ippar1r1u*) should not lead them to a hasty implementation of an *ât#ci mol1i*, "official language," that would be incomprehensible to the very people for whose benefit it was being created. It was therefore decided that the official language policy would at first be implemented, starting in 1958-59, in eight departments of government. By 1962, this was abandoned in favor of implementation in four phases (Kumaramangalam 1965: 68-73). It was acknowledged that it would be easiest to switch to Tamil as *ât#ci mol1i* at the lowest rungs of the district administration where English had hardly penetrated. It would be most difficult to ensure the use of Tamil at the highest levels of government, in the state secretariat at Madras, and this was scheduled for only the fourth phase. It is telling that no time limit was explicitly stipulated for the unilateral use of Tamil in all spheres.

Indeed, the state's troubles over the next few years show clearly that it took the plunge before it was ready. Subramaniam himself compared his government's dilemma to that of someone who did not know how to swim but realized that he could only learn by throwing himself into the water. This analogy is quite revealing, for the list of tasks to be accomplished before Tamil could actually become *ât#ci mol1i* was formidable, ranging from the technological to the ideological. For instance, Tamil could not really be used for bureaucratic communication until government offices were stocked with Tamil typewriters. This in turn depended on the standardization of the keyboard, on which there was much disagreement from the start. Further, typists had to learn to use these Tamil keyboards, and a network of training institutes, as well as economic incentives for those who underwent the training, had to be set up. The absence of skills in Tamil shorthand was also a glaring problem.

Another key requirement, of course, was the creation of a glossary of Tamil administrative terms. Here, in addition to the ongoing debate between purists and nonpurists on the relative "Tamilness" of these terms, there was the more demanding task of overcoming years of bureaucratic dependence on English, especially in higher circles of the government, and instilling in its place the new habit of using Tamil. Further, once the glossary was created, various laws and statutes had to be translated into Tamil. In certain areas, such as legal procedures, there was doubt from the very beginning whether Tamil was even capable of expressing "with precision" the language of the courts. Finally, all these measures depended on the existence of a pool of government officers and clerical staff who were equipped to use Tamil in administrative contexts. Many legislators pointed out the obvious paradox of bringing in Tamil as language of rule, even before institutionalizing its use in school and college education. But here, as late as 1963, Chief Minister Bhaktavatsalam dismissed demands for Tamil as principal medium of instruction in colleges as "not a practical proposition,...not...in the interests of national integration, not in the interests of higher education, and not in the interests of the students themselves" (quoted in Kumaramangalam 1965: 62-63). Even a casual survey of government records in the 1950s and 1960s shows that this brief treatment only touches upon the surface of the numerous dilemmas faced by the state in implementing the bill that was passed so confidently in December 1956.

So, why did the state take the plunge well-before it was remotely ready to govern in Tamil? One obvious reason is that it gave in to the continual demand for bringing in such legislation, voiced since at least the 1920s not just by Tamil's devotees but also by Congress nationalists. In 1948, two districts had been selected for a trial run; the relative lack of success of this experiment did not deter supporters of Tamil from continuing to push their cause. Up until 1956, the reality of Madras's multilinguality prevented any easy abandonment of English. Indeed, over the years from the 1920s, there had been repeated demands from various legislators that the "regional language" (which invariably meant Tamil) ought to be the language of the legislature, since a growing number of members of that august body did not know English (Sundaresan 1986). A. Ramalingam declared in March 1939, "I do not understand [anything] if English is spoken in this Assembly. I only understand Tamil. Our land is Tamilnadu. We ought to speak in Tamil." Such a demand, not to mention the continual overwriting of "Madras Presidency" as "Tamilnadu," only caused anxiety and hostility among non-Tamil-speaking legislators, which in turn mirrored the confusion that would prevail if Tamil indeed became the language of rule in a multilingual province. By late 1956, however, after the linguistic states became a political reality, the Congress government in Madras was hard pressed to defend itself successfully from the criticisms increasingly leveled against it by opposition parties for being soft on Tamil issues. Although the government resisted this accusation, there were many who pointed out that the Congress rushed through the legislation on Tamil as official language as a preelection gesture. I would also suggest that whenever the state had passed such a bill, it would have faced similar problems. For there was growing consensus that mandating the use of Tamil through legislation was the only way to ensure the Tamilization of the administration and bureaucracy. The limits of *tamil1ppar1r1u* as well as of community-spurred improvement activities are clearly revealed in this realization.

Third, the state's 1956 legislation also showed up the category of "mother tongue" for what it was: a metaphorical construct. The demand for Tamil as the language of rule drew its power from

Indianist and Dravidianist assertions that the language of the people—of their homes and their mothers—ought to be the language of government. Yet there was dawning awareness that just because a language had been imbibed through one's mother's milk, or learned at her knee, one did not necessarily "know" the language sufficiently to administer a modern state with it. Indeed, the technologies and complexities of modern government inevitably inserted a gap between the *ât#ci mol1i*, "official language," and the *tâymol1i*, "the mother tongue," although they might both be named "Tamil." So, for much of the decade following 1956, legislators and planners argued the pros and cons of ensuring that the *ât#ci mol1i* stay as close as possible to the *tâymol1i*. There were purists among the legislators (many of whom, like V. V. Ramasami and Muthukannappan, were Tamil scholars and devotees) who demanded the complete erasure of all Sanskritic and English words from the language of rule, insisting that there was little reason to ponder at length over the creation of new administrative terms, for these had existed from time immemorial since the days of the *Tirukkur1al#* and the *Cilappatikâram*. Those who countered this demand maintained that an *ât#ci mol1i* based on old Tamil would be totally incomprehensible to the people. An insistence on "pure" Tamil words was not an expression of *tamil1ppar1r1u* but of *tamil1ver1i*, "Tamil fanaticism," one legislator insisted.

The Congress government itself adopted an anti-English and pro-Sanskrit stance. Only the elimination of English words was set up as part of the government's strategy for creating the *ât#ci mol1i*, on the grounds that Sanskritic words were comprehensible to the people, and hence were "Tamil," after all. And even in this respect, the government was quite flexible, appropriating as "Tamil" all those English words (such as "revenue" or "police") that had become naturalized in popular parlance. Here, the government's position was similar to that of liberals who maintained that English words like "collector" or "radio" were so much part of the vocabulary of the Tamil speaker that these, too, were Tamil, and ought not to be eliminated in favor of some unfamiliar and panditic neologism. One cannot legislate into existence a totally new language, it was asserted. In contrast to Tamil's devotees, who insisted that their language was their life and soul, some legislators like Allapichai declared (in English):

"Language is only a vehicle of expression that we speak in....[I]t is only a vehicle of thought to express oneself better. Such being the case, there is no meaning whatsoever in insisting upon people to speak only in Tamil." Insisting that it was unfair to dismiss those who wished to speak English or Sanskritized Tamil or English-inflected Tamil as disloyal Tamilians, some legislators reiterated that the institution of Tamil as official language did not necessarily mean the elimination of other tongues from Tamilnadu. On the contrary, Tamil would benefit by drawing upon all languages to enrich itself (C. Subramaniam 1962: 19-20).

Thus in the debate on the *ât#cimol1i*, there was an important reversal of the relationship between the language and its speaker. The devotional community had defined a Tamilian as one whose "mother tongue" was Tamil. Language defined the speaker, as the latter was rendered a subject of Tamil through *tamil1ppar1r1u.* In contrast, when the state stepped in to institute the "mother tongue" as language of rule, it became clear that the speaker defined the language: "Tamil" was whatever the Tamilian spoke, be it shot through with English, Sanskrit, or any other language. Language was thus defined by the speaker: "The Tamil that the people understand is good Tamil," in Subramaniam's words. The subjection of the speaker to the language in the discourses of Tamil devotion was thus unsettled by the work of the state.

Finally, the debate on the institution of Tamil as official language and the subsequent attempts to implement it show that in spite of having been grandly (re)installed as "queen" of the Tamil state in 1956, Tamil1ttây was not really sovereign in her own kingdom. As late as 1970, the government was compelled to confess that "in no department is business conducted 100 percent in Tamil," and its devotees insist that this is true even today. Most immediately, it is the continued dependence by the state on English that limits Tamil's sovereignty. The devotional community, including adherents of Indianism, the most anti-English of its regimes, conceded that English was necessary for the development of the sciences, for keeping up with the rest of India, and for the continued participation of the Tamilian in an international world. For its devotees, however, Tamil ought to reign supreme within the Tamil home and homeland. But the government repeatedly confessed in the 1950s and 1960s that even within the Tamil homeland, the "use of English will be unavoidable" and "that we are not able to give up English." Ironically, the speeches made by numerous legislators in December 1956, when the "Tamil as Official Language Bill" was offered as a "ritual tribute" to Tamil1ttây, were replete with Sanskritized Tamil and English words. Over the next few years as well, Tamil speeches delivered in the legislature continued to be dominated by Sanskrit and English, and several Tamil scholars-cum-legislators periodically submitted resolutions calling attention to the fact that in the state's highest governing body, Tamil still did not reign. As one of them lamented, expressing his dismay in gendered terms, "Tamil is the mother, English is the companion (*tôl1i*). The mother needs the help of the companion. But the companion has displaced the mother and even become the lover [of the Tamilian], with whom she romps around, hand in hand." And in the years following 1956, English continued to rule the roost, drawing strength from arguments that Tamil was not precise enough, that it was not neat and clear enough to be used for writing government notes, that complicated scientific and technical terminology could just not possibly be expressed through it, and so on.

But it is not English alone that troubles Tamil. As long as Tamilnadu is part of the Indian union, Hindi also continues to erode Tamil's absolute sovereignty. As the official language of the nation, Hindi vies with Tamil even within its own homeland on money order and telegraph forms, on postage stamps and currency notes, as well as in military, railway, and other central government institutions that are based in the land of Tamil. Hindi has continued to be taught in schools affiliated to the central government's education board and in schools run by minorities even after 1968 when the state government legislated out the language from its schools; and it has taken up the lion's share of nationalized television broadcasts until recently. Further, it is knowledge of Hindi (and/or English), rather than of Tamil, that provides access to lucrative central government employment. Indeed, critics like Mohan Kumaramangalam argued in 1965 that "instead of the regional language becoming *more* and *more* dominant, the tendency in the non-Hindi areas [like Tamilnadu] was already beginning to slip back towards English, almost as if it were in defence against the advance of Hindi" (Kumaramangalam 1965: 51). In Kumaramangalam's reckoning, a fundamental inequity had been written into the constitutional position of Indian languages through the privileging of Hindi. In the triangular battle between Hindi, English, and Tamil, it is the latter that has suffered the gravest injuries and is facing a slow death.

Kumaramangalam's critique did not raise the possibility that Tamil might never be sovereign as long as Tamil speakers participated in the Indian union. But other critics did openly make this argument. Adithan, the founder of the We Tamils movement, wrote in his *Tamil1p Pçraracu* (The Tamil empire) that not until Tamilnadu overthrew the "imperialism" of Delhi and Hindi could Tamil truly become a sovereign language of rule (Adithanar 1965: 26-30). And the parties of the Dravidian movement used such an argument through much of the 1950s and 1960s both to empower themselves and eventually to rise to power in 1967 by battling the "demoness Hindi."

Battling the Demoness Hindi

On 23 January 1968, the Madras government decreed that the central government's three-language formula would no longer be in effect in schools under its jurisdiction; henceforth, students were not required to study Hindi. As of that date, Hindi, the putative official language of India, was deprived of pedagogical and political privilege in the state.

This legislation followed the resumption of anti-Hindi protests in December 1967 that involved considerable loss of lives and property. These protests were launched in response to the Official Languages Amendment Bill passed by the Indian Parliament on 16 December, which strengthened the position of Hindi relative to English and overturned an earlier resolution specifically stating that a compulsory knowledge of Hindi was not mandatory for central government employment.

Perceiving a direct threat to their fortunes and futures, college students in Tamilnadu mounted fierce anti-Hindi demonstrations all over the state, the more radical among them demanding immediate secession from the nation. These protests were not just directed at the central government but also threatened the very stability of the newly elected DMK government in the state. The DMK may have promised to protect Tamil from Hindi and risen to power on the strength of its anti-Hindi leadership. Nonetheless, if the protests had not been so ferocious, it might not have been compelled to legislate against Hindi in Tamilnadu (Barnett 1976: 240-49; Ramanujam 1971: 28-40).

In successfully passing the anti-Hindi legislation, the DMK did reinforce its image as Tamil's guardian. All the same, the circumstances under which Hindi was legislated against suggest that the state had, once again, succumbed reluctantly to Tamilizing itself. Indeed, even earlier, from the 1930s through the 1950s, the Congress-led state government had often been compelled by local pressures to take a position in opposition to the dictates of the party's high command in New Delhi. Soon after independence, when the central government urged all states to promote the compulsory study of Hindi in preparation for its installation as the sole official language of the union in 1965, a vigorous series of protests in 1948-49 led the Madras government to make it an optional subject. Through the 1950s, the Madras government kept the pressure on the central government to retain English alongside Hindi as official language, its education minister P. Subbarayan even appending a lengthy dissenting note to the report of the Official Language Commission in 1956 (Subbarayan 1956). Caught between the central government's demands and pressures at home, the Madras state's Hindi policy from the 1930s through 1968 was dogged by contradictions, retractions, and ultimately failure.

The 1968 anti-Hindi legislation followed a half century of intense opposition to the language. The specific occasion which sparked off the first wave of protests was an April 1938 order by the Congress government of C. Rajagopalachari ordering the compulsory study of Hindi in 125 secondary schools in the Madras Presidency. The government justified its action thus:

The attainment by our Province of its rightful place in the national life of India requires that our educated youth should possess a working knowledge of the most widely spoken language in India. Government have therefore decided upon the introduction of Hindustani in the secondary school curriculum of our province. Government desire to make it clear that Hindi is not to be introduced in any elementary school whatsoever, the mother tongue being the only language taught in such schools. Hindi is to be introduced only in secondary schools and there too only in the 1st, 2nd and 3rd forms, that is to say in the 6th, 7th and 8th years of school life. It will not therefore interfere in any way with the teaching of the mother tongue in the secondary schools....Hindi will be compulsory only in the sense that attendance in such classes will be compulsory and pupils cannot take Hindi as a substitute for Tamil, Telugu, Malayalam or Kannada, but must learn Hindi only in addition to one of these languages.

Despite the government's insistence that the "mother tongue" was in no way endangered by the Hindi policy, this is exactly how it was interpreted by many devotees of Tamil. Between late 1937 and early 1940, they spearheaded numerous anti-Hindi demonstrations which led to the incarceration of close to 1,200 and to the death of two young men. Although this particular order was withdrawn in February 1940, the Congress continued to promote Hindi in Madras schools into the 1950s, even in the face of mounting resistance. Throughout this period, the anti-Hindi cause was clearly linked to the DK and DMK's separatist demand for a sovereign Dravidian or Tamil nation. No longer content with protest marches and making speeches, protesters tarred Hindi names on official name boards, picketed stores run by North Indians, burned facsimiles of the Indian map and the Constitution (itself characterized as the material manifestation of Hindi imperialism), obstructed train services, and so on. Following the 1963 constitutional amendment that banned political parties with separatist agendas, overt demands for secession were muted in Madras, although not entirely absent. Instead, the focus was on reversing the provisions of the Constitution which decreed that on 26 January 1965, English would be replaced by Hindi as the *sole* official language of India. In the most dramatic phase of the anti-Hindi movement, launched in 1963, hundreds were arrested; schools and colleges were closed as thousands of students all over the state took to protest marches; several hundred students went on hunger fasts; and the effigy of the "demoness" Hindi, as well as Hindi books, was burned. There was extensive damage to government and private property; and many lives were lost. Not least, it was at this time that *tamil1ppar1r1u* acquired its most celebrated martyrs with the self-immolation of Chinnasami and others.

In numerous respects, these waves of anti-Hindi protests have critically shaped the contours of party politics in modern Tamilnadu, arguably more so than the anticolonial agitations against the British. A steady stream of anti-Hindi demonology from the 1930s clearly identified and vilified the putative enemies of Tamil. These included Hindi-speaking North Indians/Aryans, Tamil Brahmans, and the state government in the clutches of these Brahmans. But above all, this demonology discredited the Tamilnadu Congress party, despite numerous differences within its own ranks on the Hindi issue. Over the decades, the party found it difficult to shake loose the reputation it acquired as the "enemy" and "slayer" of Tamil1ttây, as a front for Brahman and Bania (North Indian merchant) interests, and as a stooge in the hands of "Hindi imperialists" of the North. Caught between coping with the dictates of its high command in New Delhi and stemming the growing popularity of the Dravidian movement in Madras, the Tamilnadu Congress became a victim of its attempts to broker Tamil interests in the national arena. By the same token, all of the party's rivals—the Justice Party, the DK, the DMK, the Tamil Arasu Kazhagam, the We Tamils, and others—were able to promote themselves as protectors of Tamil and as true representatives of Tamil interests, precisely by opposing the Congress's Hindi policy. These parties spearheaded the Hindi protests in the state, providing popular and organizational ballast to *tamil1ppar1r1u*'s arguments against the language even as they reaped rich political rewards in the process. To this day, one of the surest ways to gain political and electoral support in Tamilnadu is to raise the anti-Hindi standard, and it is telling that since 1967, the Congress has never returned to power in the state.

All the same, growing numbers of Tamil speakers have in recent years taken to studying the language, and Hindi propagation societies are doing a thriving business in Tamilnadu today. Indeed, except for a brief few months when the angry sentiments against the language spilled over into antagonism towards Hindi movies and songs, the latter have a popularity in Tamilnadu quite incommensurate with Hindi's pedagogical and political status in the state. It would be a mistake, therefore, to assume there has been no popular support for Hindi in Tamilnadu. Well before the state took up its cause in the late 1930s, various civic organizations began promoting Hindi in the Presidency. While the need for a common language other than English was voiced in Madras newspapers by the turn of this century, with both Hindi/Hindustani and Sanskrit being proffered as early candidates, concerted efforts to spread Hindi date to the founding of the

Dakshin Bharat Hindi Prachar Sabha (Institution for the Propagation of Hindi in South India) in 1918 by Gandhi. The Sabha ran schools, trained teachers, conducted examinations, and awarded numerous diplomas of proficiency, though well into the 1930s the Tamil-speaking area lagged behind others in the Presidency in its enthusiasm for Hindi (Nambi Arooran 1980: 186-91). The Sabha's endeavors received a boost when the Indian National Congress decreed in 1925 that all its proceedings, hitherto carried out in English, "shall be conducted as far as possible in Hindustani" and provided funds for the promotion of the language (Nayar 1969: 59-60). Through the 1920s and 1930s, the Sabha, as well as other organizations such as the Hindustani Seva Dal and the Hindustani Hitashi Mandal, petitioned the state to join in the promotion of Hindi in the Presidency and succeeded in convincing many Congress-led local governments to introduce the compulsory study of Hindi in schools in the 1930s (Irschick 1986: 212-14; Nambi Arooran 1980: 188-94). So Rajagopalachari's decision to make the study of Hindi mandatory was not a total innovation. Nevertheless, the extension of state patronage to what had hitherto largely been a civic and Congress party activity completely changed the stakes in the Hindi game, especially in the face of complaints of Tamil's devotees that the state was not doing much to promote the study of Tamil.

All the same, it would also be a mistake to argue, as the Congress did, that popular hostility towards Hindi was an illusion. For example, Rajagopalachari declared in 1938 that the opposition to Hindi did not stem from devotion to Tamil but was mounted by those "cursed with the prejudices of anti-Aryanism" and "with the hatred of Congress" (Nambi Arooran 1980: 195). Through the 1950s and early 1960s, other Congress leaders continued to insist that the DK and the DMK had duped the hapless Tamil masses by stirring up anti-Hindi sentiments in order to garner power for themselves. Yet, ironically, if there is one effort that succeeded—more so than any other undertaken by Tamil's devotees and pro-Tamil politicians—in making *tamil1ppar1r1u* visible among a general populace, it was the Hindi policy of the central and state governments. As I have already noted, the anti-Hindi movement took Tamil devotional ideas out of the narrow elite and literary circles in which they had hitherto circulated. For the first time in the 1930s, the idea that Tamil might be endangered caught on among those who were not necessarily its ardent devotees; consequently, the hitherto scholarly, elite male ranks of Tamil's devotees swelled over the years with the addition of the street poet, the petty shopkeeper, the small time pamphleteer, the college going student, and the woman. By the 1960s, even the English-speaking middle class, which had hitherto stayed out of both Tamil devotional activities and the anti-Hindi movement, was galvanized (Barnett 1976; Rocher 1963).

Equally ironically, it is the battle against Hindi, rather than any sustained activity on behalf of Tamil, which spurred the devotional community to unite in harmony, setting aside differences and dissensions. Regardless of their disagreements over the meaning of Tamil, proponents of neo-Shaivism, contestatory classicism, and Dravidianism came together in response to the threat posed by Hindi by the late 1930s. Devotees of Indianist persuasion still kept their distance from this emerging consensus, but this was to change by the late 1940s, as is apparent from the attendance at a large anti-Hindi conference held in Madras city in July 1948. Convened under the aegis of the Dravidian movement, the conference featured devotees like Bharatidasan, Annadurai, Maraimalai Adigal, Kalyanasundaram, and Sivagnanam, all-speaking on the same platform against Hindi. The presence of Bharatidasan, Annadurai, and Maraimalai Adigal was not unusual, since they had been writing and-speaking passionately against the government's Hindi policy for more than a decade. But Kalyanasundaram and Sivagnanam had built their literary and political reputations as Congress nationalists in the 1920s and 1930s, during which time they had both supported the cause of Hindi. Sivagnanam (1974: 268) recalls attending Hindi classes when he was in prison in the 1940s, although he confesses that he never did become proficient in the language. Similarly, in 1925 so concerned was Kalyanasundaram with the slow progress of Hindi in the Presidency that he called upon Tamil youth to join the Hindustani Seva Dal and help in its dissemination (Nambi Arooran 1980: 189). A native of Tiruvarur, Kalyanasundaram grew up in a poor family in Madras city where, after finishing the tenth grade, he clerked for a while and taught Tamil in local schools from 1910. At great cost to his own material welfare, he became involved in nationalist politics beginning in 1917, and he was a member of the Tamilnadu Congress as well as the Madras

Presidency Association, the party formed by "non-Brahman" nationalists to counter the Justice Party. A devout Gandhian and reformed Shaivite, Kalyanasundaram was the editor of key nationalist newspapers like *Tçcapaktan1* (1917-20) and *Navacakti* (1920-40) through which he popularized a style of writing Tamil, especially for use in politics, that was simple but refined; it was free of foreign words, both English and Sanskrit. Kalyanasundaram's *tamil1pparlr1u* in those early decades was clearly Indianist; although he was a close friend of both Maraimalai Adigal and E. V. Ramasami, his devotion to Tamil did not lead him into antagonism towards Sanskrit or Hindi. Neither was he anti-Brahman nor a supporter of the Dravidianist separatist agenda. Yet by the 1940s, Kalyanasundaram was certainly marching to a different tune. To the delight of many a Dravidianist, he came out publicly in support of the Dravidian movement and its demand for a separate Tamilnadu, declaring that in this lay the hope for a truly socialist community (Kalyanasundaranar 1949). By the 1930s, Kalyanasundaram had already become disillusioned with the Congress and its promotion of upper-caste, upper-class interests. This led him to increasing involvement in the labor movement, a cause he had adopted as early as 1918 (Kalyanasundaranar 1982). The Congress's aggressive pursuit of the Hindi policy only convinced him that not only was that party inimical to Tamil interests but so too was the language that it promoted with such enthusiasm. Thus in 1948, the same Kalyanasundaram who had worked to popularize Hindi in the 1920s dismissed it now as a language that was impoverished and that promoted the subservience of women and "Shudras." "Tamil," he declared, "has the capacity to change a monkey into a man; Hindi, on the other hand, can make monkeys out of men."

While the battle against Hindi diluted the Indianist passions of devotees like Kalyanasundaram, Sivagnanam, Suddhananda Bharati, and others, it also drew into the fray Tamil schoolteachers and scholars who, for the first time, took to the streets, courted arrest, and served prison sentences. Prior to the 1930s, few Tamil scholars had been driven to political activism by their passion for Tamil. The anti-Hindi movement changed this, however. Although Maraimalai Adigal himself did not go to prison, two of his daughters-in-law and his son, Tirunavukarasu, joined the picket lines in Madras and served prison sentences in 1938-39. Not surprisingly, when scholars and teachers like Somasundara Bharati, K. Appadurai, Mudiyarasan, and Ilakuvan took part in protest meetings, or courted arrest or were sent off to prison, they received much publicity in the opposition press, for this clearly disproved the government's claim that the anti-Hindi movement was the mischief wrought by politicians and their uneducated "rabble" followers.

The anti-Hindi movement also made Muslim participation in Tamil devotional activities more visible (Abdul Karim 1982: 250-61; More 1993). From the turn of this century, devotees who were Muslims by faith wrote eulogistic essays and verses on Tamil, an early example being Abdul Kadir Rowther's long poem in praise of the various Tamil academies of Madurai (Rowther 1907). Rowther himself was one of three Muslim poets who were members of the Madurai Tamil Sangam in its first years, and he won the admiration of his fellow devout for "his deep devotion to Tamil, his unbounded sympathy for every thing Tamil" (Rowther 1907: 1). P. Dawood Sha, another Tamil enthusiast, who received a gold medal from the Madurai Tamil Sangam, was editor in the 1920s of the journal *Dar ul Islam,* which promoted pure Tamil and criticized Muslim theologians for their poor command of the language (More 1993: 88). Also of particular interest is an essay published in the nationalist journal *Ân1antapôtin1i* by A. Mohamed Ibrahim of Papanasam, in which the author praised Tamil and Tamil1ttây by invoking the various premodern Shaiva hymns on the language (Ibrahim 1920). Later in the century, the poet K. M. Sharif (1914-94) received much praise for many of his verses on Tamil, and for his passionate editorials in the 1940s and 1950s in journals like *Tamil1 Mul1akkam* and *Cât#t#ai.* In these editorials, Sharif, a member for a while of Sivagnanam's Tamil Arasu Kazhagam, promoted many of the latter's causes: the use of Tamil in schools and government, the creation of a Tamilnadu whose borders conformed to those described in the ancient Cank#am poems, the glories of ancient Tamil culture, and so on (Sharif 1990, 1992).

In a recent essay, J. B. P. More traces the growing collaboration during the 1920s and 1930s between the Tamil-speaking Muslim leadership of the Madras Presidency and Ramasami's Self-Respect movement. This collaboration was based on the latter's rejection of Hinduism and Brahmanism, its support of lower caste conversion to Islam, and its vision of a Dravidian society which would honor Muslims. In turn, the Tamil Muslim leadership drew upon the support of the Dravidian movement in its own efforts to counter the domination of a Urdu-speaking Muslim elite in the Presidency. Whereas many among the latter supported Hindustani on the grounds that "the language is one [although] the scripts are two," Tamil-speaking Muslim leaders joined forces with the Dravidian movement in opposing Hindi. So one of them, Khalifullah, declared in the Legislative Assembly: "I may at once say that I am a Rowther myself; my mother tongue is Tamil and not Urdu. I am not ashamed of it; I am proud of it" (quoted in More 1993: 98). More documents the extensive participation of Tamil-speaking Muslims in various anti-Hindi protests and rallies in different cities and towns of the Presidency, and he rightly notes that it was "the language agitation which finally led Tamil Muslims to affirm their distinct Tamil identity," even at the cost of parting ways with their putative coreligionists who nonetheless spoke a different tongue, Urdu (1993: 102). Instead, they chose to join forces with Tamil-speaking "non-Brahmans" and "fellow" Dravidians. Clearly, in this case language bonds and ethnic ties triumphed over religious affinity.

Further, it was in the context of these anti-Hindi protests that various new technologies for demonstrating and disseminating *tamil1ppar1r1u* were deployed, beyond the elite literary journal and the scholarly publication. These included subversive acts, such as writing on Hindi exams slogans like "Down with Hindi" and "Long Live Tamil" (Nayar 1969: 199); the public and dramatic burning of facsimiles of the Constitution or the map of India; the tarring over of Hindi names and the Devanagari script on official billboards; and the self-immolations and suicides of young men. In the early years, as the Congress itself took delight in reminding everyone, the protesters appropriated many of the strategies that Indian nationalists had developed in their anticolonial struggles against the British: the peaceful picketing of schools where Hindi was taught and of government buildings and official residences, black flag demonstrations, and public processions and meetings. The Gandhian strategy of fasting was also appropriated, although with not much success or support, as we will see. In big cities and small towns alike, hundreds of anti-Hindi protest meetings were held, frequently attracting thousands. Such meetings often opened and closed with the singing of a pro-Tamil song or hymn and concluded with the staging of plays that propagated the message(s) of Tamil devotion and the Dravidian movement.

As popular as public meetings were protest marches, sometimes drawing thousands, marked by the reciting of slogans and the singing of pro-Tamil and anti-Hindi songs and ditties. Protesters walked through city streets carrying the Tamil banner (which bore the symbols of the fish, the bow, and the tiger for the ancient Tamil dynasties of the Chera, the Pandya, and the Chola); they would also carry colorful placards emblazoned with anti-Hindi and pro-Tamil slogans; and they distributed handbills publicizing the evils of Hindi and the wonders of Tamil. The most spectacular of these protest marches was the one undertaken by the *tamil1ar pat#ai,* the "Tamilian Brigade," in August-September 1938. Jointly organized by the Self-Respect movement and the Muslim League, the brigade of a hundred or so young men set out from Tiruchirapalli on 1 August, under the stewardship of Kumaraswami Pillai and Ramamirtham Ammal. During the next forty-two days, members of the brigade walked through 234 villages and 60 towns; and they addressed eighty-seven public meetings attended by at least half a million. Opposition newspapers carried daily news of the brigade's progress and noted the "rousing reception" it received in various towns and villages of the Presidency on its six-hundred-mile trek. In September 1938 it finally reached Madras, where many of its members joined the picketing activities in the city and were arrested. Not the least of the consequences of the march of the anti-Hindi brigade (which, contemporaries did not fail to note, resembled Gandhi's famous march to Dandi, and Rajagopalachari's to Vedaranyam in 1930) was the formation in smaller towns and villages of similar brigades, which took up the cause of spreading the anti-Hindi and pro-Tamil message (Ilanceliyan 1986: 114-23; Visswanathan 1983: 211-13).

The battle against Hindi also spurred the proliferation of numerous populist organizations devoted to protect Tamil from the new threat. So, at the organizational level as well, *tamil1ppar1r1u* came to be transformed during these years, as populist associations such as Tamil1 Val#ar Nilayam (Academy for Tamil Development), Tamil1ar Kal1akam (Society of Tamilians), and Tamil1ar Nalvâl1vu Kal1akam (Society for Tamilian Welfare) joined the ranks of more elite literary societies such as the Madurai Tamil Sangam, Karanthai Tamil Sangam, and the like. The founding charters of many of these organizations declared the need to cherish Tamil1ttây and the mother tongue, to protect the Tamil people, and to oppose Hindi. The Tamil1p Pâtukâppuk Kal1akam (Society for the Protection of Tamil), founded in Tirunelveli in 1937 by devotees associated with both the Shaiva Siddhanta Kazhagam and the Karanthai Tamil Sangam, issued a circular asking Tamil speakers to Tamilize their personal names and the names of their homes and workplaces, of streets and towns, of eating places, and so on. The circular ended with the words, "Do service to Tamil and secure freedom" (Visswanathan 1983: 197-99). Furthermore, in many towns and even in the occasional village, anti-Hindi leagues and Tamil societies and student associations sprung up. Although such organizations were invariably short lived, their very existence reminds us that the anti-Hindi movement promoted the percolation of Tamil devotional ideas down to the grassroots level. Because Tamil's devotees had made clear that it was the Tamilian who was going to save their language from Hindi, the Everyman began to be integrated into the devotional community and its activities in a manner not done before. The Tamilian—the ordinary Tamil speaker—became the heart and soul of Tamil devotion at last, in the context of the movement against Hindi. Indeed, opposition to Hindi came to ultimately define the loyal Tamilian, for the Tamil subject is not just anyone who is devoted to Tamil but is one who is convinced that Hindi threatens the mother/language and is prepared to take to the streets to demonstrate this conviction.

Like many an oppositional practice, the anti-Hindi movement of Tamil's devotees has had many consequences—some paradoxical, some tragic. How may we assess its success? from whose viewpoint? Their protests may have allowed Tamil's devotees to set aside various crucial differences, if only temporarily, and heal the fissures among them; they may have aroused the interest of even the disinterested in *tamil1ppar1r1u*, compelled the state to take a more sustained interest in the promotion of Tamil, and put a brake on Hindi domination. But all this has not come without its costs, the most obvious of which, of course, is that speakers of Tamil who grow up in Tamilnadu, and depend on state sponsored education, do not have the ready opportunity to learn the putative official language of India and avail themselves of the potential benefits this brings. Just as crucially, the anti-Hindi movement has re-signified the very meaning of *tamil1pparlr1u*. Increasingly in the discourse(s) of many devotees, resistance to Hindi (*inti etirppu*) has received more emphasis than laboring for Tamil (*tamil1ppan#i*). Correspondingly, the paradigmatic Tamil devotee is not necessarily the one who has worked all her life to improve Tamil but rather the one who gave up his life in the battle against Hindi. Indeed, even those who disavow *tamil1pparlr1u* are admitted into the ranks of Tamil's devotees because of their opposition to Hindi. Paradoxically, therefore, like all identities that are defined in opposition, the Tamilian self is (re)cast in terms of resistance to Hindi: "true" Tamilians are those who may or may not speak good Tamil or even care for it; but they are certainly those who gave up their bodies, lives, and souls in the battle against Hindi.

TO DIE FOR

Living for Language

It was the year 1887 in Madras city. After more than six years of laboring over the palm-leaf manuscript of the ancient epic poem *Cîvaka Cintâman#i,* Swaminatha Aiyar had just handed over the final sections of the text to his printer. For the past few years, his entire life had been wrapped up in the *Cintâman#i:* he woke up thinking about it and stayed up late into the night, deciphering and transcribing archaic words. His fingers were sore from turning over the brittle leaves of the manuscript, and his eyes ached from going over proofs by the dim light of oil lamps. He had spent most of his summer and winter vacations, and all other days he could steal from his teaching responsibilities, travelling back and forth between the printer's workshop, in Madras city, and his college and home, far south in Kumbakonam. There had been moments of great anxiety when he had been convulsed with fear he would run out of money, that the press would burn down, or that malcontents would tamper with his proofs. But all that was now in the past. He had seen the work through to its final printed form. It was only then, after all those years of laboring day and night, that he allowed himself the luxury of succumbing to his tiredness. He was still at the printer's. He laid himself down, right there and then on the floor, and slept deeply and happily. When he woke up, he saw a man standing before him. "Here, sir, is the

Pattuppât#t#u," the man said, and handed over to Swaminathan another palm-leaf manuscript. He thought, "Tamil1an1n1ai [Tamil1ttây] herself has sent [this man], commanding me to go on with my service to Tamil," and he addressed her: "O mother! You have (re)adorned yourself with the *Cintâman#i* that I, your poor devotee, gave back to you. Continue to offer me grace, so that I, your servant, can go on with my work of recovering all your other jewels." So saying, he reverenced Tamil1ttây with all his heart, and continued, he tells us, for the rest of his life trying to fulfill her wishes (Swaminatha Aiyar 1982: 612-13).

As this incident illustrates so well, the heart and soul of the practice of Tamil devotion are the deeply personal bonds of reverence, affection, and passion that tie the devout to the language, bonds that are only further reaffirmed in the stories that its devotees tell about themselves and each other. Indeed, if praise poems are one of the means through which a community of sentiment tying its devotees to Tamil is constituted, then stories that recount the hardships they faced, the resistances they encountered, and their success in overcoming these difficulties to triumph in their *tamil1ppar1r1u* are another. In many such stories, her devotees speak directly to their Tamil1ttây, complain about the numerous woes that beset them, and beseech her to grant them grace. She, too, talks with them, recalls the many afflictions that trouble her, and pleads with them to meliorate her condition. In all such accounts, the language is not an impersonal, abstract, distant entity. Instead, it is imagined as a concerned, deeply involved participant in the lives of its speakers, an intimate member of their families. So in 1942, on the eve of the Japanese invasion of Singapore, S. B. Adithan, who had a flourishing law practice there, was torn between staying on or returning to Tamilnadu. He wrote down the words "Stay on in Singapore" and "Return to Tamilnadu" on two chits, folded these up, and then picked out the one which commanded him to return home. "Adithan[ar] should return to his motherland, and serve Tamilnadu, the Tamil people, and Tamil: this was Tamil1ttây's will," his biographer concludes (Kuppusami 1969: 11). Tamil1ttây could also exercise her will to bring her straying "children" back to the fold. In the 1930s, K. Appadurai, a comparatively late convert to *tamil1ppar1r1u*, was involved in an activity that amounted to cardinal sin in the eyes of most devotees of Tamil: the teaching of Hindi. During these years, he also lost his father and his (first) wife, as well as fracturing his leg and spending months in the hospital. "This was the punishment that Tamil1ttây herself gave [Appadurai] for laboring for Hindi," his fellow devotees concluded. After this, he dedicated himself totally to Tamil, we are told (Mamani 1992: 49).

It is a measure of the intimacy between the language and its devotees that their births are imagined as Tamil1ttây's gift and blessing; their deaths, her loss. Many recall that it is their *tamil1ppar1r1u* that carried them through critical periods of their life, helping them overcome hunger and poverty, humiliation and rejection, illness and suffering. The poet Mudiyarasan spent most of his life as a poorly paid Tamil schoolteacher. Yet he notes with pride, "As long as I have Tamil in my heart, I am not poor" (Mudiyarasan n.d.: 101). Similarly, Sivagnanam writes that plagued by a terrible stomach ulcer, he carried on his daily life in a state of acute pain. Indeed, he even thought of committing suicide. "What prevented me from doing so was the deep devotion I had for Tamil, and the great desire I had for realizing a new Tamil land" (Sivagnanam 1974: 774-75). In all such stories, Tamil's devotees refer to each other by titles which remind one and all of the intimate bonds with their beloved language. Thus Maraimalai Adigal is *tamil1k kat#al*, "ocean of Tamil," or *tamil1malai*, "mountain of Tamil" Viswanatham is *muttamil1k kâvalar*, "guardian of the three Tamil(s)" Kalyanasundaram is *tamil1t ten1r1al*, "southern Tamil breeze" and Umamakeswaram (1883-1941) is *tamil1avçl#*, "great Tamil hero," to name just a few. Even as such epithets bestowed a mantle of honor generally reserved for sovereigns, deities, and other notables on Tamil's devout, they also suggest that these individuals attained meaning only in relation to Tamil.

This is also suggested by many devotees' desire to confer upon themselves and their children names that invoke Tamil and its literature. Sivagnanam named his daughter Kannagi, because she was born after he had immersed himself in the study of the *Çilappatikâram*. "After the Tamil language, I have the deepest devotion to my daughter Kannagi," he writes. If we do not even have Tamil names for ourselves, how will we make Tamil proud? he demands of his readers (Sivagnanam 1974: 775-76). Similarly, Ilakuvan, who Tamilized his given Sanskritic name, states: "They may ask what's in a name. One's name is everything. Tamilians should only bear Tamil names. Those who refuse this cannot be devotees of Tamil" (Ilakuvanar 1971: 4). Today, of course, many Tamil speakers, and not just those overtly devoted to the language, bear personal names containing the word "Tamil," such as Tamilcelvi, "daughter of Tamil" Tamilanban, "lover of Tamil" Tamilarasi, "Queen Tamil" even Tamilpitthan, "mad about Tamil."

The stories that circulate in the devotional community also dwell on the numerous small but by no means insignificant ways in which devotees lived out, on an everyday basis, their love for their language. In the 1930s, Sivagnanam, who hailed from a very poor family and whose formal education ended in the primary school, collected all the Tamil books that he could lay his hands on and ran a Tamil1ttây Library in Madras city, so that even the working-class community in which he lived could have access to the wealth of Tamil (Sivagnanam 1974: 116-17). In the late 1930s and early 1940s, when the demand for an independent Tamilnadu surfaced, the poet Pulavar Kulanthai printed the words "Tamilnadu for Tamilians" on the borders of saris and towels, and distributed these all over the Presidency (Pulavar Kulanthai 1971: 58). Somasundara Bharati named his newly built house (in his home town of Ettaiyapuram) Tamil1akam, "Abode of Tamil" (Sambasivanar and Ilankumaran 1960: 84). Although not particularly affluent herself, Dharmambal, who played a leading role in the anti-Hindi protests of the 1930s, donated her family home to the Karanthai Tamil Sangam (K. Tirunavukarasu 1991: 208). Umamakeswaram Pillai, for many years the president of Karanthai Tamil Sangam, at his own expense printed and distributed among the general populace copies of Sundaram Pillai's signature hymn on Tamil1ttây (Sambasivanar 1974: 35). And V. V. Ramasami, who was editor of the literary magazine *Ten1r1al* and a member of the Madras Legislative Council in the 1950s, began all his letters with the phrase *tamil1 velka!*, "may Tamil be victorious."

These are just a few incidents from the many stories that Tamil's devotees tell about each other. These narratives undoubtedly labor under the weight of despair that its enthusiasts experienced on behalf of their ailing language/mother. In the interstices of this rhetoric of decline and dismay, however, lurks the absolute joy or wonder that fills its devotees when they chanced upon the sweet sounds of Tamil, in song or word; when they had the good fortune of meeting a fellow devout; when they saw some sign, however small, that their beloved language was flourishing. Indeed, it is telling that in these stories, Tamil's triumphs are experienced as personal victories, just as its defeats are narrated as personal failures. Such stories obviously reaffirm the intimacy of the bonds with Tamil that manifests itself in every sphere of its devotees' lives. They also simultaneously keep alive the memory of Tamil's devotees in their community; for had not Bharatidasan insisted passionately, again and again, that there is no death for the true follower of Tamil (Bharatidasan 1958: 22)? But above all, such stories transform, through various narrative strategies, certain individuals into paragons of Tamil devotion and paradigmatic Tamilians whose lives are worthy of emulation by all good and loyal speakers of the language. These stories are therefore the sites for the production of what I characterize as the *devotional subject,* whose self merges into the imagined self of Tamil, whose life experiences are subordinated to the superior cause of the language, and whose story is the story of Tamil.

There are many models of devotional subjectivity that are produced by these stories. Because the unmarked Tamil devotee is always a male who is not Brahman, and who claims Tamil as his "mother tongue," I begin by exploring the stories of those who do not fall into this category: the stories therefore of the Tamil enthusiast who is woman, who is European missionary, and who is Brahman. I then turn to the stories of the model devotee who is poet and scholar, the devotee who is publicist and patron, the warrior devotee, and the devotee who becomes martyr to the Tamil cause. I close with the story of a man who all his life resisted being drawn into the devotional community, but nevertheless is enshrined, through the inexorable logic of *tamil1ppar1r1u,* as a paradigmatic *tamil1an1par,* "Tamil devotee."

The Woman Devotee

From the time of Vedanayakam Pillai's 1879 novel *Piratâpa Mutaliyâr Carittiram* through Bharatidasan's numerous plays in the 1940s and 1950s, to Mudiyarasan's 1964 epic poem *Pûnk#ot#i,* the Tamil reading public has been offered the image of the ideal Tamil woman as an enthusiastic devotee of Tamil. It is Vedanayakam's spirited heroine, Gnanambal, rather than the hero of his novel, who mounts a fiery attack on the infatuation with

English among lawyers of her time, producing in that process one of the earliest passionate eulogies of Tamil in devotional discourses (Vedanayakam Pillai 1879: 279-90). In a radical departure, Mudiyarasan's heroine Poonkodi even rejects marriage and motherhood, dedicating her entire life to the service of Tamil. Mudiyarasan yearned to see a woman who gave herself up to the Tamil cause, like Manimekhalai, the nun who dedicated her life to Buddhism in the ancient epic poem *Man#imçkalai* (Mudiyarasan n.d.: 94-95). Like Manimekhalai, Poonkodi, too, spurns a life of pleasure and comfort, refuses to marry her ardent suitor Komagan, immerses herself in a passionate pursuit of Tamil learning, and even goes to prison to save her beloved language from its enemies. On her deathbed in prison, Tamil1ttây appears to her in a vision, praises her for her services, and offers her blessings to her selfless daughter (Mudiyarasan 1964).

Mudiyarasan's image of the woman devotee who is not wife and mother is comparatively rare in (male) devotional discourses. In general, as custodians of Tamil, women are celebrated less for their achievements in their own right as poets, authors, or thinkers, and more for their role as the heroic mothers (*vîrattây*) of Tamil1ttây's children, especially her sons (Ramaswamy 1992a; see also Anandhi 1991b; Lakshmi 1990). In the writings of Tamil's devotees, the Tamil-speaking woman is recast as a surrogate Tamil1ttây. So M. Kathiresan Chettiar (1881-1953), professor of Tamil at Annamalai University, introduced Tamil1ttây to his readers thus: "Who is Tamil1 An1n1ai [Tamil1ttây]? Our mothers, too, are Tamil1 An1n1ai. All mothers who speak Tamil are Tamil1 An1n1ai...[at the same time], the Mother who instructs all the mothers of the world in speech and is the very embodiment of the sweetness that we call 'Tamil'—she is the person we call Tamil1 An1n1ai" (Kathiresan Chettiar 1959-60: 169).

Here, as in numerous other instances, the Tamil woman perforce came to be figured as the visible and substantial presence of intangible abstractions—the language, and the community imagined around it. As the living embodiment of Tamil, she is charged with the responsibility of reproducing (literally, as well as metaphorically) Tamil society and culture, most especially the language. Modelled on the "new woman" who emerged in middle-class imaginations everywhere in colonial India, she is appropriately educated to run a neat, disciplined, and efficient home where she nourishes her children on her pure Tamil milk, raising them to be heroic sons who would willingly go into the world to work for Tamil's welfare and fertile daughters who would become good, educated mothers themselves. Devotional writings spur women on to embrace this vision by dredging up images of the heroic mother of the Cank#am poems, who rejoices on the day she learned that the son whom her womb had given birth to, and her milk had nourished, now lay dead on the battlefield, having fought honorably for lord and land—and by extension, of course, for his language (Bharati 1988: 318-20; Nilambikai 1960: 82-91; M. Raghava Aiyangar 1986; C. S. Subramaniam 1986: 397-99).

Its female devotees did not reject either the motherhood of Tamil or their own in their writings. On the contrary, rather than seeing motherhood as "a strategy of containment," as some feminist scholars are wont to do today (Visweswaran 1990: 66; see also Lakshmi 1990), Tamil1ttây's daughters saw it as an opportunity for self-empowerment. They pursued this opportunity through appropriating the figure of Tamil1ttây, even though such an appropriation necessarily took place in the crevices of the patriarchal structures that were relegitimized by *tamil1ppar1r1u* itself. Almost without exception, its female devotees maintained that because Tamil is woman and mother, they, as women and mothers, have a better understanding of Tamil1ttây's plight and needs. They insisted that women ought not to just passively participate in Tamil devotional activities initiated by men, but ought to lead and march ahead of them (Ramaswamy 1992a: 46-48). Although such an empowerment was necessarily premised on the essentializing of the woman as mother, in this deployment of Tamil1ttây her female devotees replaced the docile mothers of male devotional discourses, who are followers, with mothers who are leaders.

In a recent essay, Janaki Nair rightly notes: "the question of female agency in history, whether that agency takes the form of consent, transgression, or subversion, can neither be wholly contained within a delineation of structures of oppression nor exhausted by accounts of female presence in history, but must be posed within specific contexts and placed along a continuum where various forms of agency may coexist" (Nair 1994: 83). And indeed, in the stories of women devotees that are circulated within the devotional community, there is a continuum which ranges from Nilambikai's conservative advocacy of women's responsibility in educating their children to Thamaraikanni's spirited call for militant warriors to battle for the Tamil cause. And in the stories of those women who during the anti-Hindi protests of the 1930s and 1940s took to the streets, organized protest marches and conferences, and even went to prison, the radical female devotee resembles the male, as she transgresses the function of the domestic paragon that has been assigned to her. These stories, even when we hear them through male voices, remind us that these women contested and subverted the patriarchal demands of *tamil1ppar1r1u,* while simultaneously appearing to give their consent to the confinement to marriage and motherhood that it demanded (Ramaswamy 1992a).

Nilambikai has been described in the biography written by her brother as a woman who came into this world solely for the purpose of serving Tamil: "she embodies *tamil1ppar1r1u;* her life is the life of Tamil; she cannot be pried apart from Tamil" (M. Tirunavukarasu 1945: 50). Born in 1903, Nilambikai's life and future as a Tamil devotee was overdetermined. The favorite daughter of Maraimalai Adigal, she was raised on the shoulders and laps of other well-known devotees such as Arasan Shanmugan (1868-1915) and Pandithurai Thevar (1867-1911), who were her father's friends and patrons. Her father appears to have taken great pride in her love for Tamil, even making her memorize, when she was thirteen, one of his essays on the duties of motherhood, which she publicly recited at a scholarly meeting in Madras. So impressed was he with his young daughter, her brother tells us, that Maraimalai Adigal declared passionately one day, "Nila's face resembles that of Shelley and Shakespeare and other great savants" (M. Tirunavukarasu 1945: 8-12).

In the devotional community, Nilambikai occupies a special niche for her role in spurring her famous father into launching his pure Tamil movement in 1916. Her brother recalls that Nilambikai bestowed pure Tamil names upon her siblings, and would use only those; she would speak and write as far as possible in pure Tamil; and she would correct anyone who used a foreign word when-speaking in Tamil (M. Tirunavukarasu 1945: 14-15). Soon after, in 1918, when she turned sixteen, Nilambikai met the twenty-eight-year-old Tiruvarangam Pillai (1890-1944), who a few years later was to set up the famous Shaiva Siddhanta Kazhagam. Her brother remembers that his entire family had come to see Tiruvarangam as a godlike figure, their father's savior and patron. It is perhaps not surprising that young Nilambikai fell in love with him, although she was not allowed to marry him for almost ten years (M. Tirunavukarasu 1945: 21-35).

Intertwined though her life may have been with those of these famous devotees, Nilambikai nevertheless strived to serve Tamil on her own as well. By the time she was in her early twenties, she had published numerous essays on the virtues of *tan1ittamil1* in the face of considerable opposition to the pure Tamil movement (Nilambikai 1960). She followed this up in 1937 with a dictionary, the first of its kind, which demonstrated the existence of pure Tamil equivalents for seven thousand Sanskrit words that had swamped Tamil (Nilambikai 1952). She also taught Tamil in girls' schools; spoke at various Shaiva conferences; and wrote extensively on the revival of Tamil, the spread of Shaivism, and the improvement of women. By all accounts, she was alarmed by what she saw as an absence of interest in Tamil among its female speakers, a concern that she voiced especially strongly in her inaugural address to the Tamilnadu Women's Conference summoned in November 1938 to register Tamil women's protest against Hindi. Of course, Nilambikai's vision for how women should help their language fell within the parameters of middle-class motherhood. They should establish *tan1ittamil1* women's colleges and bookstores, encourage widow education, and become Tamil teachers. But such public services should never compromise their primary function as educated homemakers who raised their children to be well-read, disciplined, and pure Tamil speakers (Nilambikai n.d.). She wrote and spoke ardently on such matters in spite of poor health, and in spite of having to take care of her own eight children. At least by her brother's account, she took great pride in her own motherhood, raising her children to be devout Shaivites and Tamil speakers (M. Tirunavukarasu 1945: 38-43). But it is hard to deny that the birth of eleven children over a period of about fifteen years must have taken its toll on her health, and she was only forty-three when she died in 1945, a year after her beloved husband and fellow devotee had passed on.

At the 1938 Tamilnadu Women's Conference which Nilambikai addressed, another woman spoke with great passion about the need for Tamil women to "rise up in anger" and step forth to help their ailing mother, Tamil1ttây. Her name was V. P. Thamaraikanni (1911-71). Named Jalajatchi at birth, she was raised in a family of musicians and patrons of Tamil, and later Tamilized her given (Sanskritic) name. An author of many essays and novels, she did not get actively involved in politics, because both her father and husband were government employees (Lakshmi 1984: 77-78; Rajagopalan 1989: 5-7). By the late 1930s, however, she aligned herself with Ramasami's Self-Respect movement and was a key speaker at many anti-Hindi conferences organized in Madras, Salem, Velur, Nagapattinam, and elsewhere. In 1938, she also published a short story called "Punitavati Allatu Tamil1ar Vit#utalaip Pôr" (Punithavathi, or the Tamilian fight for freedom), which features a heroine, Punithavathi, who forsook her husband and her young daughter to help Tamil1ttây, and was arrested in this process (Ramaswamy 1992a: 53-56). Thamaraikanni's spirited heroine asks, "What is the use of wealth, of freedom, and of human relationships, when I can be in the front ranks of those who serve Tamil1ttây?" (Thamaraikanni 1938: 21).

Thamaraikanni herself did not go to prison on behalf of her beloved language. But many other women did, following her impassioned speech at the November conference. This was the first time women—anywhere in the world, by some reckoning—had ever taken to the streets to battle on behalf of their "mother tongue," it is proudly claimed. By February 1939, the battle against Hindi had intensified, and official figures show that thirty six women, nine of them described as "ladies with children," were arrested and sentenced to six months' imprisonment; these figures almost doubled over the next few months (Ramaswamy 1992a: 56-57). Prison records show that many of the women had distinctly Tamil names; their ages ranged from eighteen to seventy; they were mostly illiterate and unemployed, and hailed from different parts of the Presidency. Devotional stories collapse their individuality into a larger narrative of Tamil devotion. Many of them are identified as daughters, wives, or daughters in law of well-known (male) anti-Hindi activists; as mothers, many of whom went to prison with their infant children; and as women who took pride in informing their sentencing judges that they were protesting against Hindi for the sake of their language and for the future of their children (Ilanceliyan 1986: 143-48).

Two of these women stand out. One of them is "Doctor" Dharmambal (1890-1959), who was honored in 1951 with the title *vîrat tamil1an1n1ai,* "heroic Tamil mother," for her various services to Tamil and to women's causes. Born in the small town of Karuntattankudi near Tanjavur, Dharmambal learned Tamil from Tamil scholars like Panditai Narayani Ammal when she moved to Madras. Prior to her involvement in the anti-Hindi movement, she had already made a reputation for herself as an activist concerned with women's issues, especially education, and as a practitioner of *siddha* medicine (hence her title "doctor"). In addition to leading the anti-Hindi women's protests in Madras in November 1938, she was also actively involved in the demands for better remuneration for Tamil teachers, and she spearheaded the Mân#avar Man1r1am (Student's Association) which cultivated *tamil1ppar1r1u* among the city's Tamil-speaking youth. Along with Dharmambal, two of her daughters in law, Saraswati and Sita, were arrested for participating in the protests against Hindi (K. Tirunavukarasu 1991: 200-213).

And then there was Ramamirtham (1883-1962), a native of the small village of Moovalur near Tanjavur, who was raised in a *devadasi* (temple dancer) family. With no formal education, much of Ramamirtham's life, prior to her involvement in the anti-Hindi cause, had been devoted to the abolition of the *devadasi* system. In 1921, she joined the Congress and allied herself with its radical faction headed by Ramasami. When the latter quit the Congress in 1925-26, she followed him, became a member of his Self-Respect movement, and continued her struggle for various women's causes, encouraged by Ramasami's own radical ideas on the subject (Anandhi 1991a: 741-42). Although there is little to indicate that she joined the anti-Hindi movement because she was a devotee of Tamil, she certainly threw herself into it with great enthusiasm, even though she was in her fifties. She played a key role in organizing the Tamilian Brigade, which marched on foot from Tiruchirapalli to Madras in August-September 1938, and was in charge of providing food for the protesters on their six-hundred-mile journey. On their reaching Madras, she joined in the picketing of the Hindu Theological School along with Dharmambal and others, and she was thrown into prison for six months beginning in November 1938 (K. Tirunavukarasu 1991: 168-78). Ten years later, she spoke out against Hindi again, at the 1948 anti-Hindi conference organized in Madras. While not asking them to reject their responsibility as educated mothers, she nevertheless called upon the women gathered there to take to the streets and, like their menfolk, march against Hindi. Unlike men, she suggested shrewdly, women would be treated much more benevolently by the government, and hence could be more effective in the campaign to save Tamil. Women, she claimed, have the capacity to create as well as destroy. Therefore, Tamil women should now rise up and destroy the scourge of Hindi. Her commitment to Dravidianism notwithstanding, Ramamirtham invoked the mythical epochs of Sanskritic Hinduism as well as its archetypical heroines, declaring that Sita had destroyed the *trçta* epoch and Draupadi had brought an end to the *dwâpara* age; today, Tamil women would rise and destroy the *kali* epoch created by Hindi, she asserted.

The Missionary Devotee

Along the beachfront in Madras city called the Marina are a series of statues that dot the mile-long esplanade, commemorating various personalities from the Tamil past, distant and recent: the sage Tiruvalluvar, the author of the *Tirukkur1al#* Kannagi, the heroine of the epic poem *Cilappatikâram;* the seer poetess, Auvaiyar, who wrote numerous didactic verses; Kamban, the author of the *Irâmâvatâram;* the poets Bharati and Bharatidasan; and the nationalist V. O. Chidambaram. Interspersed among these statues are three others whose plaques identify them as the "Italian savant" Veeramamunivar [Beschi] and the "English scholars," Robert Caldwell and George Pope. It is perhaps not surprising that in 1968, when the DMK government set up these statues to commemorate the Second International Tamil Conference, these three Europeans should have joined the ranks of poets and scholars who are revered within the devotional community as among the noblest of Tamil1ttây's numerous gifted sons and daughters. For a special aura surrounds those Westerners who, over the centuries, came to Tamil's home, learned the language, and spread its glories in distant lands. They have been integrated into Tamil1ttây's family as her "noble sons" they have been made honorary Tamilians. In his memoirs, after a discussion of his correspondence in 1891 with the French scholar Jules Vinson over some missing texts, Swaminatha Aiyar proudly notes that while Tamil1ttây was being cast into fire and floods in Tamilnadu, her jewels were welipreserved in a distant city like Paris (Swaminatha Aiyar 1982: 688-89). Elsewhere, he rejoices that Tamil had crossed the seas and found such love abroad (Swaminatha Aiyar 1991c: 4). Similarly, a long prose poem called *Tamil1 Val#arnta Katai* (The story of Tamil's growth) flags the contributions made to Tamil through the ages by such hallowed figures as Kumarakuruparar, Sivagnana Munivar, Meenakshisundaram Pillai, Arumuga Navalar, and Sundaram Pillai, and then notes:

And then came the scholars from foreign lands;

With his lofty Tçmpâvan#i, *the eminent Veeramamunivar raised [Tamil] to new heights;*

The noble Caldwell joyously bestowed upon Tamil a comparative grammar;

The incomparable G. U. Pope gifted [to it] his translation of the Tamil Veda, *the* Vâcakam;

He prided himself as a student of Tamil;

Scholar Winslow created its dictionary, and supported Tamil and praised it.

(Navanitakrishnan 1952: 22-23)

The text then laments, "Our Tamilians do not have the *tamil1ppar1r1u* that these [men] had. Alas ! Alas! O Tamilnadu!"

Indeed, a virtual hagiography has emerged around these figures whose "missionary" presence in the region is glossed over in favor of their role as "Christian devotees" of Tamil1ttây. Adulation of these European missionaries within devotional discourses contrasts curiously with the powerful critique of missionary linguistics in Western academic circles in recent years. For rather than innocently recovering dying languages and lost literatures, missionaries colluded with colonial power structures in reconfiguring "native" vocabularies, restructuring "indigenous" grammars in accordance with Western categories, superimposing alien ways of conceptualizing languages over conventional notions, and so on (Cohn 1985; Fabian 1986; Rafael 1988). However, Tamil's enthusiasts, and even academics in Tamilnadu today, rarely allege that these missionaries violated Tamil, though they so accuse other "foreigners," such as Brahmans and Aryans from North India. And yet some missionaries themselves acknowledged that they had been responsible for creating a new kind of Tamil. Thus

George Pope wrote in 1900 in the preface to his much lauded translation of the *Tiruvâcakam:*

> There exists now much of what is called Christian Tamil, a dialect created by the Danish missionaries of Tranquebar, enriched by generations of Tanjore, German and other missionaries; modified, purified and *refrigerated* by the Swiss Rhenius and the very composite Tinnevelly school; expanded and harmonized by Englishmen, amongst whom Bower (a Eurasian) was foremost in his day; and finally, waiting now for the touch of some heaven born genius among the Tamil community to make it as sweet and effective as any language on earth, living or dead.

Occasional antagonistic statements about these missionary devotees did surface within Tamil devotional discourses, in Indianism in particular as part of its attack on colonialism and English. Subramania Bharati complained in 1906 that while the colonial government was only too happy to extend its patronage to ("white") missionaries like Pope and to their scholarship, it did not help out Tamil scholars like Swaminatha Aiyar who had for years slaved over ancient manuscripts (C. S. Subramaniam 1986: 362). Years later, Sivagnanam carefully noted the "great service" done by Caldwell, Pope, and others, which deserves "immense praise." Nevertheless, they also sowed the seeds of separatism among Tamilians and widened the gap between Sanskrit and Tamil, he writes. Furthermore, they did not contest colonial rule nor oppose the oppression of Tamilians by the British. "Christian missionaries came to the Tamil land not to help Tamil grow but to spread Christianity," he concludes (Sivagnanam 1970: 51).

All the same, Sivagnanam also notes that "from its early past, Tamil has never been the sole possession of the people following a particular religion. From the beginning of history it has been the people's language, transcending religious differences" (Sivagnanam 1970: 48). And indeed, this statement accounts for the remarkable absence of animosity towards the European missionary among a large majority of the devout. They assert, in terms that we have now come to identify as Orientalist, that the missionary interest in Tamil only proved that even the West was mesmerized by its beauty. Moreover, these missionaries only demonstrated that devotion to Tamil transcends religious boundaries, for Hindus, Muslims, and Christians are all children of Tamil1ttây and members of the same Tamil family. Love for Tamil is a superior form of love, precisely because it does not recognize sectarian and religious differences. Christian devotees of Tamil are living proof that Tamil is a truly ecumenical language. Not surprisingly, these missionaries are appropriated by the devotional community, "converted" into honorary Tamilians, and enshrined as adopted "sons" of Tamil1ttây.

Ranking high among these adopted sons is Constantius Beschi (1680-1746/7), who was honored with the name Veeramahamunivar, "heroic great sage," by fellow Tamil scholars for his demonstrated mastery of their language. A native of Castiglione in Italy, Beschi joined the Society of Jesus in 1698, and came to Tirunelveli around 1711. Over the next few years, he served in various adjoining parishes before he moved to the general region of Tiruchirapalli where he spent most of the rest of his life (Caldwell 1881: 240-43). Tamil's adherents take delight in noting that Beschi cast off his European clothes, adopted the ochre robes and lifestyle of a mendicant, learned Tamil, and "Tamilized" his Christian name as Dairiyanathan. Beschi is best known for his pioneering work in grammar and lexicography, but his crowning achievement was the narration of the life of St. Joseph in Tamil in his poem *Tçmpâvan#i*, probably completed around 1729. Within the devotional community, Beschi's works are represented as "adding to Tamil1ttây's beauty" the *Tçmpâvan#i* in particular is "the gift to Tamil1ttây on behalf of the Christian religion" (Sivagnanam 1970: 48). Beschi died in 1747 in Ambalakadu and is buried there, but in the words of a fellow devotee, his *Tçmpâvan#i* adorns Tamil1ttây as an "unfading garland" (Sethu Pillai 1964: 10).

It is with equal affection, if not more, that the services of Reverend Robert Caldwell are celebrated. Caldwell published a number of works on the history and religious practices of southern India, many of which contain several disparaging statements on its cultural practices (Dirks 1995), but he is most remembered as the author of *A Comparative Grammar of Dravidian or South-Indian Family of Languages* (1856). Although Caldwell's assertions have not gone unchallenged in the devotional community, there is general consensus that he laid the groundwork for the tremendous groundswell of pride in Tamil in the century following his work. In the words of a fellow devotee, Devaneyan Pavanar, "Tamil's antiquity was spread all over the world by that worthy man, Caldwell; the seeds for *tan1ittamil1* [pure Tamil] were sown by [Suryanarayana Sastri]; the revered Maraimalai Adigal raised it into a plant; I am cultivating it into a tree" (quoted in Tirumaran 1992: 109). Thus Caldwell has been not only incorporated into the family of Tamil's devotees but given pride of place at its head, by one of their own.

Robert Caldwell, born in Ireland in 1814, arrived in Madras in 1838 as a missionary for the London Missionary Society. He spent most of his life in the small town of Idayankudi near Tirunelveli with the Society for the Propagation of the Gospel, and in 1877 he became bishop of Tinnevelly. A fellow devotee, R. P. Sethu Pillai, writes with affection that in the fifty odd years he worked in Tamilnadu, Caldwell went home on furlough only three times. When he went back to England the third time, his friends there begged him to stay. But he refused. "I have lived all these years for Indians. As long I am alive, I will toil for them. I will give up my life in their land." And so he did, and when he died in 1891, he was buried in Idayankudi on the grounds of the church that he had himself built. "Caldwell Aiyar worked selflessly for fifty-three years for Tamilnadu. Is he not one of Tamil1ttây's true sons?" concludes Sethu Pillai (1964: 32).

And there was George Pope (1820-1908), beloved among Tamil's enthusiasts for translating into English their most revered texts, the *Tirukkur1al#* and the *Tiruvâcakam*. Late in his life, Pope recalled a conversation he had with a "native friend in South India." He reportedly said to him: " 'I am going to live for Tamil. It shall be my great study; your people shall be my people; and I hope that my God will be theirs.' The friend replied: 'Sir, that is very delightful; but it means for you contempt and poverty.' " Tamil's devout mention with delight that although he himself had declared that "Tamil scholarship is the direct road to poverty," Pope dedicated his entire life to the "service of Tamil" (Sethu Pillai 1964: 11).

Born in Nova Scotia in 1820, Pope and his family emigrated to England, where at fourteen he resolved to become a missionary. He set sail for India in 1838, reportedly studying Tamil for the first time on his eight-month voyage over. He became so good at it that he preached his first sermon in Tamil upon landing in Madras.

Attached at first to the Wesleyan Missionary Society, he later joined the Society for the Propagation of the Gospel. His base of operations was Sawyerpuram in Tirunelveli district, where he founded a seminary. Around 1850, now married, Pope moved to Tanjavur; there, under the tutelage of the Tamil poet and fellow Christian Vedanayaka Sastri (1774-1864), he immersed himself in the study of ancient Tamil literature. This was also the most productive of his years in India, when he wrote a number of Tamil handbooks, textbooks, and dictionaries. After stints in Ootacumand and Bangalore, he returned to England in 1880 and joined Oxford University in 1884, where he taught Tamil and Telugu. It is then that he published his translations of the *Tirukkur1al#* (1886), the *Nâlat#iyâr* (1893), a partial translation of the *Man#imçkalai* (1900), and, most important, the *Tiruvâcakam* (1900). With great enthusiasm, an admirer, Saravana Pillai, greeted Pope's translation of the *Tiruvâcakam:*

> *In this world, surrounded by oceans and abounding with languages,*
>
> *Who is that great scholar who rendered into faultless English our divine Tamil* Veda's *truths in such a manner that even those who do not know the glorious Tamil may understand?*
>
> *Born as jewel of the English land,*
>
> *He has with affection embraced our precious Tamil1ttây as his foster mother.*
>
> *He is a worthy Christian preceptor.*
>
> *He is the notable who bears the name Pope*
>
> *(quoted in Sethu Pillai 1964: 18)*

Although Pope did not die in the Tamil country nor is he buried there, Tamil enthusiasts mention with satisfaction that he had insisted that his epitaph should bear the phrase *tamil1 mân#avan1*, "student of Tamil."

The Brahman Devotee

For most sections of the devotional community, and indeed for the bulk of the Tamil-speaking populace today, the very category "Brahman devotee of Tamil" would be a contradiction in terms. Yet, in the early decades of *tamil1ppar1r1u*, many who were nominally Brahman wrote and spoke enthusiastically about the glories and wonders of Tamil, about the need to improve it, and so on. In contrast to his comparatively high visibility in those early years, the Brahman devotee becomes a rare presence by the 1930s, especially as radical neo-Shaivism, contestatory classicism, and Dravidianism consolidated their explicitly anti-Brahman agendas. The Brahman adherent indeed offers a curious counterpoint to the missionary devotee; where the latter's demonstrated love for Tamil allows him to erase the stigma of foreignness and his association with the colonial power structure, the former is not able (or allowed) to transcend his primordial identity as Brahman. His putative Brahmanness makes his devotion suspect, his love for Tamil spurious.

While defense of Tamil-speaking Brahmans continues well into the century, especially within Indianism and compensatory classicism, and while they were progressively rehabilitated by the 1950s into the Tamilian community in official DMK rhetoric, a question that was repeatedly raised in the discourses of many of Tamil's devotees from the turn of the century is "Are Brahmans Tamilian?" The answer, increasingly, was an emphatic "No." Brahmans are exclusionist and caste conscious; they identify themselves with the North, with Aryan culture, and with Sanskrit. Above all, and most sacrilegiously from the radical enthusiast's point of view, they disparage Tamil, treating its high literature and culture as derivative of Sanskrit. So in 1926, Ramasami—not particularly devoted to the language himself, as we will see—insisted that Brahmans had sold out "Tamil1ttây's chastity" to traitors of Tamil by introducing Sanskrit words into it (E. V. Ramasami 1985: 84). And in *Tamil1ttây Pulampal* (The lamentations of Tamil1ttây), Tamil1ttây herself lamented that the Brahman had been borne by her womb, and had been nourished on her milk; yet he had rejected her and her other children. "Will he even call himself a son of Tamil?" she asks (Arunagirinathar 1937: 12). The message was increasingly unambiguous: Brahmans were not supporters of Tamil; they were ashamed to accept, or refused to admit, that they were Tamil speakers. As Ramasami thundered in *Vit#utalai* in 1960, "Where can we see a Brahman who is ready to declare that Tamil is his mother tongue?" (Anaimuthu 1974: 998-99). With the gathering Hindi threat, the Brahman became an even more menacing figure, colluding with North Indians to destroy Tamil1ttây (Bharatidasan 1948: 17). In August 1938, at an anti-Hindi gathering in Madras, the lead speaker, Pavalar Balasundaram, asked his audience, "What is to be done with the Brahman community which is killing our [Tamil1ttây]?"

The response to this question varied over the years; it included the progressive dislodging of Brahmans from positions of bureaucratic and political power from the 1920s with the ascendancy of the Justice Party, as well as the more radical, albeit unsuccessful, calls for Brahmanicide by Ramasami and some of his followers in the 1950s. Not surprisingly, that anomalous figure, the Brahman who did profess his love for Tamil and dedicated his life to its cause, is tainted by association with the community of which he is recognized as a nominal member. He was further tainted because his love for Tamil was generally compensatory classicist and Indianist in complexion. This meant that he was not overtly anti-Sanskritic, anti-Aryan, or anti-India, even when he expressed his passionate desire for Tamil. Instead, he insisted on seeing Tamil as coexisting with Sanskrit and Sanskritic culture; and, not surprisingly, he is increasingly peripheralized within the devotional community. Consider the fate of M. Raghava Aiyangar, a leading member of the Madurai Tamil Sangam, who between 1905 and 1910 helped edit its famed journal, *Centamil1*. In 1913, Raghava Aiyangar was appointed as the chief Tamil pandit in the committee set up to produce the multivolume *Tamil Lexicon*, and he received the prestigious title of Rao Sahib in 1936 for his efforts. In addition, he wrote several historical and literary theses in a compensatory classicist vein, many critical commentaries, and a study of the ancient grammar, *Tolkâppiyam* (Zvelebil 1992: 203-5). The latter in particular was severely attacked within the devotional community, by contestatory classicists as well as Dravidianists, for its portrayal of the sexual morality of ancient Tamilians (Maraimalai Adigal 1936b; Pulavar Kulanthai 1958: 22-23). In August 1938, at an anti-Hindi rally held in Madras, Pavalar Balasundaram fumed:

Raghava Ayyangar has written a commentary on Tolkappiyam....I shall read to you what he has written...."Tamilian women of those days were flirting with whomsoever they came across; the Aryans taught and gave them education to be chaste...." How dare he write like this? Today, it is the Brahman who plays the part of pimps....[W]ith whom have our women flirted? Can a Tamilian who keeps quiet after this claim to be a human being?...Who can put up with such an insult?...Are not the Tamilian women our mother [*sic*]?

A little earlier, in 1936, Panditai Gnanambal wrote a searing essay defending the fidelity of Tamil women and questioning the sexual morality of Brahman women and their Aryan gods. She called upon the government to confiscate Raghava Aiyangar's "traitorous text" that set out to dishonor Tamilians, especially the woman. Otherwise, she concluded, Tamilians would be compelled to rise up in anger all over Tamilnadu to protect their tarnished honor (Gnanambal 1936).

Another enthusiast whose devotion became suspect was V. V. Subramania Aiyar, editor briefly of the nationalist newspaper, the *Tçcapaktan1* (1920-21). In 1922, with the help of funds from the Congress and private patrons, Subramanian established a residential Tamil school (*tamil1k kurukulam*) first at Kallidaikurichi and then at Sheramadevi (in Tirunelveli) for the purpose of teaching students in Tamil, following the principles of the national education scheme. His intention, he explained in a 1924 editorial in the journal *Pâla Pârati*´ that he launched from the school, was "to restore Tamil to its natural state of unrivalled preeminence." He planned to do this by teaching students not only ancient arts and sciences but modern ones as well, and by imparting to them the spirit of social service. Subramanian himself resigned from the management of the school in 1925 after a scandal erupted when it was learned that Brahman students were fed separately. Soon after, he died in an accident while trying to save his young daughter from drowning (Visswanathan 1983: 45-55).

Subramanian did not start out as a Tamil devotee; on the contrary, he first made a name for himself as a nationalist who advocated violence as the principal means to secure freedom from colonial rule. Born in a small village near Tiruchirapalli in 1881, he went on to get a B.A. in history, economics, and Latin from Madras University. He worked for a few years as a lawyer in Tiruchirapalli and in Rangoon before going to London in 1907 to study for a law degree. There, he linked up with V. D. Savarkar and, over the next three years, got drawn into the circle of militant nationalists around him. On his return to India in 1910, he went to Pondicherry, where he met Subramania Bharati and became part of the poet's circle. Subramanian's devotional activities included an English translation of the *Tirukkur1al#* in 1915 and the establishment of a Tamil publishing house in 1916 (Mani 1993). In a number of essays on Tamil he published beginning in 1914, he took an Indianist stance on the language; in 1924, he even insisted (to the ire of many fellow devotees) that for its replenishment and modernization, Tamil should turn to Sanskrit, "the great treasure house." He pointed out that hostility towards Sanskrit was misplaced when even the earliest works of Tamil literature had so many words of Sanskritic origin (Subramania Aiyar 1981; Mani 1993: 116). His own Tamil was highly Sanskritic, and drew criticism even from someone like Kalyanasundaram, a fellow Indianist. Another of its devotees sarcastically asked how Subramania Aiyar could claim to restore Tamil to its "natural state of unrivalled preeminence" if his own speech was so inflected with Sanskrit (Mani 1993: 187-88).

The 1925 scandal over the Sheramadevi Tamil school, which led to Subramania Aiyar's earlier record as a "militant nationalist" being overshadowed by his putative Brahmanness, was soon followed by attacks on other Brahman adherents of Tamil. In 1926, Ramasami published an essay in his *Kut#i Aracu* in which he ridiculed his fellow "non-Brahmans" who had established the prestigious Madurai Tamil Sangam only to have that association hijacked by Brahmans and their Sanskritized Tamil (E. V. Ramasami 1985: 82-83). Soon after, in 1933, a group of Tamil enthusiasts, several among them Brahmans, organized the Tamil1an1par Makânât#u (Tamil Devotees Conference) in Madras to discuss publication of Tamil books in the sciences, the creation of new words to express modern thought, the dissemination of ancient Tamil literature among the populace, the reform of the Tamil script, and the removal of books which promoted caste consciousness from school curricula. But the conference was bitterly attacked in both the Dravidian movement press and in journals like *Centamil1c Celvi,* whose spirit was neo-Shaivite and contestatory classicist. It was seen as a means through which, among other things, Brahmans tried to pass themselves off as "devotees of Tamil," to corner the publishing market, and to introduce more Sanskrit words into Tamil in the name of "improvement." Is it not revealing, critics asked, that these Brahman enthusiasts called the conference by the Sanskritic word *makânât#u* instead of the pure Tamil *mânât#u?* These "lovers of

Tamil" (*tamil1 an1par*) were actually "deceitful lovers," it was declared. In a decade marked by the rise of the Self-Respect movement and by efforts of pure Tamil advocates to create *tan1ittamil1* scientific vocabularies, it is not surprising that the proceedings of the conference were disrupted. In 1934, members of the rival *tan1ittamil1* faction convened their own conference, the Cen1n1ai Mâkân#at Tamil1ar Mânât#u (Madras Presidency Tamilians Conference), which released proposals challenging those of the Tamil Devotees Conference (E. M. Subramania Pillai 1951-52: 141-43; Velu and Selvaraji 1989: 17-78).

All this antagonism towards Brahmans came to a head in the late 1930s during the anti-Hindi protests, not least because the author of the government's compulsory Hindi policy was a Brahman: the much-maligned Rajagopalachari, the premier of the Presidency from July 1937 to October 1939. A native of Salem district and a lawyer by profession, Rajagopalachari, like many other Brahman adherents of Tamil, started his devotional career as an Indianist. More than any of his fellow devotees, he was involved in local Congress politics from very early on, serving as a member, then as chairman, of the Salem Municipal Council from 1911 to 1919. His interest in Tamil-related activities dated to the 1910s, when he demanded the adoption of Tamil as medium of instruction in schools (Rajagopalachari 1956) and, along with some friends, in 1916 instituted the Tamil Scientific Terms Society. The early few issues of its short lived journal published various scientific terms relating to botany, chemistry, physics, astronomy, and mathematics (Irschick 1969: 303-5; Kailasapathy 1986: 32). Rajagopalachari's interest in creating scientific vocabularies in Tamil continued in subsequent years as well when he published books such as *Tamil1il Mut#iyumâ?* (Can it be done in Tamil?; 1937) and *Tin#n#ai Racâyan1am* (Chemistry on the front porch; 1946). For example, the former, a translation of an English-language physics textbook, set out to demonstrate that physics (*pautika câttiram*) could be studied in Tamil. In its preface, Rajagopalachari apologized for the preliminary quality of his efforts and called upon Tamil scholars, with more courage, time, and love for Tamil than he had been able to summon up, to continue this work (Rajagopalachari 1937). The book had a mixed reception in the Tamil devotional community, not least because of its reliance on Sanskrit roots to coin new Tamil words. This reliance was not surprising, for from the start, Rajagopalachari was a great admirer of Sanskrit and its literature, an admiration which he did not see as being at cross-purposes with his attachment to Tamil (Rajagopalachari 1962: 66-67).

His obvious involvement in Tamil "improvement" activities notwithstanding, during the anti-Hindi protests Rajagopalachari was repeatedly identified as an "enemy" of Tamil1ttây and her "destroyer." Dravidian movement newspapers circulated inflammatory cartoons showing him hurling a dagger at Tamil1ttây and disrobing her (figs. 5 and 6). The antagonism against him mounted not least because Rajagopalachari persisted in publicly disparaging the struggle against Hindi in the most elitist (and Brahmanical) terms possible, even casually dismissing the death of a young protester in 1938 when asked about it in the Legislative Assembly. "While Tamilians shed tears of blood that their hero had died, the Aryan members [of the assembly] laughed and clapped their hands," one critic declared indignantly (Ilanceliyan 1986: 173). In the 1940s, Rajagopalachari extended his support to the Tamil music movement and, by the 1960s, lent his considerable influence to the anti-Hindi protests of that decade, but all this helped little in overcoming his predominant image as the Brahman who had tried to "snuff out the life of our ancient Tamil1ttây."

Of course, not all Brahmans fared this way, and there are at least three devotees whose Brahmanness is pondered over, debated, and then set aside in favor of their incorporation into the devotional community. Thus Swaminatha Aiyar, the much revered *tamil1 tâtâ*, "grandfather Tamil," did attract some ire for his defense of Sanskritic Tamil. Nevertheless, he is praised widely for his painstaking efforts to recover and publish the ancient manuscripts of the Cank#am corpus, although a suggestion was aired in the 1950s in *Kuyil*, a journal edited by Bharatidasan, that he may have tampered with these. Similarly, V. G. Suryanarayana Ṣastri, a novelist and essayist who in 1902 was the first devotee to vehemently demand recognition of Tamil's "classical" status, is much praised. Brahman he may nominally have been, but in his *Tamil1mol1iyin1 Varalâr1u* (1903), Suryanarayana Sastri offered a spirited defense of the autonomy, originality, and uniqueness of Tamil, refusing to subordinate the language to Sanskrit in any realm. Suryanarayanan was born into an orthodox Smarta Brahman family of Vilacceri near Madurai in 1870. His father was a scholar of Sanskrit, and Suryanarayanan formally studied the language from his early youth. It was not until he went to high school, however, that his love for Tamil was really kindled, and by the time he was twenty, he was learned enough to start writing literary pieces. In 1890, he moved to Madras for his college education, and he graduated with top honors. Although he could have had any job for the asking, as a true devotee of Tamil he chose to become a Tamil pandit, low salary and all, at Madras Christian College. Over the next decade, he became renowned not just for his mastery of literary Tamil but also for his attempts to introduce innovative ideas, from English literature, into Tamil prose, plays, and poetry.

Yet he never let his admiration for English compromise his love for Tamil: indeed, his fellow devout recall with delight that as a student, when challenged by one of his English professors, he had declared that Kamban's verse from centuries before was superior to Tennyson's. Not surprisingly, for all his work he won the admiration of the famed scholar and fellow devotee Damodaram Pillai, who bestowed upon him the title *tirâvit#a câstiri,* "Dravidian Brahman scholar," a title which even in those days already appeared oxymoronic (N. Subramanian 1950). And he became a close associate of another Tamil litterateur and fellow devotee, M. S. Purnalingam Pillai, whose journal, *Òân1apôtin1i,* he helped co-edit and who declared, when Suryanarayanan died young at thirty-three in 1903, that he had become a "martyr to Tamil" (Purnalingam Pillai 1985: 347).

Suryanarayanan's reputation as Tamil adherent also rests on a singular act that has elicited much admiration from successive generations of the devout. In 1899, in an anthology in which he attempted to introduce the sonnet into Tamil poetry for the first time, he adopted the pen name "Paritimâl Kalaiòar," the pure Tamil rendering of his own given (Sanskritic) name. In his preface to the text, he was clear about why he did this; he was worried about his innovation and was keen on getting his fellow scholars' frank criticisms of his attempt. The work went on to elicit much enthusiasm, and its second edition was published with its author's Sanskritic name (N. Subramanian 1950: 81-84). Although he was hailed as a founder of the *tan1ittamil1* movement by some later devotees, his critics fault him for using his pure Tamil name only once; they also point out that his plays and novels featured characters bearing Sanskritic names, and his own Tamil was inflected with Sanskrit (Tirumaran 1992: 118-23).

And then, finally, there is the most famous of them all, Subramania Bharati. One can do little justice to Bharati in the space of a few pages, but my concern here is with considering whether his Brahmanness factors into the ambivalence with which he has been treated for a good part of this century, his hallowed status today notwithstanding. So, speaking in 1960, Ramasami demanded that if Bharati was such a great devotee of Tamil as they all say he is, how is it that in his poetry, Tamil1ttây herself declares that she is a companion of Sanskrit. How is it that he does not proclaim her autonomy from Sanskrit (E. V. Ramasami 1960: 9-10)? A few years earlier, a short piece in the Dravidianist journal *Tîcut#ar* declared,

> They say Bharati is an immortal poet....[E]ven if a rat dies in an *akrakâram* [Brahman settlement], they would declare it to be immortal....All of Tamilnadu praises him. Why should this be so? Supposedly because he sang fulsome praises of Tamil and Tamilnadu. What else could he sing? His own mother tongue, Sanskrit, has been dead for years. What other language did he know? He cannot sing in Sanskrit....[He says Tamilnadu] is the land of Aryas.

Similarly, another fellow devotee, the Dravidianist poet Pulavar Kulanthai, wrote in the 1950s that "in the name of 'nationalism,' Bharati inserted Sanskrit into Tamil, caused Tamilians to lose pride in their own community, and enslaved them to Northerners" (Pulavar Kulanthai 1958: 22).

Thus the charges against Bharati are similar to those brought against other Brahman devotees; even in claiming devotion to Tamil, he repeatedly sacrificed Tamil1ttây at the altar of Sanskrit and Aryanism. Bharati's vision of Tamil is vulnerable to such attacks, for it falls well within the parameters—indeed, it provides the defining moments—of the Indianist imagination. Yet, as Bharati's many admirers also do not fail to point out, the poet was clearly ambivalent about his Brahman status; he cut off his hair tuft and sacred thread characteristic of many orthodox Brahmans of his times, and sported a mustache; he wrote essays and poems over the years in which he was clearly critical of Brahmanical privilege (Bharati 1987: 51-52, 1988: 264-67); and intimate accounts by friends and family suggest that he hardly led a conventional Brahmanical lifestyle, thereby inviting the wrath of many in his putative community. Indeed, by the 1940s when he had been confirmed as modern Tamilnadu's greatest poet, albeit not without considerable controversy (Sivathamby and Marx 1984), many an ardent Dravidianist, like Annadurai, glossed over the issue of his Brahmanness, preferring to focus on his roles as the "people's poet" and as revolutionary social reformer (Annadurai 1948). And even an acerbic anti-Brahman critic like Bharatidasan, who was to become the poetic muse of the Dravidian movement, did not hesitate to call himself the "slave" (*tâsan1*) of Bharati, the latter's Brahmanness notwithstanding.

All the attention he has received after his death might have come as quite a surprise to Bharati, for during his own lifetime, although he had an ardent coterie of friends and admirers, his genius went largely unrecognized. In fact, towards the very end of his life, when he tried to raise money from the public to have his manuscripts published, he received hardly a response. He died in 1921, broken and dejected, and a man very much in debt (Padmanabhan 1982b: 153-59). Bharati's life—as indeed the life of many a Tamil devotee—clearly underscores one of the principal claims of Tamil devotion: namely, that even in the putative "kingdom" of Tamil1ttây, it was impossible to make ends meet as a Tamil poet or writer or journalist. It was because of this fear that his father, as Bharati tells us in autobiographical verses published in 1897 and in 1910, had compelled his son to learn that "foreign" language English, when Bharati himself would have preferred to have studied the "sweet" Tamil which Shiva favored with his grace. But, he adds, there were few who cared for such a glorious language (Bharati 1987: 1-3, 173-90). Following his father's injunction, the young Subramanian did study English; but in his spare moments in his native Ettaiyapuram, he stole off with his childhood friend and fellow devotee, Somasundara Bharati, to a nearby temple to surreptitiously read Tamil literature away from the eyes of watchful adults.

Subramanian's poetic abilities received early acclaim when he was just eleven, and he secured the title "Bharati" (the learned) from the landlord of Ettaiyapuram (Padmanabhan 1982b: 4-12). His poems did not begin to be published regularly until 1905. By then, he had graduated from high school and gotten married

(1897), spent a few years in Benaras studying Sanskrit and Hindi (1898-1902), and taught Tamil in the high school attached to the Madurai Tamil Sangam for a few months (1904). A friend who knew him in his Benaras days later recalled that he had had no idea then that Bharati was interested in Tamil literature, for he could be seen wandering around the city with a copy of Shelley's poetry. In fact, soon after he returned to Ettaiyapuram in 1902, he formed a local Shelley literary guild and even wrote a few essays under the pen name Shelleydasan, "follower of Shelley" (Padmanabhan 1982b: 16).

In late 1904, he moved to Madras to work for the nationalist daily *Cutçcamittiran1*, where his job involved translating into Tamil news received in English. The pay was poor and the work difficult, but it provided the foundation for Bharati's lifelong passion for transforming Tamil into an easy language of modern communication and politics. Under him, the *Cutçcamittiran1* began to rid itself of its reliance on English (but not Sanskritic) words, for which it had become notorious in Tamil devotional circles. Around this time, Bharati also got involved in nationalist politics; attended the annual meetings of the Congress; and published fiery essays and poems in *Cakravarttin1i*, the women's magazine that he edited in 1905-06, and in *Intiyâ*, the newspaper of which he was editor from 1906. From the start, Bharati's nationalism was heavily inflected with religious fervor, and of course, some of his most famous, and much recited, poems were on Bhârata Mâtâ. In 1908, fearing that he, too, would be caught in a general crackdown on "seditious" writers initiated by the Madras government, he fled to Pondicherry, then a French colony, and was in exile there until 1918. These were also his most productive years as poet, essayist, and journalist, and much of what we now have of his oeuvre today, including some of his most passionate statements on Tamil, belongs to this period. In 1918, he returned to British India and was thrown into prison for a brief while. At the time of his early death in 1921, he was in Madras where he had been working, once again, on the editorial board of *Cutçcamittiran1*.

Much of his later life was marked by poverty, even destitution; poor health; the burdens of taking care of his family; and the attempts to find patrons who would publish his work. Yet the stories that circulate about Bharati today emphasize that he did not let any of these stand in the way of expressing and pursuing his primary passions—devotion to India and to Tamil. Sprinkled through his personal letters to friends and relatives, which recount his many financial and health problems, are his injunctions to them to not abandon Tamil. So, in a 1918 letter to his brother that shows him clearly troubled about his many financial problems, he takes the time to insist, "Do not write me letters in English any more. However colloquial your Tamil may be, I am eager to read it. If you cannot even write in colloquial Tamil (*koccaittamil1*), write to me in Sanskrit" (quoted in Padmanabhan 1982b: 134). And in another much-cited letter to his close friend Nellaiyappar, which ends with his numerous personal problems, he writes, "Tamil! Tamil! Tamil!—think ceaselessly that it is your duty to make it prosper!" He goes on, "Oh! what can I do. I suffer when I see languages other than Tamil prosper. I will not accept that men who are not Tamilian are forging ahead, in knowledge and strength. My heart grieves when I see women who are not Tamilian look so much more beautiful" (quoted in Padmanabhan 1982b: 130). Is it any surprise that latter-day devotees rejoice over sentiments like this, and embrace Bharati as one of their own, his Brahmanness notwithstanding?

The Poet Devotee

Poetry, I have suggested, is the paradigmatic mode of practicing intimate Tamil devotion. The poet, correspondingly, is a particularly heroic figure within the regimes of *tamil1pparlrlu*, however marginalized he may be within the economies of modernity. While in the early years of Tamil devotion Bharati was the poet devotee par excellence, his putative Brahmanness set aside in favor of the passionate poetry he produced, in the later years it is his self proclaimed disciple, Bharatidasan, who is the model poet devotee. Reverenced by his fellow devotees as *pâvçntan1*, "king of verse," and as *purat#cikkaviðar*, "revolutionary poet," Bharatidasan has been the guiding muse for a whole generation of poets in the later half of this century whose verses promote agonistic and fierce *tamil1pparlrlu*, and whose ideal devotee is the warrior willing to give up his body for Tamil (Rajendran 1985: 159-283). For did he not ask, "When harm befalls the glorious Tamil, what use is this body to us?" (Bharatidasan 1948: 9)?

In his autobiographical poem entitled "I Am King of Poetry," published late in his life in 1960, Bharatidasan takes pride in the breadth and depth of his scholarship in Tamil, in his role as a teacher of Tamil, in his various poetic creations, and in his unwavering service to his mother tongue (*tâymol1it ton#t#u*) (Krishnamurthy 1991: viii-xii). This is not, however, the self-portrait of a militant warrior. That his militancy was largely confined to his subversive writings is also apparent from the numerous biographies of the poet, some critical but most hagiographic, that are available today. Named Subburathinam at the time of his birth in 1891, Bharatidasan was a native of Pondicherry. His father was an affluent merchant who fell upon hard times; but we are told that he nevertheless encouraged his son to pursue his love for Tamil, unprofitable though it might be. In 1909, instead of following in his father's footsteps as a businessman, Subburathinam decided to become a Tamil teacher, taking up his first job in a small village school near Karaikal. From then on up until 1946, he worked in various schools in the French colony. His son proudly mentions that his father frequently talked to him about the difficulties and the indignities of being a low paid Tamil teacher. At the risk of jeopardizing his job, on several occasions Subburathinam protested to local French authorities over the low salaries paid to Tamil teachers and over their right to organize; over the quality of Tamil textbooks used in schools, which promoted casteism and hierarchy among young children; and so on (Mannar Mannan 1985: 31-69).

There were two important turning points in the poet's life. Around 1909, he met Subramania Bharati, who had recently arrived in Pondicherry. Over the next two decades or so, Bharatidasan's poems were dominated by the two themes that saturate Bharati's own poetry—Hinduism and Indian nationalism (Ilango 1982; Ilavarasu 1990). He wrote many passionate songs on Hindu deities and on Bhârata Mâtâ, wore *khadi* (homespun), and kept company with the various nationalists who were part of Bharati's coterie. This is also when he published what was perhaps his earliest prose essay on Tamil, which appeared in the nationalist daily *Cutçcamittiran1* in May 1914 and expounded, in a style highly reminiscent of Bharati's Indianism, on the need for a Tamil thesaurus. Soon after Bharati's death in 1921, Subburathinam assumed the pseudonym Bharatidasan, "the follower of Bharati," a name that demonstrated his devotion to his mentor even as it allowed him to publish anticolonial tracts while holding a government job. Although he was chastised over the years for having adopted a name that both was Sanskritic and tied his poetic persona to that of the complex figure of Bharati, Bharatidasan steadfastly maintained that his mentor had been foremost in opposing caste oppression and hierarchy and that he was the first to write in a style of Tamil easily comprehensible to even the commoner. Throughout his life, he remained publicly loyal to Bharati's memory, refusing to be daunted by those who ridiculed him for having declared himself a slave (*tâcan1*) to a Brahman (Ilango 1982).

The second important transformation in his life came in the late 1920s when he was converted to Dravidianism, through exposure to Ramasami's fiery anti-God and anticaste writings and to his polemical weekly, *Kut#i Aracu.* Their passionate espousal of the "self respect" of Tamilians and fierce opposition to Brahmanism resonated with Bharatidasan's own nascent ideas on such matters (Krishnamurthy 1991: 91-92). Although he continued to publish nationalist poems in the Bharati tradition into the mid-1930s, he progressively became the poetic voice of the Dravidian movement, translating into verse many of Ramasami's rationalist, atheist, anti-Brahman, and anti-India ideas. It was during the first wave of anti-Hindi protests of the late 1930s that his writings began to reach a wider audience in the Presidency; over the next few decades, his poems were recited by protesters in anti-Hindi street marches, and his iconoclastic plays were performed at public meetings and conferences of Dravidianist parties. In contrast to many of his more militant followers, Bharatidasan himself rarely participated in such activities. He showed his devotion to Tamil primarily by writing fiery poems, plays, and movie scripts; helping local poets organize; and editing and publishing in polemical journals, such as *Putuvai Muracu* and *Kuyil,* and poetry magazines, such as *Cuppiraman#iya Pârati Kavitâ Mân#t#alam.* Fellow devotees often write with admiration that he conducted his numerous literary activities despite financial straits and political hostility. Nevertheless, when he died in 1964, his reputation as the most important Tamil poet of the post Bharati generation was well-secured, not least because of the deployment of his poetry and his plays in the political activities of the Dravidian movement in the 1940s and 1950s (Krishnamurthy 1991: 89-220).

The experiences of the poet Mudiyarasan resonate with those of Bharatidasan, his mentor and fellow Dravidianist. In his as yet unpublished reminiscences, Mudiyarasan writes that when he was a young man attending college, he heard a talk by Bharatidasan and was convinced that he too, like the famous poet, should write poems on the Tamil land, language, and community (Mudiyarasan n.d.: 151). And indeed, although not as prolific a poet or playwright as his famous mentor, beginning in the late 1940s, Mudiyarasan produced his share of verses on the beauties and glories of Tamil, which earned him the title of *kaviyaracu*, "king of poets," in 1966. Many of his poems, like Bharatidasan's, promote the image of the ideal devotee as militant warrior; his most brilliant effort, the epic *Pûnk#ot#i*, even enlists the Tamil woman in such a role. Yet, like Bharatidasan, he too rarely took an active, public part in language protests; constrained by his job as a government employee, he could spread Tamil consciousness among young Tamilians only through subversive teaching and writing.

Born in 1920 into a poor family in a small village called Periyakulam in Madurai district, he tells us that his love for Tamil was fostered by his mother, who sang sweet lullabies to him, and by a maternal uncle who, although a shopkeeper by profession, had great interest in Tamil literature. He also recalls with affection that his interest in Tamil was paradoxically further stimulated by his first Tamil teacher in primary school, who was a Brahman (Mudiyarasan n.d.: 4-5). It is clear from his reminiscences that he was struck by the urgency of the Tamil cause, growing up in an environment in which he witnessed Tamil and its speakers being demeaned everywhere, often by fellow Tamilians who were Brahman. As a student in a local college in Mayilam, he was troubled when he heard his teacher offering his prayers in Sanskrit, and he was clearly offended when he saw that Brahman students were given privileged treatment (Mudiyarasan n.d.: 21). So in 1947, when he took up his first job as Tamil teacher in Muthialpet High School in Madras, he began his classes with the invocation, "Long live Tamil." His students wrote "Long live Tamil" on the blackboard in their Sanskrit classroom, an act that, he notes, offended his Brahman colleagues (Mudiyarasan n.d.: 26-27). During the centenary celebrations of the high school, he was incensed when the invocation prayer was sung in Sanskrit; his anger only abated when his students spontaneously filled the hall with cries of "Long live Tamil" (Mudiyarasan n.d.: 31). In 1949, he moved to Karaikkudi to teach Tamil in another high school, a job that he held until his retirement in 1978; there he continued to keep vigil over Tamil. If any of his (Brahman) colleagues made fun of Tamil or Tamilians, he writes, he would pounce upon them fiercely, like a tiger (Mudiyarasan n.d.: 48).

It is apparent from his reminiscences that Mudiyarasan cherished his role as a Tamil teacher and as a molder of young minds. Although as a government employee he could not openly and publicly speak out against the state's language policies without risking his job, he practiced his devotion to Tamil subversively by encouraging his students to take pride in their language and their heritage. He was not deterred by the hostility with which such efforts were greeted by some of his senior colleagues and headmasters, who were often Brahmans. In 1966, soon after his passionate poem *Pûnk#ot#i* was proscribed, the then-Congress government tried to force him out of his job, and it was only the coming of the DMK to power in 1967 that prevented this from happening (Mudiyarasan n.d.: 57).

Mudiyarasan's frustration at not being able to participate more publicly and militantly in Tamil devotional activities is apparent throughout his reminiscences. The fear of losing his job and concern over how he could take care of his large family under those circumstances clearly restrained his desire to openly espouse his Tamil devotion. Nevertheless, he proudly recalls that in 1949, his wife joined the anti-Hindi picketing launched by the women's wing of the DK. During the anti-Hindi demonstrations of the previous year, he himself, along with some of his colleagues, had picketed the high school in which they taught, just for one day. "We are Tamil teachers.

Tamil is being harmed. We intend nothing more than showing our grief," Mudiyarasan told the authorities who questioned them (Mudiyarasan n.d.: 42-45). In the mid-1960s, when the protests against Hindi increased in intensity and scale, he recalls being accused of antinationalist and antigovernment activities in the classroom, and he was subjected to interrogation by state officials. He laments that Tamilians are their own enemies, and he writes that only when Tamil speakers appreciate the worth of their language would Tamilnadu improve (Mudiyarasan n.d.: 76-78).

The Scholar Devotee

Within the devotional community, all forms of devotion to Tamil are more or less equally valid, but a special kind of veneration and affection adheres to those who are deemed to be learned scholars (*ar1iòar*). This is quite paradoxical, for Tamil's devotees have been only too painfully aware that the world at large does not treat the Tamil scholar with any particular respect. Until recently, Tamil teachers were routinely paid less than their colleagues, were often the butt of popular jokes, and not surprisingly had a poor self-image. Yet, one model for devotion that clearly exists in the community is that of the scholar devotee who shows his passion for Tamil by pouring his life and energy into deciphering ancient manuscripts, writing books that may sell few copies but nevertheless are a labor of love, and teaching students who are largely unenthusiastic about the language. That all this he does under material conditions that range from middling to appalling is what makes the devotion of the scholar devotee particularly heroic.

Few narratives offer a more strikingly poignant portrayal of one devotee's struggle to pursue scholarship in Tamil under circumstances that were both materially daunting and socially discouraging than Swaminatha Aiyar's *En1 Carittiram* (My story). As a young man, Swaminathan recalls a visitor asking his father: " 'What does your son do?' My father replied, 'He reads Tamil.' Stunned, as if he had heard something incredible, he burst out, 'What? Tamil?' He did not stop there. 'He reads Tamil? Why could he not study English? And how about Sanskrit? If he studies English, he would benefit in this world. The study of Sanskrit will prepare him for the other world. Studying Tamil will bring him neither benefit" ' (Swaminatha Aiyar 1982: 262). The visitor was not alone in thinking thus. Several of Swaminathan's Brahman kinsmen urged him to study either Sanskrit or the more profitable English. But for him, as he wrote later, the motto of his life had been prefigured by the anonymous author of the seventeenth-century poem *Tamil1 Vit#utûtu:* "O preeminent Tamil! I exist because of you! / Even the ambrosia of the celestials, I do not desire!" (Swaminatha Aiyar 1991b: 127).

A native of Uthamadanapuram in Tanjavur district, Swaminathan was born in 1855 and raised as a devout Smarta

Brahman. His father made his (meager) livelihood through giving music performances and religious discourses in the Tanjavur hinterlands. Although supportive in most ways, his father wished that Swaminathan would follow in his footsteps and would study music and the Telugu language that was most appropriate for a career as musician. But Swaminathan tells us, "Contrary to everyone's desires, from the time I was a young man, my mind was immersed in the beauties of the goddess Tamil (*tamil1t teyvam*). More and more, it yearned for Tamil1ttây's auspicious grace (*tiruvarul#*). Sanskrit, Telugu, English—none of these held my interest. Sometimes, I even felt a deep aversion towards them....Tamil had captured my heart" (Swaminatha Aiyar 1982: 156). And Tamil had indeed captured his heart, for there appears to have been space for little else in his life, at least as it is narrativized in his reminiscences. He seems to have been attached to his parents, later even turning down an opportunity to teach in the prestigious Presidency College in Madras city so that they could spend their last days in their beloved Kaveri Valley. The birth of his first son is noted, with some joy. But in the seven-hundred-odd pages of his autobiography, his wife, Madurambikai, does not feature at all, apart from a brief mention on the occasion of their marriage in 1868. Even that important rite of passage left him unmoved. "It does not appear as if anything new has happened to me, now that I have become a householder." For a few days, before and after the occasion, he was filled with great joy, revelling in all the attention—and gifts (!)—he received. Then he soon realized that "there was little gain from all this. I have only one purpose. Tamil is my wealth. It is the food for the hunger of my mind....It was true then. It is true now." So he concludes his brief discussion of his marriage (Swaminatha Aiyar 1982: 123-30).

The absence of details about his personal life is in striking contrast to the wealth of information he provides on the world of Tamil scholarship around the turn of this century. As he tells us on several occasions, he had no worldly interests other than the desire to study Tamil and to spend his time in the company of other Tamil scholars. He got ample opportunity to do so when he apprenticed himself around 1871 to Meenakshisundaram Pillai (1815-1876), perhaps the best-known Tamil savant of his time, on whom he later published a detailed biography. His relationship with his teacher, as he presents it in his reminiscences, echoes his relationship to the language; it was marked by intense reverence, devotion, even love. He recalls how he walked once, in the hot noonday sun, to another village, about two miles away, in order to procure a manuscript that he thought his master would like to see (Swaminatha Aiyar 1982: 193-94). He lapped up eagerly even the smallest word of praise that his master would throw his way, was jealous of fellow students who he feared may make their way into his master's heart, and constantly worried about falling out of favor.

By his own reckoning, Swaminathan's life took a dramatic turn on 21 October 1880, the day he met Ramasami Mudaliar, the *munsif* (civil judge) of Kumbakonam. By then, much had happened in his life. His master had died; he himself had moved to Kumbakonam, where he had secured a job teaching Tamil in the government college; he had an infant son; and he had already begun to acquire quite a name for himself in Tamil scholarly circles. Flushed with pride over his accomplishments, he set out to meet Ramasami Mudaliar, who he had heard was a Tamil enthusiast. Quizzed on the depth of his knowledge, Swaminathan tells us that he proudly rattled off the names of the numerous texts that he had learned by heart. Ramasami Mudaliar, however, was unimpressed. "What is the use of knowing all this....These are all later works. Do you know any of the ancient ones?" he asked. A week later, he handed Swaminathan a manuscript of the ancient epic poem *Cîvaka Cintâman#i,* which he had never before seen. Humbled by the realization of how much more there was to know, he began the quest for other such old texts that changed the course of his life (Swaminatha Aiyar 1982: 528-34).

As he recalls, this of course was no easy matter. Frequently relying on word-of-mouth information about manuscript collections in remote villages, he would walk for miles down country roads, sometimes riding bullock carts which broke down, at other times taking trains (one of the few signs in his autobiography, we note, of industrial modernity). On these trips—the equivalent of other people's holy pilgrimages—he would sometimes encounter wonderful people who filled him with awe and joy because of their obvious reverence for Tamil, and because of the care with which they had maintained old Tamil manuscripts; their abodes, he writes, were "temples of the goddess Tamil (*tamil1t teyvam*)" (Swaminatha Aiyar 1982: 636-38, 690-94). More often, he came across signs of utter callousness, and with horror he recounts stories of old manuscripts being cast into fire as fuel, or thrown into the river. Our ancients tell us that Tamil survived fire and water in the past, but not any more, he writes. In many places, he ignored discomfort as well as personal disrespect. Had he been defeated by these hardships, he could never have restored Tamil1ttây's jewels back to her, he writes (Swaminatha Aiyar 1982: 640-86). Until the very end of his life, he appears not to have lost his love for these manuscripts. "My body may be tiring with age, but my mind has still not lost its devotion to these palm leaves," he observes (Swaminatha Aiyar 1991b: 120).

With the acquisition of the desired manuscripts, the battle had only barely begun. He had to labor hard to read them, struggling over the meanings of archaic words that had long been in disuse, and to understand ancient worldviews quite alien to his Shaiva and Brahmanical upbringing. There were also the challenges of printing, at a time when that technology was still fairly new (Venkatachalapathy 1994a: 274-78). Unlike many later scholars, who would leave the details to the publisher and the press, Swaminathan supervised the entire printing process from start to end, from the selection of the font to the binding of the finished product. Above all, there were financial problems. Publication of these works demanded enormous outlays of money, far in excess of his modest income as a college teacher, and he had to turn to a network of patrons—some reliable, others not so. On more than one occasion, he had to borrow money to keep the printing process going. He also spent many of his waking moments worrying over potential competitors (including fellow devotee Damodaram Pillai), who might beat him to the punch, and dealing with nasty rumors that were floated about his inabilities and inadequacies. About his troubles and worries, he writes: "In the land of *ten1r1al* [southern breeze] and sandal, our Tamil reigns, sweet and soft. I have dedicated myself to the auspicious service (*tiruppan#i*) of that glorious goddess Tamil. Thanks to the wondrous grace of that goddess, the waves of trouble of this world do not deluge me in misery" (Swaminatha Aiyar 1982: 657). Not surprisingly, when the first copies of his published *Cintâman#i* arrived from the binders, he stacked them reverentially and offered them worship. For, he writes, the text—whether published or unpublished—"appears to me as the image of a deity. My desire is only to wipe away the dust and clothe it anew so I can see it....I believe that each part of it is divinity itself" (Swaminatha Aiyar 1982: 611).

Swaminathan lived his life in the high noon of empire. Yet there are few signs of colonialism, westernization, or modernity in his reminiscences. With touching candor, he confesses to the thrill of excitement he felt as a child when he learned the English alphabet. There must be something magical about it, he notes, for even mere association with it confers so much prestige (Swaminatha Aiyar 1982: 61-62). Frequently, during the course of his travels and research, he would encounter fellow devotees—Vedanayakam Pillai, Damodaram Pillai, and others—who knew English and were obviously men of influence and power. And yet it astounded him that they continued to be enthusiastic about Tamil. Swaminathan was not alone in registering such wonder, and a special affection is accorded in the devotional community to all those who had not let their knowledge of English, or their worldly affluence, get in the way of their love for Tamil. Indeed, in the early years of *tamil1ppar1r1u,* there were quite a few "gentlemen scholars" such as J. Nallaswami Pillai and P. V. Manickam Nayakar, who, like Swaminathan, expressed their devotion to Tamil through their scholarship. But they moved in a world that appeared far removed from Swaminathan's. They had university degrees, were well-placed in the hierarchies of government, were fluent in English, and were materially well-off.

One such savant devotee whose story is told with a great deal of pride in the devotional community is Somasundara Bharati, reverentially referred to as *nâvalar,* "the eloquent." A native of Ettaiyapuram, where his father was part of the local landlord's coterie, Somasundaram was a childhood friend of Subramaṇia Bharati with whom he would read Tamil on the sly. Unlike a majority of Tamil's devotees, Somasundaram led a life of comparative ease and affluence as a lawyer, first in Tuticorin and then in Madurai. All the same, we are told that he did not let his law practice, profitable though it was, interfere with his devotion to Tamil. Even while working as a lawyer, he earned a master's degree in Tamil in 1913, and over the next few decades he published numerous essays on the language and its literature, mostly in a compensatory classicist vein (Sambasivan 1967). In 1933, when he was asked to head the Tamil department of the newly founded Annamalai University in Chidambaram, he was faced with a difficult choice, his biographers tell us. On the one hand, he had his lucrative career as a lawyer; on the other, there was service to Tamil, hardly profitable but fulfilling in so many other ways. Somasundaram did not find it difficult to make up his mind: he gave up his law practice and headed the Tamil department for five years (Sambasivanar and Ilankumaran 1960: 57-67). This is not the only instance in which his *tamil1ppar1r1u* led Somasundaram to change the course of his life. In 1937-38, when the government announced its compulsory Hindi policy, Somasundaram was one of the leading figures who spoke out against the Congress at numerous rallies; on one occasion, he even suffered a physical assault. His opposition to Hindi was all the more unusual because he had been a dedicated member of the Congress for much of his life up until then: he had organized numerous political rallies on that party's behalf and had been quite involved in nationalist politics. And yet, as he declared in his *Open Letter to the Hon. C. Rajagopalachariar*, when Tamil1ttây was in danger, how could he afford to maintain his old political convictions (Somasundara Bharati 1937)?

A very different model of scholarly devotion is offered by the life of G. Devaneyan, referred to in devotional circles as *pâvân#ar*, "the poet." The author of numerous books, essays, and poems, most of which are in the contestatory classicist idiom, Devaneyan is best known for his etymological researches on Tamil, and for his attempts to prove that Tamilnadu (or Kumari Nadu, as he called it) had been the site of the birth of humanity and that Tamil speakers were the first humans (Devaneyan 1972). Most of the trials and tribulations that Devaneyan faced in practicing his *tamil1ppar1r1u* followed from having to combat not just the difficulties of abject poverty, but the social stigma of hailing from a very low-caste family recently converted to Christianity. Born in 1902 in the small village of Shankaranayinarkoyil in Tirunelveli district, Devaneyan tells us that when he was a high school student, he had memorized all of Shakespeare's plays and desired to become an English professor at Oxford. And then in 1918-20, he read history and Tamil, and became devoted to the latter. Poverty prevented him from pursuing his higher education, and he began to work as a Tamil schoolteacher in Ambur, North Arcot. But this did not deter him from later passing the Tamil examinations administered by the Madurai Tamil Sangam in 1924 and by the

Shaiva Siddhanta Kazhagam in 1926, which gave him the title of *pulavar*, "scholar." Recognizing the value placed on formal university degrees, however, he also went on to earn a master's degree in Tamil from Madras University in 1944. Meanwhile, he held a variety of teaching jobs, mostly poorly paid in small town schools; starting in 1944, he found a period of stable security for about twelve years, teaching Tamil in Salem.

The one theme that runs through the various biographies on him, written by fellow devotees, is the stark state of poverty in which he lived; often he did not have enough money even to feed his growing family, let alone to do research and publish his works (Tamilkudimagan 1985; Tamilmallan 1989). In his letters to fellow scholars, he frequently laments over his material conditions and writes piteously about visits to bookstores where, even after striking a hard bargain that brought the price of a book down, he still could not afford to purchase it and would have to go home empty-handed (Ilankumaran 1985: 6). Although he found an outlet for publishing his books in the Shaiva Siddhanta Kazhagam, he also published quite a few of his researches at his own expense. For, as his biographers tell us, he could never let economic considerations stand in the way of his *tamil1ppar1r1u* (Tamilmallan 1989: 45-52). In a letter to a friend in 1964, Devaneyan tells him that he would go anywhere if invited to speak publicly on the linguistic problems facing Tamilians, even if he were not paid for his lecture. He was even willing to forgo being reimbursed for travel expenses, when it was Tamil's future that was at stake, for as he writes in another letter, "the life-breath of the Tamilian is Tamil" (Ilankumaran 1985: 9, 79). Such an attitude was forged fairly early in his life. For instance, in a 1937 letter to a fellow devotee, he writes, "As long as we live, we ought to not let Tamil decline" (Ilankumaran 1985: 11). On many occasions, he tells us that his duty to Tamil was to rescue it from the clutches of Sanskrit and to make the world accept what he believed to be the first principle that guided his own life: namely, that Tamil was the first language of the world and the parent of them all. It is for this purpose that he believed he had been created by God (Ilankumaran 1985: 20, 57, 80, 110).

Such statements of devotion are also interspersed with comments of despair and frustration. In 1964, he laments that if he had devoted himself as passionately to English as to Tamil, he would have been a respected professor at Oxford. "The extent to which I have grieved and suffered because of Tamil is no laughing matter" (Ilankumaran 1985: 121). On another occasion, he asked, "What does it matter if Shankaralinga Nadar fasted [to death]? What does it matter if Chinnasami immolated himself? The Tamilian will not heed or improve" (Ilankumaran 1985: 14).

The despair expressed by Devaneyan echoed that of so many devotees who came to hold that a life dedicated to the Tamil cause had brought little material comfort, and even fewer social benefits. His wife's death in 1963 after a lingering illness left him both grieving and guilt-stricken, for he had had no money to buy medicines that might have saved her life. For much of his lifetime, he had few decent clothes to wear, and on occasion he survived for days on gruel and raw onions (Ilankumaran 1985: 110; Tamilmallan 1989: 48-52).

And yet, we are told that even when he was offered a way out of such abject poverty, he refused to take it, because it involved bringing humiliation to Tamil.

In 1956, he was hired by Annamalai University to produce a Tamil etymological dictionary. He had to report his findings to a committee headed by Suniti Kumar Chatterjee, the well-known Bengali linguist who, despite not knowing Tamil, was put in this position of power. Devaneyan's opinions on Tamil and its relationship to Sanskrit were at odds with Chatterjee's, and when asked to change his views, he refused. "Why should we fear to tell the truth about Tamil? How long should we Tamilians live in fear and servitude in this fashion?....It is the duty of every researcher to reveal the truth, whatever may be its consequences. The rescuing of Tamil from its cruel subjection to Sanskrit is the purpose of my life.

This is why I have been created by God" (quoted in Tamilkudimagan 1985: 16-17). In 1961, he resigned his job (or was relieved of it, by other accounts) and returned to his former hand-to-mouth existence. In words that have been repeated many times by his fellow devotees, he is supposed to have declared, "I am poor; I have a wife and children; but I also have honor" (quoted in Tamilkudimagan 1985: 17). As his biographers tell us, rather than betray Tamil and take care of himself, he chose to live heroically, as a poor but honorable and devoted Tamilian.

The Devotee as Publicist

"In my dreams and in my thoughts, I forever think about Tamil and Shaivism. May the Lord offer me grace so that I continue to think about them" (Anbupalam Ni 1967: 56). So declared Maraimalai Adigal in a public meeting in Madras in 1949 at the end of a life dedicated to the task of publicizing the glories of Tamil. Years before, in 1912, during the early years of his career while he was travelling to numerous small towns all over the Presidency as well as Sri Lanka to spread the message of Shaivism and Tamil, he noted in his diary: "I am leading a life happier than that of a prince" (quoted in M. Tirunavukarasu 1959: 130). Service to Shaivism and to Tamil appears to have been the motto of Maraimalai's "princely" life. A devotee with ardent faith in the power of reform, Maraimalai made full use of the modernist technologies of print, associations, and public lectures to convert his fellow speakers into devotees of Tamil.

Maraimalai's use of such technologies of publicity, which were much favored by many reformers all across colonial India, may be traced back to his early youth. Growing up in the coastal town of Nagapattinam, he founded the Intu Matâpimân1am Cank#am (Society for Pride in Hindu Religion) to combat missionary attacks on Hinduism in 1892 when he was sixteen. At this time, he was an ardent believer in Vedantic and Sanskritic Hinduism (Nambi Arooran 1976: 312-13). Within a few years, however, he came under the influence of the well-known scholar Somasundara Nayakar (1846-1901), on whom he subsequently wrote a biography, and was converted to the latter's philosophy of Shaiva Siddhanta. In 1897, as a young man, he had his first encounter with the power of print when he published several essays defending his mentor's version of Shaivism against Vedantic detractors (M. Tirunavukarasu 1959: 4-19). A year later, he secured regular employment as a Tamil teacher in Madras Christian College. This did not stop him from continuing with his proselytizing activities, using weekends as well as his vacation days to give public lectures on Shaivism and Tamil; to publish his researches on Cank#am poems; and to establish reform societies such as the Caiva Cittânta Makâ Samâjam (Society for Shaiva Siddhanta), founded in 1905, and the Camaraça Can1mârkka Nilaiyam (Sacred Order of Love), founded in 1911 (Nambi Arooran 1976: 319-27).

Maraimalai's diaries and letters offer interesting glimpses of the lives of those devotees who turned into publicists and reformers dedicated to the Tamil cause. They formed associations, published books and journals, and organized literary conferences to spread the message of Tamil. These conferences were festive occasions marked by religious hymns and popular songs on Tamil, speeches on the wonders of its literature, and debates about how to go about restoring the language to its former glory. Speakers like Maraimalai were treated particularly well. On one occasion, when he visited Salem, he was taken in procession around the town and greeted by local notables; he then gave a talk for about an hour and a quarter on "the nobility and antiquity of Tamil." His talk was followed by discussions and lectures by other scholars and devotees (M. Tirunavukarasu 1959: 700-702).

Yet it is also clear from his son's account, as well as from the reminiscences of others, that Maraimalai was a demanding publicist for the Tamil cause. Fellow devotee K. A. P. Viswanatham recalls that after being invited to address the annual conference of the Shaiva Siddhanta association of Tiruchirapalli in 1921, Maraimalai presented a formidable list of demands which included detailed specifications on his lodging, provisions for worship and for his food, as well as payment of two hundred silver coins. When asked, "How many will invite you if you ask so much for service to Tamil and to Shaivism?" Maraimalai acerbically replied that while his fellow Tamilians were willing to heap thousands on actors and singers, they refuse to similarly honor Tamil scholars (Viswanatham 1989: 15-17). For Maraimalai, the honoring—both materially and otherwise—of speakers like himself was the honoring of Tamil itself.

His speeches certainly appear to have influenced at least one young man to convert to the Tamil cause. R. P. Sethu Pillai, who later became professor of Tamil in Madras University and published numerous books and essays on Tamil and its literature, many of them Indianist and compensatory classicist in sentiment, recalls a public lecture on Tamil that Maraimalai gave in the small town of Palayamkottai in June 1912. Tirunavukarasu, to whom Sethu Pillai talked later about this event, describes the impact of Maraimalai's speech on the young man: "His being pulsed with the consciousness of Tamil. 'I, too, will learn this great Tamil. I, too, will spread Tamil by lecturing and by offering my services,' he thought to himself" (M. Tirunavukarasu 1959: 162-63).

Maraimalai appears to have been paid well for his speeches. Much of the money he made on these lecture tours was ploughed back into his publication and reform activities. In a 1941 letter to a friend, he observes, "I have spent an enormous amount of wealth on Tamil" (Anbupalam Ni 1967: 24-26). Yet, like the majority of Tamil's devotees, he appears to have led a life of only middling prosperity, and the prefaces to his various books as well his letters contain frequent references to the financial hardship that he faced in continuing with his publication efforts, to the lack of appreciation for his work, and so on. Nonetheless, he worked on tirelessly, beginning most days at the crack of dawn with prayers and going to bed past midnight (Anbupalam Ni 1967: 49-51).

In 1911, at the age of thirty-five and as the sole breadwinner for his family—consisting of his aged mother, his wife, and seven children—Maraimalai decided to give up his teaching career and become an ascetic instead. In doing so, his son tells us, he was following an age-old tradition: "Having dedicated himself to the cause of Shaivism and Tamil, he donned the ascetic's robes and the lifestyle of a renouncer" (M. Tirunavukarasu 1959: 128). At least in his son's reckoning, Maraimalai's act was justifiable, his dedication to the cause of Shaivism and Tamil overriding his family responsibilities. Indeed, it is as an ascetic that Maraimalai entered the most productive period of his career as Tamil devotee; these were the "golden years of his life" (Tirunavukarasu 1959: 481). He published prodigiously and his books sold well; there were numerous requests for his presence as inaugural speaker at conferences; he became a member of the local vegetarian society and led campaigns against the performance of animal sacrifices in rural and low-caste temples. Scholars and admirers thronged to visit his home in Pallavaram, a suburb of Madras where he had taken up residence after becoming an ascetic. "Ah! How many people are now filled with Tamil devotion! They are filled with pride in their community. My work has had its impact. In the future, my books will sell abundantly, and my thoughts will spread far and wide. Tamil will flourish! Shaivism will triumph!" he remarked in contentment to his son in the 1940s (M. Tirunavukarasu 1959: 836-37; Anbupalam Ni 1967: 25). Above all, these were the years in which he earnestly pursued the *tan1ittamil1* cause, republishing pure Tamil versions of his early essays and striving to create a language that would be as free of Sanskrit words as possible. He refused to lend the prestige of his name to any publication that did not conform to his notion of Tamil, and periodically he had public disputations with fellow scholars on the purity of their language. Indeed, though his livelihood partly depended on the remuneration he received from-speaking at conferences, he refused (in a letter he wrote in English) "to attend any Tamil meeting which is not willing to maintain and advance pure Tamil. Of all the Cultivated ancient Languages, Tamil is the only one which is still living in all its pristine glory. I am strongly convinced that any mixture of foreign words in it will tend to vitiate its healthy life and hamper its vigorous growth. Please, therefore, excuse me for not attending your conference which does not seem to meet my ideal" (quoted in Ilankumaran 1991: 127).

In his personal life as well, his son tells us, he attempted to meet his ideals. After 1912, he refused to allow the participation of Brahman priests in the domestic rituals performed at home, deeming this a non-Tamil practice; after 1916, he attempted to speak only in pure Tamil; in the shrine that he built in his home in 1931 in Pallavaram, worship was offered only in Tamil; and he was a devout Shaivite, regularly visiting Shaiva temples where he would sing Tamil hymns to his heart's content and, we are told, would bring tears of joy to all those who heard him.

All the same, his devotion, like that of so many others, was not without its share of contradictions. Later in his life he was neutral, even hostile, to the cause of Indian nationalism, but in his early years, according to his diary entries, he composed nationalist songs, attended nationalist lectures, and even wrote in 1906 that he bought a bundle of *swadeshi* (nationalist) candles (M. Tirunavukarasu and Venkatachalapathy 1988: 25-30). On the incarceration of the nationalist leader Tilak, his diary entry in English dated 23 July 1907 reads, "Oh! Mother India! Are thy sons to suffer thus!" (Anbupalam Ni 1967: 40). At the same time, he also composed songs commemorating George V's accession in 1911 and joined the celebrations in Pallavaram marking that occasion. In 1912, noting that the government probably had him under surveillance, he comments on the stupidity of this, for he was after only a preacher, and he writes that he desired British rule to continue (M. Tirunavukarasu and Venkatachalapathy 1988: 35-36). He may have spent much of his public life castigating Sanskrit for its evils, but unlike those in a later generation of Tamil devotees who criticized the language without any knowledge of it, Maraimalai had formally learned Sanskrit and even translated from it into Tamil a well-known play, *Shakuntala.* In his later published writings, he may have ardently preached the inherent superiority of Shaiva Siddhanta, but in his diaries he expresses admiration for Vivekananda's Vedantic teachings and even gave a public lecture in 1909 on the *Bhagavad Gîtâ*'s importance in modernity (M. Tirunavukarasu and Venkatachalapathy 1988: 32-33). Indeed, although in a large number his writings on Tamil he may appear a classicist, in his own personal reading habits he appreciated a good number of modern works written in other languages. His love for English offers another similar contradiction. He seems to have spent a good part of his limited funds on purchasing English books to stock his personal library, and he translated numerous English classics into Tamil. His son tells us that on his many lecture tours and pilgrimages, he would carry along with him as reading material English books, rather than Tamil. He maintained his personal diary in English. When asked about this, he told his son, "My thoughts, speech, and writing are all in Tamil. To ensure that my knowledge of English does not fade away, I write my daily diary in English" (M. Tirunavukarasu 1959: 700). Such contradictions lasted until the end; when he died in September 1950, he requested that his body be cremated rather than buried in what had been deemed the authentic Tamil style (Viswanatham 1989: 22).

THE DEVOTEE AS PATRON

Among the many grievances of the devotional community was the absence of appreciative patrons who would extend their liberality and largesse to the support of Tamil and its followers. In 1897, as a young man barely fifteen, Subramania Bharati lamented to one such patron, the landlord of Ettaiyapuram:

> *Is our glorious and auspicious Tamil, sweeter than nectar, to which the great lord Shiva himself offered his grace;*
>
> *Yet there is no one around anymore to favor it;*
>
> *Its learners languish away, while lesser tongues flourish.*
>
> *(Bharati 1987: 2)*

Tamil's devotees were of course not alone in colonial India in lamenting over the deteriorating state of patronage extended to traditional arts and letters. The attrition and disappearance of royal courts and religious centers of learning, the redirection of funds towards "useful" and "modern" forms of knowledge, the rise of new bourgeois forms of consumption, and a colonial state indifferent to the promotion of India's languages and literatures—all these contributed to the generalized feeling that things were no longer as they were in the past. The nostalgia for ancient Cank#am poems that was so endemic in devotional circles was also very much a nostalgia for an age in which magnanimous kings were imagined to welcome with open arms the poor poet who wandered into their courts, lend an appreciative ear to his compositions, and shower him with food, clothing, and gold. Those were the days, its devotees sigh, when the wealthy and the notable were admirers of Tamil (and of its scholars). But today, "we lavishly heap our wealth on jewelry, cards, drinks, tobacco, entertainment...but would not spend even one paisa out of a hundred rupees to protect [Tamil1ttây]. What a shame!" (Lakshmana Pillai 1892-93: 154).

Not surprisingly, when one such patron did put in an appearance at the turn of this century, and placed his considerable wealth and influence at the service of Tamil, he came to be narrated in devotional writings as a Cank#am king reincarnate. The institution that he founded and funded in 1901, the Madurai Tamil Sangam, was itself characterized as the "Fourth" Tamil Cank#am, thus establishing a genealogical connection with the three ancient academies that are believed to have flourished in the distant past under the patronage of successive generations of Pandyan kings. Its founder-patron, Pandithurai Thevar, named at birth in 1876 Ugrapandyan (an ancient name that recalled the glory of the Pandyan kings of the Cank#am age), was the landlord (*zamindar*) of Palavanatham, a small estate in Ramanathapuram district. In the reckoning of his biographers and admirers, Pandithurai—unlike many of his *zamindari* cohort, who frittered away their life and wealth in wasteful activities—was an enthusiastic Tamil scholar and poet himself. He may have inherited his love for Tamil from his father, Ponnusami Thevar (1837-70), who also had been its patron, "like the Pandyan kings of yore," in the words of the famous Shaivite scholar Arumuga Navalar (M.

Raghava Aiyangar 1948: 51). Indeed, distressed that so many great works of ancient Tamil had yet to find their way into print, Ponnusami, who was then the chief manager of the Ramanathapuram estate of his brother, Muthuramalinga Setupati (1841-73), commissioned Arumuga Navalar to publish texts such as the *Tirukkôvaiyâr* and the *Tirukkur1al#,* which he then distributed at his own expense to scholars. Ponnusami also established a much-needed printing press for the publication of Tamil books in Ramanathapuram town (M. Raghava Aiyangar 1948: 51-53).

Raised in an environment where such value was placed on Tamil learning, Pandithurai continued this tradition of extending patronage to Tamil and also prevailed upon his more influential cousin, Bhaskara Setupati (1868-1903), the *zamindar* of Ramanathapuram, to do the same. Indeed, their "courts," we are told, were like "heaven on earth." Here, from morning till late into the night, one could hear learned disquisitions on the intricacies of Kamban's *Irâmâvatâram* or the *Tirukkur1al#* poets and musicians were frequent visitors, and "forgetting hunger and thirst," they would sing their compositions and recite poetry. In addition to throwing his court open to visiting scholars, Pandithurai also financed the publication of many ancient manuscripts, including some of Swaminatha Aiyar's (M. Raghava Aiyangar 1948: 76-95). Tamil enthusiasts narrate with pride an incident from Pandithurai's life illustrating how his devotion to Tamil led him to ensure that the reading public had access to well-published and error-free editions of their ancient texts. An Anglo-Indian lawyer of Madurai had had the temerity to publish five hundred copies of the *Tirukkur1al#,* "made easy." Pandithurai invited him over to his palace and asked to see the publication. He noted with anger that the lawyer had erred in the very first key verse of the text. Learning that only two hundred copies of the publication had been sold so far, Pandithurai purchased the remaining three hundred and burned the whole lot, rather than expose his fellow Tamilians to such a travesty (M. Raghava Aiyangar 1948: 105-7).

The scarcity of good published versions of Tamil literary works was what spurred Pandithurai to found his well-known Sangam. In one version of the story, when he was visiting Madurai and needed copies of the *Tirukkur1al#* and Kamban's *Irâmâvatâram* to prepare a lecture, he discovered that it was impossible to procure them. If these works, the heart of Tamil literature, were unavailable in Madurai, the center of Tamil learning, what fate awaited Tamil? he lamented. Resolving to do something to change this, in 1901 he summoned together various notables and scholars and spoke of the need to create a society dedicated to the improvement of Tamil (M. Raghava Aiyangar 1948: 87-89). "The rejection of our mother tongue, Tamil, and the embracing of English mostly for the sake of greater comfort, is like the rejection of our mother in favor of our newly arrived wife," he declared in his speech urging his fellow speakers to come forward and help him in his new venture.

His idea was not new. Since the 1880s, a few such societies had sprung up in the Presidency, although most were short lived. No doubt, the Madurai Tamil Sangam's own longer and more fruitful existence was the result of a convergence of factors: the liberal funding it received from Pandithurai and Bhaskara Setupati (who also used their influence to get other notables to make contributions); the supplementing of the scholarly activities of the Sangam with the establishment of a printing press, a research center, a school that conducted exams and offered degrees in Tamil, and a library (which was started with liberal donations of books from Pandithurai's and the Setupati's own collections); and the founding of a journal, *Centamil1,* in late 1902. All of these attracted to the Sangam some of the finest minds in the world of Tamil learning. But not least of the reasons for the Sangam's success was the symbolic capital that accrued from its location in Madurai; from its self-representation as continuing the traditions of the ancient academies of the Tamil land; and from the persona of its founder, Pandithurai, as a true descendant of the great *val#l#al#s*, "benefactors," of yore (Rowther 1907).

A less spectacular, but no less heroic, model of patronage is offered by the life of V. Tiruvarangam Pillai, the founder of the Shaiva Siddhanta Kazhagam, perhaps the largest publishing house devoted to printing ancient Tamil literary and religious books from its inception in 1920 to this day. Tiruvarangam's life, in stark contrast to Pandithurai's, began in a humble Vellala home in Palayamkottai in Tirunelveli district, where his family ran a general merchandise store. When his father died in 1899, the young Tiruvarangam, who was then only nine years old, went to work in Tuticorin to support his family. When he was seventeen, he sailed to Colombo where he worked for a number of years in various commercial establishments. His entrepreneurial skills must have been forged in this context, for he was able to gather together enough money in 1914 to help finance the first trip to Colombo by Maraimalai Adigal (about whose skills as a speaker and reformer there was much talk). Furthermore, he was also able to put together a handsome purse which he presented to Maraimalai and which enabled the latter to continue with his work in Madras. Over the next few years, Tiruvarangam continued to help Maraimalai's reform activities by arranging for public lectures, collecting funds, and opening bookstores in Colombo and Madras to help sell the reformer's books. In 1920, he even launched a monthly journal called *Centamil1kkal#aòciyam*, primarily for the purpose of publishing Maraimalai's commentary on the *Tiruvâcakam* (Ilankumaran 1982: 1-30).

His crowning achievement, however, was the establishment of the Kazhagam in Tirunelveli in 1920, with a branch office opening in Madras in 1921. His biographer tells us that he took the cue from Maraimalai and his circle of scholar friends, who lamented that Tamilians were quick to invest in all kinds of new ventures but none would support the publication of books of knowledge which are the very source of life (Ilankumaran 1982: 30-31). True to the spirit of *tamil1ppar1r1u*, its admirers insist that although the Kazhagam is a business venture, it has not let economic reasons override its dedication to the cause of Tamil (Ilankumaran 1991: 183). The Kazhagam's involvement in Tamil devotional activities over the past few decades has been manifold, including the support of educational institutions as well as of Tamil libraries. Additionally, it has convened numerous public conferences on various aspects of Shaiva and Tamil literature, on the creation of Tamil technical terms, on Tamilnadu history, and the like. In 1937, Tiruvarangam and his associates played a key role in the founding in Tirunelveli of the Tamil1p Pâtukâppuk Kal1akam (Society for the Protection of Tamil), which published several pamphlets and books promoting the cause of *tan1ittamil1* and protesting the government's Hindi policy. In 1923, Tiruvarangam also started the *Centamil1c Celvi*, a journal devoted to promoting the twin causes of Shaivism and Tamil that is still published today.

But over and above all this, Tiruvarangam's fame in the world of *tamil1ppar1r1u* rests on the role that the Kazhagam has played in the field of publishing: under its auspices, almost every major work in Tamil and Shaiva literature, as well as several minor and hitherto unknown ones, has been printed and made available to the public. Indeed, the image of Tiruvarangam that is remembered most fondly by fellow devotees is that of a man whose voluminous coat pockets were ever stuffed with old manuscripts and galley proofs. In 1980, V. S. Manickam, then vice chancellor of Madurai Kamaraj University, noted that if Tiruvarangam had not founded the Kazhagam, none of the following would have found their way into print: Tamil school textbooks, the Cank#am poems, the *Tolkâppiyam,* M. Varadarajan's sparkling commentary on the *Tirukkur1al#,* dictionaries and encyclopedias, and the *Centamil1c Celvi.* Consequently, "our Tamil1ttây, too, would have wandered around like a weakling able to carry only one child. [But, because of the Kazhagam], our Tamil1ttây has acquired several heads and arms, her blood has been enriched with knowledge, and her nerves and sinews have been strengthened with books. She now has the capacity to go everywhere in all directions; even shouldering the burden of fifty million of her children, she flourishes happily" (quoted in Ilankumaran 1982: 2).

The Warrior Devotee

Increasingly from the 1930s on, especially as Dravidianist sentiments began to dominate the devotional community, the *kaviòar* (poet) and the *ar1iòar* (scholar) had to make room for a new kind of devotee, the *mar1avar* (warrior), who fiercely fought in the glorious and honorable battle for liberating Tamil1ttây. Among the many devotees who so present themselves, perhaps none is as spectacular as Muthuvel Karunanidhi. His life, he writes, is a "battle," and he is the "warrior" who bravely and fearlessly takes it on (Karunanidhi 1989: 7). His reminiscences are sprinkled with numerous allusions to the Cank#am past, and there are repeated comparisons between his own efforts for the Tamil cause and the heroic deeds of ancient Tamil warriors. Like those ancient *mar1avar*s who battled to maintain their honor, he writes that he, too, was prepared to battle—and had indeed done so—to maintain the honor of Tamil and the well-being of its speakers. The four most memorable days of his life, he recalls, are the day he was born; the day he got married; the day he met his beloved leader, Annadurai; and, finally, the day he was thrown into prison for the first time during "the battle to protect [his] language" (Karunanidhi 1989: 15).

Born in 1924 into a working-class family in the small village of Tirukkuvalai near Tiruvarur in Tanjavur district, Karunanidhi's involvement in the Tamil cause began very early, when he was in high school. He was fourteen when the first wave of anti-Hindi protests began to sweep across the Presidency in the late 1930s, and he recalls being impressed with the Tamilian Brigade that marched from Tiruchirapalli to Madras in 1938 and with young men like Dhalamutthu, Natarajan, and Stalin Jegadeesan who had sacrificed themselves in the battle against Hindi. Inspired by their deeds, he organized his fellow students and marched every evening through the streets of Tiruvarur carrying the Tamil banner and shouting anti-Hindi slogans. The student procession was headed by a cart bearing a giant poster of Tamil1ttây being stabbed by Rajagopalachari (fig. 5). The students chanted a verse that young Karunanidhi himself had composed: "Let us all gather together and go to war! / Let us chase away and drive back that she devil, Hindi!" (Karunanidhi 1989: 43-44). One day during their daily march, the students encountered their Hindi teacher. Karunanidhi handed him a pamphlet of anti-Hindi songs, raised the Tamil banner, and shouted, "Let Hindi die! Long live Tamil!" He writes that even though he was just a teenager, and ought to have been scared about confronting his teacher in this way, he felt no fear for his "blood and [his] breath pulse[d] with Tamil" (Karunanidhi 1989: 42-46).

His participation in these anti-Hindi protests laid the foundation for his full-scale involvement in politics. Soon after, he dropped out of high school, became actively involved in the youth wing of the Dravidian movement, and contributed essays on rationalism, atheism, and other such issues to various party newspapers. In 1942, he founded his own newspaper, the *Muracoli*, which continues to be published to this day; and by the early 1950s, he was writing scripts for plays and movies that propagated the ideals of the movement. Later in his life he wrote, "Even if I have a mother and father, wives and children and siblings, and whether they stay with me or part from me, it is the [Dravidian] movement that I think of as my family, and I think of myself as part of it" (Karunanidhi 1987b: 1). He recalls that during several crucial moments in his life, such as the deaths of his father and of his first wife, he was off making speeches for the movement rather than at their side (Karunanidhi 1989: 96, 107). He observes (with some amusement) that when he got married the second time, his wedding took place on 15 September 1948—the same day that Ramasami had called for a renewed protest against Hindi. Friends and relatives had gathered at Karunanidhi's home. He himself was standing at the entrance, greeting his guests, when an anti-Hindi procession went by on its way to picket the local school. The processors were shouting anti-Hindi slogans: "Let Hindi die! May Tamil live!" In the roar of these slogans, he notes, the music of his wedding party could hardly be heard. He, too, joined the procession, and went off to picket the nearby school. Fortunately, he writes, he was not arrested on that day and returned home to marry his bride, who had been waiting patiently through all this (Karunanidhi 1989: 113-15).

From the early 1950s, as a key member of the newly formed DMK, Karunanidhi began to participate enthusiastically in various protests launched by that party, picketing shops run by North Indian merchants and tarring over Hindi names on public billboards. He gained early fame in 1953 when he led a group of DMK volunteers in a bid to change the name of the industrial town called Dalmiapuram to its Tamil original, Kallakudi. His narration of this event offers a clear illustration of Karunanidhi's efforts to capitalize on themes drawn from ancient heroic poetry. He writes that he and twenty-four others set out on that fateful day. "Look, the herd of Tamil lions has set out to cast aside the crown of dishonor that sits on our Tamil1ttây's head....We ran towards our mother. We erased the name Dalmiapuram. We painted on the name Kallakudi." Then, over the protests of police officials who had gathered there, he and his fellow "warriors" laid themselves down on the railroad tracks as they heard the train approaching: "One last time, I looked up at the sky! I looked around at Kallakudi; I looked to my heart's content at Tamil1ttây who nurtured me. I looked at all those standing around me...I closed my eyes. I heard the sound of the train approaching. My heart resounded with the words, 'May Tamil live long!" ' Several men lost their lives or were injured at Kallakudi, and Karunanidhi himself was sentenced to six months in prison. "We received our reward for fighting for the honor of Tamilians," he concludes (Karunanidhi 1989: 196-214).

This is not the only time Karunanidhi went to prison in the battle to save the honor of his language and his fellow speakers; he was imprisoned once again in 1965 for his role in the anti-Hindi protests of that year. He writes in the style of the *mar1avar* devotee, "I will have no greater joy than if I die on the battlefield, opposing Hindi" (Karunanidhi 1989: 476). And although he has held several public and political offices—as a member of the Legislative Assembly from 1957; as a cabinet minister in the first DMK government in 1967; and then as chief minister of the state from 1969 to 1976, 1989 to 1991, and most recently beginning in May 1996—he clearly takes pride in his persona as a "warrior" for Tamil, as someone who has been ready to put his body on the line for his fellow speakers of Tamil. As he declared later in life, in a verse that admirably captures his flamboyant presentation of self:

> *O Tamilians! O Tamilians!*
>
> *If you throw me into the ocean, I will float on it as a raft; you may climb aboard and ride the waves.*
>
> *If you throw me into the flames of a fire, I will be the burning log; you can use me in your hearth and cook your meals.*
>
> *If you dash me against the rocks, I will break into the flakes of a coconut; you can pick these up and eat them, and rejoice. (Karunanidhi 1987b: 229)*

Another devotee who presents himself, albeit less colorfully than does Karunaṇidhi, as a *mar1avar* battling for Tamil is M. P. Sivagnanam. Sivagnanam's life, like Karunanidhi's, offers an illustration of how *tamil1ppar1r1u* can bring fame and fortune, the trials and tribulations involved in its practice notwithstanding. Born in 1906 into a very poor family of the low Gramani caste in Madras city, Sivagnanam had to drop out of school early, and he helped support his family through a variety of minor jobs: rolling tobacco for country cigarettes, working as a day laborer on construction sites, and as a printer for about eight years. In 1927, he joined the Congress and rose slowly but steadily in its ranks, in spite of his low-caste, working-class background. In 1942, he was imprisoned in Amaravati for his participation in the Quit India protests. This was a turning point in his life, for there he read Cank#am poetry for the first time and came to believe that the Tamil country ought to be ruled only by Tamilians; that every

Tamilian's credo ought to be, "Tamil everywhere, everything in Tamil" that Tamil should be the first principle of their lives; and that the Tamil land should be restored to its original, "sacred," and "natural" frontiers (Sivagnanam 1974: 250-53).

Over the next two decades, he "battled" to make this vision a reality. In his autobiography suggestively entitled *En1atu Pôrât#t#am* (My struggle), Sivagnanam writes that he had to conduct this battle on several fronts. As a Tamil devotee in the regional Congress, he struggled to ensure that Tamil interests were not compromised by that "nationalist" party. By 1953, he found that his continuing membership in the party threatened his devotion to Tamil. He writes that if he had not severed his connections with the Congress, he could have become mayor of Madras, or even a cabinet minister—no small achievement for a poor boy from the slums. But "for the sake of Tamil and Tamilnadu and Tamilians," he gave all this up (Sivagnanam 1974: 709). On another front, as a "nationalist," he also conducted a series of campaigns against the Dravidian movement in the 1950s to counter any possibility of Tamilnadu seceding from India (Sivagnanam 1974: 535-55).

His fame in Tamil devotional circles rests on his attempts to popularize the poems of the Cank#am; on his efforts to commemorate the birthdays of great Tamil poets and nationalists like Bharati; and on a series of assaults he led from the late 1940s through the 1950s to ensure that the borders of the newly formed linguistic state of Madras conformed to what was imagined as Tamil1akam, "the home of Tamil," in the Cank#am age, stretching from the Tirupati hills in the north to the Cape in the south. He also fought to ensure that the city of Madras would not be lost to neighboring Andhra Pradesh, declaring in 1953, "We will save our capital if it means cutting off our heads. As long as the last Tamilian is alive, we will not surrender our rights. We will not forget our heroic heritage. Fiercely, we will rise! We will protect our Tamil1ttây" (Sivagnanam 1974: 617). And fiercely he did rise and march, and he was detained in 1953 and in 1956 by the Congress government for his role in these border campaigns. Although by the mid-1960s Sivagnanam joined ranks with the DMK party in order to fight the common battle against Hindi and was subsequently elected to the Madras Legislative Assembly, he turned down an offer to join the DMK cabinet in 1967, wishing not to be diverted from his true service to Tamil, its land, and its people (Sivagnanam 1974: 981).

THE DEVOTEE AS MARTYR

While not minimizing the sacrifices made by these better-known luminaries, the real "warriors" of *tamil1ppar1r1u* were the hundreds of relatively unknown, even anonymous, young men who, from the 1930s on, increasingly took to the streets, courted arrest, undertook fasts, died under police fire, and burned themselves alive for the sake of Tamil and Tamil1ttây. Whatever each individual's intentions and motivations may have been, their deeds are remembered, textualized, and circulated by their fellow devotees to conform to the ideal of the "Tamil martyr" (*mol1i tiyâki*). Their names are invoked again and again in poem and song, in speech and writing. Since 1967, after the DMK first came to power, buildings and streets and bridges have been named after them; commemorative statues have been installed; and pensions have been given to their survivors. And since 1968, the party has routinely celebrated 25 January as "Language Martyrs' Day." The memory of these martyrs is repeatedly used to spur Tamil speakers to take up the Tamil cause and, if need be, to sacrifice their lives for their language/mother.

If a populist political movement reaches its apogee when it gains its first martyrs, *tamil1ppar1r1u* attained that moment in 1939. Early that year, two young men, Natarajan and Dhalamutthu, died in prison, having been arrested along with numerous others for joining the anti-Hindi picketing in front of the Hindu Theological High School in Madras city. The government was quick to point out that both men had been in poor health when they had entered the prison, and that they died of cellulitis and amebic dysentery. In devotional writings, however, their deaths are presented as heroic sacrifices to the Tamil cause, and over the years these men have attained the status of devotees who selflessly gave up their lives for their language (Annadurai 1985: 34-36, 56-57; Karunanidhi 1989: 196-207; Parthasarathy 1986: 410-37). Their funeral processions in Madras city were attended by hundreds of mourners and marked by fiery speeches celebrating their martyrdom. Annadurai proclaimed that Natarajan's name and deeds had to be inscribed in gold in the history of the world. Another admirer, Kanchi Rajagopalachari, a maverick Brahman in the Justice Party and archcritic of the government, declared that never before even in the glorious history of ancient Tamilnadu had anyone sacrificed his life for his language, predicting that Natarajan's grave would become a hallowed site for all true Tamilians. Natarajan's father, we are told, declared that his son's spirit lived on in all true Tamilians and invited them to continue the battle for Tamil rights (Iraiyan 1981: 108).

Government records only tell us that Dhalamutthu Nadar was a native of Kumbakonam, an illiterate who was arrested on 13 February 1939, fell ill on 6 March, and died on 11 March. According to Tamil's devotees, he was married, and when he was arrested, the judge asked him if he would return to his hometown if he was released; he refused the conditions. Sentenced to six months' "rigorous imprisonment," he entered prison shouting "Down with Hindi! May Tamil flourish" (Iraiyan 1981: 107). Natarajan, government sources note in passing, was an illiterate twenty-year-old "Adi-Dravida" carpenter and a native of Madras. He was arrested on 5 December 1938, fell ill and was admitted to the hospital on 30 December, and died on 15 January 1939. The 22 January issue of the *Sunday Observer* carried an interview with K. Lakshmanan, young Natarajan's father, in which he declared that his son often sang religious and anti-Hindi songs at home. Three days prior to his arrest, his son had expressed his desire to go to jail for the sake of Tamil. Lakshmanan also said that when his son was hospitalized, he was told by the authorities that if he submitted an apology for his activities, he would be released from prison. But Natarajan refused. In its editorial of 22 January, the *Nakaratûtan1* declared that Natarajan, filled with "love for Tamil," preferred to die a honorable death in prison rather than agree to a dishonorable release (Ilanceliyan 1986: 171-72; Visswanathan 1983: 244-47).

Along with Dhalamutthu and Natarajan, these early protests against Hindi also produced another martyr in a young man who called himself Stalin Jegadeesan. On 1 May 1938, he started a fast, demanding the cancellation of the government's Hindi legislation. He was frequently put on display at anti-Hindi meetings, and his photograph was periodically published in sympathetic newspapers. A statement issued by him, published in the *Vit#utalai*, had him declaring that he had gone on his fast to prove to Hindi supporters that Tamil1ttây still had loyal sons: "I will return with our Tamil1an1n1ai [Tamil1ttây], or I will die," he concluded. Following his example, another man, named Ponnusami, also went on a fast on 1 June in front of Rajagopalachari's residence, sitting under a tree and carrying the Tamil banner (with its characteristic emblems of the tiger, the bow, and the fish, signifying the ancient Tamil dynasties of the Chola, Chera, and Pandya). He is reported to have declared: "I shall fast unto death; even if released from jail I shall go and fast and die in front of the Premier's house. If Jegadeesan should die...[a] thousand lives should go for it."

Some anti-Hindi leaders such as Ramasami rejected fasting as a form of protest; others such as Annadurai used the example of Jegadeesan to spur Tamil speakers to join the cause. At an anti-Hindi meeting in 1938, Annadurai thundered, "If Jegadeesan dies, I am ready to take his place, and die along with ten other persons. As soon as Jegadeesan dies, you should also be prepared to die." Jegadeesan, however, did not die; on the contrary, it was reported that he had been stealthily eating at night all along, and his fast was called off after about ten weeks (Nambi Arooran 1980: 208-10; Visswanathan 1983: 201-5).

Stalin Jegadeesan may not have given up his life for Tamil, but Shankaralinga Nadar certainly did, in the process of demanding that Madras state be renamed Tamilnadu. Nothing in the biography of Shankaralingam, as it has been documented by T. Sundararajan (1986) from information obtained from his grandson, offers a clear reason for why he took this course of action. A lifelong Gandhian, Shankaralingam was born in 1895. He was a social reformer and nationalist in his native Virudhunagar, but there seems to be little evidence of devotion to Tamil during his early years. The only possible explanation that Sundararajan himself obliquely offers is that by the 1940s, Shankaralingam was disillusioned with life, and perhaps the fast was one last effort to do something for his beloved Tamilnadu (Sundararajan 1986: 68-76). He died on 13 October 1956 after a fast of over seventy days; his demand for renaming the state was not granted until a decade later. Soon after Shankaralingam's death, in 1958-59, two young men named Ilavalakan and Arangarathinam fasted in front of radio stations in Tiruchirapalli and Madras demanding that the Sanskritic work for radio, *âkâs#vân#i,* which smacked of Hindi domination, be replaced with the pure Tamil term, *vân1oli.* Others, including K.

A. P. Viswanatham, joined in their protest, and more than sixty were arrested by 1960. Arangarathinam himself was hailed as the great hero who was a direct descendant of ancient Tamil warriors like Senguttuvan and Nedunceliyan, and Bharatidasan wrote poems and editorials celebrating his heroic act (Sambandan 1976: 120-25).

All these martyrs, however heroic and lauded, were soon overshadowed by Chinnasami, who set himself on fire in Tiruchirapalli on 25 January 1964, on the eve of municipal elections in the state. Chinnasami's self-immolation inaugurated a dramatic new form of expressing devotion and offered a spectacular new model of the true devotee of Tamil, as one who turns himself into ashes for his language/mother. Verses have been written on him, including a long poem which portrays him and his family as the archetypal heroic Tamilians (Puthumai Vannan 1968). During the 1964 elections, the DMK plastered the walls of Madras city with posters showing the charred body of Chinnasami, and in the 1967 campaign, the party staged a play on his life and death. In April 1967, soon after the party came to power, a memorial to Chinnasami was set up near Tiruchirapalli (Karunanidhi 1989: 698; M. S. S. Pandian 1992: 17; Ryerson 1988: 132-33).

In his memoirs, Karunanidhi tells us Chinnasami's story in a chapter entitled "Chinnasami, the Lion Tamilian" (Karunanidhi 1989: 498-501). A native of the small village of Kilpaluvur near Tiruchirapalli, Chinnasami had a primary school education up to the fifth grade and later worked as a day laborer. In his spare time, he avidly read Dravidianist literature and newspapers, and he had even named his only daughter Dravidacelvi, "Lady Dravida." A few days before he immolated himself, he had visited Madras, and on a chance meeting with Chief Minister Bhaktavatsalam, he implored the latter to do something to save Tamil. He was taken into custody. On 25 January, in the early dawn, he doused himself with kerosene and set himself ablaze in front of the railway station in Tiruchirapalli. He was twenty-seven. Karunanidhi writes that as the flames consumed him, he shouted, "Let Hindi die! May Tamil flourish!" Karunanidhi also quotes from a letter Chinnasami is believed to have written to a friend on the eve of his death in which he declared, "O Tamil! In order that you live, I am going to die a terrible death!" In a speech that Karunanidhi himself gave soon after Chinnasami's death at a public meeting, he declared,

"Even when his youthful face was being scorched by the flames, from the bottom of his heart, he cried out, consumed by passion for his mother tongue, 'May Tamil1ttây flourish! Down with Hindi.' He then surrendered his life." Karunanidhi concludes that in his death, Chinnasami gave truth to every Tamil devotee's reigning sentiment: "I want to die with Tamil on my lips! / My ashes should burn with the fragrance of Tamil!" (Karunanidhi 1989: 498). His wife Kamalam, it is reported, today takes pride in the fact that he was the first to immolate himself in the battle against Hindi. "[His] greatness is my wealth," she notes with tears.

A year after Chinnasami's death, in the early months of 1965, several other young men followed in his footsteps and immolated themselves. Today, in various devotional tracts, their names are repeated, over and again, almost like a litany: Sivalingam, Aranganathan, Veerappan, Mutthu, and Sarangapani. Three other young men—Dandapani, Mutthu, and Shanmugam—died after consuming poison. On January 27, an eighteen-year-old college student named Rajendran, himself the son of a policeman, was killed when police opened fire on a huge anti-Hindi protest march at Annamalai University in Chidambaram. The varying stories of all these young men have been narrativized in the devotional community to conform to the image of the selfless Tamil martyr, overwriting any individual aspirations or passions they might have had. Each of them, prior to death, professed his devotion to Tamil and lamented over Tamil's fate at the hands of Hindi. Some left behind letters (which were found sometimes beside their charred bodies) in which they proclaimed their deaths to be "in protest against the imposition of Hindi, and [as] sacrifice at the altar of Tamil" (Barnett 1976: 131); others cried out "Long Live Tamil! Down with Hindi!" as their bodies were beginning to burn. When neighbors tried to save Veerappan, he reportedly told them as the flames were consuming his body that they should use their efforts to save not him, but Tamil. Young Sarangapani died in his hospital bed, saying, it is claimed, "I have given up my life for Tamil1ttây" (Parthasarathy 1986: 412). Mallika, Aranganathan's wife, told newsmen that her husband cared for Tamil deeply, even more than for his three children and herself. For days before his death, he had been troubled about the ruin that Hindi was causing Tamil, the DMK newspaper *Muttâram* reported. Many of these young men, it is claimed, were inspired by Chinnasami's example, which they read about in DMK party newspapers. Aranganathan is believed to have immolated himself after seeing the charred body of Sivalingam. Sivalingam in turn was inspired to his act by Chinnasami's.

With the exception of Veerappan, who was a schoolteacher, and Sarangapani and Dandapani, who were college students, all the others, like Chinnasami, had had only a basic education and held low paying jobs of various kinds. Like Chinnasami again, they all came from very poor rural families, and at least in the government's reckoning, they "were also reported to be suffering from domestic troubles, illnesses, etc." Finally, they all appear to have subscribed to the ideals of Dravidianism to various degrees. Like Chinnasami, they were rank-and-file members of the DMK. Some DMK leaders publicly expressed their horror over these immolations; others attended the men's funerals.

The party has in general condoned devotion in this form and even celebrates such martyrs, if the hagiography it generates on these young men is any testimony. DMK newspapers routinely carried photographs of the charred bodies and the funeral processions of the dead martyrs, and, as already noted, the date of Chinnasami's self-immolation has become "Language Martyrs' Day." The speeches and essays of key DMK leaders are to this day sprinkled with celebratory allusions to these men. It is reported with pride that newspapers, both Indian and foreign, carried news of the immolations. The Tamil devotee had at last succeeded in drawing the attention of the rest of the world to the plight of his language/mother, by literally burning himself to death.

The Anti Devotee

Finally, I turn to the maverick figure of E. V. Ramasami, the "patriarch" (*tantai*) of the Dravidian movement, who is reverentially referred to as Periyâr (the great one) by his followers and admirers. Perhaps more than any single individual, Ramasami has had the greatest influence, by their own reckoning, on the lives of large numbers of Tamil's devotees, especially those who write in the Dravidianist idiom. Indeed, in a literary culture given to extravagant adulation and excess, praise of Ramasami is only surpassed by praise of Tamil (Pulamaidasan 1975). To quote a typical example:

You were the courageous one
in the group that sought
the welfare of southern people.
......
You mastered and embraced
the British language
as the language of science.
You blocked the ascent of Hindi
that had gained a place
in the life of my people.
You are the king who rises up
if Tamils anywhere suffer.
......
You, who always think
about developing fair Tamil
......
You…came as a son
so fair Tamil could flourish.
(quoted in Richman 1997: 198, 204)

It is ironic that his admirers wrote verses such as this, for the subject of all this adulation had very little patience with a literary form like poetry. Even more ironically, beginning in the 1940s if not earlier, Ramasami launched a sustained attack on the passionate attachment to Tamil that was the binding glue of the devotional community; in the 1950s, he even referred to the language as "primitive" and "barbaric" (Nannan 1993: 52, 138-50; E. V. Ramasami 1960: 10-11). This attack peaked in the early 1960s when he published a polemical pamphlet provocatively entitled *Tâyppâl Paittiyam* (Madness over mother's milk), in which he boldly satirized the hallowed figure of Tamil1ttây (E. V. Ramasami 1962: 7-17). Nevertheless, devotees who are admirers of Ramasami strategically overlook his denial of Tamil and present him instead as its "savior"—even as one of Tamil1ttây's true sons. Indeed, because so many of them profess to be rationalists and atheists, they can no longer call upon Hindu deities to grant protection to their adored subject, Ramasami; instead, they turn to Tamil or Tamil1ttây to do so. Typically, praise poetry on Ramasami begins with praise of Tamil. For Tamil1ttây's devotees, he is one of their own, and one of hers, as well.

And yet all along, Ramasami vigorously resisted being thus appropriated into the Tamil devotional community; hence my characterization of him as "anti-devotee." So, for instance, in July 1939 at a public meeting in Coimbatore, he announced:

The chairman says I have great devotion for our mother tongue, Tamil. He also said that I toil hard for it.... I do not have any devotion for Tamil, either as mother tongue or as the language of the nation. I am not attached to it because it is a classical language, or because it is an ancient language, or because it was the language spoken by Shiva, or the language bestowed upon us by Agastya....Such an attachment and devotion is foolish. I only have attachment to those things that have qualities that have utility. I do not praise something just because it is my language or my land or my religion or because it is something ancient.

Here, in one sweep, he vigorously set himself in opposition to every assertion made by the devout, across the various regimes of *tamil1ppar1r1u*, over the past half century. Indeed, in contrast to its devotees who imagined Tamil as a person—their goddess, their mother, even their beloved lover—Ramasami represented it as a worldly object: an instrument (*câtan1am*) for communicating one's thoughts, a tool (*karuvi*) for expressing ideas. The greatness of a language, he wrote, lay in the ease with which one could express thoughts in and through it, and the efficiency with which one could learn it; its usefulness lay in its appropriateness for any community's conditions for existence, its compatibility with the environment, and so on (Anaimuthu 1974: 963-69; Kothandaraman 1979). So, in his 1939 speech in Coimbatore, he conceded that if he had any affection (*an1pu*) at all for Tamil, it is because it had some use for its speakers. Over the following decades, he became less willing to make even this concession. Mudiyarasan recalls that at the Language Teachers Conference in 1948 over which Ramasami presided, he scribbled the words "Down with Tamil" on a piece of paper lying on the table; contrary to the spirit of the conference, Ramasami declared in his own speech, "First, Tamil has to die....Only English should reign. It is only then that the

Tamilian will improve" (Mudiyarasan n.d.: 42-43). Ramasami himself wrote a few years later that when he made a similar point at another public meeting, some Tamil "fanatics" (*molli verliyar*) asked him whose son he was. Ramasami replied that if-speaking English meant that Tamilians were children of the British, then they should also give up using other "English" products such as the radio and the telephone (E. V. Ramasami 1962: 6-7).

Indeed, in his editorials of early 1967, which were surely a commentary on recent happenings in the state, convulsed as it had been by anti-Hindi protests, he wrote: "In our land today, those who have no other means of survival invoke Tamil in order to survive. They declare in frenzy that 'Tamil has to be protected; We will labor for Tamil; We will give up our lives for Tamil.'...The people [of this land] should not be fooled by this....How can people who live in modern times be seized by this language madness (*molli paittiyam*)? The madness over language is like the madness over caste and religion" (Anaimuthu 1974: 983, 1001).

"Why should we get into a frenzy over language?" This was an interesting question to raise at a time when so many had claimed, and acted on the premise, that a life without Tamil was a life not worth living. In the numerous self-reflections that Ramasami offers on his life, "service to Tamil," that driving imperative of Tamil's devotees, hardly figures at all—yet another reason for characterizing him as "anti-devotee." Instead, the burning passion of his life, as he himself declared on many occasions, was to put an end to caste exploitation: specifically, to Brahman denigration of, and domination over, the "non-Brahman," Dravidian populace (S. Chidambaranar 1971: ix-xxxi, 15-20). It is caste and religion that were his central concerns for most of his life, not language. As he declared in the 1950s, "language is not so important for man" (E. V. Ramasami 1962: 1).

Not surprisingly, unlike any of its devotees, Ramasami makes no claims to have labored for Tamil. Born in 1879 into a middle-class merchant family in Erode, by his own reckoning he was a rebellious young man, going against the wishes of his orthodox parents on more than one occasion. He dropped out of school—not driven out by poverty, as was the case with so many of Tamil's devotees, but by choice—and started working for his father. It was not until 1915, when he was in his thirties, that he began to involve himself in civic activities; and here, too, unlike many in the devotional community, his interest lay in local politics, and increasingly in anticolonial politics. By 1920, after serving for two years as chairman of the Erode municipality, he joined the Congress, and by all accounts he ardently threw himself into promoting the end of untouchability, the virtues of *khadi* (homespun) and teetotalism, and other such staples of Gandhian nationalism. In 1924, he led a campaign in Vaikom (in present-day Kerala) to demand the rescinding of rules prohibiting Untouchables from access to roads near the local temple. He received the sobriquet *Vaikkam Vîrar,* "hero of Vaikom," for his efforts, and this campaign also consolidated his growing reputation as a man who was radically opposed to Brahmanical privilege and caste exploitation (S. Chidambaranar 1971: 1-88; Visswanathan 17-66).

Soon after, in 1925-26, he parted from the Congress, dissatisfied with the party's Brahmanical predilections, the most recent illustration of which was its support of separate dining facilities for Brahman students in Subramania Aiyar's Tamil school in Sheramadevi (discussed earlier). Over the next few years, he began to drift towards the Justice Party, the premier organization that represented "non-Brahman" interests in the Presidency, although there were considerable differences between its conservative, elite agenda and Ramasami's own rationalist, atheist, iconoclastic imperatives that found expression in the Self-Respect movement he spearheaded from this time on. He also founded, and often acted as editor of, a number of controversial and radical newspapers and journals, such as the *Kut#i Aracu, Vit#utalai, Revolt,* and so on, publications which reportedly had a transformative influence on so many of Tamil's devotees. And yet his own writings are marked by the absence of the literary flourishes and the erudite citations from ancient Tamil literature that characterize devotional writings; on the contrary, Ramasami appears to have taken an almost perverse pleasure in using colloquialisms, *koccaittamil1* (unrefined Tamil), even what some would consider vulgarisms. Ironically, or perhaps deliberately, the Tamil that he employed in his writings was inflected with Sanskrit, his polemical attacks against the language notwithstanding.

Ramasami's involvement in activities related to Tamil began in the 1930s (Nannan 1993: 11-14). In 1934-35, in essays he published in *Pakuttar1ivu* and *Kut#i Aracu,* he called for reform and rationalization of the Tamil script in order to make it more serviceable in printing and typewriting. Although not the first person to call for such a reform, nevertheless he was among the earliest to demonstrate by example: his publications began to use a modified version of the script that was eventually officially adopted by the Tamilnadu state in 1978. In the 1940s and 1950s, Ramasami also supported the demand for use of Tamil in temple worship, the Tamil music (*tamil1 icai*) movement, the call for renaming Madras state Tamilnadu, the protests over better pay for Tamil teachers, and all other such causes that were so dear to Tamil's followers (Anaimuthu 1974: 959-63; Kothandaraman 1979; Nambi Arooran 1980: 167-68; Velu and Selvaraji 1989).

Of course, his reputation and fame as devotee of Tamil rests on his spirited opposition to Hindi and on his vigorous leadership of the anti-Hindi movement from the late 1930s through the 1960s. Indeed, as early as 1926, long before the opposition to the language had grown among scholars as well as the general populace, he insisted that Hindi was being favored politically, pedagogically, and financially by the Brahman dominated Congress party at the expense of Tamil (E. V. Ramasami 1985). Over the next few decades, he vigorously flooded newspapers and magazines with powerful, and often colorful, arguments against the language; led numerous campaigns for picketing government offices, schools teaching Hindi, and business establishments run by North Indians; tarred over Hindi names on official boards in railway stations and post offices; burned the Constitution of India and the national map; and was arrested on numerous occasions for all his efforts. His admirers mention that in this process, not only did he instill Tamil consciousness into the hitherto "sleeping" Dravidian masses, but he was also responsible for politicizing women and drawing them into the Tamil cause.

Through all this, Ramasami paradoxically maintained that he was-speaking out against Hindi not because he was a devotee of Tamil, but because he saw Hindi as an agent of continuing Aryan, Brahman, Sanskritic, North Indian imperialism. During the 1930s, he was willing to concede that given their other choices—the irrational and ritualistic Sanskrit, and the "backward" Hindi—Tamilians were much better off with Tamil (Anaimuthu 1974: 968-69, 1763-825). But from the 1940s, even as he was leading the fight against Hindi, he also attacked the enormous political, symbolic, and emotional investment in Tamil made by so many of his fellow Tamil-speaking Dravidians. He ridiculed neo-Shaiva attempts to divinize the language, declaring that if Tamil society had to progress, and if Tamil had to take its place among the modern languages of the world, its intimate ties with religion had to be severed. What use was it to declare that Tamil emerged from Shiva's drum or that it could magically create a woman out of some old bones, as some of its devotees were wont to do, when the language did not have the capacity to express rational thought? he asked with brutal realism (Anaimuthu 1974: 969, 976-77; E. V. Ramasami 1960).

While he was willing to go along with the contestatory classicist and Dravidianist claim that Tamil was more ancient than and a superior language to Sanskrit, he questioned the wisdom of the proposition that the salvation of modern Tamil speakers lay in a return to the imagined perfect past of their Cank#am poems. And here, his growing disparagement of Tamil was matched only by his utter scorn for its high literature, whose "classicality" its devotees had so painstakingly constructed over the past few decades. Instead, he insisted that all of Tamil literature—with the possible exception of the *Tirukkur1al#*—was tainted with Sanskritic ritualism, casteism, gender inequalities, and irrational follies, arguing that it was the very means by which Tamilians had been, and would continue to be, enslaved to Aryanism (Anaimuthu 1974: 959-1002; Nambi Arooran 1980: 164-66; E. V. Ramasami 1960).

But above all, Ramasami attacked the feminization of Tamil as a mother figure, that construct so dear to the Indianist and Dravidianist imaginations. What is this "obstinacy" over the mother tongue when the language spoken by our mothers is itself so problematic? he demanded. "Having given birth to us, if our mother left us in the house of a Telugu speaker or a Muslim, would we not start to speak in Telugu or Urdu? Just because our mother spoke Tamil does that mean that Tamil will spurt from us all by itself?" Moreover, can the baby talk that mothers use with their infants be used by us as adults? Is this not utter foolishness? he asked (Anaimuthu 1974: 969).

Ramasami thus deconstructed the metaphorical construct of the "mother tongue" to reveal what it was, after all—a metaphor;

and in general, there was a remarkable absence in his writings of references to Tamil1ttây, "mother's milk," "mother tongue," and all such staples of *tamil1ppar1r1u*. This is not surprising, for as he asked in his provocative pamphlet, *Tâyppâl Paittiyam* (Madness over mother's milk), why is it that Tamilians insist, as if they were "children," that they would only live on their mother's milk, Tamil: " 'Mother's milk is superior' only if the mother's milk has power (*cakti*) and substance (*cattu*). When the mother, Tamil, is herself without substance and diseased, how could the child who drinks her milk improve? The mother's milk will be strong only if the mother herself is well-nourished. Is Tamil well-nourished?" (E. V. Ramasami 1962: 9-10).

Contrary to so many of her devotees who proposed that imbibing Tamil1ttây's milk cultivated in the Tamil speaker the true "Tamil" qualities of virtue and chastity, heroism and self-respect, Ramasami argued that Tamilians who had been content with drinking her milk were diseased with irrationalism, superstition, and traditionalism, so much so that one recoiled from the nasty odor of religiosity and orthodoxy that emanated from them. He went on to propose that if Tamilians took to drinking "bottled milk," that is, English, they would gain in fortitude, independence, and rationality (E. V. Ramasami 1962: 10-12). As in his antireligious and anticlassicist arguments against devotional claims, he invoked the power of modern science and rationalism to undermine the "irrational" follies of its devotees' attachment to Tamil:

> If Tamil1ttây offers her milk for scientific examination, it will be proven that there is nothing in it that provides strength or fortitude to the body, and the reality of mother's milk will be revealed. Is it not appropriate that those who praise the virtues of mother's milk should tell us what its constituents are that supposedly contribute to our well-being? Instead of so doing, they have turned...mother's milk into a capital resource with which they have deluded the people.

The pamphlet ends by announcing that through deploying the trope of mother's milk to stir the gullible Tamilians' devotion to their language, Tamil devotees had only succeeded in turning them into fools. This, Ramasami concluded, was "the real fruit of mother's milk."

Ramasami's most vehement statements about the "madness" over Tamil1ttây, or the "barbarism" of Tamil, were made in the 1950s and 1960s, when the DMK was riding the crest of the popular and political wave in the state by projecting itself as the guardian of the language. In 1949, that party had split off from Ramasami's DK, which he had created in 1944 out of the ashes of the defunct Justice Party (of which he had been president since 1938). The ostensible occasion for the split was Ramasami's (second) marriage, at seventy, to Maniyammai, a party worker forty or so years younger than him; the marriage was denounced as a betrayal of Ramasami's own dearly held principles. But other ideological differences had accumulated between Ramasami and Annadurai, his able lieutenant of many years, including their varying stances on Dravidian and Indian nationalisms, Brahmanism, and electoral politics. As the DMK became more and more vigorous in its espousal of the Tamil cause, Ramasami took an alternate route. After 1953, he even backed the Congress in spite of that party's reputation as "anti-Tamil," a reputation that Ramasami himself had helped establish in earlier years (Barnett 1976: 56-84). He also called upon Tamil speakers to abandon Tamil and to embrace English, at one point even urging, "Speak with your wives and children and servants in English! Give up your infatuation with Tamil (*tamil1p paittiyam*)....Try and live like human beings!" (Anaimuthu 1974: 989). Where the DMK was willing to concede the usefulness of English in the public sphere, Ramasami insisted that even in the private, intimate space of their homes, Tamilians should abandon their "mother" and adopt English—a stunning repudiation of a fundamental devotional premise.

Yet it would be a mistake to reduce Ramasami's iconoclastic pronouncements on Tamil to the shifting vagaries of electoral and party politics alone. His dismay over Tamil-speaking Dravidians' preoccupation with their language cannot be separated from his dominant ideological and political objective through much of the 1940s and early 1950s—the creation of a separate Dravidian nation, in opposition to the Indian nation (M. S. S. Pandian 1993). He argued that their ethnic/racial identity as "Dravidians" was, and should be, more important to Tamilians than their linguistic identity as speakers of Tamil. Unlike language—which he insisted could be picked up today and dropped tomorrow—the bond of blood was durable and distinctive. And yet, paradoxically, he had as encompassing a vision of Tamil as so many of its devotees, for in making his case for a "Dravidian nation," he suggested there was no distinction between Tamil and the other Dravidian languages: "Some of our pandits declare that these four languages emerged from one, that they are four sisters that were borne by one mother's womb. This is utter nonsense. There was only one daughter who was given birth to by Tirâvit#attây [Mother Dravida], and her name is Tamil. We have given it four different names, because the language is spoken in four different places. *But in all four places, it is Tamil that is spoken*" (E. V. Ramasami 1948: 30, emphasis mine). So, for Ramasami, "Dravidian is Tamil, Tamil is Dravidian"—a sentiment that led him to deny the existence of the non-Tamil languages and their speakers as autonomous entities, and enabled his imagination of a unitary Dravidian nation.

Why did Tamil's devotees absorb Ramasami into their ranks, despite his stunning disparagement of their object of devotion? They lionized him for his leadership of the anti-Hindi struggle: since so much of *tamil1ppar1r1u* from the 1930s defined itself in its opposition to Hindi, it follows that Ramasami's catalytic role in these protests bestowed the aura of a Tamil devotee on him. Moreover, for all his numerous slippages, contradictions, and turnabouts in politics, Ramasami consistently and fiercely opposed Brahmanism, Aryanism, and Sanskrit. Since so much of the devotional community was itself animated by such an opposition, he is seen as a fellow traveller in their own struggle against these forces. Further, Ramasami's fundamental ideological and political commitment to restore the "self-respect" and rights of Dravidians resonated with the devotees' own efforts to reinstate the lost privileges and honor of Tamil.

But above all, I would maintain that this most undevoted "Tamilian" was ensnared by the inexorable logic of *tamil1ppar1r1u*. In that logic, there is no other subject-position available to someone like Ramasami other than that of "devotee of Tamil." For, as the century progressed and especially as the Dravidianist idiom came to hold sway over the devotional community, a "Tamilian" or "Dravidian" had to be, by definition, a devotee of Tamil; no other ways of being were possible. As one of the founding fathers of the Dravidian movement, Ramasami's status as paradigmatic "Tamilian" was sacrosanct; it could not, and indeed should not, be interrogated. Inevitably, this meant that if he had to retain that status, he had to be converted into a *tamil1 an1par,* a devotee of Tamil. His protests notwithstanding, the devotional community appropriated this maverick individual and rendered him, like many others, into a subject of Tamil.

CONCLUSION

Tamil Subjects

With the analytic of devotion based on the Tamil word *par1r1u,* and with the help of Tamil1ttây, I set out to write the language question in colonial and post-colonial Tamil India differently, as a history that is not a rehearsal of Europe's linguistic nationalism(s). My attempt to write such a history, organized around the concept of language devotion with attention to notions of love, labor, and life at the service of Tamil, has certainly followed my desire not to hastily empty the culturally specific and contingent into a ready-made narrative of language-and-nationalism. But just as surely, I *had* to attempt a different history, because Tamil's own devotees have insisted from the turn of the century that there is literally nothing else in the world like their language; there is no one else like their Tamil1ttây. Yet, in so insisting, and in conducting a whole range of activities around such a conviction, they recast their language in a manner that robs it of its putative exceptionalism. Tamil's singularity and uniqueness are constituted by demonstrating that it is a "divine" language, like Sanskrit, and just as "classical" as Greek and Latin. Most important, Tamil is presented to its speakers, for the first time in its long history, as a "mother tongue," just like the languages of modern Europe. Despite considerable effort to endow her with a distinctive and different persona, even their beloved Tamil1ttây seems like other modern icons of the nation such as Bhârata Mâtâ and Britannia, when she does not resemble the mother-goddesses of conventional Hinduism.

Which is why this history of Tamil devotion is almost the same even when it is not quite, to paraphrase Homi Bhabha: in the process of talking and writing eloquently about their love and devotion for their language, Tamil's devotees, who were colonial subjects after all, began to subscribe to the reigning certitudes of linguistic nationalism. In their narratives, as in those of Herder or Fichte, the state of the language mirrors the state of its speakers; language is the essence of their culture, the bearer of their traditions, and the vehicle of their thoughts from time immemorial. It holds the key to their social solidarity and to their political health and fortunes:

National life and national progress depend upon the development of the language of a people. A study of the language of a nation reveals to us their social status, their moral and intellectual progress, their inner life, their spiritual and religious advancement, their political problems and aspirations, their love of science and arts, their commercial intercourse, their assimilation of foreign ideas and ideals, and finally, among other things, their place in the scale of nations....[T]he future salvation of our country entirely depends upon our improving our vernacular tongue.

It is clear from this statement that Tamil's devotees also become subscribers to the patrimonial imagination ushered in by colonial modernity, in which language is constituted as a tangible, material possession of its speakers. Like other kinds of property, its value and worth could be enhanced by not allowing it to decline, by continuing to develop it, and by preventing others from encroaching upon it. The life of Tamil and the lives of its speakers as a community are now imagined as inextricably intertwined in a way that they had never been before in the land in which the language had been spoken for at least two thousand years. Not least, in Tamil India as well as in Europe, this patrimonial imagination was supplemented by the conviction that language is "the improver no less than the improved" (Spadafora 1990: 196). As in other parts of colonial India, many literate Tamil speakers were convinced that their society was in a state of total decline. Taking the cue from their colonial masters, they offered numerous solutions for its "improvement": most notably, the rationalization of religion; the abolition of caste consciousness; the spread of modern, scientific education; and the "reform" of women. For its devotees, subjects of the modern linguistic imagination, the primary solution lay in their language, identified through their discursive practices as the source of antiquity, autonomy, and authenticity of its speakers, who are imagined as a singular community and a potential nation unto themselves. So, from the turn of this century, Tamil's adherents offered *tamil1ppar1r1u* as a liberating force to their fellow speakers. Energized by their devotion to their language, its speakers would be able to right all wrongs and set themselves on the road to prosperity and well-being. Though conducted around a language bearing the singular name "tamil1," *tamil1ppar1r1u* nevertheless produces an entity that is multiply imagined and contrarily fashioned. In certain contexts, Tamil is constituted in religious terms as a "divine" language favored by the gods themselves; in other cases, it is secularly imagined as a "classical" tongue, the parent of the languages of the world and the progenitor of one of its most ancient "civilizations," if not the oldest. For the devotional community as a whole, however, Tamil is increasingly "mother tongue"—the language of their mothers, their homes, and their childhood. Even here, there are differences between those who imagine Tamil as part of a larger "family" of "mother tongues," harmoniously coexisting within the framework of the Indian nation, and those who emphatically assert that it is the one and only mother/tongue to which its speakers owe total and unconditional allegiance, the language of their (Tamil) nation.

Given these varying conceptions, what appeared as a relatively straightforward agenda for "reviving" the language in order to "improve" its speakers splintered into various projects at odds with each other. Thus the "community" of devotees is shot through with difference: there were those who invested their efforts in forming associations, convening revivalist conferences, and running journals that disseminated knowledge about "divine" and "classical" Tamil among the populace; there were others who pragmatically focused on promoting its study as "mother tongue" in schools and colleges, and on its adoption as the language of government, politics, and public communication; and finally, there were the "warriors" in the trenches, willing to give up their lives to protect the integrity of their beloved language. I have also suggested that these varying devotional imaginings about the language frequently clashed with the imperatives of the modern state. In the latter's bureaucratic rationalist perspective, Tamil is an instrument and tool for governing a modern populace. But as we have seen, for its ardent followers Tamil is not merely an inanimate object but a near and dear person, their personal goddess, their compassionate mother, and their beloved lover. Increasingly from the 1950s, as many of its devotees gained political power, and even held the highest political office in the state by the late 1960s, these very contrary imaginations about Tamil came to a head, producing a series of language policies that can claim some success but are also marked by numerous contradictions, even failure.

The vast scholarly literature on language, nationalism, and modernity has rightly recognized the various strategies through which languages have been linguistically transformed through rationalization and standardization, especially through the interventions of the state and its agencies. But much less attention has been paid to the structures of sentiments in which languages come to be embedded in the new people centered ideologies of modernity. With the analytic of devotion, I have tracked the myriad ways in which Tamil came to be subjected to the love, loyalty, and reverence of those who claimed to be its devotees. Instead of assuming, as its speakers (and scholars) are wont to do, that attachment to a language, imagined in primordial terms as the "mother tongue," is natural and inevitable, I have argued that it is produced under specific historical conditions, and as such is subject to negotiation and change. Correspondingly, the power that a language exercises over its speakers, as indeed the passions that it elicits, is ideologically produced and historically contingent. Unless we pay attention to such structures of sentiment and regimes of love that coalesce around languages, it is very difficult, even impossible, to explain why and how they acquire the ability to arouse their speakers to rally around their cause, to the point of surrendering body, life, and spirit.

The linchpin in the ideologies of devotion which emerged around Tamil is the construct of "mother tongue," a label that was appropriated for the language for the first time in the closing decades of the nineteenth century and is an expression of the regimes of mimicry spawned by colonial rule everywhere. And yet, as this most European of terms played itself out in Tamil India, it was subversively taken apart not just to reveal the convergence between "language" and "motherhood" that went into its constitution in the first place, but also to mobilize all the emotive and sentimental powers that had come to be associated with the mother figure by the end of the nineteenth century. Thus one of its devotees asked of his fellow speakers in 1918, "Do you love your own mother? Then you must surely love your mother tongue" (Devasikhamani 1919: 26-27). Another,-speaking to other women in 1938, reminded them that "forgetting [our] mother tongue is akin to forgetting [our] mother" (Nilambikai n.d.: 21).

Such statements are not surprising, for Tamil's adherents insist that they did "not refer to their language as mother tongue for rhetorical reasons" (K. Appadurai 1944: 20); rather, "my knowledge of Tamil is my mother's gift. For that reason, Tamil is my mother tongue" (Sivagnanam 1974: 868). In the writings of Tamil's devotees, *tamil1*, *tâymol1i* (mother tongue), *tâyppâl* (mother's milk), and *tây* (mother) all shade into each other. It is in this context that the figure of Tamil1ttây assumes significance. Neither ubiquitous nor routinized in their discourses, her devotees strategically deployed Tamil1ttây at crucial moments to draw the attention of speakers of Tamil to the plight of their language: to elicit their passions, filial and otherwise, to cajole them to place their bodies and lives at the service of Tamil. And all such deployments, once again, drew upon the new emotive powers that had come to be invested in motherhood. For, while her devotees may insist that she is an ancient and time-honored figure, I have argued that Tamil1ttây is essentially a modern being, erupting within the regimes of *tamil1ppar1r1u* as a consequence of laminating the domain of "motherhood" onto that of "language" in late colonial India.

As the figure of the mother came to be reconfigured as a sign of the authentic, pure community, and as a metonym for "the people," and as the language they spoke was configured as the bearer of the true soul, spirit, and genius of the "community" of its speakers within the ideologies of modernity, the motherhood of language was fashioned into a weapon to contend with both British colonialism *and* Indian nationalism. In repeated circulation through the discursive activities of *tamil1ppar1r1u*, the motherness of Tamil acquires a material presence in the life-world of Tamil speakers that has rendered it natural, and hence inviolable. As recently as 1990, schoolchildren in Tamilnadu were told in an essay entitled "Devotion to Mother Tongue," which appears in their seventh grade textbook published by the government:

"Motherland" and "mother tongue" are concepts that have a relationship to "mother." Our mother tongue captures our inner sentiments and shows them to us. It is language that distinguishes humans from animals. The mother tongue is the language with which one speaks with the mother who rears and raises us from the time of birth. The mother is the first acquaintance of the child, and it is through her that the child recognizes others as well. *Just as the child has great devotion towards its mother, similarly, all of us, too, must have devotion towards our mother tongue.*

Statements like these serve to remind its speakers of Tamil's status as their mother, lest they forgot this in its naturalization as "mother tongue." *Tamil1pparlrlu* constitutes the motherness of Tamil within a context in which both their mothers and their language had been rendered foundational for the very existence of Tamil speakers as a community.

Today, there are many who continue to lament that a century of devotional activities notwithstanding, Tamil has not "improved" and is far from being the language of prestige, profit, and power that *tamil1pparlrlu* intends for it. In the words of a contemporary poet, Tamil1ttây continues to wear feathers, not ornaments (Kailasapathy 1986: 49). The rhetoric of decline that marked so many a devotional narrative in the colonial period continues to plague post-colonial discourses as well, as does the lament of critics who insist that Tamil devotion is misplaced to start with, and that "wallowing in sentimentalism" about Tamil is not really going to bring about fundamental transformations in the lives of its speakers (Ramaswamy 1992b: 421-28). And yet, if Tamil's devotees had accompanied the anthropologist Jacob Pandian in the early 1970s to a high school in Pulicat, outside Madras city, they would have undoubtedly been pleased with the responses of the teenage students there to his questions about their allegiance to Tamil. Early in the century, few had studied Tamil or known much about its history or culture; but these students echoed many of the ideas that the devotional community had been circulating over the past few decades. One of them, a young man of seventeen, even proclaimed, "There is everything in Tamil, and learning Tamil will make me possess everything I require. If any danger threatens my mother tongue, I will give my life to protect it. My life is interwoven with my mother tongue." Another, age sixteen, maintained that "more than caste, religion, and country I love Tamil. Tamil is one of the greatest languages." A Brahman student, whose mother tongue was officially Telugu, nevertheless insisted, "I consider Tamil as my mother tongue....The culture of India is better than any other cultures of the world....Tamil culture is the greatest in India." A sixteen-year-old Muslim student similarly said, "I know a little Urdu which is considered the language of Muslims, but I like only Tamil and my love for Tamil is increasing day by day....[T]he ancient Tamil kings, Chera, Chola, and Pandya protected Tamil as though Tamil was their mother" (J. Pandian 1987: 151-64).

In addition to these young voices, there are other signs that Tamil has left its mark on the political and cultural landscape of contemporary Tamilnadu. Since Indian independence, and especially since the late 1960s, the state has pursued policies that are informed, if only rhetorically, by the devotional belief that Tamil is everything. Districts, cities, urban streets, state corporations, and the like have been renamed over the past decades after Tamil historical figures, litterateurs, and devotees, inspired by Bharatidasan's lament that "in the Tamil streets of the Tamil land, there is no Tamil," as well as by Bharati's demand that "the sound of Tamil ought to thunder in its streets." Grand state sponsored architectural projects have recreated scenes from the Tamil literary and historical past. Statues of famous poets and devotees adorn city squares, public buildings, and beachfronts. Efforts to Tamilize, following normative models drawn from literature and history, are not limited to the physical landscape of Tamilnadu. In their private lives as well, many Tamil speakers have taken to adopting personal names, conducting marriages and funerals, and celebrating festivals and rituals in what is identified as the authentic Tamil way. Such activities supplement other efforts to Tamilize the public domain: today, the language of government is Tamil; the medium of education in state schools and colleges is Tamil; and television, radio, and other technologies of mass communication are in Tamil. Admittedly, the language does not have sole reign in public—it shares space with both English and Hindi; nevertheless, its presence is by no means insignificant.

Statistics generated by the colonial government in the first half of the century show a steady increase in the volume of Tamil print activity, especially in fields such as literature, religion, and the sciences. The post-colonial state in its annual administrative reports has regularly carried announcements of the steady progress of Tamil in educational and administrative domains; of the establishment of Tamil universities and academies; of the publication of new scientific and administrative glossaries, dictionaries, encyclopedias, and school and college textbooks; and so forth. Indeed, no less a critic than Annadurai was able to declare in 1945 at a public meeting held in Annamalai University: "Today, Tamilnadu welcomes all those poets who labor for Tamil, and sing for it....[W]herever one goes, one hears Tamil....Even those who vowed that they would only speak English, now claim that they will only speak in Tamil, write in Tamil, think in Tamil....[W]e can see Tamil literature, Tamil plays, Tamil music everywhere. Even those who yesterday refused are beginning today to declare that they are 'Tamilian' (*tamil1ar*)" (Annadurai 1968: 12-13).

Why is Annadurai so pleased that speakers of Tamil are at last declaring themselves "Tamilian"? A year later, K. A. P. Viswanatham wrote in an editorial: "Westerners refer to the Tamilian as 'Black Man.' His neighbors refer to him as 'Indian.' Aryans call him 'Dravidian,' and Brahmans, 'Shudra.' At the time of the *Vedas*, he was referred to as *'arakkar'* [demon]. Members of the Justice Party called him 'non-Brahman,' and for the Government, he is a 'non-Muslim.'...When there is no one to refer to the Tamilian as 'Tamilian,' will at least the Tamilian call himself 'Tamilian'?" Why was this so important for Viswanatham? And why is it that one of the chief government buildings in Madras city carries the message, boldly emblazoned across its facade, "Declare yourself a Tamilian! Stand proudly, your head held high!"? What is at stake in making such a claim?

My attempt to answer this question begins with the proposition that as the language they speak becomes subject to the discourse(s) of *tamil1ppar1r1u*, its speakers become subjects of Tamil, their state of subjection reflected in the terms *tamil1an1*, "Tamilian" (lit., "he-of-Tamil"), or *tamil1ar*, "Tamilians" (lit., "they-of-Tamil"). Admittedly the category of *tamil1an1* is an old one, and its presence in literary sources has been traced back by some scholars to at least the late first millennium (Krishnan 1984: 145-46). Nevertheless, I would insist that it assumes significance in political and social discourses only with the consolidation of the people-centered and patrimonial ideologies of language ushered in by modernity. From the turn of this century, discussions of what to do about improving Tamil have been invariably accompanied by the question, "Who is a Tamilian?" or "Who are the Tamilians?" The question is repeatedly posed, and answers repeatedly sought, because at stake is the production and definition of the modern Tamil subject. Today, in the various human sciences, not only is the concept of subject widely deployed, but there is a proliferating literature on what it means to be a subject, on the various processes of subjection, on subjectivity or the state of being a subject, and so on. Paul Smith comments on this state of affairs:

> Over the last ten or twenty years [these] discourses have adopted this term, the "subject," to do multifarious theoretical jobs. In some instances the "subject" will appear to be synonymous with the "individual," the "person." In others—for example, in psychoanalytical discourse—it will take on a more specialized meaning and refer to the unconsciously structured illusion of plenitude which we usually call "the self." Or elsewhere, the "subject" might be understood as the specifically subjected *object* of social and historical forces and determinations.

It is this last sense of the "subject"—as the "specifically subjected object of social and historical forces"—that I draw upon here in my discussion of the notion of the "Tamilian" in Tamil devotional discourses. *Tamil1ppar1r1u,* I suggest, divides the world into two: those who are Tamilians and those who are not. Speakers of Tamil are evaluated, and then transformed—*if* they qualify—through the discursive practice(s) of *tamil1ppar1r1u* into *tamil1ar,* "Tamilians," their beings and subjectivities inevitably and necessarily bound to the language. This process of subjection, moreover, proceeds categorically, epistemologically, and ontologically.

Categorically-speaking, the *tamil1an1* is the entity who is cajoled, even compelled, into being, as we see in the statements of Annadurai and Viswanatham, by *tamil1ppar1r1u.* He—and it is always "he" the term itself is gendered masculine—is the principal addressee and interlocutor in all its regimes. Minimally, a *tamil1an1* is one whose "mother tongue" is Tamil. But it is a measure of the multiplicity of conceptions about the language that reigns among its devout that no single definition of the *tamil1an1* prevails, either. For radical neo-Shaivism, all those Tamil speakers adhering to a (reformed) Shaiva religion and who are not Brahman are the true Tamilians; in classicism, Tamilians are those who are racially Dravidian and historically "the lineal descendants of the original and highly civilized Tamils of pre-Aryan times" (Maraimalai Adigal 1974b: 14). Dravidianism admits into the category all those who claim Tamil as their "mother tongue" and disavow attachment to any other language, especially to Sanskrit and Hindi. Indianism has perhaps the most ambitious logic of subjection at work and admits, like Dravidianism, that Tamilians are those who claim Tamil as their "mother tongue". All the same, it also insists that those who maintain that the Tamil land is their home—"even though their mother tongue may be another"—are also Tamilians (Kalyanasundaranar 1935: 37; Ramalinga Pillai 1953: 55-56; Sivagnanam 1974: 387). Indeed, for some devotees of Tamil, one does not even have to be born a Tamil speaker to become "Tamilian": all those who show desire for Tamil are Tamilians; all those who are devoted to it are also transformed into subjects of Tamil. Thus K. Appadurai refers to the missionary devotees, Caldwell and Pope, as *vel#l#ait tamil1ar* (white Tamilians), and writes:

> I wish to declare that all those who show devotion to Tamil ought to be considered *tamil1ar.* It gives me great pleasure to include amongst Tamilians all those who come to the Tamil land and learn and use Tamil and turn into devotees of Tamil....If asked who are the Tamilians, we could easily say that they are those who reverence Tamil1ttây. If asked who are the friends of Tamilians, they are the speakers of other languages who wish they could have been borne by Tamil1ttây's womb.

By the same token, one could be born a speaker of Tamil yet spurn the language, chasing after Sanskrit, English, or Hindi, and hence be disqualified as a Tamilian. This is the plight, of course, of the Brahman, who is not reckoned to be a Tamilian by neo-Shaivism, contestatory classicism, and Dravidianism, which chastise him for not being devoted to Tamil.

Categorically-speaking, the modern Tamil subject has also been produced through a disavowal of alternate selves, contrary allegiances, and prior commitments. Tamil's devotees repeatedly insist that a *tamil1an1* is one who, regardless of whether he is Hindu, Muslim, or Christian, claims Tamil as his mother tongue:

> Wherever you may be, whether in Burma, Malaya, Durban, Lanka, or Fiji, you are a Tamilian. Your mother tongue is Tamil. You may be a Hindu, a Muslim, or a Christian at home, in your temples and mosques and churches. There is no objection to that. But in public and on the streets, when asked, "Who are you?," do not say that you are a Brahman or Vellalan or Pillai or Mudaliar or Naidu or Servai, or that you belong to this or that religion. Do

not speak with a sectarian mind. "I am a Tamilian. Tamilnadu is mine. Wherever I am, I belong to the Tamil populace." Say so proudly with your head held high!

Thus, in the process of producing the *tamil1an1*, preexisting allegiances are recognized and set aside—in some sectors of the devotional community, even discredited—in favor of declaring one's primary loyalty to Tamil. As Kalyanasundaram reminded his fellow speakers in 1928, "If we wish to bind the people born in this [Tamil] nation into the net of unity, there is only one instrument, and that is the Tamil language....We may be attached to different religions but we cannot forget we are all Tamilians" (Kalyanasundaranar 1935: 25-26). Similarly, a decade later, Shaktidasan Subramanian, a Brahman devotee and who also edited the nationalist newspaper *Navacakti*, insisted: "There is only one *jâti* [lit., "caste"] in Tamilnadu, and that is the Tamil *jâti*. Think of yourself as *tamil1an1*" (S. Subramanian 1939: 5). As all manner of differences are thus dissolved, and other allegiances rendered illegitimate, the name of the collectivity—*tamil1ar*—becomes one's name, *tamil1an1* individualities are collapsed into a shared linguistic identity: "If they ask me 'Who are you?,' instead of referring to myself in terms of this or that caste, or this or that religion, I will declare proudly, 'I am a Tamilian.' I will not hate any other Tamilian. Even if another Tamilian hates me, I will transform him through my love" (Suddhananda Bharati 1938: 103-4).

But a *tamil1an1* is a being who is asked not just to set aside his individuality, and contrary allegiances, in favor of being a part of the collectivity of Tamilians; he is also asked to submit himself to the regime of *tamil1ppar1r1u*, to become a devotee of Tamil. Suddhananda Bharati invited the Tamilian to take the following oath: I am a Tamilian; Tamil is my mother tongue. I live only for the betterment of Tamil, of Tamilians, and of Tamilnadu. All my deeds will contribute to the glory of Tamil, of Tamilians, and of Tamilnadu. I will oppose and conquer anything that harms Tamil, Tamilians, and Tamilnadu. I may forget my life, but I will not forget Tamil. They may destroy my body, but I will not forsake Tamil....I live so that I may restore my mother back on her throne as the queen of languages.

The Tamil speaker thus (re)emerges in this discourse with his entire life project rewritten in terms of Tamil. He is repeatedly called into being, told to arouse himself from his "sleep" and serve his mother/language by Tamilizing himself: by adopting a Tamil name, by-speaking and writing and thinking only in Tamil, by marrying only a Tamil woman, by raising his children as true *tamil1ar.* His life is the life of Tamil and, correspondingly, Tamil's life is his life. For, as Bharatidasan reminded his fellow speakers in 1945:

> *The progress of our glorious Tamil1ttây is your progress.*
> *You should realize this and arouse yourself!*
> *O young Tamilian, open your eyes!*
> ......
> *Every victory that she attains is your victory!*
> ......
> *Know this! The evil that befalls Tamil1ttây befalls you as well!*
> *(Bharatidasan 1969: 9-10)*

Thus, as far as the ardent devotee of Tamil is concerned, the *tamil1an1* has no existence outside and beyond his mother/tongue, a point I will return to shortly.

The transformation of speakers of Tamil into subjects of Tamil, *tamil1ar,* also takes place epistemologically, as they come under the scrutiny of various modern knowledge practices which provide them with their "history," tell them about their true "culture," find a place for them in the evolution of human "civilization," establish their relationship to other language speakers of the world, and so on. The discourses of *tamil1ppar1r1u,* as I noted earlier, liberally draw upon the various human sciences of philology, history, ethnology, and archaeology in constructing their structures of devotion to the language. In recent years, there has been considerable discussion of the part played by these sciences in transforming men and women into objects of knowledge, and of the complicity between these (European) knowledge practices and the exercise of colonial power and control (Said 1978). In India, with colonialism came not just the English language and new linguistic habits and cultural dispositions, but new concepts for imagining the world and for securing one's place in that world. At the same time, there was a vigorous renewal of the ancient and the authentic, a revamping of "tradition" which accompanied what Thomas Metcalf (1994) has adroitly characterized as the complex interplay between essential similitude and the enduring difference between themselves and the "natives" that the colonial masters stressed in their various ideologies and institutions of rule. The colonized subject's being is in turn shot through with traces of the archaic and the new, of the "West" and the "Orient," of "tradition" and "modernity."

In producing the Tamil subject who is similarly a melange of the old and the new, Tamil devotionalism thus continues and extends a process already well under way under colonialism. In the (colonizing) knowledges which Tamil's devotees inherited (or appropriated, as the case may be), the Tamilian had already been incorporated into an European and colonial economy of signification that assigned him a linguistic label and a racial category, decided whether he possessed a "history," and determined whether his "culture" was worthy of being classified as a "civilization." In engaging such knowledge practices, if only to counter their assertions, *tamil1pparl1r1u* further ensnared the Tamilian in this colonial economy of meanings in which it mattered—politically, economically, and psychologically—whether one's language was a "classical" tongue or a mere "vernacular" whether one's religion was "rational" or "idolatrous" and whether one possessed "civilization" or was "primitive."

Perhaps nothing illustrates this process of ensnarement better than the troubling category of "Dravidian" to which the *tamil1an1* has been subjected in colonial ideologies, as well as in the discourse(s) of Tamil devotionalism. As I noted earlier, not all of Tamil's devotees agree to the use of the term "Dravidian" to refer to the Tamilian—and it is important to register the resistance, if only scattered and muted, to the global hegemony of European meanings. Some worried over it because of the negative connotations it had picked up in colonial usage; others insisted that the *tamil1an1* should be identified by a term that indicated his attachment to his language; still others protested that this was not a "Tamil" term at all and that it was foisted on the Tamilian by his colonial masters. Such protests notwithstanding, the notion that the "Tamilian" is a "Dravidian," and distinct from the Sanskrit-speaking "Aryan," has had a long and enduring life in the cultural and political discourses of the region up until today. Most ironically, this has meant that for much of this century, the *tamil1an1* has been subjected to a category that is a Europeanization of a Sanskrit term used in pre-colonial times to refer, often in a derogatory sense, to the peoples of southern India, Brahmans included (M. Srinivasa Aiyangar 1914: 1-6). To paraphrase Kwame Appiah, the overdetermined course of cultural nationalisms in India has been to make real the many imaginary identities to which Europe has subjected it (Appiah 1992: 62). The Dravidianization of the *tamil1an1*, however much it may have been a strategy of empowerment for the disenfranchised and the marginalized, is very much an instance of such an overdetermination. Last but not least, the *tamil1an1* has been transformed into a subject of Tamil ontologically as well, his very being suffused with the language. Tamil is not just a language that determines his categorical existence and life project from without, but it is also the very life force (*uyir*) that animates him from within. So, Shaktidasan addresses the young *tamil1an1* and asks him to remember: "My mind is filled with Tamil; my life is Tamil; my pulse is Tamil; my veins are Tamil; my blood is filled with Tamil; all my flesh is Tamil" (S. Subramanian 1939: 4). Another devotee echoes this sentiment in verse:

Tamil abides in me,
as my flesh
as my life
as my life force.
(quoted in K. Appadurai 1944: 29)

As the language itself is thus corporealized, its speakers come to be Tamilized. The *tamil1an1* is (re)produced substantially as the language becomes part of his very life essence, feeding his consciousness and his spirit. Incorporated as it has been into the body of the *tamil1an1*, and blended as it has with his very life and consciousness, it is impossible to separate Tamil from his being:

We can turn mountains into pits;
We can dry up the ocean bed;
We can fly speedily through the skies.

......

We can even bring the dying back to life.
The Tamilian cannot be separated from Tamil
Even for a moment, by anyone.

This incorporation of the language into the very being of the *tamil1an1* carries tremendous consequences, for in its most passionate moments, *tamil1ppar1r1u* certainly instructs Tamil speakers that devotion to their language should supersede devotion to their parents, their spouses, and children; but it also tells them that devotion to their language should transcend attachment to their own bodies and to their own lives. Even when thrown into prison for his participation in the anti-Hindi protests in 1965, the poet Perunchitran was willing to declare:

When they tell me that

This body, and all the blood and sinews and feelings that it contains, belongs to Tamil1ttây and to other tamil1ar,

I lose all my fatigue!

(Perunchitranar 1979: 66)

And decades earlier, the mystic poet Suddhananda Bharati insisted, "I may forget my own life, but I will not forget Tamil. They may destroy my body, but I will not forsake Tamil" (Suddhananda Bharati 1938: 103).

The subjection of the *tamil1an1* to Tamil is complete when he willingly agrees thus to surrender his body, his life, and his soul to his mother/language. And so it came about that in the cool dawn of a January morning in 1964, young Chinnasami burned himself alive, leaving behind a letter in which he declared, "O Tamil! In order that you live, I am going to die a terrible death!" In order to enable Tamil to live and flourish, *tamil1ppar1r1u* transforms its speakers, who ought to have been masters of the language, into its subjects, a critical reversal of the patrimonial imagination it inherited from European modernity. Their dearest possession, their language, ends up by possessing its devotees, compelling them to sacrifice to it their body, life, and spirit. It is only fitting that one of Tamil's own has the last word:

There is nothing more precious than life.

However, if any evil befalls you, my glorious Tamil1ttây!

I will not think that life is precious;

To put an end to your suffering,

I will give up my life.

(Pulavar Kulanthai 1972: 21)

BIBLIOGRAPHY

Bell, Sir Charles: *Portrait of a Dalai Lama: The Life and Times of the Great Thirteenth*, Boston, Wisdom Publications, 1987.

Cook, Elizabeth: *Holy Places of the Buddha*, Berkeley, Dharma Publishing, 1994.

Dargyay, Eva M.: *The Rise of Esoteric Buddhism in Tibet*, Delhi, Motilal Banarsidass, 1977.

Eppsteiner, Fred: *The Path of Compassion: Writings on Socially Engaged Buddhism*, Berkeley, Parallax Press, 1988.

Gombrich, Richard F.: *Buddhist Precept and Practice*, Delhi, Motilal Banarsidass, 1991.

Hakeda, Yoshito S.: *Kukai, Major Works*, New York, Columbia University Press, 1972.

Keown, Damien: *The Nature of Buddhist Ethics*, New York, St. Martin's Press, 1992.

Lalwani. K.C.: *Kalpa Sutra of Badrabahu Svami*, Delhi, Motilal Banarsidass. 1979.

Mookerjee, Satkari: *Buddhist Philosophy of Universal Flux*, Delhi, Motilal Banarsidass, 1980.

Payutto, Prayudh: *Buddhist Economics: A Middle Way for the Marketplace*, Bangkok, Buddhadhamma Foundation, 1994.

Powers, John: *Wisdom of Buddha: The Samdhinirmocana Sutra*, Berkeley, Dharma Publishing, 1994.

Sprung, Mervyn: *The Problem of Two Truths in Buddhism and Vedanta*, Boston, Reidel, 1973.

Strong, John: *The Legend of King Asoka*, Princeton, Princeton University Press, 1983.

Thomas, E. J.: *The Life of the Buddha as Legend and History*, London, Routledge & Kegan Paul, 1927.

Wells, Kenneth E.: *Thai Buddhism, Its Rites and Activities*, Bangkok, Christian Bookstore, 1960.

INDEX

A

Advantages, 78, 171.
Ambassador, 3.
Appreciation, 2, 118, 299.
Approach, 57, 58.
Architecture, 59.
Art, 11, 23, 51, 60.
Attitudes, 68, 72, 74, 131, 169, 212.

B

Buddha, 1, 2, 3, 9, 10, 11, 12, 14, 16, 17, 18, 19, 21, 22, 25, 27, 33, 37, 42, 43, 45, 46, 48, 49, 57, 58.
Buddhism, 1, 2, 3, 4, 5, 9, 10, 11, 12, 13, 14, 15, 16, 18, 19, 23, 28, 30, 33, 34, 35, 36, 37, 38, 41, 43, 44, 45, 48, 49, 50, 51, 52, 53, 54, 55, 56, 57, 58, 59, 60, 61, 62, 63, 65, 262.

C

Christians, 2, 14, 63, 64, 139, 270.
Civilizations, 80, 328.
Collections, 291, 304.
Community, 6, 13, 17, 21, 38, 41, 43, 60, 61, 64, 71, 74, 75, 76, 77, 80, 82, 85, 86, 88, 89, 94, 97, 99, 100, 102, 115, 116, 130, 131, 132, 135, 139, 140, 143, 146, 147, 148, 149, 151, 153, 154, 161, 171, 172, 176, 181, 185, 187, 188, 196, 200, 201, 212, 217, 220, 229, 236, 238, 239, 242, 244, 251, 252, 256, 258, 260, 261, 262, 264, 268, 270, 271, 273, 274, 275, 278, 279, 281, 282, 287, 289, 293, 299, 301, 306, 315, 317, 318, 320, 325, 326, 327, 328, 330, 331, 336.
Contributions, 117, 269, 304.
Conversion, 131, 225, 254.
Culture, 14, 58, 72, 76, 81, 85, 88, 89, 93, 94, 102, 103, 105, 108, 109, 110, 111, 113, 117, 119, 125, 128, 134, 144, 148, 154, 158, 172, 176, 180, 195, 196, 197, 198, 202, 222, 229, 253, 262, 274, 275, 316, 326, 331, 337, 338.

D

Development, 13, 55, 61, 62, 64, 77, 80, 129, 228, 244, 255, 327.
Devotee, 2, 12, 13, 16, 51, 87, 94, 109, 113, 121, 123, 129, 130, 131, 135, 143, 153, 155, 156, 157, 158, 159, 161, 162, 163, 164,

165, 166, 167, 169, 170, 171, 172, 176, 179, 180, 181, 183, 185, 186, 188, 189, 191, 193, 194, 195, 208, 214, 215, 219, 221, 224, 228, 230, 231, 232, 257, 258, 261, 262, 264, 265, 267, 268, 271, 272, 273, 274, 276, 279, 280, 281, 282, 284, 287, 289, 292, 293, 295, 297, 298, 299, 301, 306, 309, 310, 311, 314, 316, 318, 319, 321, 325, 326, 336, 337, 339.

Devotion, 1, 15, 54, 60, 68, 70, 71, 72, 73, 74, 75, 77, 79, 82, 84, 87, 88, 94, 113, 114, 116, 118, 126, 127, 131, 133, 135, 139, 141, 142, 143, 149, 150, 152, 153, 154, 155, 156, 158, 164, 168, 169, 170, 176, 180, 182, 184, 185, 186, 188, 192, 194, 198, 203, 204, 206, 210, 214, 218, 235, 236, 240, 244, 250, 252, 253, 255, 256, 258, 259, 261, 266, 270, 274, 276, 281, 282, 284, 285, 286, 288, 289, 291, 292, 293, 294, 295, 299, 300, 303, 310, 313, 314, 315, 316, 318, 323, 325, 326, 327, 329, 330, 331, 335, 337, 340.

Dilemmas, 66, 87, 127, 238, 242.

E

Economy, 79, 117, 146, 168, 184, 185, 229, 338.

Erotics, 155, 156, 188, 194, 195, 206.

Ethical System, 3.

F

Forbearance, 27.

Friendship, 58.

G

Governance, 75, 120, 212.

Government, 4, 35, 49, 50, 51, 54, 55, 83, 91, 92, 97, 108, 109, 114, 115, 124, 129, 138, 141, 142, 144, 145, 147, 148, 153, 154, 179, 180, 181, 182, 200, 202, 205, 208, 214, 215, 216, 217, 219, 227, 228, 232, 233, 235, 236, 237, 238, 239, 240, 241, 242, 243, 244, 245, 246, 247, 248, 249, 253, 254, 266, 268, 270, 276, 283, 286, 287, 288, 291, 293, 294, 300, 309, 310, 311, 312, 321, 328, 330, 332, 333.

I

Independence, 116, 117, 127, 128, 129, 197, 199, 226, 247, 323, 332.

Influence, 5, 13, 18, 23, 32, 33, 34, 44, 47, 51, 52, 53, 60, 92, 95, 99, 106, 109, 111, 121, 124, 134, 138, 232, 279, 293, 297, 302, 304, 316, 320.

Islam, 253, 254.

J

Joseph, 148, 271.

L

Laws, 1, 4, 22, 241.

Lexicon, 124, 275.

Literature, 6, 11, 53, 60, 62, 79, 89, 98, 105, 106, 107, 108, 109, 113, 115, 116,

120, 128, 133, 140, 141, 149, 157, 164, 166, 174, 180, 189, 197, 204, 212, 213, 216, 224, 226, 228, 232, 234, 247, 257, 288, 302, 303, 305, 306, 307, 308, 311, 316, 323, 327, 328, 333, 335, 340.
Loyalty, 9, 69, 73, 75, 116, 137, 141, 142, 150, 153, 179, 185, 188, 329, 336.

M

Majority, 203, 205, 208, 270, 293, 299.
Merchant, 93, 249, 285, 319.
Merciful, 13, 20.
Multilingualism, 66.

N

National Language, 66, 117, 118, 127.
Nature, 7, 11, 12, 19, 22, 46, 54, 56, 67, 69, 71, 81, 112, 113, 114, 198, 211.

P

Phonology, 227.
Pilgrimage, 16, 36.
Poetics, 70, 73, 150.
Poetry, 75, 77, 85, 123, 129, 151, 152, 153, 154, 155, 156, 159, 160, 162, 182, 195, 201, 202, 204, 280, 281, 282, 284, 285, 286, 287, 288, 304, 309, 311, 318, 319.
Policy, 4, 117, 127, 128, 130, 144, 147, 153, 181, 212, 215, 218, 220, 240, 247, 248, 249, 250, 251, 252, 278, 294, 305.
Politics, 66, 70, 72, 73, 74, 87, 93, 94, 97, 99, 107, 114, 115, 120, 131, 132, 133, 134, 138, 139, 150, 154, 186, 195, 198, 199, 201, 207, 214, 248, 251, 252, 266, 278, 283, 294, 307, 320, 324, 325, 328.
Preparation, 60, 247.
Press, 53, 253, 257, 277, 292, 303, 304.
Prisoners, 54.
Prominence, 87.
Promotion, 127, 153, 217, 250, 252, 256, 302.
Punishment, 22, 28, 31, 32, 38, 39, 41, 259.

R

Responsibility, 13, 262, 264, 268.
Rituals, 91, 92, 96, 121, 209, 216, 218, 223, 300, 332.

S

Sangha, 43.
Scholar, 14, 25, 32, 106, 130, 134, 163, 175, 190, 219, 221, 224, 238, 261, 268, 269, 273, 279, 280, 289, 295, 297, 302, 305, 306.
Society, 7, 14, 35, 54, 55, 59, 61, 63, 90, 93, 94, 95, 101, 102, 104, 106, 138, 139, 151, 154, 214, 217, 226, 237, 240, 254, 255, 256, 262, 271, 272, 273, 278, 297, 299, 304, 305, 322, 327.

V

Vedas, 97, 98, 165, 213, 333.
Violence, 41, 176, 185, 276.

□□□

Buddhism in South-east Asian Countries

Vol. 2

Buddhism in South-East Asian Countries

Dr. Indra Narain Singh

Prashant Publishing House
DELHI - 110094 (INDIA)

PRASHANT PUBLISHING HOUSE
C-34, 28 Foota Road, Gali No. 3
West Karawal Nagar, Delhi-110094
Phone : 9810396373, 22963970

Buddhism in South-East Asian Countries

First Published : 2009

ISBN : 978-81-908282-5-3

PRINTED IN INDIA

Published by Mr. R. K. Jha M/s. Prashant Publishing House, Delhi and Printed at H.S. Offset Press, Delhi.

Preface

Major world religion and philosophy founded in northeastern India in the 5th century BCE. Based on the teachings of Siddhartha Gautama, called the Buddha, Buddhism takes as its goal the escape from suffering and from the cycle of rebirth: the attainment of nirvana. It emphasizes meditation and the observance of certain moral precepts. The Buddha's teachings were transmitted orally by his disciples; during his lifetime he established the Buddhist monastic order (sangha). He adopted some ideas from the Hinduism of his time, notably the doctrine of karma, but also rejected many of its doctrines and all of its gods. In India, the emperor Ashoka promoted Buddhism during the 3rd century BC, but it declined in succeeding centuries and was nearly extinct there by the 13th century.

It spread south and flourished in Sri Lanka and Southeast Asia, and it moved through Central Asia and China (including Tibet, Korea, and Japan. In the 19th century, Buddhism spread to Europe and the United States, and it became increasingly popular in the West in the second half of the 20th century. Buddhism's main teachings are summarized in the Four Noble Truths, of which the fourth is the Eightfold Path. Buddhism's two major branches, Mahayana and Theravada, have developed distinctive practices and unique collections of canonical texts. In the early 21st century, the various traditions of Buddhism together had more than 375 million followers.

— *Author*

Acknowledgement

The present work has received encouragement, help and support from a large number of persons. It would be impossible to acknowledge my gratitude to everyone in this limited space.

I must above all especially express my idebtedness to Prof. Bhikshu Satyapal.

I wish to acknowledge with deep sense of gratitude, the unfailing encouragement and cooperation. I have received from my wife Aparajita, daughter Tanya and son Uday.

—Dr. Indra Narain Singh

CONTENTS

Preface

1. Buddhism in Myanmar 1

2. The Edicts of King Asoka 61

3. Buddhism in Sri Lanka 111

4. Buddhism in Thailand 174

5. Buddhist Culture, The Cultured Buddhist 198

6. Buddhist Ceremonies and Rituals of Sri Lanka 224

Bibliography 285

Index 286

1

Buddhism in Myanmar

EARLIEST CONTACTS WITH BUDDHISM

Myanmar and its Peoples

There are four dominant ethnic groups in the recorded history of Myanmar: the Mon, the Pyu, the Myanmar, and the Shan.

Uncertainty surrounds the origins of the Mon; but it is clear that, at least linguistically, they are related to the Khmer. What is known is that they settled in the south of Myanmar and Thailand while the Khmer made northern Thailand, Laos, and Cambodia their home. These two peoples were probably the first migrants to the region, apart from Indian merchants who established trading colonies along the coast. The Mon with their distinct language and culture competed for centuries with the Myanmar. However, today their influence and language is limited to remote areas of the south.

The Pyu, like the Myanmar, are a people of Tibeto-Burman origin with a distinct culture and language. They lived in the area around Prome long before the Myanmar pushed into the plains of Myanmar from the north. Their language was closely related to the language of the Myanmar and was later absorbed by it. Their script was in use until about the fourteenth century, but was then lost.

The Myanmar people began to colonise the plains of Myanmar only towards the middle of the first millennium AD. They came from the mountainous northern regions and may well have originated in the Central Asian plains.

After the Myanmar, the Shan flooded in from the North, finally conquering the entire region of Myanmar and Thailand. The Thai people are descended from Shan tribes. The northeast region of modern Myanmar is still inhabited predominantly by Shan tribes.

The Region

In the sixth century BC, most of what we now know as Myanmar, Thailand, Laos, and Cambodia was sparsely populated. While migrants from the east coast of India had formed trading colonies along the coast of the Gulf of Martaban, these coastal areas of Myanmar and Thailand were also home to the Mon. By this time, the Khmer probably controlled Laos, Cambodia, and northern Thailand, while Upper Myanmar may already have been occupied to some extent by Myanmar tribes.

As these early settlers did not use lasting materials for construction, our knowledge of their civilization remains scant. We do know, however, that their way of life was very simple — as it remains today in rural areas — probably requiring only wooden huts with palm-leaf roofs for habitation. We can assume that they were not organised into units larger than village communities and that they did not possess a written language. Their religion must have been some form of nature worship or animism, still found today among the more remote tribes of the region.

There were also more highly developed communities of Indian origin, in the form of trading settlements located along the entire coast from Bengal to Borneo. In Myanmar, they were located in Thaton (Suddhammapura), Pegu (Ussa), Yangon (Ukkala, then still on the coast), and Mrauk-U (Dhannavati) in Arakan; also probably along the Tenasserim and Arakan coasts. These settlers had mainly migrated from Orissa on the northeastern coast of the Indian subcontinent, and also from the Deccan in the southeast. In migrating to these areas, they had also brought their own culture and religion with them. Initially, the contact between the Hindu traders and the Mon peasants must have been limited. However, the Indian settlements, their culture and traditions, were eventually absorbed into the Mon culture.

G.E. Harvey, in his *History of Burma*, relates a Mon legend which refers to the Mon fighting Hindu strangers who had come back to re-conquer the country that had formerly belonged to them. This Mon tale confirms the theory that Indian people had formed the first communities in the region but that these were eventually replaced by the Mon with the development of their own civilization. As well as the Indian trading settlements, there were also some Pyu settlements, particularly in the area of Prome where a flourishing civilization later developed.

Also, it is assumed that some degree of migration from India to the region of Tagaung and Mogok in Upper Myanmar had taken place through Assam and later through Manipur, but the "hinterland" was of course much less attractive to traders than the coastal regions with their easy access by sea. A tradition of Myanmar says that Tagaung was founded by Abhiraja, a prince of the Sakyans (the tribe of the Buddha), who had migrated to Upper Myanmar from Nepal in the ninth century BC. The city was subsequently conquered by the Chinese in approximately 600 BC, and Pagan and Prome were founded by refugees fleeing southward. In fact, some historians believe that, like the Myanmar, the Sakyans were a Mongolian rather than an Indo-Aryan race, and that the Buddha's clansmen were derived from Mongolian stock.

First Contacts with the Buddha's Teachings

The source of information for many of the events related forthwith is the *Sasanavamsa*. The *Sasanavamsa* is a chronicle written in Pali by a bhikkhu, Pannasami, for the Fifth Buddhist Council held in Mandalay in 1867. As the *Sasanavamsa* is a recent compilation, many events mentioned therein may be doubted. However, as it draws on both written records, some of which are no longer available, and on the oral tradition of Myanmar, information can be included in this account with the understanding that it is open to verification.

There are many instances in the history of Southeast Asian tribes in which a conquering people incorporates into its own traditions not only the civilization of the conquered, but also their clan gods, royal lineage, and thereby their history. This fact would explain the visits of the Buddha to Thaton and

Shwesettaw in the Mon and Myanmar oral tradition, and the belief of the Arakanese that the Buddha visited their king and left behind an image of himself for them to worship. Modern historiography will, of course, dismiss these stories as fabrications made out of national pride, as the Myanmar had not even arrived in the region at the time of the Buddha. However, it is possible that the Myanmar and Arakanese integrated into their own lore the oral historical tradition of their Indian predecessors. This does not prove that the visits really took place, but it seems a more palatable explanation of the existence of these accounts than simply putting them down to historical afterthought of a Buddhist people eager to connect itself with the origins of their religion.

The *Sasanavamsa* mentions several visits of the Buddha to Myanmar and one other important event: the arrival of the hair relics in Ukkala (Yangon) soon after the Buddha's enlightenment.

The Arrival of the Hair Relics

Tapussa and Bhallika, two merchants from Ukkala, were traveling through the region of Uruvela and were directed to the Buddha by their family god. The Buddha had just come out of seven weeks of meditation after his awakening and was sitting under a tree feeling the need for food. Tapussa and Bhallika made an offering of rice cake and honey to the Buddha and took the two refuges, the refuge in the Buddha and the refuge in the Dhamma (the Sangha, the third refuge, did not exist yet). As they were about to depart, they asked the Buddha for an object to worship in his stead and he gave them eight hairs from his head. After the two returned from their journey, they enshrined the three hairs in a stupa which is now the great Shwedagon Pagoda in Yangon.

It is believed in Myanmar that the hill upon which the Shwedagon Pagoda stands was not haphazardly chosen by Tapussa and Bhallika but was, in fact, the site where the three Buddhas preceding the Buddha Gotama in this world cycle themselves deposited relics. Buddha Kakusandha is said to have left his staff on the Theinguttara Hill, the Buddha

Konagamana his water filter, and Buddha Kassapa a part of his robe. Because of this, the Buddha requested Tapussa and Bhallika to enshrine his relics in this location. Tapussa and Bhallika traveled far and wide in order to find the hill on which they could balance a tree without its touching the ground either with the roots or with the crown. Eventually, they found the exact spot not far from their home in Lower Myanmar where they enshrined the holy relics in a traditional mound or stupa. The original stupa is said to have been 27 feet high. Today the Shwedagon pagoda has grown to over 370 feet.

The Buddha's Visits to the Region

The Myanmar oral tradition speaks of four visits of the Buddha to the region. While these visits were of utmost significance in their own right, they are also important in having established places of pilgrimage up to the present day.

The Visit to Central Myanmar

According to the *Sasanavamsa,* the city of Aparanta is situated on the western shore of the Irrawaddy river at the latitude of Magwe. The *Sasanavamsa* gives only a very brief summary of the events surrounding the Buddha's visit to Aparanta, presumably because these were well known and could be read in the Tipitaka and the commentaries.

Punna, a merchant from Sunaparanta, went to Savatthi on business and there heard a discourse of the Buddha. Having won faith in the Buddha and the Teachings, he took ordination as a bhikkhu. After sometime, he asked the Buddha to teach him a short lesson so that he could return to Sunaparanta and strive for arahatship. The Buddha warned him that the people of Sunaparanta were fierce and violent, but Punna replied that he would not allow anger to arise, even if they should kill him. In the Punnovada Sutta, the Buddha instructed him not to be enticed by that which is pleasant, and Punna returned and attained arahatship in his country. He won over many disciples and built a monastery of red sandalwood for the Buddha (according to some chronicles of Myanmar, the Buddha made the prediction that at the location where the red sandalwood monastery was, the great king Alaungsithu of Pagan would build a shrine). He then sent flowers as an invitation to the Buddha and the Buddha came accompanied by five hundred arahats, spent the night in the monastery, and left again before dawn.

Sakka, the king of the thirty-three devas living in the Tavatimsa plane, provided five hundred palanquins for the bhikkhus accompanying the Buddha on the journey to Sunaparanta. But only 499 of the palanquins were occupied. One of them remained empty until the ascetic Saccabandha, who lived on the Saccabandha mountain in central Myanmar, joined the Buddha and the 499 bhikkhus accompanying him. On the way to Sunaparanta, the Buddha stopped in order to teach the ascetic Saccabandha. When Saccabanda attained arahatship, he then joined the Buddha and completed the total of 500 bhikkhus who usually traveled with the Master.

On the return journey, the Buddha stopped at the river Nammada close to the Saccabandha mountain. Here, the Blessed One was invited by the Naga king, Nammada, to visit and preach to the Nagas, later accepting food from them. The tradition of Myanmar relates that he left behind a footprint for veneration near this river, which would last as long as the Sasana (i.e. 5000 years). Another footprint was left in the rock of the Saccabandha mountain. These footprints, still visible today, were worshipped by the Mon, Pyu, and Myanmar kings alike and have remained among the holiest places of pilgrimage in Myanmar. In the fifteenth century, after the decimation of the population through the Siamese campaigns, knowledge of the footprints was lost. Then, in the year 1638, King Thalun sent learned bhikkhus to the region; fortuitously, they were able to relocate the Buddha's footprints. Since then Shwesettaw, the place where the footprints are found, has once again become an important place of pilgrimage in Myanmar. And in the dry season thousands of devout Buddhists travel there to pay respects.

The Visit to Arakan

In Dhannavati, whose walls are still partially visible today, the Mahamuni temple is located on the Sirigutta hill. In this temple, for over two millennia, the Mahamuni image was enshrined and worshipped. The story of the Mahamuni image, at one time one of the most revered shrines of Buddhism, is told in the *Sappadanapakarana,* a work of a local historian.

Candrasuriya, the king of Dhannavati, on hearing that a Buddha had arisen in India, desired to go there to learn the Dhamma. The Buddha, aware of his intention, said to Ananda: "The king will have to pass through forests dangerous to travelers; wide rivers will impede his journey; he must cross a sea full of monsters. It will be an act of charity if we go to his dominion, so that he may pay homage without risking his life."

So the Buddha went there and was received with great pomp by King Candrasuriya and his people. The Buddha then taught the five and eight precepts and instructed the king in the ten kingly duties, namely, (1) universal beneficence, (2) daily paying homage, (3) the showing of mercy, (4) taxes of not more than a tenth part of the produce, (5) justice, (6) punishment without anger, (7) the support of his subjects as the earth supports them, (8) the employment of prudent commanders, (9) the taking of good counsel, and (10) the avoidance of pride. The Buddha remained for a week and on preparing for his departure the king requested that he leave an image of himself, so that they could worship him even in his absence. The Buddha consented to this and Sakka the king of the gods himself formed the image with the metals collected by the king and his people. It was completed in one week and when the Buddha breathed onto it the people exclaimed that now there were indeed two Buddhas, so alike was the image to the great sage. Then the Buddha made a prophesy addressing the image: "I shall pass into Nibbana in my eightieth year, but you will live for five thousand years which I have foreseen as the duration of my Teaching."

The Mahamuni image remained in its original location until 1784 when King Bodawpaya conquered Arakan and had the image transported to Mandalay where a special shrine, the Arakan pagoda, was built to enshrine the three-meter image. To have this image in his capital greatly added to his prestige as a Buddhist king, as it was one of the most sacred objects in the region. The king himself went out of his city to meet the approaching image with great devotion and "through the long colonnades leading to the pagoda, there used to come daily from the Myanmar palace, so long as a king reigned there, sumptuous offerings borne in stately procession, marshalled by a minister and shaded by the white umbrella."

The Missionaries of the Third Buddhist Council

The Third Buddhist Council was held in the reign of Emperor Asoka in the year 232 BC in order to purify the Sangha, to reassert orthodox teaching and to refute heresy. But the work of the Council did not stop there. With the support of Emperor Asoka, experienced teachers were sent to border regions in order to spread the teachings of the Buddha. This dispersal of missionaries is recorded in the *Mahavamsa,* a Sinhalese chronicle on the history of Buddhism:

When the thera Moggaliputta, the illuminator of the religion of the Conqueror, had brought the (third) council to an end and when, looking into the future, he had beheld the founding of the religion in adjacent countries, then in the month of Katthika he sent forth theras, one here and one there. The thera Majjhantika he sent to Kasmira and Gandhara, the thera Mahadeva he sent to Mahisamandala. To Vanavasa he sent the thera named Rakkhita, and to Aparantaka the Yona named Dhammarakkhita; to Maharattha he sent the thera named Mahadhammarakkhita, but the thera Maharakkhita he sent into the country of the Yona. He sent the thera Majjhima to the Himalaya country and together with the thera Uttara, the thera Sona of wondrous might went to Suvannabhumi...

According to the *Sasanavamsa,* the above mentioned regions are the following: Kasmira and Gandhara is the right bank of the Indus river south of Kabul; Mahisamandala is Andhra; Vanavasa is the region around Prome; Aparantaka is west of the upper Irrawaddy; Maharattha is Thailand; Yona, the country of the Shan tribes; and Suvannabhumi is Thaton. The *Sasanavamsa* mentions five places in Southeast Asia where Asoka's missionaries taught the Buddha's doctrine, and through their teaching many gained insight and took refuge in the Triple Gem. There are two interesting features mentioned in the text. First, in order to ordain nuns, bhikkhunis, other bhikkhunis had to be present, and secondly, the Brahmajala Sutta was preached in Thaton.

The *Sasanavamsa* goes on to describe sixty thousand women ordaining in Aparanta. It states that women could not have been ordained without the presence of bhikkhunis, as in Sri Lanka where women could only be ordained after Mahinda's sister Sanghamitta had followed her brother there. In this case, the author surmises that bhikkhunis must have followed Dhammarakkhita to Aparanta at a later stage.

The Brahmajala Sutta, which the arahats Sona and Uttara preached in Thaton, deals in detail with the different schools of philosophical and religious thought prevalent in India at the time of the Buddha. The fact that Sona and Uttara chose this Sutta to convert the inhabitants of Suvannabhumi indicates that they were facing a well-informed public, familiar with the views of Brahmanism that were refuted by the Buddha in this discourse. There can be no doubt that only Indian colonisers, not the Mon, would have been able to follow an analysis of Indian philosophy as profound as the Brahmajala Sutta.

BUDDHISM IN THE MON AND PYU KINGDOMS

While there is no conclusive archaeological proof that Buddhism continued to be practiced in southern Myanmar after the missions of the Third Council, the *Sasanavamsa* refers to an unbroken lineage of teachers passing on the Dhamma to their disciples.

The Mon

In a third century AD inscription by a South Indian king in Nagarjunakonda, the land of the Cilatas is mentioned in a list of countries visited by a group of bhikkhus. Historians believe the Cilatas or Kiratas (also mentioned by Ptolemy and in Sanskrit literature) to be identical to the Mon populations of Lower Myanmar.

The inscription states that the bhikkhus sent to the Cilata country converted the population there to Buddhism. In the same inscription, missions to other countries such as Sri Lanka are mentioned. It is generally believed that most of these countries had received earlier Buddhist missionaries sent by Buddhist kings, but as civilization in these lands was relatively undeveloped, teachings as profound as the Buddha's had probably become distorted by local religions or possibly been completely lost. It is possible that these missions did not so much re-establish Buddhism, but rather purify the type of Buddhism practiced there. Southern India was then the guardian of the Theravada faith and obviously remained in contact with countries that had been converted in earlier times but were unable to preserve the purity of the religion.

As has been already mentioned, the first datable archaeological finds of the Mon civilization stem from the Mon kingdom of Dvaravati in the South of Thailand. They consist of a Roman oil lamp and a bronze statue of the Buddha which are believed to be no later than the first or second century AD. In discussing the Mon Theravada Buddhist civilization, we cannot remain in Myanmar only. For only by studying the entire sphere of influence of the Mon in this period, can a comprehensive picture be constructed. This sphere includes large parts of present day Thailand. In fact, the Chinese Buddhist pilgrim, Yuan Chwang, who traveled to India in about 630 AD, describes a single Mon country stretching from Prome to Chenla in the east and including the Irrawaddy and Sittang deltas. He calls the country Dvaravati, but the annals of the court of China of the same period mention Dvaravati as a vassal of Thaton. We can, therefore, safely conclude that the Mon of the region formed a fairly homogenous group in which the distribution of power was obviously not always evident to the outsider.

The Pyu

Lower Myanmar was also inhabited by another ethnic group, the Pyu, who were probably closely related to the modern Myanmar. They had their capital at Sri Ksetra (near modern day Prome) and were also followers of the Theravada Buddhist faith. Chinese travelers' reports of the mid-third century AD refer to the kingdom of Lin-Yang where Buddha was venerated by all and where several thousand monks or bhikkhus lived.

As Lin-Yang was to the west of Kamboja and could not be reached by sea, we can infer that the Chinese travelers must have been referring to the ancient kingdom of Prome. This is all the more likely as archaeological finds prove that only about one century later Pali Buddhist texts, including Abhidhamma texts, were studied by the Pyu.

The earliest highly developed urban settlement of the Pyu was Beikthano, near Prome. However, its importance dwindled towards the sixth century, when Sri Ksetra became the center of Pyu civilization. A major monastery built in the fourth century has been unearthed at Beikthano. The building, constructed in brick, with a stupa and shrine located nearby, is identical to the Buddhist monasteries of Nagarjunakonda, the great Buddhist center of southern India. It is situated near a stupa and a shrine, a design which is identical to the one used in South India. Bricks had been used by the Pyus since the second century AD for the construction of pillared halls, which formed the temples of their original religion. Interestingly, the Pyu bricks have always been of the exact dimensions as those used at the time of Emperor Asoka in India. But the brick laying techniques used in the monastery in Beikthano were far inferior to the ones used in their southern Indian counterparts.

For such a major edifice as the monastery at Beikthano to have been constructed, the religion must have been well established at least among the ruling class. How long it took for Buddhism to become influential in Pyu society is difficult to determine, but some historians assume that the first contacts with Asokan religious centers in India took place in the second century AD. This would allow for a period of development of two hundred years until the first important shrine was built. Despite the Indian architectural influence, the inferior brick laying techniques found in Beikthano indicate that indigenous architects and artisans, rather than imported craftsmen or Indian colonisers, were employed in the construction of monasteries and other important buildings.

It should, of course, not be forgotten that the Pyu possessed an architecture of their own and a highly developed urban culture that had evolved quite independently of Indian influences. Theravada Buddhism found a fertile ground in this highly developed civilization. It is probable that the Pyu civilization was more advanced than that of the Mon. The Pyu sites found around Prome are the earliest urban sites in Southeast Asia found to date. The urban developments and datable monuments in Thailand and Cambodia are only from the seventh century. Older artifacts may have been found in Thailand, but they were not products of indigenous people and do not prove the existence of a developed civilization.

The information we have of the state of the religion in the Mon and Pyu societies during the first four centuries AD is very limited. However, by the fifth century, with the development of religious activity in the region, information becomes more substantive. The historical tradition of Myanmar gives the credit for this religious resurgence to a well-known Buddhist scholar, Acariya Buddhaghosa.

Buddhaghosa and Myanmar

Acariya Buddhaghosa was the greatest commentator on the Pali Buddhist texts, whose *Visuddhimagga* and commentaries to the canon are regarded as authoritative by Theravada scholars. The chronicles of Myanmar firmly maintain that Buddhaghosa was of Mon origin and a native of Thaton. They state that his return from Sri Lanka, with the Pali scriptures, the commentaries, and grammatical works, gave a fresh impetus to the religion.

However, modern historians do not accept that Buddhaghosa was from Myanmar while some even doubt his existence. Despite this contention, Eliot, in his *Hinduism and Buddhism,* gives more weight to circumstantial evidence and writes:

> The Burmese tradition that Buddhaghosa was a native of Thaton and returned thither from Sri Lanka merits more attention than it has received. It can easily be explained away as patriotic fancy. On the other hand, if Buddhaghosa's object was to invigorate Hinayanism in India the result of his really stupendous labors was singularly small, for in India his name is connected with no religious movement. But if we suppose that he went to Sri Lanka by way of the holy places in Magadha

[now Bihar] and returned from the Coromandal coast [Madras] to Burma where Hinayanism afterwards flourished, we have at least a coherent narrative.

The Sinhalese chronicles, especially the *Mahavamsa,* place Buddhaghosa in the first half of the fifth century. Although he spent most of his active working life in Sri Lanka, he is also credited with imbuing new life into Theravada Buddhism in South India, and developing such important centers as Kancipura and Uragapuram that were closely connected with Prome and Thaton. Proof of this connection can be found in archeological finds in the environs of Prome which include Pali literature inscribed in the Kadambe script on gold and stone plates. This script was used in the fifth and sixth century in southern India.

All in all, Myanmar has a valid case for claiming some connection with Buddhaghosa. It is, of course, impossible to prove that he was born there or even visited there, but his influence undoubtedly led to great religious activity in the kingdoms of Lower Myanmar.

Buddhism in Lower Myanmar: 5th to 11th Centuries

From the fifth century until the conquest of Lower Myanmar by Pagan, there is a continuous record of Buddhism flourishing in the Mon and Pyu kingdoms. The Mon kingdoms are mentioned in travel reports of several Chinese Buddhist pilgrims and also in the annals of the Chinese court. In the fifth century, Thaton and Pegu (Pago) are mentioned in the Buddhist commentarial literature for the first time. They were now firmly established on the map as Buddhist centers of learning. Despite this, Buddhism was not without rivals in the region. This is shown, by the following event some chronicles of Myanmar mention.

A king of Pago, Tissa by name, had abandoned the worship of the Buddha and instead practiced Brahmanical worship. He persecuted the Buddhists and destroyed Buddha images or cast them into ditches. A pious Buddhist girl, the daughter of a merchant, restored the images, then washed and worshipped them. The king could not tolerate such defiance, of course, and had the girl dragged before him. He tried to have her executed in several ways, but she seemed impossible to kill. Elephants would not trample her, while the fire of her pyre would not burn her. Eventually the king, intrigued by these events, asked the girl to perform a miracle. He stated that, if she was able to make a Buddha image produce seven new images and then make all eight statues fly into heaven, she would be set free. The girl spoke an act of truth, and the eight Buddha statues flew up into the sky. The king was then converted to Buddhism and elevated the girl to the position of chief queen.

Until now, archaeological finds of Mon ruins in Myanmar are meager, but at P'ong Tuk, in southern Thailand, a Mon city, dating from the second half of the first millennium AD, has been unearthed. Here, excavations have revealed the foundations of several buildings. One contained the remains of a platform and fragments of columns similar to the Buddhist vihara at Anuradhapura in Sri Lanka; another, with a square foundation of round stones, seems to have been a stupa. Statues of Indian origin from the Gupta period (320-600 AD) were also found at the site. The Theravada Buddhist culture of the Mon flourished in both Dvaravati and Thaton. However, the Mon civilization in Thailand did not survive the onslaught of the Khmer in the eleventh century who were worshipping Hindu gods. In Myanmar, the Mon kingdom was conquered by Pagan. The Myanmar were eager to accept the Mon culture and especially their religion, while the Khmer, as Hindus, at best tolerated it.

The Pyu culture of this period is well documented because of archaeological finds at Muanggan, a small village close to the ancient ruins of Hmawza. There two perfectly preserved inscribed gold plates were found. These inscriptions reveal three texts: the verses spoken by Assaji to Sariputta *(ye dhamma hetuppabhava...)*, a list of categories of the Abhidhamma *(cattaro iddhipada, cattaro samappadhana...)*, and the formula of worship of Buddha, Dhamma, and Sangha *(iti pi so bhagava...)*. At the same site, a book with twenty leaves of gold protected with golden covers, was discovered. It contained texts such as the *paticca-samuppada* (dependent origination), the *vipassana-nanas* (stages of insight knowledge), and various other excerpts from the Abhidhamma and the other two baskets of the Buddhist scriptures. The scripts in all these documents are identical to scripts used in parts of southern India, and can be dated from the third to the sixth century AD.

In addition to these golden plates, a number of sculptures and reliefs were found in Hmawza. They depict either the Buddha or scenes from his life, for example, the birth of the Buddha and the taming of the wild elephant Nalagiri. The sculpture is similar in style to that of Amaravati, a center of Buddhist learning in South India. There were also unearthed remains of Brahman temples and sites of Mahayana worship of east Indian origin; hence it would appear that several faiths, of which the Theravada was the strongest, co-existed in Sri Ksetra, the then capital of the Pyu. The script used by the Pyu is indicative of major links with Buddhist kingdoms in South India rather than with Sri Lanka. And it can be surmised that the bhikkhus of the Deccan and other regions of southern India were the teachers of both the Mon and the Pyu in religious matters as well as in the arts and sciences.

The inscriptions show how highly developed scholarship of the Pali Buddhist texts must have been in Lower Myanmar even in these early days. Learning had gone well beyond the basics into the world of Abhidhamma studies. Pali was obviously well known as a language of learning, but unfortunately no original texts composed in Sri Ksetra or Thaton have come down to us. Interestingly, some of the texts inscribed on these gold plates are not identical to the same canonical texts as they are known today. Therefore, the Tipitaka known to the Pyu must have been replaced by a version preserved in a country that had no close contact with the Pyu. This could well have been Sri Lanka, as this country came to play an important role in the history of Buddhism in Myanmar through the friendship between the conqueror of Lower Myanmar, Anawratha, and the king who drove the Hindus from Sri Lanka, Vijayabahu.

The finds on the site of the ancient Pyu capital confirm the reports of the Chinese pilgrims and also the Tang imperial chronicles of China which state: "They (the Pyu) dislike taking life. They know how to make astronomical calculations. They are Buddhists and have a hundred monasteries, with brick of glass embellished with gold and silver vermilion, gay colours and red kino... At seven years of age the people cut their hair and enter a monastery; if at the age of twenty they have not grasped the doctrine they return to the lay state."

Both Buddhist cultures in the south of Myanmar, the Mon and the Pyu, were swept away in the eleventh century by armies of the Myanmar who had found a unifying force in their leader, the founder of Pagan and champion of Buddhism, Anawratha.

THERAVADA BUDDHISM COMES TO PAGAN

The Beginnings of Pagan

Pagan is believed to have been founded in the years 849-850 AD, by the Myanmar, who had already established themselves as rice growers in the region around Kyauksai near Mandalay. Anawratha began to unite the region by subjugating one chieftain after another and was successful in giving the Myanmar a sense of belonging to a larger community, a nation. The crucial event in the history of Myanmar is not so much the founding of the city of Pagan and the building of its walls and moat, but more Pagan's acceptance of Theravada Buddhism in the eleventh century. The religion was brought to the Myanmar by a Mon bhikkhu named Shin Arahan.

The religion prevailing among the Myanmar before and during the early reign of Anawratha was some form of Mahayana Buddhism, which had probably found its way into the region from the Pala kingdom in Bengal. This is apparent from bronze statues depicting Bodhisattas and especially the "Lokanatha," a Bodhisatta believed, in Bengal, to reign in the period between the demise of the Buddha Gotama and the advent of the Buddha Metteyya. Anawratha continued to cast terracotta votive tablets with the image of Lokanatha even after he embraced the Theravada doctrine.

In India, Buddhism had split into numerous schools, some of which differed fundamentally from the teachings of Pali Buddhism, which is also called Theravada Buddhism (the doctrine of the Theras). The Ari, the monks or priests of this

Mahayana Buddhist form of worship, are described, in later chronicles of Myanmar, as the most shameless bogus ascetics imaginable. They are said to have sold absolution from sin and to have oppressed the people in various ways with their tyranny. Their tantric Buddhism included, as an important element, the worship of Nagas (dragons), which was probably an ancient indigenous tradition.

At this time, the beginning of the eleventh century, the Buddhist religion among the Mon in Suvannabhumi was on the decline as people were disturbed by robbers and raiders, by plagues, and by adversaries of the religion. These most probably came from the Hindu Khmer kingdom in Cambodia and the north of Thailand. The Khmer were endeavoring to add Thaton and the other Mon kingdoms of the south to their expanding empire. Shin Arahan must have feared that bhikkhus would not be able to continue to maintain their religious practice and the study of the scriptures under these circumstances. He went, therefore, upcountry where a new, strong people were developing, prosperous and secure from enemies.

It is interesting to note that in this same period, Buddhism was under attack in other places as well. The Colas, a Hindu dynasty strongly opposed to Buddhism, arose in southern India, one of the last strongholds of Theravada Buddhism. They were able to expand their rule to include most of Sri Lanka between 1017 and 1070. The great Mon city, Dvaravati, a Theravada center in southern Thailand, fell to the Khmer, the masters of the whole of Thailand, who were Shaivaite Hindus. In the north of India, Muslim armies were trying to destroy what little was left of Buddhism there. "In this perilous period," writes Professor Luce, "Buddhism was saved only by such valiant fighters as Vijayabahu in Sri Lanka and Anawratha."

Shin Arahan Converts the King

Shin Arahan arrived in the vicinity of Pagan and was discovered in his forest dwelling by a hunter. The hunter, who had never before seen such a strange creature with a shaven head and a yellow robe, thought he was some kind of spirit and took him to the king, Anawratha. Shin Arahan naturally sat down on the throne, as it was the highest seat, and the king thought: "This man is peaceful, in this man there is the essential thing. He is sitting down on the best seat, surely he must be the best being." The king asked the visitor to tell him where he came from and was told that he came from the place where the Order lived and that the Buddha was his teacher. Then Shin Arahan gave the king the teaching on mindfulness *(appamada),* teaching him the same doctrine Nigrodha had given Emperor Asoka when he was converted. Shin Arahan then told the monarch that the Buddha had passed into Parinibbana, but that his teaching, the Dhamma, enshrined in the Tipitaka, and the twofold Sangha consisting of those who possessed absolute knowledge and those who possessed conventional knowledge, remained.

The king must have felt that he had found what had been missing in his life and a genuine alternative to the superficial teachings of the Ari monks. He built a monastery for Shin Arahan, and according to some sources, stopped all worship of the Ari monks. Tradition has it that he had them dressed in white and even forced them to serve as soldiers in his army. The Ari tradition continued for a long time, however, and its condemnation is a feature of much later times, and not, as far as contemporary evidence shows, of the Pagan era.

The *Sasanavamsa* gives an alternate version of Anawratha's conversion according to which Shin Arahan had originally come from Sri Lanka to study the Dhamma in Dvaravati and Thaton and was on his way to Sri Ksetra in search of a text when he was taken to Anawratha by a hunter. The king asked him, "Who are you?" — "O King, I am a disciple of Gotama." — "Of what kind are the Three Jewels?" — "O King, the Buddha should be regarded as Mahosadha the wise, his doctrine as Ummagga, his order as the Videhan army."

This version is interesting in that Anawratha is portrayed as being a Buddhist with knowledge of Jataka stories, such as the Mahosadha Jataka referred to above, even before meeting Shin Arahan. This assumption that he was no stranger to Buddhism is supported by the fact that earlier kings had been followers of Buddhism in varying degrees. Caw Rahan, who died about 94 years before Anawratha's accession, is said to have built a Sima and five Pagodas, and Kyaung Pyu Min built the white monastery outside Pagan. Kyaung Pyu Min is believed to have been Anawratha's father.

Anawratha Acquires the Scriptures

Through Shin Arahan, Anawratha had now found the religion he had been yearning for and he decided to set out and procure the scriptures and holy relics of this religion. For he wished his kingdom to be secured on the original teachings of the Buddha. He tried to find the scriptures and relics of his new religion in different quarters. In his enthusiasm he did not limit his quest to Thaton, but also searched among the Khmer in Angkor, and in Tali, the capital of the Nanchao, a kingdom in modern day Yunnan, in China, where a tooth of the Buddha was enshrined. But everywhere he was refused. He then went to Thaton, where his teacher Shin Arahan had come from, to request a copy of the scriptures. According to the tradition of Myanmar, Anawratha's request was refused, and unable to endure another refusal he set out with his army in the year 1057 to conquer Thaton and acquire the Tipitaka by force. Before conquering Thaton, however, he had to subjugate Sri Ksetra, the Pyu capital. From there, he took the relics enshrined in King Dwattabaung's Bawbaw-gyi Pagoda to Pagan.

Some think that the aim of his campaign was mainly to add the prosperous Indian colonies of Lower Myanmar to his possessions, while others think he may have actually been called to Thaton to defend it against the marauding Khmer. Whatever the immediate cause of his campaign in the lower country, we know for certain that he returned with the king of Thaton and his court, with Mon artists and scholars and, above all, with Thaton's bhikkhus and their holy books, the Tipitaka. Suvannabhumi and its Mon population were now in the hands of the Myanmar and the Mon culture and religion were accepted and assimilated in the emergent Pagan with fervor.

Initially the fervor must have been restricted to the king and possibly his immediate entourage, yet even they continued to propitiate their traditional gods for worldly gain as the new religion was considered a higher practice. Theravada Buddhism does not provide much in the way of rites and rituals, but a royal court cannot do without them. So the traditional propitiation of the Nagas continued to be used for court ceremonials and remained part of the popular religion, while the bhikkhus were accorded the greatest respect and their master, the Buddha Gotama, was honored with the erection of pagodas and shrines.

There were contacts between the new kings of Myanmar and Sri Lanka that are recorded not only in the chronicles of the two countries but also in stone inscriptions in South India. As the Hindu Colas had ruled Sri Lanka for more than half a century, Buddhism had been weakened and King Vijayabahu, who had driven out the Vaishnavite Colas, wanted to re-establish his religion. So in 1070, he requested King Anawratha of Myanmar, who had assisted him financially in his war against the Colas, to send bhikkhus to re-introduce the pure ordination into his country. It is interesting to note that the *Culavamsa* refers to Anawratha as the king of Ramanna, which was Lower Myanmar, also called Suvannabhumi. He was approached as the conqueror and master of Thaton, a respected Theravada center, rather than as the king of Pagan, a new and unknown country. The bhikkhus who traveled to Sri Lanka brought the Sinhalese Tipitaka back with them and established a link between the two countries which was to last for centuries.

Anawratha is mentioned in the Myanmar, Mon, Khmer, Thai, and Sinhalese chronicles as a great champion of Buddhism because he developed Pagan into a major regional power and laid the foundation for its glory. He did not, however, build many of the temples for which Pagan is now so famous as the great age of temple building started only after his reign. It is important to realize that his interest was not restricted only to Pagan. He built pagodas wherever his campaigns took him and adorned them with illustrations from the Jatakas and the life of the Buddha. Some maintain that he used only Jatakas as themes for the adornment of his religious buildings because that was all he possessed of the Tipitaka. Such a conclusion is negative and quite superficial. After all, during Asoka's time

Jatakas and scenes from the life of the Buddha were used for illustrations in Bharut and Sanchi, the great stupas near Bombay. We cannot therefore deduce that the builders of Bharut and Sanchi were acquainted only with the Jatakas. These edifying stories which teach the fundamentals of Buddhism so skillfully are singularly suited to educate an illiterate people beset by superstitions through the vivid visual means of the stone reliefs depicting these stories. It is almost unthinkable that the Mon Sangha, who taught Anawratha, had no knowledge of at least all of the Vinaya. Otherwise, they would not have been able to re-establish a valid ordination of bhikkhus in Sri Lanka.

Anawratha left behind innumerable clay tablets adorned with images of the Buddha, the king's name, and some Pali and Sanskrit verses. A typical aspiration on these tablets was: "By me, King Anawratha, this mould of Sugata (Buddha) has been made. Through this may I obtain the path to Nibbana when Metteyya is awakened." Anawratha aspired to become a disciple of the Buddha Metteyya, unlike many later kings of Myanmar who aspired to Buddhahood. Is this an indication that this warrior had remained a modest man in spite of his empire building?

PAGAN: FLOWERING AND DECLINE

Anawratha was succeeded by a number of kings of varying significance to Buddhism in Myanmar. His successors inherited a relatively stable and prosperous kingdom and consequently were able to embark on the huge temple building projects for which their reigns are still remembered.

This is the time when kings such as Kyanzitta and others built pagodas, libraries, monasteries, and ordination halls. These kings must have possessed coffers full of riches collected from their extensive kingdom which they lavished on the religion of the Buddha. Their palaces were probably built of wood as was the last palace of the Myanmar dynasty. Though the palaces must have reflected the wealth and power of the rulers, the more durable brick was not deemed necessary for such worldly buildings. This is similar to views still found in rural areas of

Myanmar today. The only structure adorned to any extent in a village is the monastery and the buildings attached to it, such as the rest house. The villagers are very modest with regard to their private houses and even consider it improper to decorate them. Their monastery, however, is given every decoration affordable.

Kyanzitta Strengthens Theravada Buddhism

Kyanzitta (1084-1113), who had been Anawratha's commander-in-chief and had succeeded Anawratha's son to the throne, consolidated Theravada Buddhism's predominance in Pagan. In his reign, such important shrines as the Shwezigon Pagoda, the Nanda, Nagayon, and Myinkaba Kubyauk-gyi temples were built.

With the three latter temples, Kyanzitta introduced a new style of religious building. The traditional stupa or dagoba found in India and Sri Lanka is a solid mound in which relics or other holy objects are enshrined. The area of worship is situated around them and is usually marked by ornate stone railings. In the new style of building, however, the solid mound had been hollowed out and could be entered. The central shrine was surrounded by halls which housed stone reliefs depicting scenes from the Buddha's life and Jataka stories. Kyanzitta's aim was the conversion of his people to the new faith. Whereas Anawratha had been busy expanding his empire and bringing relics and the holy scriptures to Pagan, Kyanzitta's mission was to consolidate this enterprise. Enormous religious structures such as the Nanda Temple attracted the populace and the interiors of the temples allowed the bhikkhus to instruct the inquisitive in the king's faith.

Professor Luce writes:

> *The Nanda (temple)... he built with four broad halls. Each hall had the same 16 scenes in stone relief all identically arranged. The bhikkhus could cope with four audiences simultaneously. The scenes cover the whole life of the Buddha. When well grounded in these, the audience would pass to the outer wall of the corridor. Here, running around the whole corridor are the*

80 scenes of Gotama's life up to the Enlightenment. The later life of the Buddha is shown in hundreds of other stone reliefs on the inner walls and shrines.

Kyanzitta's efforts for the advancement of Buddhism were not limited to his own country. For in one of his many inscriptions, he also mentions that he sent craftsmen to Bodhgaya to repair the Mahabodhi temple, which had been destroyed by a foreign king. The upkeep of the Mahabodhi temple became a tradition with the kings of Myanmar, who continued to send missions to Bodhgaya to repair the temple and also to donate temple slaves and land to the holiest shrine of Buddhism.

Kyanzitta also initiated an extensive review and purification of the Tipitaka by the bhikkhus. This was the first occasion in Myanmar's history when the task of a Buddhist Sangayana or Synod, comparing the Sinhalese and Suvannabhumi's Tipitaka, was undertaken. It is possible and even probable that this huge editing work was carried out along with visiting Sinhalese bhikkhus.

By nature of Myanmar's geographical position, external influences swept in predominantly from northern India, and therefore tantric Buddhism, dominant especially in Bengal, remained strong. However, Kyanzitta succeeded in firmly establishing the Pali Tipitaka by asking the bhikkhus to compare the ancient Mon Tipitaka with the texts obtained from the Mahavihara in Sri Lanka. In this way, he also made it clear that confirmation of orthodoxy was to be sought in Sri Lanka and not in any other Buddhist country. Though Mahayana practices were tolerated in his reign (his chief queen was a tantric Buddhist), they were not officially regarded as the pure religion. It is characteristic of Pagan that these two branches of Buddhism co-existed — the religion of the Theras, which was accepted as the highest religion — and the tantric practices, which included the worship of spirits or *nats* and gave more immediate satisfaction. Pagodas are often adorned with figures of all types of deities, but the deities are normally shown in an attitude of reverence towards the pagoda, a symbol of the Buddha. The ancient gods were not banished, but had to submit to the peerless Buddha. Tradition attributes to King Anawratha the observation: "Men will not come for the sake of the new faith. Let them come for their old gods, and gradually they will be won over."

An approach such as this, whether it was Anawratha's or Kyanzitta's, would suggest that the practice of the old religion of the Ari monks was allowed to continue and that the conversion of the country was gentle and peaceful as befits the religion of the Buddha. Although later Myanmar chronicles refer to the Ari monks as a debased group of charlatans who were totally rooted out by Anawratha, this is far from the truth. A powerful movement of "priests" who incorporated magic practices in their teachings continued to exist throughout the Pagan period, and though they may have respected the basic rules of the Vinaya and donned the yellow robe, their support was rooted in the old animistic beliefs of the Myanmar. It should not be forgotten that the Myanmar first started to settle in the area of Kyauksai in the sixth century AD and that the "man in the field" was in no way ready for such highly developed a religion as Theravada Buddhism. The transition had to be gradual, and the process that started remains still incomplete in the minds of many people, especially in the more remote areas of the hill country.

The example of Kyanzitta's son Rajakumar, however, shows how even in those early days the teachings of the Buddha were understood and practiced not only by the bhikkhus, but also by lay people and members of the royal court. Rajakumar's conduct is proof of his father's ability to establish men in the Dhamma and survives as a monument just as the Ananda temple does.

Rajakumar was Kyanzitta's only son and his rightful heir. Due to political misadventures Kyanzitta was separated from his wife and therefore not aware of the birth of his son for seven years. When his daughter gave birth to his grandson he anointed him as future king immediately after his birth. Rajakumar grew up in the shadow of his nephew, the crown prince, but neither during his father's reign nor after his death did he ever try to usurp the throne through intrigue or by force. He was a minister zealous in the affairs of state, prudent and wise. He was also a scholar of the Tipitaka and instrumental in its review, vigorously supporting his father in his objective to establish Buddhism. But he is best known for his devotion to his father in his last years when his health was failing. In order to restore the king's health he built five pagodas which to this day are called Min-o-Chanda, "The Welfare of the Old King." When the king was on his deathbed:

Rajakumar, remembering the many and great favors with which the king had nourished him, made a beautiful golden image of the Buddha and entering with ceremony presented it to the king, saying: "This golden Buddha I have made to help my lord. The three villages of slaves you gave me, I give to this Buddha." And the king rejoiced and said "Sadhu, sadhu, sadhu." Then in the presence of the compassionate Mahathera and other leading bhikkhus, the king poured on the ground the water of dedication, calling the earth to witness. Then Rajakumar enshrined the golden image, and built around it a cave temple with a golden pinnacle.

Later Kings

Rajakumar's nephew was King Alaungsithu (c.1113-67), who continued the tradition of his dynasty of glorifying the Buddha's religion by building a vast temple, the Sabbannu Temple, probably the largest monument in Pagan. During his many travels and campaigns, he built pagodas and temples throughout Myanmar. The faith that Shin Arahan had inspired in Anawratha and his successors continued to inspire Alaungsithu. Shin Arahan, who had seen kings come and go and the flowering of the religion he brought to Pagan, is believed to have died during the reign of King Alaungsithu, in about 1115.

After the death of Alaungsithu, Pagan was thrown into turmoil by violent struggles for the throne. Several kings reigned for short periods and spent most of their time and resources in power struggles. One even succeeded in alienating the great king of Sri Lanka, Parakramabahu, by mistreating his emissaries and breaking the agreements between the two countries. Eventually Parakramabahu invaded Myanmar, devastating towns and villages and killing the king. The new king, Narapati (1174-1210), blessed the country with a period of peace and prosperity. This conducive atmosphere was to allow outstanding scholarship and learning to arise in Pagan.

Kyawswa (1234-50) was a king under whom scholarship was encouraged even more, undoubtedly because the king himself spent most of his time in scholarly pursuits including memorizing passages of the Tipitaka. He had relinquished most of his worldly duties to his son in order to dedicate more time to the study of the scriptures. Two grammatical works, the *Saddabindu* and the *Paramatthabindu,* are ascribed to him. It would appear that his palace was a place of great culture and learning as his ministers and his daughter are credited with scholarly works as well.

During the twelfth century, a sect of forest dwellers also thrived. They were called *arannaka* in Pali and were identical with the previously mentioned Ari of the later chroniclers of Myanmar. This was a monastic movement that only used the yellow robes and the respect due to them in order to follow their own ideas. They indulged in business transactions and owned vast stretches of land. They gave feasts and indulged in the consumption of liquor, and, though they pretended to be practicing the teachings of the Buddha, their practices were probably of a tantric nature. It would appear that they had a considerable amount of influence at the royal court and one of the main exponents of the movement was even given the title of royal teacher. Superstition and magic were gaining dominance once again and Anawratha's and Kyanzitta's empire was slowly sliding into decadence.

The last king of Pagan, Narathihapate, whom the Myanmar know by the name Tayoupyemin (the king who fled the Chinese), repeatedly refused to pay symbolic tribute to the Mongol emperors in Peking who in 1271 had conquered neighbouring Yunnan. He even went so far as to execute ambassadors of the Chinese emperor and their retinue for their lack of deference to the king. He became so bold and blinded by ignorance that he attacked a vassal state of the Mongols. The emperor in

Peking was finally forced to send a punitive expedition which defeated the Pagan army north of Pagan. The news of this defeat caused the king and his court to flee to Pathein (Bassein). As the imperial court in Peking was not interested in adding Pagan to its possessions, the Yunnan expedition did not remain in the environs. When the king was later murdered and the whole empire fell into disarray, the Yunnani generals returned, looting Pagan. The territories were divided amongst Shan chiefs who paid tribute to the Mongols.

G.E. Harvey honors the kings of Pagan with the following words:

> *To them the world owes to a great measure the preservation of Theravada Buddhism, one of the purest faiths mankind has ever known. Brahmanism had strangled it in its land of birth; in Sri Lanka its existence was threatened again and again; east of Burma it was not yet free from priestly corruptions; but the kings of Burma never wavered, and at Pagan the stricken faith found a city of refuge.*

Contacts with Sri Lanka and the First Controversies

The contact with Sri Lanka was very important for the growth of the religion in Pagan. As was shown previously, it started with the friendship of Anawratha and Vijayabahu, both of whom fought for Buddhism: Anawratha to establish a new kingdom, Vijayabahu to wrench an old one from the clutches of the Hindu invaders. They supported each other in their struggles and then together re-established the Theravada doctrine in their respective countries, Anawratha sending bhikkhus to Sri Lanka to revive the Sangha, while Vijayabahu reciprocated by sending the sacred texts. The continued contact between the two countries was beneficial to both: many a reform movement, purifying the religion in one country spread to the other as well. Bhikkhus visiting from one country were led to look at their own traditions critically and to reappraise their practice of the Dhamma as preserved in the Pali texts. After the fall of the main Buddhist centers in southern India, centers which had been the main allies of the Mon Theravadins in the south, Sri Lanka was the only ally in the struggle for the survival of the Theravada tradition.

Leading bhikkhus of Pagan undertook the long and difficult journey to Sri Lanka in order to visit the holy temples and study the scriptures as they had been preserved by the Sinhalese Sangha. Shin Arahan's successor as the king's teacher left the royal court for Sri Lanka, returning to Pagan only to die. He was succeeded by a Mon bhikkhu, Uttarajiva, who led a pilgrimage to Sri Lanka in 1171. This was to cause the first upheaval in the Sangha of Pagan.

Uttarajiva traveled to Sri Lanka accompanied by Chapada, a novice who remained behind on the island in order to study the scriptures in the Mahavihara, the orthodox monastery of Sri Lanka and the guardian of the Theravada tradition. After ten years, he returned to Pagan accompanied by four elders who had studied with him. The Kalyani inscription, written about three hundred years later, relates that Chapada considered the tradition of the Myanmar bhikkhus impure. He had consequently taken four bhikkhus with him because he needed a chapter of at least five theras in order to ordain new bhikkhus.

It is possible that the Myanmar bhikkhus, who seemed to have formed a group separate from the Mon bhikkhus, had paid more attention to their traditional worship than was beneficial for their practice of the Dhamma. It is also possible that there was an element of nationalist rivalry between the Mon bhikkhus and the Myanmar bhikkhus. As he showed a penchant for the reform movement, the Myanmar king Narapati seems to have accepted the superiority of the Mon bhikkhus, though he did not neglect the other bhikkhus. Chapada and his companions refused to accept the ordination of the Myanmar bhikkhus as legitimate in accordance with Vinaya. They established their own ordination, following which the Myanmar bhikkhus sent a delegation to Sri Lanka to receive the Mahavihara ordination for themselves.

After Chapada's death, the reform movement soon split into two factions, and eventually each of the four remaining bhikkhus went his own way, one of them leaving the order altogether. "Thus in the town of Arimaddana (Pagan) there were four schools... Because the first of these to come was the school of the Elder Arahan from Sudhamma (Thaton) it was called the first school; while the others, because they came later, were called the later schools."

Scholarship in Pagan

It is surprising how quickly a relatively simple people absorbed the great civilization that arrived in their midst so suddenly. Even before the conquest of Thaton, Pagan possessed some ornate religious buildings, which is indicative of the presence of artists and craftsmen. It is quite likely, however, that these were Indians from Bengal and the neighbouring states.

The type of Buddhism that had come to Pagan from India was an esoteric religion, as some old legends indicate. It was the jealously guarded domain of a group of priests, who made no attempt to instruct the people but were happy if their superiority remained unquestioned by a superstitious populace.

The advent of Theravada Buddhism with its openness and its aim to spread understanding must have been quite revolutionary in Pagan and obviously the people were eager to acquire the knowledge offered to them by the bhikkhus. Mabel Bode says in her *Pali Literature of Burma:*

Though the Burmese began their literary history by borrowing from their conquered neighbours, the Talaings (Mon)— and not before the eleventh century — the growth of Pali scholarship among them was so rapid that the epoch following close on this tardy beginning is considered one of the best that Burma has seen.

The principal works of the Pagan period still extant are Pali grammars. The most famous of these is the *Saddaniti,* which Aggavamsa completed in 1154. Uttarajiva gave a copy of this work to the bhikkhus of the Mahavihara in Sri Lanka and it "was received with enthusiastic admiration, and declared superior to any work of the kind written by Sinhalese scholars."

The *Saddaniti* is still used to teach grammar in the monasteries in Myanmar and has been printed many times.

B.C. Law regards it as one of the three principal Pali grammars along with the grammars by Kaccayana and Moggallana. K.R. Norman says: "The greatest of extant Pali grammars is the *Saddaniti,* written by Aggavamsa from Arimaddana [Pagan] in Burma..." Aggavamsa was also known as the teacher of King Narapatisithu (1167-1202) and was given the title Aggapandita. Unfortunately, no other works by this author are known today.

The second famous author of Pagan was Saddhammajotipala who has been previously mentioned under his clan name of Chapada. He was a disciple of Uttarajiva and is credited with a great number of works, but in the case of some it is doubtful whether he actually composed them himself or merely introduced them from Sri Lanka. His works deal not only with grammar, but also with questions of monastic discipline (Vinaya) and the Abhidhamma, which in later centuries was to become a favorite subject of Myanmar scholars.

His work on Kaccayana's grammar, the *Suttaniddesa,* formed the foundation of his fame. However, his specialty would appear to have been the study of Abhidhamma, as no less than four noted works of his on the subject attained fame: *Samkhepavannana, Namacaradipani, Matikatthadipani,* and *Patthanagananaya.* According to the Pitaka-thamain, a history of Buddhism in Myanmar, he also devoted a commentary to the *Visuddhimagga* by Buddhaghosa called the *Visuddhimagga-ganthi.* There are no written records that refer to meditation being practiced in Myanmar before this century. However, his interest in the *Visuddhimagga* is indicative of an interest in meditation, if only in the theory rather than in the practice. Another scholar of Pagan, Vimalabuddhi, also wrote a commentary concerning Abhidhamma, the *Abhidhammatthasangahatika,* in addition to another important grammatical work, the *Nyasa,* a commentary on Kaccayana's grammar.

Other grammatical works of some importance were written, but none acquired the standing of Aggavamsa's *Saddaniti.* However, a rather peculiar work worth mentioning is the *Ekakkharakosa* by Saddhammakitti. It is a work on Pali lexicography enumerating words of one letter.

SHAN RULE

Upper Myanmar

After Narathihapate had fled Pagan in fear of the Mongol army, he was never able to re-establish his authority, even though the Mongols supported the Pagan dynasty. The Mongol court in Peking preferred a united neighbouring country under a single ruler, but in spite of its efforts Myanmar was divided into several principalities mainly under Shan tribal leaders. These self-styled princelings paid tribute to the Chinese Mongol court and were nominally its subjects. The Shan, at this time still nomadic tribes in the north, broke into an already destabilized Myanmar like a tidal wave. They penetrated the entire region as far as the Mon country and established themselves as rulers in many towns and cities. The intrigues, fratricidal wars, and murders that make up the history of their courts are innumerable.

A division of the country into Upper and Lower Myanmar is somewhat arbitrary, as, after the fall of Pagan, the two regions were composed of many competing principalities. However, there were the two principle kingdoms of Ava in Upper Myanmar and Pago (Pegu) in Lower Myanmar. Hostilities between these two prevailed, as well as with the neighbouring smaller states including the Shan fiefs of Chiang Mai and Ayutthaya in Thailand. Intrigues within and between courts were rife. Sometimes these claimed victims only within the circle of the powerful and mighty, and sometimes whole towns were looted and destroyed, and their population massacred or carried off into slavery.

But, in spite of politically unsettled conditions, the Sangha survived, because the new rulers, initially somewhat barbaric, soon accepted the religion of their subjects. Just as the Myanmar had adopted the religion and culture of the more refined Mon, so the Shan submitted to the sophisticated civilization of the peoples they subjugated. The Shan initially established their capital at Pinya in Upper Myanmar to the north of Pagan and transferred it to Ava in 1312. Ava was to remain the capital of Upper Myanmar until the eighteenth century.

The *Sasanavamsa* praises Thihathu, the youngest of three Shan brothers who wrested power from the Pagan dynasty in Upper Myanmar, as a Buddhist king who built monasteries and pagodas. He had a bhikkhu as his teacher and supported thousands of bhikkhus in his capital Pinya and later Ava. However, Pagan remained the cultural and religious capital of the region for the whole of the fourteenth century. Scholarly works were composed in its monasteries throughout this period whereas no such works are known to have been written in the new centers of power. The works of this period of scholarship were mostly concerned with Pali grammar.

Two generations later, a descendant of Thihathu secured himself a place in religious history as a great patron of scholarship. As in the courts of some previous kings, his court was also devoted to scholarly learning; and not only bhikkhus, but also the palace officials, produced treatises on religious subjects and the Pali language.

Although the political situation remained unsettled in Upper Myanmar throughout the fifteenth century, in the main, this affected only those in power and their usurpers. Consequently the Sangha appears to have flourished, while the traditional devotion to the support of the Sangha through gifts of the four requisites remained unchanged. The royal court, followed by the leading families, made great donations of monasteries, land, and revenue to the bhikkhus.

In approximately 1440, two Mahatheras from Sri Lanka settled in Ava. Here they joined a group of famous scholars, of whom Ariyavamsa was the most outstanding. The *Sasanavamsa* tells us of his great wisdom and humility in an anecdote.

The elder Ariyavamsa had studied the books of the Abhidhamma Pitaka, but felt he had not gained real understanding. Eventually he came to a bhikkhu in Sagaing who kept his mouth always filled with water in order not to have to engage in meaningless chatter. Ariyavamsa did not talk to "the Elder Water-bearer," as this bhikkhu was known in the Myanmar language, but simply performed the duties of a disciple to his teacher for two days. On the third day, the

Venerable Water-bearer spat out the water and asked Ariyavamsa why he was serving him. When Ariyavamsa told him that he wanted to learn from him, the Venerable Water-bearer taught him the *Abhidhammattha-vibhavani-tika,* a subcommentary on the *Abhidhammattha-sangaha.* After two days, Ariyavamsa grasped the meaning and his teacher asked him to write a commentary on this book in order to help others to gain understanding.

During the composition of his first work, Ariyavamsa submitted his writings to the assembled bhikkhus on every Uposatha day, reading out what he had composed and asking his brethren to correct any mistakes they found. On one occasion, a visiting bhikkhu twice made a sound of disapproval during the reading. Ariyavamsa carefully noted the passages where the sound of disapproval had occurred. On reflecting on them in the evening, he found one error of grammar where he had used the wrong gender and also a repetition, an error of style. He approached the bhikkhu who had made the sounds during the reading and out of gratitude for the correction gave him his own outer robe.

Ariyavamsa composed several works in Pali: works on the Abhidhamma, on grammatical subjects, and a study of the Jatakas. But his very important contribution to Buddhism in Myanmar was the fact that all his writing was in the Myanmar vernacular. He was probably the first bhikkhu to write treatises on religious subjects in the local idiom, thus making the religion accessible to a greater number of people. The work by Ariyavamsa still known today is a commentary on the anutika (sub-commentary) of the Abhidhamma.

Towards the end of the fifteenth century, a bhikkhu by the name of Silavamsa composed several epic poems in Pali. They were, of course, of a religious nature dealing with subjects such as the life of the Buddha, or Jataka stories. This genre was later very popular in the Myanmar language and there are many poems relating Jataka stories which were sung by bards throughout the country until recently. In the *Sasanavamsa,* however, Pannasami disapproves of bhikkhus writing or reciting poetry as he considers it to be in breach of the Vinaya rules.

He says that because of this, Silavamsa's name was excluded from the Theraparampara, a listing of eminent bhikkhus of Myanmar by ancient chroniclers.

Lower Myanmar

The Mon civilization in Lower Myanmar flourished after Pagan's importance waned, once again reliving the era of glory that it had experienced prior to Anawratha's conquest.

Wareru, the Shan ruler who had established himself in Martaban in 1287, was soon converted to Buddhism. He was a Shan peddler who had astutely wrested power from a son of the last king of Pagan, a son who had revolted against his father and founded an independent kingdom. Under Wareru's rule, scholarship in the Mon monasteries flourished and a code of law was compiled which still forms the foundation of the legal literature of Myanmar. The Mon bhikkhus based this code on ancient Hindu codes of law which had found their way into Mon tradition through Indian colonisers and merchants.

At the beginning of the fourteenth century two respected Mon theras named Buddhavamsa and Mahanaga revived the tradition of their countryman Chapada in making a pilgrimage to Sri Lanka. There, they accepted new ordination in the Mahavihara monastery, the guardian of Sinhalese orthodoxy. The bhikkhus of the Mahavihara asked those ordained in other countries to revert to the lay-state before being re-ordained as novices and full bhikkhus, as it was considered of the utmost importance that the ordination be handed down in an unbroken tradition from the time of the Buddha. This was especially significant in Myanmar where there were some reservations about the continuity of the tradition. By disrobing, a bhikkhu forgoes the seniority he has acquired through the years spent in robes and, in this case, he also states that he considers his former ordination invalid. One can imagine that such a step is not taken lightly but only after careful consideration.

The Great Reformation of the Sangha

King Dhammazedi (1472-92) takes a special place in the history of the religion in Myanmar. He unified the Sangha in the Mon country and purified the order of the bhikkhus. He recorded his great service to the country in the Kalyani inscription, which will be quoted below.

Dhammazedi was a bhikkhu of Mon origin who taught one of the queens at the royal palace in Ava. This lady, Shin Sawbu, was the daughter of the king of Pago. She had been queen to several unfortunate kings of Upper Mynamar and had beeen conveyed into the hands of the subsequent kings along with the throne. She had become disenchanted with the life of a queen and desired to return to her native land. Dhammazedi and a fellow Mon bhikkhu helped her to escape and brought her back to Pago. Eventually she became queen of Pago, but after reigning only a few years she wished to retire and do works of merit. She found that the only people worthy of the throne of Pago were her teachers, the two bhikkhus. She let fate decide which would be the future king by concealing miniature imitations of the regalia in one of the two bowls in which she offered them their daily alms food.

She handed the throne over to Dhammazedi who had received the fateful bowl and spent the rest of her life at Dagon (Yangon) building the terrace around the Shwedagon Pagoda and gilding the sacred mound. The Shwedagon became what it is today chiefly thanks to Shin Sawbu's munificence.

Dhammazedi assumed government in Pago after leaving the Order of the bhikkhus. He moved the capital closer to the Swemawdaw Pagoda and built several pagodas and shrines. His name is also connected with a collection of wise judgments and the translation of Wareru's Code of Law into the vernacular. In 1472, Dhammazedi sent a mission to Bodhgaya to repair the temple and make plans and drawings of it.

Dhammazedi had received his education in monasteries of Ava which adhered to the Sihala Sangha. The Sihala Sangha was the faction of the Sangha of Myanmar that accepted only the Mahavihara of Sri Lanka as the ultimate authority in religious questions. King Dhammazedi knew from direct experience the state of the Sangha in Lower Myanmar and was determined to improve it. Having lived as a bhikkhu for so many years, he was also singularly qualified to change the Sangha for the better.

He chose twenty-two senior bhikkhus to lead the reform movement and informed them:

Reverend Sirs, the *upasampada* ordination of the bhikkhus of the Mon country now appears to us to be invalid. Therefore, how can the religion, which is based on such invalid ordination, last to the end of 5000 years? Reverend Sirs, from the establishment of the religion in the island of Sri Lanka up to this present day, there has been existing in this island an exceedingly pure sect of bhikkhus... Receive at their hands the *upasampada* ordination... and if you make this form of the *upasampada* ordination the seed of the religion, as it were, plant it, and cause it to sprout forth by conferring such ordination on men of good family in this Mon country... Reverend Sirs, by your going to the island of Sri Lanka, much merit and great advantage will accrue to you.

At the beginning of 1476 the chosen bhikkhus with their twenty-two disciples embarked on the journey to Sri Lanka. They sailed in two ships, one taking about two months while the other needed six full months to arrive on the shore of the Buddhist island. They received the *upasampada* ordination at the Mahavihara from 17th to 20th July 1476. The return journey of the forty-four Mon bhikkhus was not so smooth, however. One group arrived home in August 1476, while the other group took three years to return to Pago and ten of the bhikkhus died en route. Following their return, Dhammazedi had a pure ordination hall*(sima)* consecrated and made the following proclamation:

May all those who possess faith and desire to receive the bhikkhu's ordination at the hands of the bhikkhus ordained in Sri Lanka come to the Kalyani sima and receive ordination. Let those who have not faith and do not desire to receive the bhikkhus ordination of the Sinhalese, remain as they are.

In order to confer the bhikkhu ordination outside the middle country (i.e. northern India), a chapter of five bhikkhus is needed, one of whom must be qualified to serve as preceptor *(upajjhaya)* and another as teacher *(acariya)*. The latter two must have spent at least ten years in robes as fully ordained bhikkhus. So if Dhammazedi wanted to have local bhikkhus ordained in the new ordination, it was necessary to find two senior bhikkhus. Since those returning from Sri Lanka had been ordained for a period of only three years, they could not act as preceptor or teacher. Local bhikkhus who had not received the ordination of the Mahavihara in Sri Lanka were unacceptable, as otherwise the ordination would again have been invalidated by one who was not of pure descent. Fortunately, the two theras who had undertaken a pilgrimage to Sri Lanka at the beginning of the century and had received the Sinhalese ordination at that time, were still alive. As a result, one was able to act as preceptor and the other as teacher of the newly ordained bhikkhus. The stage was now set for the reformation and unification of the Mon Order of bhikkhus and soon the re-ordination of almost the entire Order of bhikkhus began. The Kalyani inscription records the number of 15,666 ordinations in hundreds of ordination halls newly constructed for the purpose.

It is interesting to note how forcefully the king reformed the Order through royal decrees that would hardly be tolerated today. He declared that all bhikkhus who were, for example, practicing medicine or other arts and crafts or who even slightly infringed on the Vinaya rules would be expelled. The king as a layman, however, did not have the power to defrock a bhikkhu who had not broken one of the four Parajika rules. Dhammazedi circumvented this by threatening to punish with royal penalties the mother, father, relatives, and lay supporters of bhikkhus whose behavior was not in accordance with the rules of the Vinaya.

It goes without saying that a king who could allow himself to take such drastic measures in regard to the Sangha must have had the support of a broad section of the Order and also the people. After years spent in robes, he was keenly aware of the problems of monastic life and because of this even senior bhikkhus respected and accepted his council. We can assume that all his actions to reform the Order were firstly discussed with his bhikkhu teachers and then implemented with their blessings. There being no such thing as a Buddhist Church with a central authority, the Sangha has little possibility to regulate itself. Only the committed support of a worldly power can protect the Order of bhikkhus from those who take advantage of the respect that is given to the yellow robe.

Dhammazedi's support for the religion was so great that his fame spread well beyond the borders of Myanmar and bhikkhus from neighbouring countries such as Thailand came to his realm to receive ordination there. Though the reform movement did not spread to Upper Myanmar and cause the same mass ordinations there, it did not remain without influence in the kingdom of Ava and other principalities, and many bhikkhus came to the Mon bhikkhus to receive the Kalyani ordination.

THE MYANMAR BUILD AN EMPIRE

Shan versus Myanmar

The beginning of the sixteenth century was one of the most difficult periods for Buddhism in Upper Myanmar. While the religious fervor of Dhammazedi still lived on in the kingdom of Pago in Ava, Shan rulers were endeavoring to bring about the destruction of the Sangha. A Shan king named Thohanbwa (?1527-1543) was particularly well-known for his barbarity. He destroyed pagodas and monasteries and robbed their treasures. Although he was a king, he was uneducated and ignorant. Hence fearing the influence of the bhikkhus and suspicious of their moves, he brought about the massacre of thousands. Under these terror regimes of the Shan rulers the Myanmar did not feel safe. Many, including learned bhikkhus, fled to Toungoo, the stronghold of the Myanmar race in the south. Despite the anarchy prevailing, some respected treatises on Pali grammar were written in Upper Myanmar in these years.

Better times, however, lay ahead for Buddhism in the Golden Land. Two successive kings of Myanmar origin from Toungoo would unite the country and fulfill the duties of Buddhist kings. The wars fought by these two kings, King Tabinshwehti (1531-50) and King Bayinnaung (1551-81), were long in duration and exceedingly cruel. They succeeded in gaining control of the Mon kingdom in Lower Myanmar and the kingdom of Ava. They conquered all of what is today

Myanmar including the Shan states as far east as Chiang Mai, and made incursions into lower Thailand and Yunnan where some kings paid tribute to the Myanmar court.

Bayinnaung deferred to the Mon as far as culture and religion were concerned and dressed in Mon style. Under his royal patronage, the Mon Sangha produced scholarly works on grammar and the Abhidhamma and also helped with the collection and standardisation of a code of law based on the old Mon code compiled during Wareru's reign.

Bayinnaung not only unified the country politically, but also made Buddhist principles the standard for his entire dominion. He forbade the sacrificial slaughter of animals, a custom still practiced by the Shan chiefs, the worshippers of certain spirits, and the followers of some other religions. He built pagodas and monasteries in all the newly conquered lands and installed learned bhikkhus in order to convert the often uncivilized inhabitants to gentler ways. The main religious building of his reign is the Mahazedi Pagoda, a majestic monument to the Buddha in the capital, Pago. He also crowned the main pagodas in Myanmar with the jewels of his own crown, a custom practiced by many rulers of the country. He continued in the tradition of Dhammazedi, in supporting the Sihala Sangha and in sponsoring the ordination of many bhikkhus in the Kalyani Ordination Hall near Pago. It is said that he built as many monasteries as there were years in his life.

It remains a mystery how a king who had such deep devotion to the religion of the Buddha and who was so generous towards it could spend his life fighting campaign after campaign to expand his realm. He caused bloodshed and suffering in the conquered regions and at home people starved because farmers were drafted into the army. However this may be, Bayinnaung seems to have been able to reconcile fighting expansionist wars with being a pious Buddhist.

After King Bayinnaung, Pago rapidly lost its significance. Bayinnaung's son persecuted the Mon and consequently re-ignited racial tensions that would plague Myanmar for centuries. Later, Pago was to fall into the hands of a Portuguese adventurer who pillaged the pagodas and monasteries. Eventually the whole of Lower Myanmar, already depopulated by the incessant campaigns of Bayinnaung and his successors, was pillaged by all the surrounding kings and princelings. The country was devastated and people starved.

The *Sasanavamsa* records one major problem of the Vinaya during the sixteenth century. At the beginning of the century, the bhikkhus of Toungoo were divided over whether or not bhikkhus could partake of the juice of the toddy palm which was generally used to prepare fermented drink. The dispute was settled by a respected thera who decided that toddy juice was permissible only if it was freshly harvested.

Political Influence of the Sangha in Early Myanmar

What motivated the royal court probably remained largely a mystery to the ordinary citizens, except when they were pressed into service in the king's army. There was little sense of collective responsibility as it is cultivated in today's democracies. Everyone looked after himself and his immediate circle and governments were sometimes more of a scourge than a protection. Kings did not always provide a visible administration beyond appointing governors at whose mercy local people were. These governors often endeavored to establish independence as soon as they perceived inherent weaknesses in their masters. Many accumulated great wealth for themselves.

There was, however, one element in the policy of rulers which, with a few exceptions, remained fairly stable throughout Myanmar history. Most kings supported Buddhism and the Sangha provided a framework of continuity as no other entity could. Ray writes:

> They (the kings) were good Buddhists and never did they waver from their kingly duty of acting as the patron-guardian of the faith of the country. Moreover, whatever their numerical strength, the bhikkhus were real spokesmen of the people and the monasteries were the popular assemblies as it were; and each king that came to the throne sought to win the bhikkhus over to his side. The best insurance of a peaceful life in Myanmar was to become a bhikkhu, as they were not drafted into armies

or enslaved by conquerors and as long as the lay people had food to eat they were also fed. The bhikkhus not only provided a link between the people and those in power, they often played a role in the affairs of state. This is illustrated by an event which occurred in the middle of the seventeenth century and is related by the *Sasanavamsa*.

The king, Ukkamsika, popularly known as King Thalun, was a devoted Buddhist and thanks to him, learning flourished in Myanmar. The king's son, however, tried to dethrone his father, and Thalun, taken by surprise, had to flee accompanied only by two companions. Coming upon a river, the only vessel in sight was the boat of a samanera. The samanera agreed to take them onboard as passengers, and they ended up in the samanera's monastery where they revealed their true identities and asked for protection from their persecutors. They were referred to another monastery where lived a bhikkhu wise in worldly affairs. Following his advice, the bhikkhus formed a living wall around the monastery and, as no Buddhist will attack a man in robes, the rebels who had come to kill the king had to withdraw. Another example of the beneficial influence of the Sangha is their appeal for clemency to King Bayinnaung. Bhikkhus often tried to stay executions in accordance with the principles of *metta* (loving kindness) and *karuna* (compassion) and sometimes their efforts achieved success.

During one of Bayinnaung's Thai campaigns, the peasantry around Pago revolted and razed the royal city to the ground. Bayinnaung, after hurrying back from Ayutthaya, captured several thousand rebels and was ready to burn them alive. It was the custom then to burn deserters from the army alive and obviously rebellion was considered to be a crime of similar gravity. The bhikkhus of all races intervened on behalf of the poor wretches and were able to save all from the pyre, except for seventy ring leaders, the most serious offenders.

There are several instances in Myanmar history when bhikkhus also mediated between contending kings or princes and helped to avoid bloodshed. This was often the case when cities were besieged and both parties realised that they could not win. The king who was besieged would normally take the initiative and send his bhikkhus to the king in attack. Often the bhikkhus were authorized to negotiate on behalf of the monarch. An armistice agreed by or in the presence of bhikkhus was more likely to be honored than a promise given without their blessings. Therefore, if the two parties were sincere in their offers to negotiate, they usually requested bhikkhus to be mediators and judges.

The Spread of Abhidhamma

The seventeenth century was a period of dynamic growth in the history of Buddhism in Myanmar. Many outstanding developments took place, and principal among these were the numerous translations of texts into the Myanmar language and the great increase in the study of the Abhidhamma. It is quite possible that the two developments were inter-connected.

In the first half of the century, Manirathana Thera translated the following texts into the Myanmar language: *Atthasalini, Sammohavinodani, Kankhavitarani, Abhidhammatthavibhavini, Sankhepavannana.* Of these five, only the *Kankhavitarani,* Buddhaghosa's commentary on the Patimokkha, is not concerned with Abhidhamma. In the second half of the century Aggadhammalankara translated Kaccayana's Pali grammar, the *Abhidhammatthasangaha, Matika, Dhatukatha, Yamaka,* and the *Patthana* into the Myanmar tongue. Later, the *Nettippakarana* was also translated.

It cannot be a coincidence that nine out of twelve translated works were texts of the Abhidhamma or its commentaries. The reason for these translations must have been a developing interest in the psychology of Buddhism among the Buddhist followers who could not themselves read Pali. Whether these were only bhikkhus or whether lay people were also interested in exploring the scriptures for themselves is difficult to determine now. However, what is known is that almost every boy and many of the girls attended monastic schools, whose curriculum was probably established by this period, if not earlier. Included in the curriculum were studies of the Mangala Sutta, Metta Sutta, Ratana Sutta, and the other parittas, as well as basic literacy which included some Pali. In addition a number of the Abhidhamma texts had to be committed to memory.

The intention behind these translations and commentaries in the Myanmar language was obviously to make the words of the Buddha accessible to a wider audience who would, then, not be solely dependent on the authority of the Pali scholars.

In the later half of the century, the bhikkhu Devacakkhobhasa designed a system for the study and teaching of the *Patthana,* the last book of the Abhidhamma, which in Myanmar is believed to be the highest teaching of the Buddha. The king at the time of Devacakkhobhasa was so impressed by the bhikkhu's proficiency in these higher teachings and by his system of instruction, that he ordered the *Patthana* to be studied in all the monasteries of Myanmar. It is not unreasonable to assume that the king himself studied these teachings. Otherwise he would hardly have been in a position to appreciate them and make them compulsory reading for the Myanmar bhikkhus.

This emphasis on Abhidhamma in general and the *Patthana* in particular has survived in Myanmar to the present day. The movement, therefore, that began in the seventeenth century is still of great significance for Buddhism there. The *Patthana,* for instance, is ubiquitous in Myanmar.

The twenty-four conditions of the *Patthana* can be found printed on the fans of the bhikkhus, on calendars, and on posters. In some monasteries, the bhikkhus are woken every morning by twenty-four strokes on a hollow tree trunk, while the bhikkhu striking the tree trunk has to recite the twenty-four conditions as he does so. Even little children learn to recite the twenty-four conditions along with the suttas of protection. As the *Patthana* is the highest and most difficult teaching of the Buddha, it is believed that it will be the first to be lost. In order to slow the decline of the Sasana, many people of Myanmar, bhikkhus and lay people alike, memorize the *Patthana* and recite it daily.

In Pagan, the Jataka stories and the history of the Buddha's life were the main subjects of religious study. In later centuries, Pali grammar and the study of the Vinaya were foremost on the agenda. Dhammazedi's reform movement drew the attention back to the foundations of all monastic life, the code of conduct for the bhikkhus as laid down by the Buddha himself.

Though stricter observation of the Vinaya would have to be re-emphasised in the future, its foundation was firm enough to insure that progressive reform movements would be instigated within the Sangha and not be dependent on external impetus. How far a bhikkhu was allowed to stray from the ideal had been defined in strictures that had become integral to the Sangha. Based on this foundation of *sila* (right conduct, morality), the Sangha was now free to give increased attention to higher teachings.

The age of the Abhidhamma had dawned. The Abhidhamma remained no longer the domain of a chosen few, but began to be studied by many. The wealth of translations from the Abhidhamma would suggest that in the seventeenth century it had become so popular that it may have been taught even to lay people. The Myanmar language had developed and had been enriched with Pali terms so that it could convey the difficult concepts of Abhidhamma. civilization had matured to an extent never seen before. Myanmar was ready to study the analysis of mind and matter as taught by the Buddha. The stage was being set for the widespread practice of insight meditation *(vipassana bhavana)* in later times.

THE EIGHTEENTH AND NINETEENTH CENTURIES

In the succession of rulers of the eighteenth century some were strong and despotic, while others were ineffective and withdrawn. Some tried to expand their power and fought wars, while others appeared satisfied with existing conditions. There were several wars with Thailand and the population of Myanmar had to bear the deprivations that war invariably brings not only to the conquered, but also to the country where the conquering armies are levied.

After a war between the Mon and the Myanmar in which the Mon initially attacked and then conquered Ava itself, the Myanmar king Alaungpaya (1752-60), who believed himself a Bodhisatta, crushed Mon resistance once and for all. After Pago had fallen into his hands in 1756, Lower Myanmar was devastated and many of the Mon survivors fled to Thailand or were deported as slaves.

Like Bayinnaung, Alaungpaya established a Myanmar empire, at the same time decimating the population of the country by drafting the peasantry into the army for campaigns against Ayutthaya (Thailand) and other countries. The *Sasanavamsa* does not comment on the atrocity of war. War is perceived as it is, cruel and pitiless — but it is the affair of rulers, not of bhikkhus. The manner in which rulers conduct their affairs is entirely their responsibility. Pannasami probably took very seriously the Buddha's injunction that a member of the Sangha should not talk about rulers and royal affairs.

The *Sasanavamsa* pays much attention to a controversy which raged in monastic circles throughout the eighteenth century. At the beginning of the century, some bhikkhus began to wear their robes outside the monasteries as they were worn within them, that is, covering only one shoulder. Even when going on their daily alms round, they failed to drape the robe in the traditional way. When challenged as to the orthodoxy of this practice, they produced various interpretations and opinions, but could not validate their practice through the authority of the scriptures. Different kings endorsed one or other of the two opinions and bhikkhus of the orthodox school even died for their conviction when a king had outlawed the covering of both shoulders.

The most interesting aspect of this historical period of the religion is not so much the actual controversy as the power the king had in religious affairs. The kings of Myanmar were not normally expert in the Vinaya and yet they took the final decision in matters of monastic discipline after due consultation with the leaders of the Sangha. In the more than one hundred years that this controversy prevailed, different kings supported the orthodoxy of either view. This shows that this system is not entirely satisfactory. However, the right view which was in accordance with the Vinaya did eventually triumph due to the persistence of the majority of the Sangha. Only the worldly power was in a position to regulate the Sangha into which undesirable elements entered repeatedly. To keep the Order pure, it had to be always under careful scrutiny and bogus ascetics had to be removed. The kings of Myanmar in cooperation with the Sangharajas and the other senior bhikkhus had established a system of supervision of the bhikkhus by royal officials. In every township, the king's representatives were responsible for ensuring that the bhikkhus adhered scrupulously to the rules of the Vinaya. Bhikkhus who transgressed were taken before religious courts and punished according to the code of discipline.

The controversy concerning the correct manner of wearing the robes came up for arbitration for the last time under Bodawpaya (1782-1819), the fifth son of Alaungpaya. He decided in favor of orthodoxy and thenceforth all bhikkhus had to cover both shoulders on the daily alms round. This ruling created one unified sect throughout Myanmar under the leadership of a council of senior bhikkhus appointed by the king. These were called the Thudhamma Sayadaws and the Thudhamma sect has survived in Myanmar down to the present day.

Bodawpaya appointed a chapter of eight eminent bhikkhus as Sangharajas, leaders of the Sangha, and charged them with the duty to safeguard the purity of the Order of bhikkhus. As a direct result of the discipline and stability created by the work of these senior bhikkhus, the Sangha prospered, and consequently scholarship flourished under Bodawpaya's reign.

The name of the Mahasangharaja Nanabhivamsa is especially noteworthy in this respect. Nanabhivamsa was an eminently learned bhikkhu who had proven his wisdom even as a young man. Only five years after his ordination as a bhikkhu, he had completed a commentary *(tika)* on the *Nettippakarana.* Eight years after full ordination, at the age of twenty-eight, he became Sangharaja, and then Mahasangharaja, the title conferred by the king on the highest bhikkhu in his realm. Soon after this, he wrote his well respected "new sub-commentary" on the Digha Nikaya, the *Sadhujjanavilasini.* At the request of the king, he wrote a commentary on Buddhaghosa's *Jatakatthakatha* and several other treatises.

The king was so devoted to the head of the Sangha that he dedicated a "very magnificent five storied monastery" to him and later many other monasteries as well. According to the

Sasanavamsa, Nanabhivamsa was not only a scholar, but also practiced the ascetic practices *(dhutanga)* sitting always alone. He divided his time between the various monasteries under his tutelage and was an indefatigable teacher of the scriptures.

Scholarship flourished in the reign of King Bodawpaya and Myanmar was able, for the first time, to return thanks to Sri Lanka for nurturing the religion in the Golden Land. The bhikkhu ordination *(upasampada)* preserved in Myanmar was re-introduced to Sri Lanka where the Sasana had been interferred with by an unwise king.

The Amarapura Nikaya in Sri Lanka

In the later half of the eighteenth century, the *upasampada* ordination in Sri Lanka was barred to all except the members of the landed aristocracy. This was a result of royal decree probably issued with the support of at least a section of the Sangha. However, this was a flagrant defilement of the letter and the spirit of the Buddha's instructions. The conferring of the *upasampada* ordination is dependent only upon such conditions as the candidate being a man, free from government service, free of debt, free of contagious diseases, and upon his having his parents' consent, etc. Members of the lower castes had now only the possibility of becoming novices (samanera), a condition that created dissatisfaction. A sizeable section of ordained bhikkhus also disapproved of the royal order, but were in no position to defy it within the country. The only recourse for those of the lower castes desiring the higher ordination was therefore to travel to other Buddhist countries to ordain. At first, missions were sent to Thailand where Dhammazedi's reforms lived on through the ordination conferred to Thai bhikkhus in Pago and through the scores of Mon bhikkhus who had found refuge in Thailand from the Myanmar armies.

At the beginning of the nineteenth century, however, Sinhalese bhikkhus began traveling to Myanmar to find the pure ordination there. The fame of the then Mahasangharaja of Myanmar, Nanabhivamsa, influenced their choice. Scholarship had developed in all fields: Pali grammar, the Vinaya, the Suttanta, and the Abhidhamma. Myanmar had, after a long period of development, become the custodian of Buddhism.

The first delegation from Sri Lanka arrived in 1800 and was welcomed with a magnificent reception by King Bodawpaya himself. Nanabhivamsa, the wise Sangharaja, ordained the samaneras as bhikkhus and instructed them for some time in the scriptures. On returning to Sri Lanka, they were accompanied by five Myanmar bhikkhus and a letter from Nanabhivamsa to the Sinhalese Sangharaja. Five bhikkhus form a full chapter and apparently the Myanmar bhikkhus were permitted to ordain bhikkhus without class distinction. Even today, Sri Lanka possesses three schools, the Amarapura Nikaya, the Siyama Nikaya (Thai school), and the Ramanna Nikaya.

The Amarapura Nikaya was so called because King Bodawpaya had established his capital in Amarapura (between Mandalay and Ava) and the bhikkhus had received their ordination there. The Ramanna Nikaya was presumably founded by bhikkhus who had received ordination from Mon bhikkhus in the tradition of the Dhammazedi reforms and who had fled to southern Thailand from the wrath of the Myanmar kings. Both these schools were allowed to ordain bhikkhus without discriminating against the lower classes. Only the Siyama Sangha (the Thai ordination) continued to follow the royal command, and ordained only novices of the higher castes as bhikkhus. Missions from Sri Lanka continued to travel to Amarapura to consult with its senior theras and they were all given royal patronage and sent back with gifts of the Pali scriptures and commentarial texts.

Bodawpaya's Relationship with the Sangha

Although King Bodawpaya would appear to have been a pious and devout king, his relationship with the Sangha was somewhat problematic. He supported it at times and even used it to extend his own glory, but at times he seemed almost jealous of the respect the bhikkhus received from the people. He realised that the bhikkhus were not respected out of fear, but were held in genuine esteem and affection by his subjects. His jealousy became apparent on different occasions.

At one time, he declared that from then on the bhikkhus were no longer to be addressed by the traditional title "Hpoungyi" meaning "The One of Great Merit." This form of address was to be reserved for the king. Then again he tried to confiscate land and other goods given to the Sangha and to pagodas by previous generations. When the Sangharajas could not answer his questions to his satisfaction, he invited the Muslim clergy for a meal to test their faith. He had heard that they were so strict in the observance of their discipline that they would rather die than eat pork. Unfortunately for them, they did not display great heroism as they all ate the pork offered to them by the king. Bodawpaya is also reputed to have been beset by a form of megalomania. He wanted to force the Sangha to confirm officially that he was the Bodhisatta of the next Buddha to come in this world cycle, the Buddha Metteyya. On this issue, however, the Sangha was not to be bent even in the face of royal wrath. The bhikkhus refused, and the king was finally forced to accept defeat. Another expression of his inflated self-esteem was the Mingun Pagoda near Sagaing. It was to be by far the biggest temple ever built. Scores of slaves and laborers worked on its construction until funds were depleted. However, it was never completed and remains today as a huge shapeless square of millions of bricks.

To his credit, King Bodawpaya imposed the morality of the Five Precepts in his whole realm and had offenders executed immediately. Capital punishment was prescribed for selling and drinking alcohol, killing larger animals such as buffaloes, spreading heretical views, and the smoking of opium. Bodawpaya ruled the country with an iron fist and brought offending lay people as well as bhikkhus to heel. His successors were benevolent, but possibly they could be so only because of the fear his rule had instilled in the populace.

The Fate of Buddhism in Upper and Lower Myanmar

Bodawpaya's successor, Bagyidaw (1819-1837), was the first of the Myanmar kings to lose territory to the white invaders coming from the West. The Myanmar court was so out of touch with the modern world that it still believed Myanmar to be the center of the world and her army virtually invincible. Hence the king was not unduly disturbed when the British raj, governing the Indian sub-continent, declared war on the Kingdom of Ava in 1824 (Bagyidaw had moved the capital back to Ava). It came to a battle near the coast in which the Myanmar general Mahabandhula achieved little or nothing against modern British arms. The Indian colonial government occupied all of the Myanmar coast as far south as Tenasserim in 1826 and forced the treaty of Yandabo on King Bagyidaw. In the treaty, he was forced to accept the new borders established by the Indian government and pay compensation to the invaders for the annexation of the coast of Lower Myanmar.

However, Bagyidaw made a very important contribution to the development of the Sangha and to the literature of Myanmar in general. His predecessor, Bodawpaya, had united the Sangha by resolving the dispute relating to the draping of the robe over one or two shoulders. Bagyidaw saw the necessity of creating stability for the Sangha. He felt that this could be achieved to some extent by bestowing on it a sense of its own history. He commissioned a work on the history of the religion starting from the time of the Buddha, which was to show an unbroken succession of the pure tradition from teacher to pupil. Its purpose was to praise the diligent theras and expose the shameless ones.

This work, the *Thathana-lin-ga-ya-kyan,* was composed at the king's request by the ex-bhikkhu Mahadhamma-thin-gyan, a leading member of the committee appointed by King Bagyidaw to compile the famous *Hman-nan-ya-za-win, The Glass-palace Chronicle,* a secular history of Myanmar. The *Thathana-wun-tha (Sasanavamsa)-lin-ga-ya-kyan* was completed in 1831; and in 1897, it was printed in the form of a modern book for the first time in Yangon. Pannasami based his *Sasanavamsa* on this work. About forty percent of the *Sasanavamsa* is straight translation from the original work, about forty percent summaries and paraphrasing of the latter, and only some twenty percent Pannasami's own work. Pannasami states in his introduction to the *Sasanavamsa* that his treatise is based on the works of the ancients *(porana).* The concept of mental property or copyright had not been born and there was no moral need to refer the reader to sources except to give authority to a statement. The only references that would lend authority to a treatise would be the scriptures, their commentaries, and sub-commentaries, but not a work as recent as the *Thathana-wuntha-lin-ga-ya-kyan.*

The preface to the original work in Myanmar explains the reason for its compilation. The king's representative had many times pleaded with the author to write a history of the succession of [righteous] religious teachers so that the people would not become heretical. Apparently the king felt that the lack of a work recording the history of the pure religion in its entirety left scope for wrong views to arise. But with an authoritative record of the lineage of teachers, bhikkhus could not call on views of shameless bhikkhus of the past anymore in order to support their heresies. This is exactly what had happened again and again through the centuries and especially in the robe-draping dispute. The *ekamsikas,* the one-shoulder-drapers, had repeatedly dug out obscure teachers in order to support their point of view. This was to be made impossible once and for all.

Whether this has been successful is difficult to ascertain without a detailed study of the developments in the Sangha since the publication of this work. However, the fact that the original Myanmar chronicle was revised and translated into Pali for the Fifth Buddhist Council indicates that it was by this time considered a useful tool to put the king's authority behind a well-defined orthodox lineage, thus making it easy to refute heresy by referring to the historical teachers.

Tharrawaddy-Min

King Bagyidaw never overcame his shock over the loss of part of his realm. He was declared insane and was removed from the throne by Tharawaddy-Min (1837-1846), King Mindon's father.

In the reign of Tharrawaddy-Min, another mission from Sri Lanka visited Myanmar and was received by the Sangharaja Neyyadhammabhivamsa. Neyyadhamma instructed the two bhikkhus and the accompanying novice in the teachings and conferred the bhikkhu ordination on the novice. He is known for his critical emendation of the text of the *Saddhammapajjotika* and its translation into Myanmar. He was also the teacher of the later Sangharaja Pannasami, the compiler of the *Sasanavamsa* and one of the most influential theras at the time of King Mindon. Neyyadhamma showed the need for a recension of at least some of the Pali texts by editing the *Saddhammapajjotika.* His disciple, Pannasami, was to preside over the recension of the entire Tipitaka as Sangharaja under King Mindon.

Pagan-Min

Tharrawaddy-Min was himself deposed because of insanity by his son Pagan-Min (1846-52), the brother of Mindon-Min. Pagan-Min appointed Pannajotabhidhaja as his Sangharaja. In his tenure, scholarship received encouragement as the Sangharaja himself wrote a commentary and its sub-commentary in Myanmar on the Anguttara Nikaya. Other works of the time, all in the vernacular, are a translation of the *Saddhammavilasini* and commentaries on the Samyutta Nikaya and the Digha Nikaya. This is also the time when the author of the *Sasanavamsa* appears. He started his scholarly career with the translation into Myanmar of a commentary on the *Saddatthabhedacinta.* His next work was a comparison of the existing versions of the *Abhidhanappadipika* and the translation of his emended text.

In accord with the pre-eminence Myanmar had achieved in the Theravada Buddhist world, the kings of the country became less fierce and wars were fewer. The successors of Bodawpaya seem to have shown a genuine interest in religion as well as in improving the administration of the country. Upper Myanmar moved into a period of peace, which meant improved conditions for the bhikkhus.

The first half of the nineteenth century saw the translation of many Pali texts into the Myanmar language. Almost the whole of the Suttanta was now available in the vernacular and many commentaries and sub-commentaries on Suttanta, Abhidhamma, and the Vinaya were composed in it. This not only made it easier for bhikkhus with limited linguistic skills to study the texts, but also made them readily accessible to the laity. That people in a peaceful country have more time for the study of religion is obvious and soon Myanmar would see the first Buddhist texts printed on modern printing presses. This made it possible for a great number of people to acquire texts relatively cheaply without having to pay a scribe to copy them laboriously onto palm leaves.

Politically Pagan-Min was no luckier than Bagyidaw, as he lost the provinces of Pathein (Bassein) and Yangon (Rangoon) to the British, who were ever ready to create some pretext for war. So, in 1852, the Kingdom of Ava lost access to the sea and became increasingly dependent on the colonial power. Like his father, Pagan-Min was overthrown in a palace revolt. Although not a leader of the uprising, his brother Mindon was placed on the throne. He did not execute the deposed king as was usually the case after a revolt, but allowed him to end his days in dignity.

The Colonial Administration and the Sangha

The occupation by the British forces was of utmost significance for the Sangha as the British administration did not grant the traditional protection afforded it by a Buddhist ruler. In accordance with the colonial policy established in India, that the colonial government should be strictly secular, the new lords refused to take on the role of a Buddhist monarch and accept responsibility for the enforcing of the bhikkhus' discipline. Without this, Buddhism in Lower Myanmar soon suffered and offending bhikkhus went unpunished. The colonial administration would recognise its mistake only much later, when it was too late, and when they were not able to establish control in the Sangha any longer.

King Mindon

Even today King Mindon's reign (1852-1877) is surrounded by the mystique of a golden era in the minds of the Myanmar people. No war occurred during the twenty-five years of his tenure and the king himself is said to have been of gentle disposition and adverse to violence. He even declared a dislike for capital punishment which was customarily inflicted by sovereigns for the slightest disobedience or even disagreement. He was not only held in esteem by his subjects, but even praised by a British envoy. The colonisers' comments on the Myanmar and their kings were usually dictated by a parochial narrow-mindedness and a simplistic view that was only widened by contact with the conquered. Therefore General Fytche's words describing King Mindon are all the more impressive: "Doubtless one of the most enlightened monarchs that has ever sat on the Burmese throne. He is polished in his manner, has considerable knowledge of the affairs of state and the history and the statistics of his own and other countries. In personal character he is amiable and kind and, according to his light, religious."

King Mindon transferred the capital from Ava to Mandalay, the last royal capital before the British annexation of the whole of Myanmar in 1886. In the early years of his reign, Mindon strove to improve monastic discipline. Although a system of official investigation of complaints relating to bhikkhus' misdemeanours existed, each king had to take his own initiative in re-establishing order in the Sangha.

Mindon found that the attitude of many members of the Sangha to their code of conduct was exceedingly lax. He therefore wanted all bhikkhus of his dominions to take a vow of obedience to the Vinaya rules in front of a Buddha image. He consulted the Sangharaja who convened an assembly of mahatheras, the Thudhamma Council. As opinions regarding the vow differed, the primate's disciple, Pannasami, had to deliver a religious address in support of the king's views. He reasoned that vows were also taken by the bhikkhus at the time of ordination and that if the king sincerely desired to improve the discipline in the Order, he should be supported. All agreed, and the vow was prescribed.

The greatest challenge King Mindon had to face as a Buddhist monarch was undoubtedly his duty to look after the spiritual welfare of his subjects not only in his own dominions, but also in the parts of Myanmar occupied by the British. Moreover, he and many of the leading sayadaws of his court were increasingly aware that the British were only waiting for an occasion to annex the whole of Myanmar. Mindon's army clearly would not be able to stand up to the might of the Indian colonial government. Therefore, it was not only important to support religious activities in the occupied territories but it was also essential to prepare the religion for the time when it would have to survive without the support of a Buddhist monarch.

The British had made it clear at the outset that they would not take over the traditional role of the Myanmar kings, that of protector of the Sasana. The new masters' religion, Christianity, rapidly gained influence through the missionary schools. The schools were popular because their education provided much assistance in securing a job and favor with the colonisers. Christian religious education was a compulsory part of their curriculum.

After the conquest of Lower Myanmar, many bhikkhus had fled north in order to remain within the jurisdiction of the Myanmar kings. Many monasteries in British Myanmar were left without an incumbent and whole villages were therefore bereft of the opportunity to receive religious and general education. King Mindon, aware of this situation, tried to convince bhikkhus to return to Lower Myanmar in order to serve their people. The king's efforts proved successful and many bhikkhus returned to their places of origin. But soon it became clear that without the king's ecclesiastic officials to control the discipline of the Sangha, many bhikkhus developed a careless attitude towards their code of discipline.

The Okpo Sayadaw, from Okpo between Yangon and Pago, had stopped many bhikkhus on their way to Upper Myanmar when the movements of bhikkhus out of the conquered territories was at its peak around 1855. He assembled the bhikkhus around himself teaching that the Sangha needed no protection from the secular power if it observed the rules of the Vinaya strictly. His monastery was the birth place of a movement of strict monastic discipline. He also emphasised that mental volition was what really mattered in the religion of the Buddha and that acts of worship done with an impure intention were worthless. He obviously felt that much of the Buddhist practice had become a ritual and that the essence had been lost. In addition to this, however, his movement also challenged the authority of the king's Council of Sayadaws, the leaders of the unified Thudhamma sect, when he declared their ordination was invalid due to a technicality. As a result, he took the higher ordination anew together with his followers.

The Okpo Sayadaw was not the only critic of the Thudhamma sayadaws. In Upper Myanmar, the Ngettwin Sayadaw criticized many religious practices and maintained that a radical reassesment of religious teachings was necessary. The Ngettwin Sayadaw was also a source of inspiration for the Okpo Sayadaw and other reformers. He had been the teacher of Mindon's chief queen and had also advised the king on many occasions. Interestingly, he was a driving force in a movement in Upper Myanmar that wanted to return to the fundamentals of the religion, but more radically than the Okpo Sayadaw. The Ngettwin Sayadaw, together with many other bhikkhus, left the royal city and went to live in the forest near Sagaing. He started to preach that meditation was essential for all bhikkhus and he required an aspirant to novicehood to prove that he had practiced meditation before he would ordain him. All the bhikkhus around him had to spend a period of the day in meditation and he emphasised that meditation was of much greater importance than learning. He advised lay people to stop making offerings of flowers, fruits, and candles to Buddha images, but to meditate regularly on the Uposatha days. Of course, his instructions that offerings to Buddha images were fruitless and merely dirtied the places of worship, caused considerable unhappiness with the traditional Thudhamma Council and presumably with many ordinary people. However, the Ngettwin Sayadaw never strove to form a different sect by holding a separate ordination as did the Okpo Sayadaw. His reforms were within the community and within a Buddhist society that was presided over by a king. The Okpo Sayadaw had no place for royalty in his view of the world and did not hesitate to confront the system that was still alive, though obviously doomed.

Two other important sayadaws of King Mindon's reign deserve mention: the Shwegyin Sayadaw and the Thingazar

Sayadaw. The Shwegyin Sayadawalso tried to reform the Sangha and his movement is still very much alive and highly respected in Myanmar today. He had studied under the Okpo Sayadaw, but when he returned to his native Shwegyin near Shwebo in Upper Myanmar, he avoided controversy in never rebelling against the Thudhamma Council. He introduced two new rules for his bhikkhus, that they must not chew betel and consume tobacco after noon. He also maintained that the Sangha must regulate itself without help from the authority, but he never doubted the validity of the traditional ordination ceremony.

The Thingazar Sayadaw was one of the most popular of the great sayadaws of his time. He was also part of the movement to return to the basics of the teachings and greatly emphasised the importance of practice as opposed to mere scholarship. Though he was greatly honored by the king and made a member of the Thudhamma Council, he preferred spending long periods in solitude in the forest. In the numerous monasteries built for him by the royal family and the nobility of the country, he insisted on the practice of the purest of conduct in accordance with the Vinaya. However, he did not involve himself in disputes with the extreme reformers or the Thudhamma council. He became very popular through the humorous tales he told in sermons preached in his frequent travels up and down the country.

King Mindon had no easy task. One section of the Sangha was pressing for far reaching reforms, yet it was the king's duty to maintain a certain continuity of the traditional ways for the benefit of the people in general. What complicated the situation was the fact that the Sangha of Lower Myanmar felt more and more independent of the Buddhist monarch and his Thudhamma council of senior mahatheras. This is illustrated graphically by the Okpo Sayadaw's declaration that the Sangha needed no regulation by the worldly power. This view gained popularity also in Upper Myanmar. Luckily, King Mindon's devotion to Buddhism was genuine and he was not deterred by the difficulties confronting him. He was determined not to allow the Sangha to split into factions that were openly opposing each other. This he achieved to some extent through careful diplomacy and through the calling of a great Synod, a Sangayana, in the royal city of Mandalay.

The Sangayana, or Buddhist Council, is the most important function of the Buddhist religion. The first Sangayana was held during the first Rains Retreat after the Parinibbana of the Buddha; the texts to be regarded as authentic were determined at this time. There had been three more Sangayanas since, according to the Theravada tradition. The council convened by the great Emperor Asoka, whose missionaries brought Buddhism to Myanmar, probably provided the most inspiration for Mindon. The Fourth Council, the one prior to Mindon's council, was held in Sri Lanka in the first century BC, at the Aluvihara near Matale, for the purpose of writing down the Tipitaka, which up to that time had been passed on orally.

King Mindon himself presided over the Fifth Buddhist Council, during which all the canonical texts were recited and the correct form was established from among any variant readings. The task took more than three years to accomplish, from 1868 to 1871. When the bhikkhus had completed their great project, the king had all of the Buddhist scriptures, the Tipitaka, engraved on 729 marble slabs. The slabs were then housed each in a separate small pagoda about three meters high with a roof to protect the inscriptions from the elements. The small shrines were built around a central pagoda, the Kutho-daw Pagoda, the Pagoda of the Noble Merit. To commemorate the great council, King Mindon crowned the Shwedagon Pagoda in Yangon with a new Hti or spire.

The Fifth Buddhist Council and the crowning of the Shwedagon Pagoda reminded all the people of Myanmar of the importance of their religion, as well as of the fact that the king and the Thudhamma Council of senior monks were still the guardians of the Sasana. The authority of the Thudhamma Council was greatly enhanced also in Lower Myanmar through the synod. Although the British had not allowed King Mindon to attend the raising of the new spire onto the Shwedagon, the crowning was a symbol of the religious unity of Myanmar which persisted in spite of the British occupation. The religion was also later to become the rallying point for the Myanmar nationalists who fought for independence from the colonisers.

King Mindon's reign produced a number of scholarly works as well as translations from the Pali. Neyyadhamma, the royal preceptor, himself wrote a sub-commentary on the Majjhima Nikaya, which had been translated by one of his disciples under his guidance. A commentary in Myanmar on the Pali Jatakas was composed by Medhavivamsa and the compiler of the *Sasanavamsa,* Pannasami, put his name to a great number of works. One of the queens of King Mindon requested Pannasami to write the *Silakatha* and the *Upayakatha.* His teacher asked him to compose the *Voharatthabheda, Vivadavinicchaya, Nagarajuppattikatha.* He also wrote a commentary on Aggavamsa's *Saddaniti.* Whether all these works were composed by Pannasami or whether they were composed under his supervision and control is difficult to assess. It is interesting to note that a majority of his works were composed in Pali, which was no doubt an attempt to encourage bhikkhus not to forgo Pali scholarship now that Myanmar translations were readily available. The calling of a great Buddhist council to purify the scriptures was part of this movement towards the revival of the study of the original texts.

During King Mindon's reign bhikkhus from Sri Lanka came to Mandalay on several occasions to solve difficult questions of Vinaya and to receive the bhikkhu ordination in Myanmar. After Mindon's death in 1877, his son Thibaw ascended the throne. He was weak and of feeble intellect, and his reign was short. In 1886, he lost his kingdom to the British empire and was exiled to India.

With the complete annexation of Myanmar by the British, a historical era came to an end. Theravada Buddhism developed in Myanmar over more than two millennia. The visits of the Buddha were the first brief illuminations in a country that was shrouded in darkness. The worship of the Buddha that is thought to have resulted from these visits and from the arrival of the hair relics, may have been merely part of a nature religion. The pure religion could not endure for long in a country which was yet on the brink of civilization. Later, however, the teachings of the Buddha were brought repeatedly to those lands by various people.

The visits of the Arahats sent out after Emperor Asoka's council are historically more acceptable than the visits of the Buddha. Their teachings were understood and perpetuated possibly in Indian settlements along the coast and later in communities of people from central Asia such as the Pyu. Through their contact with India, these cultural centers of the Pyu and Mon could remain in contact with Buddhism. At first the important centers of Theravada Buddhism were in northern India and later in South India and then Sri Lanka. Through repeated contact with orthodox bhikkhus abroad, the understanding of Buddhism grew ever stronger in the minds of the people of Myanmar. The religion was distorted dozens of times through ignorance and carelessness, but someone always appeared to correct the teachings with the help of the mainstays of the Sasana abroad. Gradually the role was reversed: instead of traveling abroad for advice, the bhikkhus of Myanmar became the guardians of Theravada Buddhist teaching and their authority was respected by all. Eventually, when Theravada Buddhism had long been lost to India and its future was uncertain in Sri Lanka, it found a secure home in Southeast Asia, especially in Myanmar.

2

THE EDICTS OF KING ASOKA

INTRODUCTION

With the rediscovery and translation of Indian literature by European scholars in the 19th century, it was not just the religion and philosophy of Buddhism that came to light, but also its many legendary histories and biographies. Amongst this class of literature, one name that came to be noticed was that of Asoka, a good king who was supposed to have ruled India in the distant past. Stories about this king, similar in outline but differing greatly in details, were found in the Divyavadana, the Asokavadana, the Mahavamsa and several other works. They told of an exceptionally cruel and ruthless prince who had many of his brothers killed in order to seize the throne, who was dramatically converted to Buddhism and who ruled wisely and justly for the rest of his life. None of these stories were taken seriously — after all many pre-modern cultures had legends about "too good to be true" kings who had ruled righteously in the past and who, people hoped, would rule again soon. Most of these legends had their origins more in popular longing to be rid of the despotic and uncaring kings than in any historical fact. And the numerous stories about Asoka were assumed to be the same.

But in 1837, James Prinsep succeeded in deciphering an ancient inscription on a large stone pillar in Delhi. Several other pillars and rocks with similar inscriptions had been known for some time and had attracted the curiosity of scholars. Prinsep's inscription proved to be a series of edicts issued by a king calling himself "Beloved-of-the-Gods, King Piyadasi." In the following decades, more and more edicts by this same king were discovered and with increasingly accurate decipherment of their language, a more complete picture of this man and his deeds began to emerge. Gradually, it dawned on scholars that the King Piyadasi of the edicts might be the King Asoka so often praised in Buddhist legends. However, it was not until 1915, when another edict actually mentioning the name Asoka was discovered, that the identification was confirmed. Having been forgotten for nearly 700 years, one of the greatest men in history became known to the world once again.

Asoka's edicts are mainly concerned with the reforms he instituted and the moral principles he recommended in his attempt to create a just and humane society. As such, they give us little information about his life, the details of which have to be culled from other sources. Although the exact dates of Asoka's life are a matter of dispute among scholars, he was born in about 304 B.C. and became the third king of the Mauryan dynasty after the death of his father, Bindusara. His given name was Asoka but he assumed the title Devanampiya Piyadasi which means "Beloved-of-the-Gods, He Who Looks On With Affection." There seems to have been a two-year war of succession during which at least one of Asoka's brothers was killed.

In 262 B.C., eight years after his coronation, Asoka's armies attacked and conquered Kalinga, a country that roughly corresponds to the modern state of Orissa. The loss of life caused by battle, reprisals, deportations and the turmoil that always exists in the aftermath of war so horrified Asoka that it brought about a complete change in his personality. It seems that Asoka had been calling himself a Buddhist for at least two years prior to the Kalinga war, but his commitment to Buddhism was only lukewarm and perhaps had a political motive behind it. But after the war Asoka dedicated the rest of his life trying to apply Buddhist principles to the administration of his vast empire. He had a crucial part to play in helping Buddhism to spread both throughout India and abroad, and probably built the first major Buddhist monuments. Asoka died in 232 B.C. in the thirty-eighth year of his reign.

Asoka's edicts are to be found scattered in more than thirty places throughout India, Nepal, Pakistan and Afghanistan. Most of them are written in Brahmi script from which all Indian scripts and many of those used in Southeast Asia later developed. The language used in the edicts found in the eastern part of the sub-continent is a type of Magadhi, probably the official language of Asoka's court. The language used in the edicts found in the western part of India is closer to Sanskrit although one bilingual edict in Afghanistan is written in Aramaic and Greek. Asoka's edicts, which comprise the earliest decipherable corpus of written documents from India, have survived throughout the centuries because they are written on rocks and stone pillars. These pillars in particular are testimony to the technological and artistic genius of ancient Indian civilization. Originally, there must have been many of them, although only ten with inscriptions still survive. Averaging between forty and fifty feet in height, and weighing up to fifty tons each, all the pillars were quarried at Chunar, just south of Varanasi and dragged, sometimes hundreds of miles, to where they were erected. Each pillar was originally capped by a capital, sometimes a roaring lion, a noble bull or a spirited horse, and the few capitals that survive are widely recognized as masterpieces of Indian art. Both the pillars and the capitals exhibit a remarkable mirror-like polish that has survived despite centuries of exposure to the elements. The location of the rock edicts is governed by the availability of suitable rocks, but the edicts on pillars are all to be found in very specific places. Some, like the Lumbini pillar, mark the Buddha's birthplace, while its inscriptions commemorate Asoka's pilgrimage to that place. Others are to be found in or near important population centers so that their edicts could be read by as many people as possible.

There is little doubt that Asoka's edicts were written in his own words rather than in the stylistic language in which royal edicts or proclamations in the ancient world were usually written in. Their distinctly personal tone gives us a unique glimpse into the personality of this complex and remarkable man. Asoka's style tends to be somewhat repetitious and plodding as if explaining something to one who has difficulty in understanding. Asoka frequently refers to the good works he has done, although not in a boastful way, but more, it seems, to convince the reader of his sincerity. In fact, an anxiousness to be thought of as a sincere person and a good administrator is present in nearly every edict. Asoka tells his subjects that he looked upon them as his children, that their welfare is his main concern; he apologizes for the Kalinga war and reassures the people beyond the borders of his empire that he has no expansionist intentions towards them. Mixed with this sincerity, there is a definite puritanical streak in Asoka's character suggested by his disapproval of festivals and of religious rituals many of which while being of little value were nonetheless harmless.

It is also very clear that Buddhism was the most influential force in Asoka's life and that he hoped his subjects likewise would adopt his religion. He went on pilgrimages to Lumbini and Bodh Gaya, sent teaching monks to various regions in India and beyond its borders, and he was familiar enough with the sacred texts to recommend some of them to the monastic community. It is also very clear that Asoka saw the reforms he instituted as being a part of his duties as a Buddhist. But, while he was an enthusiastic Buddhist, he was not partisan towards his own religion or intolerant of other religions. He seems to have genuinely hoped to be able to encourage everyone to practice his or her own religion with the same conviction that he practiced his.

Scholars have suggested that because the edicts say nothing about the philosophical aspects of Buddhism, Asoka had a simplistic and naive understanding of the Dhamma. This view does not take into account the fact that the purpose of the edicts was not to expound the truths of Buddhism, but to inform the people of Asoka's reforms and to encourage them to be more generous, kind and moral. This being the case, there was no reason for Asoka to discuss Buddhist philosophy. Asoka emerges from his edicts as an able administrator, an intelligent human being and as a devoted Buddhist, and we could expect him to take as keen an interest in Buddhist philosophy as he did in Buddhist practice.

The contents of Asoka's edicts make it clear that all the legends about his wise and humane rule are more than justified and qualify him to be ranked as one of the greatest rulers. In his edicts, he spoke of what might be called state morality, and private or individual morality. The first was what he based his administration upon and what he hoped would lead to a more just, more spiritually inclined society, while the second was what he recommended and encouraged individuals to practice. Both these types of morality were imbued with the Buddhist values of compassion, moderation, tolerance and respect for all life. The Asokan state gave up the predatory foreign policy that had characterized the Mauryan empire up till then and replaced it with a policy of peaceful co-existence. The judicial system was reformed in order to make it more fair, less harsh and less open to abuse, while those sentenced to death were given a stay of execution to prepare appeals and regular amnesties were given to prisoners. State resources were used for useful public works like the importation and cultivation of medical herbs, the building of rest houses, the digging of wells at regular intervals along main roads and the planting of fruit and shade trees. To ensue that these reforms and projects were carried out, Asoka made himself more accessible to his subjects by going on frequent inspection tours and he expected his district officers to follow his example. To the same end, he gave orders that important state business or petitions were never to be kept from him no matter what he was doing at the time. The state had a responsibility not just to protect and promote the welfare of its people but also its wildlife. Hunting certain species of wild animals was banned, forest and wildlife reserves were established and cruelty to domestic and wild animals was prohibited. The protection of all religions, their promotion and the fostering of harmony between them, was also seen as one of the duties of the state. It even seems that something like a Department of Religious Affairs was established with officers called Dhamma Mahamatras whose job it was to look after the affairs of various religious bodies and to encourage the practice of religion.

The individual morality that Asoka hoped to foster included respect *(susrusa)* towards parents, elders, teachers, friends, servants, ascetics and brahmans — behavior that accords with the advice given to Sigala by the Buddha (Digha Nikaya,

Discourse No. 31). He encouraged generosity *(dana)* to the poor *(kapana valaka),* to ascetics and brahmans, and to friends and relatives. Not surprisingly, Asoka encouraged harmlessness towards all life *(avihisa bhutanam).* In conformity with the Buddha's advice in the Anguttara Nikaya, II:282, he also considered moderation in spending and moderation in saving to be good *(apa vyayata apa bhadata).* Treating people properly *(samya pratipati),* he suggested, was much more important than performing ceremonies that were supposed to bring good luck. Because it helped promote tolerance and mutual respect, Asoka desired that people should be well-learned *(bahu sruta)* in the good doctrines *(kalanagama)* of other people's religions. The qualities of heart that are recommended by Asoka in the edicts indicate his deep spirituality. They include kindness *(daya),* self-examination *(palikhaya),* truthfulness *(sace),* gratitude *(katamnata),* purity of heart *(bhava sudhi),* enthusiasm *(usahena),* strong loyalty *(dadha bhatita),* self-control *(sayame)* and love of the Dhamma *(Dhamma kamata).*

We have no way of knowing how effective Asoka's reforms were or how long they lasted but we do know that monarchs throughout the ancient Buddhist world were encouraged to look to his style of government as an ideal to be followed. King Asoka has to be credited with the first attempt to develop a Buddhist polity. Today, with widespread disillusionment in prevailing ideologies and the search for a political philosophy that goes beyond greed (capitalism), hatred (communism) and delusion (dictatorships led by "infallible" leaders), Asoka's edicts may make a meaningful contribution to the development of a more spiritually based political system.

The Fourteen Rock Edicts

Beloved-of-the-Gods, King Piyadasi, has caused this Dhamma edict to be written. Here (in my domain) no living beings are to be slaughtered or offered in sacrifice. Nor should festivals be held, for Beloved-of-the-Gods, King Piyadasi, sees much to object to in such festivals, although there are some festivals that Beloved-of-the-Gods, King Piyadasi, does approve of. Formerly, in the kitchen of Beloved-of-the-Gods, King Piyadasi, hundreds of thousands of animals were killed every day to make curry. But now with the writing of this Dhamma edict only three creatures, two peacocks and a deer are killed, and the deer not always. And in time, not even these three creatures will be killed.

Everywhere within Beloved-of-the-Gods, King Piyadasi's domain, and among the people beyond the borders, the Cholas, the Pandyas, the Satiyaputras, the Keralaputras, as far as Tamraparni and where the Greek king Antiochos rules, and among the kings who are neighbors of Antiochos, everywhere has Beloved-of-the-Gods, King Piyadasi, made provision for two types of medical treatment: medical treatment for humans and medical treatment for animals. Wherever medical herbs suitable for humans or animals are not available, I have had them imported and grown. Wherever medical roots or fruits are not available I have had them imported and grown. Along roads I have had wells dug and trees planted for the benefit of humans and animals.

Beloved-of-the-Gods, King Piyadasi, speaks thus: Twelve years after my coronation this has been ordered — Everywhere in my domain the Yuktas, the Rajjukas and the Pradesikas shall go on inspection tours every five years for the purpose of Dhamma instruction and also to conduct other business.

Respect for mother and father is good, generosity to friends, acquaintances, relatives, Brahmans and ascetics is good, not killing living beings is good, moderation in spending and moderation in saving is good. The Council shall notify the Yuktas about the observance of these instructions in these very words.

In the past, for many hundreds of years, killing or harming living beings and improper behavior towards relatives, and improper behavior towards Brahmans and ascetics has increased. But now due to Beloved-of-the-Gods, King Piyadasi's Dhamma practice, the sound of the drum has been replaced by the sound of the Dhamma. The sighting of heavenly cars, auspicious elephants, bodies of fire and other divine sightings has not happened for many hundreds of years. But now because Beloved-of-the-Gods, King Piyadasi promotes restraint in the killing and harming of living beings, proper behavior towards relatives, Brahmans and ascetics, and respect for mother, father and elders, such sightings have increased.

These and many other kinds of Dhamma practice have been encouraged by Beloved-of-the-Gods, King Piyadasi, and he will continue to promote Dhamma practice. And the sons, grandsons and great-grandsons of Beloved-of-the-Gods, King Piyadasi, too will continue to promote Dhamma practice until the end of time; living by Dhamma and virtue, they will instruct in Dhamma. Truly, this is the highest work, to instruct in Dhamma. But practicing the Dhamma cannot be done by one who is devoid of virtue and therefore its promotion and growth is commendable.

This edict has been written so that it may please my successors to devote themselves to promoting these things and not allow them to decline. Beloved-of-the-Gods, King Piyadasi, has had this written twelve years after his coronation.

Beloved-of-the-Gods, King Piyadasi, speaks thus: To do good is difficult. One who does good first does something hard to do. I have done many good deeds, and, if my sons, grandsons and their descendants up to the end of the world act in like manner, they too will do much good. But whoever amongst them neglects this, they will do evil. Truly, it is easy to do evil.

In the past there were no Dhamma Mahamatras but such officers were appointed by me thirteen years after my coronation. Now they work among all religions for the establishment of Dhamma, for the promotion of Dhamma, and for the welfare and happiness of all who are devoted to Dhamma. They work among the Greeks, the Kambojas, the Gandharas, the Rastrikas, the Pitinikas and other peoples on the western borders. They work among soldiers, chiefs, Brahmans, householders, the poor, the aged and those devoted to Dhamma — for their welfare and happiness — so that they may be free from harassment. They (Dhamma Mahamatras) work for the proper treatment of prisoners, towards their unfettering, and if the Mahamatras think, "This one has a family to support," "That one has been bewitched," "This one is old," then they work for the release of such prisoners. They work here, in outlying towns, in the women's quarters belonging to my brothers and sisters, and among my other relatives. They are occupied everywhere. These Dhamma Mahamatras are occupied in my domain among people devoted to Dhamma to determine who is devoted to Dhamma, who is established in Dhamma, and who is generous.

This Dhamma edict has been written on stone so that it might endure long and that my descendants might act in conformity with it.

Beloved-of-the-Gods, King Piyadasi, speaks thus: In the past, state business was not transacted nor were reports delivered to the king at all hours. But now I have given this order, that at any time, whether I am eating, in the women's quarters, the bed chamber, the chariot, the palanquin, in the park or wherever, reporters are to be posted with instructions to report to me the affairs of the people so that I might attend to these affairs wherever I am. And whatever I orally order in connection with donations or proclamations, or when urgent business presses itself on the Mahamatras, if disagreement or debate arises in the Council, then it must be reported to me immediately. This is what I have ordered. I am never content with exerting myself or with despatching business. Truly, I consider the welfare of all to be my duty, and the root of this is exertion and the prompt despatch of business. There is no better work than promoting the welfare of all the people and whatever efforts I am making is to repay the debt I owe to all beings to assure their happiness in this life, and attain heaven in the next.

Therefore this Dhamma edict has been written to last long and that my sons, grandsons and great-grandsons might act in conformity with it for the welfare of the world. However, this is difficult to do without great exertion.

Beloved-of-the-Gods, King Piyadasi, desires that all religions should reside everywhere, for all of them desire self-control and purity of heart. But people have various desires and various passions, and they may practice all of what they should or only a part of it. But one who receives great gifts yet is lacking in self-control, purity of heart, gratitude and firm devotion, such a person is mean. In the past kings used to go out on pleasure tours during which there was hunting and other entertainment.

But ten years after Beloved-of-the-Gods had been coronated, he went on a tour to Sambodhi and thus instituted Dhamma tours. During these tours, the following things took place: visits and gifts to Brahmans and ascetics, visits and gifts of gold to the aged, visits to people in the countryside, instructing them in Dhamma, and discussing Dhamma with them as is suitable. It is this that delights Beloved-of-the-Gods, King Piyadasi, and is, as it were, another type of revenue.

Beloved-of-the-Gods, King Piyadasi, speaks thus: In times of sickness, for the marriage of sons and daughters, at the birth of children, before embarking on a journey, on these and other occasions, people perform various ceremonies. Women in particular perform many vulgar and worthless ceremonies. These types of ceremonies can be performed by all means, but they bear little fruit. What does bear great fruit, however, is the ceremony of the Dhamma. This involves proper behavior towards servants and employees, respect for teachers, restraint towards living beings, and generosity towards ascetics and Brahmans. These and other things constitute the ceremony of the Dhamma. Therefore a father, a son, a brother, a master, a friend, a companion, and even a neighbor should say: "This is good, this is the ceremony that should be performed until its purpose is fulfilled, this I shall do." Other ceremonies are of doubtful fruit, for they may achieve their purpose, or they may not, and even if they do, it is only in this world. But the ceremony of the Dhamma is timeless. Even if it does not achieve its purpose in this world, it produces great merit in the next, whereas if it does achieve its purpose in this world, one gets great merit both here and there through the ceremony of the Dhamma.

Beloved-of-the-Gods, King Piyadasi, does not consider glory and fame to be of great account unless they are achieved through having my subjects respect Dhamma and practice Dhamma, both now and in the future. For this alone does Beloved-of-the-Gods, King Piyadasi, desire glory and fame. And whatever efforts Beloved-of-the-Gods, King Piyadasi, is making, all of that is only for the welfare of the people in the next world, and that they will have little evil. And being without merit is evil. This is difficult for either a humble person or a great person to do except with great effort, and by giving up other interests. In fact, it may be even more difficult for a great person to do.

Beloved-of-the-Gods, King Piyadasi, speaks thus: There is no gift like the gift of the Dhamma, (no acquaintance like) acquaintance with Dhamma, (no distribution like) distribution of Dhamma, and (no kinship like) kinship through Dhamma. And it consists of this: proper behavior towards servants and employees, respect for mother and father, generosity to friends, companions, relations, Brahmans and ascetics, and not killing living beings. Therefore a father, a son, a brother, a master, a friend, a companion or a neighbor should say: "This is good, this should be done." One benefits in this world and gains great merit in the next by giving the gift of the Dhamma.

Beloved-of-the-Gods, King Piyadasi, honors both ascetics and the householders of all religions, and he honors them with gifts and honors of various kinds. But Beloved-of-the-Gods, King Piyadasi, does not value gifts and honors as much as he values this — that there should be growth in the essentials of all religions. Growth in essentials can be done in different ways, but all of them have as their root restraint in speech, that is, not praising one's own religion, or condemning the religion of others without good cause. And if there is cause for criticism, it should be done in a mild way. But it is better to honor other religions for this reason. By so doing, one's own religion benefits, and so do other religions, while doing otherwise harms one's own religion and the religions of others. Whoever praises his own religion, due to excessive devotion, and condemns others with the thought "Let me glorify my own religion," only harms his own religion. Therefore contact (between religions) is good. One should listen to and respect the doctrines professed by others. Beloved-of-the-Gods, King Piyadasi, desires that all should be well-learned in the good doctrines of other religions.

Those who are content with their own religion should be told this: Beloved-of-the-Gods, King Piyadasi, does not value gifts and honors as much as he values that there should be growth in the essentials of all religions. And to this end many are working — Dhamma Mahamatras, Mahamatras in charge of the women's quarters, officers in charge of outlying areas, and other such officers. And the fruit of this is that one's own religion grows and the Dhamma is illuminated also.

Beloved-of-the-Gods, King Piyadasi, conquered the Kalingas eight years after his coronation. One hundred and fifty thousand were deported, one hundred thousand were killed and many more died (from other causes). After the Kalingas had been conquered, Beloved-of-the-Gods came to feel a strong inclination towards the Dhamma, a love for the Dhamma and for instruction in Dhamma. Now Beloved-of-the-Gods feels deep remorse for having conquered the Kalingas.

Indeed, Beloved-of-the-Gods is deeply pained by the killing, dying and deportation that take place when an unconquered country is conquered. But Beloved-of-the-Gods is pained even more by this — that Brahmans, ascetics, and householders of different religions who live in those countries, and who are respectful to superiors, to mother and fatner, to elders, and who behave properly and have strong loyalty towards friends, acquaintances, companions, relatives, servants and employees — that they are injured, killed or separated from their loved ones. Even those who are not affected (by all this) suffer when they see friends, acquaintances, companions and relatives affected. These misfortunes befall all (as a result of war), and this pains Beloved-of-the-Gods.

There is no country, except among the Greeks, where these two groups, Brahmans and ascetics, are not found, and there is no country where people are not devoted to one or another religion. Therefore the killing, death or deportation of a hundredth, or even a thousandth part of those who died during the conquest of Kalinga now pains Beloved-of-the-Gods. Now Beloved-of-the-Gods thinks that even those who do wrong should be forgiven where forgiveness is possible.

Even the forest people, who live in Beloved-of-the-Gods' domain, are entreated and reasoned with to act properly. They are told that despite his remorse Beloved-of-the-Gods has the power to punish them if necessary, so that they should be ashamed of their wrong and not be killed. Truly, Beloved-of-the-Gods desires non-injury, restraint and impartiality to all beings, even where wrong has been done.

Now it is conquest by Dhamma that Beloved-of-the-Gods considers to be the best conquest. And it (conquest by Dhamma) has been won here, on the borders, even six hundred yojanas away, where the Greek king Antiochos rules, beyond there where the four kings named Ptolemy, Antigonos, Magas and Alexander rule, likewise in the south among the Cholas, the Pandyas, and as far as Tamraparni.

Here in the king's domain among the Greeks, the Kambojas, the Nabhakas, the Nabhapamkits, the Bhojas, the Pitinikas, the Andhras and the Palidas, everywhere people are following Beloved-of-the-Gods' instructions in Dhamma.

Even where Beloved-of-the-Gods' envoys have not been, these people too, having heard of the practice of Dhamma and the ordinances and instructions in Dhamma given by Beloved-of-the-Gods, are following it and will continue to do so. This conquest has been won everywhere, and it gives great joy — the joy which only conquest by Dhamma can give. But even this joy is of little consequence. Beloved-of-the-Gods considers the great fruit to be experienced in the next world to be more important.

I have had this Dhamma edict written so that my sons and great-grandsons may not consider making new conquests, or that if military conquests are made, that they be done with forbearance and light punishment, or better still, that they consider making conquest by Dhamma only, for that bears fruit in this world and the next. May all their intense devotion be given to this which has a result in this world and the next.

Beloved-of-the-Gods, King Piyadasi, has had these Dhamma edicts written in brief, in medium length, and in extended form. Not all of them occur everywhere, for my domain is vast, but much has been written, and I will have still more written. And also there are some subjects here that have been spoken of again and again because of their sweetness, and so that the people may act in accordance with them. If some things written are incomplete, this is because of the locality, or in consideration of the object, or due to the fault of the scribe.

The Kalinga Rock Edicts

Beloved-of-the-Gods says that the Mahamatras of Tosali who are judicial officers in the city are to be told this: I wish to see that everything I consider to be proper is carried out in the right way. And I consider instructing you to be the best way of accomplishing this. I have placed you over many thousands of people that you may win the people's affection.

All men are my children. What I desire for my own children, and I desire their welfare and happiness both in this world and the next, that I desire for all men. You do not understand to what extent I desire this, and if some of you do understand, you do not understand the full extent of my desire.

You must attend to this matter. While being completely law-abiding, some people are imprisoned, treated harshly and even killed without cause so that many people suffer. Therefore your aim should be to act with impartiality. It is because of these things — envy, anger, cruelty, hate, indifference, laziness or tiredness — that such a thing does not happen. Therefore your aim should be: "May these things not be in me." And the root of this is non-anger and patience. Those who are bored with the administration of justice will not be promoted; (those who are not) will move upwards and be promoted. Whoever among you understands this should say to his colleagues: "See that you do your duty properly. Such and such are Beloved-of-the-Gods' instructions." Great fruit will result from doing your duty, while failing in it will result in gaining neither heaven nor the king's pleasure. Failure in duty on your part will not please me. But done properly, it will win you heaven and you will be discharging your debts to me.

This edict is to be listened to on Tisa day, between Tisa days, and on other suitable occasions, it should be listened to even by a single person. Acting thus, you will be doing your duty.

This edict has been written for the following purpose: that the judicial officers of the city may strive to do their duty and that the people under them might not suffer unjust imprisonment or harsh treatment. To achieve this, I will send out Mahamatras every five years who are not harsh or cruel, but who are merciful and who can ascertain if the judicial officers have understood my purpose and are acting according to my instructions. Similarly, from Ujjayini, the prince will send similar persons with the same purpose without allowing three years to elapse. Likewise from Takhasila also. When these Mahamatras go on tours of inspection each year, then without neglecting their normal duties, they will ascertain if judicial officers are acting according to the king's instructions.

Beloved-of-the-Gods speaks thus: This royal order is to be addressed to the Mahamatras at Samapa. I wish to see that everything I consider to be proper is carried out in the right way. And I consider instructing you to be the best way of accomplishing this. All men are my children. What I desire for my own children, and I desire their welfare and happiness both in this world and the next, that I desire for all men.

The people of the unconquered territories beyond the borders might think: "What is the king's intentions towards us?" My only intention is that they live without fear of me, that they may trust me and that I may give them happiness, not sorrow. Furthermore, they should understand that the king will forgive those who can be forgiven, and that he wishes to encourage them to practice Dhamma so that they may attain happiness in this world and the next. I am telling you this so that I may discharge the debts I owe, and that in instructing you, that you may know that my vow and my promise will not be broken. Therefore acting in this way, you should perform your duties and assure them (the people beyond the borders) that: "The king is like a father. He feels towards us as he feels towards himself. We are to him like his own children."

By instructing you and informing you of my vow and my promise I shall be applying myself in complete fullness to achieving this object. You are able indeed to inspire them with confidence and to secure their welfare and happiness in this world and the next, and by acting thus, you will attain heaven as well as discharge the debts you owe to me. And so that the Mahamatras can devote themselves at all times to inspiring the border areas with confidence and encouraging them to practice Dhamma, this edict has been written here.

This edict is to be listened to every four months on Tisa day, between Tisa days, and on other suitable occasions, it should be listened to even by a single person. Acting thus, you will be doing your duty.

Minor Rock Edicts

Beloved-of-the-Gods speaks thus: It is now more than two and a half years since I became a lay-disciple, but until now I have not been very zealous. But now that I have visited the Sangha for more than a year, I have become very zealous. Now the people in India who have not associated with the gods do so. This is the result of zeal and it is not just the great who can do this. Even the humble, if they are zealous, can attain heaven. And this proclamation has been made with this aim. Let both humble and great be zealous, let even those on the borders know and let zeal last long. Then this zeal will increase, it will greatly increase, it will increase up to one-and-a-half times. This message has been proclaimed two hundred and fifty-six times by the king while on tour.

Beloved-of-the-Gods speaks thus: Father and mother should be respected and so should elders, kindness to living beings should be made strong and the truth should be spoken. In these ways, the Dhamma should be promoted. Likewise, a teacher should be honored by his pupil and proper manners should be shown towards relations. This is an ancient rule that conduces to long life. Thus should one act. Written by the scribe Chapala.

Piyadasi, King of Magadha, saluting the Sangha and wishing them good health and happiness, speaks thus: You know, reverend sirs, how great my faith in the Buddha, the Dhamma and Sangha is. Whatever, reverend sirs, has been spoken by Lord Buddha, all that is well-spoken. I consider it proper, reverend sirs, to advise on how the good Dhamma should last long.

These Dhamma texts — Extracts from the Discipline, the Noble Way of Life, the Fears to Come, the Poem on the Silent Sage, the Discourse on the Pure Life, Upatisa's Questions, and the Advice to Rahula which was spoken by the Buddha concerning false speech — these Dhamma texts, reverend sirs,

I desire that all the monks and nuns may constantly listen to and remember. Likewise the laymen and laywomen. I have had this written that you may know my intentions.

The Seven Pillar Edicts

Beloved-of-the-Gods speaks thus: This Dhamma edict was written twenty-six years after my coronation. Happiness in this world and the next is difficult to obtain without much love for the Dhamma, much self-examination, much respect, much fear (of evil), and much enthusiasm. But through my instruction this regard for Dhamma and love of Dhamma has grown day by day, and will continue to grow. And my officers of high, low and middle rank are practicing and conforming to Dhamma, and are capable of inspiring others to do the same. Mahamatras in border areas are doing the same. And these are my instructions: to protect with Dhamma, to make happiness through Dhamma and to guard with Dhamma.

Beloved-of-the-Gods, King Piyadasi, speaks thus: Dhamma is good, but what constitutes Dhamma? (It includes) little evil, much good, kindness, generosity, truthfulness and purity. I have given the gift of sight in various ways. To two-footed and four-footed beings, to birds and aquatic animals, I have given various things including the gift of life. And many other good deeds have been done by me.

This Dhamma edict has been written that people might follow it and it might endure for a long time. And the one who follows it properly will do something good.

Beloved-of-the-Gods, King Piyadasi, speaks thus: People see only their good deeds saying, "I have done this good deed." But they do not see their evil deeds saying, "I have done this evil deed" or "This is called evil." But this (tendency) is difficult to see. One should think like this: "It is these things that lead to evil, to violence, to cruelty, anger, pride and jealousy. Let me not ruin myself with these things." And further, one should think: "This leads to happiness in this world and the next."

Beloved-of-the-Gods speaks thus: This Dhamma edict was written twenty-six years after my coronation. My Rajjukas are working among the people, among many hundreds of thousands of people. The hearing of petitions and the administration of justice has been left to them so that they can do their duties confidently and fearlessly and so that they can work for the welfare, happiness and benefit of the people in the country. But they should remember what causes happiness and sorrow, and being themselves devoted to Dhamma, they should encourage the people in the country (to do the same), that they may attain happiness in this world and the next. These Rajjukas are eager to serve me. They also obey other officers who know my desires, who instruct the Rajjukas so that they can please me. Just as a person feels confident having entrusted his child to an expert nurse thinking: "The nurse will keep my child well," even so, the Rajjukas have been appointed by me for the welfare and happiness of the people in the country.

The hearing of petitions and the administration of justice have been left to the Rajjukas so that they can do their duties unperturbed, fearlessly and confidently. It is my desire that there should be uniformity in law and uniformity in sentencing. I even go this far, to grant a three-day stay for those in prison who have been tried and sentenced to death. During this time their relatives can make appeals to have the prisoners' lives spared. If there is none to appeal on their behalf, the prisoners can give gifts in order to make merit for the next world, or observe fasts. Indeed, it is my wish that in this way, even if a prisoner's time is limited, he can prepare for the next world, and that people's Dhamma practice, self-control and generosity may grow.

Beloved-of-the-Gods, King Piyadasi, speaks thus: Twenty-six years after my coronation various animals were declared to be protected — parrots, mainas, *aruna,* ruddy geese, wild ducks, *nandimukhas, gelatas,* bats, queen ants, terrapins, boneless fish, *vedareyaka, gangapuputaka, sankiya* fish, tortoises, porcupines, squirrels, deer, bulls, *okapinda,* wild asses, wild pigeons, domestic pigeons and all four-footed creatures that are neither useful nor edible. Those nanny goats, ewes and sows which are with young or giving milk to their young are protected, and so are young ones less than six months old. Cocks are not to be caponized, husks hiding living beings are not to be burnt and forests are not to be burnt either without reason or to kill creatures. One animal is not to be fed to another. On the three Caturmasis, the three days of Tisa and during the fourteenth and fifteenth of the Uposatha, fish are protected and not to be sold. During these days animals are not to be killed in the elephant reserves or the fish reserves either. On the eighth of every fortnight, on the fourteenth and fifteenth, on Tisa, Punarvasu, the three Caturmasis and other auspicious days, bulls are not to be castrated, billy goats, rams, boars and other animals that are usually castrated are not to be. On Tisa, Punarvasu, Caturmasis and the fortnight of Caturmasis, horses and bullocks are not be branded.

In the twenty-six years since my coronation prisoners have been given amnesty on twenty-five occasions.

Beloved-of-the-Gods speaks thus: Twelve years after my coronation I started to have Dhamma edicts written for the welfare and happiness of the people, and so that not transgressing them they might grow in the Dhamma. Thinking: "How can the welfare and happiness of the people be secured?" I give attention to my relatives, to those dwelling near and those dwelling far, so I can lead them to happiness and then I act accordingly. I do the same for all groups. I have honored all religions with various honors. But I consider it best to meet with people personally.

This Dhamma edict was written twenty-six years after my coronation.

Beloved-of-the-Gods speaks thus: In the past kings desired that the people might grow through the promotion of the Dhamma. But despite this, people did not grow through the promotion of the Dhamma. Beloved-of-the-Gods, King Piyadasi, said concerning this: "It occurs to me that in the past kings desired that the people might grow through the promotion of the Dhamma. But despite this, people did not grow through the promotion of the Dhamma. Now how can the people be encouraged to follow it? How can the people be encouraged to grow through the promotion of the Dhamma? How can I elevate them by promoting the Dhamma?" Beloved-of-the-Gods, King Piyadasi, further said concerning this: "It occurs to me that I shall have proclamations on Dhamma announced and instruction on Dhamma given. When people hear these, they will follow them, elevate themselves and grow considerably through the promotion of the Dhamma." It is for this purpose that proclamations on Dhamma have been announced and various instructions on Dhamma have been given and that officers who work among many promote and explain them in detail. The Rajjukas who work among hundreds of thousands of people have likewise been ordered: "In this way and that encourage those who are devoted to Dhamma." Beloved-of-the-Gods speaks thus: "Having this object in view, I have set up Dhamma pillars, appointed Dhamma Mahamatras, and announced Dhamma proclamations."

Beloved-of-the-Gods, King Piyadasi, says: Along roads I have had banyan trees planted so that they can give shade to animals and men, and I have had mango groves planted. At intervals of eight *krosas,* I have had wells dug, rest-houses built, and in various places, I have had watering-places made for the use of animals and men. But these are but minor achievements. Such things to make the people happy have been done by former kings. I have done these things for this purpose, that the people might practice the Dhamma.

Beloved-of-the-Gods, King Piyadasi, speaks thus: My Dhamma Mahamatras too are occupied with various good works among the ascetics and householders of all religions. I have ordered that they should be occupied with the affairs of the Sangha. I have also ordered that they should be occupied with the affairs of the Brahmans and the Ajivikas. I have ordered that they be occupied with the Niganthas. In fact, I have ordered that different Mahamatras be occupied with the particular affairs of all different religions. And my Dhamma Mahamatras likewise are occupied with these and other religions.

Beloved-of-the-Gods, King Piyadasi, speaks thus: These and other principal officers are occupied with the distribution of gifts, mine as well as those of the queens. In my women's quarters, they organize various charitable activities here and in the provinces. I have also ordered my sons and the sons of other queens to distribute gifts so that noble deeds of Dhamma and the practice of Dhamma may be promoted. And noble deeds of Dhamma and the practice of Dhamma consist of having kindness, generosity, truthfulness, purity, gentleness and goodness increase among the people.

Beloved-of-the-Gods, King Piyadasi, speaks thus: Whatever good deeds have been done by me, those the people accept and those they follow. Therefore they have progressed and will continue to progress by being respectful to mother and father, respectful to elders, by courtesy to the aged and proper behavior towards Brahmans and ascetics, towards the poor and distressed, and even towards servants and employees.

Beloved-of-the-Gods, King Piyadasi, speaks thus: This progress among the people through Dhamma has been done by two means, by Dhamma regulations and by persuasion. Of these, Dhamma regulation is of little effect, while persuasion has much more effect. The Dhamma regulations I have given are that various animals must be protected. And I have given many other Dhamma regulations also. But it is by persuasion that progress among the people through Dhamma has had a greater effect in respect of harmlessness to living beings and non-killing of living beings.

Concerning this, Beloved-of-the-Gods says: Wherever there are stone pillars or stone slabs, there this Dhamma edict is to be engraved so that it may long endure. It has been engraved so that it may endure as long as my sons and great-grandsons live and as long as the sun and the moon shine, and so that people may practice it as instructed. For by practicing it happiness will be attained in this world and the next.

This Dhamma edict has been written by me twenty-seven years after my coronation.

The Minor Pillar Edicts

Twenty years after his coronation, Beloved-of-the-Gods, King Piyadasi, visited this place and worshipped because here the Buddha, the sage of the Sakyans, was born. He had a stone figure and a pillar set up and because the Lord was born here, the village of Lumbini was exempted from tax and required to pay only one eighth of the produce. Beloved-of-the-Gods commands: The Mahamatras at Kosambi (are to be told: Whoever splits the Sangha) which is now united, is not to be admitted into the Sangha. Whoever, whether monk or nun, splits the Sangha is to be made to wear white clothes and to reside somewhere other than in a monastery.

THAT THE TRUE DHAMMA MIGHT LAST A LONG TIME

The edicts of King Asoka are a remarkable record of one of the most remarkable events in human history: One man's efforts to rule an empire with a policy based on Dhamma. Asoka's policy had three prongs: administration based on Dhamma, instruction in Dhamma for the populace, and personal practice of Dhamma by the ruler.

The edicts are direct evidence of the second prong, and for the most part present Dhamma as a series of moral principles and rational behavior that should be common to all religions. However, a few of them are addressed to Buddhists in particular, and one of them — the Bhabru Rock Edict — deals with themes that are of interest not only to historians, but also to Buddhists of all times and places. It deals with what may be done to keep the True Dhamma alive for a long time, and Asoka's recommendation is a list of passages from the Buddhist Canon that he says all Buddhists — ordained or not — should listen to and reflect on frequently. Here is the text of the edict:

"His Gracious Majesty, King of Magadha, bows down to the Sangha and — hoping that they are free from disease and living in peace — addresses them as follows: You know well the extent of my reverence and faith in the Buddha, Dhamma, and Sangha. Whatever has been said by the Buddha has of course been well-said. But may I be permitted to point out the passages of scripture I have selected that the True Dhamma might last a long time: Vinaya-samukasa, Aliya-vasani, Anagata-bhayani, Muni-gatha, Mauneya-sute, Upatisa-pasine, and the Instructions to Rahula beginning with (the topic of) falsehood, as taught by the Blessed One.

"Reverend Sirs, I would like the reverend bhikkhus and bhikkhunis — as well as the laymen and laywomen — to listen to these passages frequently and to ponder on them. "For this reason, Reverend Sirs, I am having this enscribed so that they may know of my intention."

As might be imagined, this passage has given rise to a great deal of conjecture ever since it was deciphered in 1840. Not the least of the questions is precisely which passages from the Canon Asoka is referring to, or indeed if he was referring to a Canon anything like what we have today.

Scholars have spilt a fair amount of ink sparring over the answer and have managed to reach a consensus on the identity of four of the passages: the Aliya-vasani is the Discourse on the Traditions of the Noble Ones (ariya-vamsa) (AN 4.28); the Anagata-bhayani are the four discourses on Future Dangers (AN 5.77-80); the Muni-gatha is the Discourse on the Sage (Muni Sutta) in the Sutta Nipata (Sn.I.12); and the Instructions to Rahula are the Cula-Rahulovada Sutta (MN 61).

The other three passages have proven more intractable. A number of scholars have favored the Nalaka Sutta as the Mauneya-sute — this, in spite of the fact that there is a Moneyya (Sagacity) Sutta in the Anguttara Nikaya (AN 3.23). The Upatisa-pasine (Question of Upatissa=Sariputta) is problematic because there is no one passage of that name and because Sariputta asks so many questions in the Canon. Some scholars have proposed the Sariputta Sutta in the Sutta Nipata, but archaeological evidence — votive tablets produced beginning with the time of Asoka and originating in the Buddhist pilgrim sites — show that Ven. Assaji's answer to Sariputta's first question about the doctrine, the answer that sparked a vision of the Dhamma in Sariputta when he heard it, has long been regarded as the ideal epitome of the Buddha's teachings. This tradition may have connections with this very edict. Ask any knowledgeable Buddhists today what Sariputta's most famous question was, and they will in all likelihood answer with this one.

As for the Vinaya-samukase, this has sparked the most fanciful conjectures, because the single reference to this word in the Canon is buried in a book hardly anyone reads: the Parivara (VI.4). The reference itself says nothing more than that there are four "vinaya-samukkamsa" — innate principles of the Vinaya — but the Commentary identifies them as the four Great Standards — most likely the four mentioned in the Mahavagga, dealing specifically with Vinaya, rather than the four in the Maha-parinibbana Sutta, which deal with Dhamma and Vinaya together.

This seems to settle the question of which passages Asoka was recommending, but it raises another one: Why these? And why in this order?

Perhaps the best approach to answering these questions would be to read the passages and ponder on them, as Asoka suggested. So here they are. Most of them are self-explanatory, except for the first, on the innate principles of Vinaya, and the poem on the sage, which — being a poem — occasionally makes use of imagery that might be unfamiliar to a modern reader. Thus I include in the translation of The Sage a set of notes, drawing mostly from the Commentary, but also from other parts of the Canon and from works on ancient culture in general.

As for the Innate Principles of the Vinaya, the passage itself contains nothing unremarkable, but it seems so obvious on first reading that one might wonder why anyone would call attention to it. Actually, it is a fine example of the Buddha's farsightedness in setting up a system of teachings and rules. There are bound to be a number of things not touched on in the rules, and this number is bound to grow as culture and technology change. An unenlightened approach to these changes would say either that anything not allowed is forbidden, or that anything not explicitly forbidden is allowed. The Buddha, typically, sets forth a system of interpretation that avoids both of these extremes and helps to ensure the long life of his doctrine and discipline by setting guidelines for expanding them to cover new objects and situations as they arise.

The Innate Principles of the Vinaya

Now at that time uncertainty arose in the monks with regard to this and that item: "Now what is allowed by the Blessed One? What is not allowed?" They told this matter to the Blessed One, (who said):

"Bhikkhus, whatever I have not objected to, saying, 'This is not allowable,' if it fits in with what is not allowable, if it goes against what is allowable, this is not allowable for you.

"Whatever I have not objected to, saying, 'This is not allowable,' if it fits in with what is allowable, if it goes against what is not allowable, this is allowable for you.

"And whatever I have not permitted, saying, 'This is allowable,' if it fits in with what is not allowable, if it goes against what is allowable, this is not allowable for you.

"And whatever I have not permitted, saying, 'This is allowable,' if it fits in with what is allowable, if it goes against what is not allowable, this is allowable for you."

— Mv.VI.40.1

The Traditions of the Noble Ones

These four traditions of the Noble Ones — original, long-standing, traditional, ancient, unadulterated, unadulterated from the beginning — are not open to suspicion, will never be open to suspicion, and are unfaulted by knowledgeable contemplatives and priests. Which four?

There is the case where a monk is content with any old robe cloth at all. He speaks in praise of being content with any old robe cloth at all. He does not, for the sake of robe cloth, do anything unseemly or inappropriate. Not getting cloth, he is not agitated. Getting cloth, he uses it not tied to it, uninfatuated, guiltless, seeing the drawbacks (of attachment to it), and discerning the escape from them. He does not, on account of his contentment with any old robe cloth at all, exalt himself or disparage others. In this he is skillful, energetic, alert, and mindful. This, monks, is said to be a monk standing firm in the ancient, original traditions of the Noble Ones.

Furthermore, the monk is content with any old almsfood at all. He speaks in praise of being content with any old almsfood at all. He does not, for the sake of almsfood, do anything unseemly or inappropriate. Not getting almsfood, he is not agitated. Getting almsfood, he uses it not tied to it, uninfatuated, guiltless, seeing the drawbacks (of attachment to it), and discerning the escape from them. He does not, on account of his contentment with any old almsfood at all, exalt himself or disparage others. In this he is skillful, energetic, alert, and mindful. This, monks, is said to be a monk standing firm in the ancient, original traditions of the Noble Ones.

Furthermore, the monk is content with any old lodging at all. He speaks in praise of being content with any old lodging at all. He does not, for the sake of lodging, do anything unseemly or inappropriate. Not getting lodging, he is not agitated. Getting lodging, he uses it not tied to it, uninfatuated, guiltless, seeing the drawbacks (of attachment to it), and discerning the escape from them. He does not, on account of his contentment with any old lodging at all, exalt himself or disparage others. In this he is skillful, energetic, alert, and mindful. This, monks, is said to be a monk standing firm in the ancient, original traditions of the Noble Ones.

Furthermore, the monk finds pleasure and delight in developing (skillful mental qualities), finds pleasure and delight in abandoning (unskillful mental qualities). He does not, on account of his pleasure and delight in developing and abandoning, exalt himself or disparage others. In this he is skillful, energetic, alert, and mindful. This, monks, is said to be a monk standing firm in the ancient, original traditions of the Noble Ones. These are the four traditions of the Noble Ones — original, long-standing, traditional, ancient, unadulterated, unadulterated from the beginning — which are not open to suspicion, will never be open to suspicion, and are unfaulted by knowledgeable contemplatives and priests.

And furthermore, a monk endowed with these four traditions of the Noble Ones, if he lives in the east, conquers displeasure and is not conquered by displeasure. If he lives in the west... the north... the south, he conquers displeasure and is not conquered by displeasure. Why is that? Because the wise one endures both pleasure and displeasure.

This is what the Blessed One said. Having said this, he said further:

Displeasure does not conquer the enlightened one.
Displeasure does not suppress him.
He conquers displeasure
because he endures it.
Having cast away all deeds:
who could obstruct him?
Like an ornament of finest gold:
Who is fit to find fault with him?
Even the Devas praise him,
even by Brahma is he praised. — AN 4.28

FUTURE DANGERS: I

Monks, these five future dangers are just enough, when considered, for a monk living in the wilderness — heedful, ardent, and resolute — to live for the attaining of the as-yet-unattained, the reaching of the as-yet-unreached, the realization of the as-yet-unrealized. Which five?

There is the case where a monk living in the wilderness reminds himself of this: I am now living alone in the wilderness. While I am living alone in the wilderness a snake might bite me, a scorpion might sting me, a centipede might bite me. That would be how my death would come about. That would be an obstruction for me. So let me make an effort for the attaining of the as-yet-unattained, the reaching of the as-yet-unreached, the realization of the as-yet-unrealized.

This is the first future danger that is just enough, when considered, for a monk living in the wilderness — heedful, ardent, and resolute — to live for the attaining of the as-yet-unattained, the reaching of the as-yet-unreached, the realization of the as-yet-unrealized.

Furthermore, the monk living in the wilderness reminds himself of this: I am now living alone in the wilderness. While I am living alone in the wilderness, stumbling, I might fall; my food, digested, might trouble me; my bile might be provoked, my phlegm... piercing wind forces (in the body) might be provoked. That would be how my death would come about. That would be an obstruction for me. So let me make an effort for the attaining of the as-yet-unattained, the reaching of the as-yet-unreached, the realization of the as-yet-unrealized.

This is the second future danger that is just enough, when considered, for a monk living in the wilderness — heedful, ardent, and resolute — to live for the attaining of the as-yet-unattained, the reaching of the as-yet-unreached, the realization of the as-yet-unrealized.

Furthermore, the monk living in the wilderness reminds himself of this: I am now living alone in the wilderness. While I am living alone in the wilderness, I might meet up with vicious beasts: a lion or a tiger or a leopard or a bear or a hyena. They might take my life. That would be how my death would come about. That would be an obstruction for me. So let me make an effort for the attaining of the as-yet-unattained, the reaching of the as-yet-unreached, the realization of the as-yet-unrealized.

This is the third future danger that is just enough, when considered, for a monk living in the wilderness — heedful, ardent, and resolute — to live for the attaining of the as-yet-unattained, the reaching of the as-yet-unreached, the realization of the as-yet-unrealized.

Furthermore, the monk living in the wilderness reminds himself of this: I am now living alone in the wilderness. While I am living alone in the wilderness, I might meet up with youths on their way to committing a crime or on their way back. They might take my life. That would be how my death would come about. That would be an obstruction for me. So let me make an effort for the attaining of the as-yet-unattained, the reaching of the as-yet-unreached, the realization of the as-yet-unrealized.

This is the fourth future danger that is just enough, when considered, for a monk living in the wilderness — heedful, ardent, and resolute — to live for the attaining of the as-yet-unattained, the reaching of the as-yet-unreached, the realization of the as-yet-unrealized. Furthermore, the monk living in the wilderness reminds himself of this: I am now living alone in the wilderness. And in the wilderness are vicious non-human beings (spirits). They might take my life. That would be how my death would come about. That would be an obstruction for me. So let me make an effort for the attaining of the as-yet-unattained, the reaching of the as-yet-unreached, the realization of the as-yet-unrealized.

This is the fifth future danger that is just enough, when considered, for a monk living in the wilderness — heedful, ardent, and resolute — to live for the attaining of the as-yet-unattained, the reaching of the as-yet-unreached, the realization of the as-yet-unrealized.

These are the five future dangers that are just enough, when considered, for a monk living in the wilderness — heedful, ardent, and resolute — to live for the attaining of the as-yet-unattained, the reaching of the as-yet-unreached, the realization of the as-yet-unrealized. — AN 5.77

FUTURE DANGERS: II

Monks, these five future dangers are just enough, when considered, for a monk — heedful, ardent, and resolute — to live for the attaining of the as-yet-unattained, the reaching of the as-yet-unreached, the realization of the as-yet-unrealized. Which five?

There is the case where a monk reminds himself of this: At present I am young, black-haired, endowed with the blessings of youth in the first stage of life. The time will come, though, when this body is beset by old age. When one is overcome with old age and decay, it is not easy to pay attention to the Buddha's teachings. It is not easy to reside in isolated forest or wilderness dwellings. Before this unwelcome, disagreeable, displeasing thing happens, let me first make an effort for the attaining of the as-yet-unattained, the reaching of the as-yet-unreached, the realization of the as-yet-unrealized, so that — endowed with that Dhamma — I will live in peace even when old.

This is the first future danger that is just enough, when considered, for a monk — heedful, ardent, and resolute — to live for the attaining of the as-yet-unattained, the reaching of the as-yet-unreached, the realization of the as-yet-unrealized.

Furthermore, the monk reminds himself of this: At present I am free from illness and discomfort, endowed with good digestion: not too cold, not too hot, of medium strength and tolerance. The time will come, though, when this body is beset with illness. When one is overcome with illness, it is not easy to pay attention to the Buddha's teachings. It is not easy to reside in isolated forest or wilderness dwellings. Before this unwelcome, disagreeable, displeasing thing happens, let me first make an effort for the attaining of the as-yet-unattained, the reaching of the as-yet-unreached, the realization of the as-yet-unrealized, so that — endowed with that Dhamma — I will live in peace even when ill.

This is the second future danger that is just enough, when considered, for a monk — heedful, ardent, and resolute — to live for the attaining of the as-yet-unattained, the reaching of the as-yet-unreached, the realization of the as-yet-unrealized.

Furthermore, the monk reminds himself of this: At present food is plentiful, alms are easy to come by. It is easy to maintain oneself by gleanings and patronage. The time will come, though, when there is famine: Food is scarce, alms are hard to come by, and it is not easy to maintain oneself by gleanings and patronage. When there is famine, people will congregate where food is plentiful. There they will live packed and crowded together. When one is living packed and crowded together, it is not easy to pay attention to the Buddha's teachings. It is not easy to reside in isolated forest or wilderness dwellings. Before this unwelcome, disagreeable, displeasing thing happens, let me first make an effort for the attaining of the as-yet-unattained, the reaching of the as-yet-unreached, the realization of the as-yet-unrealized, so that — endowed with that Dhamma — I will live in peace even when there is famine.

This is the third future danger that is just enough, when considered, for a monk — heedful, ardent, and resolute — to live for the attaining of the as-yet-unattained, the reaching of the as-yet-unreached, the realization of the as-yet-unrealized.

Furthermore, the monk reminds himself of this: At present people are in harmony, on friendly terms, without quarreling, like milk mixed with water, viewing one another with eyes of affection. The time will come, though, when there is danger and an invasion of savage tribes. Taking power, they will surround the countryside. When there is danger, people will congregate where it is safe.

There they will live packed and crowded together. When one is living packed and crowded together, it is not easy to pay attention to the Buddha's teachings. It is not easy to reside in isolated forest or wilderness dwellings. Before this unwelcome, disagreeable, displeasing thing happens, let me first make an effort for the attaining of the as-yet-unattained, the reaching of the as-yet-unreached, the realization of the as-yet-unrealized, so that — endowed with that Dhamma — I will live in peace even when there is danger.

This is the fourth future danger that is just enough, when considered, for a monk — heedful, ardent, and resolute — to live for the attaining of the as-yet-unattained, the reaching of the as-yet-unreached, the realization of the as-yet-unrealized.

Furthermore, the monk reminds himself of this: At present the Sangha — in harmony, on friendly terms, without quarreling — lives in comfort with a single recitation. The time will come, though, when the Sangha splits. When the Sangha is split, it is not easy to pay attention to the Buddha's teachings. It is not easy to reside in isolated forest or wilderness dwellings. Before this unwelcome, disagreeable, displeasing thing happens, let me first make an effort for the attaining of the as-yet-unattained, the reaching of the as-yet-unreached, the realization of the as-yet-unrealized, so that — endowed with that Dhamma — I will live in peace even when the Sangha is split.

This is the fifth future danger that is just enough, when considered, for a monk — heedful, ardent, and resolute — to live for the attaining of the as-yet-unattained, the reaching of the as-yet-unreached, the realization of the as-yet-unrealized.

These are the five future dangers that are just enough, when considered, for a monk — heedful, ardent, and resolute— to live for the attaining of the as-yet-unattained, the reaching of the as-yet-unreached, the realization of the as-yet-unrealized.— AN 5.78

FUTURE DANGERS: III

Monks, these five future dangers, unarisen at present, will arise in the future. Be alert to them and, being alert, work to get rid of them. Which five?

There will be, in the course of the future, monks undeveloped in bodily conduct, undeveloped in virtue, undeveloped in mind, undeveloped in discernment. They — being undeveloped in bodily conduct, undeveloped in virtue, undeveloped in mind, undeveloped in discernment — will give full ordination to others and will not be able to discipline them in heightened virtue, heightened mind, heightened discernment. These too will then be undeveloped in bodily conduct... virtue... mind... discernment. They — being undeveloped in bodily conduct... virtue... mind... discernment — will give full ordination to still others and will not be able to discipline them in heightened virtue, heightened mind, heightened discernment. These too will then be undeveloped in bodily conduct... virtue... mind... discernment. Thus from corrupt Dhamma comes corrupt discipline; from corrupt discipline, corrupt Dhamma.

This, monks, is the first future danger, unarisen at present, that will arise in the future. Be alert to it and, being alert, work to get rid of it.

And again, there will be in the course of the future monks undeveloped in bodily conduct, undeveloped in virtue, undeveloped in mind, undeveloped in discernment. They — being undeveloped in bodily conduct, undeveloped in virtue, undeveloped in mind, undeveloped in discernment — will take on others as students and will not be able to discipline them in heightened virtue, heightened mind, heightened discernment. These too will then be undeveloped in bodily conduct... virtue... mind... discernment. They — being undeveloped in bodily conduct... virtue... mind... discernment — will take on still others as students and will not be able to discipline them in heightened virtue, heightened mind, heightened discernment. These too will then be undeveloped in bodily conduct... virtue... mind... discernment. Thus from corrupt Dhamma comes corrupt discipline; from corrupt discipline, corrupt Dhamma.

This, monks, is the second future danger, unarisen at present, that will arise in the future. Be alert to it and, being alert, work to get rid of it.

And again, there will be in the course of the future monks undeveloped in bodily conduct... virtue... mind... discernment. They — being undeveloped in bodily conduct... virtue... mind... discernment — when giving a talk on higher Dhamma or a talk composed of questions and answers, will fall into dark mental states without being aware of it. Thus from corrupt Dhamma comes corrupt discipline; from corrupt discipline, corrupt Dhamma.

This, monks, is the third future danger, unarisen at present, that will arise in the future. Be alert to it and, being alert, work to get rid of it.

And again, there will be in the course of the future monks undeveloped in bodily conduct... virtue... mind... discernment. They — being undeveloped in bodily conduct... virtue... mind... discernment — will not listen when discourses that are words of the Tathagata — deep, profound, transcendent, connected with the Void — are being recited. They will not lend ear, will not set their hearts on knowing them, will not regard these teachings as worth grasping or mastering. But they will listen when discourses that are literary works — the works of poets, elegant in sound, elegant in rhetoric, the work of outsiders, words of disciples — are recited. They will lend ear and set their hearts on knowing them. They will regard these teachings as worth grasping and mastering. Thus from corrupt Dhamma comes corrupt discipline; from corrupt discipline, corrupt Dhamma.

This, monks, is the fourth future danger, unarisen at present, that will arise in the future. Be alert to it and, being alert, work to get rid of it.

And again, there will be in the course of the future monks undeveloped in bodily conduct... virtue... mind... discernment. They — being undeveloped in bodily conduct... virtue... mind... discernment — will become elders living in luxury, lethargic, foremost in falling back, shirking the duties of solitude. They will not make an effort for the attaining of the as-yet-unattained, the reaching of the as-yet-unreached, the realization of the as-yet-unrealized. They will become an example for later generations, who will become luxurious in their living, lethargic, foremost in falling back, shirking the duties of solitude, and who will not make an effort for the attaining of the as-yet-unattained, the reaching of the as-yet-unreached, the realization of the as-yet-unrealized. Thus from corrupt Dhamma comes corrupt discipline; from corrupt discipline, corrupt Dhamma.

This, monks, is the fifth future danger, unarisen at present, that will arise in the future. Be alert to it and, being alert, work to get rid of it.

These, monks, are the five future dangers, unarisen at present, that will arise in the future. Be alert to them and, being alert, work to get rid of them. — AN 5.79

FUTURE DANGERS: IV

Monks, these five future dangers, unarisen at present, will arise in the future. Be alert to them and, being alert, work to get rid of them. Which five?

There will be, in the course of the future, monks desirous of fine robes. They, desirous of fine robes, will neglect the practice of wearing cast-off cloth; will neglect isolated forest and wilderness dwellings; will move to towns, cities, and royal capitals, taking up residence there. For the sake of a robe they will do many kinds of unseemly, inappropriate things.

This, monks, is the first future danger, unarisen at present, that will arise in the future. Be alert to it and, being alert, work to get rid of it.

Furthermore, in the course of the future there will be monks desirous of fine food. They, desirous of fine food, will neglect the practice of going for alms; will neglect isolated forest and wilderness dwellings; will move to towns, cities, and royal capitals, taking up residence there and searching out the tip-top tastes with the tip of the tongue. For the sake of food they will do many kinds of unseemly, inappropriate things.

This, monks, is the second future danger, unarisen at present, that will arise in the future. Be alert to it and, being alert, work to get rid of it. Furthermore, in the course of the future there will be monks desirous of fine lodgings. They, desirous of fine lodgings, will neglect the practice of living in the wilds; will neglect isolated forest and wilderness dwellings; will move to towns, cities, and royal capitals, taking up residence there. For the sake of lodgings they will do many kinds of unseemly, inappropriate things.

This, monks, is the third future danger, unarisen at present, that will arise in the future. Be alert to it and, being alert, work to get rid of it.

Furthermore, in the course of the future there will be monks who will live in close association with nuns, female probationers, and female novices. As they interact with nuns, female probationers, and female novices, they can be expected either to lead the holy life dissatisfied or to fall into one of the grosser offenses, leaving the training, returning to a lower way of life.

This, monks, is the fourth future danger, unarisen at present, that will arise in the future. Be alert to it and, being alert, work to get rid of it.

Furthermore, in the course of the future there will be monks who will live in close association with monastery attendants and novices. As they interact with monastery attendants and novices, they can be expected to live intent on storing up all kinds of possessions and to stake out crops and fields. This is the fifth future danger...

This, monks, is the fifth future danger, unarisen at present, that will arise in the future. Be alert to it and, being alert, work to get rid of it.

These, monks, are the five future dangers, unarisen at present, that will arise in the future. Be alert to them and, being alert, work to get rid of them. — AN 5.80

The Sage

Danger is born from intimacy,

society gives birth to dust.

Free from intimacy,

free from society:
such is the vision of the sage.
Who, destroying what's born
wouldn't plant again
or nourish what will arise:
They call him the wandering, singular sage.
He has seen the state of peace.
Considering the ground,
crushing the seed,
he wouldn't nourish the sap
— truly a sage —
seer of the ending of birth,
abandoning conjecture,
he cannot be classified.
Knowing all dwellings,
not longing for any one anywhere
— truly a sage —
with no coveting, without greed,
he does not build,
for he has gone beyond.
Overcoming all
knowing all,
wise.
With regard to all things:
unsmeared. Abandoning all,
in the ending of craving,
released:
The enlightened call him a sage.

Strong in discernment,
virtuous in his practices,
centered,
delighting in jhana,
mindful,
freed from attachments,
no constraints :: no fermentations:
The enlightened call him a sage.
The wandering solitary sage,
uncomplacent, unshaken by praise or blame.
Unstartled, like a lion at sounds.
Unsnared, like the wind in a net.
Unsmeared, like a lotus in water.
Leader of others, by others unled:
The enlightened call him a sage.
Like the pillar at a bathing ford,
when others speak in extremes.
He, without passion,
his senses well-centered:
The enlightened call him a sage.
Truly poised, straight as a shuttle,
he loathes evil actions.
Pondering what is on-pitch and off:
The enlightened call him a sage.
Self-restrained, he does no evil.
Young and middle-aged,
the sage self-controlled,
never angered, he angers none:
The enlightened call him a sage.

From the best
the middling
the leftovers
he receives alms.
Sustaining himself on what others give,
neither flattering
nor speaking disparagement:
The enlightened call him a sage.
The wandering sage
abstaining from sex,
in youth bound by no one,
abstaining from intoxication
complacency
totally apart:
The enlightened call him a sage.
Knowing the world,
seeing the highest goal,
crossing the ocean, the flood,
— Such —
his chains broken,
unattached
without fermentation:
The enlightened call him a sage.
These two are different,
they dwell far apart:
the householder supporting a wife
and the unselfish one, of good practices.
Slaying other beings, the householder
is unrestrained.

Constantly the sage protects other beings,
is controlled.
As the crested,
blue-necked peacock,
when flying,
never matches
the wild goose
in speed:
Even so the householder
never keeps up with the monk,
the sage secluded,
doing jhana
in the forest. — *Sn.I.12*

SAGACITY

Monks, there are these three forms of sagacity. Which three? Bodily sagacity, verbal sagacity, and mental sagacity.

And what is bodily sagacity? There is the case where a monk abstains from taking life, abstains from theft, abstains from unchastity. This is called bodily sagacity.

And what is verbal sagacity? There is the case where a monk abstains from lying, abstains from divisive tale-bearing, abstains from harsh language, abstains from idle chatter. This is called verbal sagacity.

And what is mental sagacity? There is the case where a monk who — with the wasting away of the mental fermentations— remains in the fermentation-free awareness-release and discernment-release, having known and made them manifest for himself right in the here and now. This is called mental sagacity.

These, monks, are the three forms of sagacity.

A sage in body, a sage in speech,
A sage in mind, without fermentation:

a sage consummate in sagacity
is said to have abandoned
everything. — the All. — AN 3.123

Sariputta's (Upatissa's) Question

Now at that time the wanderer Sanjaya was residing in Rajagaha with a large company of wanderers — 250 in all. And at that time Sariputta and Moggallana were practicing the holy life under Sanjaya. They had made this agreement: Whoever attains the Deathless first will inform the other.

Then Ven. Assaji, arising early in the morning, taking his robe and bowl, entered Rajagaha for alms: Gracious in the way he approached and departed, looked forward and behind, drew in and stretched out his arm; his eyes downcast, his every movement consummate. Sariputta the wanderer saw Ven. Assaji going for alms in Rajagaha: gracious... his eyes downcast, his every movement consummate. On seeing him, the thought occurred to him: "Surely, of those in this world who are arahants or have entered the path to arahantship, this is one. What if I were to approach him and question him: 'On whose account have you gone forth? Who is your teacher? In whose Dhamma do you delight?'"

But then the thought occurred to Sariputta the wanderer: "This is the wrong time to question him. He is going for alms in the town. What if I were to follow behind this monk who has found the path for those who seek it?"

Then Ven. Assaji, having gone for alms in Rajagaha, left, taking the alms he had received. Sariputta the wanderer approached him and, on arrival, having exchanged friendly greetings and engaged in polite conversation, stood to one side. As he stood there he said, "Your faculties are bright, my friend, your complexion pure and clear. On whose account have you gone forth? Who is your teacher? In whose Dhamma do you delight?"

"There is, my friend, the Great Contemplative, a son of the Sakyans, gone forth from a Sakyan family. I have gone forth on account of that Blessed One. That Blessed One is my teacher.

It is in that Blessed One's Dhamma that I delight." "But what is your teacher's teaching? What does he proclaim?"

"I am new, my friend, not long gone forth, only recently come to this doctrine and discipline. I cannot explain the doctrine in detail, but I can give you the gist in brief."

Then Sariputta the wanderer spoke thus to the Ven. Assaji:

Speak a little or a lot,

but tell me just the gist.

The gist is what I want.

What use is a lot of rhetoric?

Then Ven. Assaji gave this Dhamma exposition to Sariputta the Wanderer:

Whatever phenomena arise from cause:

their cause

and their cessation.

Such is the teaching of the Tathagata,

the Great Contemplative.

Then to Sariputta the Wanderer, as he heard this Dhamma exposition, there arose the dustless, stainless Dhamma eye: Whatever is subject to origination is all subject to cessation.

Even if just this is the Dhamma,

you have penetrated

to the Sorrowless (asoka) State

unseen, overlooked (by us)

for many myriads of aeons.

Then Sariputta the wanderer went to where Moggallana the wanderer was staying. Moggallana the wanderer saw him coming from afar and, on seeing him, said, "Your faculties are bright, my friend; your complexion pure and clear. Could it be that you have attained the Deathless?"

"Yes, my friend, I have attained the Deathless. "

"But how, friend, did you attain the Deathless?"

"Just now, friend, I saw Ven. Assaji going for alms in Rajagaha: gracious in the way he approached and departed, looked forward and behind, drew in and stretched out his arm; his eyes downcast, his every movement consummate. On seeing him, the thought occurred to me: 'Surely, of those in this world who are arahants or have entered the path to arahantship, this is one. What if I were to approach him and question him: "On whose account have you gone forth? Who is your teacher? In whose Dhamma do you delight?"'

"But then the thought occurred to me: 'This is the wrong time to question him. He is going for alms in the town. What if I were to follow behind this monk who has found the path for those who seek it?'

"Then Ven. Assaji, having gone for alms in Rajagaha, left, taking the alms he had received. I approached him and, on arrival, having exchanged friendly greetings and engaged in polite conversation, stood to one side. As I stood there, I said, 'Your faculties are bright, my friend, your complexion pure and clear. On whose account have you gone forth? Who is your teacher? In whose Dhamma do you delight?'

"'There is, my friend, the Great Contemplative, a son of the Sakyans, gone forth from a Sakyan family. I have gone forth on account of that Blessed One. That Blessed One is my teacher. It is in that Blessed One's Dhamma that I delight.'

"'But what is your teacher's teaching? What does he proclaim?'

"'I am new, my friend, not long gone forth, only recently come to this doctrine and discipline. I cannot explain the doctrine to you in detail, but I can give you the gist in brief.'

"'Speak a little or a lot,

but tell me just the gist.

The gist is what I want.

What use is a lot of rhetoric?'

"Then Ven. Assaji gave me this Dhamma exposition:

"'Whatever phenomena arise from cause:

their cause

and their cessation.

Such is the teaching of the Tathagata,

the Great Contemplative.'"

Then to Moggallana the wanderer, as he heard this Dhamma exposition, there arose the dustless, stainless Dhamma eye: Whatever is subject to origination is all subject to cessation.

Even if just this is the Dhamma,

you have penetrated

to the Sorrowless (asoka) State

unseen, overlooked (by us)

for many myriads of aeons. — *Mv.I.23.5*

INSTRUCTIONS TO RAHULA

I have heard that on one occasion the Blessed One was staying at Rajagaha, at the Bamboo Grove, the Squirrels' Feeding Ground.

At that time Ven. Rahula was staying at the Mango Stone. Then the Blessed One, arising from his seclusion in the late afternoon, went to where Ven. Rahula was staying at the Mango Stone. Ven. Rahula saw him coming from afar and, on seeing him, set out a seat and water for washing the feet. The Blessed One sat down on the seat set out and, having sat down, washed his feet. Ven. Rahula, bowing down to the Blessed One, sat to one side.

Then the Blessed One, having left a little bit of water in the water dipper, said to Ven. Rahula, "Rahula, do you see this little bit of left-over water remaining in the water dipper?"

"Yes sir."

"That's how little of a contemplative there is in anyone who feels no shame at telling a deliberate lie."

Having tossed away the little bit of left-over water, the Blessed One said to Ven. Rahula, "Rahula, do you see how this little bit of left-over water is tossed away?"

"Yes, sir."

"Whatever there is of a contemplative in anyone who feels no shame at telling a deliberate lie is tossed away just like that.

Having turned the water dipper upside down, the Blessed One said to Ven. Rahula, "Rahula, do you see how this water dipper is turned upside down?"

"Yes, sir."

"Whatever there is of a contemplative in anyone who feels no shame at telling a deliberate lie is turned upside down just like that."

Having turned the water dipper right-side up, the Blessed One said to Ven. Rahula, "Rahula, do you see how empty and hollow this water dipper is?"

"Yes, sir."

"Whatever there is of a contemplative in anyone who feels no shame at telling a deliberate lie is empty and hollow just like that.

"Rahula, it's like a royal elephant: immense, pedigreed, accustomed to battles, its tusks like chariot poles. Having gone into battle, it uses its forefeet and hind feet, its forequarters and hindquarters, its head and ears and tusks and tail, but will simply hold back its trunk. The elephant trainer notices that and thinks, 'This royal elephant has not given up its life to the king.' But when the royal elephant... having gone into battle, uses its forefeet and hind feet, its forequarters and hindquarters, its head and ears and tusks and tail and his trunk, the trainer notices that and thinks, 'This royal elephant has given up its life to the king. There is nothing it will not do.'

"The same holds true with anyone who feels no shame in telling a deliberate lie: There is no evil, I tell you, he will not do. Thus, Rahula, you should train yourself, 'I will not tell a deliberate lie even in jest.'

"What do you think, Rahula: What is a mirror for?"

"For reflection, sir."

"In the same way, Rahula, bodily acts, verbal acts, and mental acts are to be done with repeated reflection. "Whenever you want to perform a bodily act, you should reflect on it: 'This bodily act I want to perform — would it lead to self-affliction, to the affliction of others, or to both? Is it an unskillful bodily act, with painful consequences, painful results?' If, on reflection, you know that it would lead to self-affliction, to the affliction of others, or to both; it would be an unskillful bodily act with painful consequences, painful results, then any bodily act of that sort is absolutely unfit for you to do. But if on reflection you know that it would not cause affliction... it would be a skillful bodily action with happy consequences, happy results, then any bodily act of that sort is fit for you to do.

"While you are performing a bodily act, you should reflect on it: 'This bodily act I am doing — is it leading to self-affliction, to the affliction of others, or to both? Is it an unskillful bodily act, with painful consequences, painful results?' If, on reflection, you know that it is leading to self-affliction, to affliction of others, or both... you should give it up. But if on reflection you know that it is not... you may continue with it.

"Having performed a bodily act, you should reflect on it... If, on reflection, you know that it led to self-affliction, to the affliction of others, or to both; it was an unskillful bodily act with painful consequences, painful results, then you should confess it, reveal it, lay it open to the Teacher or to a knowledgeable companion in the holy life. Having confessed it... you should exercise restraint in the future. But if on reflection you know that it did not lead to affliction... it was a skillful bodily action with happy consequences, happy results, then you should stay mentally refreshed and joyful, training day and night in skillful mental qualities.

"Whenever you want to perform a verbal act, you should reflect on it: 'This verbal act I want to perform — would it lead to self-affliction, to the affliction of others, or to both? Is it an unskillful verbal act, with painful consequences, painful results?' If, on reflection, you know that it would lead to self-affliction, to the affliction of others, or to both; it would be an unskillful verbal act with painful consequences, painful results, then any verbal act of that sort is absolutely unfit for you to do. But if on reflection you know that it would not cause affliction... it would be a skillful verbal action with happy consequences, happy results, then any verbal act of that sort is fit for you to do.

"While you are performing a verbal act, you should reflect on it: 'This verbal act I am doing — is it leading to self-affliction, to the affliction of others, or to both? Is it an unskillful verbal act, with painful consequences, painful results?' If, on reflection, you know that it is leading to self-affliction, to the affliction of others, or to both... you should give it up. But if on reflection you know that it is not... you may continue with it.

"Having performed a verbal act, you should reflect on it... If, on reflection, you know that it led to self-affliction, to the affliction of others, or to both; it was an unskillful verbal act with painful consequences, painful results, then you should confess it, reveal it, lay it open to the Teacher or to a knowledgeable companion in the holy life. Having confessed it... you should exercise restraint in the future. But if on reflection you know that it did not lead to affliction... it was a skillful verbal action with happy consequences, happy results, then you should stay mentally refreshed and joyful, training day and night in skillful mental qualities.

"Whenever you want to perform a mental act, you should reflect on it: 'This mental act I want to perform — would it lead to self-affliction, to the affliction of others, or to both? Is it an unskillful mental act, with painful consequences, painful results?' If, on reflection, you know that it would lead to self-affliction, to the affliction of others, or to both; it would be an unskillful mental act with painful consequences, painful results, then any mental act of that sort is absolutely unfit for you to do. But if on reflection you know that it would not cause affliction... it would be a skillful mental action with happy consequences, happy results, then any mental act of that sort is fit for you to do.

"While you are performing a mental act, you should reflect on it: 'This mental act I am doing — is it leading to self-affliction, to the affliction of others, or to both? Is it an unskillful mental act, with painful consequences, painful results?' If, on reflection, you know that it is leading to self-affliction, to the affliction of others, or to both... you should give it up. But if on reflection you know that it is not... you may continue with it.

"Having performed a mental act, you should reflect on it... If, on reflection, you know that it led to self-affliction, to the affliction of others, or to both; it was an unskillful mental act with painful consequences, painful results, then you should feel distressed, ashamed, and disgusted with it. Feeling distressed... you should exercise restraint in the future. But if on reflection you know that it did not lead to affliction... it was a skillful mental action with happy consequences, happy results, then you should stay mentally refreshed and joyful, training day and night in skillful mental qualities.

"Rahula, all those priests and contemplatives in the course of the past who purified their bodily acts, verbal acts, and mental acts, did it through repeated reflection on their bodily acts, verbal acts, and mental acts in just this way.

"All those priests and contemplatives in the course of the future who will purify their bodily acts, verbal acts, and mental acts, will do it through repeated reflection on their bodily acts, verbal acts, and mental acts in just this way.

"All those priests and contemplatives at present who purify their bodily acts, verbal acts, and mental acts, do it through repeated reflection on their bodily acts, verbal acts, and mental acts in just this way.

"Therefore, Rahula, you should train yourself: 'I will purify my bodily acts through repeated reflection. I will purify my verbal acts through repeated reflection. I will purify my mental acts through repeated reflection.' That is how you should train yourself."

That is what the Blessed One said. Gratified, Ven. Rahula delighted in the Blessed One's words. — MN 61

Whether King Asoka selected these texts on his own or had the advice of his mentor, Ven. Moggaliputta-tissa, no one knows. Still it is possible to derive from them a conception of Dhamma of which Asoka approved, whether or not it originated with him. One of the main points of this selection is that Dhamma is a quality of a person, rather than of doctrines or ideas. The central passage in the selection, and its only extended poem—The Sage — paints an idealized picture of the Dhamma as embodied in the deeds, words, and attitudes of the person who practices it. Only if the Dhamma finds concrete expression in people's lives will it last.

The selection also shows something of the educational strategy Asoka might have had his Dhamma officials use in teaching his populace — Buddhist and non-Buddhist — to make the Dhamma a reality in their lives. The texts are not listed in random order. Instead, they follow a pattern to impress on their listeners first that the ideals of the Dhamma are timeless and well-tested, and that there is a need to realize them as quickly as possible. Then they analyze the ideal, present a picture of it in action, and end with the basic principles for putting it into practice.

The title of the first passage — the Vinaya samukase — is explained in the Commentary as follows: "Samukase" means that the principles are innately true, established of their own accord. Whether or not a Buddha arises to point them out, they are true in and of themselves.

The second passage, The Traditions of the Noble Ones, brings in the perspective of time that is to provide a recurring theme throughout Asoka's selections. It looks back to the past to show how venerable, time-tested, and pure the traditions of the Dhamma are.

It plays on the notion of the traditions of a noble family — unadulterated, not open to criticism or suspicion — that were so important in ancient India. It even plays on words: The traditions of a family were supposed to enable those who followed them to conquer their enemies (ari), while the noble traditions taught by the Buddha enable one to overcome one's true enemy, displeasure (arati) in the mind.

Turning from the past to look at the future, the third set of selections — the four discourses on future dangers — presents a warning. The practice of the Dhamma should not be put off to a later date, because there is no certainty that the future will provide any opportunities for practice. First, there are the dangers of death, aging, illness, famine, and social turmoil in one's own life. Secondly, there are the dangers of degeneracy in the religion, when those who are supposed to practice it ignore the noble traditions and teachings, and instead do many unseemly, inappropriate things simply for the sake of material comfort. The point of this set of passages, of course, is to give a sense of urgency to one's practice, so that one will make the effort to take advantage of the teachings while one can.

The Sage, taking up the theme of danger, goes on to present an ideal of inner safety in the present tense, an ideal already embodied in the lives of those who have practiced the religion in full. It shows the actions and attitudes of one who finds his happiness not in relationships — and the home-building and food-raising they entail (all of which in Buddhism are viewed as symbolic of the round of death and rebirth) — but instead in the peace that comes in living a solitary life, subsisting on whatever food one may receive as alms, free to meditate in the wilderness.

The next passage — Sagacity — analyzes this ideal into three qualities of body, speech, and mind; and the sixth passage shows the ideal in action: Ven. Assaji, simply by the graciousness of his manner, inspires Sariputta the wanderer to follow him; and with a few well-chosen words, he enables Sariputta to gain a glimpse of the Deathless. This is thus no empty ideal.

This passage also contains what has long been recognized as the most succinct expression of the Four Noble Truths — suffering, its cause, its cessation, and the path to its cessation — just as the discourse on Sagacity contains one of the most succinct expressions of the goal of training one's actions in body, speech, and mind.

The final passage shows how this goal may be brought about, focusing on the development of two qualities — truthfulness and constant reflection — that underlie every stage of the practice. Although the earlier passages focus on the monk as the ideal, this one shows that the practice builds on qualities that anyone — lay or monastic; man, woman, or child — can develop within. It also ends with a return to the theme of time, and the timelessness of the Dhamma: Whoever in the past, future or present develops purity — or sagacity —

in thought, word or deed, will have to do it in this way, and this way only. There is no other.

It is possible to search in Asoka's selection for passages that may have had personal meaning for him — the reference to the Deathless as the Sorrowless (asoka) state; the image of the peacock, the emblem of his dynasty; the image of the elephant who has given its life up to the king — but he himself would probably have preferred that Buddhists reflect on these selections to see what passages have meaning for them. The fact that the Dhamma is alive today is due in no small measure to his efforts. Buddhists today can carry on his work by doing as he asked: Reading and reflecting often on these selections and consistently applying the principles of truthfulness and self-examination to their own lives.

3

BUDDHISM IN SRI LANKA

A SHORT HISTORY

State of Sri Lanka before the Introduction of Buddhism

Buddhism was introduced to Sri Lanka in 236 b.e. (cir. 250 BCE) and became the national religion of the Sinhalese from that date. It is, however, necessary for a proper study of the history of Buddhism in the island to consider the state of the island and its social and political developments and the culture and character of the people immediately preceding this period. This will enable us to get a clear understanding of the manner in which such a far-reaching revolution in the beliefs, manners, customs and character of a people was effected by the introduction of this new religion and the progress in literature, art and culture that has been manifested through its influence.

Early Traditions

According to the early chronicles relating the historical traditions of Sri Lanka, a prince named Vijaya and his followers who came from India and landed in Lanka on the day of the Parinibbaana of the Buddha were the first human inhabitants of this island. When they came the island was occupied by "yakkhas" (sprites, demons). "Yakkhas" and "naagas" are also said to have inhabited Lanka in the time of the Buddha. A legend relating the existence of a great civilization before this time, under a king named Raavana, is also current though the early chronicles make no mention of it.

The Vijaya legend of these chronicles is taken by modern historians as a poetic expression of the actual aryanization of

Sri Lanka in about the sixth century BCE The term "yakkhas and naagas" may refer to the aborigines who occupied the island before their arrival. No traces of an advanced civilization, however, have yet been discovered to support the Raavana legend. Archaeologists have discovered chert and quartz implements and tools at various sites, believed to have been used by aborigines of Sri Lanka, and they indicate that these people were a primitive tribe who lived by hunting. These aborigines have not left traces of a strong political organization. or an advanced culture. The present Veddas are believed to be their descendants.

Colonization by Prince Vijaya and his Followers

Vijaya and his 700 followers are described in the Lankan chronicles as a set of adventurous young men who, when they were banished from their Indian homeland Laala (or Laata), came in search of new land for settlement. Other legends, some of which are even older, relating how the first aryan inhabitants came to settle down in Lanka are found in several Pali and Sanskrit works. Most of them show that the settlement of early aryan settlers is due to the enterprise of the pioneering merchant mariners who came to this island for pearls and precious stones. Historians thus do not lay much reliance on the details of the Vijayan legend but they accept Vijaya as the first traditional ruler of the newcomers — the Sinhalese.

Vijaya, who was a Kshatriya, landed in Lanka, according to the chronicles, on the day of the Parinibbaana of the Buddha. He allied himself with an aboriginal princess named Kuveni and married her and with her influence soon became the master of the country. Later he drove Kuveni away and obtained a princess from Maduraa whom he made his queen. Maidens of high birth came from the Pandyan kingdom as wives of his followers.

Vijaya ruled from his settlement Tambappanni and his ministers founded other settlements like Anuraadhagaama, Upatissagaama, Ujjeni, Uruvelaa and Vijitapura. Thus the earliest settlements that were founded in the time of King Vijaya were located along the river banks in the northwestern region of Lanka like the Malvatu-oya and the Kalaa-oya.

Political Development and Social Organization after Vijaya

Vijaya died after a rule of 38 years. Since he had no son to succeed him, before his death he sent messengers to his brother Sumitta in Sihapura to come and rule here. Sumitta sent his youngest son Panduvaasudeva, since he himself was king of Sihapura and was also too old. Panduvaasudeva, Vijaya's nephew, arrived one year after Vijaya's death during which period the ministers of Vijaya ruled the country. When Panduvaasudeva came he brought with him 32 sons of ministers.

The early chronicles preserve an episode which connects the Sakka family of the Buddha with the sovereignty of Lanka from the time of King Panduvaasudeva. According to this account, Bhaddakaccaanaa, who also arrived in Lanka with 32 other maidens shortly after Panduvaasudeva arrived, was the daughter of Pandu Sakka, who himself was the son of Amitodana, an uncle of the Buddha.

Panduvaasudeva ruled for 30 years and was succeeded by his eldest son Abhaya, who ruled for 20 years. Abhaya's successor was Pandukaabhaya, the son of his sister Ummaadacitta. Pandukaabhaya was a great ruler in whose reign Anuraadhapura developed into a great city with well-marked boundaries. After a long reign of 70 years, Pandukaabhaya was succeeded by his son Mutasiva who ruled for 60 years. Mutasiva's second son, Devaanampiya Tissa, succeeded him in 250 BCE, that is, 236 years after the accession of Vijaya.

These 236 years could be reckoned as a separate period in the history of Sri Lanka for it formed the background for the offical introduction of Buddhism, which occurred during the opening years of the next ruler, King Devaanampiya Tissa. During this period the aryan colonists founded settlements along the fertile river banks almost throughout the island. They chose the river banks because they were mainly agriculturists. Thus the regions watered by the Malvatu-oya, Kalaa-oya, Valave-ganga, Kirindi-oya, Menik-ganga and Kumbukkan-oya, the Kelani-ganga and some regions around the Mahaveli-ganga soon became populated. Anuraadhapura became a well-organized city with boundaries marked, lakes dug and hospitals and other buildings constructed. In the south, Mahaagaama (Maagama), became the center of activity. The majority of the aboriginal inhabitants were absorbed into the new community through intermarriage while a few withdrew to the Malayadesa, the highlands.

Pre-Buddhist Religion in Sri Lanka

It is evident from the chronicles relating the early history of Sri Lanka that before the introduction of Buddhism in the reign of King Devaanampiya Tissa (250-210 BCE) there was no single religion which was widely accepted as the national religion of the country. Nevertheless, there was a wide range of religious beliefs and practices, different from one another, and each individual seems to have freely observed his religion according to his belief.

A noteworthy feature of the pre-Buddhist religion of Sri Lanka is that it was a mixture of the aboriginal cults and the beliefs of the aryan newcomers.

The worship of yaksas and yaksinis was a widely prevalent aboriginal custom of pre-Buddhist Lanka. King Pandukaabhaya, the grandfather of Devaanampiya Tissa, provided shrines for many of these spirits and also gave them sacrificial offerings annually. Some of these yaksas and yaksinis mentioned by name are Kaalavela, Cittaraaja, Vessavana, Valavaamukhi and Cittaa. Vyaadhadeva, Kammaaradeva and Pacchimaraajini, though not known as yaksas and yaksinis, also belong to the same category of aboriginal spirits. Trees like the banyan and palmyrah were also connected with the cults of these spirits showing that tree-worship was also prevalent.

Many scholars agree that these yaksas and other non-human beings are none but the spirits of the dead relatives and tribal chiefs who, the people believed, were capable of helping friends and harming enemies. This belief, as is widely known, formed one of the main features of the primitive religion and is extant even today.

Accounts relating the pre-Buddhist history of Sri Lanka also show a considerable influence of the religious trends of India on the society of Lanka. Several niganthas (Jainas) such as Giri, Jotiya and Kumbhanda lived in the reign of Pandukaabhaya and hermitages were constructed for them and other ascetics like aajivakas, brahmans and the wandering mendicant monks. Five hundred families of heretical beliefs also lived near the city of Anuraadhapura. The brahmans occupied a high place in society and their religious beliefs were also respected. The worship of Siva too may have been prevalent.

The account in the *Mahaava.msa* of the settling of the adherents of various sects by King Pandukaabhaya does not specifically mention the presence of any adherents of Buddhism among them. But the work refers to three visits of the Buddha to Sri Lanka, a statement which, though not corroborated by other evidence, has not been disproved. Legendary accounts also claim that two stuupas — the Mahiyangana and the Girihandu — were constructed before the introduction of Buddhism. Among the newcomers too there could have been some members who were acquainted with Buddhism, especially as Bhaddakaccaanaa, who arrived with 32 other maidens in the guise of nuns, was a close relative of the Buddha.

Emperor Asoka and Buddhism in India

Buddhism as a form of religious expression gained ascendency in India during this period. Emperor Asoka was crowned, according to the chronicles, in the year 218 of the Buddhist era (i.e., 268 BCE). Like his father Bindusaara and grandfather Candragupta, Asoka was a follower of the brahmanical faith at the beginning of his reign. In the early years of his reign he followed an expansionist policy and in the eighth year of his coronation he conquered Kaalinga, in the course of which 100,000 were slain and 150,000 taken prisoners. But the carnage of the Kaalinga war caused him much grief and the king was attracted towards the humanistic teachings of Buddhism. According to the Sri Lanka chronicles, it was a young novice named Nigrodha who converted Asoka.

After the conversion of this great emperor Buddhism flourished under his patronage. He inculcated the teachings of the Buddha and set up edicts of morality at numerous places of his vast empire so that his subjects would adhere to them and his successors might follow him. He himself followed those morals and set an example to the others. The king is reputed to have built 84,000 stupas. The monks were lavishly provided with their requisites.

The king even permitted his son Mahinda and daughter Sanghamittaa to join the Order when they were twenty and eighteen years of age respectively. These two illustrious disciples became noted for their piety, attainments, learning and profound knowledge of the Dhamma.

Vast numbers joined the Order in the reign of Asoka solely to share the benefits showered on it by the king, and such people were not only lax in their conduct, but also held doctrines counter to the teachings of the Buddha.

It was this dissenting element that led to the holding of the Third Buddhist Council under the patronage of King Asoka in order to purify the Buddhist religion (Saasana). It was at this Council held by a thousand theras (elders) under the leadership of Moggaliputta Tissa, at Paataliputta, that the Pali Canon of the Theravaada, as it exists today, was finally redacted.

At this Council was also taken the important, decision of sending missionaries to different regions to preach Buddhism and establish the Saasana there. Thus the thera Moggaliputta Tissa deputed Majjhantika Thera to Kaasmira-Gandhaara, Mahaadeva Thera to Mahisamandala, Rakkhita Thera to Vanavaasi, Yona-Dhammarakkhita Thera to Aparaantaka, Dhammarakkhita Thera to Mahaarattha, Mahaarakkhita Thera to Yonaloka, Majjhima Thera to Himavanta, theras So.na and Uttara to Suvannabhuumi, and Mahinda Thera with theras Itthiya, Uttiya, Sambala and Bhaddasaala to Lanka, saying unto the five theras: "Establish ye in the delightful land of Lanka the delightful religion of the Vanquisher."

The Mission to Sri Lanka

Mahinda was thirty-two years old when he undertook the mission to Sri Lanka. He had adopted the religious life at the age of twenty, mastered the doctrines and attained the highest spiritual life, i.e., arahantship. Pondering on the fitting time to come to Lanka, he perceived that Mutasiva, the ruler at that time, was in his old age, and hence it was advisable to tarry until his son became ruler. In the meantime Mahinda visited his relatives at Dakkhinaagiri and his mother at Vedisagiri along with his companions. His mother Devi, whom Asoka had married while he was yet a prince, was living at Vedisagiri at that time. Having stayed for six months at Dakkhinaagiri and a month at Vedisagiri, Mahinda perceived that the right time had come, for the old ruler was dead and his son Devaanampiya Tissa had become king.

Devaanampiya Tissa was the second son of Mutasiva. He was a friend of Asoka even before he became king but the two had not seen each other. The first thing that Devaanampiya Tissa did when he became king was to send envoys to Asoka, bearing costly presents. The envoys, when they returned, brought among other things the following message from Asoka:

"Aha.m Buddhañ ca Dhammañ ca Sanghañ ca sara.na.mgato upaasakatta.m vedesi.m Saakyaputtassa saasane tvamp'imaani ratanaani uttamaani naruttama citta.m pasaadayitvaana saddhaaya sara.na.m bhaja."

"I have taken refuge in the Buddha, his Doctrine and his Order, I have declared myself a lay-disciple in the religion of the Saakya son; seek then, O best of men, refuge in these best of gems, converting your mind with believing heart."

This message of Asoka was conveyed to King Devaanampiya Tissa in the month of Vesakha and it was the full-moon day of the following month Jettha (Sinh. Poson) that Mahinda fixed for his arrival in Sri Lanka. Among the companions of Mahinda were the theras Itthiya, Uttiya, Sambala and Bhaddasaala, the saamanera Sumana who was the son of Sanghamittaa, and the lay-disciple Bhanduka who was the son of a daughter of Devi's sister and had become an anaagaami (once-returner) on hearing a sermon of Mahinda preached to Devi.

Arrival of Mahinda

Thus on the full-moon day of the month of Jettha in the year 236 b.e. (i.e., 250 BCE) Mahinda and his companions, departing from Vedisagiri, rose up in the air and alighted on the Silakuuta of the pleasant Missaka hill, presently Mihintale, eight miles east of Anuraadhapura. The thera alighted here for he had perceived that he would meet the king there on that day.

The first meeting of the king of Lanka and the thera Mahinda is graphically described in the chronicles of Sri Lanka. The full-moon day of Jettha was a day of national festival in Lanka. Men and women were engaged in amusing themselves. The king with a large party of followers went to Mihintale hills on a hunting expedition.

There he saw the theras with shaven heads dressed in yellow robes, of dignified mien and distinguished appearance, who faced him and addressed him not as ordinary men addressing a king but as those to whom a king was their inferior. The conversation impressed the king and his immediate surrender to the wisdom and piety displayed by the thera was complete. Mahinda Thera in reply to the king's inquiry as to who they were and whence they had come, said:

"Sama.naa maya.m Mahaaraaja Dhammaraajassa saavakaa tav'eva anukampaaya Jambudiipaa idhaagataa."

"We are the disciples of the Lord of the Dhamma. In compassion towards you, Mahaaraaja, We have come here from India."

When he heard these words of the thera, the king laid aside his bow and arrow, and approaching the thera, exchanged greetings with him and sat down near him. Mahinda then had a conversation with the king, and realizing that the king was intelligent enough to comprehend the Dhamma, preached the Cuulahatthipadopama Sutta.

At the end of the discourse the king and his retinue of forty thousand people embraced the new faith. Having invited the missionaries to the city the king left for his palace. Mahinda spent his first day in Sri Lanka at Mihintale where he solemnized the first ecclesiastical act by admitting to the Order the lay-follower Bhanduka who had accompanied him from India.

Entry into the Capital

On the invitation of the king, Mahinda and the other theras arrived at Anuraadhapura the following day. Going forward to meet the theras, the king respectfully led them into the palace where he himself served them with dainty food. After the meal Mahinda preached the Petavatthu, the Vimaanavatthu and the Sacca-sa.myutta to the royal household.

The people of the city who heard of the theras flocked near the palace-gate to see them and the king prepared a hall outside the palace so that the townspeople could see the theras. On this occasion Mahinda preached the Devaduuta Sutta (Majjhima Nikaaya, No. 130).

This hall too was not spacious enough for the vast gathering and seats were prepared for the theras in the Nandana-garden in the royal park, where Mahinda preached the Baalapandita Sutta, (Majjhima Nikaaya, No. 129).

In the evening the theras expressed their desire to go back to Mihintale. The king, who wished them to stay in his capital, granted to the Sangha the royal park Mahaamegha for their residence. The king himself marked the boundaries by plowing a furrow. Thus was established the Mahaavihaara which became the earliest celebrated center of the Buddhist religion. Having spent twenty-six days in the Mahaamegha Park, the thera returned to Mihintale for the rain-retreat (*vassa*). This was the beginning of the Cetiyagiri-vihaara, another great monastic institution of early Buddhist Sri Lanka.

Sanghamittaa and Women Disciples

Many women of Sri Lanka, headed by Queen Anulaa, desired to enter the Order of disciples and thus it came about that emissaries led by the king's nephew Arittha were sent to Emperor Asoka to obtain the help of female disciples to enable the women of Lanka to obtain ordination.

Sanghamittaa, the sister of Mahinda Thera, who had entered the Order and had received ordination, was sent out to Lanka at the request of the king and the people and on the recommendation of Mahinda Thera.

The message sent by thera Mahinda to Emperor Asoka pleased him very much, for in it he realized that the mission to Lanka had been eminently successful and the king and the people of Lanka had accepted the new doctrine with enthusiasm.

Arrival of the Sacred Bo-Tree

Emperor Asoka decided on sending a token of the Great and Enlightened One to the land of Lanka and prepared a branch of the Sacred Bodhi Tree under which the Lord attained enlightenment. He planted the branch in a golden vessel and, when it had taken root, conveyed it to the ship, depositing it in the ship. He also sent a large number of attendants to accompany the tree. The chronicles mention that these were selected from the brahmans, nobles and householders and consisted of 64 families. Sanghamittaa Therii and her attendants embarked on the same ship as well as the ambassadors and messengers who came from Lanka.

The ship sailed from Taamralipti (Tamluk) and arrived at the port in Lanka in seven days. The port was known as Jambukola and was situated in the north of the island. The king of Lanka on hearing of the arrival of the ship had the road from Jambukola to the capital city of Anuraadhapura gaily decorated. He arrived in state and himself took charge of the Sacred Bodhi Tree. This tree was planted in the Mahaamegha garden of Anuraadhapura with great festivities and tended with honor and care. Up to this date it flourishes as one of the most sacred objects of veneration and worship for millions of Buddhists.

The Firm Establishment of the Saasana

Arittha, the king's nephew who had obtained the king's permission to enter the Order of monks on his return from India, did so with five hundred other men and all became arahants. With the ordination of Anulaa and the other women both the Bhikkhu-saasana and the Bhikkhuni-saasana were established in the island. Separate residences for monks and nuns were built by the king.

The Thuupaaraama-cetiya enshrining the right collar-bone and other bodily relics of the Buddha was built, and the Sacred Bodhi Tree was planted for the devotion of the laity. When these acts of religious devotion were accomplished, the king asked Mahinda Thera whether the Saasana had been firmly established in the island, to which the latter replied that it had only been planted but would take firm root when a person born in Sri Lanka, of Sinhalese parents, studied the Vinaya in Sri Lanka and expounded it in Sri Lanka.

Arittha Thera had by this time become noted for his piety and his learning and on an appointed day, at a specially constructed preaching hall, in the presence of numerous theras, the king and the chiefs, Arittha Thera was invited to give a discourse on the Vinaya in the presence of the thera Mahaa Mahinda. And his exposition was so correct and pleasing that there was great rejoicing as the condition required for the firm establishment of the Saasana was fulfilled by him.

Progress of Buddhism in Lanka

Devaanampiya Tissa ruled in Sri Lanka for forty years. It was in the first year of his reign that Buddhism was introduced and from that time the king worked for the progress of the new faith with great zeal. Apart from the Mahaavihaara, the Cetiyapabbatavihaara, the Thuuparaama and the Sacred Bodhi Tree, he established numerous other monasteries and several Buddhist monuments. The chronicles mention that he built monasteries a yojana from one another. Among these monuments the Isurumuni-vihaara and the Vessagiri-vihaara are important centers of worship to this day. He is also credited with the construction of the Pathamaka-cetiya, the Jambukola-vihaara and the Hatthaalhaka-vihaara, and the refectory.

Thousands of men and women joined the Order during his reign. The king not only built vihaaras for their residence but also provided them with their requisites. It was not only in the capital city that Buddhism spread in his reign but even in distant regions like Jambukola in the north and Kaajaragaama and Candanagaama in the south.

The remarkable success of Mahinda's mission and the rapid spread of the religion in a very short time were mainly due to the efforts of Mahinda and the unbounded patronage of King Devaanampiya Tissa. Apart from them the people of Lanka too were eminently ripe at this period for receiving and adopting the teachings of the Buddha. The people in the land were prosperous, their wants were few, and these were supplied by the fertile soil. There was prosperous trade, for merchants came from all lands to barter goods; their art was well developed, for in the leisure people enjoyed they were able to build cities and tanks, great and small, and to perform works both of utility and artistic value. Contentment reigned supreme. Where such conditions existed the people were ready to embrace new ideals that had the prospect of helping their culture and elating their thoughts and activities, and as such the new doctrine preached by Mahinda Thera fell on a fertile soil, where it soon rose to its full height. Hundreds of thousands of men and women rose to high spiritual attainments on hearing the new message and thus the Law of the Blessed One was firmly established.

The Passing Away of Mahinda and Sanghamittaa

Both Mahinda and Sanghamitta survived Devaanampiya Tissa. Mahinda lived to the age of 80 years and Sanghamittaa to the age of 79 years. They spent nearly 48 years in the island. The former died in the eighth year and the latter in the ninth of the reign of King Uttiya, brother and successor of Devaanampiya Tissa. Uttiya performed their funerals with great honor and built stuupas over their relics. The king himself died in the following year, 286 b.e., after a reign of ten years.

The hierarchy of the disciples was continued in pupilary succession. Arittha Thera succeeded Mahinda Thera; he was in turn succeeded by Isidatta, Kaalasumana, Diighanaama and Diighasumana.

Invasion of Tamils and Restoration of the Saasana by King Dutthagaamani

Twenty years after the death of Uttiya foreign usurpers from South India seized Anuraadhapura. Two of them, Sena and Guttika, reigned together for twenty-two years and another Tamil usurper, Elaara, reigned for forty-four years. The lack of interest of these Tamil rulers in the Buddhist faith and the vandalism of their supporters evidently retarded the progress of the religion. Furthermore, the Sinhalese rulers were not free to work for the religion during these periods of political unrest. Nevertheless, the people held strongly to their new religion and showed no signs of laxity.

It was a young prince from Maagama of the southeastern principality of Ruhuna who restored the lost glory of the Sinhalese and their religion. He was Abhaya, known to posterity by a nickname which means "disobedient," Dutthagaamani. He was a descendant of Mahaanaaga, who had established himself at Maagama when his older brother Devaanampiya Tissa was ruling at Anuraadhapura. Kaakavanna Tissa and Vihaaramahaadevi were his parents.

After a thorough preparation for war Dutthagaamani defeated and killed Elaara in battle and became the ruler of Anuraadhapura. Thus the sovereignty of the Sinhalese rulers of Anuraadhapura was once more established.

Dutthagaamani reigned for twenty-four years. The advancement of the Buddhist religion was his main concern. The Ruvanveli-saaya, the most celebrated stupa in Sri Lanka, was his greatest work. The magnificent edifice of nine storeys and nine hundred chambers, called the Lohapaasaada, "the Brazen Palace," was constructed by him for the use of the monks. Mirisaveti-daagaba was another of his works.

Dutthagaamani was not only a supporter of Buddhism but was also a zealous follower himself. Many episodes in the Pali commentaries depict him as a pious monarch. Under his patronage there flourished several learned monks during his reign.

Social and Cultural Development due to Buddhism

It is well to find out the social and cultural development of the Sinhalese during the two centuries following their acceptance of the Buddhist religion. We have many incidents and stories in the Sri Lanka chronicles from which a definite idea regarding these conditions can be inferred. For instance, the *Rasavaahinii*, a Pali work composed in the thirteenth century of the Christian era, contains over a hundred stories of the life of the people during this early period. According to these stories, among the Sinhalese there do not appear to have been any caste divisions. Brahmans are mentioned as living apart in their own villages, and they were more or less counted as foreign to the Sinhalese. The members of the royal families were held in a class by themselves, and those of such families who aspired to the kingdom had to marry a member of a royal family or at least from a Brahman family. The rest of the people were grihapatis (householders with settled abodes).

The Candaalas (despised) were those without a fixed abode; they were despised on account of being tramps and vagrants with no fixed residence. In some cases the word Candaala was used in a self-deprecatory manner in order to indicate unworthiness. There is the instance of Prince Saali, son of King Dutthagaamani, who fell in love with a village artisan's daughter, Devi (Asokamaalaa). In addressing the prince she said that she was a Candaali as she did not belong to a family into which a member of the royal family was allowed to marry. The two divisions of people merely appear to be those who had a fixed abode and those who had no fixed abode. There were at this time no special caste divisions for trades or occupations, for a householder or members of a family were, in general, expected to engage themselves in one of the three occupations, as traders, as artisans or as cultivators.

Prince Dighaabhaya, when appointed as governor of Kasaatota, required attendants and asked each chief family of a village to send one of its sons for service and sent a messenger to Sangha, the chief of the village. The chief called together his seven sons. The elder six asked him to send the youngest to the king's service as he was idling his time at home without engaging in any work. "We six are engaged in such occupations as trade, industries and cultivation and work hard at our occupations." Again, in another story, the father, a chief of a village, addressing his daughter regarding her husband, tells her that her husband is living in idleness, and like her brothers should engage himself in an occupation such as cultivation, industry and commerce. Thus it appears all trades were common, and the same family engaged in work as artisans, tradesmen and cultivators without distinction.

The religion of the Sinhalese during this period was purely and entirely Buddhist and the stories indicate much practical activity in religious affairs, both in endowment and maintenance of religious institutions and the practice of religious principles.

The Orders of bhikkhus and bhikkhunis flourished during this period; a very large number of men and women entered the religious Orders. Some of the vihaaras (monasteries) had thousands residing in them.

There were also large numbers who were practicing meditation in forests and rock caves. They were well supported by the laity. There were four classes of disciples: the novices (saamanera), bhikkhus (fully ordained), theras (elders) and mahaatheras (chief elders.) There are no Sangharaajas (heads of the entire Sangha) mentioned in any of the stories and no interference by kings or ministers in appointment or in giving ranks to the members of the Order. The affairs of the Sangha were managed by the monks themselves under well established rules of the Vinaya.

There appear to have been large numbers of disciples who had attained to the state of arahant, i.e., saints who had gained emancipation. In addition practically every man or woman was an upaasaka or upaasikaa, a devotee who regularly performed religious duties. The bhikkhus lived in their vihaaras during the rainy season and at other seasons traveled far and wide in the country, visiting villages, other vihaaras, and as pilgrims worshipping at shrines. Both laymen and bhikkhus are frequently mentioned as going on pilgrimages to Gayaa in India to worship at the sacred Bodhi Tree there. These parties of pilgrims sometimes crossed over to Southern India and walked all the way to Gayaa, taking about six months on the journey; sometimes they went by sea and landed at Taamralipti at the mouth of the Ganges and reached Gayaa in half the time.

The canonical scriptures had not been committed to writing at this time though writing was known. The bhikkhus learned the Dhamma and many committed to memory the scriptures or parts of them, thus preserving the tradition by frequent rehearsal. That the art of writing was probably introduced to Sri Lanka only after the introduction of Buddhism seems deducible from the circumstance that so far, no pre-Buddhist writing, lithic or other, has been identified. The earliest lithic records date back to the time of King Uttiya, successor of Devaanampiya Tissa.

The bhikkhus were the instructors of the people. This was practically a duty. The Dhamma was expounded individually on every occasion and sermons to congregations were also held from time to time. There is mention of the periodical expounding of the Dhamma at a temple. Each temple in a district sometimes took its turn once a year to preach the Ariyava.msa Sutta, which was continued each time for seven days; the gatherings on these occasions appear to be very large as in instances mentioned it is said that the crowds were so great that large numbers usually had to stand outside the hall for the whole night and listen to the Dhamma, the audience including bhikkhus and the laity. There is also mention of discourses by lay preachers well versed in the Dhamma employed by the king at halls of preaching.

It is not clearly stated whether brahmans who lived in brahman villages practiced their own religion. Mention is made of sannyaasis or yogis who practiced asceticism and sometimes lived in cemeteries scantily clad, with bodies covered with ashes, and as the story says, pretending to be saints while at the same time they led sinful lives. There is no mention of brahman temples or places of worship.

Women had a very high status in society during this period. Practically in every strata of society the position of women showed no distinction from that of men. They freely took part in every activity of life and their influence is well marked. Their character is depicted in most favorable terms; they were gentle, courteous and good natured, hospitable, tender and intelligent, ever ready to help others, to preserve the honor of their families, devoted to religion and country with untrammelled freedom of action. The position of women is further seen from the fact that monogamy was a definite institution. There is no mention of any other form of marriage. Women had freedom to choose their husbands.

Vattagaamani Abhaya

After the death of King Dutthagaamani his younger brother Saddhaatissa ruled for eight years and did a great deal for Buddhism. He was succeeded by his sons Thuulatthana, Lanjatissa, Khallaata Naaga and Vattagaamani Abhaya, in succession. The period of Vattagaamani Abhaya, also known as Valagambahu, is noteworthy in the history of early Buddhism in Sri Lanka. Five months after his accession to the throne, in 103 BCE a brahman named Tiya (or Tissa) from Ruhuna, South Lanka, revolted against him. At the same time a Tamil army led by seven Tamil chiefs landed at Mahaatittha and waged war against the king. The Tamil army vanquished Tiya and defeated Vattagaamani in battle after which the latter fled and lived in exile for fourteen years.

These fourteen years of Tamil domination were disastrous to the cause of Buddhism, especially because the country was also ravaged by an unprecedented famine during that period. Food was so scarce during that time that even cases of cannibalism are said to have occurred. Many thousands of monks and laymen died of starvation. The monasteries were deserted. The Mahaavihaara of Anuraadhapura was completely abandoned and the Mahaathuupa was neglected. Trees grew in the courtyards of vihaaras. 12,000 arahants from the Tissamahaaraama and another 12,000 from the Cittalapabbata-vihaara passed away in the forest due to lack of food. While thousands of monks died in the country, many left the country and went to India.

As a result of the death of most of the learned monks there was even the fear that some parts of the scriptures would be lost. The Mahaaniddesa of the Sutta Pitaka, for instance, was on the verge of being lost, for this text was known by only one monk at that time. The monks, in their earnestness to preserve the teachings of the Buddha, subsisted on roots and leaves of trees and recited the scriptures, lest they should forget them. When they had the strength they sat down and recited and when they could no longer keep their bodies erect they lay down and continued their recitation. Thus they preserved the texts and the commentaries until the misery was over.

The First Schism

After Vattagaamani Abhaya regained the throne he demolished the monastery of a nigantha (Jain ascetic) named Giri for having mocked him when he was fleeing. He built a Buddhist monastery called the Abhayagiri-vihaara over it, which he presented to a monk named Kupikkala Mahaa Tissa who had helped the king in his exile. Later, the monks of the Mahaavihaara imposed the punishment of expulsion on Tissa on the charge of improper contact with lay families. Tissa's pupil Bahalamassu Tissa, who resented the punishment imposed upon his teacher, was likewise expelled from the Mahaavihaara. He then went away with a following of five hundred monks and lived at Abhayagiri-vihaara, refusing to return to the Mahaavihaara. There was thus a group of monks who broke away from the Mahaavihaara and lived separately in the Abhayagiri-vihaara, but they did not yet disagree with each other either in the theory or the practice of the Dhamma.

The actual schism occurred only when monks of the Vajjiputta sect in India came to Sri Lanka and were received at the Abhayagiri, not long after Tissa and his followers occupied that monastery. Tissa and his followers liked the new monks and adopted their doctrines. Thenceforth they came to be known as the Dhammaruci sect, after the name of the great Indian monk who was the teacher of the newcomers to Abhayagiri. There was no official suppression of the new sect, presumably because the king was in their favor, but the Mahaavihaara monks opposed them as unorthodox and heretical. From this time the Abhayagiri existed as a separate sect opposed to the Mahaavihaara.

Writing of the Sacred Books

It is stated in the early chronicles that after the acceptance of Buddhism by the people in Lanka and after the formation of a hierarchy of disciples who were Sinhalese, a council was held under Mahinda Thera, where all the leading theras were present and the teachings were recited and authoritatively laid down, as was done in the third convocation held in India under the direction of Emperor Asoka. Theravaada was thus established in Sri Lanka and according to tradition and custom the various parts of the Tipitaka were learned by the members of the Order, committed to memory, and preserved as oral traditions. It was seen how, during the famine that broke out in the time of King Vattagaamani Abhaya, a great strain was put on the continuance of this form of preserving the teachings of the Tipitaka. When conditions became normal, the members of the Order considered that they could lose the teachings if any similar calamity or calamities were to occur in the future, and they decided that the time had arrived for committing these teachings to writing so that they might be preserved for future generations. The advent of schisms about this time might also have weighed strongly in favor of this decision.

Thus the members of the Order assembled at the Mahaavihaara at Anuraadhapura, took counsel together, and with the permission and encouragement of the king a convocation was held. The teachings were recited and scribes were engaged to commit to writing, on palm leaves, the Pali canonical texts (the Tipitaka) consisting of Vinaya, Sutta and Abhidhamma, and the Sinhalese commentaries. According to the *Nikaaya Sangraha*, a Sinhalese work of the fourteenth century dealing with the history of the Buddhist order, after the convocation at the Mahaavihaara at Anuraadhapura, the selected number of reciters and scribes, 500 in all, went to Alulena (Aluvihaara) cave temple close to Matale, in the central province. There in retirement they completed the work assigned to them and thus for the first time brought out in book form the teachings of the Buddha.

The Growth of Dissentient Schools

About two centuries after the formation of the Dhammaruci sect at the Abhayagiri-vihaara, in the days of King Vohaarika Tissa (214-36 a.c.), the monks of the Abhayagiri-vihaara adopted the Vaitulyavaada. Thereupon the monks of the Mahaavihaara, having compared it with their own texts, rejected the Vaitulya doctrines as being opposed to traditional doctrine. The king, who had them examined by a learned minister named Kapila, burnt them and suppressed the Vaitulyavaadins.

Despite the suppression by Vohaarika Tissa, the Vaitulyavaadins began to assert themselves again and a few years later, in the time of King Gothaabhaya (Meghavanna Abhaya, 253-266 a.c.), the Dhammaruci monks of Abhayagiri again accepted Vaitulyavaada. When this happened, about three hundred monks left the Abhayagiri-vihaara to reside at the Dakkhinavihaara, founding a new sect known as Saagaliya.

The king, having assembled the bhikkhus of the five great monasteries of the Theriya Nikaaya (Mahaavihaara Nikaaya), had the Vaitulya books examined, ordered the books to be destroyed, and expelled the Vaitulya monks. Sixty of them left for the Chola country in South India.

The struggle did not end here, for the adherents of the new doctrine were firmly established in South India and they planned to undermine the Mahaavihaara Nikaaya in Sri Lanka. With this object a very learned monk by the name of Sanghamitra came to Sri Lanka and obtained the post of tutor to the king's two sons. Sanghamitra gained considerable influence over the young pupil, Mahaasena, and was able to instil into him the new doctrine and make him a follower of his views. When Mahaasena ascended the throne, the opportunity looked forward to by the Vaitulyans came. The new king became a great supporter of his tutor and as such persecuted the Mahaavihaara monks. The king, at the instigation of Sanghamitra Thera, ordered that no one should give food to the monks of the Mahaavihaara. The Mahaavihaara, as a result, had to be abandoned for nine years. The supporters of Sanghamitra destroyed the buildings of the Mahaavihaara and carried away their material to construct new buildings for the Abhayagiri-vihaara.

Two persons, a minister and a queen, came forward this time to suppress Vaitulyavaada and save the Mahaavihaara. The minister, Meghavannaabhaya by name, managed to persuade the king to rebuild the Mahaavihaara. The queen caused Sanghamitra to be put to death and burned the Vaitulya books.

But the king, who was yet favorable towards the followers of Sanghamitra, built and gave the Jetavana-vihaara to a monk named Tissa. Tissa, who was later charged by the Mahaavihaara monks of a grave offense, was expelled from the Order. The monks of the Sagaliya sect at Dakkhina-vihaara then came to reside in the Jetavana-vihaara. In the reign of Silaakaala (522-35) a Vaitulyan book called the *Dharmadhaatu*, which was brought to Sri Lanka from India, was kept at the Jetavana-vihaara and venerated. Thus from this time the monks of

Jetavana-vihaara too became adherents of Vaitulyavaada. In the reign of King Aggabodhi I (575-608) a great monk and teacher named Jotipaala, coming from India, so exposed the fallacies of the Vaitulya doctrines that in his day they fell into disrepute and disappeared from Sri Lanka. Since that time the monks of the Abhayagiri and Jetavana vihaaras who adhered to Vaitulyan doctrines, abandoned their pride and lived in submission to the monks of the Mahaavihaara.

Intercourse with India was so frequent that from time to time other unorthodox doctrines occasionally found favor with certain monks, but these had no marked effect on the general progress or the stability of the Mahaavihaara Nikaaya.

For nearly three centuries after the time of Aggabodhi I the chronicles make no mention of the Vaitulyavaada or any other heretical teaching, until in the reign of King Sena I (833-53) a monk of the Vaajraparvata Nikaaya came to Sri Lanka from India and introduced Vaajiriyavaada, converting the king to his doctrines. It was at this time that teachings like the Ratnakuuta-suutra were also introduced to Sri Lanka and another heresy called Nilapata-darsana appeared. Sena II (853-87), who succeeded Sena I, managed to suppress these new doctrines. From his time until the Chola conquest in the early eleventh century there is no mention of any heretical sect in Sri Lanka. However, a survey of the religious monuments of that period clearly shows that their teachings survived side by side with the teachings of the Theravaada.

The Nature of the New Doctrines

It is opportune here to enquire about the nature of the new doctrines that were mentioned in the previous chapter as having been introduced into Sri Lanka from time to time since the first century a.c. It was the monks of the Vajjiputra sect in India who were the first to introduce a new teaching. The Vajjiputra sect is mentioned in the Sri Lanka chronicles as one of the groups that parted from the Theriya Nikaaya after the Second Buddhist Council to form a new sect. They thus evidently held some views different from those of the orthodox teachings. Buddhaghosa mentions in the Pali commentaries that the Vajjiputrakas held the view that there is a persistent personal entity, which is opposed to the accepted theory of *anattaa* of the Theravaada teachings. They also believed that arahants may fall away from their attainment.

These followers of the Vajjiputraka doctrines, residing at the Abhayagiri-vihaara, became adherents of the Vaitulya doctrines about two centuries afterwards, and until the beginning of the seventh century Vaitulyavaada became closely associated with Abhayagiri-vihaara and Jetavana-vihaara.

Like the Vajjiputra sect the Vaitulyavaada is mentioned in the *Nikaaya Sangraha* as one of the sects that arose in India after the Second Buddhist Council. The *Nikaaya Sangraha* also states that the Vaitulya Pitaka was composed by heretic brahmans called Vaitulyas who entered the Order in the time of King Asoka to destroy Buddhism. It has been noticed that the terms Vaitulya, Vaipulya and Vaidalya are commonly used as a designation for Mahaayaana suutras and hence the term Vaitulyavaada is used in the Sri Lanka chronicles to denote Mahaayaanism in general without having a particular Buddhist school in view.

The Vaitulyavaadins were considered even more heretical than the Vajjiputrakas. The Pali commentaries mention some of their heretical views. They held the view that the Buddha, having been born in the Tusita heaven, lived there and never came down to earth and it was only a created form that appeared among men. This created form and ânanda, who learned from it, preached the doctrine. They also held that nothing whatever given to the Order bears fruit, for the Sangha, which in the ultimate sense of the term meant only the path and fruitions, does not accept anything. According to them any human pair may enter upon sexual intercourse by mutual consent. The *Diipava.msa* used the term Vitandavaada in place of Vaitulyavaada and the Pali commentaries mention them as holding unorthodox views regarding the subtle points in the Dhamma, particularly the Abhidhamma.

Buddhaghosa also refers to the Vaitulyavaadins as Mahaasuññavaadins. The philosophy of the Mahaayaana as expounded by the great Mahaayaana teacher Naagaarjuna was Suunyavaada. Thus the fact that the first appearance of

Vaitulyavaada in Sri Lanka took place shortly after Naagaarjuna's teachings spread in South India, and that Vaitulyavaada is also identified with Suunyavaada of Naagaarjuna, suggests that it was the teaching of Naagaarjuna that was received by the monks of Abhayagiri-vihaara in the days of Vohaarika Tissa.

The book called *Dharmadhaatu,* which was brought to Lanka in the reign of Silaakaala, is described in the chronicles as a Vaitulyan book. The monks of the Abhayagiri-vihaara and the Jetavana-vihaara are connected with the honors paid to it. It has become evident that a book named *Dharmadhaatu* was known and held in high esteem in the tenth century in Lanka and it is quite probable that this book was a Mahaayaanistic treatise dealing with the doctrine of the three bodies of the Buddha found among the teachings of the Mahaayaana.

Vaajiriyavaada was introduced in the reign of King Sena I by a monk of the Vajraparvata Nikaaya. Scholars have pointed out that the Vaajiriyavaadins are identical with the Vajrayaanists, a school of Buddhism which flourished in eastern India about this time and which was an exponent of the worst phases of Tantrism. The *Nikaaya Sangraha* describes their writings as "secret teachings" and the Guudhavinaya, i.e., the "secret Vinaya," is one of the compositions of the Vajrayaanists.

The *Nikaaya Sangraha* mentions that about this time the Ratnakuuta-suutra was introduced to Sri Lanka. In the Chinese Canon the second of the seven classes of the Mahaayaana-suutras is called the Ratnakuuta. The Niilapata-darsana, which was also introduced about this time, was also an extreme form of Tantrism. Blue has been a color often favored by Tantrists.

The Śacred Tooth Relic

An important event in the early history of Buddhism in Sri Lanka is the arrival of Buddha's Tooth Relic, the left eye-tooth, from India about 805 b.e. (311 a.c.), during the time of King Sirimeghavanna, son and successor of King Mahaasena. Ever since this Sacred Tooth Relic was received in Sri Lanka it has been a national treasure of great value and a tangible token of the attachment of the Sinhalese to the doctrine of the Blessed

Tathaagata. King Sirimeghavanna held a great festival for the Tooth Relic and decreed that it should be brought every year to the Abhayagiri-vihaara and the same ceremonial should be observed. Today it is enshrined in golden caskets in the Temple of the Tooth Relic (Daladaa Maaligaawa) in Kandy, which has become the center of devout pilgrims from all over the island and from Buddhist lands elsewhere.

Ancient customs and ceremonies are scrupulously kept up, offerings are made daily, and in honor of the Sacred Relic an annual festival lasting fourteen days is held in Kandy every year during August. The Perahera, or procession, on these occasions is conducted by the temple authorities with elephants, lights, music and dancers, and is witnessed by thousands of devotees. Chiefs in full ancient attire accompany the procession. Large tracts of land have been set apart as fees for services at this temple and the tenants of these lands have various services apportioned to them. The exhibition of the Sacred Relic itself takes place at rare intervals when tens of thousands of pilgrims find their way to the Temple to worship and view the Relic. A medieval chronicle, chiefly of the eastern part of the island, mentions the existence of the right eye-tooth and its enshrinement in Somavati Cetiya in pre-Christian times.

The Sacred Tooth Relic was in the possession of King Guhasiva of Kaalinga before it was brought to Sri Lanka. When he was about to be defeated in battle he entrusted it to his daughter Hemamaalaa: Hemamaalaa with her husband Dantakumaara brought the Sacred Tooth to Lanka and handed it over to King Sirimeghavanna at Anuraadhapura. From this date the Sacred Tooth Relic became the care of the kings of Lanka, who built special temples for it. During the many vicissitudes of the fortunes of the kings of Lanka, the Sacred Relic was conveyed from place to place where the fortunes of the king happened to take him. Replicas of the Sacred Tooth were made at various times and were owned by princes claiming the throne. About the year 1071 King Anawrahta (Anuruddha) of Burma sent various presents to King Vijayabaahu I of Sri Lanka and in return received a duplicate of the Sacred Tooth Relic, which he received with great veneration, and a shrine was built for it in Burma. The Portuguese, in one of their expeditions to Sri Lanka, claim to have captured the Sacred Tooth Relic at Jaffna in the year 1560. Jaffna was an outlying port away from the strongholds of Sinhalese kings and the relic said to have been found by the Portuguese in a temple at Jaffna appeared to be one of the several duplicates which had been made at various times. On this question Prof. Rhys Davids wrote in the *Academy* of September 1874: "Jaffna is an outlying and unimportant part of the Ceylon kingdom, not often under the power of the Sinhalese monarchs, and for some time before this it had been ruled by a petty chieftain; there is no mention of the Tooth brought by Dantakumaara having been taken there — an event so unlikely and of such importance that it would certainly have been mentioned had it really occurred. We have every reason to believe therefore that the very Tooth referred to in the *Daañhaava.msa* is preserved to this day in Kandy."

In 1815 the British occupied Kandy. As usual the Sacred Tooth Relic had been taken to the mountains for security and one of the earliest tasks of the Agent of the British Government in the Kandyan Province was to arrange for the bringing back of the Relic with due ceremony. The houses and streets of Kandy were decorated, the surface of the streets whitened, and the Relic was brought in a magnificent procession. In 1818 there was a rebellion in the Kandyan provinces and the Sacred Tooth Relic was taken away from Kandy and hidden in a forest. After the suppression of the rebellion the British were able to find the Sacred Tooth Relic and bring it back to Kandy. The Sacred Tooth Relic continued to be in the custody of the British Government till 1853, when by order of the Secretary of State for the Colonies, the charge was given over to the Diyawadana Nilame (lay custodian) and the chief monks of Malwatte and Asgiriya monasteries in Kandy.

Buddhaghosa Thera and the Compilation of the Pali Commentaries

The compilation of the Pali Atthakathaa (commentaries) by Buddhaghosa Thera is another important event in the annals of Sri Lanka, which marks the progress of Buddhism. As has already been stated, the Pitakas or the teachings of the Buddha which were being handed down orally were committed to writing in 397 b.e. (89 BCE) and the commentaries on these, composed in Sinhalese, were also committed to writing at this time. Since this period much by way of exegetical works in Sinhalese was added from time to time and during the next five hundred years literary activity progressed considerably. By about 896 b.e. (410 a.c.), when King Mahaanaama reigned at Anuraadhapura, the fame of Buddhist literature in Sri Lanka was well recognized throughout India and tradition mentions Sinhalese Buddhist monks visiting India, China and other countries and introducing the literature produced in Sri Lanka. Monks from India and China also visited Anuraadhapura during this time to procure Buddhist books.

It was about this time that Buddhaghosa Thera came to Sri Lanka in the reign of King Mahaanaama (410-432). Mahaanaama succeeded to the throne 79 years after the death of King Sirimeghavanna, during whose reign the Sacred Tooth Relic was brought to Sri Lanka, and three rulers, namely Jetthatissa II, Buddhadaasa and Upatissa I, reigned in between. The story of Buddhaghosa is given in detail both in the *Mahaava.msa* and the Sinhalese works composed in later times. According to these sources Buddhaghosa was a brahman youth who was born in the vicinity of Buddha Gayaa and became well known as an exponent of Veda and philosophy. He was such a proficient scholar that in his youth he was able to assert his knowledge among the great scholars of the time. He traveled from place to place, from one seat of learning to another, from one set of teachers to another, triumphantly asserting his knowledge and scholarship.

At a well-known Buddhist monastery at Tamluk, he met Revata Mahaathera, one well versed in the doctrines and philosophy of Buddhism. There he entered into discussions and found not a peer but one superior to him in knowledge and understanding. This made him join the Order of Buddhist monks as a pupil of Revata Mahaathera. At this vihaara he studied Buddhist philosophy diligently and produced a treatise on Buddhism, *¥aa.nodaya*; he also planned to compose commentaries on the Abhidhamma and the suttas. His teacher at this stage advised him to go to Anuraadhapura before undertaking this work, as he said that in Lanka were preserved not only the Tipitaka, the teachings of the Buddha himself, but also the Sinhalese commentaries and various expositions of the teachings which were very valuable and of high repute.

Buddhaghosa Thera proceeded to Sri Lanka and stayed at the Mahaapadhaanaghara of the Mahaavihaara. He then asked the monks at Anuraadhapura for access to books for the compilation of commentaries. The learned theras at Anuraadhapura tested his knowledge and ability by setting him a thesis on which he compiled the well-known *Visuddhimagga*. They were so pleased with this work that he was given facilities for his projected work and books were placed at his disposal for the preparation of Pali commmentaries.

The old Sinhalese commentaries from which Buddhaghosa drew material for the compilation of his Pali commentaries are occasionally named in his works. The Mahaa (or Muula) Atthakathaa occupied the foremost position among them while the Mahaa-paccari Atthakathaa and the Kurundi Atthakathaa were also important. These three major works probably contained exegetical material on all the three Pitakas. Apart from these there were other works like the Sankhepatthakathaa, Vinayatthakathaa, Abhidhammatthakathaa and separate commentaries on the four âgamas or Nikaayas, namely, the Diigha Nikaaya Atthakathaa, Majjhima Nikaaya Atthakathaa, Samyutta Nikaaya Atthakathaa, and the Anguttara Nikaaya Atthakathaa. References to numerous other sources like the Andhakatthakathaa, the âcariyaa (or Teachers), and the Poraanaa (or Ancient Masters) are also found in Buddhaghosa's works.

Utilizing the copious material of these commentaries and other sources, which sometimes contained conflicting views and contradictory assertions, Buddhaghosa compiled his Pali commentaries including all authoritative decisions, sometimes giving his own views but leaving out unnecessary details and repetitions as well as irrelevant matter. The first of such commentaries was the *Samantapaasaadikaa* on the Vinaya

Pitaka. The *Kankhaavitaranii* on the Paatimokkha of the Vinaya Pitaka was compiled later. These books were followed by the commentaries on the four Nikaayas, the *Sumangalavilaasinii* on the Diigha Nikaaya, the *Papañca-suudanii* on the Majjhima Nikaaya, the *Saaratthappakaasinii* on the Samyutta Nikaaya, and the *Manorathapuura.nii* on the Anguttara Nikaaya. The *Dhammapadaññhakathaa* on the Dhammapada, the *Jaatakaññhakathaa* on the Jaataka, and the *Paramatthajotikaa* on the Khuddaka Nikaaya, are also ascribed to him. On the books of the Abhidhamma Pitaka, Buddhaghosa compiled the *Aññhasaalinii* on the Dhammasanganii, the *Sammohavinodanii* on the Vibhanga, and the *Pañcappakara.naññhakathaa* on the other five books.

The voluminous literature which Buddhaghosa produced exists to this day and is the basis for the explanation of many crucial points of Buddhist philosophy which without them would have been unintelligible. His commentaries become all the more important since the old Sinhalese commentaries gradually went out of vogue and were completely lost after the tenth century. Buddhaghosa's activities gave an impetus to the learning of Pali in Sri Lanka which resulted in the production of many other Pali commentaries and other literary works, and also established the pre-eminence of Sri Lanka as the home of Theravaada Buddhism.

The Pali Chronicles

Some time before and after the compilation of the Pali commentaries by Buddhaghosa two important literary works of a different type were produced in Sri Lanka. They are the *Diipava.msa* and the *Mahaava.msa*, described in the foregoing pages either as the Sri Lanka chronicles or the Pali chronicles. These two works are the earliest extant literary records giving a continuous history of the activities of the kings of Sri Lanka from pre-Buddhistic times up to the end of the reign of King Mahaasena. Both works are composed in Pali metrical verses.

The *Diipava.msa* is the earlier of these two chronicles. It is not a compilation of one individual author but is the outcome of several previous works to which additions have been made from time to time, taking its present form about the fourth century a.c. The chronicle does not name any author but it has been held by some scholars, from the abundant material it contains about nuns, that the *Diipava.msa* is a work compiled and continued by nuns from time to time.

The *Diipava.msa* consists of 22 chapters. They contain accounts of the three visits of the Buddha to Sri Lanka, the ancestry of the Buddha, the three Buddhist councils and the different Buddhist schools which arose after the Second Council, the activities of King Asoka, the colonization of Sri Lanka by Vijaya, his successors, the introduction of Buddhism in the reign of King Devaanampiya Tissa and the activities of his successors, especially Dutthagaamani, Vattagaamani and Mahaasena. The narrative ends with the reign of Mahaasena (276-303).

The *Diipava.msa* has obtained its material from different sources of which the Sihala *Mahaava.msatthakathaa* (also called the Sihalatthakathaa or Poraanatthakathaa or merely Atthakathaa) was pre-eminent. Besides this there were several other sources like the Uttaravihaara Mahaava.msa, Vinayatthakathaa and the Dipava.msatthakathaa. By these names were known the records collected and preserved in the Mahaavihaara and the other monasteries.

The *Mahaava.msa*, which is the better work in its comprehensiveness, arrangement of facts and high literary standard, was compiled by a thera named Mahaanaama either in the late fifth century or the early sixth century a.c. It also covers the same period of history and its material is drawn from the same sources as the *Diipava.msa*, but it contains much more additional material presented in a better form.

The *Mahaava.msa* contains 37 chapters in all. They deal mainly with the same events as those of the *Diipava.msa*, but there are much longer accounts and greater details of the activities of several kings such as Pandukaabhaya and Dutthagaamani and events like the establishment of Buddhism and the rise of new schools.

These two chronicles contain many myths and legends. Yet they are among the primary sources for the reconstruction of the early history of Sri Lanka for they contain a great deal of historical facts, especially in the narratives dealing with the period after the 2nd century BCE, corroborated by epigraphical, archaeological and other evidence.

The *Mahaava.msa* has been continued in later times, at three stages, giving a connected history of the island up to modern times. This continuation of the chronicle, which is in three parts, is called the *Cuulava.msa*. The first part brings the history down to the twelfth century, the second part to the fourteenth century and the third part to modern times.

Political Unrest and the Decline of Buddhism

The political situation in Sri Lanka from about the middle of the fifth century a.c. until the third quarter of the eleventh century a.c. was not favorable towards the progress of Buddhism. This period of Sri Lankan history is marked with continuous warfare between the reigning king and his rival claimants or the foreign invaders. Often when the reigning king was defeated in battle he fled to India and came back with a Tamil troop to regain his lost throne, and as a result the Tamils who thus settled down in Sri Lanka from time to time also became an important element even powerful enough to seize political power for themselves.

Such a political situation evidently did not give the rulers an opportunity to work for the religion and as a result the community and the monasteries were neglected. Some rulers like Aggabodhi III and Daathopatissa I even resorted to the evil practice of robbing monasteries of their gold images, precious gems and other valuables which had accumulated there for centuries, for the purpose of financing their military operations when the royal treasury had become empty.

Daathopatissa I also removed the gold finial of the Thuupaaraama and the gem-studded umbrella of the cetiya. Relic chambers of stuupas were opened and valuable offerings were removed. Their Tamil soldiers were allowed to burn down monastic buildings like the Sacred Tooth Relic Temple and take away the valuables. The Pandya and the Chola invaders from South India who also attacked Sri Lanka several times during this period ransacked the monasteries and carried away vast treasures. These conditions necessarily worsened when Sri Lanka passed into the hands of the South Indian Cholas in 1017 and remained a part of the Chola empire until 1070.

Amidst this political unrest and the resultant religious decline several events important in the history of Buddhism in Sri Lanka occurred. In the reign of Moggallaana I (495-512) the Sacred Hair Relic of the Buddha was brought to Sri Lanka from India and the king placed it in a crystal casket in an image house and held a great festival. The writing of the *Mahaava.msa* by a Mahaavihaara monk is ascribed to the reign of his successor Kumaara Dhaatusena (512-520). In the reign of Silaakaala (522-535) the Mahaayaana book, the Dharmadhaatu, was brought to Sri Lanka and in the reign of Aggabodhi I (575-608) the monk Jotipaala defeats the Vaitulyavaadins in a public controversy. Apart from these special events several rulers purified the Saasana and repaired the old and neglected monasteries. They also encouraged the recital of Dhamma.

Vijayabaahu I and the Revival of Buddhism

In the year 1070 Vijayabaahu I succeeded in defeating the Cholas and becoming the king of Sri Lanka. Residing at Polonnaruwa, which he made the capital of his kingdom, he turned his mind to the noble task of repairing the damage that had been inflicted upon the national religion by the invaders. The great religious edifices, the pirivenas and the monasteries which were in utter destruction were restored and new ones were built. But the greatest of his tasks was the restoration of ordination of monks.

When he found that the five ordained monks required to carry out an ordination ceremony could not be found in the whole island, he sent an embassy to his friend and ally, King Anuruddha (i.e., Anawrahta) of Burma, soliciting his help in restoring the Saasana in Sri Lanka. King Anuruddha sent a number of eminent theras who re-established the Saasana in Sri Lanka and instructed a large number of monks in the three Pitakas and the commentaries. The king also brought about a reconciliation of the three Nikaayas of the Mahaavihaara, Abhayagiri and Jetavana and restored their ancient monasteries to them. Thousands of laymen joined the Order.

The religious revival inaugurated by King Vijayabaahu led to a great intellectual re-awakening and a large number of religious literary works in Pali and Sanskrit were written. King Vijayabaahu also encouraged learned men to come and settle down in Sri Lanka and also induced his courtiers to engage in literary pursuits. These activities suffered temporarily with his death in 1110, but were revived after the accession of Paraakramabaahu the Great in 1153.

Revival of Buddhism under Paraakramabaahu the Great

King Paraakramabaahu the Great (1153-1186) ascended the throne after a great struggle with rival claimants and even after his accession he had to suppress many rebellions. Being a great leader of men he was able to restore order and even carry his prowess as a conqueror to foreign lands including South India and Burma. He rebuilt the city of Polonnaruwa. King Paraakramabaahu also undertook the restoration of the ancient capital city of Anuraadhapura which had been neglected and abandoned after the Cholas had captured and devastated it about a century and a half earlier. The four great thuupas were overgrown with trees, and bears and panthers dwelt there. The king restored all the important monuments at Anuraadhapura and the entire Mihintale monastery.

But the most important task which the king performed for the establishment of the Saasana was its purification and the unification of the Sangha. In spite of the activities of King Vijayabaahu I there were by this time members of Sangha who were unfit to lead the monastic life. Some of the monks are said to have even supported wives and children. With a learned thera named Mahaa Kassapa of Udumbaragiri Vihaara (Dimbulaagala near Polonnaruwa) at its head, the king convened a Council of the leading monks of the dissentient schools and was convinced that the teachings of the Mahaavihaara were correct and their claims were in keeping with the Dhamma. Consequently with great care and patience, the king made investigations into the members of the schismatic schools. Many of the unworthy monks were persuaded to leave the Order and those who were not open to persuasion were expelled. Some monks were made to return to the status of novices. After that the three fraternities of the Mahaavihaara, the Abhayagiri-vihaara and the Jetavana-vihaara remained united.

Subsequent to this purification of the Sangha the king, with the assistance of the leading monks, proclaimed a code of regulations for the guidance of the bhikkhus. After the proclamation of that code the internal discipline of the Sangha was in the hands of the monks themselves and the king acted only when a necessity arose. The code of regulations enforced by King Paraakramabaahu became a royal proclamation. It gave directions for the proper observance of the Vinaya rules and dealt with the procedure that should be followed by his subjects who had become or who wished to become lay pupils, novices and subsequently ordained monks. The king also caused this proclamation to be engraved on the rock surface of the Uttaraaraama, presently known as Gal-vihaara, which exists to this day. It is now known as Polonnaru-katikaavata or the Paraakramabaahu-katikaavata.

The great interest taken by the king in the affairs of the religion coupled with internal peace and prosperity brought about a revival of Buddhist learning which created a rich literature during this period.

Compilation of Religious Treatises

It has been mentioned earlier that Buddhaghosa Thera compiled the Pali commentaries to many of the texts of the Tipitaka in the early part of the fifth century. Buddhaghosa was, however, not able to compile commentaries to all the books of the Tipitaka due perhaps to the fact that the illness of his teacher Revata in India caused him to leave Sri Lanka before he finished the entire work. Fortunately, there were several other scholars who took up the work left undone by Buddhaghosa, and in the succeeding years they compiled commentaries to the rest of the texts of the Pali Canon.

Thus the commentator Dhammapaala Thera compiled the commentaries to the Udaana, Itivuttaka, Vimaanavatthu, Petavatthu, Theragaathaa, Theriigaathaa and Cariyaapitaka of the Khuddaka Nikaaya; all these commentaries are known by the name *Paramatthadiipanii*: Upasena Thera compiled the

Saddhammappajjotikaa on the Niddesa. Mahaanama Thera compiled the *Saddhammappakaasinii* on the Patisambhidaamagga, and Buddhadatta Thera compiled the *Madhuratthavilaasinii* on the Buddhava.msa. The author of the Visuddhajanavilaasinii, which is the commentary on the Apadaana, is not known. Of these commentators Buddhadatta was a contemporary of Buddhaghosa; Upasena and Mahaanaama flourished about the latter part of the sixth century, and Dhammapaala about the latter part of the tenth century.

The political disturbances from the time of King Dhaatusena until the reign of Vijayabaahu I greatly hampered literary activities and as a result only a few religious works were composed during this period. About the end of the tenth century, a thera named Khema wrote an expository work on the Abhidhamma, called the *Paramatthadiipanii*. To the same period belongs also the Pali *Mahaabodhiva.msa*, which gives primarily the history of the Sacred Bodhi Tree at Anuraadhapura and the ceremonies connected with it. A poem entitled *Anaagatava.msa* on the future Buddha Metteyya is also ascribed to this period. To the tenth or the early part of the eleventh century belongs a Pali poem of 98 stanzas, called the Telakañaahagaathaa, in the form of religious exhortations of a great elder named Kalyaaniya Thera, who was condemned to be cast into a cauldron of boiling oil.

King Vijayabaahu I, in whose reign occurred a great intellectual re-awakening, was himself a great patron of literature and a scholar of high repute. Many Sinhalese works including a Sinhalese translation of the Dhammasanganii are attributed to him but not one of them exists today. About this time a monk named Anuruddha composed the *Anuruddhasataka*, the *Abhidhammattha-sangaha*, the *Naamaruupa-pariccheda* and the *Paramattha-vinicchaya*. The first is a Buddhist devotional poem of 101 stanzas, in elegant Sanskrit. The second work is a compendium on the teachings of the Abhidhamma and is held in high esteem by all Buddhists of the southern school. The third and fourth are two short works in verse on the Abhidhamma, giving the reader a general idea of the subjects dealt with in the Abhidhamma Pitaka.

The reign of King Paraakramabaahu the Great ushered in another great epoch of literary activity. Three great scholarly monks flourished in his reign, namely, Mahaa Kassapa of Dimbulaagala Vihaara, Moggallaana Thera and Saariputta Thera. Mahaa Kassapa was the author of a Sinhalese paraphrase (*sanne*) to the *Samantapaasaadikaa*, which is now lost. He is also reputed to have written a sub-commentary to the *Abhidhammattha-sangaha*. It is probable that he was also the author of several other works such as the *Mohavicchedanii*, which is a treatise on the Abhidhamma, and *Vimativinodanii*, which is a commentary on the Vinaya. Moggallaana, a contemporary of Mahaa Kassapa, was the author of the Pali grammar, *Moggallaana Vyaakara.na*. He is also credited with the authorship of the *Abhidhaanappadiipikaa*, which is the only ancient Pali dictionary in Sri Lanka.

Saariputta was the most prominent scholar of the reign of Paraakramabaahu the Great. A clever Sanskrit scholar as he was, Saariputta compiled two works on Sanskrit grammar. Another work by him, the *Vinayasangaha*, was a summary of the Vinaya Pitaka. This work was known by several titles and was widely known in Burma. On this work Saariputta himself wrote a sub-commentary (*ñiikaa*) and a Sinhalese paraphrase. The most comprehensive and therefore important work of Saariputta is the masterly sub-commentary called the *Saaratthadiipanii*, which he composed on Buddhaghosa's commentary on the Vinaya, the *Samantapaasaadikaa*. The immense and valuable information it contains shows that his knowledge was extensive and profound even as that of the great commentator Buddhaghosa.

He further wrote a Sinhalese paraphrase to the *Abhidhammattha-sangaha* of Anuruddha Thera and this paraphrase is still held in high esteem by modern scholars. Saariputta is also credited with the authorship of two other ñiikaas, the *Saratthamañjuusaa* on the *Manorathapuura.nii* and the *Liinatthappakaasinii* on the *Papañcasuudanii*, which are commentaries on the Anguttara and Majjhima Nikaayas, respectively, by Buddhaghosa. To this period also belong the ñiikaas on the other three Nikaayas of the Sutta Pitaka, collectively known as the *Saratthamañjuusaa-ñiikaa*. It should be mentioned here that the ñiikaas named above formed one of the major groups of Pali literature compiled during this period. As described in the *Saddhamma-sangaha,* a Pali work of the 14th century, Mahaa Kassapa and a large congregation of monks who assembled at the Jetavana Vihaara at Polonnaruwa decided to compose exegetical commentaries since the existing sub-commentaries on the old Atthakathaas were unintelligible. Acting on this decision they compiled ñiikaas, namely, the *Saaratthadiipanii* on the Vinaya Pitaka, the *Saratthamañjuusaa* in four parts on the first four Nikaayas of the Sutta Pitaka, and the *Paramatthadiipanii* in three parts on the Abhidhamma Pitaka.

These ñiikaas or sub-commentaries were works containing expositions of points in the Atthakathaas compiled by Buddhaghosa and other commentators, which needed further elucidation for their correct interpretation. There were ñiikaas compiled from time to time subsequent to the compilation of the commentaries, and what the council headed by Mahaa Kassapa performed was the bringing of these various ñiikaas together and making a synthetic summary of them. Though the *Saddhamma-sangaha* does not give any prominence to the part played by Saariputta at this council, it is well known that several ñiikaas were compiled either by him or under his supervision.

Several religious works written in Sinhalese also belong to this period. The Sinhalese exegetical works on which the Pali commentaries were based were preserved in the Mahaavihaara as late as the tenth century. Likewise there were the collections of Jaataka stories and the stories connected with the verses of the Dhammapada, in the Sinhalese language. A collection of stories from which the Pali *Rasavaahinii* drew material and a work called the *Siihalaññhakathaa Mahaava.msa*, on which the Pali chronicles were based, also existed in Sinhalese. None of these works is now extant. Several Sinhalese religio-literary works which were composed in or about the twelfth century are popular even today. Among them are the *Sasadaavata*, which is a poem on the Sasa Jaataka; the *Muvadevdaavata*, which is a poem on the Makhaadeva Jaataka; and the *Kavsilumina*, which is a poem on Kusa Jaataka. Gurulugomi's *Amaavatura* and *Dharmapradiipikaava* and Vidyaacakravarti's *Butsara.na* are also generally ascribed to the twelfth century.

Decline of Buddhism after Paraakramabaahu I and Restoration by Paraakramabaahu II

After the death of Paraakramabaahu the Great there was much internal disturbance in the country caused by rival claimants to the throne and invasions by foreigners. As a result Buddhism was on the decline again. Paraakramabaahu's immediate successor, Vijayabaahu II, promoted trade and religious relations between Burma and Sri Lanka but was slain after a year's rule by a usurper. The usurper was, however, slain five days later by Nissankamalla, who thereafter reigned for nine years (1187-96). Nissankamalla was a great benefactor of Buddhism. He built several notable religious edifices in Polonnaruwa, his capital. Some of these, like the Ruvanveli-daagaba (now called Rankot-vehera), the beautiful Vatadaa-ge, the Sacred Tooth Relic Temple (Hetadaage), and the Nissankalataa-mandapa exist to this day. He made occasional tours in his kingdom, visiting places of religious significance like the Sumanakuuta (Sri Paada, or as called by the English, Adam's Peak) and the Dambulu-vihaara. He built alms-houses at several important places and purified the Saasana by expelling corrupt bhikkhus from the Order.

The period of two decades that followed the death of King Nissankamalla was one of the most disturbed periods in Sri Lanka, during which time occurred several assassinations of rulers and invasions by foreigners. In 1214 a foreigner named Megha invaded, defeated the Sinhalese ruler and reigned for 36 years (1215-51). His reign was one of the most disastrous for Buddhism, for he plundered the monasteries and made them over to his soldiers to dwell in. The people were persecuted by torture and were forced to adopt a different faith. He also destroyed libraries containing many valuable books. The situation was temporarily saved by Paraakramabaahu II, who ruled from Dambadeniya from 1236 while Maagha was still dominating north Lanka. Paraakramabaahu II, who was a ruler of great learning, earned for himself the title Kalikaala Sahitya Sarvajña Pandita. He made efforts to restore the Saasana by bringing over monks from the Chola country in South India and holding a festival to admit monks to the higher ordination. He established several monasteries and pirivenas and encouraged learning. The king also held a great council of monks under the leadership of the great thera Aranyaka Medhankara and purified the Saasana. Subsequently, like Paraakramabaahu I, he formulated rules for the proper conduct of the monks, the code of these rules being known by the name Dambadeni Katikaavata. At Palaabatgala he constructed a great monastery for the hermit-monks who were full of virtue and were able to undergo strict austerities. Two succeeding kings, Vijayabaahu IV (1270-72) and Paraakramabaahu III (1287-93), took much interest in maintaining Buddhism and consolidating the efforts of their predecessor.

The Literary Revival

The religious revival brought about by Paraakramabaahu II continued until about the fifteenth century, though there was not much political stability in the country during that period. The outstanding feature of the period is the compilation of a large number of religio-literary works. Paraakramabaahu II himself obtained teachers from India to teach Lankan monks. He persuaded his younger brother Bhuvanekabaahu to become a scholar and be a teacher to many thousands of elders. The king's minister Devapatiraaja was a great patron of learning. To Paraakramabaahu II is ascribed the authorship of the Sinhalese translations to the *Visuddhimagga* and the *Vinaya Vinicchaya*, the Sinhalese poem *Kavsilumi.na*, the masterpiece of Sinhalese poetry, based on the Kusa Jaataka, and the Sinhalese prose work *Daladaa-sirita*. In the reign of Paraakramabaahu II lived the thera Dharmakirti who was the author of the Pali poem Daathaava.msa and the first part of the *Cuutava.msa*.

The *Thuupava.msa* on the erection of stuupas in Lanka, the *Hattha-vanagalla-vihaara-va.msa* on the history of the ancient vihaara at Attanagalla, the *Rasavaahinii* which is a collection of stories about ancient India and Sri Lanka, the

Samantakuuta-va.n.nanaa on the Buddha's visit to Sumanakuuta (Adam's Peak), the *Kesadhaatuvamsa* on the history of the hair-relics of the Buddha, the *Paarami-mahaasataka* on the ten perfections (*paraamitaa*), the *Saddhamma-Sangha* which gives an account of the history and development of Buddhism in Lanka, are several of the religious works of merit composed in Pali from the time of Paraakramabaahu II until the fifteenth century.

A large number of Sinhalese works on religious subjects too belongs to this period. The *Saddharmaratnaavalii*, which narrates the stories of the Pali Dhammapadatthakathaa in Sinhalese, the *Puujavalii* which relates the honor and offerings received by the Buddha, the *Pansiya-panas-jaataka* based on the Pali Jaataka commentary, the Sinhala *Bodhiva.msa* on the history of the Bodhi Tree, the *Elu-Attanagaluva.msa* which is a translation of the Pali work, the *Saddharmaalankaara*, based on the Pali *Rasavaahinii*, the *Guttilakaavyaya* based on the Guttila Jaataka, the *Kaavyasekharaya*, based on the Sattubhatta Jaataka, the *Budugu.naalankaaraya*, which narrates the dispelling of the calamity in Vesaali by the Buddha, and the *Loveda-sangaraava*, containing religious instructions for the laity, are the standard works among them.

Embassy from Burma to Obtain Ordination

As a result of this religious revival, the reputation of the Sangha in Sri Lanka became so well established that in the year 1476 King Dhammaceti of Burma decided to send twenty-two selected bhikkhus to Lanka to obtain ordination and bring back to Burma the traditions of Lanka. He sent these bhikkhus with numerous presents in charge of two ministers, Citraduuta and Raamaduuta.

They came in two ships. The first ship with eleven bhikkhus and their attendants, in charge of the minister Citraduuta, arrived in Colombo and the other ship in charge of Raamaduuta with eleven bhikkhus and attendants arrived at Weligama on the southern coast of Lanka. These deputations were received with due ceremony and given a cordial reception by King Buvanekabaahu VI (1470-78), who reigned at Kotte (Jayawardhanapura), six miles from Colombo.

The king of Burma sent the following message to the chief theras of Lanka: "My Lords, I am sending many articles to be offered to the Sacred Tooth Relic, etc. and I request you to make an endeavor to offer these to the Sacred Tooth Relic.

May the noble ones obtain facilities for the twenty-two bhikkhus and their pupils and the two ministers, Citraduuta and Raamaduuta, who are attending on these bhikkhus to assist them in worshiping, honoring and viewing the Sacred Tooth Relic if they are so fortunate as to get an opportunity to do so; after which may the Noble Ones be pleased with their endeavor to enable the twenty-two bhikkhus and their pupils to be ordained in the community of succession from Mahaavihaara fraternity founded by the great thera Mahinda by selecting such bhikkhus who hold an established high reputation and giving the ordination of Upasampadaa in the Siimaa (ordination hall) in the river Kalyaani, which has been made sacred by its association with our Great Lord."

The request made by the king of Burma was duly granted, the bhikkhus were ordained in the Siimaa in the Kalyaani River. The minister Raamaduuta with twenty bhikkhus and thirty-three pupils, duly ordained, returned to Burma. The other minister, Citraduuta, and his party of bhikkhus were shipwrecked and six of these bhikkhus met with their death. The remaining ones reached their country.

Establishment of Mahaavihaarava.msa in Burma

In Burma King Dhammaceti built an ordination hall, known as Kalyaani Siimaa, and the bhikkhus ordained there went by the name of Kalyaaniva.msa. At a later period ordination of this Nikaaya was carried to Siam from Burma.

The connection with Burma at this period has an important bearing on the fortunes of Buddhism in Sri Lanka, for through these embassies the books that existed in Lanka were taken to Burma, Siam and Cambodia and the Mahaavihaara Nikaaya was established in these countries. This helped Lanka to reobtain the books and the ordination at a subsequent period, when ordination had disappeared in the island and the books were lost.

The Arrival of the Portuguese and the Persecution of Buddhism

The political stability that was maintained by Paraakramabaahu II and his successors until about the fifteenth century began to weaken by the end of that century. At this time the Sinhalese king who ruled at Kotte was the head of a very small territory. The interior regions of the country were in the hands of several petty chiefs who did not care about the religion or the welfare of the people. The Moors on the other hand controlled the trade of the coastal regions. Economically too the country had sunk to such a very low level that by this time Sri Lanka had become dependent on India even for food.

Such was the condition when the Portuguese, who were engaged in discoveries and conquests in the East and were in pursuit of Eastern trade, landed in Lanka in 1505, when Vira Paraakramabaahu VIII (1484-1508) was ruling at Kotte. The Portuguese promised him military aid against his rivals and great riches from the trade which they proposed to establish. They then gained a foothold in Lanka by erecting a fortress on the rocky beach in Colombo and establishing many trading settlements. Before long the entire coastal region passed into the hands of the Portuguese and the kings of Kotte were entirely at the mercy of their allies. They even made several assaults on the interior of the country in order to become masters of the whole island.

The Portuguese arrived in Colombo in 1505 and, gradually occupying all maritime provinces, remained in their possession up to 1658. The Lanka chronicles as well as the records of their friendly historians describe them as cruel, inhuman, rapacious, bigoted and savage persecutors of Buddhism in their endeavor to impose their own faith — Roman Catholicism — on the people of Sri Lanka.

A few decades after the arrival of the Portuguese, King Bhuvanekabaahu VI (1534-1551), who ruled at Kotte, sought the assistance of his allies, the Portuguese, to ensure the succession of his grandson Dharmapaala to the throne. For this purpose an ivory image of Dharmapaala was sent to Portugal where a coronation of the effigy was held by the Portuguese emperor. When the Sinhalese ambassadors returned they were accompanied by a party of Franciscans who, under the direction of the Portuguese emperor and with the permission of the king of Kotte, preached the Christian Gospel in Lanka. Thus for the first time Christian communities were organized in the maritime provinces of Lanka. Dharmapaala, who had become a baptized Christian under the name of Don Juan Dharmapaala, as an expression of thankfulness to the Portuguese gave them a deed of gift (*sannas*) after his accession, transferring to them the Daladaa Maaligaawa (i.e., the Temple of the Tooth), the temple at Kelaniya and all the temple revenues in the island for the maintenance of the missionary establishments.

Thus there was the necessary assistance given to the Portuguese by the rulers of Kotte to suppress the national religion of the Sinhalese and propagate their own religion — Catholicism. With this support they set about their task. In their conversions they adopted two distinct methods, namely, inducement by offices and other temporal favors, and brutal punishment where inducement failed. People who wished to obtain high offices under them and who wished to earn the goodwill of those in power readily adopted the new faith and took up new Biblical names. Others who hesitated to give up their national faith and showed resistance were brutally punished.

There are lurid accounts of men thrown into rivers to be eaten by crocodiles, babies spitted on the soldiers' pikes and held up before the parents, or crushed between millstones before the eyes of their mothers who later were to be tortured to death. Those who dared to worship in public or wear the yellow robe were put to death. Buddhist monasteries and institutions were destroyed and their treasures looted. Libraries were set on fire. Thus did the period of Portuguese rule become one of the darkest periods of Buddhism in Sri Lanka.

Persecution of Buddhism by Raajasinha I

The Portuguese were not the only enemies of Buddhism at this period. King Raajasinha I (1581-1592), who was the son of Mayaadunne, a brother of Bhuvenekabaahu VI, ruled from Sitawaka when the Portuguese were holding power at Kotte.

A gallant leader as he was, Raajasinha succeeded in gaining the confidence of the Sinhalese who opposed the Portuguese rule and winning several battles against the Portuguese, the battle at Mulleriyaawa being the most famous. But, as the chronicles mention, his popularity was shortlived. The foolish king, in his thirst for power, slew his old father with his own hands. Later, being seized with the fear of his crime, Raajasinha sought the advice of the monks for setting himself free from the sin. When the monks explained to him that it was too great a crime to be absolved, the king was provoked to anger.

He then became a follower of the Saivites, in whose advice he took refuge, and became an enemy of Buddhism. The chief Buddhist elder was stoned to death, and many other monks were buried neck-deep in the earth and their heads plowed off. Some others were put to the sword. The sacred edifices and the monasteries were pulled down, and the sacred books were reduced to ashes. The lands which had been endowed in earlier times to the monastic establishments were taken away and Sri Paada, the Sacred Footprint of the Buddha on Adam's Peak, was handed over to the Saivites. Those monks who managed to escape from the king's wrath disrobed themselves and fled.

Vimala Dharmasuriya's Attempt at Restoring Buddhism

In 1592, the year in which Raajasinha died, a Sinhalese ruler, Vimala Dharmasuriya I, ascended the throne of the hill capital, Kandy, and ruled for twelve years. Though he had been educated by the Portuguese and was originally favored by them, the king soon after his accession turned against them out of his love for the country and the religion.

Vimala Dharmasuriya I was a great patron of Buddhism of that time. After his wars with the Portuguese he set his heart on repairing the damage done by Raajasinha. Several Buddhist monuments were restored. Finding that there was hardly a single monk left in the country who was properly ordained, Vimala Dharmasuriya sent an embassy to the country of Arakan (now part of Burma) to obtain monks to restore ordination in Sri Lanka. The mission was successful; several monks led by the elders Nandicakka and Candavisaala came to Kandy and in the year 1597 an ordination ceremony was held in the

Udakukkhepa Siimaa at Getambe, near Kandy, many men of noble families entering the Order on this occasion. The king also built a storeyed pavilion and, bringing back the Sacred Tooth Relic from the Delgamuvihaara where it was hidden, deposited it in the pavilion. The control of Sri Paada was taken from the Saivites and handed over to the Buddhist monks.

Successors of Vimala Dharmasuriya I and the Arrival of the Dutch in Sri Lanka

Vimala Dharmasuriya was succeeded on the throne of Kandy by Senarat, a man zealous in religious works. In his reign the Portuguese invaded Kandy and the king carried away the Sacred Tooth Relic to Mahiyangana for safety. Senarat's son and successor Raajasinha II (1634-1687) was a great warrior but was not zealous. In his reign ended the Portuguese rule in the maritime provinces of Lanka, a feat which the king accomplished with the aid of the Dutch in June 1658.

It was as early as 1602 that the Dutch visited the court of Kandy, in the reign of Vimala Dharmasuriya I, seeking an alliance. In 1612 a treaty was agreed upon between the Dutch and King Senarat, the then king of Kandy, and in accordance with this agreement, in 1638 Raajasinha II sought Dutch assistance against the Portuguese. From that time the two European nations fought each other until in 1658 the Portuguese were expelled from the country and the Dutch came to occupy those regions which formerly were occupied by the Portuguese. They remained in possession until 1796, in which year they were ousted by the British.

The Dutch, whose religion was Protestant Christianity, followed a policy which was in marked contrast to that of the Portuguese. Extension of commerce was their main concern and since peace was essential to achieve this end, they even endured with subdued humbleness and patience whatever insult and provocation came from the Sinhalese. They even assisted the Sinhalese in two embassies to Siam which were sent to obtain monks to establish higher ordination in Sri Lanka.

The Dutch, however, had an established system of education throughout their territories. The school building was both church and school, the schoolmaster was both teacher and representative of the religion. Services were held regularly at these places; births and marriages were registered according to Christian rites. When the agent of the Church was so disposed, he was able to get those who did not attend church punished for the alleged offense. All civil rights and inheritance depended on a person's church affiliation. No person who was not a Christian could hold even a minor office under government, no person who was not a Christian could get married legally or register the birth of a child.

There was, however, one redeeming feature of this system. The organization was so extensive that they had to employ Sinhalese as their teachers and agents of religion. The vast majority of these Protestant agents were at heart Buddhists; they were Christians only in the sense of their office. The people themselves followed this plan: they were Buddhists inwardly but were officially Christians, for the purpose of registering their marriages, the births of their children, for holding office, etc. Thus the efforts of the Dutch in the propagation of their religion did not affect Buddhism much. On the other hand the Portuguese, where they had priests and where they had established churches under the direct control of these priests, were able to look after the congregations and gradually established their religion in such centers. Most of them were zealous and earnest in their duties and took a genuine interest in the welfare of their flocks.

Vimala Dharmasuriya II and his Successors

When the Dutch were occupying the maritime provinces, several Sinhalese rulers of the Kandyan kingdom made attempts to restore Buddhism. One of them was Vimala Dharmasuriya II (1687-1706), son and successor of Raajasinha II. He constructed a three-storeyed pavilion for the Sacred Tooth Relic. The king also made a pilgrimage to Sumanakuuta (Adam's Peak) on foot. Seeing that the state of the Order of monks was unsatisfactory again to such an extent that not more than five ordained monks were found in the whole country, the king sent an embassy to Arakan and obtained monks for an ordination ceremony. With the help of these monks an ordination ceremony was held at Getambe, at the place where a similar ceremony had been held formerly in the reign of Vimala Dharmasuriya I. At this ceremony thirty-three novices were given higher ordination and another one hundred and twenty persons were admitted to the Order.

Vimala Dharmasuriya II was succeeded by his son Sri Viraparaakrama Narendrasinha (1706-1739), a just ruler, mindful of the welfare of the religion. He constructed a two-storeyed building for the Sacred Tooth Relic, provided the monks with their requisites, and induced several members of the laity to enter the Order. However, during his reign many a monk had resorted to scandalous practices.

His successor Sri Vijaya Raajasinha (1739-1747), also a pious ruler, induced many a young person to join the Order and also held several religious festivals. He spent money on getting religious books written, caused preaching halls to be constructed at several places, and took measures to educate the people in the doctrine. Discovering that the Order of the Sangha was almost extinct in the island, he sent two missions to Siam, with the help of the Dutch who lent a ship for the voyage. The first expedition proved disastrous due to shipwreck, and before the second mission returned the king died. Thus his attempt to restore higher ordination failed.

The Reign of Kirti Sri Raajasinha

Sri Vijaya Raajasinha was succeeded by King Kirti Sri Raajasinha, whose reign proved to be one of the most inspiring periods for Buddhism in that century. At the time of his accession the Order of monks had sunk to very low levels of degeneracy. There was not a single monk in the whole island who had received the higher ordination. There were plenty of novices (i.e., saamaneras), but apart from a few skillful and pious ones among them the majority were leading a life unbecoming to monks. They set aside the study of Dhamma and Vinaya and resorted to the study of astrology, medicine and devil worship, led scandalous lives and engaged in cultivation of land and in trade. The older saamaneras ordained only the sons of their relatives so that they could obtain the immense wealth which the generations of kings and ministers had dedicated to the service of the Order. Kirti Sri Raajasinha was determined to set right this state of affairs. With the aid of the Dutch who gave a vessel for the voyage, the king sent an embassy to King Dhammika of Siam and re-established the higher ordination in Sri Lanka. Several hundreds were ordained and education was fostered. The king also proclaimed a code of conduct (*katikaavata*) for the guidance of the monks.

Velivita Sri Saranankara

In all these religious activities of King Kirti Sri Raajasinha he was inspired and guided by a great personality, a saamanera who was distinguished for his piety, enthusiasm, learning and determination. He was Velivita Pindapaatika Sri Saranankara. Born in 1698 at Velivita, a village near Kandy, he became a novice at the age of sixteen as a pupil of an elder saamanera called Suuriyagoda. With great effort and devotion he studied the Pali language and the doctrine, for which purpose he traveled from place to place in search of books and tutors. Later he went about preaching the Dhamma, thus encouraging others to rise up for the welfare of the religion. These activities of Saranankara Saamanera soon made him popular as a teacher of great renown who devoted his life to his own welfare and that of others, a poet, preacher and controversialist.

Apart from his skill as a scholar he was also known for his austere practices. When he went round the country learning or preaching, he depended for his sustenance on the ancient practice of a bhikkhu, called *pi.n.napaata*, gathering his food from house to house in his almsbowl. For this he became known as Pindapaatika Saranankara. When King Vimala Dharmasuriya II reigned he was a saamanera, but his sincere devotion had pleased the king so much that he made a gilt casket set with seven hundred gems and presented it to Saranankara Saamanera, with many books. This king also provided the monk with the requisites and induced him to write several literary works.

When King Sri Vijaya Raajasinha came to the throne it was at the request of Saranankara Saamanera that the king sent two embassies to Siam. In the reign of King Kirti Sri Raajasinha, Saranankara Saamanera offered his fullest cooperation in his activities in the revival of Buddhism and the king depended upon the saamanera for guidance, advice and inspiration. He urged the king to send the embassy to Siam and himself wrote the messages that were taken to the Siamese king and the Sangharaaja of that country. The king's ministers who constituted the embassy were chosen on his advice and this mission was successful mainly due to his exertions. After the return of the embassy Saranankara Saamanera was given higher ordination and was appointed Sangharaaja of Sri Lanka, the highest office conferred on a monk.

The activities of Saranankara Thera not only restored the higher ordination and the purity of the Sangha but also brought about a literary revival as a result of the impetus given by him to the study of the Pali language and the Buddha's teachings.

Saranankara Thera himself compiled several important religious works such as the *Munigu.naalankaara*, a Sinhalese poem in praise of the Buddha, the *Saaraartha Sangraha*, a treatise on various doctrinal teachings in Buddhism. *Abhisambodhi-alankaara*, a Pali poem in a hundred stanzas on the life of the Buddha from the time of Dipankara up to his enlightenment, the *Madhuraartha Prakaasanii*, which is a Sinhalese commentarial paraphrase to the Pali *Mahaabodhiva.msa*, and the *Ruupamaalaa*, a work on Pali grammar. Several others who were pupils of Saranankara Thera also composed many literary works. The great monk died in 1778 a.c. at the age of 81.

The successors of Sri Saranankara Thera are known as belonging to the Syaamopaali Nikaaya, now popularly called the Siyam (Syaama) Nikaaya. Only those who belonged to what was regarded as the highest caste could obtain higher ordination in that Nikaaya. In the year 1799 a saamanera named Ambagahapitiya ¥aanavimalatissa, who did not belong to that caste, went to Amarapura in Burma to obtain higher ordination and on his return he established the Amarapura Nikaaya in 1803. Subsequently, in 1863 Ambagahawatte Sri Saranankara Thera established the Raamañña Nikaaya. These three Nikaayas exist up to this day, with no doctrinal differences between them.

The Arrival of the British and the End of Sinhalese Rule in Sri Lanka

King Kirti Sri Raajasinha, whose reign, as was seen above, was one of the most fruitful for the cause of Buddhism, was succeeded by his brother Raajaadhi Raajasinha. A scholar of Pali, Sanskrit and Sinhalese as he was, the king himself composed the beautiful Sinhalese poem *Asadisa-daa-kava* and worked for the religion by taking necessary steps to preserve the purity of the Saasana. His nephew, Sri Vikrama Raajasinha, was the next and last king of Lanka. This ruler, who was in constant fear of the intrigues of his Adigar Pilima Talawe and his allies, had recourse to intoxicating drinks, hoping thus to forget his sorrows, and tortured all his enemies with appalling cruelty. There was general unrest in the kingdom and these conditions were evidently not conducive to the progress of Buddhism.

It was in 1796, during the reign of Raajaadhi Raajasinha, that the Dutch, who were defeated in battle, surrendered their territories to the British colony and Sir Frederick North was sent as the first British governor.

Before long North realized that the opportunity would come soon for them to possess the whole island, for Pilima Talawe, the Adigar of King Sri Vikrama Raajasinha of Kandy, disclosed his plans to ruin the king to the British governor himself. However, this plan of Pilima Talawe was revealed to the king, and the Adigar was beheaded in 1812. Ehelepola, who became the next Adigar, was detected in an attempt to organize a general rebellion against the king, and as punishment, the king tortured his wife and children cruelly. Subsequently the king punished all whom he suspected and as a result, unrest and disorder became the order of the day.

In these circumstances, Ehelepola appealed to the British for help. In January 1815 a British army marched to the capital city of Kandy and took the Sinhalese king captive. On the 2nd of March 1815, at a solemn assembly of the Kandyan chiefs and the monks, the king was deposed and his dominions were vested in the British Crown. Thus ended the glamour of the Kingdom of Kandy which had withstood the invasions and attacks of the Portuguese and the Dutch and for some time the English. Thus ended too the line of the Buddhist kings of Lanka who for 2301 years, from the accession of Vijaya in 486 BCE, brought glory and fame to their country and religion.

The British Attitude towards Buddhism

It was seen in the previous chapter how the British occupied the low-country of Lanka in 1796 and the Kandyan territories in 1815. These territories remained in their hands until 1948, in which year Sri Lanka regained her independence.

Mention has already been made of the solemn assembly of the 2nd of March 1815 held in Kandy. At this assembly a treaty was signed between the British rulers and the Kandyan chiefs, by which the chiefs handed over the country to the British and the British promised to safeguard Buddhism, declaring its rites and ceremonies sacred and inviolate.

The inclusion of this clause referring to Buddhism in the very treaty by which the chiefs handed over the country to the British is very significant. On the one hand, it indicates how concerned the Sinhalese leaders were about the future of Buddhism even in the hour of their misfortune. On the other hand, the British had obviously considered that its omission would bring disastrous results.

However, the British attitude towards Buddhism soon caused dissatisfaction among the Sinhalese chiefs. The chiefs and the Buddhist monks realized that the British had no desire to respect the clause of the treaty relating to Buddhism, and that they were keen to convert the people to their own faith.

During the early years after the signing of the treaty the British governor took part in the annual ceremonies connected with the Sacred Tooth Relic and appointed the chief theras, as had been done by the Sinhalese kings in former times. This created resentment on the part of the Christian missionaries in Sri Lanka and the Christian authorities in England, and soon both practices were dropped, severing whatever connection they had with Buddhism. From 1847 the bhikkhus were required to elect and appoint their own chiefs and in 1853 the British government handed over the Tooth Relic from their custody to the Diyawadana Nilame and the chief monks of the Malwatte and the Asgiriya monasteries.

While thus violating the treaty of 1815 the British rulers even prohibited the Buddhists from enjoying some of the privileges that were granted to the followers of the Christian faith. Thus, for instance, even as late as 1805 no child could be legally registered without previous baptism by a Christian minister, and the clergy did not solemnize the marriage of unbaptized individuals. Further, only those who adopted the Christian faith were favored with government employment. This attitude of the British made vast numbers of Buddhists adopt the new faith without any understanding of its teachings. These people saw in Christianity "not only happiness in the world which is to come, but, what was more important to them, the promise of this life as well!"

Some of the British governors in their attempt to disrupt the Buddhist organization even tried to bring about disunity between the monks and the laity and also to win over some of the leading Buddhist monks to their side. For they realized that the monks were the main obstacle to their conversions and that as long as the monks and the laity remained united their attempts would not meet with great success.

Lastly, the British rulers gave all possible support to the Christian missionaries to carry out their educational and missionary activities. How these missionary bodies attempted the Christianization of Lanka will be discussed in the next chapter.

The Christian Missionary Activities

From the beginning of the period of British rule several Christian missionary bodies engaged themselves actively in missionary activities in Sri Lanka. The Baptists had already started their activities in 1792. They were followed by the Wesleyan Methodists in 1814, the Americans in 1816, and the Church of England in 1818. These missionary bodies received every encouragement and assistance from the government.

The establishment of missionary schools in various parts of the island was one of the principal undertakings of these missionary bodies. These schools were manned and managed by the missionary societies with the assistance of the British government and were partly financed by public funds. The schools attracted large numbers of Buddhist children because they were the centers where young men were trained for high government offices. Hitherto the temple had been the village school and the monks were the instructors of the village children in secular learning as well as in spiritual wisdom. But under the British government temple education could not provide the learning necessary for government employment. Thus the Buddhist parents who wished to see their children in high government offices willingly sent them to the new missionary schools.

In these schools the children were molded according to the requirements of the missionary bodies. The authorities did not insist that one should become a Christian before admission, but each student was required to learn the Christian religion and to participate in the morning and evening religious services in the school. They had no opportunity of participating in their own religious observances. Almost every school had its own church. The lessons imparted to these children were arranged with a view to undermining their Buddhist religion. The teaching of the Buddha was criticized and condemned and the Buddhist practices were ridiculed. Buddhism was held up as a religion of the vulgar masses as opposed to the Christianity of civilized people.

This disparagement in course of time naturally had its expected result. People gradually began to give up their national faith for the new faith which they were trained to think of as more refined and cultured. It now became the fashion to adopt the Christian faith and Christian names and customs. Even those who did not embrace Christianity became indifferent to their own religion. When they grew up they did not even mind their conversion to any religion.

The missionaries also did not neglect the education of the girls. Convents were opened up with boarding facilities and in them the girls were brought up and educated with the utmost care until they were married in due time, with the sanction of the Christian guardians. The following table enumerating the assisted schools in Sri Lanka in 1886 belonging to the different denominations shows the extent of missionary activities in Lanka in the sphere of education:

NUMBER OF ASSISTED SCHOOLS IN 1886

	English	Bi-lingual	Vernacular	Total
Wesley Miss.	18	18	170	206
Rom. Cath.	25	5	175	205
C.M.S.	28	18	178	224
Amer. Miss	8	9	116	133
Baptist	1	5	32	38
Private	7	5	13	25
Hindu	0	0	5	5
Buddhist	0	1	11	12

Apart from the Christianization carried out through schools these missionary bodies sought conversion by distributing books and pamphlets which criticized and ridiculed the Buddhist religion and sang the praises of Christianity. For this purpose the missionaries themselves studied the doctrines of Buddhism and the Buddhist literature and also the Sinhalese language, thus enabling them to write tracts in Sinhalese attacking the Buddhist religion and extolling the virtues of Christianity. Christian preachers went about from village to village distributing these books and pamphlets and denouncing Buddhism and exhibiting the supremacy and the divine origin of Christianity.

Mohottiwatte Gunaananda Thera and the Buddhist Re-awakening

When the Christian missionaries were thus active in towns and villages propagating their gospel and converting the Buddhists to their faith, the Buddhist monks were not able enough to offer much resistance. When the villagers assembled in the temple on Poya (*uposatha*) days, they attempted to refute the arguments of the Christian preachers in the course of their sermons, but this method was not very effective. It was at this time, about 1860, that a young Buddhist saamanera named Mohottiwatte Gunaananda appeared on the scene and challenged the Christian missionaries to meet him in open-debate. This young novice had obtained his early education in Christian schools and had thus studied the Christian scriptures and was also well versed in the Buddha's teachings. He went from village to village making public speeches and held meetings in several Christian strongholds, often challenging the Christian clergy to face him in open debate. Soon he earned a great reputation for his eloquence and people flocked in thousands to hear him.

The Christian clergy at first took no notice of the challenge of this monk, but later, quite confident of their success they accepted the challenge. This resulted in three public controversies, one at Udanvita in 1866, another at Gampola in 1871 and the last at Panadura in 1873.

The Panadura controversy, which lasted for a week, was the most important of them all. It was the culmination of his efforts and it led to a Buddhist reawakening. The controversy was to take place in the presence of leading Sinhalese Christians and Buddhists. Rules were laid down so that the meeting could be held in a fair manner. The leading English newspaper of the time, *The Ceylon Times*, sent a special representative to report the proceedings. A complete report of all the speeches corrected by the speakers themselves was published in English day by day. The controversy ended with victory for the Buddhists. The Buddhist orator not only replied effectively to the fallacies of the Christian speakers, but also enlightened them on the principles and tenets of the Buddhist doctrine. When the Christians retired from the debate defeated, the Buddhists were overjoyed. Festivities were held in every temple to mark their triumph and the effigy of Gunaananda Thera was carried in procession in every village.

The triumph of the Buddhists over their Christian adversaries at the Panadura controversy flushed into their veins vigor and enthusiasm to work for the recovery of their lost glory.

Colonel Olcott and Buddhist Activities

An American scholar named Dr. Peebles, who happened to be in Sri Lanka on a visit about the time of this Panadura controversy, was so impressed with it that he published its proceedings in book form on his return to America. The attention of Colonel Henry Steele Olcott was first drawn towards Buddhism by this report of the controversy which he happened to read in a public library in America. Olcott was an American by birth who had spent his early life as a very successful farmer and a colonel of both the army and the navy. At an early age of 43 years in 1875 he gave up all worldly fortunes and together with Madame Blavatsky formed the Theosophical Society for the quest of truth in all religions. Having read the reports of the Panadura controversy, he realized the importance of the teachings of the Buddha and in 1880 he came over to Lanka along with Madame Blavatsky to gain a first-hand knowledge of Buddhism. When his studies soon convinced him of the teachings of the Buddha, he embraced Buddhism and worked for the upliftment of the Buddhists in Lanka.

Olcott showed the Buddhist leaders of Sri Lanka that if Buddhism was to raise its head against the Christian missionary activities, they should open up Buddhist schools to educate their children. Under his guidance and leadership, and with the support of all the leading Buddhist monks, the lay Buddhist leaders in Sri Lanka at that time founded the Buddhist Theosophical Society on 17th June 1880. The primary objects of the society were the establishment of Buddhist schools, and the bringing together of Buddhist workers in a cooperative body without distinction of caste or position for the purpose of promoting the welfare of the Buddhists of Lanka.

At the time of Olcott's arrival there were only three Buddhist schools in Sri Lanka which obtained government grants, one at Dodanduwa, another at Panadura, and the third at Bandaragama. In 1897, twelve years after the establishment of the society, there were 25 boys' schools, 11 girls' schools, and 10 mixed schools founded by the society. In 1903 there were 174 schools under the management of the society with an attendance of about 30,000 children. In 1940 the number of schools had risen to 429. Olcott and his supporters went from village to village appealing to the people to donate subscriptions for the maintenance of these schools, and funds were readily forthcoming. Several leading educationists of his day made his educational plans a great success. Mention should be made among them of C. W. Leadbeater, Bowles Daly, F. L. Woodward, A. E. Bultjens and Mrs. M. M. Higgins. Mrs. Higgins was particularly responsible for the successful education of the Buddhist girls. The leading Buddhist schools of the present day such as Ananda and Nalanda Colleges in Colombo, Dharmaraja in Kandy, Mahinda in Galle, Dharmasoka in Ambalangoda, Visakha in Bambalapitiya, and Museus in Colombo are outstanding examples of the success of his efforts.

Olcott pointed out to the Sinhalese Buddhist leaders of his time that they should have their own publications to give publicity to Buddhist and national opinion. For this purpose the Buddhist Theosophical Society started the Sinhalese newspaper, *Sarasavisandarasa*, in December 1880, and later its English supplement, *The Buddhist*, now a monthly of the YMBA, Colombo. Colonel Olcott worked hard to win back for the Sinhalese their lost rights. It was as a result of his efforts that the Buddhists of Lanka gained freedom to hold their Buddhist processions and that the full-moon day of Vesak was declared a public holiday. The present Buddhist flag is also a creation of Olcott which he appealed to the Buddhists to hoist on all important Buddhist occasions. His efforts also resulted in the appointment of Buddhist registrars of marriages.

Of the Panadura controversy and the consequent arrival of Colonel Olcott, it could justly be said that these two events jointly closed down a dark period in Lankan Buddhism and ushered in a new bright era.

This noble personality who awakened the Sinhalese Buddhists and showed them the path on which they should proceed passed away in 1907 while he was in India.

Other Activities of the Buddhist Renaissance Movement

Apart from meeting the Christian opponents in open debate, Mohottivatte Gunaananda Thera and his companions had planned other devices to counteract the anti-Buddhist propaganda of the Christian missionaries and revive the Buddhist faith in the country. One of these devices was the establishment of a printing press whereby they could reply to the criticisms of the Christians and also publish books for the study of Buddhism.

Thus the first press, controlled by Sinhalese Buddhists, was established in 1862 under the name of Lankopakaara Press. It was a donation by the king of Siam. In the same year Mohottivatte Gunaananda Thera established the Sarvajña-saasanaabhivurddhi-daayaka Press at Kotahena, near Colombo. Consequently the Lakrivikirana Press was established in 1863 and the Lankabhinavavisruta Press in 1864.

In the meantime learned monks of the period, with the assistance of lay followers, brought about a revival of Buddhist learning. Pioneers among them were the venerable Hikkaduve Sri Sumangala, who founded the Vidyodaya Pirivena of Maligakanda in Colombo in 1874 and the venerable Ratmalaane Sri Dhammaaloka, who founded the Vidyaalankara Pirivena of Peliyagoda in Colombo in 1875. In these two great centers of learning a vast number of monks and lay people received education and in a short time the fame of these two pirivenas spread even in foreign countries.

The scholars whom these two centers produced opened up other pirivenas in different parts of the country and also contributed to Buddhistic studies by compiling and editing numerous books. It was also about this time that devoted scholars from foreign countries who happened to be in Sri Lanka evinced a great interest in Buddhism, its culture and literature, and created an interest in their kinsmen in the West through their valuable treatises. Turner, Tennant, Childers, Rhys Davids and Geiger were but a few among them.

Anagaarika Dharmapaala and the Buddhist Cultural Revival

A different type of revivalistic activity was carried out by a group of lay Buddhist leaders just at this time, the foremost of this group being Anagaarika Dharmapaala. The fame of this great personality lies in his successful effort of reforming the Buddhist society in Sri Lanka, which had fallen into a very low moral state, and also in his activities in India for the purpose of reviving Buddhism in that country and for winning back the Buddhist sacred places there for their rightful owners, the Buddhists. We are presently concerned only with his social reformation in Sri Lanka.

Anagaarika Dharmapaala, formerly known as David Hewavitarana, was born in 1864 as the eldest son of a leading businessman in Colombo who had migrated to the capital city from Matara in south Lanka. The father, mother and the grandfather of the child were devoted Buddhists who were close associates of the venerable Hikkaduve Sri Sumangala Thera. At home the child was thus brought up in a Buddhist environment though he received his education in Christian schools. Those were the days when Mohottiwatte Gunaananda Thera was engaged in verbal battles against the Christian missionary activities, and young Dharmapaala had not only listened to the orations of the great speaker with much inspiration, but also had become a favorite of the monks by his constant visits to the temple at Kotahena. When Colonel Olcott and Madame Blavatsky arrived in Lanka in 1880, Dharmapaala, then a youth of 16 years, naturally became a great favorite of the two foreigners through his association with Gunaananda Thera.

The speeches and activities of Colonel Olcott greatly inspired the young enthusiast. In 1883, consequent upon a brutal assault on a Buddhist procession by a Catholic mob at Kotahena, Dharmapaala left his Catholic school and in the following year became a member of the Buddhist Theosophical Society in Colombo, of which his grandfather was the president. At the age of 20 Dharmapaala obtained permission from his father to leave home and lead a celibate life as he wished to devote all his time to the welfare of the Saasana. From that time he stayed at the headquarters of the Buddhist Theosophical Society.

In 1886 when Colonel Olcott returned to Sri Lanka after a short stay abroad and planned to go round the country addressing public gatherings and collecting money for the

Buddhist Educational Fund, Anagaarika Dharmapaala joined him as his interpreter. For this purpose he obtained leave from the Education Department where he was working as a junior clerk and subsequently vacated his post in order to dedicate all his life to the good of the religion.

As the interpreter of Colonel Olcott, Dharmapaala gained immense experience as a speaker. He now traveled throughout the country with or without his companion, Olcott.

Those were the days when the Buddhists of Lanka were reluctant to declare themselves Buddhists, for Buddhism was considered to be the faith of the unurbanized masses. It was the fashion at that time to become a Christian, to study English and other allied subjects, to adopt a foreign name and to imitate the dress of the foreigners and their customs and manners. Buddhism and Buddhist culture were subjected to ridicule and were the heritage of villagers in the interior.

Anagaarika Dharmapaala was the foremost among those who rose against this mentality of the Buddhists. Through his public speeches and numerous articles in newspapers and journals he vehemently opposed the habit of imitating foreigners in religion, names and customs. He emphatically pointed out that this tendency to imitate was a clear manifestation of a lack of the primary element of self-esteem. In keeping with his preaching he himself changed his name from David to Dharmapaala. The people listened to his sermons and attentively read his articles in journals and newspapers and were convinced of the truth of his philosophy. Gradually there came about a cultural revival. The people began to take pride in their religion, their language and their customs.

Above all, several younger men of his time joined the Buddhist forward movement to guide the destinies of future generations of Buddhists in Sri Lanka.

This great personality, who indefatigably gave his services for the revival of Buddhism in Lanka, India and other parts of the world, in his last days entered the Order as the venerable Devamitta Dhammapaala Thera. He passed away in the year 1933, while he was in India. To perpetuate his memory Sri Lanka and India celebrated his birth centenary in 1964-65.

Buddhism in Sri Lanka in the First Half of the Twentieth Century

The leading men in the Buddhist community at the beginning of the twentieth century were inspired by the activities of Anagaarika Dharmapaala and they formed into organized bodies for the promotion of the Buddhist revivalistic movement. Among them were great personalities such as Sir D. B. Jayatillake, F. R. Somnayake, Valisinha Harishchandra and W. A. de Silva. To them the Buddhist revival was the national revival.

These prominent men, whose names have gone into history, became active members of leading Buddhist associations like the Buddhist Theosophical Society (founded 1880), the Colombo Young Men's Buddhist Association (1898), the Maha Bodhi Society (1891), and the Ceylon Buddhist Congress (1918), and worked with remarkable success to achieve the aims and objects of those organizations. Through such organizations these Buddhist leaders were able to unite and bring together all Buddhists in Sri Lanka, to inspire them to be active, to collect funds for educational and other religious purposes, to give the Buddhist children a sound religious and secular education, to do a great deal of social work and to raise the spiritual and moral standard of the people.

A great deal of literary work was produced during this period. The Vidyodaya and the Vidyaalankaara Pirivenas and their affiliated institutions, which numbered about 200, had produced many scholars who edited several canonical and commentarial works in the early twentieth century. Simon Hewavitarana, the youngest brother of Anagaarika Dharmapaala, had left a large legacy which was to be used for the printing and publishing of Pali books, and this greatly facilitated the production of books at this time. From about 1930 many modern scholars, both monks and laymen, have edited and published many more texts of Pali Buddhism and have also compiled several secondary works on the different aspects of Buddhism. To name these scholars and their publications is not necessary since they and their works are very well known.

A great enthusiasm was also created for the rebuilding of ancient Buddhist shrines in the old capitals of Sri Lanka. The Ruwanveli Daagaba was the first to receive attention. The other shrines too were renovated one by one and today the old city of Anuraadhapura has once more become a sacred city with the Catholic Church and the commercial sites which were in the city being moved to other places.

Sri Lanka has not only reorganized her Buddhist activities within the country but has also taken a leading part in sending *Dhammaduutas*, "messengers of the Dhamma," abroad. In 1950 the World Fellowship of Buddhists was set up in order to bring all Buddhist countries together, and several conferences were held in the subsequent years.

It is a very significant fact that this revival of Buddhism in the twentieth century was accelerated towards the middle of that century as a result of the Sinhalese Buddhist leaders of the time gaining control of the reins of government. Ultimately in 1948 Sri Lanka regained its independence after a period of British rule of 133 years. The Buddhist leaders who worked indefatigably for the cause of Buddhism were also the Sinhalese national leaders who led the struggle for liberation from foreign rule. It was therefore to be expected that when these leaders gained national freedom and took over the reins of government from the British rulers, they were mindful of their national faith and its culture and therefore took the necessary steps to set things right so that Buddhism would once more receive its rightful place.

The Buddha Jayanti and After

In the year 1956, on the 23rd of May, which was the Vesak full-moon day of that year, the Buddhists in Sri Lanka and other parts of the world celebrated the Buddha Jayanti. That was the 2500th anniversary of the Buddha's Parinibbaana, a day specially significant to the Buddhists the world over on account of the tradition that it constitutes half the life-span of the Saasana and that from that year the Dhamma would flourish and spread far and wide.

The history of Buddhism in Sri Lanka from the closing years of the last century has clear indications that the prophecy, as far as Lanka is concerned, is coming true. In other parts of the world too it is seen that more and more people who were not Buddhists by birth are becoming interested in Buddhism.

The government of Sri Lanka, on its part, undertook numerous activities in commemoration of the Buddha Jayanti. A committee of leading Buddhist monks and laymen was appointed to advise the government on all matters relating to the Buddha Jayanti celebrations. Arrangements were made to translate the Tripitaka into Sinhalese and compile an *Encyclopaedia of Buddhism* in English and one in Sinhalese as well. It was also decided to compile other books dealing with the biography of the Buddha, his teachings and the history of Buddhism. The completion of the renovation of the Daladaa Maaligawa (the Temple of the Tooth) in Kandy, before the Buddha Jayanti and to aid the reconstruction of the Mahiyangana Thupa were among its other undertakings. A substantial grant was also given to the organization which was handling the construction work of a Sanghaaraama for the Buddhist monks at the University of Ceylon, Peradeniya. Arrangements were made to hold a World Buddhist Conference in Colombo in the following year.

From the Buddha Jayanti year it was noticeable that the Buddhists in Lanka applied themselves more keenly to the practice of morality taught in Buddhism while showing interest in the celebration of Buddhist festivals. More and more people observe the eight precepts on the Poya days and young children are given a sound religious education. The government on its part has given the necessary encouragement for this religious re-establishment. In January 1959 the Vidyodaya and the Vidyaalankaara Pirivenas were made two universities. The private Buddhist and Christian schools were taken over in December 1960 and are now managed by the government. The four Poya days of the month (i.e., full and new moon, and the two quarter moon days) were made the weekend holidays in 1966, instead of Sundays as in previous times. It has also been planned to start a new Bhikkhu University in Anuraadhapura.

Sri Lanka has today about 6.5 million Buddhists, which is about sixty-five percent of her total population. There are nearly

6,000 Buddhist monasteries all over the island with approximately 15,000 monks. Almost all the monasteries in the island have their Dhamma schools where Buddhist children are given religious instruction on the Poya days (previously on Sundays). The Colombo Young Men's Buddhist Association conducts an island-wide examination annually for the pupils of these Dhamma schools. The children are provided with free books, by the Ministry of Cultural Affairs and prizes are given to those who pass these examinations, including one on the Dhammapada, and this association spends annually a large sum of money on the religious education of children. In 1956-57, 163,180 children sat for the Dhamma examination.

The foregoing account will tell the reader of the vicissitudes that this great religion, Buddhism, had to face during its history of over 2,000 years in this isle of Sri Lanka. It had its tidal ebb and flow. During the four centuries of foreign domination Buddhism withstood all the assaults that almost crushed it.

Since Sri Lanka gained its independence in 1948, there has been a revival of the Buddhist religion and culture in the country, and this reawakening was particularly noticeable when the Buddha Jayanti was celebrated in 1956.

The progress achieved since the eighties of the last century may well be called remarkable. Yet, to the Buddhists of Lanka, this should not be a cause of complacency, for which there is no room in a world of change. It remains the duty of the present generation and the coming ones to preserve and strengthen these achievements against the corrosive forces of a materialist age, and to work devotedly so that the Buddha's message of Wisdom and Compassion may take still firmer and deeper roots in Lanka and also spread its beneficial influence over the world.

4

Buddhism in Thailand

ITS PAST AND ITS PRESENT

People all over the world who are interested in Buddhism and keep in touch with its news and activities must have heard of the Buddha Jayanti celebrations held a few years ago in all Buddhist countries, including India and Japan. It was in 1957 or, according to the reckoning of some Buddhist countries, in 1956, that Buddhism, as founded by Gotama the Buddha, had completed its 2,500th year of existence. The Buddhist tradition, especially of the Theravada or Southern School such as now prevails in Burma, Ceylon, Cambodia, Laos and Thailand, has it that on the completion of 2,500 years from its foundation, Buddhism would undergo a great revival, resulting in its all-round progress, in both the fields of study and practice. Buddhists throughout the world, therefore, commemorated the occasion in 1956-57 by various kinds of activities such as meetings, symposia, exhibitions and the publication of Buddhist texts and literature.

As to whether or not the tradition mentioned above has any truth behind it, the future alone will testify. However, judging from news received from all corners of the globe, it is no exaggeration to say that mankind is taking an ever-increasing interest in Buddhism. As a matter of fact, since the end of the Second World War interest in Buddhism as evinced by people in Europe, America, and Australia has reached a scale unheard of before. Any casual perusal of journals on Buddhism in any of these continents will convince the readers of this statement. It is a matter worth noticing that after the end of the First

World War also, Buddhism made great headway in Europe and elsewhere. This phenomenon can perhaps be best explained by the fact that mankind's spiritual thirst is more sharpened by calamities like war, and that in times of distress mankind realizes Truth better.

The Land of Yellow Robes

Thailand is perhaps the only country in the world where the king is constitutionally stipulated to be a Buddhist and the upholder of the Faith. For centuries Buddhism has established itself in Thailand and has enriched the lives of the Thais in all their aspects. Indeed, without Buddhism, Thailand would not be what it is today. Owing to the tremendous influence Buddhism exerts on the lives of its people, Thailand is called by many foreigners "The Land of Yellow Robes," for yellow robes are the garments of Buddhist monks. In view of the increasing interest the world is taking in Buddhism and in view of the fact that Thailand is one of the countries where Buddhism still exists as a living force it will not, perhaps, be out of place to know something of the story of how this great faith reached that country.

BUDDHISM IN THAILAND: ITS PAST

Different opinions exist about when, exactly, Buddhism reached that part of the world now officially known as Thailand. Some scholars say that Buddhism was introduced to Thailand during the reign of Asoka, the great Indian emperor who sent Buddhist missionaries to various parts of the then known world. Others are of the view that Thailand received Buddhism much later.

Judging from archaeological finds and other historical evidence, however, it is safe to say that Buddhism first reached Thailand when the country was inhabited by a racial stock of people known as the Mon-Khmer who then had their capital, Dvaravati, at a city now known as Nakon Pathom (Sanskrit: Nagara Prathama), about 50 kilometers to the west of Bangkok. The great pagoda at Nakon Pathom, Phra Pathom Chedi (Prathama cetiya), and other historical findings in other parts of the country testify to this fact as well as to the fact that

Buddhism, in its varied forms, reached Thailand at four different periods, namely:

I. Theravada or Southern Buddhism

II. Mahayana or Northern Buddhism

III. Burma (Pagan) Buddhism

IV. Ceylon (Lankavamsa) Buddhism

We shall now proceed to study each of these periods in detail.

Theravada or Southern Buddhism

That the first form of Buddhism introduced to Thailand was that of Theravada (The Doctrine of the Elders) School is proved by various archaeological remains unearthed in the excavations at Nakon Pathom, such as the Dharma Chakra (Wheel of Law), the Buddha footprints and seats, and the inscriptions in the Pali language, all of which are in rocks. Such objects of Buddhistic veneration existed in India before the introduction of the Buddha image, which appeared later as a result of Greek influence. Buddhism, therefore, must have reached Thailand during the 3rd century B.C., and it must have been more or less the same form of Buddhism as was propagated by the great Buddhist Emperor Asoka. This form of Buddhism was known as Theravada or Hinayana (The Lower Vehicle) in contradistinction to the term Mahayana (The Higher Vehicle); the two schools having sprung up soon after the passing away of the Buddha. When worship of the Buddha image became popular in India, it also spread to other countries where Buddhism had already been introduced. This is borne out by the fact that many Buddha images, especially those of the Gupta style, had been found in the ruins of Nakon Pathom and the neighboring cities. Judging from the style of the Buddha images found, it can also be assumed that the early Buddhist missionaries to Thailand went from Magadha (in Bihar state, India).

To support the view that the first form of Buddhism introduced to Thailand was that of the Theravada School as propagated by Emperor Asoka, we have evidence from the

Mahavamsa, the ancient chronicle of Ceylon. In one of its passages dealing with the propagation of the Dhamma, the Mahavamsa records that Asoka sent missionaries headed by Buddhist elders to as many as nine territories. One of these territories was known as Suvarnabhumi where two Theras (elder monks), Sona and Uttara, were said to have proceeded.

Now opinions differ as to where exactly this land of Suvarnabhumi is. Thai scholars express the opinion that it is in Thailand and that its capital was at Nakon Pathom, while scholars of Burma say that Suvarnabhumi is in Burma, the capital being at Thaton, a Mon (Peguan) town in eastern Burma near the Gulf of Martaban. Still other scholars of Laos and Cambodia claim that the territory of Suvarnabhumi is in their lands. Historical records in this connection being meager as they are, it would perhaps be of no avail to argue as to the exact demarcation of Suvarnabhumi. Taking all points into consideration, one thing, however, seems clear beyond dispute. That is Suvarnabhumi was a term broadly used in ancient times to denote that part of Southeast Asia which now includes Southern Burma, Thailand, Laos, Cambodia and Malaya. The term Suvarnabhumi is a combination of the words *suvarna* and *bhumi*. Both are Sanskrit words; the former means gold and the latter stands for land. Suvarnabhumi therefore literally means Golden Land or Land of Gold. Keeping in view the abundance of nature in that part of Asia just referred to, the term seems but appropriate.

The reason why scholars of Thailand express the view that the capital of Suvarnabhumi was at Nakon Pathom was because of the archaeological finds unearthed in the area surrounding that town. Nowhere in any of the countries mentioned above, not even at Thaton in Burma, could one find such a large and varied number of ancient relics as were found at Nakon Pathom. By age and style these archaeological objects belong to the times of Emperor Asoka and the later Guptas. Even the Great Stupa (Phra Pathom Chedi) at Nakon Pathom itself is basically identical with the famous Sañchi Stupa in India, built by Asoka, especially if one were to remove the *shikhara* or upper portion. Many Thai archaeologists are of the opinion that the shikhara was a later addition to the pagoda, a result, so to say, of the blending of the Thai aesthetic sense with Indian architectural art. Moreover, the name Pathom Chedi (Pali: Pathama Cetiya) means "First Pagoda" which, in all probability, signifies that it was the first pagoda built in Suvarnabhumi. This would easily fit in with the record of the Mahavamsa — that Theras Sona and Uttara went and established Buddhism in the territory of Suvarnabhumi at the injunction of Emperor Asoka. Taking cognizance of the fact that Asoka reigned from 269 to 237 B.C., we can reasonably conclude that Buddhism first spread to Thailand during the 3rd century B.C. It is interesting to note in this connection that the history of the penetration of Indian culture to Southeast Asia also started more or less during the same period.

Mahayana or Northern Buddhism

With the growth of Mahayana Buddhism in India, especially during the reign of King Kanishka who ruled over Northern India during the second half of the first century A.D., the sect also spread to the neighboring countries, such as Sumatra, Java, and Kambuja (Cambodia). It is probable that Mahayana Buddhism was introduced to Burma, Pegu (Lower Burma) and Dvaravati (now Nakon Pathom in Western Thailand) from Magadha (in Bihar, India) at the same time as it went to the Malay Archipelago. But probably it did not have any stronghold there at that time; hence no spectacular trace was left of it.

Starting from the beginning of the fifth century A.D. Mahayana Buddhist missionaries from Kashmir in Northern India began to go to Sumatra in succession. From Sumatra the faith spread to Java and Cambodia. By about 757 A.D. (Buddhist Era: 1300) the Srivijaya king with his capital in Sumatra rose in power and his empire spread throughout the Malay Peninsula and Archipelago. Part of South Thailand (from Surasthani downwards) came under the rule of the Srivijaya king. Being Mahayanists, the rulers of Srivijaya gave much encouragement and support to the propagation of Mahayana Buddhism. In South Thailand today we have much evidence to substantiate that Mahayana Buddhism was once prevalent there. This evidence is in the form of stupas or chetiyas and images, including votive tablets of the Buddhas and Bodhisattas (Phra Phim), which were found in large number, all of the same type as those discovered in Java and Sumatra. The chetiyas in Chaiya (Jaya) and Nakon Sri Thammarath (Nagara Sri Dharmaraja), both in South Thailand, clearly indicate Mahayana influence.

From 1002 to 1182 A.D. kings belonging to the Suryavarman dynasty ruled supreme in Cambodia. Their empire extended over the whole of present-day Thailand. Being adherents of Mahayana Buddhism with a strong mixture of Brahmanism, the Suryavarman rulers did much to propagate and establish the tenets of the Northern School. There is an interesting stone inscription, now preserved in the National Museum at Bangkok, which tells us that in about 1017 A.D. (B.E. 1550) there ruled in Lopburi, in central Thailand and once a capital city, a king from Nakon Sri Thammarath who traced his ancestry to Srivijaya rulers. The king had a son who later became the ruler of Kambuja (Cambodia) and who, more or less, kept Thailand under the suzerainty of Cambodia for a long time. During this period there was much amalgamation of the two countries' religions and cultures. The stone inscription under consideration probably refers to one of the Suryavarman kings who had blood relationship with the Srivijaya rulers.

From the inscription just referred to we also learn that at that period the form of Buddhism prevalent in Lopburi was that of Theravada, and that Mahayana Buddhism, already established in Cambodia, became popularized in Thailand only after Thailand had come under the sway of Cambodia. There are no indications, however, that the Mahayana School superseded the Theravada in any way. This was due to the fact that Theravada Buddhism was already on a firm basis in Thailand when the Mahayana School was introduced there. That there were monks of both schools, Theravada and Mahayana, in Lopburi during those days, is indicated in a stone inscription in the Cambodian language, found in a Brahmanic Temple within the vicinity of Lopburi city itself.

Much of the Brahmanic culture which survives in Thailand till today could be traced to its origin from Cambodia during this period. Many of the Cambodian kings themselves were zealous adherents of Brahmanism and its ways of life. This period, therefore, can be termed Mahayana Period. Sanskrit, the sacred language of the Hindus, took its root deep in Thailand during these times.

Burma (Pagan) Buddhism

In 1057 A.D. King Anuruddha (Anawratha) became powerful in the whole of Burma, having his capital at Pagan (Central Burma). Anuruddha extended his kingdom right up to Thailand, especially the Northern and Central parts, covering areas now known as Chiengmai, Lopburi, and Nakon Pathom. Being a Theravada Buddhist, Anuruddha ardently supported the cause of Theravada which Burma, like Thailand, at first received directly from India through missionaries sent by Emperor Asoka. However, at the time under consideration, Buddhism in India was already in a state of decline, and as contact between Burma and India was then faint, Theravada Buddhism, as prevalent in Burma at that time, underwent some changes and assumed a form somewhat different from the original doctrine. This, at a later stage, became what is known in Thailand as Burma (Pagan) Buddhism. During the period of King Anuruddha's suzerainty over Thailand, Burmese Buddhism exercised great influence over the country, especially in the North where, owing to proximity, the impact from Burma was more felt.

It is significant that Buddhist relics found in North Thailand bear a striking Theravada influence, whereas those found in the South clearly show their Mahayana connections dating back from Srivijaya days. To a great extent this is due to the fact that, in their heyday of suzerainty over Thailand, the Burmese under Anuruddha were content with Upper Thailand only, while leaving the South practically to be ruled by their Khmer (Cambodian) vassals whose capital was at Lopburi.

From the beginning of the 2nd century B.C. the Thai people, whose original homeland was in the valleys between the Huang Ho and the Yangtze Kiang in China, began to migrate southwards as a result of constant friction with the neighboring tribes. In the course of their migration which lasted for several centuries, they became separated into two main groups. One group went and settled in the plains of the Salween River, Shan States, and other areas and spread on as far as Assam. This group of Thais is called Thai Yai (Big Thai). The other main group moved further South and finally settled in what is today termed Thailand. The latter group of Thais is called Thai Noi (Small Thai). The Thais in present-day Thailand are actually the descendants of these migrant Thais. Of course, in the course of their migration which, as said above, continued off and on for a long time, there had been a great deal of mixture of blood through intermarriage which was only natural. We should always bear in mind that there are several ethnic groups scattered through the length and breadth of Southeast Asia from times immemorial. But even today we can trace the language affinity of the Thais living in widely scattered areas such as Assam, Upper Burma, Southern China, Shan States, Laos, North Vietnam, and Thailand.

After struggling hard for a long time the Thais were able to establish their independent state at Sukhothai (Sukhodaya) in North Thailand. This was probably about 1257 A.D. (B.E. 1800). It was during the period of their movement southwards that the Thais came into contact with the form of Buddhism as practiced in Burma and propagated under the royal patronage of King Anuruddha. Some scholars are of the opinion that as Mahayana Buddhism had spread to China as early as the beginning of the Christian Era, the Thais, while still in their original home in China, must have already been acquainted with some general features of Buddhism. As the Thai migrants grew in strength their territory extended and finally they became the masters of the land in succession to Anuruddha, whose kingdom declined after his death. During the succeeding period, the Thais were able to exert themselves even more prominently in their southward drive. Thus they came into close contact with the Khmers, the erstwhile power, and became acquainted with both Mahayana Buddhism and Brahmanism as adopted and practiced in Kambuja (Cambodia). Much of the Brahmanic influence, such as religious and cultural rites, especially in the court circles, passed on from Cambodia to the Thais during this period, for Hinduism was already firmly established in Cambodia at that time. Even the Thai scripts, based on Cambodian scripts which, in turn, derived their origin from India, were invented by King Ram Kamhaeng of Sukhothai during the period under consideration.

Of the period under discussion it may be observed in passing that Northern Thailand, from Sukhothai District upwards, came much under the influence of Burma (Pagan) Buddhism, while in the central and southern parts of the country many Mahayana beliefs and practices, inherited from the days of the Suryavarmans and the Srivijayas, still persisted.

Ceylon (Lankavamsa) Buddhism

This is the most important period in the history of the spread of Buddhism to Thailand, for it witnessed the introduction to that country of that form of Buddhism which remains dominant there until today.

About 1153 A.D. (B.E. 1696) Parakramabahu the Great (1153-1186 A.D.) became king of Ceylon, known in ancient days as Lanka. A powerful monarch and a great supporter of Theravada Buddhism, Parakrāmabahu did much to spread and consolidate the Dhamma of the Lord in his island kingdom. He it was who caused (according to some scholars of Southern Buddhism) the Seventh Buddhist Council to be held under the chairmanship of Kassapa Thera, of Dimbulagala in order to revise and strengthen the Doctrine and the Discipline (Dhamma and Vinaya).

As a result of the efforts of King Parakramabahu the Great, Buddhism was much consolidated in Ceylon and the news spread to neighboring lands. Buddhist monks from various countries, such as Burma, Pegu (Lower Burma), Kambuja, Lanna (North Thailand) and Lanchang (Laos) flocked to Ceylon in order to acquaint themselves with the pure form of the Dhamma. Thailand also sent her Bhikkhus to Ceylon and thereby obtained the *upasampada vidhi* (ordination rite) from Ceylon, which later became known in Thailand as Lankavamsa. This was about 1257 A.D. (B.E. 1800). Apparently the early batches of Bhikkhus, who returned from Ceylon after studies, often accompanied by Ceylonese monks, established themselves first in Nakon Sri Thammarath (South Thailand), for many of the Buddhist relics bearing definitely Ceylonese influence, such as stupas and Buddha images, were found there. Some of these relics are still in existence today. News of the meritorious activities of these monks soon spread to Sukhothai, then the capital of Thailand, and King Ram Kamhaeng who was ruling at the time, invited those monks to his capital and gave them his royal support in propagating the Doctrine. This fact is recorded in one of the King's rock inscriptions, dated about 1277 A.D. Since then Ceylon (Sinhala) Buddhism became very popular and was widely practiced in Thailand. Some of the Thai kings, such as King Maha Dharmaraja Lithai of Sukhothai dynasty and King Borom Trai Lokanath of the early Ayudhya Period, even entered the Holy Order or Bhikkhu Sangha according to the ordination rite of Lankavamsa Buddhism by inviting a patriarch from Ceylon, Maha Sami Sangharaja Sumana by name, to be the presiding monk over his upasampada (ordination) ceremony. Many monasteries, stupas, Buddha images and even Buddha footprints, such as the well-known one at Sraburi in central Thailand, were built in accordance with the usage popular in Ceylon. The study of Pali, the language of Theravada or Southern Buddhism, also made great progress, and in all matters dealing with the Dhamma the impact of Ceylon was perceptibly felt.

However, there had been no antagonism between the different forms of Buddhism already in existence in Thailand and the Lankavamsa which had been introduced later from Ceylon. On the contrary they seemed to have amalgamated peacefully, and all had adjusted themselves to one another's benefit. This is evident in all religious rites and ceremonies of Thailand. Indeed, somewhat characteristic of the Buddhists, there had been a spirit of forbearance in all matters. For instance, even today Brahmanic rites thrive side by side with Buddhistic ceremonies in Thailand and Cambodia, especially in the royal courts.

History repeats itself. Years after, when in Ceylon under King Kirtisri (1747-1781 A.D.) the upasampada ordination was lost due to a decline of Buddhism and upheavals in the country, Thailand (during the reign of King Boromkot, 1733-1758 A.D.)

was able to repay the debt by sending a batch of Buddhist monks, under the leadership of Upali and Ariyamuni Theras, who in the course of time established in Ceylon what is known as the *Siyamopali Vamsa* or *Siyam Nikaya,* or Siamese Sect, which still is a major sect in that country. Upali worked and died in Sri Lanka, the country he loved no less than his own.

Today, for all purposes, Thailand can be termed a Theravada Buddhist country. There are, of course, a few Mahayana monks and monasteries, but they are mostly confined to foreign communities, chiefly the Chinese. All, however, live at peace and cooperate with one another.

So much for the past of Buddhism in Thailand.

BUDDHISM IN THAILAND: ITS PRESENT

According to the census taken in 1960 the population of Thailand numbers 25,519,965. Of this number 94% are Buddhists (the rest are mostly Muslims and Christians). This fact itself demonstrates more than anything else how influential Buddhism is in Thailand. In their long history of existence the Thais seem to have been predominantly Buddhists, at least ever since they came into contact with the tenets of Buddhism. All the Thai kings in the recorded history of present-day Thailand have been adherents of Buddhism. The country's constitution specifies that the King of Thailand must be a Buddhist and the Upholder of Buddhism.

The term "The Land of Yellow Robes" has not been inappropriately applied to Thailand, for two things strike most foreigners as soon as they set foot in that country. One is the Buddhist temple with its characteristic architecture, and the other is the sight of yellow-clad Buddhist monks and novices who are to be seen everywhere, especially in the early hours of dawn when they go out in great numbers for alms. The two sights inevitably remind the foreigners that here is a country where Buddhism is a dominant force in the people's life. Indeed, to the Thai nation as a whole, Buddhism has been the main spring from which flow its culture and philosophy, its art and literature, its ethics and morality, and many of its folkways and festivals.

For clarity and convenience we shall divide the study of the present state of Buddhism in Thailand into two parts, namely the Bhikkhu Sangha or the Holy Order, and the Laity.

The Bhikkhu Sangha or the Holy Order

The Bhikkhu Sangha or the Holy Order of Buddhist monks has been in existence in Thailand ever since Buddhism was introduced there. According to the 1958 census there were in the whole kingdom of Thailand 159,648 monks; 73,311 novices; and 20,944 monasteries or temples. These are scattered throughout the country, particularly more numerous in the thickly populated areas. The Bhikkhu Sangha of Thailand, being of Theravada or Southern School, observes the same set of discipline (Vinaya) as the Bhikkhu Sanghas in other Theravada countries such as Ceylon, Burma, Laos, and Cambodia. In spite of the fact that the government allots a yearly budget for the maintenance and repair of important temples and as stipends for high ranking monks, almost the entire burden for the support of the Sangha and the upkeep of the temples rests with the public. A survey entitled "Thailand Economic Farm Survey" made in 1953 by the Ministry of Agriculture of the Government of Thailand gives the religious cash expenses of the average Thai rural family per year as ranging from 5 to 10 per cent of its total annual cash income. It may be added here that the report concerns the average Thai rural family, and not the urban dwellers, the majority of whom, in Thailand as elsewhere, are less inclined to religion than the country folks.

Two Sects or Nikayas

There are two sects or Nikayas of the Buddhist Order in Thailand. One is the Mahanikaya, and the other is the Dhammayuttika Nikaya. The Mahanikaya is the older and by far the more numerous one, the ratio in the number of monks of the two sects being 35 to 1. The Dhammayuttika Nikaya was founded in 1833 A.D. by King Mongkut, the fourth ruler of the present Chakri Dynasty who ruled Thailand from 1851 to 1868 A.D. Having himself spent 27 years as a Bhikkhu, the King was well versed in the Dhamma, besides many other branches of knowledge, including Pali, the canonical language of Theravada Buddhism. The express desire of the King in founding the Dhammayuttika sect was to enable monks to lead a more disciplined and scholarly life in accordance with the pristine teachings of the Buddha. The differences between the two Nikayas are, however, not great; at most they concern only matters of discipline, and never of the Doctrine. Monks of both sects follow the same 227 Vinaya rules as laid down in the Patimokkha of the Vinaya Pitaka (the Basket of the Discipline), and both receive the same esteem from the public. In their general appearance and daily routine of life too, except for the slight difference in the manners of putting on the yellow robes, monks of the two Nikayas differ very little from one another.

Organization of the Sangha

Formerly, and in accordance with the Administration of the Bhikkhu Sangha Act (B.E. 2484, A.D. 1943), the organization of the Sangha in Thailand was on a line similar to that of the State. The Sangharaja or the Supreme Patriarch is the highest Buddhist dignitary of the Kingdom. He is chosen by the King, in consultation with the Government, from among the most senior and qualified members of the Sangha. The Sangharaja appoints a council of Ecclesiastical Ministers headed by the *Sangha Nayaka*, whose position is analogous to that of the Prime Minister of the State. Under the Sangha Nayaka there function four ecclesiastical boards, namely the Board of Ecclesiastical Administration, the Board of Education, the Board of Propagation and the Board of Public Works.

Each of the boards has a Sangha Mantri (equivalent to a minister in the secular administration) with his assistants. The four boards or ministries are supposed to look after the affairs of the entire Sangha. The Ecclesiastical Ministerial Council which, by the way, corresponds to the Cabinet, consists of ten members, all senior monks of the Sangha. In addition to this, there is a Consultative Assembly (*Sangha Sabha*), equivalent to the National Assembly, the members of which number 45, selected from various important monasteries. The Sangha Sabha acts as an Advisory Body to the Ecclesiastical Ministerial Council. Below the Sangha Sabha the administration of the

Sangha continues to correspond to the secular administration of the country. All monks and novices (*samaneras*) have to live in monasteries which are scattered throughout the country. Each monastery has its abbot appointed by the Ecclesiastical Ministerial Council in consultation with local people. It may be pointed out here that all religious appointments in Thailand are based on scholarly achievements, seniority, personal conduct and popularity, and contacts with monks further up in the Sangha.

There is a Department of Religious Affairs in the Ministry of Education which acts as a liaison office between the Government and the Sangha. In general the Department of Religious Affairs works in cooperation with the Ecclesiastical Ministerial Council on all matters affecting the Sangha. For instance, it issues all legal directives concerning the entire community of monks; it keeps record of the Sangha's property, such as lands etc.; it maintains facts and figures with respect to monks and monasteries. The Religious Affairs Department also prepares the annual budget for the upkeep of the Sangha functionaries and the maintenance and repair of temples etc. It may be added here that all temples and monasteries are State property.

In 1962, the Administration of the Bhikkhu Sangha Act of 1943 was abolished; a new one was enacted instead. By virtue of the new act, the posts of Sangha Nayaka, Sangha Mantris, and Sangha Sabha were abolished. In place of these there is a *Mahathera Samagama* (Council of the Elders) headed by the Sangharaja himself and consisting of not less than four and not more than eight senior monks (*mahatheras*) of the two sects (*nikayas*). The Mahathera Samagama, in collaboration with the Department of Religious Affairs, directly governs the entire Sangha.

Education of Monks

As is well known, the original idea of men's entering monkhood during the Buddha's time or shortly later, was to attain liberation from worldly existence in accordance with the teaching of the Master. Such an idea, of course, springs from man's feeling of aversion to things mundane. In other words, in those far-off days, men entered monkhood with the sole intention of ridding themselves of life's miseries and of obtaining spiritual freedom or Nirvana. Instances of such self-renunciation are found in the holy books of the Buddhists. With the passage of time, as is only natural, many of the ideals and practices of the early followers of the Buddha underwent modifications. Today, over 2,500 years after the passing away of the Buddha, though the ideal of becoming a Bhikkhu still remains very lofty among Buddhists of all lands, in practice it must be admitted that there have been many deviations from the Master's original admonitions with regard to the whys and wherefores of man's entering monkhood. Generalization of any subject matter is often dangerous but it will not be far from truth to say that today, in Thailand as in other Buddhist countries, the practice of Buddhist males entering monkhood is to a considerable extent prompted rather by the dictation of custom, the wish for education and other external considerations than by the desire to attain emancipation. Yet there are also many who join the Sangha through genuine love for a religious life and religious studies, or out of the wish to be of service to Buddhism and their country. Finally, in the Thai Sangha also those are not entirely lacking whose life is vigorously devoted to the aim of ultimate emancipation and to the guidance of others towards that goal. There have been, and still are, saintly and able meditation masters in Thailand, with a fair number of devoted disciples in Sangha and laity. There are also still monks — the so-called *thudong* bhikkhus — who follow the ancient way of austere living embodied in the "strict observances" or *dhutangas.*

In view of the above facts, there are two categories of Buddhist monks in Thailand. One comprises those who become monks for long periods, sometimes for life, and the other those who enter the Order temporarily. To serve in the monkhood even for a short period is considered a great merit-earning attainment by the Thai Buddhists. Even kings follow this age-old custom. For instance, the present ruler, H.M. King Bhumibol Adulyadej, also observed the custom for a period of half a month some time ago. Government officials are allowed leave with full pay for a period of four months in order to serve in monkhood. The idea is to enable young men to gain knowledge of Buddhism and thereby to become good citizens. Life as a monk gives them practical experience of how an ideal Buddhist life should be. In rural districts the general tendency is still to give more deference to those who have already served in monkhood. Such people are supposed to be more "mature" than those who have not undergone the monk's life. Moreover, in Thailand *wats* (monasteries and temples) used to be and are still regarded as seats of learning where all men, irrespective of life's position, could go and avail themselves of education benefits. This is especially so in the case of economically handicapped males of the countryside. Instances are not lacking in which people have climbed high up on life's status ladder after obtaining education while in monkhood. There are neither religious restrictions nor social disapproval against monks' returning to lay life if and when they find themselves unable to discharge their duties as monks.

Cases exist in which, for some reason or the other, men have entered monkhood more than once, although such practice cannot be said to be in the esteem of the public. Looked at from this viewpoint, the institution of entering monkhood in Thailand, apart from being a way of gaining moral and spiritual enlightenment, is a social uplift method by which those not so fortunately placed in life could benefit. Judged from the ideal of adopting a monk's life as enunciated by the Buddha, whether or not such practice is commendable, is a different story. The fact is that even today when modernism has penetrated deep into Thailand, about one half of the primary schools of the country are still situated in wats. With sex and crimes on the increase in the country, the cry for living a better Buddhist life is being heard more and more distinctly in Thailand today.

The traditional education of monks and novices in Thailand centers mainly on the studies of the Buddhist Doctrine (Dhamma) and Pali, the language in which the Theravada scriptures are written. Of the former, the study of the Doctrine, there are three grades with examinations open to both monks and laymen. Those passing such examinations are termed *Nak Dhamm,* literally meaning one who knows the Dhamma. The latter, i.e., the study of Pali, has seven grades, starting with the third and ending with the ninth grade. Students passing Pali examinations are called *parian* (Pali: *pariñña* = penetrative knowledge); in the Thai language the word *parinna* is used to mean academic degree. For example, monks and novices passing the first Pali examination are entitled to write "P. 3" after their names.

Generally the Dhamma and the Pali studies go hand in hand and take at least seven years to complete. The stiffness of the two courses, especially that of the Pali language, can be guessed from the fact that very few students are able to pass the highest grade, the Parian 9, in any annual examination. In the good old days when living was less competitive than now, passing of even the lower Dhamma and Pali examinations used to be of much value in securing good government posts. But now things are quite different; even those successful in the highest Pali examination, the 9th Grade, find it difficult to get suitable employment.

Of late there has developed a new outlook in the education of monks in Thailand. With the rapid progress of science and with the shrinking of the world, Buddhist leaders of Thailand, monks as well as laymen, are awakened to the necessity of imparting broader education to members of the Sangha, if the Sangha is to serve the cause of Buddhism well, "for the gain of the many, for the welfare of the many." As a result of the new outlook there now function in Bangkok two higher institutes of learning exclusively for monks and novices. One is the Mahachulalongkorn Rajvidyalaya, and the other is the Mahamongkut Rajvidyalaya. Both are organized on a modern university footing and both seem to be making satisfactory progress towards that direction. Inclusion in the curriculum of some secular subjects not incompatible with monks' discipline (Vinaya) is among the notable features of these two institutes; the aim is to give an all-round education to monks in order to enable them to be of better service to the cause of Buddhism amidst modern conditions.

So much for the education of 'long-term' monks. As for those who enter the Order temporarily, mostly for a period of three rainy months during the Vassa, or Buddhist Lent, the education is brief and devoted to the main tenets and features of Buddhism only. As pointed out above, such people enter monkhood either by their own genuine desire for knowledge of the Dhamma, by the dictum of custom or, as generally is the case, by the two reasons combined. Monks of this category return to lay life again as soon as the Lent is over. This is the reason why accommodations in monasteries (wats) are usually full during the Lenten period. Nowadays, owing to the pressure of modern life, the custom of temporarily entering monkhood is not so rigorously observed by people living in urban areas as by those in the countryside. The custom has its parallel in Burma, Cambodia, and Laos where Theravada Buddhism prevails.

Wats and Monks

The word "wat" means monastery and temple combined. It is the residence of monks and novices. There are about 21,000 wats in the whole of Thailand. In Bangkok alone there are nearly two hundred wats. Some big wats in Bangkok have as many as 600 resident monks and novices. Wats are centers of Thai art and architecture. Thai culture, to a considerable extent, flows from wats. Wat-lands and constructions thereon are donated by royalty, wealthy people and the public in general. The wat is the most important institution in Thai rural life. The social life of the rural community revolves around the wat. Besides carrying out the obvious religious activities, a wat serves the community as a recreation center, dispensary, school, community center, home for the aged and destitute, social work and welfare agency, village clock, rest-house, news agency, and information center. A wat is headed by a *Chao Avas* (the abbot) who is responsible for the maintenance of the wat discipline, the proper performance of religious services and rituals, and the general welfare of the inmates. Besides monks and novices, there are also the "temple boys" in wats, who assist monks and novices in various ways, such as bringing and arranging food, cleaning dormitories, washing yellow robes, etc. Usually these boys are related to resident monks in one way or another, and their stay is free of charge. Most of them are students whose homes are far away and who would, otherwise, find it impracticable to get education. This is especially so in Bangkok where accommodation is difficult to get and where all higher seats of learning of the country are situated. The census taken in 1954 reveals that there are as many as 119,044 temple boys in Thailand, which indeed is not a small figure. The institution of the wat, in itself a gift of Buddhism, therefore contributes in no small measure to the social welfare and progress of the Thai Buddhists. The benefits in this respect, of course, are more apparent among the lower strata of society than in the case of the fortunate few on the top.

Apart from engaging themselves in doctrinal studies and observing disciplinary rules (Vinaya) in general, monks are expected to be "friends, philosophers, and guides" of the people. Preaching to masses face to face or over the radio is one of the commonest ways by which monks help the promotion of moral stability among various members of the society. It may not be out of place to reiterate the fact that Buddhism lays great stress on the necessity of leading a morally good life in order to obtain happiness in life here and hereafter. In most of the ceremonies and rituals, whether private or public, monks' cooperation and benediction are indispensable. Indeed, in the life of the average Thai Buddhists, from the cradle to the grave, monks are persons to whom they constantly turn for moral support.

The role of monks in rural districts is even more important, for there the local wat is not only the religious but also the social center of the community. It is at the wat that people come together and experience a sense of comradeship. Religious rituals and ceremonies held at wats are always accompanied by social activities: they are occasions for people, especially the young, to enjoy themselves in feast, fun and festivities. This aspect of the religious service helps the common folks to relax and satisfies their needs for recreation. Not a few matrimonial alliances started from contacts at wat premises. Acting as a moral and ethical example, monks are the most venerated persons in the countryside Thai society, remaining very close to the hearts of the people. In times of crisis, it is to monks that people bring their problems for counsel and encouragement. With few exceptions, the Sangha has well justified this attitude of respect and honor shown to it on the part of the laity and, on the whole, has lived up to the dignity of the Faith.

The Laity

Throughout its over 2,500 years of existence Buddhism has been closely connected with the lay community. In Pali the word for a male lay devotee is *upasaka*; *upasika* is its female equivalent. In the history of Buddhism, right from the time of its founder, there had been numerous upasakas and upasikas whose faith in the Teachings of the Master had contributed largely to the dissemination of the Doctrine. Names of the Buddha's munificent followers like Anathapindika, Visakha, Asoka, Kanishka, etc., are on the lips of Buddhists even today. Without the patronage of Emperor Asoka, Buddhism probably could not have spread so far and the course of its history might have been different. In India, the land of its birth, as well as in most of the countries where its Message has been accepted, Buddhism has received unstinted support from people of all classes, especially the ruling class. History of the movements of Buddhism in China, Japan, Burma, Ceylon, Tibet, etc., amply justifies this statement. In the case of Thailand too, ever since its introduction to that country, Buddhism has been warmly received and patronized by kings and commoners alike. It is well-known that many of the Thai rulers, not satisfied with being mere lay-devotees, got themselves ordained into monkhood and became famous for their erudition in the Dhamma. King Mongkut, Rama IV, probably stands out as most distinguished among this class of royal devotees. The custom of Thai males entering the Sangha also contributes much to the better understanding and cooperation between the lay community and the monkhood. After all, personal experience is better than mere theoretical knowledge.

The Buddha himself, in one of his discourses, exhorted his followers to discharge their duties well so as to enable the Dhamma to endure long in the world. One of the duties of the lay followers, as taught by the Master, is to look after the needs of monks. Hence it is the traditional practice with lay followers in all Buddhist countries, especially those following Theravada

Buddhism, to see that monks do not suffer from lack of the four requisites, namely food, clothing, shelter, and medicine. Although in the present age of competitive economy, when life in any field is not so easy, nobody can say in fairness that monk-life in Thailand suffers greatly from shortage of the above four requisites. As Bhikkhus are not allowed to follow any occupational activities, it is clear that they entirely depend on the laity for their existence. In return for this spontaneous support offered them by the public, monks are expected to live exemplary lives for the benefit of themselves as well as of those who look to them as teachers and guides. We have already seen what moral influence monks have upon the people.

Cooperation between the laity and the Bhikkhu Sangha in Thailand is close and spontaneous. To a very great extent this is due to the fact that in an average Thai family some of its members are certain to be found who have for some time served in the Sangha. To the masses yellow robes are symbol of the Master, and Bhikkhus are upholders of the Dhamma, to be deferred to in all circumstances. It is interesting to note that Bhikkhus or Samaneras found guilty of committing crimes are formally divested of their yellow robes before legal action is taken against them by the State, and this is done invariably under permission of the chief monk or the abbot.

"To do good" (*kusala kamma*) is a cardinal point in the teachings of Buddhism. Consequently the idea of performing meritorious deeds is very deeply ingrained in the minds of Buddhists. Ways of doing good or making merit (*puñña*) among the Thai Buddhists are numerous. A man gains merit each time he gives alms to monks or contributes to any religious rituals. To get ordination into monkhood even for a short period, of course, brings much merit. Besides, there are other ways of merit-earning, such as releasing caged birds or freeing caught fishes, plastering gold leaf on Buddha statues or religious monuments, contributing to the construction of a new temple or the repair of an old one, etc. "The Law of Karma" that each action has its corresponding result and the belief in rebirth are two important factors in molding such attitude towards life among the Buddhists. Though *Nibbana* (Sanskrit: Nirvana), the highest bliss in Buddhism, is aspired to by all good Buddhists, the vast majority of them still think it is not so easy to reach and that they will be reborn again in this world, in heaven or some other world, or — at the very worst — in hell. Hence, as long as they live they must try to do good in order to ensure good results in this very life as well as in the life to come. "Be a light unto yourself. Each man must strive for his own salvation"— these were the Master's words. In view of this, Theravada Buddhism is often said to have individualistic temper. Nevertheless, it is very tolerant, as the long history of its existence will prove. Indeed, the characteristic tolerance of Buddhism, for instance in Thailand, has always permitted the absorption of many beliefs and practices from other sources which have often served to supplement or expand its concepts or to fill gaps. Animism and Brahmanism may be cited in this connection; the two being important supplements of popular Buddhism in Thailand. A foreign writer has rightly observed that the attitude of the Thai masses towards their religion is of an easy-going nature. They do not bother to distinguish among the various components of their religion; for them it is all of a piece. Only the sophisticated few are concerned with doctrinal logic and purity. Of course, they too know much about its legends, its festivals, its ideals, and its general message that "good will render good." On the whole it can be said that the Thais enjoy their religion. Religious observances are to them as social and recreational as sacred occasions. And for the vast majority, Buddhism suffices in that it enables them to feel and believe and enjoy.

Buddhist Organizations and the Revival of Buddhism

Organizations among the lay Buddhists of Thailand are recent establishments. Prominent and oldest among them is perhaps the Buddhist Association of Thailand, under Royal Patronage, which now is about 30 years old, having been established in 1933. Having its head office in Bangkok, it maintains branch organizations in almost all major districts of Thailand. Its membership is open to both sexes, irrespective of class, creed, and color. The aim and object of the Buddhist Association of Thailand is to promote the study and practice of Buddhism and to propagate its message in and outside Thailand. Besides arranging regular lectures and discussions on topics concerning the Dhamma, the Association also publishes a monthly journal in the Thai language on the teachings of the Buddha.

Another organization is the Young Buddhists Association which came into being at the close of the Second World War. As its name implies, the Young Buddhists Association takes care of the interest of the young in matters concerning Buddhism. Its primary object is to encourage the young to imbibe the tenets of Buddhism and to live a virtuous life. Chief among its activities are arranging regular lectures and discussions on the Dhamma, issuing publications on subjects dealing with Buddhism in general, and sponsoring meetings of the young on the platform of Buddhism. The Young Buddhists Association also has branches in the districts.

As said earlier the end of the Second World War saw a great revival of interest in Buddhism throughout the world. Even in countries like Thailand where the Doctrine of the Awakened One has been traditionally accepted for generations, people seem to be increasingly eager to know more about the Dhamma. Strange as it may seem, this is partly due to the interest the Occidental World has taken in Buddhism.

In times past religion has been more or less regarded in Thailand as "solace of the old." But with the impact of the West in most matters and with the general interest shown towards Buddhism by Western intelligentsia, the Buddhists of Thailand, especially the younger generations who came into contact with the West, began to evince an inquisitive attitude towards their religion — a heritage which they have all along accepted as their own but which they have cared little to know about its true value. This is no attempt to belittle the exceedingly great importance the Thais attach to their religion. But human nature being what it is, the saying "Familiarity breeds contempt" is in most cases not very far wrong. In the Thai language also we have a proverb "*klai kleua kin dang*" which may be rendered in English as "to have the folly to resort to alkali when one is in possession of salt."

Having taken root on the soil of Thailand for centuries Buddhism has naturally attracted many appendages to its fold, some of which are not quite in conformity with the teachings of the Master as contained in the Canon (Tipitaka). Many leaders of Buddhistic thought in Thailand have, therefore, come forward to try to purify the Dhamma of the many impurities that have crept into it. Notable among the reformatory groups are the Dhammadana Association in Jaiya, South Thailand, under the leadership of Buddhadasa Bhikkhu, and the Buddha Nigama of Chiengmai (North Thailand) started by Paññananda Bhikkhu. The two organizations are showing good efforts in the field of awakening the Buddhists of Thailand to the pristine teachings of the Buddha as treasured in the Pali Tipitaka. The mission is admittedly a difficult one but already a promising start has been made in this direction. Much will also no doubt depend on how things transpire in other spheres of human activities, chiefly economic, social and political. The present is an age of conflict — conflict between mind and body, between spirit and matter. Man must find harmony between the two if peace be his aim in life. And to this task of finding harmony within man Buddhism could contribute in no small measure.

5

Buddhist Culture, The Cultured Buddhist

BUDDHIST CULTURE

For over twenty-five centuries, Buddhist ideas and ideals have guided and influenced the lives and thoughts of countless human beings in many parts of the world. As lay Buddhists, our own experiences and discoveries in life are not enough to give a true perspective on life. To bring ourselves closer to the ideal of a well-balanced man or woman, we need to acquire, at least in outline, what is called a cultural grounding in the Buddha-Dhamma.

Culture reveals to ourselves and others what we are. It gives expression to our nature in our manner of living and of thinking, in art, religion, ethical aspirations, and knowledge. Broadly speaking, it represents our ends in contrast to means.

A cultured man has grown, for culture comes from a word meaning "to grow." In Buddhism the arahant is the perfect embodiment of culture. He has grown to the apex, to the highest possible limit, of human evolution. He has emptied himself of all selfishness — all greed, hatred, and delusion — and embodies flawless purity and selfless compassionate service. Things of the world do not tempt him, for he is free from the bondage of selfishness and passions. He makes no compromises for the sake of power, individual or collective.

In this world some are born great while others have greatness thrust on them. But in the Buddha-Dhamma one becomes great only to the extent that one has progressed in ethical discipline and mental culture, and thereby freed the mind of self and all that it implies. True greatness, then, is proportional to one's success in unfolding the perfection dormant in human nature.

We should therefore think of culture in this way: Beginning with the regular observance of the Five Precepts, positively and negatively, we gradually reduce our greed and hatred. Simultaneously, we develop good habits of kindness and compassion, honesty and truthfulness, chastity and heedfulness. Steady, wholesome habits are the basis of good character, without which no culture is possible. Then, little by little, we become great and cultured Buddhists. Such a person is rightly trained in body, speech, and mind — a disciplined, well-bred, refined, humane human being, able to live in peace and harmony with himself and others. And this indeed is Dhamma.

In order to grow we also have to be active and energetic, diligent in wholesome conduct. There is no place for laziness and lethargy in Buddhism. We must be diligent in cultivating all aspects of the Dhamma in ourselves at all times. If we develop as good individuals, we automatically become cultured members of our society, mindful both of rights and duties. Buddhism addresses itself only to the individual thinking person. It has nothing to do with mass movements, for "masses" are just collections of individual men and women. Any true social development must therefore begin with the transformation of each individual person.

In this way the ethical dilemmas of an economically developing country like Sri Lanka, with a background of Buddhist culture, are resolved, for a true lay Buddhist will aim at personal progress in worldly matters only on the foundation of the Noble Eightfold Path. Progress by way of *adhamma* — unrighteousness — well inevitably bring in its trail disaster, pain, and suffering to individual, community, and nation.

Such a misguided policy implies disbelief in kamma and its effects. Reject kamma and one is rootless. Rejection is the result of blinding greed for quick material gain and sensual pleasures, conjoined with delusion about the true nature and destiny of man and life. It also signifies acceptance of the philosophy of expediency — that one should "get the most that one can" out of this single fleeting life on earth guided largely by one's instincts, subject to the laws of society, which the affluent and powerful often circumvent with impunity. Such a short-sighted and mistaken view ultimately leads to individual and social tensions, to restlessness and conflict, and to the spread of indiscipline, lawlessness, and crime.

Buddhism distinguishes between emotions that are constructive, such as *metta* and *karuna,* and those that are destructive: anger and jealousy, for instance. It encourages the cultivation of the former to eliminate the latter. Human beings can both think and feel. When the Buddha taught the Dhamma, sometimes he appealed to reason, sometimes to the emotions, and sometimes to the imagination, using such means of instruction as fables, stories, and poetry. Buddhist culture, too, manifests in other forms than that of a fine character, such as in the field of literature — the Jatakas, the Theragatha and Therigatha, for examples — philosophy, art, architecture, and sculpture.

Art is basically a medium of human communication. It can help in the education of the emotions and is one of the civilizing agencies of humankind. The work of the artist, whether painter, dramatist, sculptor, or writer, is worthy of study because it has a certain expressiveness that both reveals and stimulates fresh insights. The artist sees new meanings in objects and experience that ordinarily escape the rest of us, and thus he creates new values and insights in life.

Rightly viewed as the expression of the good life, and as an aid to living it — and not for mere enjoyment and appreciation — art can therefore ennoble us. For example, the tranquillity and peace that one sees in the Samadhi statue of the Buddha elevates the mind, stimulates confidence, and induces reverence for the Dhamma. In all Buddhist lands, the images of the Buddha and the Bodhisatta have become the typical form of artistic expression.

Buddhist culture is perennial and so is as fresh today as it was in the Buddha's time 2500 years ago. It is also self-sufficient, self-consistent, and self-sustaining. Based as it is on eternal verities, verifiable by individual experience, it is never obsolete, and animates the progress that seems to kill it. Nor does its content change with context.

The impact of Buddhism on world culture was truly significant. In it, there is no intellectual error, based as it is on reason and on the bedrock of personal experience. It is free from moral blindness, for its ethics is truly lofty, guided by a rational basis for such an ethic, namely, personal evolution in terms of one's own kamma. It engendered no social perversity — hate and intolerance were for none, limitless loving-kindness and compassion were for all. The doors to deliverance were open to anyone who wished to enter them. Its thrilling message of reason, universal benevolence, flaming righteousness, social justice, hope, and deliverance in this very existence by one's own exertion — all had a fertilizing and liberating influence on thought and action wherever Buddhism spread.

To the thinking person, Buddhism offered a rational, practical, and balanced way of deliverance from all life's sorrows, and the certainty of the perfectibility of man, here and now solely by one's own effort. To the humanist it gave an all-embracing compassionate vision, inspiring ameliorative action as a pre-condition for the realization of the highest spiritual attainments.

Even to have a general idea of its achievements, in the manifold ways it has expressed itself in society, is an education in the art of living. Buddhism gives perspective to the whole of life. Nothing in life is seen as more important than it really is. A cultured Buddhist can tell the good from the bad, the right from the wrong, the true from the false. He can weigh the evidence skillfully, and his Buddhist cultural background makes his judgment a wise one.

The Balanced Personality

The Buddha-Dhamma is not a fiction to be read and forgotten. It deals with life — with real life, the life that you and I lead every day, the value and worth of which is greatly enhanced when the Dhamma is translated into action and built into our character by constant effort and practice.

The ultimate aim of the Buddha-Dhamma is Nibbana — emancipation from suffering. The immediate objective is to help us to understand and solve the problems that confront us in our daily life, to make us well-rounded, happy, and balanced men and women, able to live in harmony with our environment and our fellow beings. Balance, however, though it is an aim worth striving for, is not easily struck in the contemporary world, with its false ideologies and illusory values.

In contrast to the relative, often false values of our age, the Buddha's teaching is a revelation of true and absolute values. Its truth can be tested and tried in one's own experience. Buddhism teaches clear thinking, self-control, and mental culture as means to these ends. One who builds his daily life upon this firm foundation of appropriate knowledge and clear-sighted ideals is assured of progress and success even as a layman.

The Buddha-Dhamma is, then, a guide to daily life, and its basic principles are of great practical value in the art of living. The householder, while involved in his responsibilities and commitments, will not lose sight of the ultimate goal, Nibbana. Rather, he should consider lay life as a preparation and training ground for its realization.

The Discourse on Blessings (Maha-Mangala Sutta) states that one of life's true blessings is to have "a mind properly directed" *(attasammapanidhi).* This means that one must discover one's proper place in the world, decide on a proper aim, and find the proper way to achieve it. A happy and balanced person is one who has a worthy aim in life, a clear course of action to follow, and a simple but sound philosophy of life as a guide. "Philosophy" here is a keen desire to understand the nature and destiny of man in the universe. Without a philosophy, life is stale, flat, unprofitable, and meaningless. A philosophy enables one to live harmoniously with the world and one's fellow beings by a process of adjustment based on true knowledge.

In Buddhism, mind predominates over matter. A characteristic feature of mind is purpose. To make the best use of our life and our kammic inheritance we must choose a practical aim in life and devise a plan to achieve this aim. Then we will become what we want to be.

The more we find out about ourselves by means of self-observation and self-analysis, the better will be our chances of self-improvement. In addition, we should ask ourselves how far and to what degree we are generous, even-tempered, natural, kind, considerate, honest, sober, truthful, heedful and observant, industrious, energetic, cautious, patient, tolerant, and tactful. These are some of the qualities of a well-adjusted Buddhist. We should try to improve ourselves where necessary — a little practice every day is all that is needed. We should be aware that the more often we perform a right action, the more easily will it become a habit. By force of habit it ultimately becomes part of our character.

Sati or bare attention is an important aspect of mindfulness. *Sati* is the objective seeing of things stripped bare of likes and dislikes, bias and prejudice. It is viewing things and events as they really are — the naked facts. The ability to do this is a sign of true Buddhist maturity. The principle of bare attention should be applied vigorously to everyday thinking. The results will be: clearer thinking and saner living, a marked reduction in the pernicious influence of mass media propaganda and advertisements, and an improvement in our inter-personal relationships.

A well-balanced Buddhist, therefore, must make up his own mind, form his own opinions, and arrive at his own conclusions in facing life's difficulties according to Buddhist principles. He must not be a moral and intellectual coward. He must be prepared to stand alone, to go his own way irrespective of what others think or say. Of course he will take advice — it is no interference with one's freedom to seek advice from a more experienced and knowledgeable person — but the decision should be his own.

Seeing the relationship between craving and suffering, we must maintain a certain degree of detachment from worldly things and, in addition, regulate our lives by strictly observing the Five Precepts. Thereby we preserve the well-being of our whole personality, both here and in the hereafter, by living in harmony with the universal laws governing our mental and moral life. The development of moral and ethical character *(sila)* is a prerequisite for mind-control and for obtaining the wisdom needed to attain Nibbana.

Change being inherent in life, disappointments and disasters are likely to happen, and when they do come, we should meet them with equanimity and a balanced response. This is evidence of right understanding, of seeing clearly that everything happens because of causes, that effects correspond to their causes, and that we ourselves are responsible for generating the causes — if not in the present life, then in some past life. Likewise, we should be able to overcome unfounded, irrational, and exaggerated fears and worries as we obtain some degree of emotional control. Thus the apparent injustices of life, grievances both personal and social, emotional maladjustments, and so on, are all explained fully and rationally by the twin principles of kamma and rebirth. There is another reason the Buddhist preserves his philosophical demeanour. He has strength derived from other unseen resources — his store of wholesome actions, the qualities of his character, the happiness derived from meditative practices, all of which are independent of material things. Thus he is the owner of an increasingly self-reliant and self-sufficient mind. He has learned simplicity of life and wants; material things have now become his servants and not his master. He is free from the tyranny of external things. He has realized that while seen things are temporary and passing, the unseen is real. In sum, he now possesses a calm, controlled, and contented mind. And contentment, says the Buddha, is the greatest wealth, one of the four sources of happiness:

Health is the highest gain.

Contentment is the greatest wealth.

The trusty are the best kinsmen.

Nibbana is the highest bliss.

— Dhammapada, v. 204

By understanding, he thus learns to adjust himself to new circumstances without rancor or bitterness.

If we have *saddha,* confidence in the Buddha-Dhamma based on knowledge, we must act on it. Every true Buddhist should constantly practice the four great efforts (the sixth step of the path), namely: to overcome and avoid unhealthy states of mind, and to stimulate and maintain healthy states of mind such as thoughts of *metta* and *karuna.* These states not only protect the practitioner, but help others as well.

We must acquire the habit of questioning whether a thought or action done is honest or not, for honesty with ourselves is the one sure way to mental health. In addition, we should set apart a few minutes every day for the purpose of quiet reflection or meditation, for reviewing the day's happenings, and to see how far we may have deviated from the essential principles of the Master's Teachings in order to avoid future lapses.

We might also read a passage of the Buddha's discourses daily. This useful habit would enable us to forget our little worries and troubles, develop our minds, and put our whole life into perspective.

In these ways, as lay disciples of the Buddha, we grow in all aspects of Dhamma, molding our whole personality, instructing the intellect, training the emotions, and disciplining the will in the interests both of ourselves and of others.

Knowing Oneself

In the ultimate sense, to know oneself is to understand one's changing personality truly and fully so that one distinguishes clearly the real from the unreal. Then one lives every moment of one's life keenly aware of each thought, word, and deed. Some self-knowledge however, is necessary even for a Buddhist layman with a more limited objective in life: personal progress in worldly matters, based on the foundation of the Noble Eightfold Path.

The human being in the Buddhist sense is a flux of mind and matter, of five component groups each of which is impermanent and changing. Nothing whatever of a lasting nature can be found within them or behind them. Each conflux is energized by craving, and is capable of doing both good and evil. Viewed in another way, a human being is the sum total of his or her thoughts and actions in this and in previous lives. At birth, we bring with us an inheritance of instincts, as well as other qualities such as intelligence, temperament, an embryonic character, and a body. Later on, many factors combine to shape our present character. More important than upbringing and education at home and school, and the qualities of our kammic inheritance, is what we do with these factors. Character decides this.

Character is not static. It changes from day to day. Every willed action affects it for good or bad; mind is responsible for actions. Character uses the intelligence, temperament, and instincts with which we are born. The strongest force which molds a person's character is his ideal which, in the case of a Buddhist, is the arahant ideal. Such an ideal co-ordinates our warring impulses, unifies our personality, and eliminates wastage and conflict. Any activity that brings us nearer to this ideal is skillful while anything that takes us away from it is unskillful. A worthy aim should be achieved by worthy means.

The wisest course to adopt is to develop further the good points in one's kammic inheritance and to deal with any weaknesses. Apart from this, if we are to be happy, secure, and successful in life, we must rely on ourselves and hold ourselves responsible for our actions — or inaction. The Buddhist law of kamma teaches us not only self-responsibility for our deeds, but also that the results *(vipaka)* of past deeds can be nullified partly or wholly by present skillful, energetic action. We must forget the past, assume responsibility for present action, and determine to shape our life in the way we want according to the principles of the Buddha-Dhamma. In this way we can face the future with confidence.

To do this realistically, we have to accept the fact that there are some unalterable things in life. Thus the three basic marks of conditioned existence — impermanence, suffering, and non-self — cannot be changed. Illness and decay are unavoidable, and death is our final destiny. The only remedy is to accept these facts and learn to live with them, without grumbling and worrying, and devote our limited time and energy to things we can change and improve.

There are, for instance, character traits and instinctive impulses — tendencies to acquisition, aggression, self-assertion, sex, and fear — that can be controlled and even uprooted by a process of understanding, adjustment, and sublimation. The key elements in this process are observance of the Five Precepts and the systematic practice of mindfulness. To use mindfulness as a key to self-improvement one must see oneself as an impartial observer would and mentally note: "This character trait is present in me. It is part of me, but it can be changed. What must I do to remedy it *now?*" The sensible attitude is to recognize what can be altered and to remedy unwholesome traits and habits by discipline and training. In both accepting and adjusting, one may have to abandon previous ideas, habits, and ways of living, but the sooner this is done the more effectively it will lead to our welfare and happiness.

Further, to make the best use of our powers and potentialities, we should draw up an objective evaluation of all our qualities and capacities by patient self-analysis and self-observation. Special attention should be given to the emotional qualities, for the emotions are generally a stronger force than the intellect. Man is far from being the rational creature he is supposed to be. He often acts quite contrary to his own true interests. His rational decisions are often subverted by gusts of passion and emotion, passing whims and fancies, apathy and laziness.

To know oneself, then, is to understand that there is room for change. We can change for the good by deliberate action, using the raw material of our kammic endowment based on an ideal. This means that one should develop a philosophy of life, and such a philosophy presupposes a purpose which, for a Buddhist, is growth in the Dhamma.

BUDDHISM AND OTHER RELIGIONS

The Buddha-Dhamma, or Buddhism, can be related to other religions in many ways. Here, only a few main points of comparison will be sketched.

Buddhism is a graduated system of moral and mental training with Nibbana, the highest happiness, as its goal. It is founded upon the principle of causality, the law of cause and effect in the moral domain, that is, in the field of human behavior. Above all, it is a path to liberation from suffering, a goal to be won by cultivating the Noble Eightfold Path in its three stages of morality, concentration, and wisdom *(sila, samadhi, pañña).*

Religion lays down the general lines of conduct by which a person will live his daily life; it lays down rules in such matters as respect for the lives of others, intoxicating liquors, marriage, divorce, and means of livelihood. For the believer it thus colors his or her whole attitude towards matters like birth, sex, family limitation, death, and the afterlife. Transgression of the religious code entails feelings of guilt, so the religion that one follows has a profound influence, shaping one's entire outlook on life as well as one's attitudes, whether in wholesome ways or in unwholesome ways.

Against this background, we can now see how the Buddha-Dhamma is related to other religions.

As stated earlier, the Buddhist way to Nibbana is the Noble Eightfold Path. The question then arises as to whether arahantship — perfect holiness — or Nibbana is possible outside this path. The Buddha's answer to Subhadda's question, just before he passed away, clarifies our problem: "In whatever teaching, O Subhadda, there exists the Noble Eightfold Path, there is the first saint *(sotapanna),* there is the second saint *(sakadagami),* there is the third saint *(anagami),* there is the fourth saint *(arahant).* An arahant is a perfect saint. Elsewhere there are mere semblances of saints." As the Noble Eightfold Path is found only in Buddhism, in the Buddha's own words "the other teachings are empty of true saints."

They therefore err who say that all spiritual paths lead to the same summit and that the view from the top is identical for all. The reason is simple: the Buddha saw the true nature of things clearly and completely with his own independent supramundane insight — his perfect enlightenment — and so his teaching is an exact reflection of reality, while other religious teachers had only an imperfect view of reality, with eyes dimmed by various forms and degrees of ignorance *(avijja).*

This, however, does not imply that Buddhism is intolerant of other religions. Neither the Buddha nor his followers ever imposed his system of thought or his way of life on anyone who would not accept it of his or her own volition. Acceptance was a purely voluntary matter. Even if accepted, how much of it one should practice is one's own responsibility. But regardless of one's personal inclinations, the universal moral laws operate objectively — action being followed by due reaction, deeds by their fruits. The Buddha merely reveals the laws of life, and the more faithfully we follow them, the better it is for us, for then we act according to the Dhamma.

This peaceful policy of non-compulsion and tolerance, characteristic of the Master's teaching, is born partly of compassion and partly of understanding human nature and the nature of truth. If the vision of some is dimmed as to the merits of the teaching it is one's duty to help them to see. But one must stop there: one should not coerce others or persecute those who refuse to accept one's own beliefs. Wisdom, the ability to see things as they truly are, cannot be imposed on others from the outside. It must grow from within the individual, out of the developing sensitivity and refinement of human nature. This takes time. At any given period only few will be capable of genuinely appreciating, understanding, and realizing the Buddha's teaching, as human beings vary widely in their intellectual, moral, and spiritual capabilities. Unethical conversions are therefore unheard of in Buddhism.

Buddhist tolerance, however, should not mean apathy and indifference. That would be a misinterpretation of the term. When erroneous statements about Buddhism were made by people in the Buddha's time, the Master kindly corrected them. He even expelled his cousin Devadatta from the Sangha when occasion demanded it to preserve the purity of the Doctrine and the unity of the Sangha. Yet the Buddha was the perfect example of tolerance and compassion. Likewise monk and laity should be always watchful and should emulate the Buddha. Otherwise their case would go by default, for which they alone are to be blamed. Today various proposals are being made to create an all-embracing system of religion, the idea being simply to absorb all other religions into one's own. However, a universal religious consciousness can never be created because: (1) the various religions have fundamentally different conceptions of reality; (2) the concept and content of the good life vary between different religions — the good means one thing to a Buddhist, and another to a Christian, and yet another to a Muslim; and (3) no adherent of a religion wants his religion to be absorbed by another body. Is it not deeply rooted in human nature to believe that no other religion in the world compares with one's own?

Taking Buddhism specifically — and in detail — it is unique, a thing apart from all other religions in the world. It teaches the formula of conditioned arising *(paticca-samuppada)* and its reversal by human effort; craving as the creator of life instead of a creator God; a becoming *(bhava)* without a self *(atta);* personal evolution according to the quality of one's own deeds *(kamma);* an impersonal moral order *(kamma-niyama)* with moral values and moral responsibility; free will, within limits, and therewith the possibility of a good life; survival after death by the continuity of the individual life-flux without transmigration of an individual, immutable, immortal soul; and a transcendental reality (Nibbana), realizable here and now solely by one's own effort. As such, there are major and unbridgeable differences between Buddhism and the other world religions and spiritual philosophies. The attempt to find a common denominator in the uncommon, or to adapt the Dhamma so that it does not differ from the other religions, must necessarily fail. It will only end in the debasement of the Buddha-Dhamma or in its total extinction by painless absorption.

The idea of a universal religion is both unrealistic and impracticable, a mere mirage and an idle delusion. In contrast, over 2500 years ago, the Buddha offered another way of relating religions to each other based on mutual respect yet maintaining the separate identity of each religion. To practice this method one need not become a Buddhist. It is also very practical, effective, and does no violence or offense to anyone. It is simply to cultivate regularly four basic social and ethical attitudes: (1)

metta — a friendly feeling of loving-kindness to all beings in every situation regardless of race, creed, or caste; (2) *karuna*— compassion for all who suffer, and to take practical steps whenever possible to eliminate or alleviate those sufferings; (3) *mudita* — altruistic joy, to be happy in others' happiness, in their prosperity and success, thereby counteracting feelings of jealousy and unhealthy rivalry between individuals and groups; and (4) *upekkha* — equanimity, the maintenance of an even mind when faced with the ups and downs inherent in life. By practicing these virtues daily, a Christian becomes a better Christian, a Hindu a better Hindu, a Muslim a better Muslim. All of these qualities convey a universal message that make the practitioners universal human beings. Surely, this is universalism in religion par excellence.

This is the most satisfactory way of living harmoniously with one's fellow men and women of all faiths, fostering inter-religious goodwill and avoiding religious conflicts. By pursuing this policy for over 2500 years, there have been no religious wars in Buddhism. It is also the best method of relating the Buddha's Teaching to other religions.

Buddhism, to repeat, is unique — a thing apart from all other religions in the world. While at all times maintaining its separate identity, it should peacefully coexist with other religions, following a policy of live-and-let-live. Such a policy has paid rich dividends in the past and will continue to do so in the future. Monks and laypersons in Sri Lanka should remember this, for the good of the Sasana and the well-being of the country.

In addition, every Buddhist should:

1. live his daily life in accordance with the Master's Teaching by observing the Five Precepts, thereby showing to all that the Buddha-Dhamma yet lives and daily rules his life;
2. support only genuine bhikkhus who observe the rules of discipline (Vinaya) to ensure the purity of the Sangha;
3. give with discrimination to Buddhist causes and to humanitarian projects, as cautioned by the Buddha —

to the most deserving the things most needed, as funds are limited;

4. help make known abroad his message of wisdom and compassion.

A TASTE OF THE HOLY LIFE

An Account of an International Ordination in Myanmar

"Ehi bhikkhu!" "Come, monk!" With these simple but portentous words, the Buddha founded the Sangha, the Order of bhikkhus, which has preserved and practiced his doctrine from that day to this.

With that *"Ehi bhikkhu!"* the Buddha conferred ordination upon the first monk, the Venerable Kondañña, at Isipatana near Benares. At the conclusion of the Buddha's first discourse Kondañña had asked to be ordained, and the Buddha, simply by calling him a bhikkhu, transformed him into one. The Buddha went on to say: "The Dhamma has been well expounded. Practice the holy life rightly to make an end of suffering." That was the ultimate, the highest aim of becoming a monk then as it is now: liberation from all *dukkha,* the suffering of repeated becoming in the cycle of rebirth, *samsara.*

During the Buddha's life, and since, the procedure to become a Buddhist monk evolved into a series of steps often involving large numbers of bhikkhus and lay people. Modern ordination ceremonies clearly express the interdependent relationship of monks and lay people supporting each other in their efforts to put an end to suffering. The bhikkhus, by their conduct, must inspire faith in the lay people. The householders in turn show deep respect for the Order by honoring the individual bhikkhus who in turn determine to make themselves worthy of the respect and support they receive from the laity.

The Buddha could only ordain a few bhikkhus with the phrase *"Ehi bhikkhu."* Such instantaneous ordination required that the man had cultivated certain *paramis* (perfections, good qualities) in the past. Chief amongst the good kammas needed for the Buddha to accept someone as a monk in this way, tradition says, was having been a bhikkhu in previous lives and/or having helped others to ordain. This is one of the reasons why laymen in Myanmar ordain temporarily, and why they obtain such lavish help from lay people, notably their families, when they undertake temporary ordination.

Because they are closely based on the Vinaya Pitaka, the ordination ceremonies in the different Theravada countries are almost identical. Whether the bhikkhus expect to remain in robes for the remainder of their lives or are "temporary" monks (a common practice in Myanmar and Thailand) makes no difference to the procedure. But national variations, especially in the lay aspects of the events, do lend color and specific points of interest to the solemn ceremony.

In January 1994 a mass ordination of foreign men was held in Yangon, Myanmar (the former Rangoon, Burma) under the combined auspices of the Myanmar Department of Religious Affairs and the International Meditation Centre, Yangon. This event, unusual in its location, scale, and international scope, will be described below along with a summary of the week these men were in robes.

All the detailed arrangements of place, transport, requisites, and the like had been made by the hosts beforehand for seven boys aged 9-14 to become samaneras or novices and forty-nine foreign men and one Myanmar to take the full *upasampada* ordination. They would remain in robes for about a week, in accordance with the Myanmar custom of temporary ordination. In that land it is considered essential for every Buddhist male to become a samanera as a boy and a bhikkhu as a man at least for some short period of his life, for the reason explained above and to earn a very high kind of merit, *puñña*. All those in this group who were to be ordained were meditation students of Mother Sayamagyi and Sayagyi U Chit Tin, direct disciples of the late Sayagyi U Ba Khin, renowned lay teacher of Vipassana meditation in Myanmar. They were associated with the International Meditation Centers in that tradition around the world, and the small original IMC, atop a low hill in suburban Yangon's diplomatic area, was the focus for most of the activities.

The shaving of heads, preliminary to every ordination, was set up just outside the wall surrounding the Light of the

Dhamma Pagoda at the Centre. About six life-long bhikkhus from the preceptor's monastery came to help shave the heads of the ordinands. Shaded from the hot afternoon sun by a permanent awning, the men doused their heads with water from plastic buckets, then the brown-haired Europeans, blond Americans, black-and grey-haired Asians and Australians sat on low stools. Two people, including the man's wife if she was available, held a piece of white cloth beneath the candidate's chin to catch the locks of hair as they fell from the blade. The bhikkhus swiftly used the straight razors the foreigners had imported, while guiding the movements of their assistants through gesture when they did not share a common language.

The men were meditating, on the parts of the body or the breath or the significance of ordaining. Well aware that this was the start of an important ceremony, everyone quietly reflected on its value. It took perhaps an hour before all were shorn. As a man's head was finished, he took a shower and changed into fresh clothes in preparation for the *pabbajja* ("going forth," the preliminary ordination) ceremony which was to take place that evening in the Center's Dhamma Hall. The organizers knew that the men would be hungry so they were given an early evening meal since they would not be able to eat again that day after they had taken the novice's Ten Precepts, the sixth of which requires abstaining from food after midday.

It had already been a long day of celebration and religious activity. Early in the morning the children in the group, four girls and seven boys, had been dressed as princesses and princes in gilt and silk costumes that included fanciful high crowns, sequined *lungis* with long trains for the girls, makeup and decorations imitating precious jewelry. The princes were going to become samaneras, novices, in the evening and the dressing up was part of the build up, so they would enjoy themselves and keep happy memories of the day. The royal attire also symbolized the renunciation of the princely life by the Bodhisatta Siddhattha — the future Buddha — when he went forth from the palace to find the way to liberation.

Before 8 am, the children were lifted up into the backs of small open pickup trucks and seated on upholstered chairs by the individuals from the Centre who had been assigned to be their foster parents for the day. The real parents, perhaps a bit nervous about how their children would behave, carried the bundle of their sons' robes along with some small white orchids. It was a landmark event in the lives of these Western Buddhist families. The boys' trucks were adorned with tall golden umbrellas proclaiming the ordination procession to passers by. The rest of the group followed in cars and coaches. They moved at a stately pace through Yangon to the Shwe Dagon Pagoda, where several hairs of the Buddha are enshrined. At the head of the motorcade a uniformed Myanmar band standing in a truck played the typical raucous music of the land and sang about the Great Renunciation. A dancer performed in the jerky bent knee and elbow style of Southeast Asia. This too was part of the traditional way to celebrate the boys' going forth.

The 130-strong group found the route up to Shwe Dagon, Myanmar's most revered Buddhist site, clear of other devotees. Single file, barefoot, contented and chatting a little, each carrying a purple orchid spray offering, they proceeded up the series of long escalators to the level of the walkway. This is situated perhaps halfway between ground level and the peak of the spire with the golden umbrella. The wide band is paved in marble and much of it is covered with pagodas, cetiyas, and sculptures, notably of the stylized lions who seem to be guardians of the sacred shrine. There were many bhikkhus and lay families at the pagoda although it was not crowded. They showed mild curiosity about the large group of outsiders. The international contingent was dressed for the occasion in proper Myanmar attire, the men in plaid *lungis* and short white jackets, the women in heavy woven cotton *lungis* all of one pattern in various dark colors. The group was led by their teachers and the princes and princesses as it respectfully and mindfully circumambulated the golden dome. The atmosphere was informal and comfortable, the meditators appreciating the beauty and peace of the scene.

After a short meditation session in a side chamber, they left Shwe Dagon and drove to an audience with the fifteen leading sayadaws, renowned senior bhikkhus, who were in office by turns from among the country's State Sangha Maha Nayakas, the Central Executive Body of the Sangha. The group had been allotted a narrow window in the busy schedules of the sayadaws, the Central Executive Body of the Sangha, to pay respects. The theras sat on chairs in the front of the room with an ornate shrine behind them, and were formally introduced in English to the meditators. The foreigners, the teachers and Myanmar hosts accompanying them all paid respects to the sayadaws by bowing with their foreheads to the floor. They then repeated "Namo Tassa Bhagavato" and other devotional verses after the chief sayadaw.

The focus of events shifted to the meditation centre for the rest of the day. In the early afternoon there was an ear-boring ceremony for the four girls aged 5-13. Since the Order of bhikkhunis (nuns) has died out and, according to Theravada orthodoxy, cannot be revived for lack of bhikkhunis to ordain others, girls in Myanmar undergo this simple ritual, generally when a brother is becoming a samanera. At IMC's Dhamma Hall, there was some chanting as the girls sat proudly before the assembly in their slightly rumpled princess outfits. A Myanmar woman doctor put earrings in each girl's ears and they were free to change out of the fancy but inconvenient clothes. For the girls this was the conclusion of their ceremony.

The head shaving of boys and men followed as already described. After their supper, the men came into the Dhamma Hall, their skulls shining, where they were seated on the rugs in rows in age order, facing a line of senior sayadaws. They received a bundle of brown robes neatly rolled together and tied with the red cloth belt worn by Myanmar bhikkhus. Everyone else sat at the back of the hall meditating and observing the proceedings. The ceremony, which had been explained in advance, went on in a combination of Pali, Myanmar and English. Small groups of the samaneras-to-be offered their robes to their preceptor, who accepted them; then they requested the robes back from him so they could go forth, and he returned the robes. Now they all changed out of their lay clothes into the robes. (The shirts and *lungis* were put in labeled bags to be washed and ironed by wives or female volunteers and returned at the time of disrobing.) Most of these men (and one of the boys) had ordained previously, and many had done so several times. But they were all anxious to have another opportunity to practice the strict purity of a member of the Sangha in Myanmar, the land they cherished as the home of the pure Buddha Dhamma which they had been practicing, some for over twenty years. They each formally requested to be ordained as novices and then took the Ten Precepts from U Pandicca, their preceptor, and underwent a few other short formalities. They were given their bhikkhu names from a list considered appropriate for the day of the week of their birth. There was a short discourse of advice for the samaneras and the sayadaws chanted several *paritta suttas* (discourses of protection), for the well being of all. With that, the novitiation was complete.

Later in the evening there was the usual group meditation in the Dhamma Hall, with the new samaneras seated at the front, in order of seniority, which in almost all cases was age. The boys formed the last row and behind them were laymen, two or three from abroad, the rest from Myanmar. Next came the foreign women who had also come for the two weeks at the Centre, about forty-five of them. Filling the back to capacity were Myanmar ladies. This formal meditation hour was repeated three times a day for the two weeks the foreigners were in Yangon.

The men's full ordination *(upasampada),* their entry into the life of bhikkhus, took place on Sunday the 9th of January. The *upasampada* had to be in a monastery, so with the sponsorship and help of the Myanmar Department of Religious Affairs, the ordinations took place at Kaba Aye. This complex had originally been constructed to accommodate thousands of members of the Buddhist Sangha who gathered in Myanmar from all over the world in the mid-1950s to recite and purify the Pali canon at the Sixth Great Buddhist Council.

Because of the large number of people to undergo full ordination at the Kaba Aye ordination hall *(sima),* they were divided into morning and afternoon batches. The motorcade left IMC right after breakfast. The men and boys had been offered their first meal as samaneras in their dining room at the Centre. After the food had been placed on the low round tables and the samaneras had all sat on mats on the floor, upasakas, while bowing, gently lifted each laden table up several inches, symbolically offering the food to the novices in Myanmar fashion.

When they reached the Kaba Aye *sima,* shoes were left in the buses and the samaneras, followed by the laypeople, formed a procession from the gateway. The *sima* is a large circular structure surmounted by a small golden pagoda. The line was led by five Burmese men dressed in fantastic gilt deva costumes holding ten foot tall white cloth sunshades dangling with small metallic Bodhi leaves. The sayadaws, samaneras and lay meditators walked slowly up a red carpet runner on the broad flight of stairs, into the *sima.*

The interior is 150 feet in diameter with a truly colossal golden Buddha statue on a nearly fifteen foot high throne at the front. It is flanked slightly below by statues of the two Chief Disciples, the Elders Sariputta and Maha-moggallana, paying respects among various devotional objects: a tasteful grand scale shrine. The ceiling must be thirty feet high, supported on six massive columns decorated with bands of mirror inlay. A frieze goes around the perimeter, level with the Buddha's throne, composed of some hundred bhikkhu statues, perhaps half life-size, seated in meditation. Screened doors open outside at equal intervals; thick carpets cover the floor for the comfort of all; low, movable, decorative section dividers separate the Sangha from householders and men from women. The foreign women sat behind Mother Sayamagyi at the left and watched the proceedings while the samaneras were seated in the central section of the *sima* several meters away from and facing their preceptor and other sayadaws participating in the ordination ceremony. Laymen occupied another back section.

When everyone had settled in the proper place, the ceremony began. In groups of three, starting with the eldest samaneras, the foreigners approached the elder monks to seek full ordination. From the remote viewpoint of the lay people, it was difficult to understand everything that was going on, but following details was not essential as they were there to witness the event and share in the making of good kamma. The samaneras could understand as they had been trained beforehand. They were being asked the questions put to prospective bhikkhus ever since the Sangha became fully organized in the Buddha's lifetime: about their health, their sex, whether they were free and not in debt, if they were really human beings, etc. They replied appropriately. When they had all completed the answers, the groups again went up to the theras to request full ordination. When they had been accepted into the Order, each trio moved to join the Myanmar lifetime bhikkhus seated just to the side of the sayadaws conducting the proceedings. At times permanent bhikkhus had to bodily manipulate the foreigners into their proper places because they could not communicate through the language barrier.

The afternoon proceedings were similar except that a large number of outsiders also came to the *sima* to participate in the meritorious actions of supporting an ordination and of giving alms to the new monks afterwards. The atmosphere was quite special, generated by the commitment the men were making to the pure Buddha Dhamma and by the intention of everyone in the crowd to create *kusala,* good deeds, by participating in the proceedings.

The Deputy Minister for Religious Affairs spent several hours observing the ordinations and the Minister himself came to lead off the offering of *dana* to the newly ordained monks outside the *sima* in the late afternoon. The general public too was welcome to participate in these activities. Many who had just read about it in the newspaper came, having bought some small item to donate, or put some cash into an envelope to give (the standard way around the fact that monks are not supposed to touch gold or silver, i.e. money). All the International Meditation Centers (Yangon, U.K., U.S.A., Austria, and Western and Eastern Australia) had their own tables loaded with a particular item to be given to the monks. These had been purchased in Myanmar out of funds donated by members of the centers. Also various associations of the city participated in this *dana,* Yangon University lecturers, for example, came together.

In all, many hundred laypeople lined the path from the ordination hall to the street, standing and waiting in the hot sunshine, or patches of shade.

Inside the building, the bhikkhus were grouped by nationality behind labeled placards carried by young men. Each monk had a Myanmar layman bearing a tall white sunshade behind him and two of them on each side. These pairs of upasakas carried large white sacks. As *dana* items piled up on the monks' bowls, they carefully placed them in the bags, making sure they did not touch the ground. All these male workers wore badges for identification.

The senior sayadaws emerged first and slowly filed through the crowd, looking neither right nor left but just before them, not acknowledging the laypeople making their donations into the big black lacquer almsbowls. The feeling in the area switched from anticipation to reverence for the Sangha, respect for this institution which protects and follows the Buddha's teachings to the full. As the newly ordained bhikkhus passed through the line of donors, they responded to this awe for the robes they were now honored to wear, keenly aware of their obligation to conduct themselves as proper monks. Only in this way would they be worthy of the respect they were being shown, not let down their teachers and hosts, and not disillusion the laity, who were so sincere in their honor.

The laypeople slipped off their shoes, picked up a packet from the table behind them, and with both hands, carefully placed it in the bowl of the monk as he passed in front of them. (The women took extra care not to touch or brush against any bhikkhu or his robes in the crowd.) The giving was done systematically, rotating through each small cluster so that every lay person had equal chance to earn merit. The almsround right after monks have been ordained is considered sure to bring donors extra merit. The new bhikkhus looked radiantly pure, with their shaven heads, lowered eyes, and restrained demeanor.

The final event of this day was held from five to six in the evening in Moguk Hall nearby in the same Kaba Aye complex. Here about a thousand lay devotees, mostly local, sat on the floor while the sayadaws and the junior monks sat on chairs at the front of the room facing them. The golden shrine was behind the bhikkhus. They recited Namo Tassa Bhagavato, the Refuges and the Precepts after the head sayadaw of the Kaba Aye monastery, and then a libation ceremony of pouring out water was held to symbolize sharing the merits made that day. This was invisible to most of the lay people but was held in the front of the hall using several sets of silver vessels.

A tired, happy serenity was felt at IMC afterwards, born of the knowledge that so much *kusala* had been generated by so many people that day.

For the remainder of the week of the ordination course, the new bhikkhus stayed at the meditation centre. They lived in their own dormitories at one end of the grounds, under the watchful eye of their assistant preceptor, the Venerable U Chanda Siri, who had also helped in all the earlier ordinations organized by the IMCs. They made good use of their time in robes free of worldly affairs by meditating many hours a day—observing the breath to develop sharp *samadhi* and then applying the concentrated mind to the sensations rising and vanishing in their bodies to penetrate the *anicca* (impermanent)— and so *dukkha* (unsatisfactory) and *anatta* (impersonal) — nature of mind and body as deeply as they could. All was done as taught in the tradition of Sayagyi U Ba Khin, in strict accordance with the teachings of the Buddha.

Every evening there was a confession also in the hall. As there were so many bhikkhus, U Chanda Siri heard the confessions of half of the men and one of the older of the foreigners heard the confessions of the remainder. The bhikkhus got up from their seats on the floor, straightened their robes and worked their way to the front of the hall in pairs to recite the short Pali catechism admitting to miscellaneous errors and accepting admonition to try to do better in the future. In this orderly way it took about twenty minutes to finish all of the monks each evening. Sometimes the confession was followed by a short discourse by U Chanda Siri or one of the meditation teachers. One talk was about the *"dullabhas,"* or states difficult to obtain, the most rare of which is being a bhikkhu. Another was an explanation of the origins of the questions the samaneras had to answer before being ordained as full bhikkhus. Those had been instituted by the Buddha in response to specific situations which arose, just as all the rules for the Sangha had been.

Following the bhikkhus' confession, the young samaneras came forward to recite the Refuges, Ten Precepts, etc., after U Chanda Siri. He was very particular that they pronounce each syllable in exactly the correct way, and they would repeat difficult words over and over until the result was as perfect as the preceptor wanted. The samaneras had their own bedroom and activities which included daily visits to the Shwe Dagon Pagoda.

The bhikkhus were fed in a separate upstairs dining hall on choice Myanmar and Chinese vegetarian food. Often some special dish — such as ice cream — had been donated by someone. People were always looking for more ways to earn merit by helping the bhikkhus, and other meditators, at the Centre. The Myanmar Buddhists exhibit great generosity, cultivating the *dana parami.*

The offerings the bhikkhus had received at the *sima* were sorted out by lay people one evening. The cash was totaled up and donated to certain pagodas and monasteries in Yangon, and the monks could take whatever they wanted of the remainder. Most of the things actually went out to vicars (monasteries) where lifetime bhikkhus would have more use for them than foreigners returning to lay life in their own countries in a few days.

The week as bhikkhus was interspersed with several events. One morning a *pindapata* (almsround) was held at IMC itself. Monks from U Pandicca's monastery had come to wrap the temporary monks' robes in the complex way, modestly covering the neck and both shoulders, appropriate for "going among the houses." The line of donors wound around the pagoda and Dhamma Hall. This time most of the items were food, since it was before noon. The atmosphere was more like a community event since the Centre was "home" to all the participants. The lay people again were dressed in fine Myanmar clothes to honor the bhikkhus. One afternoon, Myanmar TV conducted interviews with six of the bhikkhus, and two of the foreign laywomen, in the Dhamma Hall. (Actually, TV crews, local and Japanese, had been covering most of the events of the ordination week and everyone was familiar with bright lights — from external sources — while they were meditating in the Dhamma Hall.) The questionnaire which had been given to the interviewees was quite serious and the bhikkhus especially had a good opportunity to express their views on the situation of Buddha Dhamma in the West and in Myanmar and about what they had personally gained from practicing this meditation. If the interviews were shown in full, some profound Buddha Dhamma would have come over that most unlikely of media.

The boys took off their robes on Saturday the 15th; the bhikkhus did so precisely a week after the ordination. On that Sunday afternoon the confession was held early, at four, and immediately afterwards they agreed aloud that they were prepared to return to lay life. They then requested to be regarded as samaneras. They removed the robes and changed back into their lay clothes and then asked to be recognized as laymen again — in both Pali and English. Finally U Chanda Siri gave them a discourse as laymen, urging them to cooperate in spreading the Buddha Dhamma in their own countries and always to follow the advice of Mother Sayamagyi and their other teachers.

The temporary bhikkhus returned to lay life with satisfaction at having done what is so hard to do: to be a good Buddhist monk. They were glad to have had even that short chance to know life without the entanglements, the "dust" as the Buddha called it, of household affairs. Some of them were a bit sorry at its ending. Most will probably try to take ordination again in this lifetime to earn still more merit. Their families were joyous to see how they had matured from the experience. Everyone had the assurance that comes from the performance of meritorious deeds dedicated towards purification of mind and the attainment of Nibbana, the cessation of all suffering.

6

Buddhist Ceremonies and Rituals of Sri Lanka

INTRODUCTION

Sri Lanka is generally regarded as the home of the pure Theravada form of Buddhism, which is based on the Pali canon. This school of Buddhism emphasizes the Four Noble Truths as the framework of Buddhist doctrine and the Noble Eightfold Path as the direct route to Nibbana, the final goal of the Teaching. However, side by side with this austere, intellectually sophisticated Buddhism of the texts, we find in Sri Lanka a warm current of devotional Buddhism practiced by the general Buddhist populace, who may have only a hazy idea of the Buddhist doctrine. Thus in practical life the gap between the "great tradition" of canonical Buddhism and the average person's world of everyday experience is bridged by a complex round of ceremonies, rituals, and devotional practices that are hardly visible within the canonical texts themselves.

While the specific forms of ritual and ceremony in Sri Lankan popular Buddhism doubtlessly evolved over the centuries, it seems likely that this devotional approach to the Dhamma has its roots in lay Buddhist practice even during the time of the Buddha himself. Devotion being the intimate inner side of religious worship, it must have had a place in early Buddhism. For Buddhism, devotion does not mean submitting oneself to the will of a God or taking refuge in an external Saviour, but an ardent feeling of love and affection *(pema)* directed towards the Teacher who shows the way to freedom from suffering. Such an attitude inspires the devotee to follow the Master's teaching faithfully and earnestly through all the hurdles that lie along the way to Nibbana.

The Buddha often stressed the importance of *saddha,* faith or confidence in him as the Perfect Teacher and in his Teaching as the vehicle to liberation from the cycle of rebirth. Unshakeable confidence *(aveccappasada)* in the Triple Gem — the Buddha, the Dhamma, and the Sangha — is a mark of the noble disciple, while the Buddha once stated that those who have sufficient confidence in him, sufficient affection for him *(saddhamatta, pemamatta)* are bound for heaven. Many verses of the *Theragatha* and *Therigatha,* poems of the ancient monks and nuns, convey feelings of deep devotion and a high level of emotional elation.

Although the canonical texts do not indicate that this devotional sensibility had yet come to expression in fully formed rituals, it seems plausible that simple ritualistic observances giving vent to feelings of devotion had already begun to take shape even during the Buddha's lifetime. Certainly they would have done so shortly after the Parinibbana, as is amply demonstrated by the funeral rites themselves, according to the testimony of the Maha-parinibbana Sutta. The Buddha also encouraged a devotional attitude when he recommended pilgrimages to the four places that can inspire a faithful devotee: the places where he was born, attained Enlightenment, preached the first sermon, and attained Parinibbana (D.ii,140).

The Buddha did discourage the wrong kind of emotional attachment to himself, as evidenced by the case of Vakkali Thera, who was reprimanded for his obsession with the beauty of the Buddha's physical presence: his was a case of misplaced devotion (S.iii,119). Ritualistic observances also pose a danger that they might be misapprehended as ends in themselves instead of being employed as means for channelling the devotional emotions into the correct path. It is when they are wrongly practiced that they become impediments rather than aids to the spiritual life. It is to warn against this that the Buddha has categorized them, under the term *silabbata-paramasa,* as one of the ten fetters *(samyojana)* and one of the four types of clinging *(upadana).* Correctly observed, as means and not as ends, ritualistic practices can serve to generate wholesome states of mind, while certain other rituals collectively performed can serve as a means of strengthening the social solidarity among those who share the same spiritual ideals.

Thus ceremonies and rituals, as external acts which complement inward contemplative exercises, cannot be called alien to or incompatible with canonical Buddhism. To the contrary, they are an integral part of the living tradition of all schools of Buddhism, including the Theravada.

A ritual may be defined here as an outward act performed regularly and consistently in a context that confers upon it a religious significance not immediately evident in the act itself. A composite unity consisting of a number of subordinate ritualistic acts may be called a ceremony. Such observances have become inseparable from all organized religions. And owing to the fear, awe, and respect that characterize man's religious psychology, such acts assume a solemnity and a sanctity of their own.

Ritual acts undertaken and performed by the Buddhists of Sri Lanka may be broadly classified under three heads:

(i) Acts performed for the acquisition of merit (e.g., offerings made in the name of the Buddha) calculated to provide a basis for achieving Nibbana, release from the cycle of becoming *(samsara);* such acts of merit are, at the same time, expected to offer semi-temporal rewards of comfort and happiness here and in the heavenly worlds in future lives. These supplementary forms of religious activity have arisen out of a natural need to augment the more austere way followed by the world-renouncing disciples.

(ii) Acts directed towards securing worldly prosperity and averting calamities through disease and unseen forces of evil, e.g., *pirit* chanting, *bodhi-puja,* etc.

(iii) Those rituals that have been adopted from folk religion. Hence these are mainly semi-religious in character like the *tovil* ceremonies. They derive their power and authority primarily through the superhuman power of the Buddha and also through the hosts of spirits, who are, as it were, commanded by invoking the power of the Buddha or of the Three Refuges — the Buddha, Dhamma and Sangha — as a whole.

Almost all the religious activities that have a ceremonial and a ritualistic significance are regarded as acts for the acquisition of merit (Sinh.: *pinkama,* from Pali: *punnakamma,* Sanskrit: *punyakarma).* In this sense, all the religious activities of lay Buddhism can be explained as being oriented towards that end. Accordingly, the first two types of rituals basically have a merit-generating character and thereby receive religious sanction. For instance, the idea of acquisition of merit through a religious act and its transference to the deities and soliciting their help has the scriptural sanction of the Maha-parinibbana Sutta itself (D.ii,88-89). Here the Buddha says that wise men, when residing in a particular area, first offer alms to religious recluses and then transfer the merits to the deities of the area, who help them in return. This seems to indicate the early beginning of adoring *vatthu-devata* or local deities in Buddhism.

Merit (Pali: *punna:* Sinh.: *pin)* earned by the performance of a wholesome act is regarded as a sure way of obtaining a better life in the future. The performance of these is also a means of expiation in the sense that the meritorious deeds have the effect of countering and hindering the operation of unwholesome *kamma* previously acquired and inherited. Thus the range of merit is very wide.

For the ordinary householder, Nibbana is a goal to be achieved through a gradual process of evolution extending over many lives, and therefore until he achieves that sublime state at some future date he continues to perform these acts in order to lead a happy life. All merit-generating rituals are performed mainly with this end in view.

Initiation and Worship

Initiation

Buddhism lacks any ceremony or ritual of initiation or admission like the *upanayana* in Hinduism or baptism in Christianity. The traditional method of becoming a Buddhist is to repeat the formula of the Three Refuges *(tisarana)* and the Five Precepts *(pañcasila),* when they are formally administered by a Buddhist monk. The formula of refuge is as follows:

Buddham saranam gacchami

I go to the Buddha as my refuge.

Dhammam saranam gacchami

I go to the Dhamma as my refuge.

Sangham saranam gacchami

I go to the Sangha as my refuge.

This avowal of confidence in the Triple Gem *(tiratana)* is repeated for a second time (e.g., *dutiyampi Buddham saranam gacchami,* etc.), and a third time *(tatiyampi).* Next, the convert repeats in the following manner the Five Precepts which are meant to regulate his moral life:

(1) *Panatipata veramani sikkhapadam samadiyami.* I undertake the precept to abstain from destroying life

(2) *Adinnadana veramani sikkhapadam samadiyami.* I undertake the precept to abstain from taking things not given.

(3) *Kamesu micchacara veramani sikkhapadam samadiyami.* I undertake the precept to abstain from sexual misconduct.

(4) *Musavada veramani sikkhapadam samadiyami.* I undertake the precept to abstain from false speech.

(5) *Suramerayamajjapamadatthana veramani sikkhapadam samadiyami.* I undertake the precept to abstain from taking distilled and fermented liquors that cause intoxication and heedlessness.

By this method a hitherto non-Buddhist lay person becomes a lay disciple *(upasaka)* of the Buddha. It has to be noted here that what is meant by taking refuge in the Buddha, the Dhamma, and the Sangha is the placing of confidence in the attainments of the Buddha as a Teacher and in the efficacy of the Dhamma as a reliable means to liberation. The term "Sangha" here refers to the *Ariya Sangha,* comprising the four pairs of noble ones, i.e., the four practicing for the fruits and the four established in the fruits *(cattari purisayugani attha purisa-puggala)*. In this ceremony of initiation there is no recognition of salvation through the grace of a god or saviour as in theistic religions. One goes for refuge as a way of expressing one's determination to follow the Buddha's path to liberation, but one must also realize that the task of walking the path is one's own responsibility.

While this is the method of formal admission of a new entrant into Buddhism, there are also certain ritualistic practices observed when a child is born to Buddhist parents. The baby's first outing would be to a temple. When the baby is fit to be taken out of doors the parents would select an auspicious day or a full-moon day and take the child to the nearest temple. They would first place the child on the floor of the shrine room or in front of a statue of the Buddha for the purpose of obtaining the blessings of the Triple Gem. This is a common sight at the Dalada Maligawa — the Temple of the Sacred Tooth Relic — in Kandy. At the time of the daily religious ceremony *(puja)* of the temple, one can observe how mothers hand over their babies to an officiating layman *(kapuva)* inside the shrine room, who in turn keeps it for a few seconds on the floor near the Relic Chamber and hands it back to the mother. The mother accepts the child and gives a small fee to the *kapuva* for the service rendered. This practice too could be described as a ritual of initiation.

Personal Worship

For the adherent of Buddhism, the ritual of worship is essentially a respectful recognition of the greatness of the Buddha as a spiritual teacher. The ritual also implies an expression of gratitude to the Buddha for having discovered and revealed to humankind the path leading out of the mass of worldly suffering. Both these factors in combination make this ritual an expression of devotion as well.

The most common daily ritual of the Buddhist is that of personal worship, which many devout Buddhists perform daily in their homes. On the communal level the ritual is observed on the *poya* days at a temple or a monastery.

A distinction may be made between simple respectful salutation *(panama* or *panamana)* and the ritualistic worship *(vandana)* accompanied by offerings of increasing complexity including food, drink, and clothing. The former type is only an expression of respect and reverence as when a person clasps his hands in the gesture of worship in front of a religious symbol (e.g., a Buddha-statue, a Bodhi-tree, a *dagaba,* etc.) and recites a simple phrase like the well-known *Namo tassa* formula (see below); nowadays the term *sadhu* has become quite popular with the Sinhala Buddhists for this purpose.

In the ritualistic form of worship the articles of offering (mainly flowers) are first respectfully placed on the altar in front of a statue of the Buddha or a *dagaba* or any other place of religious significance where such worship is performed. Next, the devotee clasps his hands in the gesture of worship *(anjali-kamma)* and solemnly recites various stanzas and formulas, thereby making the offerings formally valid. Every act of Buddhist worship begins with the well-known formula of homage to the Buddha, *Namo tassa bhagavato arahato sammasambuddhassa* ("Let my obeisance be to the Blessed One, the Honorable One, the Fully Enlightened One"), which is repeated thrice. This is followed by the Refuge formula and the Five Precepts given earlier.

The next step is paying homage to the Three Gems in three separate formulas, which recount nine virtues of the Buddha, six virtues of the Dhamma, and nine virtues of the Sangha. These formulas are extracted from the Pali Nikayas and have become the standard formulas with which the Three Gems are worshipped.

The physical posture adopted by the devotees when performing these acts of worship may vary according to the solemnity of the occasion or the degree of the devotion of the worshipper. In the most respectful form of worship, e.g., when worshipping a *dagaba* in which the relics — a bone, hair, bowl, etc., of the Buddha — are enshrined, one touches the ground with five parts of the body (Sinh.: *pasanga pihituva,* i.e., knees, elbows, and forehead). The two postures of squatting *(ukkutika)* and kneeling (with one or both knees) are also popular. The cross-legged posture *(pallanka)* and the standing position are also sometimes adopted. Whatever be the posture taken, it should be accompanied with hands clasped together in adoration (Sinh.: *andilibanda,* Pali: *anjalim panametva).*

Of the many articles of offering used at present in this kind of worship in Sri Lanka, flowers have become the most important and popular. They constitute the minimum requirement at any form of Buddhist worship. One can observe how the devotees arrange the flowers in various patterns on the altar. The color *(vanna),* smell *(gandha),* and quality *(guna)* of the flowers are taken into account when selecting them for offering. Before being offered, the flowers are "bathed" with filtered water *(pan).* Sometimes they are arranged in a tray *(vattiya)* and offered. A flower's blooming upon contact with light is regarded as symbolic of the attainment of Enlightenment, hence flowers become quite a fitting article for offering to the Buddha, the Enlightened One.

As was mentioned earlier, an essential part of the ritual of offering flowers is the recital of the following Pali stanza, whereby the offering is made valid:

Vannagandhagunopetam

etam kusumasantatim

pujayami munindassa

siripadasaroruhe.

Pujemi Buddham kusumena 'nena

punnena 'metena ca hotu mokkham

Puppham milayati yatha idam me

kayo tatha yati vinasabahavam.

"This mass of flowers endowed with color, fragrance, and quality I offer at the lotus-like feet of the King of Sages. I worship the Buddha with these flowers: by the merit of this may I attain freedom. Even as these flowers do fade, so does my body come to destruction."

It is of interest to note that this stanza incorporates the Buddhist idea of the impermanence *(anicca)* of all phenomena.

Merit-acquisition is also regarded as contributing towards the attainment of Nibbanic freedom.

Another popular offering of much importance is that of lighted lamps, usually of coconut oil *(dipa-puja* or *pahan-puja).* As the Buddha is regarded as the dispeller of the darkness of ignorance, when lighted lamps are offered in his name this metaphorical contrast between the light of knowledge and the darkness of ignorance is taken as the theoretical basis for the ritual. This kind of symbolism being too deep for the vast majority of ordinary people, their motive for this ritual is usually the desire to acquire merit or to avert the evil influence of a bad planetary conjunction. However, it is the former idea that is implied in the traditional stanza used by the Buddhists of Sri Lanka for this offering:

Ghanasarappadittena
dipena tamadamsina
tilokadipam sambuddham
pujayami tamonudam.

"With this lamp lit with camphor that dispels all darkness, I worship the Perfectly Enlightened One who is a lamp unto the three worlds and is the dispeller of darkness."

The epithets *tilokadipa* ("lamp unto the three worlds") and *tamonuda* ("dispeller of darkness") as applied to the Buddha are significant in this context. The stanza itself seems to testify to the popularity of the offering of camphor *(ghanasara)* in early times. But nowadays, even when coconut oil has replaced camphor, the stanza has survived without change.

The offering of lighted lamps had been a popular ritual even in ancient times. The Bodhi-tree and the *dagaba* (also referred to as *stupa, cetiya,* or *caitya)* are the two main objects or places where the ritual is usually performed. The offering of lamps is one of the main aspects of the worship of the Bodhi-tree *(bodhi-puja).* As it was under a Bodhi-tree that the Buddha attained Enlightenment, it is quite natural that lamps be lit under that tree, not only in memory of the great event, but also as a ritual whereby the devotee could expect to obtain a ray of that light of wisdom attained by the Great Sage. Thus the entire ritual becomes a spiritual exercise, the merits of which are transferred to all other beings, gods, humans, and spirits *(bhuta)*. *Dagabas* constitute another place where this popular offering is made. Consequently, along with the flower-altar, the lamp-stand too has become a necessary adjunct of the *dagabas.* One can also see that the Bodhi-tree in most temples is surrounded by a platform built of brick or stone in which niches are made to hold lighted oil lamps. The niches are meant to shelter the lamps from wind and rain. In any Buddhist temple there are many other places where lamps can be lit in that way. Sometimes special lamp-stands are constructed for the purpose. Of special significance is the lamp called the *dolosmahe-pahana* (twelve-month lamp), sometimes found in Buddhist temples and *devalayas.* It is called thus because it is expected to keep burning all-year round.

Special light offerings are also made on auspicious occasions. On full-moon days when devotees flock to the temples, lamps are lit in large numbers, for it is the custom among the Sri Lankan Buddhists invariably to take flowers and coconut oil on their visits to the temple as two indispensable articles of worship. There are also occasions when devotees light and offer a particular large number of lamps for special purposes, such as redeeming a vow *(baraya)* or on special occasions like Vesak Day. Many Buddhists perform the ritual of light offering *(pahan-puja)* to counter evil planetary influences. In order to obtain maximum results from the ritual, the devotees make it a point to purify themselves completely before attending the ceremony by bathing and wearing fresh, clean clothes. Coconut oil used as an illuminant is specially prepared for the purpose and taken separately from the coconut oil used for household purposes. Wicks are prepared from a clean, white, fresh cloth. Sometimes the inhabitants of an entire village co-operate in holding a mass-scale lamp offering. For instance, they may offer 84,000 lighted lamps in memory of the 84,000 elements of the Dhamma *(dhammakkhandha)* comprising the Buddha's Teaching.

This important Buddhist ritual was practiced even in ancient Sri Lanka. King Dutugemunu (2nd century B.C.) is recorded to have lit one thousand lamps with ghee as the illuminant and with white wicks burning perpetually in twelve sacred places in Anuradhapura (Mhv. xxxii,37). King Vasabha (1st century A.C.) is also said to have lit one thousand oil lamps at Cetiyapabbata, Thuparama, Mahathupa (Ruvanweli-dagaba), and the Bodhi-tree (Mhv. xxxvi,80).

Today, this ritual has become so popular and elaborate that the annual Vesak festival commemorating the birth, Enlightenment, and Parinibbana of the Buddha has become more or less a festival of lights. Vesak lanterns of various kinds and shapes are lit in Buddhist homes on this day. Pandals well illuminated with multi-colored electric bulbs, depicting various scenes from the Master's life and from the Jataka stories, also constitute a type of light offering to the Buddha.

Yet another aspect of the ritual of light offering is the burning of camphor near the object of worship like *dagabas*, Buddha statues, etc. Camphor gives out a fragrant smell as it burns, and is also regarded as having a very pure flame, although its smoke has a strong blackening effect. Camphor-burners have been found in ancient temples, showing that this was an ancient practice.

The offering of food and drink is still another aspect of the ritual of worship. When food is offered to the Buddha in a religious place it is usually done in front of a Buddha-image. If it is the morning meal that is offered, it would be something suitable for breakfast, usually milk-rice *(kiribat)*. If it is lunch, it would be the usual rice-and-curry meal and is invariably offered before noon. At the Dalada Maligawa in Kandy and the Sri Mahabodhi in Anuradhapura, these rituals are performed regularly and with meticulous care and also somewhat elaborately, accompanied by other subsidiary rituals like the beating of drums. It is an important part of this ritual that whatever food is offered in this manner should be separately prepared with special care and should not be tasted before the offering. The stanza that is popularly used for the offering of food runs as follows:

Adhivasetu no bhante

bhojanam parikappitam

Anukampam upadaya
patiganhatumuttama.

"O Lord, accept with favor this food which has been ritualistically prepared. Receive it, O Noble One, out of compassion."

As regards the offering of drinks and beverages, it is customary to offer these prepared from fruit-juices. Unlike the solid foods, these may be offered in the afternoon, in keeping with the meal habits of the Buddhist monks. Offering of incense generally consists of joss sticks, these being the most easily available. Otherwise this offering is made by putting certain kinds of sweet-smelling powders or incense into glowing charcoal so that it smokes well. A kind of resin, known locally as *sambrani*, is the variety generally used.

The chew of betel *(dahat-vita)* is yet another item of offering. This is mostly for consumption after meals, and consists of betel leaves, arecanut, and certain other items like cloves, nutmeg, cardamons, etc. which give a pleasant smell and a pungent taste when chewed. For every kind of offering there are separate stanzas like the one quoted earlier for food. These stanzas are composed in Pali, which is supposed to be the language in which the Buddha preached his doctrine.

When visiting the temple the object of worship that ranks first is the *dagaba* enshrining the bone-relics of the Buddha. There are three categories of worshipful objects: (i) bodily relics, consisting of the bones collected after cremation *(saririka);* (ii) those articles the Buddha used, e.g., the alms-bowl, Bodhi-tree, etc. *(paribhogika);* and (iii) those memorials that have been erected on his account as a mark of remembrance *(uddesika),* e.g., images, paintings, etc. The devotee is expected to worship these in due order, reciting the appropriate stanzas and making at least an offering of a few flowers.

An important aspect of the worship of the *dagaba* and the Bodhi-tree is the custom of circumambulation *(padakkhina)* as a mark of respect. Usually three rounds are done, always keeping the object of worship to the right side and with the hands clasped together in adoration. As regards *dagaba* worship in Sri Lanka, the local Buddhists have a separate stanza for worshipping each of the sixteen sacred places hallowed by the Lord Buddha on his three visits to the island. There is also a popular stanza that covers in a general manner all the three categories of worshipful objects mentioned above:

Vandami cetiyam sabbam

sabbathanesu patitthitam,

saririkadhatu mahabodhim

buddharupam sakalam sada.

"Forever do I worship all the dagabas situated all over, all the bodily relics, the Mahabodhi (tree), and Buddha-images."

The worship of the *dagaba* or *stupa* is an important merit-acquiring act of devotional Buddhism in Sri Lanka as also in other Buddhist lands. The first such *dagaba* to be constructed after the official introduction of Buddhism into the country by the arahant Mahinda was the Thuparama at Anuradhapura, which enshrines the collar-bone of the Buddha. It was constructed by the first Buddhist ruler of Sri Lanka, King Devanampiya Tissa, in the 3rd century B.C. Since then *dagabas* have become so popular among the local Buddhists that almost every village temple has a *dagaba* as an indispensable feature. A special ritual connected with the *dagaba* is the enshrining of relics, which is done with much ceremony at a specially selected astrologically auspicious moment called *nakata* (Skt. *naksatra).* A similar ritual is that of pinnacle-setting *(kot-palandavima),* which is the concluding stage in the construction of a *dagaba.*

It should be mentioned here that scriptural sanction for *dagaba* worship is found in the words of the Buddha himself in the Maha-parinibbana Sutta (D.ii,142), where he has enumerated four categories of individuals worthy of *dagabas.* These are the Tathagata, a Paccekabuddha, a disciple of the Tathagata, and a universal monarch *(raja cakkavattin).* The worship and offerings made to the Buddha's body after his passing away may also be cited as an instance in this connection.

The most important item that comes within the *uddesika* kind of sacred object is the Buddha-image, which is found in every temple in its image-house *(viharage).* In addition to the central image or images, the inside walls of the temple — and sometimes the ceiling as well — are covered with paintings depicting events from the Buddha's life, as well as from his past lives as a Bodhisatta, recorded in the Jataka stories. An important ceremony associated with the Buddha-image is the ritual of painting its eyes *(netra-pinkama),* which is performed with much care on an auspicious occasion as the last item of its construction. Until this is done the image is not considered an adequate representation of the Buddha.

Group Worship

Collective worship of the Buddha is generally performed in a public place of worship so that anyone who wishes may participate: in a temple before the shrine room, at a *dagaba,* a Bodhi-tree, or any other such place. The devotees stand in a row in front of the place of worship and pass the items of offering from hand to hand towards the shrine room, *dagaba,* or the Bodhi-tree. These offerings usually consist of bowls or vases of flowers, incense, joss sticks, beverages, fruit drinks, medicinal items, oil-lamps, etc. Here no distinction of age, position, or sex is observed. All participate in a common act of merit *(pinkama).* A bhikkhu or a number of bhikkhus may sometimes head the line.

The commonest of the *Buddha-pujas* is the one performed in the evening, around 6 p.m., known as the *gilampasa Buddha-puja* or the Buddha-offering consisting of medicaments and beverages. If the *Buddha-puja* is done in the morning it would be one consisting of milk-rice *(kiri-ahara)* or any other item of food suitable for breakfast. The mid-day food *(dana)* also may be offered in this manner. The mid-day meal is offered to the Buddha when lay people bring food to the monastery to offer as alms to the bhikkhus. First, under the guidance of a bhikkhu, they perform the offering to the Buddha, who is represented symbolically by relics and an image; thereafter the food is offered to the resident bhikkhus. It is the established tradition that in whatever circumstances alms are offered to the bhikkhus, the first portions are offered to the Buddha beforehand. The variations in the kinds of food offered are in keeping with the meal habits of the Buddha and his monk-disciples, who refrain from taking solid food and milk-foods after mid-day.

Once the offerings are placed in the appropriate place, lamps lit, and incense burnt, stanzas are recited for each kind of offering made so that the offerings become valid. This is done by a bhikkhu who first administers the Refuges and Precepts (explained earlier) and then recites the relevant stanzas (in Pali) aloud, while the other participants, with their hands clasped in adoration, repeat them in chorus after the bhikkhu. Sometimes this kind of public *Buddha-puja* is accompanied by drumming and horns, called *hevisi-puja* or offering of music, which usually accompanies many Buddhist functions. As the final item of the programme, one of the participating bhikkhus delivers a short sermon explaining the significance of the occasion.

It may also be mentioned here that this kind of public *puja* is performed as a general act of merit-acquisition on religiously important days such as the full-moon days or in remembrance of important dead personages. In the latter case the ritual is held on the death anniversary of the person concerned. It is believed that the dead person can partake of the merits transferred to him *(pattidana)* from his new existence and thereby obtain relief from any unfortunate realm in which he might have been born. If the ritual is performed for such a purpose, the participating monk would specially mention this fact and transfer the merits earned.

Whatever be the purpose for which the ceremony is held, the concluding part is marked by certain features which are of further interest. One is the usual practice of the transference of merit to all beings, including gods and spirits, by reciting the appropriate stanzas. Another is the general aspiration *(patthana)* that the participants make to the effect that by the merits earned from the ritual they may not be born into the company of foolish and unworthy friends but into the company of wise and virtuous men until they attain Nibbana. They also do not fail to add the final attainment of Nibbana to this list *(idam me punnam asavakkhayavaham hotu:* "May this merit bring about the extinction of defilements in me").

Yet another popular aspiration which has a greater social significance is the following:

Devo vassatu kalena — sassasampatti hotu ca

phito bhavatu loko ca — raja bhavatu dhammiko.

"May the rains come in time

So that the harvests may be abundant:

May the world be prosperous,

May the rulers be righteous."

The ritual is concluded by asking for pardon for whatever lapses may have occurred inadvertently:

Kayena vaca cittena pamadena maya katam

accayam khama me bhante bhuripanna tathagata.

"O Lord, Tathagata of extensive wisdom, may you excuse me for whatever transgressions might have been done by me through body, speech, or mind due to negligence."

Sometimes a similar request is made to the Dhamma and the Sangha as well. However, as the idea of pardoning one's sins is foreign to Buddhism, this kind of request would be meaningful only if the devotee does so with full understanding as an expiatory act, as a means of self-reformation, for the Buddha, unlike the God of theistic religions, cannot forgive sins.

Another kind of *Buddha-puja* is the one regularly done in temples and Buddhist *devalayas.* It is the daily offering of food and drink *(murutan puja)* made to the Buddha by the temple authorities. At the Dalada Maligawa (Temple of the Tooth) in Kandy and the Sri Mahabodhi at Anuradhapura offerings of this kind are made on a solemn and grand scale. These two places assume this significance because they are the two most deeply venerated sacred places for the Buddhists of Sri Lanka. The breakfast, noon meal, and the evening drinks are all offered regularly at fixed hours accompanied by drumming and horn playing *(tevava).* Often, the public also make their own offerings.

Another important Buddhist ritual is the honoring of the Buddha with what appears to be a relic of the musical performance held in order to revere and pay homage to the sacred memory of the Master. The historical beginning of this form of worship can be traced as far back as the time of the Buddha. A passage in the Maha-parinibbana Sutta (D.ii,159) records that after his passing away, while the body of the Buddha was lying in state for seven days at Kusinara in the capital of the Mallas, complete musical performances inclusive of dance, song, and orchestration *(nacca, gita, vadita)* were held in his honor.

This undoubtedly was an unreserved expression by the lay patrons of their deep veneration for the Master. Of this kind of offering, all that seems to have survived is drumming and some light dancing engaged in by the drummers themselves to the drum-beat and horns. In Sri Lanka the ritual is performed by the professionals belonging to the drummer *(berava)* caste and as an offering it is popularly known as *sabda-puja* or the "offering of sound."

This orchestration is collectively called *hevisi* and usually consists of two drums (called *davul),* a twin-drum with one face for each and turned upwards *(surappattuwa* or *tammattama),* and a horn-like instrument called *horanava* referred to earlier. Drumming of this type, with a bigger number of drummers, is an essential part of Buddhist processions as well. This kind of drumming also takes place at other Buddhist ceremonies, such as *pirit* chanting and alms-giving, to be described below.

At important temples where offerings of food are made to the Buddha and the deities at meal times, drumming is performed to coincide with the offering and continues until the ritual of offering is over. This kind of regular service is known as *tevava.* The ritual may also be held on Poya days, especially the full-moon day, in temples as a special offering to the Buddha. An important point to be noted in this *pujava* is that while the other kinds of offering are made by the worshipper himself, in this case he hires professionals to make the offering on his behalf. But in big temples like the Dalada Maligawa at Kandy, payments in money are not usually made as the drummers have the hereditary right to the tenure of the temple lands in return for which these services are performed.

The Bodhi-Puja

The veneration of the Bodhi-tree (pipal tree: *ficus religiosa)* has been a popular and a widespread ritual in Sri Lanka from the time a sapling of the original Bodhi-tree at Buddhagaya (under which the Buddha attained Enlightenment) was brought from India by the Theri Sanghamitta and planted at Anuradhapura during the reign of King Devanampiya Tissa in the third century B.C. Since then a Bodhi-tree has become a necessary feature of every Buddhist temple in the island.

The ritualistic worship of trees as abodes of tree deities *(rukkha-devata)* was widely prevalent in ancient India even before the advent of Buddhism. This is exemplified by the well-known case of Sujata's offering of milk-rice to the Bodhisatta, who was seated under a banyan tree on the eve of his Enlightenment, in the belief that he was the deity living in that tree. By making offerings to these deities inhabiting trees the devotees expect various forms of help from them. The practice was prevalent in pre-Buddhist Sri Lanka as well. According to the *Mahavamsa,* King Pandukabhaya (4th century B.C.) fixed a banyan tree near the western gate of Anuradhapura as the abode of Vessavana, the god of wealth and the regent of the North as well as the king of the *yakkhas.* The same king set apart a palmyra palm as the abode of *vyadha-deva,* the god of the hunt (Mhv. x,89, 90).

After the introduction of the Bodhi-tree, this cult took a new turn. While the old practice was not totally abandoned, pride of place was accorded to the worship of the pipal tree, which had become sacred to the Buddhists as the tree under which Gotama Buddha attained Enlightenment. Thus there is a difference between the worship of the Bodhi-tree and that of other trees. To the Buddhists, the Bodhi-tree became a sacred object belonging to the *paribhogika* group of the threefold division of sacred monuments, while the ordinary veneration of trees, which also exists side-by-side with the former in Sri Lanka, is based on the belief already mentioned, i.e., that there are spirits inhabiting these trees and that they can help people in exchange for offerings. The Buddhists also have come to believe that powerful Buddhist deities inhabit even the Bodhi-trees that receive worship in the purely Buddhist sense. Hence it becomes clear that the reverence shown to a tree is not addressed to the tree itself. However, it also has to be noted that the Bodhi-tree received veneration in India even before it assumed this Buddhist significance; this practice must have been based on the general principle of tree worship mentioned above.

Once the tree assumed Buddhist significance its sanctity became particularized, while the deities inhabiting it also became associated with Buddhism in some form. At the same time, the tree became a symbol representing the Buddha as well. This symbolism was confirmed by the Buddha himself when he recommended the planting of the Ananda Bodhi-tree at Jetavana for worship and offerings during his absence (see J.iv,228f.). Further, the place where the Buddha attained Enlightenment is mentioned by the Buddha as one of the four places of pilgrimage that should cause serene joy in the minds of the faithful (D.ii,140). As Ananda Coomaraswamy points out, every Buddhist temple and monastery in India once had its Bodhi-tree and flower altar as is now the case in Sri Lanka.

King Devanampiya Tissa, the first Buddhist king of Sri Lanka, is said to have bestowed the whole country upon the Bodhi-tree and held a magnificent festival after planting it with great ceremony. The entire country was decorated for the occasion. The *Mahavamsa* refers to similar ceremonies held by his successors as well. It is said that the rulers of Sri Lanka performed ceremonies in the tree's honor in every twelfth year of their reign (Mhv. xxxviii,57).

King Dutugemunu (2nd century B.C.) performed such a ceremony at a cost of 100,000 pieces of money (Mhv. xxviii,1). King Bhatika Abhaya (1st century A.C.) held a ceremony of watering the sacred tree, which seems to have been one of many such special *pujas*. Other kings too, according to the *Mahavamsa,* expressed their devotion to the Bodhi-tree in various ways (see e.g., Mhv. xxxv,30; xxxvi, 25, 52, 126).

It is recorded that forty Bodhi-saplings that grew from the seeds of the original Bodhi-tree at Anuradhapura were planted at various places in the island during the time of Devanampiya

Tissa himself. The local Buddhists saw to it that every monastery in the island had its own Bodhi-tree, and today the tree has become a familiar sight, all derived, most probably, from the original tree at Anuradhapura through seeds. However, it may be added here that the notion that all the Bodhi-trees in the island are derived from the original tree is only an assumption. The existence of the tree prior to its introduction by the Theri Sanghamitta cannot be proved or disproved.

The ceremony of worshipping this sacred tree, first begun by King Devanampiya Tissa and followed by his successors with unflagging interest, has continued up to the present day. The ceremony is still as popular and meaningful as at the beginning. It is natural that this should be so, for the veneration of the tree fulfills the emotional and devotional needs of the pious heart in the same way as does the veneration of the Buddha-image and, to a lesser extent, of the *dagaba*. Moreover, its association with deities dedicated to the cause of Buddhism, who can also aid pious worshippers in their mundane affairs, contributes to the popularity and vitality of Bodhi-worship.

The main center of devotion in Sri Lanka today is, of course, the ancient tree at Anuradhapura, which, in addition to its religious significance, has a historical importance as well. As the oldest historical tree in the world, it has survived for over 2,200 years, even when the city of Anuradhapura was devastated by foreign enemies. Today it is one of the most sacred and popular places of pilgrimage in the island. The tree itself is very well guarded, the most recent protection being a gold-plated railing around the base *(ranvata)*. Ordinarily, pilgrims are not allowed to go near the foot of the tree in the upper terrace. They have to worship and make their offerings on altars provided on the lower terrace so that no damage is done to the tree by the multitude that throng there. The place is closely guarded by those entrusted with its upkeep and protection, while the daily rituals of cleaning the place, watering the tree, making offerings, etc., are performed by bhikkhus and laymen entrusted with the work. The performance of these rituals is regarded as of great merit and they are performed on a lesser scale at other important Bodhi-trees in the island as well. Thus this tree today receives worship and respect as a symbol of the Buddha himself, a tradition which, as stated earlier, could be traced back to the Ananda Bodhi-tree at Jetavana of the Buddha's own time. The *Vibhanga Commentary* (p.349) says that the bhikkhu who enters the courtyard of the Bodhi-tree should venerate the tree, behaving with all humility as if he were in the presence of the Buddha. Thus one of the main items of the daily ritual at the Anuradhapura Bodhi-tree (and at many other places) is the offering of alms as if unto the Buddha himself. A special ritual held annually at the shrine of the Anuradhapura tree is the hanging of gold ornaments on the tree. Pious devotees offer valuables, money, and various other articles during the performance of this ritual.

Another popular ritual connected with the Bodhi-tree is the lighting of coconut-oil lamps as an offering *(pahan-puja),* especially to avert the evil influence of inauspicious planetary conjunctions. When a person passes through a troublesome period in life he may get his horoscope read by an astrologer in order to discover whether he is under bad planetary influences. If so, one of the recommendations would invariably be a *bodhi-puja,* one important item of which would be the lighting of a specific number of coconut-oil lamps around a Bodhi-tree in a temple. The other aspects of this ritual consist of the offering of flowers, milk-rice, fruits, betel, medicinal oils, camphor, and coins. These coins (designated *panduru)* are washed in saffron water and separated for offering in this manner. The offering of coins as an act of merit-acquisition has assumed ritualistic significance with the Buddhists of the island. Every temple has a charity box *(pin-pettiya)* into which the devotees drop a few coins as a contribution for the maintenance of the monks and the monastery. Offerings at *devalayas* should inevitably be accompanied by such a gift. At many wayside shrines there is provision for the offering of *panduru* and travelers *en route,* in the hope of a safe and successful journey, rarely fail to make their contribution. While the coins are put into the charity box, all the other offerings would be arranged methodically on an altar near the tree and the appropriate stanzas that make the offering valid are recited. Another part of the ritual is the hanging of flags on the branches of the tree in the expectation of getting one's wishes fulfilled.

Bathing the tree with scented water is also a necessary part of the ritual. So is the burning of incense, camphor, etc. Once all these offerings have been completed, the performers would circumambulate the tree once or thrice reciting an appropriate stanza. The commonest of such stanzas is as follows:

Yassa mule nisinno va
sabbari vijayam aka
patto sabbannutam Sattha
Vande tam bodhipadapam.
Ime ete mahabodhi
lokanathena pujita
ahampi te namassami
bodhi raja namatthu te.

"I worship this Bodhi-tree seated under which the Teacher attained omniscience by overcoming all enemical forces (both subjective and objective). I too worship this great Bodhi-tree which was honored by the Leader of the World. My homage to thee, O King Bodhi."

The ritual is concluded by the usual transference of merit to the deities that protect the Buddha's Dispensation.

Poya Days

In their religious observances the Sri Lankan Buddhists have adopted from Indian tradition the use of the lunar calendar. The four phases of the moon are the pre-new-moon day, when the moon is totally invisible, the half-moon of the waxing fortnight, the full moon, and the half-moon of the waning fortnight. Owing to the moon's fullness of size as well as its effulgence, the full-moon day is treated as the most auspicious of the four phases. Hence the most important religious observances are held on full-moon days and the lesser ones in conjunction with the other phases. In the Buddhist calendar, the full moon, as the acme of the waxing process, is regarded as the culmination of the month and accordingly the period between two full moons is one lunar month.

The religious observance days are called *poya* days. The Sinhala term *poya* is derived from the Pali and Sanskrit form *uposatha* (from *upa* + *vas:* to fast) primarily signifying "fast day." Fasting on this day was a pre-Buddhist practice among the religious sects of ancient India. While the monks use the monthly moonless day (called *amavaka* in Sinhala) and the full-moon day for their confessional ritual and communal recitation of the code of discipline *(Patimokkha),* the lay devotees observe the day by visiting temples for worship and also by taking upon themselves the observance of the Eight Precepts.

A practicing Buddhist observes the *poya* day by visiting a temple for the rituals of worship and, often, by undertaking the Eight Precepts. The Eight Precepts include the Five Precepts (see above, pp.5-6), with the third changed to abstinence from unchastity, and the following three additional rules:

(6) to abstain from solid food after mid-day;

(7) to abstain from dancing, singing, music, and improper shows, and from ornamenting the body with garlands, scents, unguents, etc.;

(8) to abstain from the use of high and luxurious beds and seats.

If one decides to observe the Eight Precepts, one would wake up early, bathe and clad oneself in clean white garments, and go to the nearest temple. The incumbent monk administers the precepts to the entire group assembled for the purpose. Thereafter they would spend the day according to a set timetable which would include sermons, *pujas,* periods of meditation, and Dhamma discussions. At meditation centers there will be more periods of meditation and fewer sermons and *pujas.*

The observance of the Eight Precepts is a ritualistic practice of moral discipline quite popular among the Sinhala Buddhists. While the Five Precepts serve as the moral base for ordinary people, the Eight Precepts point to a higher level of training aimed at advancement along the path of liberation. The popular practice is to observe them on full-moon days, and, among a few devout lay Buddhists, on the other phases of the moon as well.

The *poya* observance, which is as old as Buddhism itself, has been followed by the Sinhala Buddhists up to the present day, even after the Christian calendar came to be used for secular matters. Owing to its significance in the religious life of the local Buddhists, all the full-moon days have been declared public holidays by the government. Another noteworthy fact about this day is that every full-moon *poya* has assumed some ritualistic significance in one way or other.

The first and the foremost of the *poya* holy days is the full-moon day of *Vesak* (May), commemorating the birth, Enlightenment, and passing away of the Buddha. The significance of Vesak is further heightened for the Sinhala Buddhists, as Sri Lankan tradition holds that it was on the Vesak Poya Day, in the eighth year after his Enlightenment, that the Buddha paid his third visit to Sri Lanka, journeying to Kelaniya on the invitation of the Naga King Maniakkhika (Mhv. i,72ff.). Consequently, Kelaniya has become a very popular place of worship and pilgrimage, the center of worship there being the celebrated *dagaba,* enshrining the gem-set throne offered to the Buddha by the Nagas (dragons). An annual procession is held there to commemorate the event.

Both in importance and in temporal sequence, the next significant *poya* is the full-moon of *Poson* (June), which is specially noteworthy to the Sri Lankan Buddhists as the day on which Emperor Asoka's son, the arahant Mahinda, officially introduced Buddhism to the island in the 3rd century B.C. Accordingly, in addition to the normal ritualistic observances undertaken on a *poya* day, on Poson day devotees flock to Anuradhapura, the ancient capital city of the country, for it was there that arahant Mahinda converted the then ruler, King Devanampiya Tissa, and his court to Buddhism, thereby setting in motion a series of events that finally made Sri Lanka the home of Theravada Buddhism. Even today, on Poson Poya, Anuradhapura becomes the center of Buddhist activity. Mihintale, the spot where the momentous encounter between the Elder and the King took place, accordingly receives the reverential attention of the devotees. The two rituals of pilgrimage and the observance of the Eight Precepts are combined here. Processions commemorative of the event, referred to as Mihundu Peraheras, are held in various parts of the country.

The next *poya* is *Esala* (July), which commemorates several significant events in the history of Buddhism. The most prominent of these is the Buddha's preaching of his First Sermon, the Dhammacakkappavattana Sutta, to the five ascetics at the Deer Park, near Benares, thereby inaugurating his public ministry. The other noteworthy events connected with this day include the conception of the Bodhisatta in the womb of Queen Maya, his Great Renunciation, the performance of the Twin Miracle *(yamaka-patihariya),* and his preaching the Abhidhamma for the first time in the Tavatimsa heaven. An additional factor that enhances the value of this *poya* to Sri Lanka is the first local ordination of a Sri Lankan, when Prince Arittha, the nephew of the king, entered the Order at Anuradhapura, under arahant Mahinda, following the introduction of Buddhism. On this day there also took place the laying of the foundation for the celebrated *dagaba,* the Mahathupa or the Ruwanvelisaya and also its enshrinement of relics by King Dutugemunu. It is owing to the combination of all these events that the Sinhala Buddhists fittingly observe the day ceremonially by holding Esala festivals throughout the island, giving pride of place to the internationally famous Kandy Esala Perahera.

* * *

The term *perahera,* primarily meaning "procession," signifies a popular Buddhist ceremony replete with many rituals, commencing and culminating respectively with the *kap*-planting and the water-cutting ceremonies. These two ceremonies are respectively the introductory and the concluding rites of the annual Esala festivals, held in July and August in various parts of the island. They are essentially connected with the Buddhist deities, either to invite their blessings or to give thanks to them for favors received. During this period every year, such religious festivals are held in almost all the religious centers of Sri

Lanka where there are abodes dedicated to various Buddhist deities. However, the festival *par excellence* of this category is the Kandy Esala Perahera, which is connected with the Temple of the Tooth and the abodes *(devalayas)* of the four Buddhist deities, Vishnu, Kataragama, Natha, and the Goddess Pattini. The main feature of all these festivals held during this period is the elaborate procession held on the lines of the Kandy Esala Perahera.

Both the *kap*-planting and water-cutting ceremonies are performed by the lay officiating priests *(kapuralas)* of the *devalaya* concerned, who are traditionally the experts regarding the details of their performance. These details are generally regarded as secret and are not divulged to the profane public.

The preliminary rite of *kap*-planting consists of planting a shaft, usually fashioned from a felled young jak tree, which must have borne no fruit. When cut, this tree exudes a white sap which is regarded as a symbol of prosperity. Even felling the tree is done with several attendant rituals at an auspicious time: the trunk is divided into four, one for each of the *devalayas,* where it is carried with drums and attendance. On the day of the new moon, at an auspicious hour *(nakata),* the "kaps" thus prepared are set up in the ground in a special place decorated with leaves, flowers, and fruits. For five nights small processions are conducted within the *devalaya* precincts around the consecrated *kaps.* Sometimes benedictory stanzas are chanted by monks.

This rite of *kap* is a kind of vow that the Esala festival, consisting mainly of the *perahera,* will be held; it is also an invitation to the deities to be present during the festival, providing the necessary protection for its successful performance. In this sense it is this ritual that inaugurates the festival.

The water-cutting ceremony *(diya-kapum-mangalyaya),* which is the concluding ritual of the Esala festival, is performed in the early hours of the day following the final *perahera.* The officiating lay-priest *(kapurala)* proceeds on a caparisoned elephant to a selected place along a river bank. He would either go to a selected spot in the river by boat or wade through the water to a particular spot and after drawing a magic circle on the water with the sword he carries, he "cuts" the water and fills the vessel he carried there with water from that spot. Before doing so he empties the water that he took in this same manner the previous year. He then returns to the *devalaya,* and the vessel of water is kept there until the following year. The ritual is repeated annually in an identical manner. This is believed to be a rain-making ceremony of sympathetic magic, which type of ritual is quite common in agrarian societies the world over. The Buddhists seem to have adopted this to suit their purposes.

* * *

The annual Esala Perahera in Kandy, held in honor of the Sacred Tooth Relic of the Buddha, is the most colorful traditional procession in the country. It is the prototype of the other *peraheras* held elsewhere in the island in such places as Kataragama, Aluthnuwara, Lankatilaka, Bellanwila, Devinuwara, etc. The Kandy Perahera is itself the latest expression of the annual festival in honor of the Tooth Relic that has been held with state patronage from the time the relic was brought to Sri Lanka from India in the 4th century A.C. Although periodically there have been intermittent breaks due to unsettled political conditions, the festival was never neglected intentionally. This had been so even during colonial times. Respected as the palladium of Sinhala royalty, the Relic had been accommodated in different parts of the country, depending on the change of the capital city. Ultimately it came to stay in Kandy, which was the last royal seat of the Sinhala people.

Esala Poya assumes prominence for yet another ritual of the Sri Lankan Buddhists. This is the annual rains retreat of the monks, *Vassa,* which commences on the day following the Esala full moon (discussed in Chap. 8). On the next *poya* day, *Nikini* (August), those monks who failed to commence the normal *Vassa* on the day following Esala Poya, are allowed to enter the "late *Vassa.*"

The *poya* that follows Nikini is *Binara* (September), which assumes solemnity as marking the inauguration of the Order of Bhikkhunis (nuns) with the ordination of Queen Mahapajapati and her retinue. Next follows the *Vap Poya* (October), which concludes the final month of the three-month rains retreat. During the following month *kathina* robes are offered to the monks who have duly completed the *Vassa.* The high esteem in which this ritual is held by the Sinhala Buddhists may be gauged from the fact that the month is popularly referred to as the "month of robes" (see Chap. 8). The November full moon, called *Il,* signifies the terminal point for the *kathina* ritual. It is also the day for commemorating such events as the despatch of the first sixty disciples by the Buddha on missionary work, the prospective Buddha Metteyya being declared a sure Buddha-to-be by Gotama Buddha, and the passing away of the arahant Sariputta, the Buddha's foremost disciple.

The *Unduwap Poya* that follows in December is of great moment to Sri Lanka as commemorating two memorable events connected with the visit of Theri Sanghamitta, sister of arahant Mahinda, from India in the third century B.C. (Mhv.iv,18-19). The first of these events was the arrival at Anuradhapura of a sapling of the sacred Bodhi-tree at Buddhagaya, brought to Sri Lanka by Sanghamitta. The planting of this tree is the origin of the *Bodhi-puja* in the country (see Chap. 4).

The other memorable event commemorated by this *poya* is the establishment of the Order of Nuns *(bhikkhuni-sasana)* in Sri Lanka by the Theri Sanghamitta when she ordained Queen Anula and her entourage of 500 women at Anuradhapura. Records indicate that the Bhikkhuni Sangha thus established flourished during the Anuradhapura period (third century B.C. to eleventh century A.C.), but disappeared after the decline of that kingdom. Historical records are silent as to the reasons for its extinction, but they do report how the Sinhala Bhikkhuni Sangha helped in the establishment of the Order of Nuns in China. In the 5th century a group of Sinhala nuns headed by the Bhikkhuni Devasara went to China to confer higher ordination there and the Bhikkhuni Sangha thus established survives there to this day. The Sinhala Buddhists commemorate this *poya* day with *peraheras,* observance of the Eight Precepts, and meetings. The day is designated Sanghamitta Day. Nowadays the *dasasil matas* (ten-precept nuns) take an active part in initiating these commemorative functions.

Next follows the *Durutu Poya* (January) when the Sinhala Buddhists commemorate the first visit of the Buddha to the island. According to the *Mahavamsa,* nine months after his Enlightenment, the Buddha visited present Mahiyangana in the Badulla District, where stands the *dagaba* by that name enshrining the Buddha's hair relics and the collar bone (Mhv.i,197). The Buddhists remember the event by holding an annual *perahera.* This much-venerated *dagaba* is also of consequence as the first edifice of this type to be constructed here, originating the ritual of *dagaba* worship in Sri Lanka.

The *poya* that follows, *Navam Poya* (February), celebrates the Buddha's appointment of the two arahants, Sariputta and Moggallana, as his two chief disciples. It also marks the Buddha's decision to attain Parinibbana in three months' time. The *Medin Poya* in March is hallowed by the Buddha's first visit to his parental home after his Enlightenment, during which he ordained the princes Rahula, Nanda, and many others as monks. The month that follows is called *Bak* (pronounced like "buck"), which corresponds to April. In this month it is not the full-moon day but the new-moon day that invites attention as signalizing the Buddha's second visit to Sri Lanka, when he visited Nagadipa on the day preceding the new-moon day *(amavaka:* Mhv.i,47) in the fifth year after his Enlightenment.

The above brief account of the twelve *poya* days demonstrates how the *poya* day has become intimately connected with the life of the Buddha and consequently with the principal events of early Buddhist history. The Sri Lankan Buddhists, quite accustomed as they are to commemorate such events with rituals and ceremonies in full measure, have maintained these traditions up to the present.

The Pirit Ceremony

Pirit (or *paritta)* is a collective term designating a set of protective chants or runes sanctioned by the Buddha for the use of both laymen and bhikkhus. *Pirit*-chanting is a very popular ceremony among the Buddhists of Sri Lanka. As the term itself implies it means a safety rune *(paritta* = protection), the ceremonial recital of which is regarded as capable of warding off all forms of evil and danger *(vipatti),* including disease, the evil influence of the planets, evil spirits, etc. These may be real dangers to the safety of persons and property as well as superstitiously believed-in calamities. In addition to this curative and positive aspect, *pirit* is also chanted for the attainment of general success *(sampatti, siddhi)*. In the domestic and social life of the Sri Lankan Buddhist no important function can be considered complete without this ceremony. However, the ceremony may vary from the simple to the highly elaborate, depending on the occasion and the status of the sponsor.

The essence of the *pirit* ceremony consists in the ritualistic chanting of certain Pali texts selected from the canonical scriptures. These extracts are found collected and arranged in a particular order in the Book of Parittas, or *Pirit-Pota*, known in Pali as *Catubhanavara*. It contains 27 extracts, including such suttas as the Ratana, Mangala, Metta, Atańatiya, etc.

The use of protective spells — variously known as *paritta, rakkha, mantra, dharani, kavaca*, etc. — against various dangers has been a common practice among the Indians from very early times. The Buddha himself is said to have adopted the practice on several occasions. The public recitation of the Ratana Sutta at Vesali is the best known instance. The Khandha Paritta, Atanatiya Sutta, and the Metta Sutta are some *parittas* that have received the sanction of the Buddha himself. As the *parittas* generally embody statements of truth as taught in Buddhism their recitation is regarded as an "asseveration of truth" *(saccakiriya)* whereby evil can be averted. The Ratana Sutta is a good example of this kind of *paritta*. It draws its power by wishing the listeners safety after affirming the excellent qualities of the Three Gems of Buddhism — the Buddha, Dhamma, and the Sangha. The power of virtue *(sila)* contained in the Mangala Sutta and the power of loving kindness *(metta)* contained in the Metta Sutta are two other aspects that make *pirit* effective. The power of the sound waves resulting from the sonorous and rhythmic recitation and also from particular combinations of certain letters and syllables also play a part in exercising this beneficial influence. The vibrating sound waves produced by the sonorous and mellifluous chanting adds to the effect of the truths enunciated. The ceremonial recitation with various ritualistic observances (discussed below) and with the presence of the Triple Gem in the form of the relic casket representing the Buddha, the *Pirit-Pota* representing the Dhamma, and the reciting bhikkhus representing the Sangha, are additional factors that are regarded as increasing the efficacy of *pirit* chanting.

Among the laity of Burma and of Sri Lanka the book of *parittas* is more widely known than any other Pali book. Any Buddhist, educated or not, knows what it is and holds it in honor and respect. Even in ancient times the blessings of the *pirit* ceremony were sought in times of national calamities just as in Vesali at the time of the Buddha. King Upatissa (4th century: Mhv. xxxvii,189), Sena II and Kassapa V (ibid, li,80; 1ii,80) are three such Sinhala monarchs who had the ceremony performed under such circumstances. The incorporation of the item called *dorakada-asna,* as shall be seen, shows that it is a ritual that has gradually been elaborated in course of time.

The simplest form of the *pirit* ceremony is held when what is called the *mahapirita* (great or major *pirit)* — the Mangala, Ratana, and Metta Suttas and a few benedictory stanzas — is chanted by a few monks, usually three or four, three times with a break in between. The three times may consist of the morning and evening of one day and the morning of the following day, or the evening of one day and the following morning and evening. The monks are conducted to the particular household and the chanting takes place in any room of the house according to choice.

The monks sit around a table on which a clean white cloth is spread and flowers and puffed rice are strewn. A pot of filtered water is also placed in the center of the table and one end of a ball of three-stranded thread is twisted around it. The thread then passes through the hands of the reciting monks and is next held by the person or the persons on whose behalf the chanting is being done. These would be seated on a mat on the ground in front of the reciting monks. The water in the pot, designated *pirit*-water *(pirit-pan),* and the sacred thread *(pirit-nula),* become sanctified through the chanting and are used thereafter as a protection against evil. The thread is used by tying a piece around the arm or the wrist, and the water by drinking it or sprinkling it, according to requirements. In the simplest form, the ceremony is called *varu-pirita* or *vel-pirita (varu* or *vel* in Sinhala meaning half-day session) as the ceremony is confined only to a portion of the day and only the *mahapirita* is chanted.

But the full-fledged *pirit* ceremony is a much more elaborate ritual. This also has two main forms — one lasting for one whole night and the other for one week or even longer. The former is the more usual form as a domestic ceremony while the latter is held on special occasions, especially for public purposes. Whatever the form may be, when this kind of chanting is undertaken, a special pavilion called the *pirit mandapaya* is constructed for the purpose. If the ceremony is to be performed in a private home, this pavilion is put up in a central room of the house. Generally it would measure about twelve by twelve feet and is gaily decorated with tissue paper, tinsel, etc. Its roof is covered with a white canopy from which are hung small cuttings of arecanut flowers, betel twigs, tender twigs of the iron-wood *(na)* tree, etc. Two water pots on which opened coconut racemes are kept are placed on either side of the entrance. Two lighted coconut-oil lamps are also placed upon the coconut racemes.

In the center of the pavilion is a table (usually a round one) on which a clean white cloth is spread. Upon it are strewn puffed rice *(vilanda)*, broken rice (sun-sal), white mustard *(sudu-aba)*, jasmine buds *(saman kakulu)*, and panic grass *(itana)*. These five varieties, known as *lada-pas-mal*, are regarded as having a sanctifying and purifying power in combination and are hence used for ritualistic purposes at Buddhist ceremonies. In the center of the table is the filtered water pot around which the three-stranded sacred thread is twisted. This thread is drawn round the interior of the pavilion and when the chanting commences it is held by the chanting monks and given over to be held by the person or persons for whose benefit the ceremony is held. A palm-leaf copy of the *Pirit-Pota*, regarded as more sanctified than the printed one, occupies a significant place on the table, representing the Dhamma, the second member of the

Buddhist Trinity. Consequently, while the printed copy is used for the legibility of its script, the palm-leaf copy is regarded as indispensable on the table. The other important item that is brought inside the pavilion is the casket containing the bone-relics of the Buddha *(dhatu-karanduwa),* representing the Buddha. This is placed on a separate decorated table on a side within the pavilion.

In the seating arrangement for the monks, two chairs, centrally placed near the table, are referred to as *yuga-asana* or "seats for the duel." During a greater part of the all-night recital, two monks occupying these two seats continue the chanting, taking it in relays, instead of the full assembly. A post called *indra-khila* or *raja-gaha* is planted securely and fastened between these twin chairs. This post, resembling a mace in more ways than one, is attractively decorated and serves as a symbol of authority and protection for the officiating monks. This is generally erected only when the ceremony lasts for a week *(sati pirita)* or longer.

Even when the ceremony is held in a private home, the temple is inevitably connected with every stage of the ritual. The temple authorities are responsible for assigning the required number of monks. On the evening of the day on which the chanting takes place, a few members from the particular household go to the temple in order to conduct the monks. The monks would come in a procession in single file in order of seniority, attended by drumming. At the head of the procession is carried the relic casket, borne on the head of a layman, under an umbrella or a canopy. The beating of drums continues throughout. As the monks enter the home, a layman washes their feet while another wipes them. They walk to the pavilion on a carpet of white cloth *(pavada)* and take their seats around the table. The relic casket, *Pirit-Pota,* and the bhikkhus thus come together, representing the Triple Gem, the Buddha, the Dhamma, and the Sangha, respectively.

Before the commencement of the ceremony proper, the usual time of which is around 9 p.m., the monks are welcomed and requested to perform the ceremony by being offered a tray in which betel leaves, arecanut, cardamons, nutmeg, etc., are nicely arranged, the ingredients being those taken for the chew of betel. This invitation is usually extended by the chief householder if it is in a private home. Otherwise some leading lay devotee would do it. One of the senior monks present would accept the invitation on behalf of the entire Sangha and, in order to make the invitation formally valid, he would get the lay devotee to repeat after him the following Pali stanza requesting the monks to begin the ceremony:

Vipattipatibahaya — sabbasampattisiddhiya

sabbadukkhavinasaya — parittam brutha uttamam

"Please recite the noble *pirit* for the avoidance of all misfortune, for the attainment of all success, and for the destruction of all suffering."

Next he would explain the significance of the occasion in a short address. This is followed by ceremonial drumming *(magulbera vadana),* as a ritualistic preamble to the ceremony, serving both as an invitation to the gods and an offering of sound *(sadda-puja).* The monks too commence the chanting by reciting a stanza that invites all the divine beings of the universe to the ceremony:

Samanta cakkavalesu Atragacchantu devata Saddhammam Munirajassa Sunantu saggamokkhadam

"May the divine beings of the entire universe come here to hear the good doctrine of the King of Sages that confers both heavenly happiness and the freedom of Nibbana."

From the commencement of the chanting until its conclusion the following morning, the pavilion is not vacated. The *mahapirita* (explained earlier), with which the chanting begins, is chanted in a rhythmic manner by all the monks, numbering about ten or twelve, seated in order of seniority. The rest of the discourses are chanted by two or four monks. The ceremony is concluded the following morning with the recital, once again, of the *mahapirita* at which ceremonial drumming takes place once more. This drumming is also performed at the recital of important discourses like the Dhammacakkappavattana Sutta and the Atanatiya Sutta. Once the chanting is concluded, convenient lengths of the thread, sanctified by the chanting, are snapped off and tied around the wrists or the arms of those assembled. A little of the sanctified water is given to everyone for drinking. When the ceremony continues for several days (e.g., one week: *sati-pirita),* the chanting must continue night and day without a break. When the set of suttas constituting *pirit* is completed, chanting is recommenced from the beginning and in this manner they are recited over and over again until the session is concluded. Both to begin and to end the session, the *mahapirita* is recited in chorus by all the monks on each day at sunrise and sunset.

An important ceremony connected with the seven-day (and longer) *pirit* ceremony is known as *dorakada-asna,* which seems to have entered the *pirit* ceremony during the Kandyan period (18th century). The theme of this ritual is to invite all the deities residing in the vicinity and request them to partake of the merits derived from the *pirit* ceremony and to help dispel all evil and bring about prosperity to everybody.

This ritual involves several stages commencing from the morning of the last day of the *pirit* ceremony, i.e., the seventh day if it is a seven-day ceremony. The first stage is the preparation of the message to be taken to the neighbouring temple where the abodes of the gods *(devalayas)* are also found. For this purpose several palm leaves (talipot), on which the message is to be written, are brought to the chanting pavilion in a ceremonial procession and handed over to a monk who has been previously selected to write the message. Next, this particular monk writes down the auspicious time for the messenger of the gods *(deva-dutaya)* to set out to the *devalaya* and reads it aloud, to be sanctioned by the assembled monks. Once this is done another monk, also previously selected, reads aloud a text written in a highly ornate stilted style, enumerating the temples and *devalayas* at which the deities are requested to be present at the *pirit* chanting that evening. This text is called the *vihara-asna.* Until these preliminaries are gone through, the other monks keep holding the sacred thread. After this, the monk who was appointed to write the message begins to write it while the other monks retire.

The message contains the invitation — which is a command from the Sangha *(sanghanatti)* and hence not to be turned down — addressed to all the deities residing at the religious places enumerated in the *vihara-asna* to come and partake of the merits of the week's *pirit* chanting. The message is prepared in quadruplicate. These are then hung on a pole and handed over to a young boy, specially selected for the task and richly attired as befits a messenger of the gods. Mounted on a caparisoned elephant and escorted by men with swords, he carries the message in a procession to the *devalaya.* This procession is called the *devaduta-perahera,* "the procession of the gods' messenger," and has many features like dancers, drummers, mask-dancers, stilt-walkers, etc.

At the *devalaya,* the bhikkhus and the *deva-dutaya* first go near a Buddha-statue and pay homage, after which they proceed to the building where the statues of the gods are and chant the Metta Sutta. The gods concerned are usually Vishnu and Kataragama (Skanda). This is followed by ceremonial drumming *(magul bera)* as an invitation to the gods, and next a monk reads out the message aloud. The four messages are given to the lay officiating priest of the *devalaya* (known as *kapurala)* to be hung in the four cardinal directions inside the *devalaya.* These are meant for the Regents of the Four Quarters — Datarattha (east), Viruda (south), Virupakkha (west), and Vessavana (north) — who are requested to come to the ceremony with their assemblies. The procession now returns.

Until the monks arrive for the *pirit* chanting, the *devadutaya* is kept confined and guarded. Once the monks arrive and take their seats inside the pavilion, a dialogue takes place between the *devadutaya* and a monk, the purpose of which is to reveal to the assembled gathering that the task of the messenger, which was to invite the gods to partake of the merits, has been done and that all the gods have arrived. The *devadutaya* makes this statement standing and guarded by the swordsmen, at the entrance *(dorakada)* to the chanting pavilion within which the monks have taken their seats. It is this statement of the *devadutaya* which thus comes to be called the *dorakada-asna,* meaning "the message read at the threshold." The gist of this statement, written in the same kind of stilted language as the *vihara-asna* referred to earlier, is that all the gods invited have arrived for the *pirit* ceremony so that they may dispel all misfortune and bring about prosperity to all.

After the *dorakada-asna,* another monk, standing within the pavilion, reads out a similar text called the *anusasana-asna,* wherein all the gods assembled are requested to rejoice in the merits of the entire ceremony. This monk holds in his hand a round-handled fan made of the talipot leaf, elaborately decorated, a symbol of authority and high ecclesiastical position. These three ritualistic texts mentioned in the foregoing account (i.e., *vihara-asna, dorakada-asna,* and the *anusasana-asna)* were all composed during the Kandyan period (18th century) when ceremonies and rituals, especially those connected with the gods, became more popular than during the earlier periods.

It is also worth noting, that this ceremony of *dorakada-asna* has, in addition to its religious and ritualistic significance, considerable dramatic and theatrical value as well, for the whole event, from the preliminaries of the morning to the grand finale of the *anusasana* in the evening, contains much impersonation, mime, and dialogue. In this connection we may note that as early as the time of Buddhaghosa (5th century A.C.) there were Buddhist rituals with such theatrical features as is shown by the exorcist ritual of reading the Atanatiya Sutta described in the Digha Nikaya Commentary (iii, 969-70).

The recital of the *Jayamangala Gatha,* a set of eight benedictory stanzas extolling the virtues of the Buddha, may also be cited as a popular custom partly related to the chanting of *pirit.* This is usually done on important occasions like a marriage ceremony, when setting out on an important journey, or when inaugurating any venture of significance. This custom is inevitably observed at what is called the *Poruva* ceremony when, after a couple to be married ascends a small decorated platform *(poruva),* they are blessed for future prosperity. The recital is usually done by an elderly person who, for the occasion, assumes the position of an officiating priest. At public functions a bevy of young girls clad in white uniforms also do the recital. The contents of the stanzas recited clearly show that the ritual is intended to bring happiness and prosperity to the persons concerned or the successful completion of the project. Accordingly these verses have come to be called "the stanzas of success and prosperity," *Jayamangala Gatha,* and have become quite popular among all sections of the Buddhists. While the origin of these stanzas is shrouded in mystery, it can be stated with certainty that they were composed in Sri Lanka by a devoted Buddhist poet. The earliest available reference to them is during the Kandyan period when they are given in a list of subjects that a monk should study. This shows that they had become well established during the 16th and 17th centuries; hence they must have been composed at least a century earlier. These stanzas are regarded as efficacious because they relate eight occasions, each based on a beautiful story, when the Buddha triumphed over his powerful opponents.

The chanting of what is called *set-pirit* by a few bhikkhus at the inauguration of new ventures or at receptions and farewells to important public personages has also become quite common. The chanting usually consists of a sutta like the Mangala, Ratana, or Metta Sutta, and a few benedictory stanzas. *Set-pirit* is broadcast by the Sri Lanka Broadcasting Corporation every morning as the first item of its programme.

Almsgiving and Funerals

The Almsgiving

The ceremony of *pirit*-chanting is very often accompanied by another important ceremony, that of almsgiving. It is generally known as *sanghika-dana,* meaning "the alms given to the community of monks." Such a ceremonial almsgiving is often preceded by an all-night *pirit* ceremony. Even otherwise this ceremony too is usually performed on important occasions in the same way as the *pirit* ceremony, associated with such events as house-warming, setting out on a long journey, a marriage, birth, or death anniversaries, and so forth.

At least four monks who have obtained higher ordination *(upasampada)* must participate for the *dana* to become valid as a full-fledged *sanghika-dana.* Such *danas* were held even during the Buddha's time, the Buddha himself participating in very many of them. Of the many items of offering that *dana* or the act of generosity could include, food is usually regarded as the most important and the formal meal offering accordingly is done with much ceremony and ritual. The monks are conducted from the temple in procession with drumming as in the case of *pirit.* A layman leads the procession, with the relic casket *(dhatu-karanduva),* representing the Buddha, borne on his head under an umbrella or canopy. As they approach the particular household they are received by the host. As the monks step into the house, one person washes their feet, while another wipes them. This part of the ceremony is the same as in the case of the *pirit* ceremony.

The monks are then conducted to the cushioned seats arranged on the floor against the wall. Alms are first offered to the Buddha in a separate bowl, and are placed on a separate table on which the relic casket, containing a bone-relic of the Buddha, has been set. All the items of food are served in plates and placed on mats or low tables before the seated monks. A senior monk administers the Three Refuges and the Five Precepts (see pp. 5-6) to the assembled gathering, as this has become the established custom with which any Buddhist function commences. After he has given a short address on the significance of the occasion, the food is formally presented by getting the chief householder to repeat a Pali statement: *imam bhikkham saparikkharam bhikkhusanghassa dema* ("These alms, along with other requisites, we offer to the whole community of monks"). Next, the food is served and once the monks have finished eating (which should be before noon) the other requisites *(parikkhara),* referred to in the statement quoted, are also offered.

The most important item among these offerings is what is traditionally known as "the eight monastic requisites" *(ata-pirikara):* the alms-bowl, three robes, belt, razor, water-strainer, and sewing needle. This offering is regarded as especially meritorious. As it is an expensive item and therefore difficult to offer to all the monks, generally one *ata-pirikara* is offered to the chief monk and other items such as books, towels, pillow-cases, umbrellas, etc., are presented to the other monks.

Once this is over, another monk administers what is called *punnanumodana* or "thanks-giving" wherein all those who were connected with the ceremony are requested to partake of the merits *(punna)* for their future good. The participants are also called upon to transfer the merits they have thus acquired for the well-being of their dead kinsmen and friends as well as for the sustenance of beings in the *deva* worlds, i.e., the deities, who are expected to protect the donors out of gratitude. The relic casket and the monks are conducted back to the temple in the same manner as they were brought and the proceedings are concluded.

A related ritual that cannot be ignored as regards the ceremony of almsgiving is the custom of getting the neighbours and friends also to serve into the alms-bowl that is offered to the Buddha. On the morning of the day on which the almsgiving takes place a separate bowl is kept on a table for this purpose. This is called the *Buddha-pattare,* or the Buddha's alms-bowl. Alms served into it are regarded as offered to the Buddha himself. The neighbours would come with plates of rice prepared in their homes and serve into it. This rice is also taken when the bowl of food is prepared for offering to the Buddha, near the relic casket at the time of the *dana* proper, the purpose here being to get the neighbours and outsiders also to participate in this merit-making ceremony.

Funerals

Among Buddhists death is regarded as an occasion of major religious significance, both for the deceased and for the survivors. For the deceased it marks the moment when the transition begins to a new mode of existence within the round of rebirths. When death occurs all the kammic forces that the dead person accumulated during the course of his or her lifetime become activated and set about determining the next rebirth. For the living, death is a powerful reminder of the Buddha's teaching on impermanence; it also provides an opportunity to assist the deceased person as he or she fares on to the new existence.

Both aspects of death — the message of impermanence, and the opportunity to help the departed loved one — find expression in the Buddhist funeral rites of Sri Lanka. Naturally, the monastic Sangha plays a prominent role in the funeral proceedings. One of the most important parts of the funeral rites is the ritual called "offering of cloth on behalf of the dead" *(mataka-vastra-puja)*. This is done prior to the cremation or the burial of the body. Monks are assembled in the home of the dead person or in the cemetery. The proceedings begin with the administration of the Five Precepts to the assembled crowd by one of the monks. This is followed by the recitation in chorus of the well-known stanza:

Anicca vata sankhara, uppadavayadhammino.

Uppajjitva nirujjhanti tesam vupasamo sukho.

Impermanent alas are formations, subject to rise and fall.

Having arisen, they cease; their subsiding is bliss.

Next follows this ritual, which consists of the offering of a length of new white cloth to the monks. The cloth, called a *pamsukula* — literally, a dust-heap cloth — is intended to be cut into pieces and then stitched into a robe.

After offering it, the close relatives of the deceased sit together on a mat, assume a reverential posture, and together they pour water from a vessel into a cup placed within a plate until the cup overflows. While the water is being poured, the monks intone in unison the following stanzas extracted from the Tirokuddha Sutta of the Khuddakapatha:

Unname udakam vattam yatha ninnam pavattati

evameva ito dinnam petanam upakappati.

Yatha varivaha pura paripurenti sagaram

evameva ito dinnam petanam upakappati.

Just as the water fallen on high ground flows to a lower level,

Even so what is given from here accrues to the departed.

Just as the full flowing rivers fill the ocean,

Even so what is given from here accrues to the departed.

The context shows that the pouring of water in this manner is a ritualistic act belonging to the field of sympathetic magic, symbolizing the beneficial inheritance of the merit transferred by the living to the dead, as a kind of *dakkhina* or offering. The entire ritual is hence an act of grace whereby merit is transferred to the departed so that they may find relief from any unhappy realm wherein they might have been born.

Another funeral rite is *mataka-bana* or "preaching for the benefit of the dead." The usual practice is to conduct a monk to the house of the dead person, generally on the third day (or occasionally on any day within a week) after the funeral and to request him to preach a sermon suited to the occasion. Accordingly he preaches a suitable sermon for about an hour's duration to the assembled audience, which inevitably consists of the deceased's relatives and the neighbours of the household. At the end of the sermon, the monk gets the relatives to recite the necessary stanzas to transfer to the deceased the merits acquired by organizing the event. Following this, a gift is offered to the monk, and the invitees are also served with refreshments.

Three months from the date of death, it is customary to hold an almsgiving *(sanghika dana)* in memory of the deceased and thence to repeat it annually. As in the case of the rituals mentioned earlier, here too the purpose is to impart merit to the deceased. Hence it is called the offering in the name of the dead *(mataka-dana).* The basis of the practice is the belief that if the dead relative has been reborn in an unhappy existence (i.e., as a *peta* or unhappy spirit), he or she would expect his or her living relatives to transfer merit in this manner as these departed spirits or *petas* are incapable of performing any meritorious deed on their own. Even their hunger and thirst, which is perpetual, subside only in this manner. Hence they are referred to as "living on what is given by others" *(paradatta-upajivi).* This custom can be traced to the Buddha's own time when King Bimbisara was harassed by a group of his departed kinsmen, reborn as *petas,* because the king had failed to give alms to the Buddha in their name. Once this was fulfilled as requested by the Buddha, the *petas* became happy and ceased to give any more trouble (KhpA. 202f; PvA.19ff). This was the occasion on which the Buddha preached the Tirokuddha Sutta referred to earlier, which further says that once these rites are performed, these contented spirits bless the donors in return. These rites, it may be mentioned here, resemble the *sraddha* ceremonies of the Hindus in some ways. And it is also significant that, according to the Buddha himself, only the dead relatives who have been reborn as *petas* are capable of receiving this benefit (A.v, 269ff.).

Monastic Ceremonies

Vassa and Kathina

The *Vassa,* a three-month rains retreat, was instituted by the Buddha himself and was made obligatory for all fully ordained bhikkhus; the details are laid down in the Mahavagga of the Vinaya Pitaka (3rd and 4th chapters). The retreat extends over a period corresponding to the North Indian rainy season, from the day following the full moon of July until the full-moon day of October; those who cannot enter the regular *Vassa* are permitted to observe the retreat for three months beginning with the day following the August full moon. From the time Buddhism was introduced to Sri Lanka by the arahant Mahinda, the observance of *Vassa* — *Vas* in Sinhala — has been one of the mainstays of monastic life in the island. During the *Vas* the monks are expected to dwell permanently in their temples and suspend all traveling. If unavoidable circumstances necessitate traveling, they are allowed to leave their residences on the promise that they will return within a week *(sattahakaraniya).* On the first day of the retreat the monks have to formally declare that they will dwell in that manner in the selected monastery or dwelling.

The *Vassa* is also a time for the lay Buddhists to express their devotion to the cause of Buddhism by supporting the Sangha with special diligence, which task they regard as a potent source of merit. It is customary for prominent persons to invite monks to spend the *Vas* with them in dwellings specially prepared for the purpose. In this latter case the host would go and invite the monk or monks formally. If the monks accept the invitation, the hosts would prepare a special temporary dwelling in a suitable place with a refectory and a shrine room. On the first day of the *Vas* they would go with drummers and dancers to the monastery where the invitees reside and conduct them thence in procession. The hosts would assume responsibility for providing all the needs of the monk or monks during this period, and they attend to this work quite willingly as they regard it as highly meritorious. If no special construction is put up, the lay supporters would invite the monks to observe the retreat in the temple itself.

At the close of the *Vas* season, the monks have to perform the *pavarana* ceremony. At this ceremony, held in place of the Patimokkha recitation, each monk invites his fellows to point out to him any faults he has committed during the *Vas* period. On any day following the day of *pavarana* in the period terminating with the next full-moon day, the *kathina* ceremony is held. Different monasteries will hold the *kathina* on different days within this month, though any given monastery may hold only one *kathina* ceremony. The main event in this ceremony is the offering of the special robe known as the *kathina-civara* to the Sangha, who in turn present it to one monk who has observed the retreat. The laity traditionally offer unsewn cloth to the monks. Before the offering takes place, the robe is generally taken, with drumming, etc., around the village in the early hours of the morning. Once the robe is given to the Sangha, certain monks are selected to do the cutting, sewing, and dying of the robe — all in a single day. Public contributions are very often solicited to buy the robe if it is not a personal offering.

This ceremony, which is performed with keen interest and devotion, has today become an important occasion of great social and religious significance for the Buddhist laity. This seems to have been so even in historical times when many Sinhala kings made this offering with much interest and devotion (e.g., Mhv. xliv,48, xci, etc).

Monastic Ordination

There is deep ritualistic significance in the two stages of monastic ordination called *pabbajja* and *upsampada.* The former is the initial admission into the homeless life as a novice or *samanera,* which can be granted to any male over the age of seven or eight, provided certain conditions are satisfied. The ritual proper consists in shaving the hair and beard, donning the dyed robes, whose color ranges from yellow to brown, and then taking from the selected preceptor *(upajjhaya)* the Three Refuges in the Buddha, Dhamma, and Sangha, and the Ten Precepts *(dasa sikkhapada):* abstinence from (i) destroying life, (ii) theft, (iii) unchastity, (iv) lying, (v) fermented liquor, spirits, and strong drinks which cause intoxication and heedlessness, (vi) eating solid food after midday, (vii) dancing, singing, music, and improper shows, etc., (viii) adorning and beautifying the person by the use of garlands, scents, and unguents, (ix) using high and luxurious beds and seats, and (x) receiving gold and silver, i.e., money. The ceremony is performed on an auspicious day at the monastery where the ordination is sought. Thus the postulant becomes a novice.

The full or higher ordination *(upasampada)* is more formal and difficult. The higher ordination ceremony should be conducted in a prescribed and duly consecrated "chapter house" *(sima,* or Sinh.: *poya-ge),* without which the ritual is not valid. If the candidate possesses the necessary qualifications like knowledge and intelligence and he is above twenty years of age, he may formally apply for admission and appear before a chapter of bhikkhus. Before admission he is made to put away the yellow robes and wear the clothes of a householder and face an interview at which he would be thoroughly examined as to his fitness for admission. If he successfully passes the test, he is led aside, reclothed in mendicant robes, and called back. Bearing his alms-bowl, he once again appears before the Sangha and goes through certain formalities after which, if all the monks agree, he is declared admitted.

Uposatha Observance

This refers to the ritual of confession performed by the monks on the new-moon and the full-moon days, when the Disciplinary Code, the Patimokkha, is recited. This is a set of 227 rules, to be observed by the members of the Buddhist Order. When each of the seven sections of the rules is recited amidst the assembled Order, if any among those present has infringed any of those rules, he should confess and undergo any punishment prescribed. Silence implies absence of guilt.

Bali and Tovil Ceremonies

Bali

Bali is the ceremony wherein the presiding deities of the planets *(graha)* are invoked and placated in order to ward off their evil influences. The belief in the good and evil influence of the planets according to the time and place of one's birth is quite widespread in Sri Lanka. The first thing done at the birth of a child is to cast the horoscope, which has to be consulted subsequently at all the important events of his or her life. When a calamity like a serious illness comes upon such a person, the horoscope would inevitably be consulted, and if the person is under a bad planetary influence, the astrologer would recommend some kind of propitiatory ritual. This could be a minor one like the lime-cutting ritual *(dehi-kapima)* or a major one like a *bali* ceremony, depending on the seriousness of the case. If it is a *bali* ceremony, he might also recommend the specific kind of *bali* suitable for the occasion.

The term *bali* signifies both the ritual in general and also the clay representations of the planetary deities which are made in relief on frameworks of bamboo and painted in appropriate colors. The ritual consists of dancing and drumming in front of the *bali* figures by the *bali* artist *(bali-adura),* who continuously recites propitiatory stanzas calling for protection and redress. The patient *(aturaya)* sits by the side of the *bali* figures.

The *bali* artist is helped by a number of assistants working under him. The knowledge and art of performing the ritual are handed down in traditional families. The retentive power of these artists is remarkable, for they can continue to recite the appropriate formulas and verses from memory for days.

The *bali* ceremony is a mixture of Buddhism and folk religion. This cult of the planets and the allied deities has become an important element in the popular living Buddhism of the island. The origins of this type of *bali* ritual have to be traced to the Kotte Period of the 15th and 16th centuries, when it was introduced into the island from South India by some Hindu brahmans from that region. However, mainly owing to the efforts of the celebrated Buddhist monk of the period, Ven.

Vidagama Maitreya Thera, this ritual was recast with a Buddhist significance, both in form and content, in that all the verses and formulas used in the ritual are those extolling the virtues of the Triple Gem — the Buddha, Dhamma, and Sangha — and of the Buddhist deities. It is these spiritual qualities that are invoked to bring redress. The entire ritual is thus made subservient to Buddhism.

The ceremony begins after paying homage to the Buddha, the Dhamma, and the Sangha. Even during the course of the ceremony this homage is paid at important junctures. The majority of the stanzas recited as benedictory verses by the artist extol the virtues of the Triple Gem or refer to the Buddha's previous existences as a Bodhisatta. The verbal part of the entire ritual consists mainly of the recitation of these verses and the pronouncement of the blessing: "By the power of those virtues let the evil influence of the planets disappear." It is believed that this kind of pronouncement of blessings becomes effective only if they are made at such an elaborate ceremony like *bali*. As in the case of the *pirit* ceremony described earlier, the spiritual qualities of the Buddha are regarded as superior to any worldly powers like those of the planets and stars as in the present instance, and consequently the ceremonial and ritualistic pronouncement of those qualities is believed to counteract those evil forces. Those propitiatory recitations also include the panegyrics *(stotras)* praising those planetary deities.

The preparation for the *bali* ceremony takes a day or two. Plantain stems, tender coconut leaves, coconut and arecanut racemes, powdered resin, limes, betel, torches made by wrapping clean rags around dry reeds *(vilakku* and *pandam),* coconut oil, flowers of different colors, and burnt offerings are among the main items needed. Plastic clay and reeds will be needed in large quantities to cast the *bali* figures. Life-size images of the planetary deities are moulded from these and painted beautifully in bright colors. Each planetary deity has its own dress, colors, diagram *(mandala),* support *(vahana),* weapon, etc. It is the nine planets *(navagraha)* that are generally propitiated: the sun *(ravi),* moon *(candra),* Mars *(kuja),* Mercury *(budha),* Jupiter *(guru),* Venus *(sukra),* Saturn *(sani),* and Rahu and Ketu, the ascending and the descending nodes of the moon respectively. When everything is ready, with the *bali* figures propped up leaning against a wall and the patient seated by a side facing the figures, the chief *bali* artist starts the proceedings by taking the Five Precepts and reciting a few benedictory stanzas while the drummers start drumming. This takes place in the evening. After these preliminaries it is more or less customary for the chief artist to retire to the side, while one or two of his assistants would appear on the scene to perform the more vigorous part of the ritual, consisting mainly of dancing and reciting.

The dancing artist wears an attractive and colorful dress consisting of white tights, a red jacket adorned with white beads, anklets, pads of jingling bells around his calves, and an elaborate headdress. In one hand he takes a *pandama* or lighted torch adequately fed with coconut oil. While reciting formulas and dancing to the beat of the drum, he throws handfuls of powdered resin into the burning *pandama,* setting up flares of flames which are regarded as very powerful in driving away the invisible evil spirits *(bhuta).* In addition to the virtues of the Triple Gem, his recitation would also include legends and anecdotes taken from the Buddha's and Bodhisatta's lives. Sometimes references to previous Buddhas are also made. Planetary deities are eulogized and requested to stop troubling the patient.

Coconut-oil lamps, an incense burner, water pots with full-blown coconut racemes *(pun-kalas)* are among the items inevitably found on the scene. Offerings done on altars made of plantain trunks and tender coconut leaves will also be found. A number of such altars called *pideni-tatu* may be set up; these are for the departed kinsmen of the family *(nati-peta)* who are expected to stop harassing the living after receiving these offerings, which generally consist of rice, seven selected curries cooked together *(hat-maluwa),* burnt offerings *(pulutu),* colored flowers, betel leaves, five kinds of seeds, etc. A live cock, with its legs tied together so that it cannot run about, is placed in a corner as an offering to the evil spirits. This is a kind of scapegoat, for all the evil influences of the patient are supposed to be transferred to this bird, which is released on the following morning. The ceremonies actually end early in the morning when the artists carry the clay images *(bali* figures) and the altars of offerings or *pideni-tatu* and leave them at the cross-roads that the evil spirits who give trouble are believed to frequent.

Tovil

Tovil or "devil-dancing" is another ritualistic healing ceremony that primarily belongs to folk religion. As in the case of the *bali* ceremony, here too many Buddhist elements have crept in and it has become a ceremony purporting to fulfill, at the popular level, the socio-religious needs of the simple rural Buddhists.

Tovil is essentially a demonic ritual mainly exorcistic in character, and hence a healing ceremony. In its exorcist form it is meant to curb and drive away any one or several of the innumerable hosts of malevolent spirits, known as *yakkhas,* who are capable of bringing about pathological states of body and mind. *Petas* or departed spirits of the malevolent type, referred to as *mala-yakku (mala* = dead) or *mala-peta,* are also brought under the exorcist power of *tovil.* While some of these could be subdued by the chanting of *pirit* (described earlier), there are some for whom methods of a more drastic type have to be adopted. The most popular of such methods is the *tovil* ceremony.

As was pointed out earlier in relation to rituals in general, *tovil* is also an important aspect of folk religion that has been adopted by the Sinhala Buddhists. In the case of *tovil* too, religious sanction is conferred on folk-religious elements that have crept into normative Buddhism, supplementing, as it were, whatever is lacking in it to satisfy the religious needs of the masses. The Buddha is the chief of living beings, who include the *yakkhas* and other related non-human beings that figure in *tovil.* Although they have the power to make their victims ill in various ways — such as by possession, gaze, etc.— they have to leave them once propitiatory offerings of food, drink, etc., are made to them. Even the mere mention of the Buddha's virtues is enough to frighten them. Moreover, the chief of the *yakkhas,* Vessavana *(Vesamuni),* is one of the four regents of the universe *(maharaja)* and as such a devoted follower of the Buddha. The ordinary *yakkhas* that trouble human beings have to obey his commands. Thus, in all rituals connected with *tovil,* it is in the name of the Buddha and Vessavana that the *yakkhas* are commanded to obey the orders of the exorcist. And in the rich folklore that deals with *tovil,* there are many anecdotes that connect every ritual or character with some Buddha of the past or with some Buddhist deity.

The Atanatiya Ritual

It is of interest to find a purely Buddhist form of an exorcist ritual that has been practiced by the Buddhists of Sri Lanka from very early times. This is the recital of the Atanatiya Sutta (of the Digha Nikaya) in order to exorcise an evil spirit that has taken possession of a person. The commentary to the sutta (DA.iii, 969), dating at least as far back as the time of Buddhaghosa (c. 6th century A.C.) or even earlier, gives a detailed description of how and when to recite it. According to this description, first the Metta, Dhajagga, and Ratana Suttas should be recited. If the spirit does not leave by such recital, the Atanatiya Sutta is to be recited. The bhikkhu who performs the recital should not eat meat or preparations of flour. He should not live in a cemetery, lest the evil spirits get an opportunity to harass him. From the monastery to the patient's house, he should be conducted under an armed guard. The recitation of the *paritta* should not be done in the open. Thoughts of love for the patient should be foremost in the reciter's mind. During the recital too he should be under armed guard. If the spirit still refuses to leave, the patient should be taken to the monastery and the recital performed in the courtyard of the *dagaba.*

Many preliminary rites are recommended before such a recital. These include getting the patient to offer a seat to the bhikkhu who is to recite the *paritta,* the offering of flowers and lamps to the *dagaba,* and the recitation by the bhikkhu of a set of benedictory stanzas, called *(Maha)-mangala-gatha.* A full assembly of the deities should also be summoned. The person possessed should be questioned as to his name, by which is implied the identity of the spirit who has taken possession of him. Once the name is given, the spirit, but visibly the patient, should be addressed by that name. It should be told that the merits of offering incense, flowers, alms, etc. are all transferred to him and that the *mangala-gatha* just referred to have been recited in order to appease him *(pannaharatthaya:* as a gift) and that he should therefore leave the patient in deference to the Sangha *(bhikkhusangha-garavena).* If the spirit still refuses to leave, the deities should be informed of his obstinacy and the Atanatiya Paritta should be recited after declaring that as the spirit does not obey them, they are carrying out the order of the Buddha.

It is significant that this is a purely Buddhist ritual of considerable antiquity performed on lines similar to those in *tovil.* But the difference between the two should also be noted. When *tovil* is performed to cure a person possessed by a spirit, the spirit is ordered to leave the patient after accepting the offering of food and drink *(dola-pideni).* But in the case of the Atanatiya ritual, it is the merits earned by making offerings to the Buddha that are transferred to the spirit. Another significant difference is that the Atanatiya recital, in keeping with its purely Buddhist spirit, is much milder and more restrained than its *tovil* counterpart. The latter, however, is much more colorful and theatrical owing to its complex and essentially secular character. From the purely curative aspect, too, there is another attractive feature in *tovil:* when the spirit leaves the patient it does so leaving a sign of its departure, like breaking a branch of a tree, making a sound like a hoot, etc. It is perhaps because of these attractive features that *tovil* has become more popular in the island, replacing the truly Buddhist ceremony of the Atanatiya recital.

Nowadays in Sri Lanka, *tovil* has become the most popular form of cure adopted for spirit possession as well as other pathological conditions consequent on this. When a person is ill and medical treatment does not respond, the suspicion arises that it is due to some influence of an evil spirit. The person to be consulted in such a case is the exorcist known as *kattadiya* or *yakadura* or *yaddessa* who would discover and identify the particular evil spirit causing the disease and perform the appropriate *tovil*. There are also certain forms of *tovil* performed as pregnancy rituals (e.g., *rata-yakuma)* and others as means of eradicating various forms of evil influences like the evil eye, evil mouth, etc. (e.g., *gara-yakuma)*.

The devil-dancers start their ceremony by first worshipping the Buddha, Dhamma, and Sangha, as in the case of the *bali* ceremony. The *yakkhas* — who constitute one of the main classes of malevolent spirits placated in devil-dancing — are believed to become satisfied with the offerings made by people through *tovil* and cease harassing them. The *yakkhas* like Riri, Sanni, Kalukumaraya, Suniyan, Mahasohon, Maru, etc. are some of the main spirits placated. There are eighteen main *yakkhas* in this category, each representing a particular kind of illness, and in *tovil* these demons are represented by the devil-dancers themselves, who wear their specific masks and other apparel in keeping with the traditional forms ascribed to these spirits. It is believed that by dancing, chanting, and acting the part of the demons after assuming their likenesses through masks and other paraphernalia, the demons possessing the patient would leave him. The sound waves created by the drum-beat and the chanting of stanzas accompanied by rhythmic dancing in keeping with these sounds are all performed to a set pattern traditionally laid down.

The collective effect of the ceremony is believed to cure the patient's illness. Thus this dancing in *tovil* is a therapeutic ritual. The impersonation of the demon by the dancer is regarded as tantamount to the actual presence of the demon who becomes placated through offerings, recitations, chanting, miming, etc. When the spirits are threatened and asked to leave the patient, they are asked to do so under the command and in the name of the Buddha.

The ceremony known as *rata-yakuma* is performed to make barren women conceive, or for the pre-natal care of pregnant women, and to ensure the safe delivery of children. One of the episodes mimetically performed by the exorcist in this ceremony shows how barren women, according to a Buddhist legend preserved among the Sinhala people, offer cloths to the past Buddha Dipankara, the fourth in the line of twenty-eight

Buddhas accepted by Theravada Buddhists; they obtain children through the merits of the act. Among the rituals specially connected with women may be mentioned those devil-dancing ceremonies that invoke the *yakkha* called Kalukumaraya in Sinhala. He is very often associated with another group of *yakkhas* called *rata-yakku,* whose leader is a female named Riddi-bisava. Another pregnancy ritual that deserves mention here is the one known as *kalas-tabima* (lit. setting apart a pot). When the first signs of pregnancy appear in a woman, a new clay pot is filled with certain ingredients and kept apart with the solemn promise that once the child is safely delivered a *tovil* will be performed. The ritual known as *hat-adiya* (seven steps) in the *tovil* ceremony called *suniyam-kapima,* signifies the seven steps the Bodhisatta Siddhattha is said to have taken just after he was born.

Two important facts that emerge from this brief description of *tovil* is the theatrical value present in these rituals and the way in which religious sanction has been obtained for their adoption by the Buddhists.

Goddess Pattini

The large number of rituals and ceremonies connected with the goddess Pattini also come under Buddhist practices. This goddess, believed to be of South Indian origin, has become the most popular female deity of the Sinhala Buddhists (see below, pp. 65-66). While Hindu goddesses like Lakshmi, Sarasvati, and Kali are also worshipped by the Buddhists, only Pattini has separate abodes among the Buddhists. The most important of the rituals connected with Pattini is the *gam-maduwa,* which is an all-purpose ceremony. As this ceremony is usually held after the harvest by offering the first portion of paddy harvested, this is also a ceremony of first-fruit offerings. A *gam-maduwa* has many interludes dramatized mainly from rich legendary lore about the goddess Pattini. *Kohomba-kankariya,* or the ritual of the god Kohomba, is a ceremony similar to the *gam-maduwa* but performed more as an expiatory ritual.

Two other ceremonies of this type are *pan-madu* and *puna-madu.* All these are different forms of the same type of ritual with slight differences. They are generally referred to as *devol-*

madu or occasions for the propitiation of the gods. The general purpose of such *devol-madu* is the attainment of immunity from disease and evil influences and the achievement of success, especially agricultural, for the entire village. A point that is sociologically important is that as they are big communal gatherings they also fulfill the social needs of the village folk. As they are performed in public places to bless the community as a whole and turn out to be social get-togethers, they bear a corporate character. When it is decided that such a ceremony should be held, all the village folk would forget their differences and work together to make it a success. Further, while it mainly serves as a ritual to propitiate the deities, it is a form of entertainment as well. Serving as it does the socio-religious needs of the masses, it becomes a big social event for the entire village.

Gara-demons

Gara-demons *(gara-yakku* (plural);*-yaka* (singular)) are a group of demons twelve in number whose female aspects are called the *Giri* goddesses. Their chief is called *Dala-raja* who is represented as having three hooded cobras over his head, ear-ornaments, two protruding tusks, and a torch in each hand. When referred to in the singular as *gara-yaka* it is he that is intended and when performing the ritual it is the mask pertaining to him that is generally used as representing the group. These demons are not inimical to humans but are regarded as removing various kinds of uncleanliness and evil influences. Accordingly it is customary among the Sinhala Buddhists to perform the ritual called *gara-yak-natuma* (dance of the *gara-yakku)* at the end of religious ceremonies like annual *peraheras, tovil* ceremonies, etc. This is to ward off what is called *vas-dos* in the terminology of the folk religion, the effects of evil-eye, evil mouth, evil thoughts, etc. The malicious influences of these evil forces have to be eliminated before the participants return to their normal activities. And for this it is these demons that have to be propitiated. Accordingly, they are invited to come and take away their prey, promising not to harm the participants thereafter. A dancer impersonates the *gara-yaka* by wearing the appropriate mask just referred to and in the dialogue that takes place between him and another dancer, he promises to comply with the request if certain things are given to him. These include drinks, food, sweets, and money. These items are given and he departs in peace. The ceremony is held annually at the Vishnu Devalaya in Kandy after the annual Esala Perahera. It goes on for one week from the last day of the Perahera and is referred to as *vali-yak-natuma.*

Worship of Devas

Deva Worship

Besides the ceremonies and rituals like *pirit, sanghika-dana, kathina,* etc., that can be traced in their origin to the time of the Buddha himself, there is another popular practice resorted to by the average Sri Lankan Buddhist which cannot be traced to early Buddhism so easily. This is *deva*-worship, the worship of deities, in what are popularly called *devalayas* or abodes dedicated to these deities. This practice cannot be described as totally un-Buddhistic, yet at the same time it does not fall into the category of folk religious practices like *bali* and *tovil* adopted by popular Buddhism.

The word *deva,* meaning "god" or "deity" in this context, signifies various classes of superhuman beings who in some respects are superior to ordinary human beings through their birth in a higher plane. As such, they are capable of helping human beings in times of difficulty. There is also another class of such superior beings who were originally extraordinary human beings. After their death, they have been raised to the level of gods and are worshipped and supplicated as capable of helping in times of need. These are the gods by convention *(sammuti-deva)* or glorified human heroes like the Minneriya Deviyo, who was glorified in this manner in recognition of his construction of the great Minneriya Tank at Polonnaruwa, or God Vibhishana, one of the four guardian deities of Sri Lanka. Both these categories of deities are, however, subject to the samsaric laws pertaining to birth and death. Thus it is seen that *deva*-worship is based on the theory that a superior being can help an inferior being when the latter needs such help. In addition to their role as helpers in need, an additional duty ascribed to the *devas* is the safeguarding of the Buddha-sasana, i.e., the Buddhist religion. This also has its origin in the story of the Buddha himself when the four divine regents of the universe mounted guard over him and helped on various occasions of the Bodhisatta's life from his conception onwards. The benevolence of the deities is also extended to the protection of the faithful followers of the Buddha's teachings as exemplified by Sakka, the good Samaritan in many Buddhist stories.

In Sri Lanka there are four deities regarded as the guardians of the Buddha-sasana in the island: Vishnu, Saman, Kataragama, and Vibhishana. Although Vishnu is originally a Hindu god, the Buddhists have taken him over as a Buddhist deity, referring to him also by the localized designation Uppalavanna. And so are Siva, specially under the name Isvara, and Ganesha under the name Ganapati or the more popular appellation Gana-deviyo. In the *devala*-worship the devotees make offerings to these deities and solicit their help for special purposes, especially in their day-to-day problems. A noteworthy feature in this practice is the presence of a mediator between the deity and the devotee, a priest called *kapurala,* or *kapu-mahattaya* or simply *kapuva,* the equivalent of the Hindu *pusari.* This figure has been copied from South Indian Hindu practices, for even in North India the devotees appeal directly to these higher powers without the help of such an intermediary.

By *devala* offering is meant the offering of food and drink as well as gifts of cloth, coins, gold, and silver often accompanied by culogies addressed to the particular resident deity and recited by the *kapurala.* In many Buddhist temples in Sri Lanka there are *devalayas* dedicated to various deities. *Devala*-worship of this type is a ritual that has gained popularity among the local Buddhists since the Polonnaruwa period (12th century). In the present day it has acquired a vital place in the religious life of the Buddhist masses. This is one of the aspects by which the "great tradition" of Nikaya Buddhism has been supplemented by popular elements. This shows that if Buddhism is to prevail as a living force among all classes of its adherents, it has to make provision for the popular demands related to the day-to-day life of the common populace. It is customary for many Sri Lankan Buddhists to visit a *devalaya* of one of the deities and make a vow that if the problem at hand (i.e., illness, enemies, etc.) is solved, they will make an offering to the deity concerned. Offerings are made even without such a special request. Whatever the case may be, this practice has become a ritual of propitiation through the *kapuralas*.

The main duties of the *kapuralas* are to look after the *devalayas* in their charge, to perform the prescribed rituals, and to offer in the inner shrine the offerings brought by devotees. The *kapurala* is given a fee for his services. Once the ritual is over, a part of the offerings is given back to the devotee for him to take home and partake of as having a sacramental value. The offerings normally consist of milk-rice, coconuts, betel, camphor, joss-sticks, fruits, along with flowers, garlands, flags, etc. All these are arranged in an orderly manner in a basket or tray and handed over respectfully to the *kapurala,* who takes it inside and offers it at the statue of the main deity inside the inner room. The devotees wait outside with clasped hands while the *kapurala* makes his pleadings on their behalf.

The statement he recites, called *yatikava* in Sinhala, is a panegyric of the deity concerned and it constitutes a humble and respectful request to bring succour to the devotee in his particular predicament. After this the *kapurala* emerges from the inner shrine room and blesses the devotees by using his thumb to place on their forehead a mark of a paste made from saffron, sandalwood, and other ingredients. This mark, the symbol of sanctification, is known as the *tilaka*.

This form of ritualistic propitiation of deities is a clear adaptation of the Hindu system where the very same method is followed, though more elaborately.

The Gods

Kataragama. *Devalayas* dedicated to the different deities are scattered all over the island. God Kataragama (Skanda) in southern Sri Lanka is by far the most popular, as he is considered to be the most powerful deity capable of granting the requests of the worshipper. It is for this reason that he has acquired territorial rights throughout the island. *Devalayas* dedicated to him are found in many places in the island, some of which are maintained by the Hindus. Ganesha. The elephant-shaped god Ganesha, regarded as the god of wisdom and the remover of obstacles, is also very popular among the Buddhists under the names Ganapati or Gana-deviyo. He is worshipped as the chief of obstacles (Vighnesvara) because it is believed that he is responsible for creating and removing obstracles. He does this through troops of inferior deities or demi-gods considered as attendants of Siva, present almost everywhere, who are under his command. It is in this sense that he is called Gana-pati (chief of hosts), which is the epithet popular among the Buddhists. The *devalayas* dedicated to him are mostly run by the Hindus. The Buddhists worship him either through his statues, found in many Buddhists temples, or by visiting the Hindu *kovils* dedicated to him. As the god of wisdom and of learning, he is propitiated at the time a child first reads the alphabet. As the chief of obstacles, as their creator as well as remover, the Hindus begin their *devala*-ritual by making the first offering to him.

Another popular aspect of his worship in some parts of Sri Lanka can be observed along the main roads, especially in the North-Central Province, where his statue is placed near trees and propitiated by travelers so that they may have a safe journey. The propitiation usually consists of breaking a coconut in his name, offering a coin *(pandura),* etc.

Natha. Natha is purely a Buddhist god, apparently the local counterpart of the all-compassionate Mahayana Bodhisattva Avalokitesvara. He is referred to in Sri Lanka by the abbreviated form Natha. His cult, as that of Natha, had become quite popular during the Kotte period (14th and 15th centuries), while references to him are found as early as the 9th and 10th centuries as shown by archaelogical evidence. The center of the cult was Totagamuwa near Hikkaduwa in the Galle District. Two of the more ancient *devalayas* dedicated to this deity are found at Kandy and at Vagiriya. The premises of the Kandy *devalaya,* opposite the Temple of the Tooth, are considered especially lucky and sacred, for the important royal rites like choosing a name for the king, putting on the royal sword, etc., were held there. It was Natha's all-pervading compassion that seems to have been appealed to by the local devotees. Vishnu. The important Hindu god Vishnu has also assumed a special Buddhist significance in the island. He is identified with the god Uppalavanna of the *Mahavamsa,* to whom Sakka, the king of the gods, is said to have entrusted the guardianship of Sri Lanka at the request of the Buddha before his passing away. This god is said to have arrived in the island to fulfill this mission. The name Uppalavanna means "the color of the blue water-lily." As Vishnu is of the same color, Uppalavanna became identified with Vishnu, and in the wake of the Mahavamsa tradition, he became, as Vishnu, the protector of the Buddha-sasana in Sri Lanka. The calculated omission of the name Vishnu in the *Mahavamsa* in this connection may be viewed as an attempt at total localization of the divinity with a view to harmonize him with the cultural fabric of the island. His main shrine is at Devinuwara (Dondra), at the southern tip of the island, where an annual Esala (July-August) festival is held in his honor. If the identification is correct his cult can be traced to the earliest phase of the history of the island and has been popular up to the present day.

Pattini. Goddess Pattini, referred to above (see p.59), is prominent as the most popular female Buddhist divinity; she has her *devalayas* scattered throughout the country. Her cult goes back at least to the second century A.C. The then ruler, King Gajabahu, is said to have introduced the worship of this divinity into the island from South India. The legend about her life is told in the Tamil poem *Silappadikaram.* According to the myths current in the island about her, she had seven incarnations, being born seven times from water, the tusk of an elephant, a flower, a rock, a fire (or peak), cloth, and a mango. Hence she is designated as *sat-pattini, sat* meaning seven. There are colorful stories woven around these births. The story about her unswerving fidelity to her fickle husband Kovalan (or Palanga) in her birth as Kannagi, is quite popular among the local Buddhists as attested by the existence of many Sinhala literary works dealing with the story (e.g., *Vayantimalaya, Pattinihalla, Palanga-halla,* etc.).

Her favors are sought especially at times of pestilences like chicken pox, measles, etc. and also by women who desire children. It is customary for the Sri Lankan Buddhists to visit her *devalaya* and worship her with offerings after recovery from infectious diseases. The banishment of evil influences and the attainment of prosperity in general and good harvests are other purposes behind the ceremonies performed in her honor. She also plays an important part in the ceremonies connected with the offering of first fruits.

Devalayas dedicated to her are found in many parts of the island, the one at Navagamuwa, about fifteen miles from Colombo on the old Avissavella Road, being the most important. The sanctity of this place seems to go back to the time of King Gajabahu.

Sakka. Sakka, the king of the gods, has been an important figure in the Buddhist affairs of Sri Lanka. Tradition connects him with the Buddha himself in connection with the landing of Vijaya and his followers in the island in the 6th century B.C. On this occasion, at the Buddha's request, Sakka is said to have entrusted Vishnu with the guardianship of Buddhism in the island. It was Sakka too who sought arahant Mahinda and requested him to come over to the island when the time became opportune for its conversion (Mhv. xiii,15,16,17).

Saman. Another important deity in the island is Mahasumana, Sumana or Saman, the guardian or the presiding deity of Sri Pada mountain or Sumanakuta (Adam's Peak), which the Buddhists treat as sacred on account of its bearing the impression of the Buddha's left foot, which he left on his third visit to the island. (Mhv.i,77ff.).

God Saman is recorded as having met the Buddha on the latter's first visit to the island when he visited Mahiyangana to drive away the *yakkhas*. Saman became a stream-entrant *(sotapanna)* after listening to the Buddha, who gave him a handful of hairs with which he erected the *dagaba* at Mahiyangana (Mhv.i,33). He is regarded as the chief deity of the area surrounding the sacred mountain as well as of the hill-country in general. Accordingly his main shrine is at Ratnapura, where an annual festival is held in his honor.

Vibhishana. Another deity, somewhat similar to Saman, is Vibhishana, who is regarded as the brother of the pre-historic King Ravana of Sri Lanka. His main shrine is at Kelaniya, as a part of the famous Buddhist temple there. Dadimunda. Another deity who likewise came into prominence during the

Kandyan period (17th and 18th centuries) is Dadimunda (Devata Bandara) who, according to the prevalent tradition, landed at Dondra (Devinuvara) in South Sri Lanka from South India. He proceeded to Alutnuvara in the Kegalla District, taking up permanent residence there in a temple, which he himself got constructed. This is the chief shrine of this deity and here too an annual festival is held. He is regarded as a general of Vishnu and accordingly, at the main Vishnu shrines in the island, he also has his shrine on a side (e.g., Dondra, Kandy, etc.). Another interesting tradition says that he was the only deity who did not run away in fear at the time of Bodhisatta Siddhattha's struggle with Mara. While all the other deities took flight in fright, he alone remained fearless as the Bodhisatta's only guardian. He is portrayed in the attire of a Kandyan chief with his special attribute, a walking stick *(soluva)*. His Kandyan dress symbolizes his suzerainty over the Kandyan area.

Huniyan Deviyo. The patron deity of the sorcerers in Sri Lanka is Huniyan or Suniyan, who has been promoted from the status of a demon to that of a deity. He is also regarded as the deity presiding over a village area bounded by its boundaries *(gam-kotuwa)*, in which role he is designated as *gambhara-deviyo* (deity in charge of the village). In many of the composite *devalayas* he too has his shrine, the one at Lunava, about seven miles from Colombo close to the Galle Road, near the Lunava railway station, being his chief *devalaya*.

Besides these deities so far enumerated there are many other minor figures who are too numerous to be mentioned here. What is important is that in the case of all these deities, the method of propitiation and worship is the same as explained earlier and every such deity is in charge of a particular aspect of life. And all of them are faithful Buddhists, extending their respective powers not only to the Buddha-sasana but also to those who follow it faithfully. As Buddhists, none of these is regarded as superior or even remotely equal to the Buddha. They all are followers of the Buddha, who has transcended the round of rebirth *(samsara)*, while they are still within *samsara*, hoping to achieve release from it by following the Buddha's Teaching.

BIBLIOGRAPHY

Bell, Sir Charles: *Portrait of a Dalai Lama: The Life and Times of the Great Thirteenth,* Boston, Wisdom Publications, 1987.

Cook, Elizabeth: *Holy Places of the Buddha,* Berkeley, Dharma Publishing, 1994.

Dargyay, Eva M.: *The Rise of Esoteric Buddhism in Tibet,* Delhi, Motilal Banarsidass, 1977.

Eppsteiner, Fred: *The Path of Compassion: Writings on Socially Engaged Buddhism,* Berkeley, Parallax Press, 1988.

Gombrich, Richard F.: *Buddhist Precept and Practice,* Delhi, Motilal Banarsidass, 1991.

Hakeda, Yoshito S.: *Kukai, Major Works,* New York, Columbia University Press, 1972.

Keown, Damien: *The Nature of Buddhist Ethics,* New York, St. Martin's Press, 1992.

Lalwani. K.C.: *Kalpa Sutra of Badrabahu Svami*, Delhi, Motilal Banarsidass. 1979.

Mookerjee, Satkari: *Buddhist Philosophy of Universal Flux,* Delhi, Motilal Banarsidass, 1980.

Payutto, Prayudh: *Buddhist Economics: A Middle Way for the Marketplace,* Bangkok, Buddhadhamma Foundation, 1994.

Powers, John: *Wisdom of Buddha: The Samdhinirmocana Sutra,* Berkeley, Dharma Publishing, 1994.

Sprung, Mervyn: *The Problem of Two Truths in Buddhism and Vedanta,* Boston, Reidel, 1973.

Strong, John: *The Legend of King Asoka,* Princeton, Princeton University Press, 1983.

Thomas, E. J.: *The Life of the Buddha as Legend and History,* London, Routledge & Kegan Paul, 1927.

Wells, Kenneth E.: *Thai Buddhism, Its Rites and Activities,* Bangkok, Christian Bookstore, 1960.

INDEX

A

Agriculture, 185.
Appreciation, 200.
Approach, 24, 84, 100, 102, 224, 262.
Architecture, 11, 184, 191, 200.
Art, 63, 111, 122, 125, 178, 184, 191, 198, 200, 201, 202, 269.
Artists, 19, 29, 269, 272.
Asoka, 8, 11, 18, 58, 61, 62, 63, 64, 65, 66, 82, 83, 84, 101, 103, 107, 108, 110, 115, 116, 117, 119, 120, 128, 132, 139, 175, 176, 177, 178, 180, 193.
Attitudes, 108, 109, 208, 210.

B

Buddha, 3, 4, 5, 6, 7, 8, 9, 10, 13, 14, 15, 16, 18, 19, 20, 21, 22, 23, 24, 25, 26, 33, 34, 39, 43, 44, 49, 50, 54, 55, 56, 58, 59, 60, 65, 76, 81, 82, 84, 108, 111, 112, 113, 115, 116, 117, 120, 121, 127, 129, 132, 133, 136, 137, 139, 141, 144, 149, 153, 158, 162, 165, 171, 172, 173, 174, 176, 183, 186, 188, 189, 193, 194, 196, 197, 198, 200, 201, 202, 204, 205, 206, 207, 208, 209, 210, 211, 212, 214, 215, 217, 218, 219, 221, 222, 223, 224, 225, 226, 227, 228, 229, 230, 231, 232, 234, 235, 236, 237, 238, 239, 240, 241, 242, 243, 244, 247, 250, 251, 252, 253, 254, 256, 259, 260, 261, 262, 263, 265, 266, 268, 270, 272, 273, 274, 275, 278, 279, 282, 283, 284.
Buddhism, 1, 7, 8, 9, 10, 11, 12, 13, 14, 15, 16, 17, 18, 20, 21, 22, 23, 24, 25, 27, 29, 30, 33, 34, 38, 40, 42, 43, 48, 49, 53, 57, 58, 59, 60, 61, 62, 64, 109, 111, 113, 114, 115, 116, 121, 123, 125, 126, 127, 128, 132, 133, 135, 136, 138, 139, 140, 141, 142, 147, 148, 149, 150, 151, 152, 153, 155, 156, 158, 159, 160, 162, 163, 165, 166, 167, 168, 169, 170, 171, 172, 173, 174, 175, 176, 178, 179, 180, 181, 182, 183, 184, 185, 186, 188, 189, 190, 191, 192, 193, 194, 195, 196, 197, 198, 199, 200, 201, 202, 207, 208, 209, 210, 211, 224, 226, 227, 229, 236, 239, 241, 242, 243, 247, 248, 253,

266, 269, 270, 272, 278, 279, 283.

C

Christians, 155, 164, 167, 184.
Collections, 146, 199.
Community, 16, 56, 64, 114, 140, 150, 170, 187, 191, 192, 193, 199, 222, 261, 262, 277.
Complexity, 230.
Concentration, 208.
Contributions, 267.
Conversion, 18, 22, 24, 115, 162, 163, 283.

D

Devotee, 125, 193, 224, 225, 230, 232, 235, 239, 257, 279, 280.
Devotion, 8, 25, 32, 39, 57, 69, 71, 73, 120, 157, 224, 225, 229, 230, 242, 243, 266, 267.
Dhamma, 4, 7, 9, 14, 18, 24, 27, 28, 64, 65, 66, 67, 68, 69, 70, 71, 72, 73, 75, 76, 77, 78, 79, 80, 81, 82, 83, 84, 89, 90, 91, 92, 93, 94, 100, 101, 102, 103, 107, 108, 109, 110, 116, 118, 125, 126, 128, 132, 141, 142, 156, 157, 171, 173, 177, 182, 183, 185, 189, 190, 191, 193, 194, 196, 197, 198, 199, 200, 201, 202, 205, 206, 207, 208, 209, 210, 211, 212, 214, 216, 217, 219, 222, 223, 224, 225, 227, 228, 230, 233, 239, 246, 253, 254, 255, 256, 268, 270, 275.
Dilemmas, 199.

E

Economy, 194.
Education, 35, 55, 154, 157, 162, 163, 164, 166, 167, 168, 169, 170, 172, 173, 186, 187, 188, 189, 190, 191, 192, 200, 201, 206.

F

Forbearance, 73, 183.
Friendship, 15, 27.

G

Government, 35, 47, 50, 53, 55, 66, 135, 155, 160, 161, 162, 165, 171, 172, 185, 186, 187, 188, 190, 247.

I

Independence, 40, 59, 160, 171, 173.
Influence, 1, 10, 11, 13, 26, 38, 40, 41, 55, 111, 112, 114, 126, 130, 173, 175, 176, 179, 180, 181, 182, 183, 194, 201, 203, 208, 232, 244, 253, 269, 270, 274.
Inscriptions, 14, 15, 20, 23, 58, 61, 63, 176, 183.

K

Kamma, 194, 199, 201, 204, 206, 210, 219, 227, 230.

L

Language, 1, 2, 15, 32, 33, 42, 43, 44, 52, 62, 63, 99, 150, 161, 162, 167, 173, 180, 183, 184, 185, 187, 189, 193, 194, 200, 201, 218, 223, 239, 263.
Laws, 200, 204, 209, 278.

Literature, 9, 13, 29, 34, 52, 63, 64, 114, 139, 150, 152, 157, 158, 160, 178, 182, 189, 199, 224.
Loyalty, 66, 72.

M

Mahavamsa, 8, 13, 61, 177, 178, 241, 242, 252, 282.
Mass Movements, 199.
Merchant, 5, 13, 112.
Merciful, 75.

N

Nibbana, 7, 21, 194, 202, 204, 207, 208, 210, 223, 224, 225, 226, 227, 238, 257.

P

Pagan, 3, 5, 13, 14, 16, 17, 18, 19, 20, 21, 22, 23, 24, 25, 26, 27, 28, 29, 30, 31, 32, 34, 43, 52, 53, 176, 180, 182.
Pilgrimage, 5, 6, 28, 34, 37, 63, 155, 242, 243, 247, 248.
Poetry, 33, 148, 200.
Preparation, 123, 137, 202, 214, 258, 270.
Prisoners, 65, 68, 78, 79, 115.
Prominence, 146, 250, 283.
Promotion, 65, 68, 79, 80, 170, 192.
Punishment, 7, 49, 53, 73, 128, 152, 159, 268.
Pyu Kingdoms, 9, 13.

R

Rahula, 76, 82, 83, 103, 104, 107, 252.
Responsibility, 40, 45, 53, 65, 206, 209, 210, 229, 267.
Rituals, 20, 64, 191, 192, 194, 224, 225, 226, 227, 234, 243, 246, 248, 249, 252, 260, 265, 272, 273, 275, 276, 278, 280.

S

Sangha, 4, 8, 14, 18, 21, 27, 28, 31, 32, 34, 35, 37, 38, 39, 40, 41, 44, 45, 46, 47, 48, 49, 50, 51, 53, 54, 55, 57, 76, 80, 82, 91, 119, 124, 125, 132, 142, 143, 149, 156, 158, 183, 185, 186, 187, 188, 190, 193, 194, 209, 211, 212, 216, 217, 218, 219, 220, 222, 225, 227, 228, 230, 239, 251, 253, 254, 256, 257, 259, 264, 266, 267, 268, 270, 274, 275.
Scholar, 12, 25, 30, 47, 136, 144, 145, 148, 157, 159, 165.
Shan Rule, 31.
Social Life, 191, 253.
Society, 11, 56, 62, 65, 95, 96, 114, 115, 126, 165, 166, 168, 170, 192, 199, 200, 201.

T

Theravada, 10, 12, 13, 14, 15, 16, 17, 20, 22, 24, 27, 28, 29, 52, 58, 59, 60, 174, 176, 179, 180, 182, 183, 184, 185, 186, 189, 191, 193, 195, 213, 216, 224, 226, 247, 276.

V

Violence, 53, 77, 210.

□□□